Oxford University Committee for Archaeology
Monograph No. 17

Minsters and Parish Churches

The Local Church in Transition 950–1200

Edited by
John Blair

Oxford University Committee for Archaeology
1988

Published by the Oxford University Committee for Archaeology
Institute of Archaeology
Beaumont Street
Oxford

Distributed by Oxbow Books
10 St. Cross Road, Oxford OX1 3TU

© Oxford University Committee for Archaeology and individual authors, 1988

ISBN 0 947816 17 8

Typeset at Oxford University Computing Service
Printed in Great Britain at the Alden Press, Oxford

Contents

Preface

List of Abbreviations

I.	Introduction: from Minster to Parish Church *(John Blair)*	1
II.	The English Parish Church in the 11th and Early 12th Centuries: a Great Rebuilding? *(Richard Gem)*	21
III.	The Anglo-Saxon Gilds *(Gervase Rosser)*	31
IV.	Parishes, Churches, Wards and Gates in Eastern London *(Jeremy Haslam)*	35
V.	The Mother Churches of Hampshire *(P. H. Hase)*	45
VI.	The Fragmentation of the Minster *Parochiae* of South-East Shropshire *(Jane Croom)*	67
VII.	Some Aspects of the *Parochia* of Leominster in the 12th Century *(Brian Kemp)*	83
VIII.	The Secular College as a Focus for Anglo-Norman Piety: St. Augustine's Daventry *(M. J. Franklin)*	97
IX.	The Churches of Canterbury Diocese in the 11th Century *(Tim Tatton-Brown)*	105
X.	Church and Parish in Norman Worcestershire *(C. J. Bond)*	119
XI.	Architectural Sculpture in Parish Churches of the 11th- and 12th-Century West Midlands: Some Problems in Assessing the Evidence *(J. K. West)*	159
XII.	The Round Towers of East Anglia *(Stephen Heywood)*	169
XIII.	The Parish Church in Norfolk in the 11th and 12th Centuries *(Neil Batcock)*	179
XIV.	Churches in York and its Hinterland: Building Patterns and Stone Sources in the 11th and 12th Centuries *(Richard K. Morris)*	191
	Index of People and Places *(Compiled by John Blair)*	201
	Select Subject Index *(Compiled by John Blair)*	214

Contributors

Neil Batcock
    The Hollies, New Road, Reepham, Norwich, NR10 4LP

John Blair
    The Queen's College, Oxford, OX1 4AW

C. J. Bond
    2 Stone Edge Batch, Tickenham, Clevedon, Avon, BS21 6SF

Jane Croom
    National Monuments Record, Fortress House, 23 Savile Row, London W1X 1AB

M. J. Franklin
    Wolfson College, Cambridge, CB3 9BB

Richard Gem
    The Bothy, Mentmore, nr. Leighton Buzzard, LU7 0QQ

P. H. Hase
    20 Tenth Street, Hong Lok Yuen, Tai Po, New Territories, Hong Kong

Jeremy Haslam
    5 Barton Orchard, Bradford-on-Avon, Wilts.

Stephen Heywood
    43 Warwick Street, Norwich, NR2 3LD

Brian Kemp
    Dept. of History, University of Reading, Whiteknights, Reading, RG6 2AA

Richard K. Morris
    The Centre for Archaeological Studies, The University of Leeds, Leeds, LS2 9JT

Gervase Rosser
    School of History, University of Birmingham, P.O. Box 363, Birmingham, B15 2TT

Tim Tatton-Brown
    7 Orchard Street, Canterbury, CT2 8AP

J. K. West
    1 Florence Road, London N4 4BU

Preface

This volume grew out of a conference, entitled 'The English Parish Church in the 11th and 12th Centuries', held in April 1985 under the auspices of the Oxford University Department for External Studies. During the weekend it became clear that several local studies, independent of each other and embodying different approaches and techniques, were making rapid advances in understanding one major historical phenomenon: the emergence of the English parish church. Of the twelve speakers, eight have contributed to this volume. The other six chapters were subsequently commissioned from scholars whose work was known to be relevant to the central theme. The result is, we hope, a book considerably more integrated than most collections of conference papers.

The OUDES has supported the preparation of the book, and I am very grateful to Trevor Rowley for his original encouragement, to Mélanie Steiner for drawing figures, to Shirley Hermon and Lynda Rowley for typing, to Clive Bown and Elizabeth Gardner for proof-reading, and above all to Jean Cook for her help in arranging publication. The contributors, notably Patrick Hase, made valuable comments on the first draft of my introduction. The community at Buckfast Abbey provided much-needed seclusion during critical stages in the editorial process. Especial thanks are due to Pat Lloyd for her quick and accurate typing, which has greatly eased the editor's task.

John Blair
The Queen's College, Oxford
March 1987

Abbreviations

Antiq. J.	*The Antiquaries Journal*
Archaeol. J.	*The Archaeological Journal*
Arch. Cant.	*Archaeologia Cantiana*
Barlow, *Church 1000–66*	F. Barlow, *The English Church 1000–1066* (2nd edn., London, 1979).
BIHR	*Bulletin of the Institute of Historical Research*
Blair, *Early Medieval Surrey*	J. Blair, *Landholding, Church and Settlement in Early Medieval Surrey* (Surrey Arch. Soc. forthcoming).
Blair, 'Local Church in Domesday'	J. Blair, 'The Local Church in Domesday Book and Before', in J.C. Holt (ed.), *Domesday Studies* (Boydell, 1987), 265–78.
Blair, 'Minsters in Landscape'	J. Blair, 'Minster Churches in the Landscape', in D. Hooke (ed.), *Anglo-Saxon Settlements* (Oxford, forthcoming).
Blair, 'Secular Minsters'	J. Blair, 'Secular Minster Churches in Domesday Book', in P.H. Sawyer (ed.), *Domesday Book: a Reassessment* (London, 1985), 104–42.
Brett, *English Church*	M. Brett, *The English Church under Henry I* (Oxford, 1975).
Brit. Lib.	The British Library, Dept. of MSS.
Brooke & Keir, *London*	C.N.L. Brooke and G. Keir, *London 800–1216: the Shaping of a City* (London, 1975).
Campbell, 'Church in Towns'	J. Campbell, 'The Church in Anglo-Saxon Towns', *Studies in Church History*, xvi (1979), 119–35.
Cart. H.T.A.	*The Cartulary of Holy Trinity Aldgate*, ed. G.A.J. Hodgett (London Rec. Soc. vii, 1971).
C & S	*Councils and Synods, with other Documents Relating to the English Church: I: AD 871–1204*, eds. D. Whitelock, M. Brett and C.N.L. Brooke (i–ii, Oxford, 1981).
DB	*Domesday Book, seu Liber Censualis Willelmi Primi Regis Angliae*, eds. A. Farley et al. (I–IV, Rec. Comm., 1783–1816).
ECWM	H.P.R. Finberg, *The Early Charters of the West Midlands* (Leicester, 1960).
EHD	*English Historical Documents: I: c. 500–1042*, ed. D. Whitelock (2nd edn. London, 1979).
Eng. Hist. Rev.	*The English Historical Review.*
Franklin, 'Identification of Minsters'	M.J. Franklin, 'The Identification of Minsters in the Midlands', *Anglo-Norman Studies*, vii (1985), 69–88.
Franklin, 'Minsters and Parishes'	M.J. Franklin, 'Minsters and Parishes: Northamptonshire Studies' (unpbl. PhD thesis, University of Cambridge, 1982).
Gilbert Foliot	*The Letters and Charters of Gilbert Foliot*, eds. A. Morey and C.N.L. Brooke (Cambridge, 1967).
Haslam, *Towns*	J. Haslam (ed.), *Anglo-Saxon Towns in Southern England* (Chichester, 1984).
JBAA	*Journal of the British Archaeological Association*
Knowles & Hadcock	D. Knowles and R.N. Hadcock, *Medieval Religious Houses: England and Wales* (2nd edn., London, 1971).
Lennard, *Rural England*	R.V. Lennard, *Rural England 1086–1135* (Oxford, 1959).
Med. Arch.	*Medieval Archaeology*
Mon. Ang.	W. Dugdale, *Monasticon Anglicanum* (revised and extended by J. Caley et al.: i–vi (in 8 vols.), London, 1817–30).
Morris, *CBA*	R. Morris, *The Church in British Archaeology* (C.B.A. Research Rep. xlvii, 1983).
PRO	Public Record Office
Reading Cartularies, i	*Reading Cartularies*, i, ed. B.R. Kemp (Camden 4th ser. xxxi, 1986).
S.	P.H. Sawyer, *Anglo-Saxon Charters: an Annotated List and Bibliography* (Royal Hist. Soc., 1968). (Charters are cited by number).
SC	*The Cartulary of Shrewsbury Abbey*, ed. U. Rees (i–ii, Aberystwyth, 1975).
Stenton, 'Norman London'	F.M. Stenton, 'Norman London', in *Preparatory to Anglo-Saxon England* (1970), 23–47.
Stringer, *Earl David*	K.J. Stringer, *Earl David of Huntingdon 1152–1219: a Study in Anglo-Scottish History* (Edinburgh, 1985).
Taxatio	*Taxatio Ecclesiastica Angliae et Walliae Auctoritate Papae Nicolai IV*, ed. J. Caley (Rec. Comm., 1802).
Taylor & Taylor	H.M. and J. Taylor, *Anglo-Saxon Architecture* (i–iii, Cambridge, 1965, 1978).
TRHS	*Transactions of the Royal Historical Society*
VCH	*The Victoria History of the Counties of England* (cited by county and volume).
Worcester *B.A.A.*	*Medieval Art and Architecture at Worcester Cathedral: British Archaeological Association Conference Transactions* i (1978).

I. Introduction: from Minster to Parish Church

John Blair

A uniting theme for these essays is the critical change in English parochial organisation which occurred between the 10th and 12th centuries. With their different emphases and approaches — documentary, topographical, archaeological and architectural — all contributions bear upon a sequence of development, now widely accepted in its main lines, which can be summarised thus: (i) a system, general in Anglo-Saxon England, of large parishes served by teams of priests operating from important central churches (the 'old minsters'); (ii) the rapid proliferation, between the 10th and 12th centuries, of 'local' or 'private' churches with resident priests; (iii) a major campaign, during the 11th and 12th centuries, of stone church-building at a local level; and (iv) the eclipse of the minsters, the division of their parishes between local churches and the crystallisation of the modern parochial system, a process which was under way in the 11th century and complete by the 13th. Recent local studies (notably by Brian Kemp, Patrick Hase and Michael Franklin, three of the present authors) have done much to elucidate the complexities of this process, but historians are only slowly abandoning the anachronistic back-projections which so distorted earlier work on the formation of English parishes. Perhaps with this volume the new approaches will 'come of age'.[1]

This introduction is intended as a framework for the succeeding chapters. The approach, the interpretation and much of the material are my own, and it may be that no one of the authors would agree with all my conclusions. Nonetheless, the consensus between these studies is impressive, and far outweighs the disagreements: evidence from different regions, seen by a series of fresh eyes, is pointing strongly to the same conclusions. I have therefore drawn heavily on the contributions, and have tried to emphasise points of contact between them. The geographical coverage is reasonably wide, though with a concentration on the West Midlands and gaps in south-western and north-western England: thus two of the areas in which the strongest traces of a minster-type system survived are not discussed.

Two words, much used in this book, require comment at the outset: 'minster' (*monasterium*) and 'parish' (*parochia*). Insofar as *mynster* is the vernacular Old English for *monasterium*, 'minster' and 'monastery' are synonymous. But 'monastery' is today a loaded word, connoting a community of monks following a monastic rule, devoted to worship, contemplation and learning and remote from parochial cares. The much looser Anglo-Saxon usage, which allowed the word to describe houses of priests as well as of monks, reflects the wider range of functions which were in some sense 'monastic'. In the 8th century Bede's Jarrow, and the 'decadent' establishments which he decried, were alike *monasteria*; in the early 10th, when there were few strict monasteries, King Æthelstan could order that 'every Friday at every minster all the servants of God are to sing fifty psalms for the king'.[2] The Tenth-Century Reformation drew a firm line between 'true' monasteries and the mass of 'secular' minsters, but produced no corresponding change in terminology; indeed, in the 11th century both *mynster* and *monasterium* could be used for any kind of religious establishment with a church. The present papers generally use 'minster' or 'mother church' for major churches which had at some time housed communities of priests but were not monastic in the strict sense in the 11th and 12th centuries, whether or not they had been controlled by monks or nuns at an earlier stage in their history.

Parochia originally meant a bishop's diocese; until the mid 12th century it was used more commonly in this sense than either for 'minster parish' (which in Old English was simply *hyrnesse*, a general term for 'obedience' or 'lordship') or for 'parish' as understood today. For clarity, we have here followed the artificial but now accepted usage of Latin *parochia* for minster parish, and English 'parish' for the institution in its modern sense.

The System of Minster Parochiae

A hypothesis for English parochial organisation in the 7th and 8th centuries has been presented in detail elsewhere.[3] Briefly, it is argued that each kingdom acquired, within a generation or so of its conversion, a coherent network of *parochiae* established by acts of royal and episcopal policy. The central churches were of diverse kinds: monasteries in the strict sense, double houses, and straightforward communities of priests. But the likelihood is that all or most establishments called *monasteria* either performed or supported pastoral work within defined territories:[4] their public rôle helps to explain the speed and efficiency of their creation. This process owed much to existing systems of government and exploitation: many minsters were founded near royal vills, their *parochiae* coterminous with the territories which the vills controlled.

Several of the present papers accept such a scheme as the background to 10th- and 11th-century changes. Patrick Hase shows (pp. 45–8) that a network of four or five minsters around Southampton Water must have been founded under the West Saxon kings Cædwalla and Ine, probably with the advice of Archbishop Theodore and his bishops: here and in north Surrey were 'ancient royal estates, each connected with a collegiate mother church and a hundred, with jurisdictional and religious districts which were essentially coterminous, forming a system covering the whole area.... It is clear that this system was in existence by 700 or a little later'. In Shropshire (pp. 67–8), Jane Croom is equally clear that royal *villae* and *regiones* constituted a coherent matrix within which the (often substantial) endowments of Much Wenlock and other early minsters were created, and in relation to which their *parochiae* were defined. Other authors, less clear about early units and boundaries, still emphasise the high correlation between monasteries mentioned in the 7th and 8th centuries and mother churches with wide parochial authority in the 11th and 12th centuries: Leominster in Herefordshire (Ch. VII); Lyminge, Dover, Folkestone and Reculver in Kent (Ch. IX); Worcester, Evesham, Pershore, Hanbury, Ripple, Fladbury and Bredon in Worcestershire (Ch. X).

Such correlations are testimony to the enduring strength of the primary minsters, which even the drastic changes of the 9th to 12th centuries could not wholly destroy. The main theme of this book is the replacement of the old system by the new, but it is important to remember the signs, usually associated with the oldest and most deep-rooted minsters, of their continuing rôle among local communities into the 11th century and beyond.[5] The *scrifcorn* which Leominster was still receiving in the 13th century (pp. 87–8) may recall a time when the minster-priests were responsible for 'shriving' the inhabitants of their large *parochia*. Many of the lesser churches of late 11th-century Kent received their baptismal oil from their head minsters, not direct from Canterbury (pp. 105, 116–17). As late as the 1090s, a Hampshire thegn negotiated the foundation of a church with the 'elder' of his local minster, not with the bishop (p. 56). Processions from daughter churches to the minster often preserved memories of a time when the locals genuinely looked to it as their spiritual centre (cf. pp. 58, 60, 65–6 notes 70–1). Many ex-minsters retained large parishes and abnormal clerical staffs, for instance the 'archpriest' and his two colleagues who served three parochial altars in St. Martin's Dover until 1536 (p. 111). Such residual 'team ministries' needed the support provided by parish gilds, which, as Gervase Rosser here shows, are one of the strongest and clearest links from the Anglo-Saxon minsters to the parochial life of late medieval England: 'The teams of priests who manned the old-style minsters were clearly well-suited to serve the intercessory needs of the laity who formed the gilds. Those needs remained a constant from the 10th to the mid 16th century' (p. 31). Indeed, the lines of social and devotional continuity must often run from the 7th century to the 16th, and they underlie many of the changes described below.

It is no accident that the chapters which convey least sense of a pre-existing minster framework deal with areas of Viking settlement, in East Anglia and Yorkshire (Chs. XII–XIV). Whether this reflects genuine regional contrasts, or merely differences in later developments, in the available evidence or in the preconceptions of local studies, is an important question for the future. Norfolk and Suffolk certainly had minsters in the 10th century (cf. Fig. 1). Of Yorkshire, Richard Morris writes (p. 197) that 'the intermediate category of old minsters which is so characteristic of late-Saxon ecclesiastical geography in parts of southern and western England seems to be missing'; some churches stand out as 'superior' in the 12th century, but on present evidence it is impossible 'to suggest whether such churches could be the vestiges of a network of minsters which had once been more extensive and was largely 'weathered down' in the 9th and 10th centuries, or the products of a more recent, limited programme of founding or upgrading'. In either case, this comment is a useful reminder that not all minsters were 'primary': the 9th, 10th and 11th centuries all brought some new foundations which were more in the tradition of the 'old-style' minsters than of the 'new-style' local churches.

Minsters in a Changing World, 800–1100[6]

The bias of our post-Gregorian sources obscures the fact that the minster community survived great social change to remain, until the late 11th century, a normal and accepted branch of the religious life. Equally, such communities were subject to all the pressures of a fast-changing society. Just as the first minsters had been founded by kings and endowed from early *regiones*, so new systems of local government and land-tenure, and above all a developing territorial aristocracy, brought new kinds of domination and patronage. The 'scandal' of religious communities controlled by laymen, which so outraged later monastic reformers,[7] was in fact an essential part of the process by which parochial organisation grew and changed before the era of the one-priest church.

The 'private minsters' of 8th- and 9th-century princely families are most clearly visible in Worcester diocese. Thus in 804 the will of Æthelric son of Æthelmund begins: 'These are the names of those lands which I will give to the place [i.e. minster] which is called Deerhurst, for me and for Æthelmund my father, if it befall me that my body shall be buried there: Todenham, and Stour, Shrawley and *Cohhanleah*; on condition that that community carries out their vows as they have promised me'.[8] The successes of 9th-century bishops of Worcester against such lay domination[9] were unusual; in Kent, where Archbishop Wulfred (805–32) fought it at great cost and trouble, his successor ceded control of the minsters to King Egbert in 838.[10] The immunity from royal exactions which the later Mercian kings gave to some minsters[11] implies the reverse as a normal fact of life; in the late 9th century, for instance, the Hwiccian minsters were responsible for stabling the king's horses.[12]

King Alfred certainly countenanced such lordship: he gave three minsters to Asser, and his will asks for 'the community at Cheddar to choose ... [my son Edward as their lord] on the terms which we have previously agreed', and that 'the community at Damerham be given their landbooks and their freedom to choose such lord as is dearest to them'.[13] Land re-acquired by Wenlock in 901 had been 'previously surrendered to the king's lordship in order to purchase the liberty of the minster' (below, p. 73). At Abingdon later tradition blamed King Alfred for annexing the minster to an *aedificium regale*, but the wickedness of the action may have been less obvious in Alfred's day than from a post-Reform perspective: his grandson Æthelstan was to hold important courts at Abingdon, which brought prestige to the community as well as to the king.[14] Insofar as they regularly accommodated the king's household and provided a setting for assemblies and councils, there is a sense in which royal minsters were also ancillary royal palaces.[15]

Although the old view that the minsters perished for good in the Viking raids is clearly wrong, the late 9th century was for many of them a time of loss, disruption and change. Alderman Alfred expresses the general insecurity in his bequest (971×89) 'to be divided among the minsters of God's churches in Surrey and Kent so long as they survive'.[16] During the 9th and early 10th centuries many communities seem to have changed in composition from double houses of nuns and monks, or nuns and priests, to colleges of male canons.[17] Much Wenlock, originally a double monastery ruled by an abbess, was in 901 a *congregatio* under a male *senior*, though probably still with some female members (p. 71); but by the mid 11th century it was evidently a straightforward community of priests. If pre-Viking minsters had often had dual functions, the monastic was certainly less resilient than the parochial.

But these changes do not betoken mere decay. Recent work has emphasised the work of Alfred and his children in transforming and revitalising the network of pastoral minsters, just as they transformed older secular divisions into the 10th-century shires and hundreds. Cases of 'hundredal minsters', of *parochiae* congruent with hundreds, may often reflect a comprehensive re-fashioning by Alfred, Edward the Elder or Æthelflæd which produced a new generation of mother churches.[18] In a convincing extension of this hypothesis, Jeremy Haslam argues (Ch. IV) that Alfred's rebuilding of London, and the foundation of other urban *burhs*, involved the creation of urban 'sub-minsters' exercising normal mother-church functions in *parochiae* which were often coterminous with wards. Thus 'the wards and sub-minsters in London and probably other towns can be argued as being the urban equivalents to the new hundreds and hundredal minsters' (p. 39).

It is undeniable that in the long run the land-base of minsters came to be vastly diminished: their estates are quantified in scores and hundreds of hides in the late 7th and 8th centuries, in ones and tens of hides in Domesday Book. Much land alienated in the 9th-century disruptions was probably never restored; 10th-century kings took church estates for political and strategic purposes, and from the 990s Danegeld must have weighed as heavily on secular minsters as it did on the reformed monasteries.[19] But to imagine a fixed body of resources in inexorable decline may be over-static; it is possible that some 9th- and 10th-century endowments were more of the nature of *precariae*, to be depleted or replenished by secular lords as occasion required.[20] The trend is not in one direction only, and at all dates it is possible to see minsters getting richer or poorer. Burgred of Mercia's grant to Worcester in 864 of five hides in Oxfordshire, reserving a 30s. payment to Eynsham church, suggests the permanent disendowment of a once-wealthy minster; Eynsham retained little land of its own at its re-foundation in 1005.[21] By contrast, Stoke-by-Nayland in Suffolk shows the same process two centuries later: the estates which Ealdorman Ælfgar and his daughters gave it during *c.* 950–1000 (Fig. 1) had largely disappeared by the end of Cnut's reign.[22] In the continuum of endowment and expropriation, it is arguable that the decisive downwards trend did not begin until quite late in the Anglo-Saxon period.

At all events, thegnly wills from the second half of the 10th century normally include bequests to secular minsters (Figs. 1–2). The Suffolk wills of Ealdorman Ælfgar and his daughters Æthelflæd and Ælfflæd[23] have small bequests to communities at Bury, Sudbury, Hadleigh and Mersea, but show special devotion to the family minster at Stoke-by-Nayland. Ælfgar (946×51) gives Æthelflæd the use of estates 'on condition that she does the best she can for the community at Stoke for the sake of my soul and of our ancestors' souls'. Æthelflæd in her turn leaves several estates to Stoke (962×91), while Ælfflæd (1000×2) expresses in clear language the special link between the family and the minster:

> And I humbly pray you, Sire, for God's sake and for the sake of my lord's soul and for the sake of my sister's soul, that you will protect the holy foundation at Stoke in which my ancestors lie buried, and the property

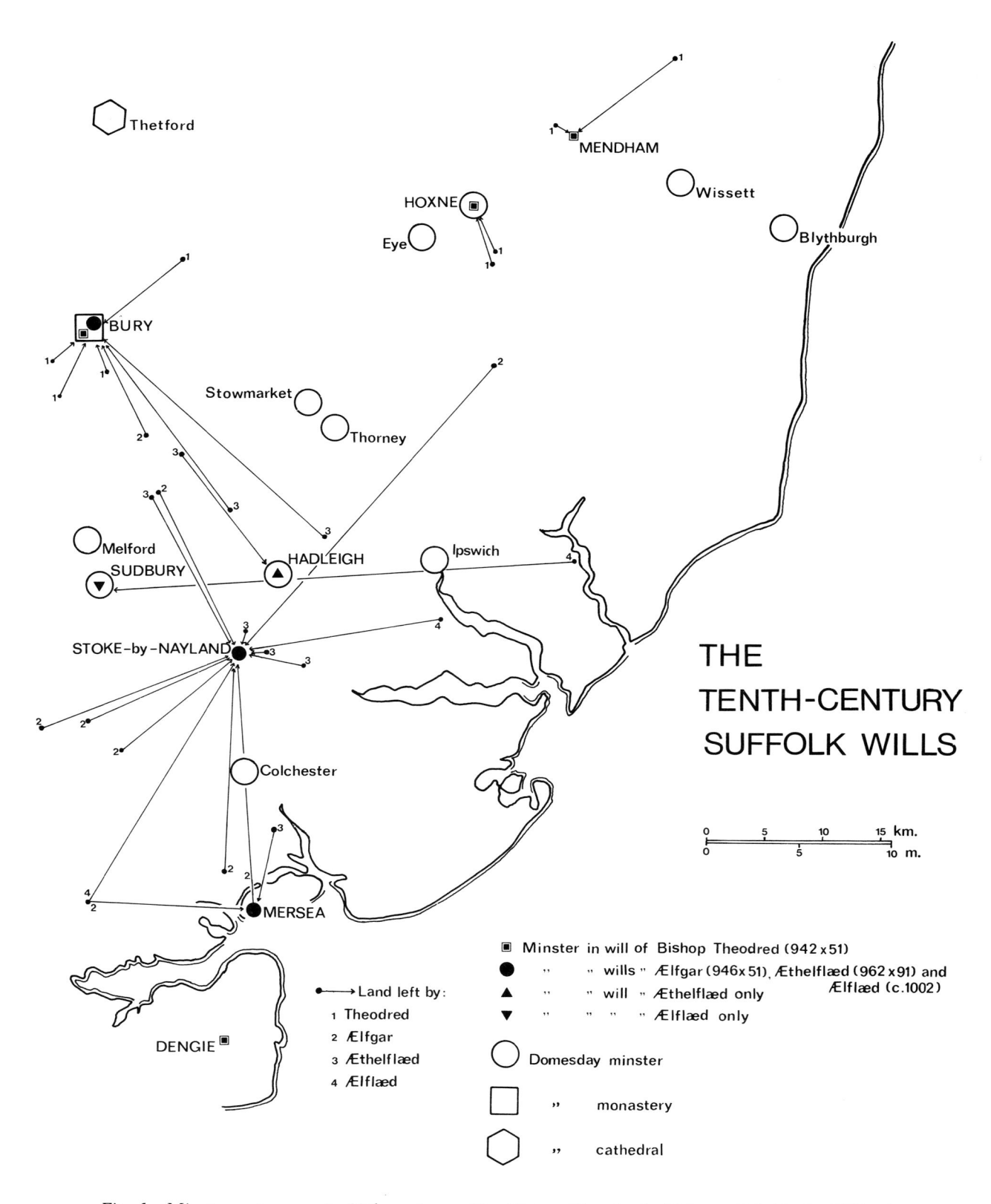

Fig. 1 Minster patronage in 10th-century wills: Bishop Theodred, Ælfgar, Æthelflæd, Ælfflaed.

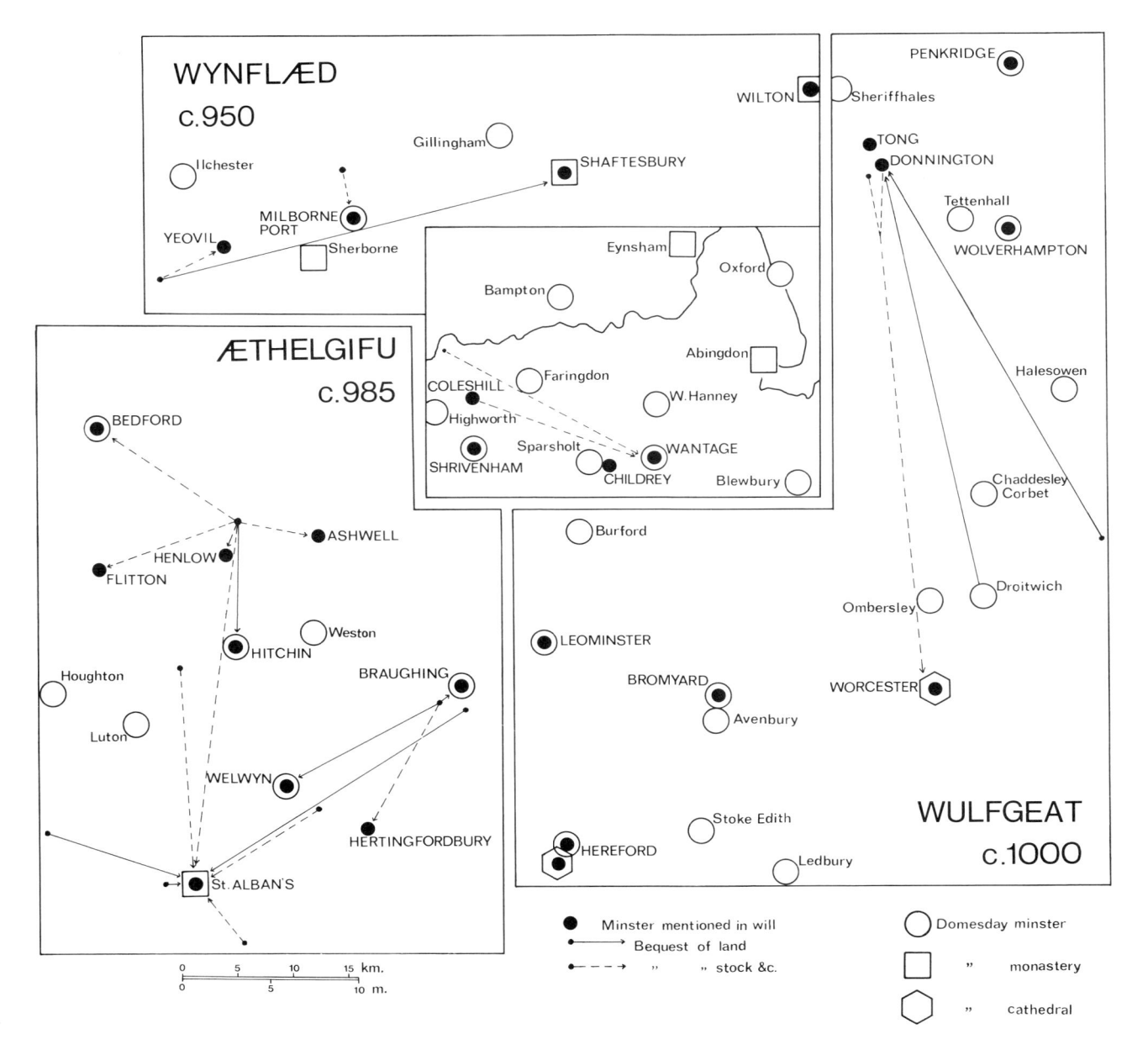

Fig. 2 Minster patronage in 10th-century wills: Wynflæd, Æthelgifu, Wulfgeat of Donington.

which they gave to it as an immune right of God for ever: which property I grant exactly as my ancestors had granted it, that is the estate at Stoke to the holy foundation with everything that belongs to the village there, and the wood at Hatfield which my sister and my ancestors gave.[24]

The wills of Wynflæd (*c.* 950), Æthelgifu (*c.* 985) and Wulfgeat of Donington (*c.* 1000)[25] show small gifts of money, stock and land distributed more evenly among the local minsters. In these cases there is a 50 to 80 per cent correlation between minsters mentioned in the will and minsters identifiable in Domesday Book in the immediate locality; the wealthy widow Æthelgifu seems to have left stock and food-rents to nearly all the minsters of her native Hertfordshire. There is no sign that such bequests were compulsory, though Wulfgeat's grant of *sawelscættas*, probably to Donington minster, was presumably the render of that name enjoined in the 10th-century legislation. The pattern is curiously reminiscent, on a larger scale, of the thousands of late medieval wills which leave tiny bequests to neighbouring parish churches. It is quite clear that in the late 10th century the local minsters were still familiar and respected, and enjoyed regular small bequests from neighbours of thegnly rank and conventional piety both inside and outside their *parochiae*.

The Monastic Reform and the 'anti-monastic reaction' do not seem to have changed this pattern significantly.[26] Propagandists for the monks, who put expellers of secular clerks on the side of the angels and cast their supporters as villains, leave an impression that these were entrenched and exclusive positions. In fact, ordinary testators saw nothing incongruous in patronising both the monks and the clerics: of the ten wills between c. 970 and c. 1000 with bequests to monasteries, eight also have bequests to secular communities. Æthelgifu was munificent to St. Albans while not forgetting the eight local minsters; Ælfflæd, whose will expresses such eloquent devotion to her ancestral minster at Stoke-by-Nayland, was married to the 'pro-monastic' Ealdorman Byrhtnoth.

During c. 990–1086 some minsters are known to have been re-founded or endowed by great magnates (notably Leofric and Godiva at Leominster, Wenlock, Stow and Chester, cf. p. 71), others by lesser thegns;[27] but the relations between communities and patrons are ill-recorded. A notable feature of Edward the Confessor's reign is the annexation of royal minsters as endowments for household chaplains,[28] and this may reflect a more general practice. Leofgifu's will of c. 1040[29] certainly shows lay control of canonries: 'I desire that Æthelric the priest and Ælfric the priest and Æthelsige the deacon shall have the minster at Colne as their lord granted it to them; and it is my wish that Ælfric the priest shall be in the same position in which Æthelnoth was; and may he be guardian over the minster who is over all others'. In such cases, the difference between a private minster and a group of household priests may not have been enormous, and the communities could well have had some involvement in the daily life of their lords' manors. Here there is a possible area of contact between the old centralised ministries and the new world of manorial priests.

It can hardly be doubted that the patronage of these late Anglo-Saxon proprietors extended to buildings. If so, it would have been operating at a time when work on the cathedrals and abbeys was in recession, and the 'Great Rebuilding' of little churches had scarcely begun (Ch. II). When Bishop Herman of Ramsbury spoke of mid 11th-century England as being 'filled everywhere with churches' through 'the most ample liberality of kings and rich men' (p. 21), he was surely thinking partly of royal minsters such as the magnificent St. Mary-de-Castro at Dover (p. 110), and comital or thegnly minsters such as Stow, Nether Wallop and Kirkdale.[30] It may be that churches of this type and status, concentrated in the period c. 975–1080, preceded and initiated the much more widespread building boom among ordinary churches during c. 1050–1150 (pp. 7, 9–10). This suggests a context for Richard Morris's observation (p. 192) that an abnormally high proportion of Yorkshire churches with 'Saxo-Norman' fabric have Anglo-Saxon 'monastic' backgrounds. Appropriately, it was probably the great clerk Regenbald, one of the most notable survivors from Anglo-Saxon into Anglo-Norman England, who rebuilt in the 1080s the Somerset minster of Milborne Port (Fig. 3):[31] in Richard Gem's words (p. 27) 'a restatement of older insular ideas in a more up-to-date dress...: a truly Anglo-Norman fusion'.

Fig. 3 Milborne Port, tower arch: a fusion of the Anglo-Saxon and Norman traditions, perhaps built by Regenbald c. 1080. (Courtesy Conway Library, Courtauld Institute of Art.)

Two chapters in this book illustrate the assimilation of secular minsters into post-Conquest society.[32] Patrick Hase presents the evidence, unique apart from the Waltham Holy Cross texts,[33] for the parochial ministry and internal life of a community at Christchurch (Hants.) during the 1080s and 1090s (Ch. V). This 'mixed system in which elements of communal life and individual life are both notable, but in which the communal life, with its full *horarium*, tends to be the more significant', was clearly based on one of the Continental rules for canons, probably the Enlarged Rule of Chrodegang. Most of the land provided communal income, and although peripheral estates were allocated to individual canons they remained, unlike formal 12th-century prebends, under the control of the community.[34] This picture may well be typical of the larger and 'stricter' English minsters throughout the 11th century. The college at Daventry discussed by Michael Franklin (Ch. VIII) was much younger, founded either just before or just after the Conquest within an existing *parochia*. This makes it all the more interesting that the canons of Daventry had a parochial ministry, which was transferred to one and perhaps more daughter churches after the college was refounded as a Cluniac priory in *c*. 1108.

These cases show that secular colleges in their own right, and to a more limited extent the parochial organisation which had once been their main *raison d'être*, still had a place in Anglo-Norman England. But the writing was on the wall. On the one hand, the rising tide of Gregorian Reform was soon to leave the seculars in despised and friendless isolation. On the other, the old order was fast losing ground to a less centralised system of pastoral care.

The Rise of Pastoral Localism

This shift to a locally-based parochial system is merely one sign of a critical change in the whole organisation of rural life. Recent work has emphasised a stage, spanning the late 9th to mid 11th centuries, when complex estates and territories based on royal, ecclesiastical or aristocratic centres fragmented into self-contained local manors, the land-base of a broader thegnly class.[35] To take two local studies, both published in 1985: Dr. Hooke shows how multiple estates in the West Midlands, at Tredington and *Wican*, broke up from the 960s onwards with the leasing-off of component townships; while Dr. Stafford sees the 10th and 11th centuries as 'a period witnessing a virtual revolution in landholding throughout the East Midlands', in which 'a group of small-scale landowners, whose only record is that left in the place-names, gave concentrated attention to their new lands; their pride in them was expressed in building activity, in churches and in memorial building'.[36]

A parallel process, elucidated above all by Christopher Taylor, is the formation and planning of villages. While the initial nucleation was probably a spontaneous result of population growth and the coherence of agrarian communities, a good case can be made for seigneurial influence on the emergence of regular settlements and field-systems during the 10th and 11th centuries.[37] Just as many churches adjoin manor-houses, so many others are integral components of villages. Like the small towns (with their own new and often multiple parishes) which were emerging in late-Saxon England, the manor-houses and villages reflect a reorganisation of rural life at a higher level of economic development.

In short, local communities were becoming more internally-focussed and coherent, and the community of the parish was no exception. French historians have recognised for some time that the re-structuring of seigneurial power accompanied, and probably stimulated, a re-structuring of rural life. Georges Duby wrote in 1953 of the Mâconnais that 'la chevalerie ... est au XIIe s. une collection de familles; de même, la société rurale devient progressivement une collection de communautés d'habitants, les paroisses'.[38] More recently, Robert Fossier has argued for Europe in general that 'l'encellulement des hommes s'est brusquement généralisé aux Xe et XIe siècles; ... durant plus d'un demi-siècle, de 990 à 1060, il s'agit d'une véritable révolution sociale'; and that 'la fixation du cadre paroissial est un des phénomènes liés à la "révolution" du XIe siècle: elle accompagne à la fois les démembrements et remembrements fonciers dont la campagne est le lieu'.[39] English historians have been slow to realise that the origins of our own churches and parishes must be seen in the same context of developing local lordship and emergent local communities.

This process could have more than one stage. Just as many large manors created in the 10th century were subdivided into smaller ones before Domesday Book, so churches of more than ordinary local status may sometimes have been founded to serve them, with parishes which fragmented in their turn.[40] The period *c*. 975–1025 evidently saw a distinct phase of parochial development: new churches, operating a scaled-down version of the old system, which can be defined as 'sub-minsters' or 'superior' estate churches. This category may have been the one most prominent in the first-phase 'Great Rebuilding' (cf. pp. 6, 9–10, 26–7); it probably includes many of the one-hide or 20*s*. churches in Domesday Book,[41] and some architecturally imposing or well-endowed churches without discernable *parochiae*.[42] Its existence emphasises the relatively late advent of the truly local church.

The argument that 'ordinary' churches and priests were rare before the late 10th century, but then became rapidly more common, is a negative one and as such hard to prove. But the lack of written evidence for a ministry based on one-priest churches, the assumption of sources before the age of Ælfric and Wulfstan that priests lived in communities, the signs that old-established local chapels were normally served from a central minster, all point in one direction.[43] So do the excavations, which are consistently revealing 'first-phase' churches and graveyards of the 10th and 11th centuries:[44] the sites at Barton Bendish and Thetford discussed by Neil Batcock (pp. 179–88) are in this respect typical.It may be added that of the twelve pre-1100 dedication inscriptions known from English churches, four (all at minsters) are 7th or 8th century, and the remaining eight date from between *c*. 980 and *c*. 1100.[45] Admittedly church archaeology is in its infancy, but future discoveries will need to take a very unexpected course if they are to change this general picture.

Most local churches seem to have originated through

seigneurial foundation (either lay or ecclesiastical), through devolution from minsters, or through corporate initiative. These were not mutually exclusive categories. The term 'proprietary church' is not meaningless, but it suggests boundaries between private and public, between manorial lords' churches and churches controlled by some external authority, which may be too sharply drawn. We should not assume that 10th- and 11th-century landowners built churches only for reasons of proprietorship and status, or that nobody would found what he could not control thereafter. Simply for convenience, people needed local churches; a lord who could arrange for himself and his tenants to have one might well rest content, whether he or the local minster had paid to build it and whether his priest or the minster's served it.

Lay wills of the period c. 970–1060 suggest a process by which household priests were provided, at first on a very informal basis, with individual churches, which gradually acquired permanent endowments of land and some kind of independent status.[46] Thus a community of priests in a great man's household (perhaps not vastly different in kind from a 'private minster') might become localised in churches on his various manors, the centres of incipient local parishes. Alternatively, if the local minster was independent and powerful, a lord might negotiate for one of its community to serve a new church on his land. Here the *locus classicus* is the narrative, discussed by Patrick Hase (pp. 54–6), of the foundation of a chapel at Milford, Hants., in the 1090s. Ælfric the Small, lord of Milford, built it by agreement with the 'elder' of Christchurch minster, who arranged for one of his own priests to serve it in return for half a virgate and a guarantee of the minster's parochial rights. The priest was to say mass in the chapel (waiting a reasonable time for Ælfric, 'he being the greater man'), and would eat at Ælfric's table before returning to Christchurch. The importance of this case cannot be over-stressed, for it almost certainly reflects pre-Conquest practice, and makes explicit what in numerous other cases can only be conjectured.

Such arrangements represent co-operation rather than encroachment. But other church-founders pursued more aggressive, separatist aims which brought emergent localism into conflict with vested interests. Encroachment began when manorial lords founded, without the leave of their local minsters, churches which usurped their parochial authority and reduced their revenues. The rights principally threatened were tithe, an expanding asset in an expanding economy, and the soul-scot which, according to a law of 1014, was to be paid for each corpse 'at the open grave'.[47] It is symptomatic that Æthelstan's ordinance of 926 × c. 930 enjoins reeves to pay their tithes, and to see that those under them do likewise and that church-scot, soul-scot and plough-alms go to their lawful recipients:[48] this new legal rigour speaks of an established order under threat.

Proprietorship, tithe and burial are all linked in the first clear statement that private churches had become a force to be reckoned with: Edgar's second code (960 × 2).[49] A thegn who has on his bookland a church with a graveyard should give it a third of his demesne tithes; if, however, it has no graveyard, he must 'pay to his priest from the [remaining] nine parts what he chooses'. As well as demonstrating that the diversion of payments and offerings from minsters to private churches was starting to cause concern, this passage suggests that the right to take corpses for burial, both as a source of mortuary payments and as a test of parochial jurisdiction, was becoming contentious. To judge from the sudden plethora of carved tombstones in the 10th and 11th centuries, private manorial churches had begun to rival minsters as favoured burial-sites for the thegnly classes.[50] This was different from the long-established practice of burial in outlying graveyards controlled by the minsters,[51] for it implied parochial independence. Æthelred's code of 1008, which states that 'if any body is buried elsewhere, outside the proper parish (*rihtscriftscire*), the payment for the soul is nevertheless to be paid to the minster to which it belonged',[52] protects the minster's rights and revenues even when the corpse is physically absent. 'Some priests are glad when men die', writes Ælfric in c. 1006, 'and they flock to the corpse like greedy ravens when they see a carcass, in wood or in field; but it is fitting for [a priest] ... to attend the men who belong to his parish (*hyrnysse*) at his church; and he must never go into another's district to any corpse, unless he is invited'.[53] These sentiments come from the same generation and milieu as the tract on status which lists a church among the normal attributes of the thriving *ceorl* worthy to be called a thegn.[54]

So far the drift towards local churches has been presented as a matter of thegnly initiative. Such is the inevitable bias of the sources; yet it is doubtful if the gentry could have achieved so drastic a re-structuring of parochial organisation without a basic shift of perceptions in society at large. Hitherto the minster had been the devotional centre to which all its parishioners looked; now, increasingly, they desired to receive the sacraments in life, and to lie in death, among their neighbours and relatives. Far more village churches may have been endowed corporately than we shall ever know. Twelfth-century cases, such as the Worcestershire and Northamptonshire churches maintained from the smallholdings of *rustici* and *cotmanni*, or the church of Exhall (Warws.) endowed by the local *probi homines*,[55] are analogous to 11th-century East Anglian practice recorded in Domesday Book.[56] Lord and tenants may often have combined in an enterprise which the former found socially advantageous, and the latter convenient. In turn, the habit of local church-going evidently created a feeling that visits to the minster were rather a nuisance. The church of Whistley (Berks.), dedicated c. 1080 because of the difficulty of getting to Sonning in winter to hear the office,[57] epitomises a new order of priorities (cf. pp. 32, 138).

As Gervase Rosser points out (p. 32), an unstated function of 11th-century religious gilds may have been to build and repair local churches. Despite their close links with the service of minster parishes, gilds could also embody a sense of local identity which ran counter to the minster system. The federation of Devon parish gilds, some of which were headed by local priests, 'may indicate a transition period of ambivalent loyalties, divided between the old minster and the nascent parish' (p. 31). Insofar as gilds still embodied a pre-Christian ethic of violence and vendetta (p. 32), it is even possible that they heightened the social fragmentation of the old *parochiae* by promoting inter-vill rivalries. A 12th-century inquiry into the lost rights of a minster at Lanow, Cornwall, reports: 'We have heard from old people that these [tithes] were alienated from Lanow church partly because the men of the said vills feared to come to Lanow church because of blood-feuds arising from a murder, whereas [St.] Teath's church was close at hand'.[58] The implication, that visiting the minster was dangerous, suggests that some organisation such as a minster-based gild was keeping the feud alive. But perhaps this was just an excuse: it is clear that the defaulters preferred to hear mass, and pay their tithes, at the rival church nearer their own villages.

From the early 11th century, the 'village priest' seems to become increasingly common. The great programme of vernacular education associated with Ælfric of Eynsham and Archbishop Wulfstan is surely directed at this new phenomenon:[59] the *uplendisca preost*, ignorant, isolated, cut off from even the basic standards of learning and discipline which he would formerly have attained through membership of a minster community. The ecclesiastical hierarchy was now making provisions, and setting standards, more relevant to the new system than to the old. Reformed monasteries were diligent builders of churches on their manors;[60] Ælfric forbade any priest to 'have two churches at once, for he cannot discharge the full service in both places together'.[61] The undoubted importance which many minsters still retained in 1066 was based on the past; the parochial order of the future is epitomised by Domesday Book's recurrent *est ibi presbiter*.

The 'Great Rebuilding'[62]

The triumph of this new order has an enduring monument in stones and mortar. Between 1050 and 1150 the English Church acquired new building-stock on a scale unparalleled either before or since, providing local communities with the simple but durable structures still encapsulated in perhaps two-thirds of our parish churches. As Richard Morris writes (p. 191), 'there was only one period during which the construction of such buildings in stone was practised as a general, national activity'. He shows (pp. 192–5, Fig. 85) how the extensive re-use of earlier masonry in the fabric of Yorkshire churches reflects circumstances peculiar to this phase of activity: clearance of Roman ruins in the expanding city of York, answering a sudden and unprecedented demand for material before freestone quarrying regained significant proportions. 'Outside York, the re-use of Roman stone seems to have lessened early in the 12th century, and to have ceased altogether by around 1150. Thereafter quarrying took over.' This analysis, which is likely to apply equally to other regions, suggests that for several decades demand outstripped the capacity of industry to respond with a regular supply.

It is traditional to see 'Saxon' parish churches as the later manifestations of a long tradition, and 'Norman' ones as marking some kind of fresh start. Here Richard Gem's contribution (Ch. II) is of the highest importance, for it demonstrates that both are essentially products of the 'Great Rebuilding'. His crucial distinction between style and technology shows how dangerous it is to claim that the biggest group of 'Anglo-Saxon' churches are actually pre-Conquest. During *c*. 1070–90 the distinctive technology of the new Romanesque architecture, in general use on the great building projects, had little influence on the small ones. The Taylors' criteria for identifying late Anglo-Saxon ('Period C') churches are mostly 'technological rather than stylistic' (p. 24), whereas stylistic features often derive from the Romanesque repertoire of the 1050s onwards. In the period of maximum activity, 'many minor churches remained the preserve of masons trained in insular pre-Romanesque traditions, who might be attracted by some of the decorative features of the new architecture but who did not understand it as a comprehensive system of building' (p. 27). The adoption of the new technology, which made churches recognisably 'Norman', could result from diverse and often incidental influences between patrons and craftsmen: it is less important than the first abrupt expansion of building in an insular idiom. Richard Morris likewise sees the 'Anglo-Saxon' churches of Yorkshire and Lincolnshire 'not as the last in a waning series, but as the *first* essays in a new tradition of stone-built village churches' (p. 197; cf. Fig. 84).

It will take time for concepts so radically different from the Taylors' (whose great corpus was only finished in 1978) to be assimilated. This volume embodies a range of different approaches, which sometimes leave it unclear how far the contrasts between areas are genuine, and how far a product of individual authors' predispositions towards 'late' or 'early' dating. It is interesting to compare the two East Anglian papers, notably in their continuing debate about the 'Anglo-Saxon cathedral' at North Elmham (pp. 175–7 note 7 and p. 190 note 4). Stephen Heywood (Ch. XII) shows that the round towers of East Anglia, so widely regarded as quintessentially Anglo-Saxon monuments, are all post-Conquest and probably mostly 12th-century. Neil Batcock (Ch. XIII) is more inclined to push proto-Romanesque features back into the immediately pre-Conquest years; he suggests that Norfolk was a 'late starter', but saw a massive campaign of building and rebuilding from the mid 11th century (p. 179). In fact this is very much in line with the later chronologies now being proposed elsewhere: Norfolk may be exceptional less for its timescale than for 'the practice of doubling, or trebling, the number of churches within a single village' (pp. 180–1). In Canterbury diocese, Tim Tatton-Brown notes that virtually every parish church was rebuilt in the half-century after Lanfranc's arrival; the 'standard' local churches are the majority listed in the late 11th century as paying 28*d* at Easter, and 'at many of them there still survive the remains of the standard two-celled building' (p. 111). The Worcestershire churches discussed by James Bond show a marked lack of 'Anglo-Saxon' features (p. 120), possibly suggesting that the 'Great Rebuilding' did not reach this rather isolated region until the new technology was becoming widely disseminated: Wulfstan's noted activity in the dedication of new churches in his diocese (pp. 23, 134) may imply that they had been notably lacking before.

In the last analysis, the remarkable coherence of the process outweighs regional differences. This was the age of the mass-produced church: groups of neighbouring buildings sharing standardised plans and modular dimensions[63] imply teams of masons working at a rate which bred such repetitive uniformity. The change was not merely architectural, but one of status. The new stone buildings are physical counterparts to the glebes which we can see being given to churches in the late Anglo-Saxon wills, and attached to them in Domesday Book. No longer ephemeral or informal, the local church was now a fixed point in the landscape, maintained from permanent endowments and the focus of a nascent parish community.

Conflict and Confusion: parochial authority in Anglo-Norman England

The incubation period of the modern parochial system, between the Conquest and the 1150s, is the one about which it is least easy to generalise: so much depends on individual cases. This state of affairs resulted from the decline of the minsters combined with the lack of any formal structure to replace them. Their parochial rights, which must have survived rather unevenly by 1066, were in many cases rapidly diminished thereafter.[64] But for minsters which enjoyed influential protection, these rights were rigorously upheld. A writ of William I orders that the churches built under Andover mother church must be destroyed or held by its proprietors, and one of Henry I (probably 1114) that the churches of five royal manors in Yorkshire 'are not to lose their parishes which they had in the time of King Edward on account of the sokes which I gave thence to certain of my barons'.[65] The *acta* of Henry I's bishops, which show little conception of the emergent local parishes, are nonetheless quite clear about the superior rights of ancient mother churches. In the late 11th century the bounds of Christchurch's *parochia* were defined with precision, and in 1123 the locals remembered in impressive detail what Leominster's had once been (pp. 60, 83; Figs. 11, 20). So by 1100 there were some *parochiae* in which minster rights had lapsed to the local churches, others in which they persisted: patronage and individual circumstances, not general principles, decided their fate.

At the same time, local 'parishes' were still inchoate and fluid. This is not to say that worshippers at a local church had no sense of their parish community: it has already been suggested that they almost certainly did. But until, in Christopher Brooke's words, 'the canon law laid its cold hand on the parishes of Europe, and froze the pattern which has in many parts subsisted ever since',[66] that community lacked legal definition and geographical stability. The distinction between minster parish and local parish is important, for we must be clear with which level of parochial authority any specific document is concerned. Thus Martin Brett writes: 'it seems by 1135 that the building of a new church, and so the creation of a new ecclesiastical circumscription, was usually accompanied or followed by an exact definition of the rights of the old church and the new, while occasional efforts were made to define the relations between churches which already existed';[67] but in fact his charters are concerned with protecting the parochial rights of old minsters, not those of parish churches in the later sense. The record of a dispute in 1114 between the priest of Carisbrooke minster and the patron of a daughter church (p. 61) is revealing: 'Almetus the priest claimed that the church of Chale was within the *parochia* of St. Mary of Carisbrooke. Hugh Gernun said that the men of his fee were not parishioners either of the church of Carisbrooke or of anywhere else but that, by ancient custom, alive they could go to whatever church they wished, and dead they could go wherever they wished for burial.' In the event, Hugh lost; but the fact that he regarded this claim of parochial anarchy as a sensible one shows how far England was from being divided up into a tidy network of parishes. Except for those people over whom a minster could successfully claim rights by ancient authority, parochial obedience was determined, when it was determined at all, by short-term and secular considerations.

This period saw a rapid decline both in the community life and in the pastoral importance of minsters, not so much a direct result of the Conquest as a feature of the years *c*. 1080–1120. Christchurch (Hants.), which again provides the most explicit evidence, was reduced by Ranulf Flambard's appropriation of resources 'from a genuinely communal mother church, with tightly controlled dependents, to what was little more than a single, very rich living for a single clerk, assisted by hired chaplains' (p. 50). In Shropshire, Jane Croom points out (pp. 71–2, 74–5) that the neighbouring minsters of Morville, Shifnal, Wenlock, Burford, Bromfield and Stanton Lacy were all still in some sense collegiate in the 1080s, perpetuating what was recognisably a minster network over a considerable territory; but except for Bromfield, which lasted in a modified form until 1155, all seem to have been disbanded within a generation. It looks as though the breakup of the pastoral minsters, gradual until William II's reign, suddenly became rapid.

In this the separatist activities of church-founding lords were important, but not the universal cause: *parochiae* which were not encroached upon from without showed a strong tendency to fragment from within. It is suggested above that chapels founded by manorial lords may often have been served on a regular basis by minster-priests; elsewhere, as at Bromfield in Shropshire, the priests seem to have divided the *parochia* into chapelries for their own convenience.[68] During the early 12th century, such cases encouraged devolution. Minster-priests seem to have established prebends at the chapels, adopted them as their main bases, and become parish clergy by degrees; Michael Franklin shows this happening at Daventry's chapel of Welton (pp. 101–2).

In perhaps a larger number of cases, manorial lords continued to build new churches in which they installed their own priests. Where the local minster had become moribund they evidently did as they pleased; where it was strong or well-protected they had to compromise. The early 12th century provides a small group of episcopal *acta*, often clumsy and experimental in their formulation, which safeguard minsters by emphasising the subject status of new chapels.[69] In 1107 × 29, Bishop Giffard of Winchester declares that he has 'dedicated the church of Ashtead as a chapel subject, with all customs pertaining to it, to the church of Leatherhead; and I forbid any priest to presume to sing mass in it except by licence of the priest of Leatherhead, to which that chapel belongs together with a virgate of land which Laurence gave him at the dedication, and with all tithes of the demesne and of peasants'.[70] The licence of 1108 × 23 by which a layman founds a chapel in an Oxfordshire *parochia* (cf. Fig. 5) is notable both for its detailed conditions and for its clear definition of the new 'parish' in terms of lordship:[71]

> This is an agreement between William bishop of Exeter and Richard de la Mare concerning Alvescot chapel, which is made in the parish of Bampton church; which bishop allows Richard to cause the same chapel to be dedicated on these conditions: That this chapel shall forever be subject to its mother church of Bampton. Also, that the men of Richard's land shall hear service there in such a way that no other parishioner of Bampton shall be received there. Also, that the corpses of the dead from Richard's land shall be carried to Bampton mother church. Also, that the clerk who serves the chapel shall come to the mother church on these feasts: on the feast of St. Beornwald, at Christmas, on Palm Sunday, on Easter Day, on the Rogation Days, at Pentecost and at the Navitity of St. John Baptist. Because the bishop has allowed the chapel to be consecrated on these conditions, the chapel and he who has it shall render yearly two sextars of wheat to Bampton mother church...

These cases are, at least ostensibly, non-contentious, but it was sometimes necessary to bring an adulterine church to heel. In a charter of 1121 × 38 the bishop of Chester defines the relations between Chesterfield minster and Wingerworth church 'which the church of Chesterfield claims to have been wrongfully built within the bounds of its parish'.[72] The lord of Wingerworth is to lay the church key on the altar of Chesterfield as a mark of submission; Wingerworth church will then be 'a mother church with all those parishioners belonging to that township', but will pertain to Chesterfield 'as a daughter to her mother' and will be served by a clerk sent by the parson of Chesterfield. The concern is always to regulate, not to suppress. Vested rights must be upheld, but there is no negation of what is now the normal way of life. A local community can reasonably expect the convenience of its own church; as the 12th century passes, the long trudge to the minster through mud and snow becomes ever more an anomaly and a cause of grievance.

These various types of origin — devolution from the centre, co-operation between minster and lay lord, and private foundation under sufferance — can make one minster's daughter churches of rather diverse origin. A good example of this is the *parochia* of Bibury, a Gloucestershire minster first recorded in 899 (Fig. 4).[73] In 1151 it was given to Oseney Abbey as 'the church of Bibury with all its appurtenances in chapels and tithes'.[74] Of the three chapels, Aldsworth and Barnsley are first mentioned explicitly in *c.* 1184, Winson not until 1276,[75] but on architectural evidence it seems likely that all had existed by 1151.[76] The chapels remained subject to Bibury's burial jurisdiction,[77] but in other ways their status varied. Barnsley was the most independent: in the third quarter of the 12th century it already had a rector, and a dispute settlement of the 1180s left its lay patron with a degree of control.[78] Aldsworth was served by a vicar or chaplain, subject to Bibury, whose revenues were established in an agreement of *c.* 1195, and although this arrangement lapsed the chapel seems always to have had a resident priest.[79] But Winson was to all appearances a chapel-of-ease pure and simple, served by a curate from Bibury and with virtually no separate identity before the Reformation.[80] While it is unknown whether these chapels were founded from the centre or by the individual manorial lords, there seems a clear difference

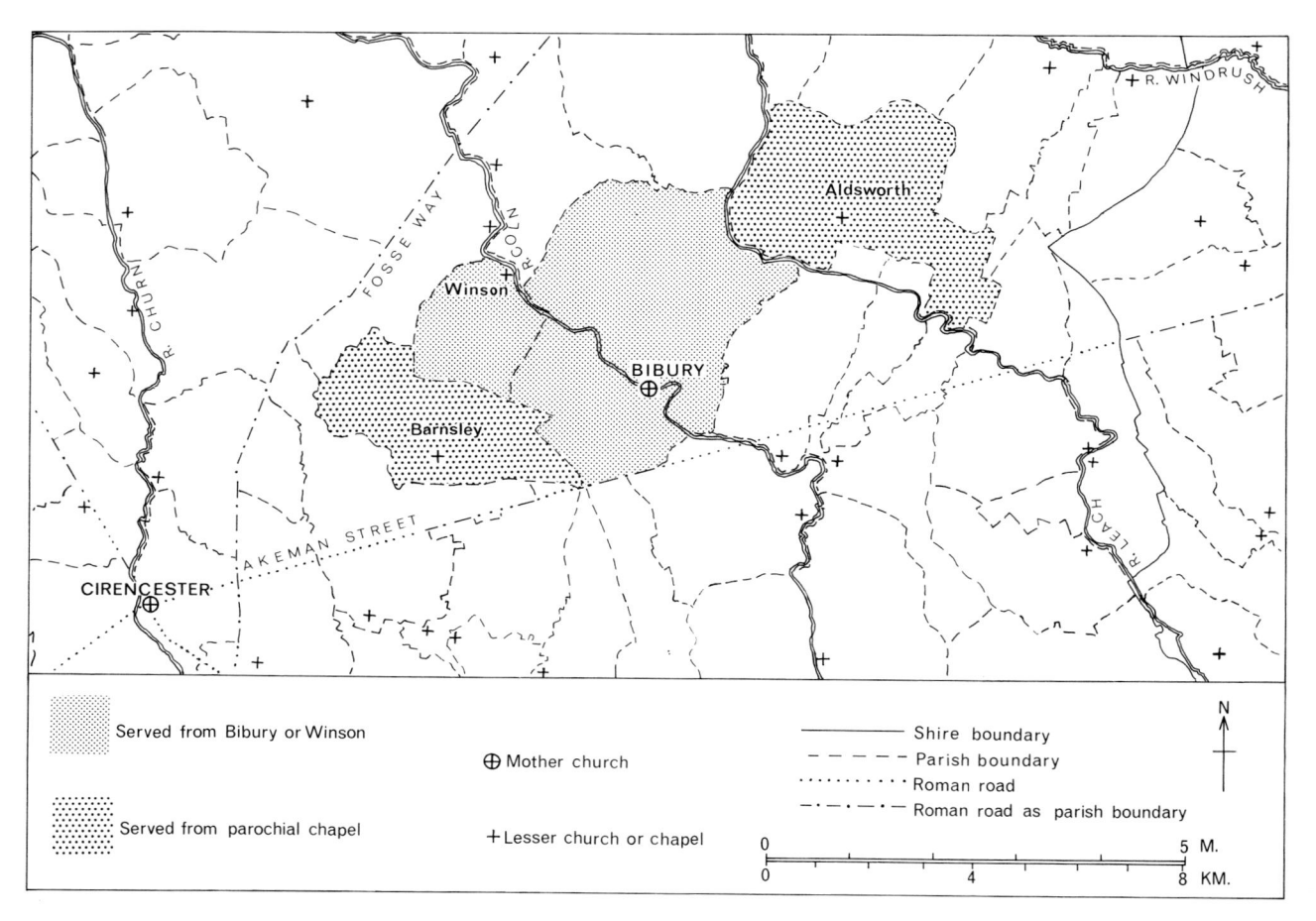

Fig. 4 *The recorded* parochia *of Bibury, Glos. (On topographical grounds, it seems likely that the original* parochia *extended from the Fosse Way westwards to the Oxfordshire border eastwards.)*

between Winson, which was a mere out-station of the former minster, and Barnsley and Aldsworth, which had their own priests in the 12th century. The same result — a localised ministry — was achieved in different ways.

The minsters which retained significant rights in their *parochiae* were mainly those controlled by bishops and monasteries. Brian Kemp remarks of Leominster that 'it must be doubtful whether the mother church's rights would have been so effectively and consistently maintained had the ancient church not come into the possession of so powerful a royal abbey as Reading' (p. 92): on acquiring it in 1121/3 the monks began a concerted campaign to recover and record its former rights. A similar process can be seen at Christchurch in the 1140s, when a vigorous, reforming dean collected evidence to establish the extent of the *parochia* and the obligations of daughter churches (pp. 51–2). This anxiety to rescue ancient and half-forgotten relationships from oblivion, and to set them down on parchment, is the first sign that order was starting to be rebuilt. But much had already been lost: the rights which were so widely confirmed during Henry II's reign were only those which proprietors had managed to pull back out of the anarchic years. This period, then, determined what survived to be perpetuated in the more extensive records of the late middle ages — in other words, most of the evidence now extant for reconstructing minster *parochiae*.

The main regular payments to minsters were church-scot (Leominster's *scrifcorn*, pp. 87–8) and tithe. The former was one of the oldest and strongest signs of ancient minster status: thus Pershore continued to take the church-scot from the two-thirds portion of its estates which Edward the Confessor had given to Westminster Abbey (p. 133).[81] By contrast, divisions of tithe could take complex forms.[82] Since Edgar's law had allowed a thegn to give one-third of his demesne tithes to his own church, the other two-thirds still going to the minster, it is not uncommon to find ex-minsters receiving two-thirds tithe portions from land in their former *parochiae* but outside their 'rump' parishes. On the other hand, many Norman lords ignored this arrangement: even when (by an inversion of the original principle) the manorial church was considered to have a *right* to one-third of the demesne tithes, the two-thirds or minster portion was alienated with a free hand. The monks of Reading found it easy to retain Leominster's tithe-rights over land which was in their secular lordship, but for some of the private manors in the *parochia*, where tithe had been given away to extraneous religious bodies, it was necessary to strike *ad hoc* bargains; in two cases they had to be content with a one-third portion, Leominster's due as parish church rather than as minster (pp. 84–7). Rights to tithe came to be widely regarded as the main test of parochial authority: a jurisdictional definition which could sometimes conflict with geographical ones. In 1069 William I gave the minster of Bampton (Oxon.) to Exeter cathedral 'with all the king's tithes', which was later understood to mean that the *parochia* comprised all land which had the legal status of ancient demesne; in 1318, some locals thought that the parish boundary ran along ancient landmarks, others that it was 'distinguished by fee'.[83] The tangle of intermixed tithe-rights, often claimed by distant proprietors for forgotten reasons, could be as baffling to contemporaries as it is to modern historians.

The distributions of chrism made by Canterbury cathedral and by Leominster (pp. 84, 105–8) show that in these cases baptism was widely practised at subordinate churches. Brian Kemp comments that among Leominster's mother-church rights 'baptism is strangely never mentioned' (p. 84), but this may not be so unusual:[84] in England, unlike most European countries, baptism never acquired strong jurisdictional overtones.[85] Romanesque fonts are common, and can sometimes be found in chapels of known subordinate status (pp. 133, 149–50). While this is clearly not incompatible with control by the mother church, it does suggest that attitudes to the location of baptism were relatively relaxed.

Burial-rights, on the other hand, were jealously guarded and often contentious. Their importance was part financial, part jurisdictional: the soul-scot (in later parlance mortuary) that came with the corpse, and the recognition of status which this payment, and the burial itself, implied. Thus the claim of St. Peter ad Vincula in London to soul-scot from an adjacent extra-mural area is strong evidence that this had once formed part of St. Peter's parish (p. 39). The soul-scots of the prosperous were worth more than those of the poor, and there may have been something of a social convention that men of status were buried at the minster; it is worth noting here that the Abbotsbury gild had been responsible for bringing members' corpses back to the minster cemetery (p. 31). At all events, rank in life seems to have influenced the extent to which physical presence was required after death. In the early 12th century, all inhabitants of Milford (Hants.) were to be buried at Christchurch except slaves and cottars, who could be buried at Milford chapel on payment of 4*d*; the only people who could be buried at Boldre, another of Christchurch's chapels, were 'cottars and slaves of the manor on which that church is founded, who were so poor that they did not have the wherewithal to allow them to be carried to Christchurch' (pp. 56, 60). Some similar provision must be recalled in the 13th-century verdict that all land-holding persons within a wide range of Pershore were buried there, whereas the landless, for whom no mortuaries were payable, were buried at Little Comberton (p. 133). Compromises between rival churches could include new burial arrangements, which were sometimes eccentric: the cemetery at Humber in the Leominster *parochia*, consecrated in 1148 × 54, was only ever to receive one corpse (p. 89), while an agreement of 1163 × 86 imposed on the inhabitants of Cleeve (Herefs.) the inconvenient duty of alternate burial at Ross and Wilton.[86] Brian Kemp also draws attention to two cemeteries *ad refugium* consecrated in 1148 × 54, which were not for burial at all but for 'the refuge of the poor in times of hostility' (p. 89). But as the 12th century passed, a feeling may have grown that insistence on the carriage of corpses over long distances was rather unreasonable, and that tradition should make some concessions to convenience.[87] A cemetery was allowed at Hatfield (Herefs.) in 1131 × 48 'as an augmentation of the cemetery at Leominster', with burial offerings and bequests still paid 'as though the dead were buried in the principal cemetery of Leominster' (pp. 88–9). Even when, in the early 13th century, a Leominster corpse was illicitly buried outside the *parochia*, the archdeacon persuaded the prior not to insist on an exhumation for the eminently practical reason that it 'would by now be stinking and horrible to look at' (p. 88).

The Mould Hardens, 1150–1200

Not surprisingly, the confirmation and recording of ancient rights during the second quarter of the 12th century was accompanied by their progressive formalisation. Relationships which had once had a social and pastoral rationale became fixed and largely financial. Reading Abbey's determination to exploit Leominster to the full produced a bundle of rights which were immutable by virtue of being clear-cut. The gradual devolution of the Christchurch (Hants.) clergy to chapels scattered through the *parochia* was made permanent by Henry of Blois, whose vicarage ordinances confirmed them as parish priests established on their own endowments; the rights of the mother church were reduced to a substantial but fixed pension (pp. 57–8).[88] The foundations were now being laid for a new and comprehensive parochial order.

It was in the mid to late 12th century that the slow but steady advance of the Gregorian Reform was at last making itself felt at a local level, above all in the attack on lay control of churches and tithes.[89] The passage of spiritual property from lay into monastic hands reached proportions unequalled before or since, not only because of the enthusiasm with which the hierarchy encouraged such gifts, but also because growing restrictions made churches less attractive to their lay 'owners'. In turn, the development of

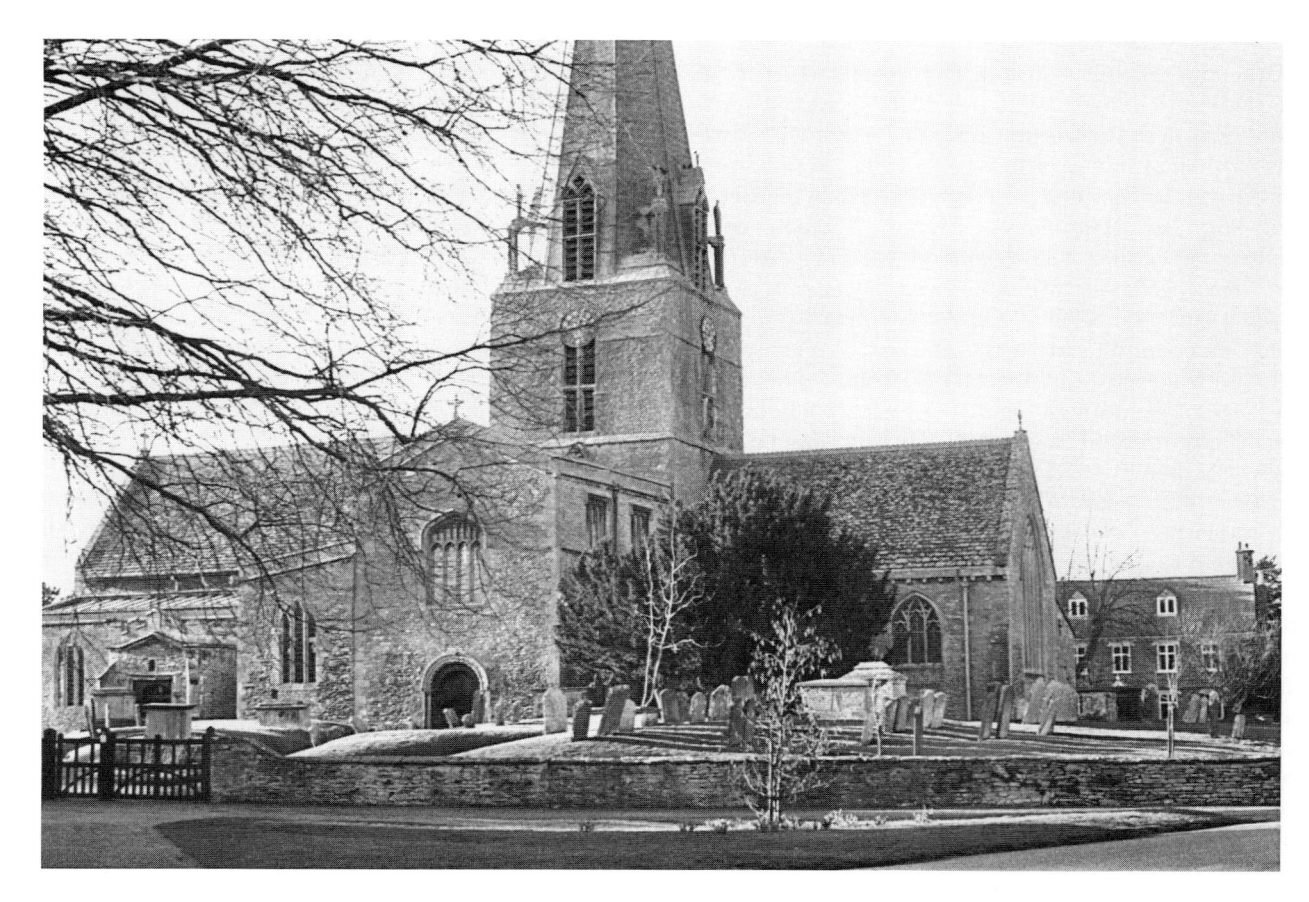

Fig. 5 Bampton, Oxon.: an important late-Saxon minster, lavishly rebuilt in the 12th and 13th centuries. The mounding-up of the graveyard reflects a burial monopoly which continued to be exercised over the large parochia *until the late middle ages.*

perpetual vicarages in monastically-owned churches subjected parochial arrangements to new safeguards and controls.[90] It was now common for a church to be in different hands from the manor which it had always served, a circumstance which must have encouraged the definition of its parish in terms distinct from those of land-lordship. The confirmations and settlements following the Anarchy,[91] initiating the rapid growth of the secular law under Henry II, contributed further to an intellectual and legal climate in which the confusions of the early 12th century would no longer do.

The key figures were Henry II's bishops: more versed than the previous generation in the new learning, more aware of the latest trends in canon law, more determined to put theory into practice. They applied to their dioceses the developing case-law of papal decretals, which defined relations between clergy, patrons and laity with ever greater precision.[92] Their *acta* apply maturer legal concepts, and clearer general principles, to dispute-settlement and the confirmation of rights: in confirming and adjudicating the bishops defined, and in defining they controlled and regulated.[93] Old anomalies were ironed out; *ecclesia* and *capella* became firmer designations of status, and it was no longer so easy for a chapel to become a church. By now there were precise territorial boundaries, not merely for ancient *parochiae* but between the parishes of village churches. In a settlement of 1184,[94] ratifying an agreement said to have been made 1123 × 48, the bishop of Lincoln establishes a boundary between Holbeach and Whaplode along two named streams. People living between this line and Whaplode are to pay tithes and offerings to Whaplode church and be buried there; people living on the other side are to tithe and be buried at Holbeach. An exception is made for four tenants on the Holbeach side who are to go to Whaplode church: a perfect illustration of the origins of those small parochial outliers which so often survived to appear on 19th-century maps. The historian writing of this period can abandon such terms as 'local churches' and 'manorial churches', and refer in a strict sense to 'parish churches'.

By 1150 the huge majority of later medieval parish churches existed; by 1200 the parochial system had crystallised. This final phase brought architectural developments which, while turning in new directions, also looked back to the old order. Several authors in this book note the frequency with which ex-minsters are perpetuated as grand 12th-century churches, either cruciform or in some other way imposing (Figs. 5, 10,

33, 53–4):[95] this comment is made in much the same terms by Tim Tatton-Brown for Kent, by James Bond for Worcestershire and by Richard Morris for Yorkshire (pp. 109–11, 138–41, 199 note 51). Stottesdon church (Salop.) had ceased to be collegiate by the late 12th century, yet it was provided with an exceptionally splendid Romanesque font (Fig. 19). Especially thought-provoking is Jeffrey West's analysis (p. 164) of Blockley (Glos.), an ex-minster lavishly rebuilt in c. 1150–75; his comment that 'the value of the manor in which a church is founded or the status of a pre-existing church replaced after the Conquest may have as much importance in matters of size, plan or decoration as the status and wealth of the patron or donor', and his question 'is there any evidence to demonstrate the proposition that churches of minster status rebuilt during the 11th and 12th centuries are distinguished by elaborate decoration?', should be pursued further. Certainly this may be one of the ways in which ex-minsters retained a residual pre-eminence in their former territories.

Jeffrey West also suggests the possibility of a 'significant change in the amount and quality of architectural decoration towards the end of the 12th century, that is after the main ecclesiastical provision of rural churches had been achieved' (p. 164). It may indeed be that as patrons found themselves operating within an essentially complete and stable system, they felt more able to divert resources from essentials to embellishments. At a manorial level, status in the hierarchy did not necessarily determine lavishness of decoration: the humble chapel at Aston Eyre has the finest piece of Romanesque sculpture in Shropshire, presumably given by its patron Robert fitz Aer (pp. 77–9, Fig. 17). But the days were passing when a church's fabric was controlled by a single lord or patron. Increasingly, from the mid 12th century onwards, monastic appropriators rebuilt chancels and parishioners added aisles (analysed here in the case of Worcestershire, p. 144). As Gervase Rosser notes (p. 33), the parish was now acquiring a corporate identity of its own, exercising duties formally imposed on it by canon lawyers. The physical transformation which most parish churches experienced during the late 12th and 13th centuries symbolises the triumph of their public status.

But the system still had an infrastructure which was more amorphous and fluid. Just as churches had originally been subordinate to minsters, so in turn they acquired chapels of their own. The difference is that chapels founded after the mid 12th century had little chance of ever becoming independent, or of establishing stable territories which could be defended at law. This does not mean that they were unimportant: their very informality enabled them to respond to continuing social change within the rigid parochial framework. A distinction is perhaps to be drawn between (a) parochial chapels, subject to their mother churches but with resident curates and sometimes fonts and graveyards; (b) chapels-of-ease, lacking any kind of independent status but open to all; and (c) private chapels, restricted to individual families with their servants and tenants.[96] But even the last category had a pastoral rôle, and may indeed have been the most flexible form of ecclesiastical provision in a changing world. In Lincolnshire and Surrey it has been shown that the proliferation of manorial or demesne chapels was influenced by local settlement conditions, especially the growth of communities in areas of late or dispersed settlement.[97] The present studies include two cases (pp. 132, 91) where the unusually complete survival of a *parochia* resulted in a three-tier structure: Martley and Eye were respectively chapels of Worcester and Leominster minsters, but functioned as parish churches in all but name, with chapels under them. The Christchurch *parochia* even provides a four-tier instance: Buckland chapel was in the 'parish' of Lymington, which was founded as a chapel of Boldre, which was dependent on the minster (p. 66). Influenced by the same economic changes, the internal organisation of these ancient *parochiae* developed along similar lines to that of the new parishes.

Because of their humble status, chapels were never systematically recorded; they also fell easy victims to later settlement changes. A striking product of recent local studies has been the realisation that huge numbers of chapels have simply vanished, leaving no more than slight archaeological traces or the occasional passing reference.[98] In Worcestershire, 'at least 180 parochial chapels of various types are documented ... between the 11th and 16th centuries, and of these over a hundred do not survive' (p. 138); in Shropshire, such chapels formed a diverse, ill-defined mass of which 'many would appear to have been short-lived and most have completely disappeared' (p. 79). This elusive substratum, of which historians are only beginning to become aware, must have been vitally important in the religious life of the medieval countryside. Our three photographs of chapels converted into houses (Figs. 6, 32, 78) may help to encourage a promising branch of fieldwork.

One case of a fully-fledged parish which is recorded in all its complexity makes a fitting conclusion. In 1220 the proprietors of the ex-minster at Godalming (Surrey) compiled a detailed survey of its rights (Fig. 7).[99] The mother church itself had moved from the ancient minster site to an 11th-century chapel, more conveniently sited in the town, which was appropriately enlarged. Dependent on this new centre were the ex-minster at Tuesley, now also a chapel, and Chiddingfold chapel with a chapel of its own at Haslemere. In addition, two of the three private estates within the old royal manor possessed their own chapels. At Hurtmore was a timber chapel dedicated to All Saints, granted two years previously to the summoner of the Guildford chapter, who paid a rent to the mother

Fig. 6 St. Leonard's chapel, Clanfield, Oxon. This improbable-looking building was a roadside chapel dependent on Bampton minster (Fig. 5), abandoned during the later middle ages. See Oxoniensia, *1 (1985), 209–14.*

church. A chapel of St. Nicholas, owing three days' weekly service (presumably of one tenant), stood in the manorial *curia* of Catteshall. But for the survival of this one exceptional source, it would have been impossible to guess at so elaborate a structure. Such cases reveal the hidden dimension to a parochial system which, fully-formed and stable though it appears by 1200, still had its inner complexities.

Notes

1. The following is a very selective bibliography of earlier work: W. Page, 'Some Remarks on the Churches of the Domesday Survey', *Archaeologia*, 2nd ser. xvi (1915), 61–102; D.H. Gifford, 'The Parish in Domesday Book' (unpublished London PhD thesis, 1952); R.V. Lennard, *Rural England* (Oxford, 1959), 396–404; B.R. Kemp, 'The Mother Church of Thatcham', *Berks. Arch. J.* lxiii (1967–8), 15–22; B.R. Kemp, 'The Churches of Berkeley Hernesse', *Trans. Bristol & Glos. Arch. Soc.* lxxxvii (1968), 96–110; P.H. Hase, 'The Development of the Parish in Hampshire' (unpublished Cambridge PhD thesis, 1975); Barlow, *Church 1000–66*, 159–208; C.N.L. Brooke, 'Rural Ecclesiastical Institutions in England: the Search for their Origins', *Settimane di Studio del Centro Italiano di Studi sull' Alto Medioevo*, xxviii.2 (Spoleto, 1982), 685–711; Franklin, 'Minsters and Parishes'; Blair, 'Secular Minsters'; Franklin, 'Identification of Minsters'; Blair, *Early Medieval Surrey*, Chs. IV–VI; Blair, 'Local Church in Domesday'; Blair, 'Minsters in Landscape'.
2. *C & S*, 54.
3. Blair, 'Minsters in Landscape'.
4. For the likelihood that communities of monks often supported or controlled priests, or themselves participated in pastoral work, see ibid. footnotes 7–12.
5. See also Blair, 'Secular Minsters', 137–42.
6. See also Blair, 'Secular Minsters'.
7. See especially Bede's strictures in his letter to Egbert: *EHD*, 805–6.
8. S.1187 (*EHD*, 512–13); J. Campbell (ed.), *The Anglo-Saxons* (London, 1982), 122–3 for context.
9. C. Dyer, *Lords and Peasants in a Changing Society* (Cambridge, 1980), 13–16.
10. N. Brooks, *The Early History of the Church of Canterbury* (Leicester, 1984), Ch. IX.
11. Campbell op.cit. note 8, 138–41.
12. S.215 (*EHD*, 533).
13. S. Keynes and M. Lapidge, *Alfred the Great* (Harmondsworth, 1983), 97, 175, 178; S.1507.
14. Alan Thacker, in St. Æthelwold commemoration essays, forthcoming. The 10th-century church at Abingdon seems to have belonged to a group of buildings derived from the Carolingian palace chapel at Aachen and with strong royal associations: see R. Gem, 'Towards an Iconography of Anglo-Saxon Architecture', *Jnl. of Warburg and Courtauld Insts.* xlvi (1983), 8–9.
15. I owe this point to Dr. Thacker.
16. S.1508. (However, *EHD*, 538, prefers to translate 'as long as they choose to remain monasteries'.)
17. Cf. Wimborne (Dorset), where there were still nuns in 901 but which was allegedly re-founded for secular canons by Edward the Confessor: *VCH Dorset*, ii, 108–9. However, the survival of nunneries has not been adequately investigated, and may prove more general than has been thought: cf. Kemp, 'Berkeley Hernesse' op.cit. note 1, 98, 101–2.
18. Cf. Page, op.cit. note 1, 66 ff; Blair, 'Secular Minsters', 118–19 and footnotes 55–7. Cf. Kemp, 'Thatcham' op.cit. note 1, 19, for Pershore (Worcs.) described as *mater ... ecclesia hundredi* in 1121 × 36.

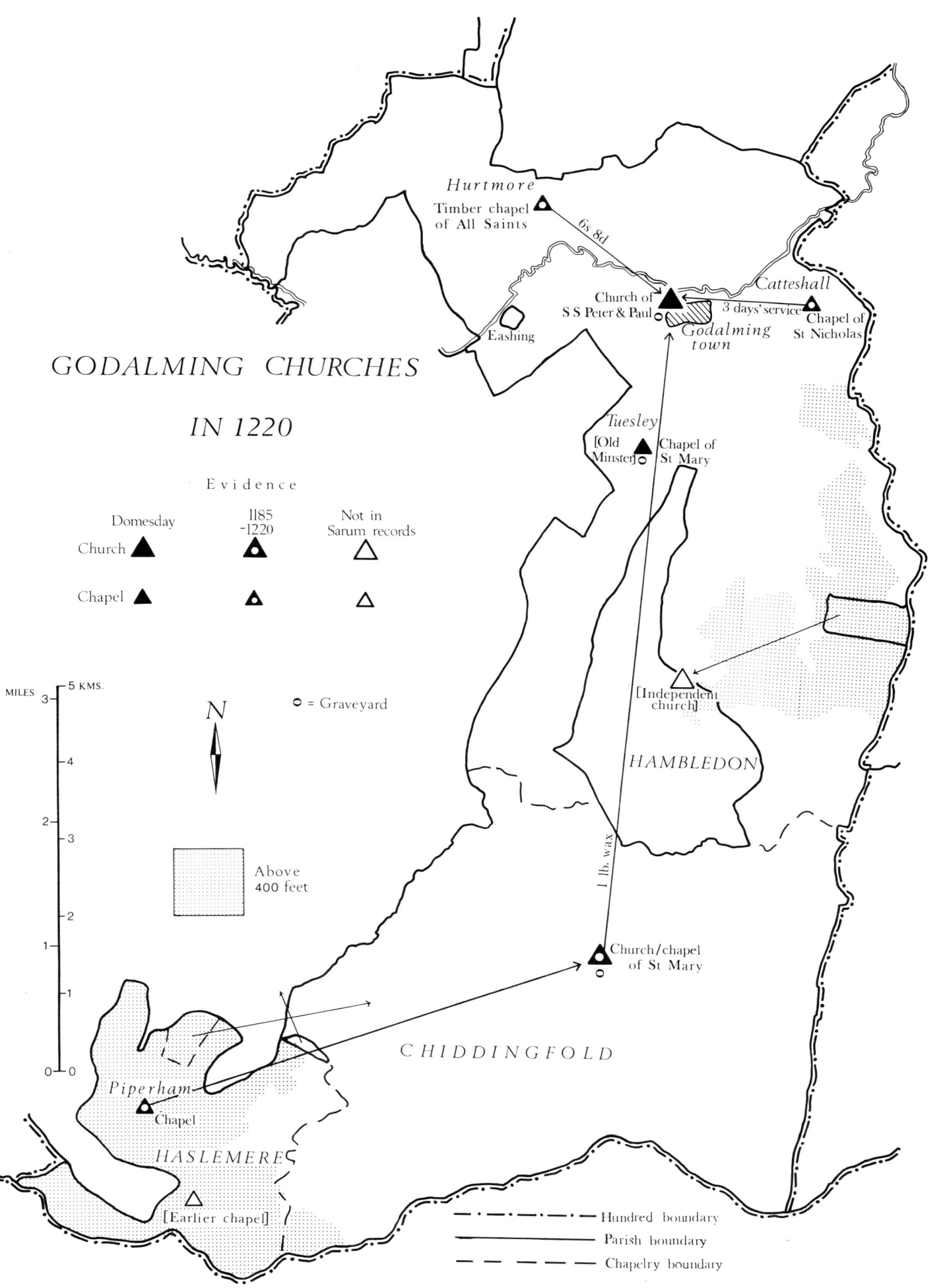

Fig. 7 The parochia *of Godalming, Surrey. (After Blair,* Early Medieval Surrey, *based on survey printed* The Register of St. Osmund, *ed. W.H.R. Jones, i (Rolls Ser. lxxviii, 1883), 296–8.)*

19. For these possible pressures on minster resources see R. Fleming, 'Monastic Lands and England's Defence in the Viking Age', *Eng. Hist. Rev.* c (1985), 247–65; M.K. Lawson, 'The Collection of Danegeld and Heregeld in the Reigns of Æthelred II and Cnut', *Eng. Hist. Rev.* xcix (1984), 721–38.
20. As with some aristocratic endowments of German monasteries; I am grateful to Professor Karl Leyser for this suggestion.
21. S.210; S.911.
22. C. Hart, 'The Mersea Charter of Edward the Confessor', *Trans. Essex Arch. Soc.* 3rd ser. xii (1980), 94–102.
23. S.1483, 1494, 1486.
24. Translation from D. Whitelock, *Anglo-Saxon Wills* (Cambridge,1930), 39.
25. S. 1539; *The Will of Æthelgifu*, eds. D. Whitelock, N. Ker and Lord Rennell (Roxburghe Club, Oxford, 1968); S.1534.
26. Cf. Blair, 'Secular Minsters', 119–20.
27. Ibid. 120–3.
28. Ibid. 124–5; Campbell, 'Church in Towns'.
29. S.1521; translation from Whitelock op.cit. note 24, 77.
30. Taylor & Taylor, 214–17, 584–93; R. Gem and P. Tudor-Craig, 'A "Winchester School" Wall-Painting at Nether Wallop, Hampshire', *Anglo-Saxon England* ix (1981), 115–36; Taylor & Taylor, 357–61, and below p. 196.
31. Blair, 'Secular Minsters', 134–5.
32. Cf. Ibid. 125–37.
33. *The Foundation of Waltham Abbey*, ed.W. Stubbs (Oxford and London, 1861).
34. On rules and prebends see Blair 'Secular Minsters', 116–18, 123–5; J. Barrow, 'Cathedrals, Provosts and Prebends: a Comparison', *Jnl. of Ecclesiastical Hist.* xxxvii (1986), 536–64.
35. For some expressions of this view see E. Miller, 'La Société Rurale en Angleterre (X^e–XIIe Siècles)', *Settimane di Studio del Centro Italiano di Studi sull'Alto Medioevo*, xiii (Spoleto, 1966), 111–34; Blair, *Early Medieval Surrey*; several papers in D. Hooke (ed.), *Anglo-Saxon Settlements* (forthcoming).
36. D. Hooke, *The Anglo-Saxon Landscape: the Kingdom of the Hwicce* (Manchester,1985), 106–11; P. Stafford, *The East Midlands in the Early Middle Ages* (Leicester, 1985), 29–39.
37. See especially C. Taylor, *Village and Farmstead* (London, 1983); R.A. Dodgshon, *The Origin of British Field Systems: an Interpretation* (London & New York, 1980); several papers in T. Rowley (ed.), *The Origins of Open Field Agriculture* (London, 1981).
38. G. Duby, *La Société aux XIe et XIIe Siècles dans la Région Mâconnaise* (Paris, 1953), 290.
39. R. Fossier, *Enfance de l'Europe* (Nouvelle Clio 17, Paris, 1982), 288, 346. See also S. Reynolds, *Kingdoms and Communities in Western Europe 900–1300* (Oxford, 1984), Ch. IV.
40. The ideas in this paragraph crystallised during correspondence with Dr. Hase after the submission of his paper, and I am very grateful to him for the following additional comments: 'In the 10th century, great royal estates did not often in Hampshire break up into one-vill units, but often into two or three blocks, each of three or four vills: the further breakup into single vill units, if it happened at all, was usually an 11th century development. Ecclesiastically, too, the 10th century developments in Hampshire seem to be more the breakup of an old minister *parochia*, not into single-vill parishes, but into two or three parishes based on the new secular units, with each new parish covering several vills, and with the further breakup into single-vill parishes coming, if it came at all, in the 11th to 12th centuries.... It seems to me that the 975–1025 parochial developments tend to be the building of new parish churches on a reduced minster type basis, by the very greatest men only (earls and religious houses), but that single-vill parochial developments by the ordinary upland thegn are conspicuous by their absence.' Thus large *parochie* were first split into smaller ones, 'the new minsters taking soulscot and churchscot from the older ones (and possibly glebeland as well), and functioning in the older way, but over a much smaller area, and presumably with a much reduced complement of priests to man them.'
41. Cf. Blair, 'Secular Minsters', 106, and comments by Hase below p. 63 note 27.
42. Churches such as Nether Wallop (Hants.), Breamore (Hants.) and Worth (Sussex) may be relevant here; for another likely case see J. Blair and B. McKay, 'Investigations at Tackley Church, 1981–4', *Oxoniensia*, l (1985), 25–45.
43. For a fuller discussion of all this evidence see Blair, 'Local Church in Domesday', 267–8, and J. Blair's review of Morris, *CBA*, in *JBAA* cxxxix (1986), 168–9; Cf. Blair, 'Minsters in Landscape'.
44. Blair, 'Local Church in Domesday', 268 note 15.
45. J.Higgitt, 'The Dedication Inscription at Jarrow and its Context', *Antiq. J.* lix (1979), 367–70.
46. Fully discussed in Blair, 'Local Church in Domesday', 269–71.
47. *C & S*, 393.
48. *C & S*, 44–6.
49. *C & S*, 97–8.
50. See Stafford op.cit. note 36, 174–5; J.T. Lang, 'The Hogback: a Viking Colonial Monument', in S.C. Hawkes, J. Campbell and D. Brown (eds.), *Anglo-Saxon Studies in Archaeology and History*, iii (1984), 85–176; C.D. Morris, 'Pre-Conquest Sculpture of the Tees Valley', *Med.Arch.* xx (1976), 140–6.
51. For outlying graveyards dependent on minsters at an earlier date, see Blair, 'Minsters in Landscape'.
52. *C & S*, 352.
53. *C & S*, 295–6.
54. *EHD*, 468, note 7.
55. R. Lennard, 'Two Peasant Contributions to Church Endowment', *Eng. Hist. Rev.* lxvii (1952), 230–3; Brett, *English Church*, 130.
56. Blair, 'Local Church in Domesday', 270–1, notes 25–6.
57. *Chronicon Monasterii de Abingdon*, ed. J. Stevenson, ii (Rolls Ser. iib, 1858), 18–19. Dr. Kemp points out (pers. comm.) that 'Whistley' church is either now lost or represented by the present church of Hurst, which in 1220 was a chapel *non dedicata* in Sonning *parochia* (*The Register of St. Osmund*, ed. W.H.R. Jones, i (Rolls Ser. lxxviii, 1883), 280).
58. W.M.M. Picken, 'The Manor of Tremaruustel and the Honour of St. Keus', *Jnl. of the Royal Inst. of Cornwall* n.s. vii (1973–7), 226.
59. For this point I am grateful to Mr. Peter Kitson.
60. For instance the Chertsey Abbey churches discussed Blair, *Early Medieval Surrey*, Ch. V; cf. M. Deanesly, 'The Late Old English Church: Bishops and Pastoral Care', in *Sidelights on the Anglo-Saxon Church* (London, 1962), 104–36.
61. *C & S*, 301.
62. See also Blair, 'Local Church in Domesday', 272–4.
63. E.g., Blair, *Early Medieval Surrey*, ch. V for two-cell churches around Godalming; [D.G. Buckley (ed.)], *Four Church Excavations in Essex* (Essex County Council Occasional Paper 4, 1984), 59, for apsidal churches in Essex.
64. Blair, 'Secular Minsters', 125.
65. *Eng. Hist. Rev.* c (1985), 283; *Regesta Regum Anglo-Normannorum* ii, No. 1046.
66. C.N.L. Brooke, 'The Missionary at Home', *Studies in Church History*, vi (1970), 72.
67. Brett, *English Church*, 223.
68. Blair, 'Secular Minsters', 128–31, and the other cases cited there.
69. The best general discussion of these *acta* is in Brett, *English Church*, 122–31.
70. *Cartularium Monasterii Sancti Johannis Baptiste de Colecestria*, ed. S.A. Moore (Roxburghe Club, London, 1897), i, 78.
71. Exeter Cathedral, Dean and Chapter MS 3672 p.33.
72. *The Registrum Antiquissinum of the Cathedral Church of Lincoln*, ii, ed. C.W. Foster (Linc. Rec. Soc. xxviii, 1933), 7–9.
73. S.1279.

74. *The Oseney Cartulary*, ed. H.E. Salter, v (Oxford Hist. Soc. xcviii, 1935), 1–2; cf. M.G. Cheney, *Roger, Bishop of Worcester 1164–1179* (Oxford, 1980), 106, 281–2, 334.
75. *Oseney Cartulary*, v, 35, 24, 9.
76. See *VCH Gloucs*. vii, and D. Verey, *The Buildings of England: Gloucestershire: the Cotswolds* (Harmondsworth, 1970).
77. *VCH Gloucs*. vii, 11, 19.
78. *Oseney Cartulary*, v, 24; *VCH Gloucs*. vii, 19, 11.
79. *Oseney Cartulary*, v, 36–7; *VCH Gloucs*. vii, 11.
80. *VCH Gloucs*. vii, 42; *Oseney Cartulary*, vi, 232.
81. However, Dr. Hase points out (pers. comm.) that there are several cases in Hampshire of religious houses without any hint of rectorial rights receiving church-scot, having probably annexed it from the old minsters during the early to mid 12th century.
82. Cf. Franklin, 'Minsters and Parishes', 13–14; Blair, 'Secular Minsters', 125; B.R. Kemp, 'Monastic Possession of Parish Churches in England in the Twelfth Century', *Jnl. Eccles. Hist.* xxxi (1980), 142.
83. J. Blair, 'Parish Versus Village: the Bampton/Standlake Tithe Conflict of 1317–19', *Oxfordshire Local History*, ii.2 (1985), 36–7.
84. As Dr. Kemp points out (pers. comm.), cases in which baptismal rights are at issue between mother and daughter churches are not unknown: cf. *Reading Cartularies*, i, 352, and *Landboc sive Registrum Monasterii de Winchelcumba*, ed. D. Royce, i (Exeter, 1892), 67.
85. Blair, 'Minsters in Landscape'.
86. J.S. Barrow, 'The Bishops of Hereford and their Acta' (unpublished Oxford DPhil thesis, 1982), No. 9.
87. This is explicit in the Wells synodal statutes of 1258 (?) (*Councils and Synods, with other Documents Relating to the English Church:II: AD 1205–1313*, eds. F.M. Powicke and C.R. Cheney (Oxford, 1964), 602, which order the consecration of cemeteries at all chapels not already having them and lying more than two miles from their mother churches. Cf. Blair, *Early Medieval Surrey*, ch. VI.
88. Cf. Kemp op.cit. note 82, 153–6.
89. See for instance Brooke op.cit. note 66; C.R. Cheney, *From Becket to Langton* (Manchester, 1956); G.W.O. Addleshaw, *Rectors, Vicars and Patrons in Twelfth and Early Thirteenth Century Canon Law* (St. Anthony's Hall Publication No. 9, York, 1956); Kemp op.cit. note 82.
90. Kemp op.cit. note 82.
91. E.g., the papal mandate of 1154×9 ordering that chapels erected in Reading Abbey's parishes during the war are not to prejudice the rights of the parish churches, 'since what is done in an emergency ought to cease when the emergency is over': *Reading Cartularies*, i, No. 147.
92. See works cited in note 89.
93. For a local study see Blair, *Early Medieval Surrey*, Ch. VI.
94. K. Major, 'Conan son of Ellis', *Assoc. Archit. Soc. Reps. & Papers* xlii (1934), 13–14.
95. Cf. however Franklin, 'Identification of Minsters', who points out that several Northamptonshire minsters were evidently not cruciform; and P.H. Hase's view (pers. comm.) that '12th-century parish churches in Hampshire which were ex-minsters do not show any particularly striking elaboration in form or finish'.
96. For these definitions I am indebted to Dr. Hase.
97. D.M. Owen, 'Chapelries and Rural Settlement', in P.H. Sawyer (ed.), *Medieval Settlement* (London, 1976), 66–71; Idem, *Church and Society in Medieval Lincolnshire* (Lincoln, 1981), 5–19; Blair, *Early Medieval Surrey*, Ch. VI.
98. E.g. Blair, *Early Medieval Surrey*, Ch. VI.
99. *The Register of St. Osmund*, ed. W.H.R. Jones, i (Rolls Ser. lxxviii, 1883), 296–8 (discussed Blair, *Early Medieval Surrey*, Ch. VI). Cf. the equally fine survey of Sonning at the same date (*Reg. St. Osmund* i, 275–83).

II. The English Parish Church in the 11th and Early 12th Centuries: A Great Rebuilding?

Richard Gem

The 'Great Rebuilding' and the Romanesque Style

Goscelin of St-Bertin, in a well-known passage, recounts how Bishop Herman of Ramsbury when he visited Pope Leo IX in 1050 told him about 'England being filled everywhere with churches, which daily were being added anew in new places; about the distribution of innumerable ornaments and bells in oratories; about the most ample liberality of kings and rich men for the inheritance of Christ'.[1] It is a picture that suggests a comparison with the often-quoted passage in Ralph Glaber who, looking back over the early decades of the 11th century, could see as it were 'the whole world shaking off the robes of ages and putting on a white mantle of churches'. But such a comparison, while raising the interesting question of parallel developments in England and the Continent in the 11th century, should be treated with caution. Ralph, writing towards the middle of the century in Burgundy, was able to survey Continental developments over his lifetime: but Herman and Goscelin, while perhaps sharing a similar perspective of Lotharingia and Flanders, did not come to England before c. 1042 and 1058 respectively,[2] and hence are witnesses to the insular scene only in and following the middle of the century.

We know indeed that political and economic circumstances were substantially different in England and on the Continent in the early 11th century,[3] and there are therefore no *a priori* reasons for supposing a directly comparable architectural development before the latter part of the century: the two regions must thus be treated initially as independent problems — but always with a view to asking finally how England relates to the culture of Europe as a whole.

Insofar as Ralph Glaber was conscious of a considerable expansion of church building in the early 11th century, he was a witness to a phenomenon that was a vehicle for (but not wholly identical with) the creation of Romanesque architecture. The early stages of this process remain to us rather obscure in detail and their elucidation is beyond the scope of this paper, but the general lines of the development are reasonably clear. In the territories ruled by the German emperors, the 10th century had seen prodigious activity in the erection of large numbers of major cathedral and monastic churches in a style still essentially pre-Romanesque. This current continued without interruption into the early 11th century, but in some of the buildings that marked its climax in the second quarter of the century Romanesque features started to appear. In France on the other hand there is less indication of major activity in the 10th century, and Ralph Glaber may have been correct in seeing a revival as belonging essentially to the early 11th century. When the revival came it made use of ideas deriving from a variety of sources and, by at latest the second quarter of the century, had begun to weld these decisively into a group of Romanesque styles. Thereafter in France the new Romanesque architecture attained a remarkable development, from its Early phase, through a Classic phase in the late 11th and early 12th centuries, and on into the Late Romanesque and Early Gothic of the mid and late 12th century. In this process there was scarcely a single major church in France that was not wholly reconstructed: it seems legitimate, borrowing a phrase, to talk of the activity of this period as a 'Great Rebuilding'.

In England the picture, insofar as we can discern it, is different again, at least for the early stages of the development. The latter part of the 10th century saw indeed a considerable body of architecture created for the new reformed monasteries, but this did not by and large rival the achievements of contemporary Germany, although there were isolated attempts to do so. The early years of the 11th century, however, saw an interruption in the level of architectural patronage — at least insofar as this affected the major religious houses — and a revival did not come again until the middle years of the century. Herman and Goscelin may have been witnessing a new phenomenon, therefore, when reporting to the pope in 1050 the widespread construction of new churches in England.

Following the Norman Conquest, this process in England gathered pace to attain, in the last years of the 11th century and opening years of the 12th, a momentum equalled scarcely anywhere in Europe. Thus the Great Rebuilding of cathedral and monastic churches, which elsewhere was drawn out over a century or more, in England was largely achieved within half a century. Thus William of Malmesbury, looking back over the sixty years between himself and the Conquest, observed how all around 'you may now see, in every village, town and city, churches and monasteries rising in a new style of architecture.'[4]

Within the context of this Great Rebuilding we can see only one certain example of the Romanesque style in England before the Conquest, at Westminster Abbey from c. 1050 onwards. Elsewhere there appear only 'proto-Romanesque' elements in the decoration of buildings (as at Stow, Lincs.), or wholly pre-Romanesque traditions of planning (as in Wulfric's rotunda at St Augustine's Abbbey, Canterbury). Following the Conquest, however, there was a rapid transformation of the situation: from c.. 1070 onwards England became not so much a passive receiver of Romanesque ideas, but more one of their most active proponents.[5] This state of affairs has often led to the popular view that Romanesque architecture in England is adequately summed up by the name 'Norman': it may be argued, however, that this term hinders rather than clarifies our understanding of 11th-century developments, since it makes English Romanesque appear absolutely as the product of the Conquest, rather than of a variety of diverse factors.

Major Trends and Minor Churches

Everything that has been stated above is preparatory to the main themes of this paper, for the picture sketched is that relating to major churches. But what of minor churches: do they share a similar pattern of development (as William of Malmesbury perhaps hints in his reference to village churches)? The question, unfortunately, is more difficult to answer than to pose, for a variety of reasons. In the first place (and this is perhaps especially true of the Continental material) minor churches have been less intensively studied than major ones. Secondly, minor churches seldom have documented dates, and if we try to date them stylistically we are in danger of prejudging the very issues that are under consideration. Put another way, whereas it may be possible to use stylistic analysis to describe particular groups of minor churches, and even to relate these to major buildings, it is not possible without further information to convert relative stylistic dates into absolute chronological ones — unless we make largely unjustified assumptions about the time-lag between stylistic developments in major and minor buildings. The intention of this paper, therefore, is to move a little further towards the solution of a particular problem, or group of inter-related problems. Given the premise that the 11th and 12th centuries in England, and in Western Europe as a whole, saw a Great Rebuilding of major churches, can we see a similar Rebuilding of minor churches? If we can, then can we further see in these minor churches a stylistic progression that is comparable to that in the major churches — a progression that carries architecture across a Romanesque 'threshold'? And can we go on to determine whether these stylistic developments are or are not synchronous at the different levels? Depending on the answers, we may be able to make important deductions about the whole social context within which the minor buildings were produced: involving considerations of patronage, craft organisations, technological skill, exploitation of resources, the local economy and many other factors. In the following paper I hope to open up the general field, and then to go on to look at one or two specific areas which I think can contribute to a deeper appreciation of the problems involved and to their solutions.

Was There a Great Rebuilding of Minor Churches?

The question as to whether there was a Great Rebuilding of minor churches sometime in the 11th and 12th centuries is one of the most difficult to answer objectively because of the absence of comprehensive statistics, or even an adequate sample. The problem is not, however, one of identifying whether or not minor churches existed in any number, for there is abundant evidence for this from a variety of sources. Already at the beginning of the 11th century Æthelred's law-code of 1014 (VIII Æthelred 5.1)[6] defines the differing status of churches in terms of the fines to be paid for violating their sanctuary: head minsters (at £5), rather smaller minsters (120s.), still smaller minsters (60s.) and field-churches (30s.). Likewise, Cnut's code of 1020 × 3 (I Cnut 3a)[7] defines the same four categories, but specifies that the field-church is one without a graveyard, whereas the next ascending catogory of minster does have a graveyard. The same code elsewhere (I Cnut 11) legislates for the apportionment of tithe between old minster churches, churches with graveyards and proprietary churches without graveyards. Such categorisation, however, was not an 11th-century innovation and can be traced back at least as far as Edgar's law code of 960 × 2 (II and III Edgar 1.1–2.2)[8] where are defined three categories for tithing purposes: old minsters to which the parishes belong, churches with graveyards on the bookland of thegns, churches without graveyards. Moving forward in time to William I's code (Leis Willelme 1.i)[9] there is again a classification in terms of the fine for violating sanctuary, but now it is only threefold: cathedral, monastic or other religious churches (100s.); parochial mother churches (20s.); chapels (10s.).

Such legislation suggests that there was already by the 10th and early 11th centuries a well-developed provision of churches below the level of the cathedrals and great monasteries. Indeed, it has been argued recently by Morris[10] that this provision had begun already in the 8th century and had continued sporadically thereafter through the entire period from the 8th to the 11th centuries: there may have been some intensification in the 10th and 11th centuries, but the process was certainly not, he argues, one concentrated into the few decades preceding the Conquest. Morris goes on to point out that by 1066 the Domesday Book commissioners were able to record some 2,000 churches and chapels, while some 550 others are to be inferred from the existence of priests. But even these statistics are known to be incomplete, and it may be that the greater number of churches that comprised the later medieval parochial system had already come into existence before the end of the 11th century — taking in both the lesser old minsters and the newer thegns' churches with graveyards to form a new category of parochial mother churches.

The evidence then seems to suggest that the *provision* of minor churches was a phenomenon that went back well before 1000 and that the 11th century itself merely saw the completion of the development. If this is so, however, it still does not bring an answer to the question of whether there was a Great Rebuilding in the 11th and 12th centuries. As with the major churches (many of which went back in origin well into the Anglo-Saxon period but which were themselves rebuilt in the late 11th and early 12th centuries, alongside the numerous new foundations); so also those minor churches which went back in origin to before 1000 could themselves have been rebuilt later in the 11th and 12th centuries, at the same time as new foundations were bringing the parochial provision up to its complement. The motivation for this rebuilding could have been much the same in the cases of the major and minor churches: namely, that by 11th- and 12th-century standards the earlier buildings were often considered inadequate in size and dignity — with the additional factor that at parochial level many more early churches must have been of timber construction.

Goscelin of St-Bertin tells us what he thought of old churches when measured up to the standards of the new age: 'I greatly dislike little buildings ... and so, if given the means, I would not allow buildings, although much esteemed, to stand, unless they were, according to my idea, glorious, magnificent, most lofty, most spacious, filled with light and most beautiful.[11] This was the ideology of the new architecture of the 11th and 12th centuries, and it was a direct attack upon older-established English ideas. But to what extent was it an ideology that was put into practice in relation to minor churches rather than to cathedrals and abbeys? In respect of this it is perhaps significant that Bishop Wulfstan of Worcester (1062–1095), who is represented as an unwilling implementer of the new ideology in the rebuilding of his cathedral, was nontheless the builder or rebuilder of many churches throughout his diocese.[12] At the same time lay noblemen were building or rebuilding proprietory churches which Wulfstan proceeded to dedicate for them.[13] By and large, however, we cannot expect an answer to this question from the documentary sources: rather we must turn to an examination of the buildings themselves.

In a number of recent archaeological examinations of parish churches it has been possible to demonstrate that a small church of a probable date before 1000 was replaced in the 11th or 12th century by a larger building (which in turn became the core of the later medieval fabric). Examples of this are Asheldham and Rivenhall (Essex), Raunds (Northants.), Barton-on-Humber (S. Humberside) and Wharram Percy (N. Yorks.).[14] But there is not enough such evidence as yet to be statisically significant, and it is likely to be a very long time before a sufficient number of parish churches are excavated to alter this situation. This means that we are thrown back upon studying the standing buildings without knowing anything, except in a few cases, about the possible prior structures that underly them. Nontheless it would be possible, theoretically at least, to carry out a survey of all medieval parish churches so that a statistical assessment could be made: of the numbers retaining a core earlier in date than 1000; of those apparently built anew or rebuilt at different stages of the 11th and 12th centuries and determining the later medieval development; and of those entirely rebuilt after 1200. But this theoretical possibility largely breaks down in practice because of the enormous difficulty in actually dating the fabric of the majority of churches before the later part of the 12th century. It is to this difficulty that I now turn.

Problems of Dating Minor Churches

In the absence, except in rare cases, of documentary dating or of other independent evidence, we are generally thrown back upon stylistic or other typological analyses for the dating of minor churches. But even in trying to construct relative chronologies these methods are fraught with difficulties, which must be recognized from the outset.

Visual analysis of a building (which will always need to go hand-in-hand with more 'archaeological' or structural analysis) may itself take more than one form. It may seek to examine the *style* of a building, that is, its general form and its decoration insofar as these are the result of aesthetic choice. Or alternatively it may examine the *technology* of the building, that is, its general form and methods of construction insofar as these are the product of a particular craft-training or competence on the part of the builders. Again, the appearance of a building may be influenced by factors such as the availability of *materials*, by *economic* considerations, or by the intervention of the *patron* who wishes the design to express a particular intention. Above all, each and every building is intended to house a particular *function*. All these factors have their implications for the appearance a building ultimately takes, and each needs to be distinguished from the others if confusion is not to ensue. Yet all too often we read analyses of buildings that do precisely confuse technology with style, style with function and so on.

Before turning to specific examples it may be worthwhile to examine a little further the general implications of these theoretical considerations. Between 1000 and 1200 the basic functional requirements of a parish church cannot have altered greatly — unless an increase in scale was required to cope with an expanding population. Therefore we may imagine that throughout this period the builders had in this respect a fairly consistent specification: the variables lay much more in other areas. In the first place there was the new ideology of the patrons who wanted constantly bigger and better churches — an ideology we have noted already. Then there was the response of the professional builders to this demand: they were developing an improved technology and a better exploitation of resources to enable them to construct the new churches; and at the same time, and no doubt encouraged by the patrons, they were creating a new aesthetic style. These changes in the first instance affected only major churches; but in the long run minor churches also would come to benefit from the new technology and the new style.

However, it is precisely because the interaction between major buildings and minor buildings can have come about in a number of different ways that we are in difficulty when explaining any particular case. Some of the possible scenarios are these:

i. An important patron who has workmen engaged on a major building sends some of them to work on a parish church for which he also has a responsibility;
ii. A mason who has been engaged on a major building project that has been completed looks round for alternative employment and contracts to build a parish church;
iii. A mason who has been trained in the old ways, and does not understand the new technology, nonetheless has an eye for the decorative details of the new buildings and tries to reproduce them in his own way;
iv. A younger mason perhaps, who has not himself worked on a major new building project but yet appreciates the new technology, tries to adapt his own work to the new standards.

In each case the results are likely to be quite different in appearance, but each may be contemporary in construction — and the more primitive looking could sometimes even be later in date than the more sophisticated.

The implications of all these problems in dating are considerable, as we can see by looking at the great corpus of Anglo-Saxon churches written by the Taylors.[15] The intention of this from the outset was to include not only churches of pre-Conquest date, but all churches up to *c.* 1100 which displayed features of Anglo-Saxon workmanship. The majority of features that are there held to be characteristic of Anglo-Saxon workmanship are technological rather than stylistic, and the result might have achieved a consistent catalogue of genuinely pre-Conquest buildings, together with those erected by Anglo-Saxon masons continuing to work up till *c.* 1100 (or perhaps somewhat later). But matters are not so straightforward, for in some cases a building is included because a Romanesque stylistic feature is handled in a primitive way, and this is assumed to be synonymous with Anglo-Saxon — which is a questionable assumption. At other times buildings are included which the authors say they have no conclusive evidence for assigning to a late Anglo-Saxon rather than an early Norman date — and the reason for their inclusion thus remains uncertain.

Very frequently one of the conclusive reasons for the Taylors including a particular building in their corpus is that it contains more than one period of work and that an earlier phase demonstrably precedes one that can be dated as 'Early Norman'.[16] A similar argument, indeed, is used for defining the basic list of features characteristic of Anglo-Saxon workmanship: that is, they occur fairly consistently in contexts that demonstrably precede an early Norman phase. However, while not wishing to dispute that we can by these means make a broad distinction between Anglo-Saxon architecture and developed Romanesque architecture, I cannot for a moment accept the possibility of making fine distinctions in 11th-century chronology by these means. We simply cannot date 'Early Norman' features at parish church level in the clear-cut way that the Taylors seem to think possible.

I say this, not to denigrate the important work done by the Taylors, but only to suggest that if we are looking at the problems of parish churches through the 11th and 12th centuries we must adopt a quite different approach to that which may yield results when our interest is focussed exclusively on Anglo-Saxon architecture. I doubt in fact whether it is possible to produce, with the tools available, an entirely consistent catalogue of Anglo-Saxon churches of the 11th century, or even one of all churches (Anglo-Saxon and 'Norman') earlier than 1100. The only sort of catalogue that could be fairly confident of completeness for the 11th century would be one running through to 1150 or 1200 — which would transfer the ragged edge to a later date.

What then are the problems that we should be isolating in our attempt to assemble the data into chronological patterns (that is, relative chronology in the first place and absolute chronology afterwards)? In the first place we need to make a clear distinction between technological and stylistic developments. We have, thanks to the Taylors, come to appreciate many characteristic features of Anglo-Saxon technology, and have become aware of other features of disputable pre-

Conquest or post-Conquest form. We need now to move on to examine the stages by which the new technology of the 11th and 12th centuries moved down from major buildings to parish level, and to consider the extent to which it was there accepted or rejected. At the same time, but without confusion, we need to look at the problem of the adoption of the Romanesque style in minor buildings. In so doing we must avoid isolating the earliest phases of this stylistic process from the later phases; and we need to seek an understanding of the dividing line between what is archaic in the sense of genuinely early, and what is primitive in the sense of folk art.

The New Technology

One of the major characteristics of 11th- and 12th-century architecture in France was the development and spread of a new technology in masonry buildings. At the beginning of the period there was a diverse tradition of building techniques, inherited in part from Antiquity and encompassing *petit appareil* masonry and brick banding, and in part representing such universal characteristics as rubble construction with only sparing use of dressed stonework. In some cases these techniques continued to be employed for great churches through a large part of the 11th century, but elsewhere they gave way to a more consistent use of ashlar masonry. Thus at Jumièges (Normandy), where the church of St. Peter had been built largely in rubble at the beginning of the 11th century, by the middle of the same century the church of St. Mary was being constructed with a systematic use of medium-to-large-sized blocks of ashlar. The latter was the technique apparently adopted in the decades following 1050 for the earliest constructional phases at Westminster Abbey – the first major Romanesque church in England.

But Jumièges was not the end of the story, for the classic Romanesque style of Normandy, that represented by the great abbeys in Caen, shows a further development. The blocks of ashlar were reduced in size to a modest and consistent dimension and were laid with fairly thick joints with ribbon pointing between them. This technique is one that can be paralleled in other regions, and especially in the Loire valley – from where it could have been introduced to Normandy. At St-Etienne in Caen the ashlar is used fairly prodigally, but elsewhere ashlar of similar character is restricted to the dressings while the main wall is of rendered rubble (as at Cerisy-la-Forêt, where the rubble is laid with frequent herringbone courses).

In England the Caenais type of masonry was certainly introduced in the 1070s, as can be seen in the two great Canterbury churches of Christ Church and St. Augustine's, and it continued to be widely used (often in conjunction with rubble walling) up until *c.* 1090 or 1100 when a finer-jointed masonry started to be laid. But what evidence is there for this specific Caenais technology being used in England below the level of the major churches? The answer is very little. One specific instance is the collegiate chapel of St. Nicholas at Bramber, Sussex, built probably in the early 1070s by William de Braose adjacent to his castle. The character of this building, considered in association with its early date, is likely to indicate the employment of masons from Normandy (who perhaps worked also on the castle, the surviving gatehouse of which is constructed of flintwork laid largely in herringbone technique).

The very absence, however, of any large number of minor churches constructed with a technology comparable to the major churches of *c.* 1070 to 1090 can mean one of two things: either, that there were few parish churches constructed in the decades following the Conquest; or, that minor churches were constructed but in a different technology. The plausibility of the latter alternative is increased by the fact that old-fashioned technology was sometimes used on the major buildings themselves. Thus at Exeter, the castle gatehouse of perhaps the 1070s or '80s is of an overall form that may be Norman, but the upper stages provide examples of triangular-headed windows and doorways that derive from Anglo-Saxon technology and must indicate the employment of at least one native English mason on the work. Later in date at Durham Cathedral can be found examples of double-splayed windows, which may again suggest a continuity with Anglo-Saxon technology – although double-splayed windows were of widespread occurence also on the Continent (albeit in contexts that are generally, but not exclusively, pre-Romanesque).

As an hypothesis to be tested further I would suggest, therefore, that minor churches of the last third of the 11th century were only in isolated instances built in an ashlar technology closely comparable to that of the major buildings. In the majority of cases their technology is more likely to be related to an earlier tradition of rubble construction with only a sparing use of ashlar dressings – a tradition that to a limited extent survived into the late 11th century even in major buildings, but which was more characteristic of an earlier date in both Normandy and England. If this hypothesis were true then we should have to follow into the 12th century the search for a closer technological accommodation between minor and major buildings – and this will be considered further below.

The Romanesque Style

The study of the Romanesque style, as of its associated technology, is a vast subject from which it is possible here to isolate only one or two trends that are relevant to minor church buildings. These are: the development of piers and jambs from a plain rectangular form to a composite form with decorative colonnettes; and the development of arches from a plain rectangular form to a moulded form.

The pre-Romanesque tradition on the Continent employed almost exclusively plain rectangular jambs and arches (though a jamb might occasionally receive a column *en délit*) and this tradition can be seen surviving into the 11th century. However, by the second quarter of the century a different, Romanesque, tradition was firmly establishing itself. In this tradition we can see (as in the crypt of Auxerre Cathedral, begun *c.* 1023 × 1035) the jambs and piers transformed by the addition to the reveal of a half-columnar shaft constructed in ashlar masonry coursed in with the pier. The arch itself retains a plain rectangular arris, but the soffit has a roll moulding corresponding to the half-column of the pier. From Burgundy or the Loire valley this new style spread into Normandy, as for example in the abbey of Bernay (probably of the second quarter of the 11th century). The details at Bernay are largely similar to Auxerre except that there are arches of two orders with, in one instance, a diminutive roll moulding in the angle between the orders.

On the available evidence the development had proceeded no further than this before the middle of the 11th century, and several features that we regard as typically Romanesque are first seen after 1050. Thus at Le Mont St-Michel (where the crossing piers were built *c.* 1048 × 1058) the transepts show a roll moulding on the arris of an arch, with a colonnette on the angle of the jamb below to support it. In the nave gallery of the same building an arris roll is to be seen outlined by a cavetto moulding. These trends reached their apogée in St-Etienne at Caen, begun *c.* 1064 and probably still under construction into the 1080s (and thus substantially a post-Conquest building), where arris roll mouldings and angle colonnettes are used consistently for the majority of the larger arches. The cavetto moulding outlining the arris roll, however, only makes a more timid appearance in the west portals, while the soffit roll is confined to the arches of the central crossing.

In England it should probably be assumed that Westminster Abbey was similar to the nave of Jumièges in having (alternate) compound piers with four attached half-columns, but in lacking angle colonnettes or any arch mouldings. It is thus first in the major buildings of the 1070s that we can see a wide range of decorative pier and arch forms introduced — and in these cases specifically the Caenais type, as for example at St. Augustine's Abbey, Canterbury. The Anglo-Norman English took up this tradition with particular zest and developed it to its ultimate expression, as in the early 12th-century nave of Ely or as at Durham. They also availed themselves swiftly of the new fashion for additional carved decoration to archways, beginning with the chevron that first appeared in England and Normandy around the turn of the century.

But if the main line of this development in major buildings from Westminster onwards is reasonably clear, the same cannot be said of minor buildings. How far if at all, had any of the Continental developments affected England in the second quarter of the 11th century? And how quickly did ideas transfer from major to minor buildings in the second half of the century? We cannot, in the absence of sure dates for the key buildings, give any final answers; but some options seem more plausible than others.

A key monument in all this is the church of Stow (Lincs). The actual origins of the church are uncertain, but *c.* 1053 × 1055 Earl Leofric established there a cathedral-type chapter, while according to the generally reliable local historian Henry of Huntingdon Leofric also built (which should probably be interpreted as *re*built) the church.[17] Following the Conquest Bishop Remi founded an abbey at Stow *c.* 1091, but this was suppressed *c.* 1093–4. The existing church has a nave and chancel entirely rebuilt in the 12th century, but earlier fabric survives in the vicinity of the crossing and transepts. The actual arches of the crossing are elaborately moulded in a mature Romanesque way with arris rolls and double cavettos; these are quite impossible before a date around the time of the Conquest but would fall happily into place a generation afterwards: they must surely date therefore to the time and patronage of Bishop Remi *c.* 1091. In this case it is therefore highly instructive to compare Stow with the approximately contemporary work of Bishop Remi on Lincoln Minster. The latter shows a use of arris rolls and cavettos that is quite orthodox by Norman canons, and is likely to be the work of Norman-trained masons. The mouldings of Stow, however, though taking the arris role and cavetto as a starting point, have developed these in a way that no Norman mason would have countenanced: they must be the work of an English mason (albeit one working for a Norman patron) who conceivably could have received a not very thorough training in the cathedral workshop at Lincoln before being sent to Stow.

But the crossing arches at Stow do not exhaust the question of Romanesque influences. The piers of the arches, which are clearly of a different phase of construction, are also susceptible of a Romanesque interpretation insofar as they use bold half-columnar shafts to flank the piers, while both the half-columns and jambs are constructed in ashlar.[18] However, the ashlar is not laid in the standard Caenais way, nor are there any half-columns attached to the reveals of the jambs. If the piers at Stow in fact date to *c.* 1050 then a Romanesque influence upon their design seems a possible explanation — but is not conclusive.

Stow was a building at the top level of patronage and so wider influences on its design are not inexplicable. Stow in turn could then have influenced lesser churches such as Skipwith where similar stylistic features appear. But what of minor buildings like Wittering (Cambs.) and Clayton (Sussex)? At Wittering we can see a similarity to Stow in the use of half-columnar mouldings on the face of the wall; but the moulding on the reveal of the jamb and continuing round the soffit of the arch is a different matter, for it directly parallels Continental Romanesque forms of the second quarter of the 11th century. Is there in fact a Continental connection or merely a fortuitous resemblance? The latter seems a very unsatisfactory explanation; while, on the other hand, it may be thought that the sort of mason who built the small church of Wittering (whose technique of handling stone proclaims him certainly English) was not likely to be in the class of international travellers. If Wittering is related to Continental developments, therefore, it seems essential to postulate an intermediary in the form of a major building directly subject to Continental influence and transmitting it on to minor buildings like Wittering — or Clayton, or Sompting.[19]

The questions raised above about the dating of some Romanesque minor churches that have sometimes been claimed as pre-Conquest apply *a fortiori* to those churches which reflect Continental developments not of the second but of the third and fourth quarters of the 11th century. Thus the phase of rebuilding at Hadstock (Essex) which accounted for the crossing arches and north doorway[20] shows the influence of a milieu where angle colonnettes and arris roll mouldings had developed, and a date before the third quarter of the 11th century is unlikely. Nevertheless at Hadstock the ashlar of these features is handled in a distinctly un-Norman way, while the windows in the rubble walling are of double-splayed type. The likely explanation is again perhaps an English mason deriving decorative ideas from a major post-Conquest building.

At Bosham (Sussex)[21] the inserted chancel arch has been claimed as Anglo-Saxon despite the fact that its inspiration is thoroughly Norman, with its grouping of half-columns and angle colonnettes in the jambs, and its mouldings to the arch with soffit roll, angle rolls and cavettos. The masonry also, with its regular coursing, shows an approach to the technology associated with Romanesque architecture. Nevertheless, some of the details of the design are singular: the bases, capitals and imposts, and the proportions of the mouldings. It is difficult to imagine a Norman mason as responsible, and an Englishman seems likely — working not before *c.* 1090 (and presumably under the patronage of Bishop Osbern). Thus in style and context there is a close parallel to the later phase at Stow.

Most of the minor buildings I have referred to in the previous few paragraphs suggest a similar context: that is, one in which a first generation or so of major Romanesque buildings was erected in a style that copied or developed from Continental orthodoxy; while many minor churches remained the preserve of masons trained in insular pre-Romanesque traditions, who might be attracted by some of the decorative features of the new architecture but who did not understand it as a comprehensive system of building. However, this fairly simple situation did not remain the case for long, because after a generation or so the architects of the major churches were growing tired of orthodoxy and were looking round for new ideas. Thus the designers of great buildings like Durham Cathedral and Ely Cathedral[22] moved in the direction of a new decorative programme which seems to have some affinity with pre-Conquest sensibilities. The changed situation would have presented interesting possibilities at the level of minor churches, for the gap between them and major churches could have seemed lessened, and the opportunity presented for a fusion — for a restatement of older insular ideas in a more up-to-date dress. But is there evidence for this in practice? I think that there is, and that this interpretation explains such buildings as Langford (Oxon.) and Milborne Port (Somerset).

Milborne Port is a building which is manifestly dated to the late 11th century by its sculptured decoration.[23] It was, moreover, the church of a royal manor and was held before and after the Conquest by the important royal clerk Regenbald,[24] so a high level of patronage may have been involved. In many ways the architecture is fairly orthodox by Continental Romanesque standards — as for instance in the south portal with its colonnettes and roll mouldings. But in other ways it is less orthodox: for example, in the flattening of the roll mouldings of the crossing arches, and in their band capitals. The external decorative arcading of the chancel suggests a parallel with the Anglo-Saxon chapel at Bradford-on-Avon, while the demolished west facade had intersected triangular arcading suggesting a glance back at Anglo-Saxon buildings like the apse of Wing, but its reinterpretation in terms of Romanesque intersected arcading. The transept stair turret has a riot of *opus reticulatum* masonry which, while paralleled in other major Romanesque buildings in England, may first have been used at Westminster Abbey. Again, the plan involving a cruciform building with a crossing tower wider than the nave relates to a pre-Conquest tradition (for example, probably Stow). The important point about Milborne Port, however, is that all these features are welded together into an articulate and satisfying whole: a truly Anglo-Norman fusion has been achieved.

If such a competent fusion was achieved in the best minor buildings by the end of the 11th century, we may go on to ask what the result would look like if something similar were attempted but less competently executed? Might it not be confusingly similar to the buildings of the previous generation that showed an awkward co-existence between pre-Conquest and Romanesque elements? If so, then it would make it very difficult to assign many individual buildings to a precise period: a 'primitive' conjunction of features not always being the result of an early date.

This area of real uncertainty is not, I believe, one that

bedevils only our study of the 11th century. It is as much, I suggest, a problem of the 12th — but one which we have not really started to define. Thus in the 12th century splendid parish churches such as that at Brook (Kent), which was clearly built by the cathedral workshop from Canterbury in the early years of the century, are always going to be found in a minority. The simpler buildings are going to be much more reticent in indicating their date by their style or their technology — which may confuse the unwary into claiming an Anglo-Saxon date.

A 12th-Century Case-Study

In the final section of this paper I would like to illustrate with reference to a particular region the real difficulty of pinning down a clearly-defined threshold between pre-Romanesque and Romanesque in the late 11th and early 12th centuries. The region is the north-western part of the former East Riding of Yorkshire.

I have referred above to the church of Skipwith, the west tower of which I believe to be (below the Gothic bell-chamber) an homogeneous construction of the middle years of the 11th century;[25] and I have referred to the possibility of some Early Romanesque influence in the mouldings of the tower arch. Despite this, the character of the masonry — betokening the gathering of available materials rather than systematic quarrying — belongs firmly to the technological stage associated with pre-Romanesque architecture. Skipwith then represents the level of evolution on the eve of the Norman Conquest of the region.

Following the Norman Conquest the first generation of major churches ringed the region but did not actually penetrate into it: York Minster, Lastingham Abbey, St. Mary's Abbey at York, Selby Abbey. It was only in the second quarter of the 12th century that this situation changed with the foundation of the Augustinian and Arrouaisian houses of Bridlington Priory (by 1113 × 1114), Kirkham Priory (c. 1122, or 1122 × 1130), Warter Abbey (c. 1132) and North Ferriby Priory (c. 1140?); then in the 1150s came the Cistercians, Gilbertines and Benedictine nuns. But where did this situation leave the development of minor churches? There are various indicators, as was realised by John Bilson, whose important papers on this subject have not universally received the credit they properly deserve.[26]

One of the key monuments is the church of Weaverthorpe, which is proclaimed by an inscribed sundial to have been built by one Herbert of Winchester. This Herbert must have been either the father or son of the name, who conjointly were granted the manor of Weaverthorpe c. 1108 × 1114 by Archbishop Thomas of York. Subsequently William, the brother of the younger Herbert, gave the church of Weaverthorpe to the canons of Nostell Priory, probably at the time of its foundation c. 1120 × 1122.[27] The likely outside dates for the construction of the church, therefore, would seem to be between 1108 and 1122 (unless, as may seem perhaps less likely, the church were rebuilt only following the donation to Nostell). The 12th-century church comprised an unaisled nave, a rectangular chancel and a west tower, constructed in neat and regular ashlar masonry which certainly belongs to the new technology. The chancel and tower arches, the doorways and the windows are all of austere unmoulded character, and only in the bell-chamber openings do any decorative colonnettes occur.

The austere character of the tower of Weaverthorpe is closely comparable to that of the nearby church of Kirby Grindalythe, although the latter has a more ornate west doorway with colonnettes. A church at Kirby Grindalythe was given by Walter Espec to Kirkham Priory, perhaps at the time of the latter's foundation c. 1122 (or 1122 × 1130);[28] but as with Weaverthorpe there remains perhaps a question as to whether this was the surviving building or whether the church was rebuilt subsequent to the donation to Kirkham.

The tower of Weaverthorpe, however, must also be compared and contrasted with that at Wharram-le-Street, which has been claimed as of Anglo-Saxon date against Bilson.[29] The manor of Wharram-le-Street was held in 1086 by Nigel Fossard but at that time seems to have been deserted. Nigel, however, must have built up the estate again for, following his death, his son Robert was able to donate the church and other property for endowing a prebend in York Minster for the canons of Nostell Priory. This donation may be dated between Robert's succeeding his father c. 1120, and Henry I's charter to Nostell, probably issued in January 1122, which confirms the donation. Thus Nostell acquired Wharram-le-Street at much the same time as Weaverthorpe: but what are the implications of this for the fabric?

The early fabric of Wharram-le-Street church comprised an unaisled nave and chancel and a west tower. It is not possible to be certain whether the tower and west wall of the nave are in bond, but the character of the openings in the tower is distinctively different from the chancel arch and south nave doorway. The tower is constructed of neat rectangular blocks of Calcareous Gritstone, but without the regularity of Weaverthorpe. At ground level is a west doorway which I believe (against Taylor) to be integral with the surrounding walling and which is of mature Romanesque form: with angle colonnettes to the jambs, and with arris roll and cavetto to the arch — though the arch has a curious recessed soffit. The capitals of the doorway and tower arch are comparable with examples elsewhere that may be dated no earlier than the second half of the 11th century (Kirkdale, N. Yorks.; Broughton, Humberside; Netheravon, Wilts.). The bell chamber of the tower has twin openings, surrounded by stripwork, which are clearly comparable with St. Mary Bishophill Junior in York (an undated building), but which here are equally clearly contemporary with the ground-floor doorway.

What is the date of this package of features at Wharram-le-Street? Here I believe that John Bilson's analysis was essentially right. He compared the details of the west portal at Wharram with the chancel arch of St. Rule's church at St. Andrews and suggested that they were built by the same masons. At Wharram he pointed out that the treatment of the west portal was impossible in a Yorkshire context before the 1090s, while at St. Andrews he associated St. Rule's chapel with Bishop Robert (elected 1124), a one-time canon of Nostell. This is not the place to set forth an extended justification for Bilson's analysis and dating of St. Rule's against Taylor's, but I believe the former to be well-founded and to constitute evidence for an approximately contemporary stylistic date for Wharram-le-Street — that is, in the 1120s. To make sense then of the hypothesis that it was the Nostell connexion that accounts for the similarities between Wharram and St. Rule's, it would be necessary to suppose that the actual date of Wharram is immediately following the donation to Nostell *c.* 1120 × 1122, rather than preceding this event.

We are now led to the conclusion that the towers of Weaverthorpe and Kirby Grindalythe (whether before or after their respective donations to Nostell and Kirkham) and of Wharram-le-Street are more-or-less contemporary. If this is so, the manifest differences between them must be indicative of the fact that our stylistic chronologies (which might place Wharram a generation or more before the other two churches) simply do not correspond at all closely to absolute chronology. Absolute chronology does not necessarily bear out the niceties of an evenly-spaced stylistic progression.

These considerations may be relevant in examining another church that might be considered to have a similar *historical* context to Kirby Grindalythe, but which stylistically belongs to a different world. The church of Garton-on-the Wolds, which was recorded in Domesday Book, was one of those apparently given to Kirkham Priory by Walter Espec at the time of the foundation *c.* 1122, and was confirmed to the Priory by a charter of 1130 × 1139.[30] According to the tradition of Rievaulx Abbey it was the Rector of Garton, Walter Espec's uncle William, who in fact urged his nephew to found Kirkham Priory as well as Rievaulx and Warden Abbeys. A close connection between Kirkham and Garton might thus seem plausible. A date in the 1130s has often been accepted for the church of Garton,[31] perhaps in part on the basis of Walter Espec's charter (though this constitutes no real evidence), and there is nothing impossible about this stylistically. Like Weaverthorpe, Wharram-le-Street and perhaps Kirby Grindalythe, the church of Garton is a three-celled building with chancel, nave and west tower. However, whereas the former buildings were characterised by their stark sobriety, Garton is marked by its rich decoration, especially on the portals with their triple orders of colonnettes and chevron ornament, all executed in beautiful ashlar masonry. This makes the point that if the former buildings are to be dated to the 1120s and Garton to the 1130s then some dramatic new factor must have intervened between them.

Was the new factor leading to architectural change the advent of new architects into the region with the inception of building work on the great religious houses in the 1120s? Unfortunately these major buildings are known only in rather sketchy detail. At Kirkham Priory the first church was in plan very simple, with an unaisled nave and deeply projecting transepts; but in the superstructure at least some decorative detail appeared, as is indicated by the surviving part of the east doorway from the nave into the cloister. Whether or not the church of the canons of Kirkham provided any precise parallels to the ornament of Garton, it may be argued that the reformed religious orders opened up the region to architectural development and that, even when they eschewed elaborate ornament in their own monastic buildings, such ornament (emanating from more uninhibited centres such as York) came in as part of the same process of development as and when this affected the parish churches.[32]

Conclusion

If the thesis argued here for the East Riding is approximately correct then it has wide implications for the study of minor churches. It means that at parochial level there was a tendency to retain old-fashioned traditions, long after these had been left behind in national and international circles. Change only came slowly: first, in isolated instances in response to particular circumstances of patronage; secondly, at a general level when the weight of example of major church building could no longer be ignored. However, since the extent and chronology of major church building varied significantly from region to region, we can expect no uniform pattern for minor buildings as between, say, Yorkshire and Sussex, or Kent and Norfolk. There will be widely diverse regional patterns found. Some of these patterns are the subject of other papers in this volume, and these may be used in the evaluation of the hypothesis here put forward.

In terms of major churches the Great Rebuilding was a phenomenon with a very specific programme, concentrated into the first two or three generations following the middle of the 11th century — although it was extended thereafter by the fresh wave of building for the reformed religious orders. However, at parochial level, whereas there was in the 11th and 12th centuries much rebuilding of already established churches (and perhaps less in the way of the foundation of new ones), it was spread out in a rather diffuse way. This diffuse character was something that was not only chronological but also stylistic and technological. Thus, while in South-East England we might find in the 1070s an isolated parish church that was thoroughly 'Norman' in style and technology, yet in the North we might still find in the 1120s a building that retained features of pre-Conquest origin. This late appearance of such features can either represent a straightforward survival of traditions at a lower cultural level than the major buildings — a simple 'folk art' — or it can reflect a continued currency of those traditions provided by an assimilation of Norman and Anglo-Saxon elements at the highest cultural level.

Notes

1. *Historia Translationis Sancti Augustini*, ed. Migne, *Patrologia Latina*, clv, col. 32.
2. F. Barlow (ed.), *Life of King Edward the Confessor* (London, 1962), xlv–xlviii.
3. R.D.H. Gem, 'A Recession in English Architecture during the Early 11th Century and its Effect on the Development of the Romanesque Style' *JBAA*, xxxviii (1975), 28–49.
4. William of Malmesbury, *Gesta Regum*, ed. W. Stubbs, ii (Rolls ser. xl, 1889), 306.
5. R.D.H. Gem, 'L'Architecture pré-Romane et Romane en Angleterre', *Bulletin Monumental*, cxlii (1984), 233–272. Bibliographical references will there be found for many of the major churches discussed here.
6. *C&S*, 389–90.
7. *C&S*, 472 note 4.
8. *C&S*, 476–7, 97–8.
9. B. Thorpe, *Ancient Laws and Institutes of England* (London, 1840), 201.
10. Morris, *CBA*, 65–71.
11. Goscelin, *Liber Confortatorius*, ed. C.H. Talbot, *Studia Anselmiana*, fasc. xxxviii (*Analecta Monastica*, 3rd ser., Rome, 1955), 93.
12. William of Malmesbury, *Vita Wulfstani*, ed. R. R. Darlington, Camden Soc. xl (1928), I.14, III.10, 14.
13. Ibid., II.17, 22.
14. Morris, *CBA*, Fig. 24.
15. Taylor & Taylor.
16. Ibid., 736–7.
17. Henry of Huntingdon, *Historia Anglorum*, ed. T. Arnold (Rolls Ser. lxxiv, 1879), 196. The church is documented before this at least as early as the time of Bishop Æthelric, 1016–1034, and its foundation may in fact have been considerably earlier again than this.
18. Gem. op.cit. note 5, Fig. 13. This figure also shows the pier profiles of several of the buildings discussed below.
19. This argument is further developed in R.D.H. Gem, 'The Early Romanesque Tower of Sompting Church, Sussex', *Anglo-Norman Studies*, v (1982), 121–128; idem, 'The "Lewes Group" of Wall paintings: Architectural Considerations', Ibid. vi (1983), 236–7.
20. W. Rodwell, 'The Archaeological Investigation of Hadstock Church, Essex, an Interim Report', *Antiq. J.*, lvi (1976), 55–71. See also E. Fernie, 'The Responds and Dating of St Botolph's, Hadstock', *JBAA*, cxxxvi (1983), 62–73, where a date in the 1060s or '70s is suggested.
21. R.D.H. Gem, 'Holy Trinity Church, Bosham', *Archaeol. J.*, cxlii (1985), 32–6.
22. J. Bony, 'Durham et la Tradition Saxonne', in S. Crosby et al., *Etudes d'Art Mediéval Offertes a Louis Grodecki* (Paris, 1981), 1–29. See also Gem op.cit. note 5.
23. G. Zarnecki, '1066 and Architectural Sculpture', *Proc. British Acad.*, lii (1966), 98–9.
24. Blair, 'Secular Ministers', 134.
25. Taylor & Taylor, 855, seeks to rebut the criticism made by the present author (R.D.H. Gem, 'The Origins of the Early Romanesque Architecture of England', unpublished Cambridge University PhD Thesis, 1973, 405, n.18) that his theory of the double-splayed ground floor windows having been adapted from an earlier single-splayed form was implausible. Against Taylor it may be argued that the monolith from which the external head of the window is cut is above the level that any head for a single-splayed window must have been sited if the position of the latter were fixed by projecting the inner splay through the outer face of the wall: Taylor's attempt to counter this involves an external embrasure to his hypothetical early window that is as deep as the supposedly later outer splay. If the theory of the alteration to the windows is rejected then there is no substantial evidence for more than one Anglo-Saxon phase in the tower — which all the other evidence suggests is unitary.
26. J. Bilson, 'Weaverthorpe Church and its Builder', *Archaeologia*, lxxii (1922), 51–70; Idem, 'Wharram le Street Church, Yorkshire, and St Rule's Church, St. Andrews', Ibid. lxxiii (1922–3), 55–72. The documentary references cited by Bilson are not further cited below. [On Wharram-le-Street cf. also below, p. 196: *Ed.*]
27. On the foundation of Nostell see: J. Wilson, 'The Foundation of the Austin Priories of Nostell and Scone', *Scottish Hist. Rev.*, vii (1910), 156–7; J.C. Dickinson, *The Origins of the Austin Canons and their Introduction into England* (London, 1950), 120–121; W.E. Wightman, 'Henry I and the Foundation of Nostell Priory', *Yorks. Archaeol. Jnl.* xli (1963–6), 57–60.
28. Dickinson, op.cit. note 27, 123.
29. Taylor & Taylor, 647–653, where it is argued that the two arches in the tower are inserted into an earlier fabric.
30. *Cartularium Rievallense*, ed. J.C. Atkinson, Surtees Soc. lxxxiii (1887), No. 216 (cf. 347). The charter is dated 1130 × 1139 by the mention of Archibishop Thurstan and Bishop Geoffrey of Durham; despite its appearance therefore it is some years later than the foundation date of Kirkham argued for by Dickinson.
31. For example, N. Pevsner, *The Buildings of England: Yorkshire East Riding* (Harmondsworth, 1972).
32. For some interesting aspects of the later 12th-century development see L.A.S. Butler, 'The Labours of the Months and "the Haunted Tanglewood": Aspects of Late 12th-Century Sculpture in Yorkshire', *Proc. Leeds Philos. Lit. Soc., Lit. Hist. Sect.*, xviii (1982), 79–95.

III. The Anglo-Saxon Gilds

Gervase Rosser

'These are the terms which Urki and the gild-brothers at Abbotsbury have agreed on for the praise of God and the honour of St. Peter and the need of their souls ...' Urki's gild was founded in the second quarter of the 11th century; it is one of a small group of 10th- and 11th-century gilds for which statutes are extant.[1] These associations hold a certain interest for those who would trace the history of English parishes between c. 1000 and c. 1200. The character of the bulk of available sources has dictated that most accounts of medieval religious practice have concentrated upon the Church in its institutional aspect. Ecclesiastical government generated a mass of materials of irresistible richness for the study of ecclesiastical government. The rôle of the layman, both as participant in and as active influence upon the life of his church, is inevitably harder to document. The nature of this rôle in the period in question is, however, to some extent illuminated by the evidence of the gild statutes which form the subject of the present brief discussion.

The five gilds of before c. 1100 whose constitutions survive vary from one another, but share significant features in common. The activity of each was focussed upon a minster church, respectively Abbotsbury (Dorset), Bedwyn (Wilts.), Cambridge and (in two cases) Exeter.[2] Yet the motivation to form a society appears to have come in every case from among the laity, who moreover comprised a preponderance of the membership. The composition of the gilds is a little obscure, even in the documented cases. Urki's gild, under his noble patronage, accommodated two ranks of membership. A similar division was observed in the older (10th-century) gild at Exeter. The Cambridge society was a gild of thegns, which allowed an inferior place in the hall to retainers. The fourteen village gilds of Devon recorded in c. 1100 seem less aristocratic; some were gathered under the village priest. All the sets of gild ordinances evince a major concern with the provision of funeral rites and memorial masses for members after their deaths. The members of the Abbotsbury gild and those of the Cambridge gild whose statutes were set down in c. 1000 undertook to fetch home the body of a deceased brother; in the former case 'the minster' was the stipulated destination. The brethren of Abbotsbury made contributions (of candle-wax or money) to the minster there before the feast of St. Peter; those of Cambridge sent offerings to the monastery of St. Etheldreda at Ely. In the early 10th century the Bedwyn gild guaranteed 'five masses or five psalters for the soul' of a departed member; at the same period the gild at Exeter retained a mass-priest who sang 'two masses at each meeting, one for the living friends, the other for the departed'; and later, towards 1100, inhabitants (male and female) of a number of Devon villages, themselves affiliated to the episcopal minster of Exeter, made regular contributions to the canons in return for prayers.[3] The teams of priests who manned the old-style minsters were clearly well-suited to serve the intercessory needs of the laity who formed the gilds.[4] Those needs remained a constant from the 10th to the mid 16th century, and later medieval parish gilds were instituted with the express intention of providing additional mass-priests.[5] Such, for instance, was the gild of Corpus Christi, St. Mary and All Saints founded in 1343 in the church of St. Martin in Leicester. The brothers and sisters of this Leicester gild supported at first one and later two chaplains praying continually for their lay employers; the list of the founders was kept at the altar.[6] At the end of the middle ages the Stratford-upon-Avon gild of the Holy Cross retained no less than five priests in the town chapel, which with the parish church of Old Stratford served a large area including seven additional hamlets.[7] The circumstances, and the associated reasons for the maintenance of the gilds, appear to have been in significant respects similar in the 10th and 11th centuries to those, better documented, prevailing in the later period.[8]

The Devon village gilds of c. 1100 reflect in their association with the cathedral at Exeter the continuing attraction of a great mother church, even to fairly remote country-dwellers with local chapels of their own.[9] A dozen or so separate gilds, scattered throughout the diocese, belonged to this federation centred in Exeter. Abbreviated lists of members survive, and in several cases these lists are headed by the priest of the district.[10] No doubt the cathedral was an infinitely more impressive building than the village chapels. Yet the century-and-a-half after 1050 saw greater attention paid to the local churches, many of which, originally perhaps of wood, were rebuilt in stone at this time. The federation of Devon gilds aound 1100 may indicate a transition period of ambivalent loyalties, divided between the old minster and the nascent parish.[11] On the other hand, the wide affiliation may, in this case at least, have survived in modified form into the high middle ages to coexist with mature parochial gilds. The former appears to have been perpetuated in the Exeter gild of the Kalendar brethren; the gild of this name, first recorded under Henry I, survived later changes until the Protestant Reformation.[12] Certainly the later period could show other instances of a regional hierarchy of gilds, the majority being confined to the parishes while a single great gild drew its membership from a far wider catchment area.[13]

If one reason for the formation of later gilds was to supplement the provision of masses, another was to construct or repair the churches in which they were offered.[14] None of the surviving early gild statutes refers to this activity in connection with the minster churches to which these relate; but it is probable that at least some of the dozens of new chapels and parish churches erected in the course of the 11th and 12th centuries were paid for in this way. Some of the new churches were doubtless in private hands from the start; others meanwhile are known to have owed their beginnings to cooperative enterprise.[15] In a later instance, a chapel was erected in c. 1349 by a fraternity of neighbours at Baslow (Derbs.) because of the inconvenient distance of the parish church of Bakewell.[16] For the decades around 1100, when this situation must have been repeated many times throughout the country, documentation is almost entirely lacking. But when the construction of a church at Whistley (Berks.) in c. 1080 was justified on the grounds that the mother church of Sonning, three miles away across the River Loddon, was difficult of access from the vill, we may suspect the operation of collective pressure brought to bear by the villagers.[17] In East Anglia, at the time of Domesday Book, groups of burgesses are recorded in possession of small urban churches, whose construction may well have been a collaborative work.[18] Whether these burgesses elected their priests, in the manner of certain Italian and German parishioners, remains uncertain.[19] Later on, however, gild priests were indeed elective, being subject to appointment (and dismissal) by the lay membership of the gilds.[20]

The later medieval gilds were never wholly contained within the official structure of the parishes. Rather, the two kinds of organisation coexisted, at times though by no means always in harmony.[21] The Anglo-Saxon gilds also, on the evidence surviving, stood in an ambiguous relation to the great minster parishes and to the Church at large. Clearly the minsters benefited from lay fraternities prepared to subsidise the central teams of clergy and to ensure the return of the dead to the mother church for burial and the payment of dues. On the other hand the available statutes express in addition different concerns, less obviously sympathetic to the Church. Here the gilds betray their pre-Christian origins.[22] This pagan inheritance is most obvious in the activities surrounding the communal feast, a virtually universal feature of all gilds. Members solemnly undertook to provide the wherewithal on these occasions to render the company drunk as lords.[23] Since at least Carolingian times the uproar of gild festivities had occasioned scandal;[24] in the 12th century Walter Map wrote scornfully of 'drinking houses, called in English *ghildhus*', where these jollifications took place.[25] Worse still, in the eyes of hostile critics like Hincmar of Rheims, was the atmosphere of violence which surrounded the gild feasts. The statutes of the Anglo-Saxon gilds do indeed assume an alarming potential for aggression between their members. In particular, the Cambridge ordinances of c. 1000 consist largely of rules relating to blood-feud.[26] Although Saxon custom recognised the right of gild-brotherhoods to act in place of the kin-group in pursuit of a vendetta,[27] the oaths sworn among such leagues were naturally viewed with suspicion by both secular and ecclesiastical authorities. Carolingian capitularies had condemned them; in c. 1240 the archbishop of Bordeaux for similar reasons pronounced all such fraternities 'enemies of ecclesiastical liberties'.[28]

It is clear, therefore, that relations between the gilds and the newly emergent ecclesiastical administration of the 11th and 12th centuries were neither simple nor entirely comfortable. Nevertheless, the gilds of the period are better understood not as licensed pretexts for drunkenness and slaughter but on the contrary as a means of containing the impulse to violence. The emphasis of the statutes under consideration is upon the preservation of peace within the society; heavy penalties were imposed for illegitimate fighting or casting of insults. Certain gilds extended this concern beyond the sphere of their memberships. The 7th- and 9th-century laws of Ine and Alfred already recognised the existence of gilds capable not only of promoting solidarity among their members, but also of acting in the king's name to apprehend thieves and murderers.[29] By the late 11th century associations of *cnihtas* were recorded in the cities of London, Canterbury and Winchester, in addition to the thegns' gild of Cambridge; it is possible and even likely that all of these urban gilds were performing local administrative functions on behalf of the crown.[30] The Dorset gild of Urki, protégé of Canute and housecarl of the Confessor, should perhaps be seen in the same light; the formation of a fellowship gave Urki the opportunity to bind in loyalty to himself the free men of the locality into which he had been intruded.[31]

At this point it becomes difficult to distinguish between the gilds as agents of royal authority and as promoters of Christian peace. Almsgiving, for example, which was enjoined upon members of the gilds of Abbotsbury and Cambridge, was a Christian imperative enshrined in the Saxon law codes;[32] while the social harmony upheld in the gild statutes was hardly less a religious than a royal ideal.[33] The Cambridge gild of thegns of c. 1000 should be seen in the same context as the 'Peace of God' associations of contemporary continental Europe.[34] Both exemplify pagan practices (above all the blood-feud) infused at the same period with a new leaven of Christianity.[35] The result, in the case of the gilds, was to transform purely secular drinking clubs into agencies of divine peace. The transformation was never complete; there was always an element in gild membership justly challenged by the jibe: 'If it were not for the feasting, few or none would come'.[36] Yet to others the language of the 11th-century gilds offered a practical rôle in promoting a more Christian society, and by the same token an enhanced sense of personal dignity.

The rôle of the laity in the gilds at this period deserves to be underlined. In the two centuries between 1000 and 1200 the monastic monopoly on the Christian life was broken.[37] New opportunities were recognised for lay men and women to lead religious careers in the world. Manifestations of this change are manifold: the formation of 'third' and military religious orders; the career and social concern of a Valdès of Lyon; the sermons of Honorius of Autun addressed severally to the different classes of lay society; the representations of artisanal crafts which took their place in the cosmic order on the west façade of Chartres cathedral. The Gregorian emphasis upon the distinctiveness of the clergy as a class served also to differentiate the laity as a separate *ordo* with its own part to play in God's universe.[38] In the new world which had been created by the beginning of the 13th century the gilds in their various forms would have many parts to play.[39] In the earlier period, these Christian fellowships had helped to prepare the laity for the responsibilities which would come to them from c. 1100 onwards as members of the new parishes.[40] In the course of the 12th and 13th centuries, lay parishioners would be formally invested by canon lawyers with duties of maintenance of the church fabric, the support of the clergy and the distribution of alms.[41] These arts, and others more convivial, had been learned before 1100 through participation in the gilds.

Notes

1. *EHD*, 603–7; B. Thorpe, *Diplomatarium Anglicum Aevi Saxonii* (London, 1865), 605–14.
2. The older set of Exeter statutes survives in a leaf of a gospel-book from Exeter of the earlier 10th century; the regulations of the Cambridge gild are entered on a leaf of another gospel-book, probably from Ely (with which place the gild was associated): *EHD* loc.cit. The very holy context in which these records are preserved should be borne in mind in relation to what follows.
3. Thorpe, op.cit. note 1, 608–10.
4. The point is made by Blair, 'Secular Minsters', 141. The multi-priest establishments of the 12th century and earlier explain the prominence in that period of gilds of priests. See 'The laws of the Northumbrian priests' (c. 1020) in *EHD*, 471–6; D. Whitelock (ed.), *Anglo-Saxon Wills* (Cambridge, 1930), 24–27, 126–27 (the will of ealdorman Æthelmær, c. 983, leaving bequests to a 'mass priests' gild' and to a 'deacons' gild' at Winchester); and G.G. Meersseman, *Ordo Fraternitatis. Confraternite e Pietà dei Laici nel Medioevo*, Italia Sacra, xxiv–xxvi (Rome, 1977), 169–77 (mid 12th-century gild of London clerks). London in the later middle ages once again contained a gild of chantry and other priests, the 'Papey': see John Stow, *A Survey of London*, ed. C.L. Kingsford, 2 vols (Oxford, 1908), i, 146, 161, ii, 293; and T. Hugo, 'The Hospital of Le Papey, in the City of London', *Transactions of the London and Middlesex Archaeological Society*, v (1877), 183–221.
5. e.g. C.M. Barron, 'The Parish Fraternities of Medieval London', in C.M. Barron and C. Harper-Bill (eds.), *The Church in Pre-Reformation Society* (London, 1985), 13–37, esp. 23–24.
6. P.R.O., C47/39/71.
7. J. and L. Toulmin Smith (eds.), *English Gilds* (Early English Text Society, old ser., xl, 1870), 221–22. In Northampton in 1460, the chaplains of the various gilds founded in the church of All Saints formed themselves into a college: *VCH Northants.*, ii, 180–81. See also note 4.
8. An additional motive evinced in the early 10th-century gild at Exeter was the desire to encourage pilgrimages to Rome: 'at a pilgrimage south, each man is to contribute fivepence'. Certain gilds of the later medieval period, notably a group in Lincoln, would show a like concern. See Toulmin Smith, op.cit. note 7, 172, 180 (reference to such a gild allegedly founded in 1279), 182.
9. Although the redaction of the notices of these gilds of Devon and its borders dates from the time of Bishop Osbern, 1072 × 1103, the situation they describe is most unlikely to have arisen after the Conquest. Cf. Barlow, *Church 1000–66*, 197–98; Campbell, 'Church in Towns', esp. 133–34.
10. Thorpe. op.cit. note 1, 608–10.
11. On the development of the parish as a focus of local solidarity in the 11th and 12th centuries, see G. Duby, *La Société aux XIe et XIIe Siècles dans la Région Mâconnaise* (Paris, 1953), 285–90; and S. Reynolds, *Kingdoms and Communities in Western Europe, 900–1300* (Oxford, 1984), 79–100, ch. IV, 'The Community of the Parish'.
12. See N. Orme, 'The Kalendar Brethren of the City of Exeter', *Report and Transactions of the Devonshire Association for the Advancement of Science, Literature and Art*, cix (1977), 153–69. Although Dr. Orme does not consider the possibility of continuity from the Devon gilds of c. 1100, a connection is nevertheless highly probable. The mortuary list of the Kalendars drawn up early in the 14th century and printed by Orme contains many names of Anglo-Saxon origin, including some apparently identical with names recurring in the short lists of c. 1100 (e.g. Ordric the priest of Cullompton in c. 1100 may be recalled in the memorial list at Orme, 165).
13. e.g. the Corpus Christi gild at Boston: D.M. Owen, *Church and Society in Medieval Lincolnshire*, History of Lincolnshire, v (1981), 127. The link expressed by the offerings of the Cambridge thegns' gild to the great church of St. Etheldreda at Ely may have been perpetuated in the particular submission of later Cambridge guilds to the tutelage of the bishop of Ely. Cf. M. Bateson, (ed.), *Cambridge Gild Records*, Cambridge Antiquarian Society, 8° Publications, xxxix (1903), xxxiii, 105, 109, 119.
14. e.g. *English Historical Documents*, iv, ed. A.R. Myers (London, 1969), 741–44; Owen, op.cit. note 13, 114. For lay confraternities founded by churchmen for this purpose, see C.R. Cheney, 'Church-Building in the Middle Ages', repr. in *Medieval Texts and Studies* (Oxford, 1973), 346–63, at 360

15. (Winchester, 1202; Worcester, 1226); and Meersseman, op.cit. note 4, 108–12 (Urgel, 1096; Tarragona, 1129).
15. C.N.L. Brooke, 'The Church in the Towns, 1000–1250', *Studies in Church History*, vi (1970), 59–83; Campbell, 'Church in Towns'.
16. P.R.O., C47/38/44. Again, in the mid 14th century the chapel of St. John the Baptist was constructed at Henley-in-Arden (Warws.), whence it had been difficult to reach the parish church of Wootton Wawen. In this case the gild is not documented before 1408. It could have existed before, however, and subsequently at any rate gild and chapel were so closely identified that they were both seized together by the crown at the dissolution of the chantries: *VCH Warwicks*. iii, 206–12.
17. Lennard, *Rural England* 296, 297–98. For a *confratria* of neighbours formed to rebuild their church at Louvres (Oise) in *c*. 1250 see Reynolds, op.cit. note 11, 92. Cf. also Owen, op.cit. note 13, 6.
18. Barlow, *Church 1000–66*, 192–93; Brooke, art.cit. note 15, 78; Reynolds, op.cit. note 11, 95.
19. Reynolds, op.cit. note 11, 95.
20. e.g. A.G. Rosser, 'The Guild of St. Mary and St. John the Baptist, Lichfield: Ordinances of the late Fourteenth Century', *Staffordshire Record Society* (forthcoming).
21. See J. Bossy, *Christianity in the West 1400–1700* (Oxford, 1985), 62–63: 'We should not regard the parish as necessarily a pre-existing datum into which fraternities were going to have to fit themselves somehow...'
22. The fundamental study on continuity in the gilds from their pagan beginnings is E. Coornaert, 'Les ghildes médiévales (V^e–XIVe siècles). Définitions. Evolution', *Revue Historique*, cxcix (1948), 22–55, 208–43. See also O.G. Oexle, '*Conjuratio* et *ghilde* dans l'Antiquité et dans le Haut Moyen Age: Remarques sur la Continuité des Formes de la Vie Sociale', *Francia*, x (1982), 1–19.
23. See e.g. the heavy fine imposed upon him of the Abbotsbury gild 'who undertakes a brewing and does not do it satisfactorily'.
24. Coornaert, art.cit. note 22, *passim*.
25. Walter Map, *De Nugis Curialium*, ed. M.R. James and others (Oxford, 1983), 154–58; Reynolds, op.cit. note 11, 76. For the gildhall at Winchester, where the *chenictes* 'drank their gild' in the time of Edward the Confessor, and where a church (presumably for the gild) was built, see M. Biddle (ed.), *Winchester in the Early Middle Ages*, Winchester Studies, I (Oxford, 1976), 335–36. Urki himself provided the hall for the use of his Abbotsbury gild.
26. *EHD*, 603–5.
27. F. Seebohm, *Tribal Custom in Anglo-Saxon Law* (London, 1902), 323–24.
28. Coornaert, art.cit. note 22, 33f.; P. Michaud-Quantin, *Universitas: Expressions du Mouvement Communautaire dans le Moyen Age Latin* (Paris, 1970), 188. The oath sworn on relics is referred to explicitly in the Cambridge gild statutes. The latent threat which the gilds perennially represented to public authority is stressed by Oexle, art.cit. note 22.
29. Coornaert, art.cit. note 22, 36. Cf. also the ordinances of the 10th-century 'peace-gild' of the London district: *EHD*, 423–27.
30. Brooke & Keir, *London*, 96–98 (some kind of defensive role envisaged for the Saxon gild of London *cnihtas*: cf. present ch. IV); W. Urry, *Canterbury under the Angevin Kings* (London, 1967), 124–31 (noting the royal portreeve's headship of the merchant gild); Biddle, op.cit. note 25, 335–36 ('...The king was lord of the city [sc. Winchester] and these gilds may have been linked with the organization of town life'). There is no evidence among the English gilds of a political independence such as was enjoyed to a dangerous degree by certain gilds in 11th-century Byzantium. Cf. S. Vryonis, 'Byzantine *Democratia* and the Guilds in the Eleventh Century', *Dumbarton Oaks Papers*, xvii (1963), 287–314.
31. *EHD*, 606–7.
32. M. Deanesly, *The Pre-Conquest Church in England* (2nd edn, London, 1963), 342–45.
33. e.g. 'The gild-brother who insults another deliberately inside the gild is to make amends to the whole fellowship with his entrance fee, and afterwards to the man whom he has insulted' (Abbotsbury). The Abbotsbury statutes end with a prayer to St. Peter.
34. On which see H.E.J. Cowdrey, 'The Peace and the Truce of God in the Eleventh Century', *Past and Present*, xlvi (1970), 42–67.
35. For the attempt to graft notions of Christian chivalry onto a secular warrior ethic in the same period, see M. Keen, *Chivalry* (New Haven and London, 1984), esp. 44–63, ch. iii, 'Chivalry, the Church and the Crusade'.
36. Michaud-Quantin, op.cit. note 28, 184.
37. See esp. M.D. Chenu, *Nature, Man and Society in the Twelfth Century*, tr. J. Taylor and L.K. Little (Chicago, 1968), 261–62 and chs. 6 and 7, *passim*.
38. Meersseman, op.cit. note 4, 216–45.
39. In the later, better-documented period, the gilds' variety was infinite, and a single association would change in character from one generation to the next. This flexibility was one of the strengths of the gilds.
40. There is no satisfactory study of the 12th-century parishioners. Cf. the resigned remarks of Brett, *English Church*, 233. Bolder is the sketch of E. Mason, 'The Rôle of the English Parishioner, 1100–1500', *Jnl. of Ecclesiastical History*, xxvii (1976), 17–29; but the picture of the 'demoted' layman of the 12th century is drawn over-darkly. The broad trend noted above fostered greater rather than less lay participation.
41. See statutes of the 13th-century English Church: *Councils and Synods, with other Documents Relating to the English Church: II: AD 1205–1313*, eds. F.M. Powicke and C.R. Cheney (Oxford, 1964), i, 512–13, 647, 650, 1002–8.

IV. Parishes, Churches, Wards and Gates in Eastern London

Jeremy Haslam

It is a curious fact that no aspect of urban history has been so much neglected until recent years as its ecclesiastical history.[1]

Introduction

The subject of this paper is the interrelationship between the ecclesiastical and civil geography of the eastern part of the City of London, including the immediately extra-mural area, in the early medieval period. It is intended, first, to use both topographical and historical evidence to reconstruct the patterns of churches and their parishes in their relation to the City walls, gates, streets and wards; and second, to draw inferences from these relationships about the functions of these units in both the ecclesiastical and civil life of the City. Although this study must be viewed in relation to similar phenomena on the north and west sides of the City — and indeed in other early medieval towns — it provides in microcosm a set of data and inferences from which a more general model for the early development of both civil and ecclesiastical institutions within English towns can be formulated.

The development of urban churches and parishes in medieval towns has been discussed elsewhere, and the evidence from London itself has also been surveyed.[2] As is beginning to be appreciated, the use of topographical evidence — i.e. the spatial relationship between these churches and parishes and other components of the townscape — represents a primary source of evidence from which more general processes and functions can be inferred.[3] A similar methodology was utilised in William Page's study of early medieval London,[4] although many of his premises and conclusions have been largely superseded by more recent developments in the understanding of processes affecting the growth of early medieval towns.

It seems clear, from the evidence discussed by Brooke and Keir, that the London churches and parishes existed in essentially their late medieval form by the 12th century, and that it was the 11th, and possibly the 10th, century in which this pattern became established.[5] There is, however, enough evidence for the existence of several older churches in various parts of the City[6] to suggest that this pattern was formed (as in other parts of the country and in other towns) by the fragmentation of larger parishes or *parochiae*, and that these early churches could have formed a series, possibly a system, of sub-ministers with their own burial, baptismal and other rights.[7] Although a general examination of this pattern cannot be undertaken here, the existence and function of two of these possible secondary minsters in the eastern part of the City will be examined below.

The eastern City

As both Biddle and Hudson, and Brooke and Keir, have realised,[8] the pattern of churches outside the City walls provides one of the best sources of evidence for the reconstruction of the history of the suburbs; indeed, nowhere is this more true than in the western suburbs of London.[9] In an important sense, however, the converse is also the case: the analysis of the topography and history of the wards, streets, gates, walls and suburbs provides a body of evidence which is crucial for the interpretation of the ecclesiastical pattern, in both its spatial and functional aspects. A key to this interpretation, as it affects the eastern part of the City, is the development of the Cnichtengild and the Portsoken, and the history of the Priory of Holy Trinity Aldgate, in the 12th century and earlier.

These bodies have been discussed at length by Brooke and Keir,[10] although the possibilities of further interpretation have by no means been exhausted. The central fact is the foundation of the Augustinian Priory of Holy Trinity Aldgate in 1107–8 by Queen Matilda, who had obtained the gate and soke of Aldgate from Henry I with her acquisition of the manor of Waltham.[11] This was built on a site just inside Aldgate which had been, significantly, the site of an earlier church dedicated to the Holy Cross and St. Mary Magdalen, in which the canons of the Priory of Holy Cross at Waltham had had substantial rights.[12] The canons of Waltham had also had ecclesiastical rights in the area round the church, the whole of the later Queen's soke of Aldgate (within the walls). That these ecclesiastical rights extended over the area of the soke outside the walls can be inferred from the creation of St. Botolph's parish in this area only subsequent to, and arguably consequent upon, the foundation of the Priory (see below).

The connection of the Portsoken with the Cnichtengild is also significant. From the analysis of Brooke and Keir it appears that the Cnichtengild were a 'cross section of the city patriarchate of whatever occupation', who were beholden to a higher lord (?the king), whose primary function was military, and whose original duties would have been 'to defend the city against attack from the east'.[13] This group had rights over the Portsoken, the area of land outside the walls which at least in the 12th century and later occupied the parish of St. Botolph, which stretched from the north of Aldgate southwards to the river (see Fig. 8).[14] The rights and privileges of the Cnichtengild were given over to the prior of Holy Trinity Aldgate in 1125, 'the culmination of a period in which it had a close liaison' with the Priory,[15] by which time the Cnichtengild had become merely an association for religious purposes of some of the leading citizens of London.[16]

These facts lend themselves to a reconstruction of earlier processes and functional interrelationships beyond what has been put forward by Brooke and Keir. There are perhaps three aspects of this reinterpretation. First, from the fact of Holy Trinity's foundation as a Priory of Augustinian canons on the site of an earlier church, and from the fact that it had rights over an extensive area both within and wlthout the walls, it can be inferred that, like many other Augustinian houses, it took over the rights and spiritual jurisdiction of an earlier mother church, which was dedicated to St. Mary Magdalen. The existence of a graveyard which was newly laid out in the late Saxon period, recently excavated near the site of the church, suggests that this church was given burial rights.[17] Although there is no evidence that this church had had either secular canons or baptismal rights, its endowments and income from the area of the soke of Aldgate must have been on a scale sufficient to provide the new Priory with an adequate economic base. It seems likely that its spiritual jurisdiction extended over the area immediately outside Aldgate, part of the later St. Botolph's parish (see below). From this it can in turn be inferred that the *parochia* of this church would have been more or less exactly coterminous with the ward of Aldgate in both its intra-mural and extra-mural aspects (see Fig. 8).

A second point of reinterpretation is the origin of St. Botolph's church. Brooke and Keir have suggested[18] that it was built subsequent to the acquisition by the Priory of the rights of the Cnichtengild over the area of the Portsoken in 1125 (see below). However, a possibly more appropriate context for its foundation could have been the creation of the Priory itself in 1107–8. At this time a new church with parochial functions would have been required to serve the extramural areas of the Portsoken, formerly served by St. Mary Magdalen, the predecessor of Holy Trinity Priory. This would explain the reference in the charter of 1125 to St. Botolph's church being already in existence, and would also fit with the suggested derivation of its dedication from St. Botolph's Priory at Colchester, of which the first prior of Holy Trinity had been a canon before moving to London. This being so, the new parish of St. Botolph would have initially comprised the extra-mural part of the earlier parish of St. Mary Magdalen. It will be argued below that to this would have been added the extra-mural part of the original parish of St. Peter ad Vincula, when this area was given to Holy Trinity Priory in 1125 as part of the Portsoken.

A third point of reinterpretation is the origin and function of the Cnichtengild. Brooke and Keir have suggested that this body was formed in the reign of Edgar.[19] Given that its original function was defensive, this raises the problem of why its formation was deemed necessary at the very time when England was no longer threatened by Viking invasions. It seems more reasonable to postulate that the mid 10th-century Cnichtengild was the successor (albeit possibly in a form altered to accommodate the mercantile and/or social elements) to a group of city dwellers whose formal organisation could be associated with the defence of the eastern walls and gate in a rather earlier period of hostilities. The obvious context for this is the programme for the 'restoration' and redefence of London initiated by King Alfred in and after 886.[20]

The existence of such an organisation seems to be required by the evidence at this time of the massive conscription of the population as a whole, which has been forcefully stated by Professor Brooks.[21] As he has stressed, the population was divided into three groups, the duties of one of which was to guard the *burhs* (the *burhwaru*). That this was the context for the creation, in London at least, of an organised levy is furthermore suggested by the evidence of the early history of the Cnichtengild itself as given in the Cartulary of Holy Trinity Priory. This says that 'Thirteen knights in the days of Edgar besought of the king a certain land on the east side of London, abandoned by the inhabitants as being too burdensome, that he would grant them the same land'.[22] Although somewhat legendary in form, this seems likely to have preserved a memory of rather earlier public duties for the manning and repair of the wall, which in the peaceful conditions of the mid 10th century had become too onerous and possibly even anachronistic.[23]

This in turn raises the question of the origin of the wards themselves. Brooke and Keir have placed their formation in the middle of the 10th century.[24] This conclusion is, however, based on the premise that the origin of the wards must be associated with the origin of the Cnichtengild, assumed to be of mid 10th-century origin (see above). As presented, this is something of a circular argument. It also sidesteps the question as to how or why the wards (and indeed the Cnichtengild itself) were brought into being. If it is accepted, as Stenton has asserted, that the wards were the 'essential link between the military and civil administration',[25] it

Fig. 8 - Parishes and wards in east London.

also raises the question of why it was necessary to have created them in a period of peace. It seems therefore more reasonable to postulate that they were formed, like the predecessors of the Cnichtengild, in the period of the 'restoration' of the City under King Alfred. Just as the creation of the new streets and *hagae* can be seen as the essential physical expression of the newly-created urban order, so the formation of the wards can be seen as the essential means by which the public duties for the manning and repair of the defences were both defined and organised on a territorial basis. Indeed, if they did not exist at this time in very much their later 11th- or early 12th-century form,[26] it would be necessary to postulate just such an organisation to account, for instance, for the success of the defences of London against Viking attack in the wars of the 890s.[27] Furthermore, the nature of the wards as 'hundreds in miniature, with hundred courts and hundredal jurisdiction'[28] carries the implication that this capability for internal organisation is a reflection of the basic mechanism with which they were originally endowed, by which the public responsibilities for defence were carried out in practice.

It is in this context that the origin of the church of St. Mary Magdalen, the predecessor of Holy Trinity Priory, can possibly be viewed. An important aspect of Alfred's political response following the destruction of monasteries and churches by the Vikings throughout the 9th century was the revitalisation both of learning and of the ecclesiastical order.[29] This policy of ecclesiastical renewal appears to have been continued by his son Edward the Elder in Wessex (and later in Mercia) and his daughter Æthelflæd in western Mercia. The former continued Alfred's practice of founding churches in new *burhs*,[30] of which a good example is the foundation by Alfred of the New Minster at Winchester as the new parochial centre for the *burh*, which was brought to completion by Edward the Elder.[31] Æthelflæd also founded minsters in a number of her newly-founded *burhs*, such as at Gloucester and Chester.[32]

There is thus some justification for proposing the general hypothesis that an integral part of Alfred's burghal policy — which was continued and indeed expanded by Edward and Æthelflæd after him — involved the creation of new ecclesiastical institutions. These must have served both the advancement of learning (possibly in the form of the setting-up of schools),[33] as well as the provision of ecclesiastical facilities to the newly-populated urban centres. Given the provision of the New Minster at Winchester for this purpose, it would be expected that London would have been treated with no less concern, especially since its 'restoration' by Alfred was effected with the close cooperation of Archbishop Plegmund of Canterbury and Bishop Wærferth of Worcester.[34] Since the pattern of London's churches does not conform to the model of the coexistence of an Old Minster and a New Minster in the late Anglo-Saxon period (as at Winchester, Chester and Gloucester), some other arrangement should be sought. From the large size of the new *burh*, and from the arguments set out above for the creation of the wards by Alfred, it could reasonably be inferred that the 'restoration' of London involved the creation of several such 'new minsters', each given burial, tithe and possibly baptismal rights, whose *parochiae* were coterminous with the wards themselves. It can therefore be postulated that the church of St. Mary Magdalen was one of these 'new minsters', created to serve the ecclesiastical needs of the inhabitants of the ward of Aldgate.

This close spatial, temporal and functional link between the minster *parochia* and the ward of Aldgate places the relationship between the ward with its church and the manor of Waltham in a new perspective. The soke and gate of Aldgate was held at the time of Domesday by the bishop of Durham as part of this manor, which he had acquired in about 1075 from William I.[35] Earlier in the century the manor had been in the possession of Tofig the Proud, who had 'founded' the church (later the abbey) of Waltham during the reign of Cnut, from whom he had probably acquired the manor.[36] From the fact that Tofig was a staller of London[37] it can reasonably be argued that Aldgate was connected with Waltham by the early 11th century at the latest. However, the church at Waltham was sited at the central place of a large estate of some 40 hides at the time of Domesday, which had arguably been in royal hands before the early 11th century. It can be inferred that, as in many other cases, there would have been an early minster attached to the royal estate centre; it is therefore unlikely that this church would have been a new creation at the time of Cnut. The possible formation of a double *burh* at Waltham by Alfred in 895 also hints at its earlier importance.[38] Page has suggested that it was Tofig who created the soke of Aldgate,[39] but this again raises the question of why this should have occurred during a period of peace. The connection between the two falls more naturally into the crucial period in the late 9th century when, it can be suggested, the ward and gate of Aldgate would have been attached to the manor of Waltham, then probably an important royal estate centre, which would in some way have been made responsible (doubtless with the inhabitants of the ward itself) for its defence and upkeep.[40] The sub-minster at Aldgate would possibly also have been in some way ecclesiastically dependent upon the postulated early minster at Waltham. This latter suggestion would explain the notification by Queen Matilda in 1108 (which was confirmed by Henry I in 1108 and 1121-2) that the church was to be 'quit of subjection to any church', the implied reference to Waltham being explicitly stated in a further confirmation by Henry III.[41]

This general model of an early relationship between urban wards and parochial sub-minsters can be applied to other Anglo-Saxon *burhs*. A similar relationship has been argued by the writer in the case of the church and parish of St. Mary at Cricklade.[42] Though small in size, it seems not unlikely that its origin and function would have been similar to that of the larger ward and *parochia* of Aldgate. Another case is Wareham, where the presumed *parochia* of the early minster church (Lady St. Mary) has become attenuated by the carving out of it of the large parishes of Holy Trinity and St. Martin's.[43] These two parishes have extensive intra- and extra-mural portions, and their churches are placed on the main north-south route through the town near the south and north gates respectively. This pattern can best be interpreted by the hypothesis that these were two sub-minsters of similar origin and function to those already discussed. A very similar process can be inferred in the case of Oxford. Though the development of its parishes requires further analysis, the creation of one or possibly several sub-minsters at an early stage in the development of the *burh* would explain the large size of the parishes of churches near its gates in the later medieval period compared to that of the early minster of St. Frideswide's.[44] Other examples could be multiplied. In general, however, the wards and sub-minsters in London and probably other towns can be argued as being the urban equivalents to the new hundreds and hundredal minsters which were being created by the kings in the late 9th and early 10th centuries in both Mercia and southern England.[45]

The relationship between St. Mary Magdalen's church and *parochia* and the ward, gate and walls, which is suggested by this model, is paralleled by the church of St. Peter ad Vincula in the Tower of London to the south. Brooke and Keir have again called attention to some crucial written evidence for the church and its parish in the 12th century. This relates to the attempts by several successive rectors of St. Peter's to exercise various rights over the extra-mural area of East Smithfield to the east of the Tower (see Fig. 8). These included mortuary rights and the right to claim soul-scot, all of which were granted to St. Botolph's church only after extensive litigation.[46] Brooke and Keir have interpreted these episodes merely as implying the fluidity of boundaries in a 'sparsely populated area where customs could be forgotten and peasants bullied'.[47] However, the significance of this could be rather that in the 12th century the rectors of St. Peter's thought, in spite of contrary claims of St. Botolph's church, that they had a just claim to the spiritual dues of this area: in other words, that in their view it belonged to St. Peter's parish. It demonstrates, contrary to the view of Brooke and Keir, not only the tenacity and conservatism of custom and perceived ecclesiastical rights in the face of new developments (in this case, the extension of the new St. Botolph's parish to the whole of the area of the Portsoken), but also the importance of anciently recognised boundaries.

What it also demonstrates is the general importance of extra-mural areas to urban churches, however seemingly 'rural' they were. The actions of the rectors of St. Peter's implies that at one time the parish of this church comprised an extra-mural as well as an intra-mural part. It is a matter of general observation that parishes in a medieval town which comprise both extra- and intra-mural portions are invariably connected by gates. It follows from this that, at the time when these two parts of St. Peter's parish formed a unity, there must have been a gate in the City wall to the south of Aldgate which connected the two halves of the parish. The only intrusive element in this part of the City is the Tower of London. The logical conclusion of these observations is that the construction of King William's first castle in 1067, and subsequently the White Tower itself, blocked and/or destroyed this gateway, thereby separating St. Peter's church from the extra-mural part of its parish.

This raises some fundamental questions concerning the topography and early development of medieval and Roman London, of which only a few aspects can be brought out here. The dual hypothesis of the existence both of a pre-Conquest gateway on the site of the Tower, and of the pre-Conquest origin of St. Peter's church, does however make sense of a number of topographical observations, of which the following are amongst the more important.

1. The gateway provides an eastern terminus for the routeway along Eastcheap and Great Tower Street. This was arguably one of the most important elements of the pre-Conquest town, a probable mid-Saxon market street complementary to Cheapside in the western part of the walled town,[48] and a direct link along Canon Street, past St. Paul's and through Ludgate to the middle Saxon trading emporium or *wic* recently recognised as having existed to the west of the walled area along the Strand.[49] Furthermore, Great Tower Street led to the only entrance to the Tower of London from the City until the late 13th century.[50] This situation is explicable on the hypothesis that the construction of the Tower blocked an already well-established route which passed through a gate where the extension of Great Tower Street met the City wall (see Fig. 8). This provides a further reason for the siting of the Tower in this part of the City, in that it corresponds to the siting of Baynard's and Montfichet's Castles by Ludgate.[51] The existence of a gate at this position also explains the change in the line of the city wall at this point, as at Aldgate and Bishopsgate.

2. From the fact that Eastcheap-Great Tower Street extends the line of Roman Canon Street eastwards it can be inferred that, as with all the other gates in the city walls (except Moorgate), the pre-Conquest 'St. Peter's Gate' had a Roman predecessor. In its relation to Aldgate this would mirror the relation of Ludgate to Newgate on the western side of the defences. It would also provide a western terminus for the Roman road leading to the City along the line of Ratcliffe Highway,

connecting *inter alia* the Roman settlement at Ratcliffe and a 3rd-century signal tower at Shadwell.[52]

3. It explains the fact that St. Peter's church was left outside the earliest identifiable defended enceinte of the Tower of London.[53] This formed an awkward trapezoid shape, which can best be explained by the supposition that St. Peter's church already existed on its present site before the Tower was built.

The evidence thus points to the existence, before the Conquest, of a large parish in the south-east corner of the City with both intra- and extra-mural areas which lapped around an early medieval gateway of Roman origin, its church placed inside the gate on an important routeway out of the City.[54] The former unity of this area is emphasised by the fact that the northern side of St. Peter's parish within the walls mirrors a pronounced break in the line of the eastern boundary of the extra-mural St. Botolph's parish (see Fig. 8).[55] The best explanation for the claims by the 12th-century rectors of St. Peter's to burial rights and soul-scot from East Smithfield is that these dues had been paid to St. Peter's both before the creation of St. Botolph's parish in the early 12th century, and also before its parish was split by the insertion of the Tower. This is therefore evidence of its relative importance before the Conquest.

Given the existence of a gateway in this quarter, it is necessary to postulate the existence of a ward which, as has been argued by Brooke and Keir and is also demonstrated above in relation to Aldgate (see above), would have been a discrete area responsible for the upkeep of both gate and walls. Here again the relationship of the later parishes and wards provides crucial evidence. The next church westwards from St. Peter's, situated on Great Tower Street itself, is All Hallows, which from structural evidence has been claimed as late 7th century.[56] From its suggested foundation by St. Eorcenwold, bishop of London in the later 7th century,[57] it could be inferred that it formed one of the early 'sub-minsters' proposed above, although the uncertainties over its date make any such inferences somewhat tentative. St. Dunstan's church, further west on St. Dunstan's Hill, would have been dedicated no earlier than the late 10th century. From its position on a side street of probably late Saxon origin, it could be inferred that this church is later than All Hallows. If the early date of All Hallows is accepted, its *parochia* can be reconstructed as comprising at least the area of these three later parishes. St. Dunstan's and All Hallows' parishes are for the most part coterminous with Tower ward (although the latter comprises part of St. Olave Bread Street parish, created no earlier than the early 11th century,)[58] with St. Peter's parish coterminous with the Tower precincts.

This civil and ecclesiastical pattern could have been produced in two ways: either the whole area — Tower Ward and St. Peter's Gate ward and three parishes — originally comprised one ward and one minster *parochia*; or the early minster *parochia* was divided into two wards, with a new sub-minster founded at St. Peter's in a similar way to the development proposed above for Aldgate ward. If (as seems more probable) the latter is the case, each of these wards would have had a minster church: All Hallows in Tower ward, St. Peter's in 'St. Peter's Gate ward', and St. Mary Magdalen in Aldgate ward. A similar relationship could have obtained between Bishopsgate Ward, arguably another ward of late 9th-century origin, and St. Helen's Bishopsgate, which Page suggested[59] was a pre-Conquest minster church. On the model proposed for Aldgate, it can reasonably be argued that St. Peter's church, like St. Mary Magdalen's, was a new sub-minster founded by King Alfred in the late 9th century at the same time as the creation of the ward, and that it was at this time that it would have been given burial, soul-scot and possibly other rights. It would also not be unreasonable to postulate that its dedication to St. Peter ad Vincula could have been suggested by Alfred himself as a result of his earlier visit to Rome.[60] The importance of this church implied in this reconstruction would fit with its location on a major route near an important gateway, both arguably in existence at least as early as the late 9th century.

Conclusions

The evidence and inferences put forward above allow an explanatory model for the development of the eastern part of early medieval London. The growth of this pattern consists essentially of four stages:

1. The formation of an early minster (All Hallows) covering much if not most of the eastern part of the City:[61] 7th to 9th centuries.

2. The formation of three wards, two of them each centred on a gate, and the other covering a length of the city wall along the river, as part of a scheme of defence for the *burh* of London as a whole. This would have been accompanied by the provision of a new minster in each of the wards by the gates (St. Mary Magdalen by Aldgate and St. Peter ad Vincula by St. Peter's Gate), their *parochiae* coterminous with the wards themselves: late 9th century.

3. The creation of the new ward of Portsoken with the formation of the Cnichtengild, this new unit comprising the extra-mural areas of Aldgate and St. Peter's gate wards and their *parochiae*: mid 10th century.

4. The subdivision of the sub-*parochiae* into smaller parishes, wlth little regard for either the original ward or *parochia* boundaries: mid or late 10th to early 12th centuries. In the eastern part of London the pre-Conquest pattern appears to have been broken by two major events: (a) the blocking of St. Peter's Gate by the insertion of King William's castle (1067) and the White Tower (1080s), resulting in the severing of St. Peter's parish; and (b) the foundation of the Priory of Holy

Trinity Aldgate and the creation of the new parish of St. Botolph to cover the ward of Portsoken: early 12th century.

Some of the underlying premises of this model can be mentioned here. First, the various programmes of burghal foundation or 'restoration' in the late 9th century (continued by Edward the Elder in the early 10th) involved not only a civil but also an ecclesiastical dimension; that is, they involved the founding of new churches with newly-created parishes to serve the spiritual needs of the new urban populations. Secondly, the origin of the wards, which were public, self-governing administrative units, must be looked for in a period in which the defence of the City was in process of organisation or reorganisation, that is, most probably in the late 9th century under Alfred. It also entails a rather different relationship between the wards and parishes than is put forward by Brooke and Keir.[62]

Thirdly, this model assumes a stability of parochial boundaries, and the tenacity on the part of interested parties to protect their rights over these areas, which is perhaps rather greater than Brooke and Keir were prepared to admit.[63] In particular, it is argued that the eastern boundary of the 12th-century St. Botolph's parish and the Portsoken, far from being a relatively new feature in the later medieval period as they have implied,[64] is in fact probably the most ancient of all. It must have formed the eastern boundary of the wards of 'St. Peter's Gate' and Aldgate at least as early as the late 9th century, and was the common boundary with the ancient *parochia* of St. Dunstan's Stepney. It also formed the eastern boundary of Bishopsgate ward (see Fig. 8).[65] Although this hypothesis cannot be argued here, there are grounds for believing that, with the rest of the extramural city boundary in its earliest form, it represents the boundary of a territory around London of early Saxon if not Roman ancestry.[66]

Fourthly, this model postulates a rather different process of transformation from the primary minsters of the Conversion period to the network of parishes and churches of the mid 12th century than is assumed, for instance, by Brooke and Keir. In the eastern area of London it is suggested that there were several tiers of minsters and 'sub-minsters'. The primary minster, St. Paul's, can be considered to have been the mother church to a secondary minster, All Hallows. This in turn was the mother church to (at least) two tertiary minsters — St. Mary Magdalen Aldgate and St. Peter's, the parishes of both these churches being carved out of its *parochia*. The formation of these minsters and sub-minsters implies a degree of ecclesiastical control and direction exercised by the bishop and probably also the king. This system to a large extent became eroded with the formation of smaller parishes out of the larger *parochiae* in the later 10th and 11th centuries (St. Dunstan's and St. Olave's possibly being of later 10th- and mid 11th-century date respectively).[67] That these and other parishes cut across the early *parochiae* boundaries implies, as Brooke and Keir have pointed out,[68] a weakening of ecclesiastical authority.

Fifthly, this model provides an explanation for the apparent conflict between the preservation of rights of ancient minsters over burial and other dues, evident in most other places, and the situation in London in the 12th century, when it was stated that citizens could be buried where they wished.[69] This statement, however, was addressed in the 12th century to the Priory of Holy Trinity with reference to the creation at this time of the new parish of St. Botolph. It might therefore be taken as showing that this was a new development from a situation in which burial rights had been limited to early minsters, and when the parochial functions of one of these minsters (St. Mary Magdalen) had been superseded. There was, therefore, not 'one law for the country, another for the town';[70] rather, the ecclesiastical development of both town and country followed very similar courses at similar times.

Acknowledgements

Much of the research for this paper was made possible by a generous research grant from the Leverhulme Trust in the period 1982–4. I am also grateful to both John Blair and Tony Dyson for many helpful comments on an earlier draft.

Notes

1. Brooke & Keir, *London*, 99.
2. A. Rogers, 'Parish Boundaries and Urban History: two Case Studies', *JBAA*, 3rd ser. xxxv (1972), 46–64; Campbell, 'Church in Towns'; C.N.L. Brooke, 'The Missionary at Home: the Church in the Towns, 1000–1250', *Studies in Church History*, vi (1970), 59–83. See also several studies in Haslam, *Towns*. For London, see Brooke & Keir, *London*, esp. Ch. 6.
3. Brooke and Keir were certainly aware of the possibilities of this approach, and advocated the use of a variety of different kinds of evidence (29, 143 and passim).
4. W. Page, *London: its Origin and Early Development*, (London, 1923), e.g. in Ch. 4.
5. Brooke & Keir *London*, 128–48.
6. Ibid., 137–38.
7. This general hypotheis has been put forward and discussed by Page op.cit. note 4, 159–61.
8. M. Biddle and D. Hudson, *The Future of London's Past* (Rescue Publication no. 4, Worcester, 1973); Brooke and Keir, *London*, 143.
9. As Brooke and Keir have demonstrated (143–47 and passim). It is hoped to extend the present analysis to the western part of the suburbs in due course.
10. Ibid., 96–100, 145–47, 314–25.
11. Page op.cit. note 4, 153. The connections of Aldgate with Waltham are discussed further below.
12. Brooke & Keir, *London*, 318 and passim, and note 17 below. For

the relationship of this church to Waltham, see below. See also *Cart. H.T.A.*, 223–33.
13. Brooke & Keir, *London*, 97–8.
14. Brooke & Keir state (98) that this included land 'as far south of the river as they could throw their lances'. It is clear however from the relevant passage in *Cart. H.T.A.* (No. 871 p. 167) (and noted for instance by Stow) that this was the distance a lance could be thrown *into* the river from the northern shore — i.e. to a notional boundary in the centre of the river.
15. Brooke & Keir, *London*, 146 note 2.
16. Stenton, 'Norman London', 32–3.
17. The dedication of the earlier church to St. Mary Magdalen must be primary to that to the Holy Cross, which was derived from the 11th-century dedication of the church at Waltham. For the excavation of the graveyard, see *Med. Arch.* xxix (1985), 174.
18. Brooke & Keir, *London*, 146 note 2.
19. However, Stenton, *Norman London*, 16, implies the possibility of its existence prior to Edgar's reign.
20. M. Biddle and D. Hill, 'Late Saxon planned Towns', *Antiq. J.*, li (1971), 70–85; M. Biddle and D. Hudson, op.cit. note 8, 22–4; A. Dyson and J. Schofield, 'Saxon London', in Haslam, *Towns*, 296–301. See also note 23, below.
21. N.P. Brooks, 'England in the 9th Century: the Crucible of Defeat', *TRHS*, 5th ser. xxix (1979), 1–20.
22. Translation that of H.A. Harben, *A Dictionary of London* (London, 1918), 481–83; see also *Cart. H.T.A.*, No. 871, p. 167.
23. There is some archaeological evidence for the disuse and virtual abandonment of the defences of Anglo-Saxon *burhs* in the mid to late 10th century. For Hereford, see R. Shoesmith, *Excavations on or close to the Defences (Hereford City Excavations 2*, C.B.A. Research Rep. xlvi, 1982), esp. 82–3 (stage 4) and passim. For Cricklade, see J. Haslam, 'Excavations at Cricklade, 1975', *Wiltshire Arch. Mag.* forthcoming. For Southampton, see P. Holdsworth, 'Saxon Southampton', in Haslam, *Towns*, 340. The origin of the Cnichtengild as a body would however also fit the circumstances of the late 10th or early 11th century, when once again the major *burhs* were being reorganised for defence. I am grateful to Tony Dyson for suggesting this.
24. Brooke & Keir, *London*, 168.
25. Stenton, *Norman London*, 29.
26. Ibid., 34–6; Brooke & Keir, *London*, 155, 162–70 and passim. It can be inferred from an analysis of the pattern of the wards that the 'primary' wards were fewer in number and somewhat larger, having subsequently been divided internally.
27. F.M. Stenton, *Anglo-Saxon England* (3rd edn., Oxford, 1971), 263–69.
28. Brooke & Keir, *London*, 170.
29. Brooks, op.cit. note 21, 14–17.
30. Some of the evidence for this is discussed in J. Haslam, 'The *burh* of *Wigingamere*', forthcoming.
31. M. Biddle (ed.), *Winchester in the Early Middle Ages* (Winchester Studies i, Oxford, 1976), 314. It has been claimed that a new minster at Exeter was founded by Æthelstan: see J. Allan, C. Henderson, and R. Higham, 'Saxon Exeter', in Haslam, *Towns*, 392–3; and C.G. Henderson and P.T. Bidwell, 'The Saxon minster at Exeter', in S.M. Pearce (ed.), *The Early Church in Western Britain and Ireland* (British Arch. Reps. cii, Oxford, 1982). There are, however, grounds for postulating that this was an earlier foundation by King Alfred and/or Edward the Elder in the late 9th or early 10th century.
32. For Gloucester, see C. Heighway, 'Saxon Gloucester', in Haslam, *Towns*, 371–75; C. Heighway, 'Excavations at Gloucester, 5th interim report', *Antiq. J.*, lx.2 (1980), 217–20. For Chester and Gloucester, see A.T. Thacker, 'Chester and Gloucester: Early Ecclesiastical Organisation in two Mercian Burhs', *Northern History*, xviii (1982), 199–216. For other examples such as Derby, Shrewsbury, Stafford and Hereford, see Campbell, 'Church in Towns', 125–26, and Blair, 'Secular Minsters', 140–42. For the suggested foundation by Offa of a new minster in the late 8th-century *burhs* of Bedford and Cambridge, see J. Haslam, 'The ecclesiastical Topography of Early Medieval Bedford', *Bedfordshire Archaeology* xvii (1985), and J. Haslam, 'The Topography and Development of Saxon Cambridge', *Proceedings of the Cambridge Antiquarian Soc.* lxxii (1984), 13–29. A further example of a new minster created by Edward the Elder as part of a new *burh* is possibly St. Mary's Southwark. This was certainly a major minster in the later 11th century and later, and probably replaced an early minster at Bermondsey. Its origin in the early 10th century is an inference from these and other observations, reinforced by the association of new minsters with *burhs* shown more clearly in other places mentioned above. I am grateful to John Blair for advice on this question.
33. In this context it is perhaps significant that Fitzstephen mentions Holy Trinity Priory as one of the three major schools in London in the 12th century, though Page (op.cit. note 4, 169) argues that he was mistaken.
34. T. Dyson and J. Schofield, op.cit. note 20, 296–97; T. Dyson, 'Two Saxon Land Grants from Queenhithe', in J. Bird, H. Chapman and J. Clark (eds.), *Collectanea Londiniensia* (London and Middlesex Arch. Soc. Special Paper No. 2, 1978), 200–215.
35. *VCH Essex*, v, 155–56.
36. Ibid.
37. Page op.cit. note 4, 136.
38. Anglo-Saxon Chronicle, *sub anno*; *VCH Essex*, v, 165–66.
39. Page op.cit. note 4, 136.
40. This interpretation of Waltham's early importance differs from that recently put forward by Blair 'Secular Minsters', 123. In the writer's view, Maitland's original hypothesis of the defensive function of properties in towns connected to rural estates in Domesday Book and earlier (the 'garrison theory') has been unduly neglected since Tait's insistence on the primacy of their economic function (J. Tait, *The Medieval English Borough* (Manchester, 1936), 26–7).
41. *Cart H.T.A.* Nos. 4, 5, 998 and 1004.
42. J. Haslam, 'A "Ward" of the *Burh* of Cricklade', *Wilts. Arch. Mag.* lxxvi (1981), 77–81.
43. L. Keen, 'The Towns of Dorset', in Haslam, *Towns*, 224–27 and figs. 75 & 77. Keen, however, has suggested that the small parish of Lady St. Mary is secondary to the larger parishes. If, as he states, Lady St. Mary is the original minster, this interpretation is not acceptable.
44. H.E. Salter, *Map of Medieval Oxford* (Oxford, 1934), map 5; *VCH Oxon.* iv, 1979, map on p. 30. See also H.M. Cam, 'The Hundred Outside the North Gate of Oxford', in *Liberties and Communities in Medieval England* (Cambridge, 1944), 107–23.
45. Blair, 'Secular Minsters', 118–19 and refs. cited there. See also R.E. Rodes, *Ecclesiastical Administration in Medieval England* (University of Notre Dame Press, 1977), 24–31 and *passim*; and Franklin, 'Minsters and Parishes', esp. pp. 10, 311–17, 332–33, 339 and *passim*.
46. Brooke & Keir, *London*, 145–46. See also *Cart. H.T.A.* Nos. 964, 966, 969, and 971. The right of St. Peter's to soul-scot can be inferred from its claim to three sheep from a deceased woman in 1166 (*Cart. H.T.A.* No. 969). This is particularly significant for the arguments (below) of the importance of the church before the Conquest, since soul-scot, with church-scot, is of very early origin, its possession 'a fundamental endowment of ... ancient minsters' (Stenton, op.cit. note 27, 153–4).
47. Brooke & Keir, *London*, 146.
48. Biddle and Hudson op.cit. note 8, 21. T. Tatton-Brown, in 'The Topography of Anglo-Saxon London', *Antiquity*, lx (1986), 21–30, p. 25, suggests a late 9th-century origin for the market at Eastcheap.
49. For the importance of this routeway through Saxon London, see T. Tatton-Brown's recent topographical analysis, op.cit.

note 48. For the *wic*, see M. Biddle, 'London on the Strand', *Popular Archaeology*, July 1984, 23–27; and A. Vince, 'The Aldwych: Mid-Saxon London Discovered', *Current Archaeology*, xciii (August 1984), 310–12. The early importance of Ludgate had already been pointed out by John Clark in 'Cadwallo, King of the Britons, the Bronze Horseman of London', in Bird, Chapman and Clark (eds.) op.cit. note 34, 195–96. Clark's observations are it seems now fully vindicated by the confirmation of Biddle's and Vince's hypotheses: see R. Whytehead, 'The Jubilee Hall Site Reveals New Evidence of Saxon London', *Rescue News*, xxxvii (summer 1985). East Smithfield probably represents an extra-mural market area of pre-Conquest origin outside this gate, comparable to West Smithfield to the north-west of the walled area.

50. H.M. Colvin (ed.), *The History of the King's Works*, (HMSO, London, 1963), 712. See also T. Dyson, 'The Topographical Development of the Custom House Area', in T. Tatton-Brown, 'Excavations at the Custom House Site, City of London, 1973, pt. 2', *Trans. London and Middlesex Arch. Soc.* xxvi (1975), 103–170, esp. 110–13.
51. Stenton, *Norman London*, 24–8. See also Colvin, op.cit. note 50, 707.
52. G. Black, *The Archaeology of Tower Hamlets* (Inner London Archaeology Unit, no date [c. 1980]), 5 and Fig. 5; T. Johnson, 'A Roman Signal Tower at Shadwell, E1 — an Interim Note', *Trans. London and Middlesex Arch. Soc.* xxvi (1975), 278–80.
53. *Med. Arch.* viii (1964), 255 and Fig. 83. St. Peter's church is not, however, marked on the accompanying plan.
54. The foundation of St. Peter's church has usually been assigned, on no good evidence, to the early 12th century: see for instance J. Bayley, *The History and Antiquities of the Tower of London* (1830), 113–14; Harben, op.cit. note 22, 470; and J.F.M. Llewellyn, 'The Tower and the Church', in J. Charlton (ed.), *The Tower of London: its Buildings and Institutions* (Dept. of Environment, London, 1978), 132.
55. As Stow (i, 121) and latterly Harben (op.cit. note 22, 93) have pointed out, this area included all of East Smithfield, the hospital of St. Katherine and the extra-mural Tower Liberties, the eastern boundary of which area was Nightingale Lane. The bounds are fully set out in Strype's edition of Stow (1720, I. ii, 26). St. Katherine's Hospital (founded 1148), the house of St. Clare of the Minoresses (founded 1293, later the parish of Holy Trinity Minories), and the precincts of the abbey of St. Mary Graces (founded 1349), were all taken out of the original ward of Portsoken and the parish of St. Botolph. These are not shown on the plan, Fig. 8. See Harben op.cit., 481–3 and passim. For details of the topography of the area, see M.B. Honeybourne, 'The Extent and Value of the Property in London and Southwark Occupied by the Religious Houses...', unpublished M.A thesis, University of London, 1930; and M.B. Honeybourne, 'The Abbey of St. Mary Graces, Tower Hill', *Trans. London and Middlesex Arch. Soc.* n.s. xi (1954), 16–26.
56. Taylor & Taylor, i, 399–400. This date is, however, open to question, since the structural features could easily be as late as 10th century. I am indebted to John Blair for these comments.
57. Ibid.; Brooke & Keir, *London*, 137 and note 3.
58. Brooke & Keir, *London*, 138, 141, 415. The dedication to St. Dunstan could have been given in the later 10th or early 11th century to a church of earlier origin. Note for instance the example of St. Dunstan's Stepney, clearly dedicated in the later 10th century or later, but (as a mother church at the central place in a large episcopal estate) probably far older than this. See K. McDonell, *Medieval London Suburbs* (Chichester, 1978), 136.
59. Page op.cit. note 4, 161.
60. The dedication, St. Peter 'in chains', commemorates St. Peter's escape from prison; a church with this dedication was built by the emperor Theodosius in Rome. The dedication is one of only nine known in this country, though in other dedications to St. Peter the suffix could have become lost in the course of time. See F. Arnold-Forster, *Studies in Church Dedications* (London, 1899), i, 54–5. It must be said that the dedication has nothing to do with the proximity of the church to the Tower, as suggested by J.E. Oxley, 'The Medieval Church Dedications of the City of London', *Trans. London and Middlesex Arch. Soc.* xxxi (1980), 117–25, p. 119. Note also the suggestion of Dr. David Hill (lecture, March 1986), that the idea of the rectilinear street pattern of London and other *burhs* could also have been derived by Alfred from his familiarity with a prototype in Rome.
61. If the early date of All Hallows is accepted, its suggested foundation by Bishop Eorcenwold may be an early example of an episcopal *Eigenkirche*, discussed for instance by Franklin, 'Minsters and Parishes', 333. This may have been placed within a large estate of 24 hides, which possibly included much or all of the eastern side of London and the estate of Stepney, which probably formed an early endowment to the bishop by King Æthelberht of Kent in the early 7th century.
62. Brooke & Keir, *London*, 168–69 and passim.
63. Ibid., 146.
64. Ibid., 162, 169. They suggest that the boundary of the 'suburbs', i.e the extramural area over which the city had jurisdiction, expanded outwards with the increase in population. This view was shared by Harben (op.cit. note 22, 349, 346 and passim), and Page (op.cit. note 4, 178–9).
65. Immediately to the east of this was the medieval parish of St. Mary Matfelon, taken out of St. Dunstan's Stepney in the 14th century: see McDonell op.cit. note 58, 141.
66. This boundary appears however to have been altered in some details to reflect the creation of the two wards around Aldgate and St. Peter's Gate, and probably also Bishopsgate, arguably in the late 9th century.
67. Brooke & Keir, *London*, 141–42.
68. Ibid., 142.
69. Ibid., 161.
70. Ibid.

V. The Mother Churches of Hampshire

P. H. Hase

The earliest English parochial system, based on collegiate mother churches each serving perhaps ten or more villages, is a subject of great interest both in itself and for the innumerable ways the system has influenced details of English local life down to the present day. Its main outlines have been known for some time, but there remain at least four major areas where further clarification would still be of value. These are, first, the question of when the mother churches were founded and how far the foundations were the result of a systematic policy rather than merely haphazard acts of piety; secondly, the question of when, why, and how the earlier system broke down to be replaced by the familiar modern parochial system; thirdly, what the internal life of the mother churches was like, what regimen was followed, and what *horarium*, how the income was handled, and what degree of community life was to be found at the mother church; and finally, how the priests of the mother church handled the cure of souls of the villages under their care, and what their relationships were with any churches or chapels built in those villages.

This paper does not claim to answer any of these questions, but only to suggest certain conclusions on them drawn from the evidence surviving on mother churches in Hampshire.[1] It is divided into four sections, one dealing with each of the four areas of interest mentioned above. An appendix gives translations of some of the more interesting documents.

The Origins of the System

In 686, Cædwalla, king of the West Saxons, in the course of his conquest of the kingdom of Wight, captured the last two princes of its royal family. Cyneberht, abbot of the monastery at *Hreutford* ('Reed Ford', later Redbridge), interceded with Cædwalla, and was permitted to spend the night with the two youths, converting and baptising them before their inevitable execution the following morning.[2] There can be little doubt that Cyneberht's monastery was at Eling, on the western bank of the crossing of the Test at Redbridge, Five centuries later, Stone, in Exbury parish, the probable place where the young princes were captured, was still considered to be within the *parochia*[3] of Eling, although Eling church lies 10 miles to the north.[4] Much of the *parochia* comprised the great royal night's farm estate of Eling, and the church is shown in Domesday as connected with that estate.[5] The royal hundred of Redbridge was also connected with this manor. Eling means 'The ætheling's (land)', suggesting a royal connection of some antiquity.

Five miles to the east of Eling, at the mouth of the River Itchen, lies Southampton, a major market for merchants in the first years of the 8th century.[6] Excavation has shown that Old Southampton was built on the west bank of the Itchen, and consisted of a number of streets running north-south for about 200 yards, from a junction with roads to Redbridge and Winchester to the north to an area of flat land beside the Itchen to the south, which was probably the beaching place for trading ships. The town seems to have been first established in the middle of the 7th century. One of the most important sites in the town, the corner where the main street opened out into the beaching place of the trading ships, was occupied by the cemetery and buildings of the church of St. Mary Extra Southampton.[7] In the 11th and 12th centuries this church was the mother church of the whole lower Itchen valley. It must have been completed by about 725; a number of cemeteries north of the town all seem to have gone out of use between 700 and 725, presumably because the church cemetery was by then available. St. Mary's was a collegiate minster, granted land at Hinton Ampner twenty miles away in 990–2,[8] and remaining collegiate to the Reformation.[9] The church was closely connected with the major royal manor of Stoneham (which was split up and most of it alienated in 1045). The royal hundred of Mansbridge was also connected with this royal estate.[10]

Nine miles north-east of Southampton lies Bishops Waltham, in the upper valley of the River Hamble. About 710 St. Willibald entered the monastery at Waltham and was educated there.[11] In the early 12th century the church at Bishops Waltham, which was built immediately adjacent to the centre of the great episcopal manor of Waltham,[12] was the mother church of the whole Hamble valley. Connected with this manor was the major episcopal franchisal hundred of Waltham.[13] However, the estate had not been episcopal from time immemorial, for before 904 it had been royal. King Edward the Elder exchanged it for the episcopal estate of Portchester at that date, probably because Portchester had proved too inviting to the Norsemen, and thus of too high a strategic value not to be in royal hands.[14]

45

Eight miles south of Bishops Waltham is Titchfield. The church of Titchfield retains in its structure substantial remains of a mid Anglo-Saxon minster, including the whole of the original west front to the roofline, and a west entrance *porticus*. The two eastern corners of the original nave may also survive. The most recent dating of this building puts its construction in the late 7th or early 8th centuries, i.e. in the period 675–725.[15] A charter of 982 mentions the 'community of Titchfield', suggesting that this church, too, was collegiate.[16] In the 12th century it was the mother church of the lower Meon valley. The church is not mentioned in Domesday, but it was attached to the royal manor of Titchfield by 1232 when it was granted with the estate to the newly-founded monastery of Titchfield.[17] This was probably originally a royal night's farm estate as Domesday book states that it had never gelded, although only a remnant of the estate survived to 1086.[18] The royal hundred of Titchfield was connected with this royal manor.

Between Eling and Southampton lies Nursling. According to his *Life*, St. Boniface entered a monastery at *Nhutscelle* for his education a little before 700.[19] *Nhutscelle* is usually identified with Nursling.[20] A mother church here seems unlikely: the site is too close to Eling (3 miles) and Southampton (5 miles) for a respectably sized *parochia* to be fitted in, unless a mother church there was built at the extreme southern tip of its *parochia*. There are no later signs of tenurial significance at Nursling, which was regarded as a detached portion of the Old Minster's main franchisal hundred of Buddlesgate from before 1086.[21] Ecclesiastically, also, there are no later signs suggesting past significance: from the earliest reference to it Nursling church was only ever a poor and simple manorial church.[22]

Three miles north of Nursling, however, is Romsey, where a major nunnery was founded in 907 by King Edward the Elder. Within the nunnery the parochial altar in the north aisle was served until the Reformation by a small college of prebendaries.[23] These prebendaries were primarily responsible not for the service of the nuns, but for the parochial cure of souls. This fact suggests that the nunnery was founded in a pre-existing collegiate parochial minster. It is possible, therefore, that Boniface's monastery was at Romsey, and that Nursling was originally the name of the whole eastern bank of the lower Test; that is, the whole area from Romsey to Nursling, centred, not on the modern Nursling, but on Romsey. It is unlikely that Boniface entered Cyneberht's monastery at Eling; although Eling and Nursling are so close, they are separated by the broad marshes of the lower Test, and are unlikely ever to have been combined in one land unit or to have been known by one name:[24] *Nhutscelle* must, therefore, refer to somewhere on the eastern bank of the Test. By the date of Domesday Book no trace of any royal manor or hundred survived in the Romsey-Nursling area. Presumably there must once have been one, to provide the source of the 14 hides held by the nuns of Romsey in Romsey before 1066: all, probably, part of the original 907 grant.[25] It is probably fair, therefore, to take the nuns' estate, and their franchisal hundred, as representing a previous royal estate and hundred, although firm evidence for this is lacking.[26]

Of these churches, Southampton and Romsey remained collegiate to the Reformation. At the other churches no evidence of collegiate status survives of a date later than 686 for Eling, 710 for Waltham, and 982 for Titchfield. None of these latter churches seems collegiate in Domesday Book, and they were certainly not so in the 12th century. Probably their corporate life ceased at various dates in the last generations before the Conquest. However. it seems clear that, whatever their later status, they were all collegiate at the date of their foundation and for presumably at least the following two hundred years.

Thus in the area around Southampton Water (Fig. 9) we can see four or five mother churches, all originally collegiate minsters. and all dating from the late 7th or early 8th centuries. Each is connected with an ancient royal estate and with a royal hundred, certainly in the case of Eling, Southampton, Bishops Waltham and Titchfield, and probably in the case of Romsey. The *parochia* of Southampton can be shown to march with that of Bishop's Waltham, and that of Bishop's Waltham with that of Titchfield. Between the demonstrable *parochiae* of Southampton and Eling is a gap of about 1½ miles which may represent the southernmost tip of a *parochia* of Romsey/Nursling. No royal estates in the area are known either from Domesday Book or from Anglo-Saxon records, other than those connected with these mother churches. The only hundreds are those connected with the estates with mother churches.

No other mother churches in Hampshire can be as closely dated as those around Southampton Water, but it can be shown that every other certain or probable mother church discernible in the 11th or 12th centuries was at least connected with an ancient royal estate and royal hundred in the same way as the churches there.[27]

A similar position can, however, be shown in the westernmost part of Surrey, where the three contiguous hundreds of Farnham, Woking, and Godley are closely connected with the three mother churches of Farnham (founded 685 × 7), Woking (probably founded before 686 and in existence at the latest by 715), and Chertsey (founded 666 × 74),[28] whose *parochiae* were, in the 12th century, to a large degree coterminous with the hundreds. Woking was connected with a major royal estate in the same way as the Southampton Water mother churches, but the other two churches were not so clearly connected with continuing royal estates: Chertsey was founded before Surrey finally became part of Wessex, on land granted to St. Eorcenwold by the sub-king of Surrey, Frithuwold, and the whole of

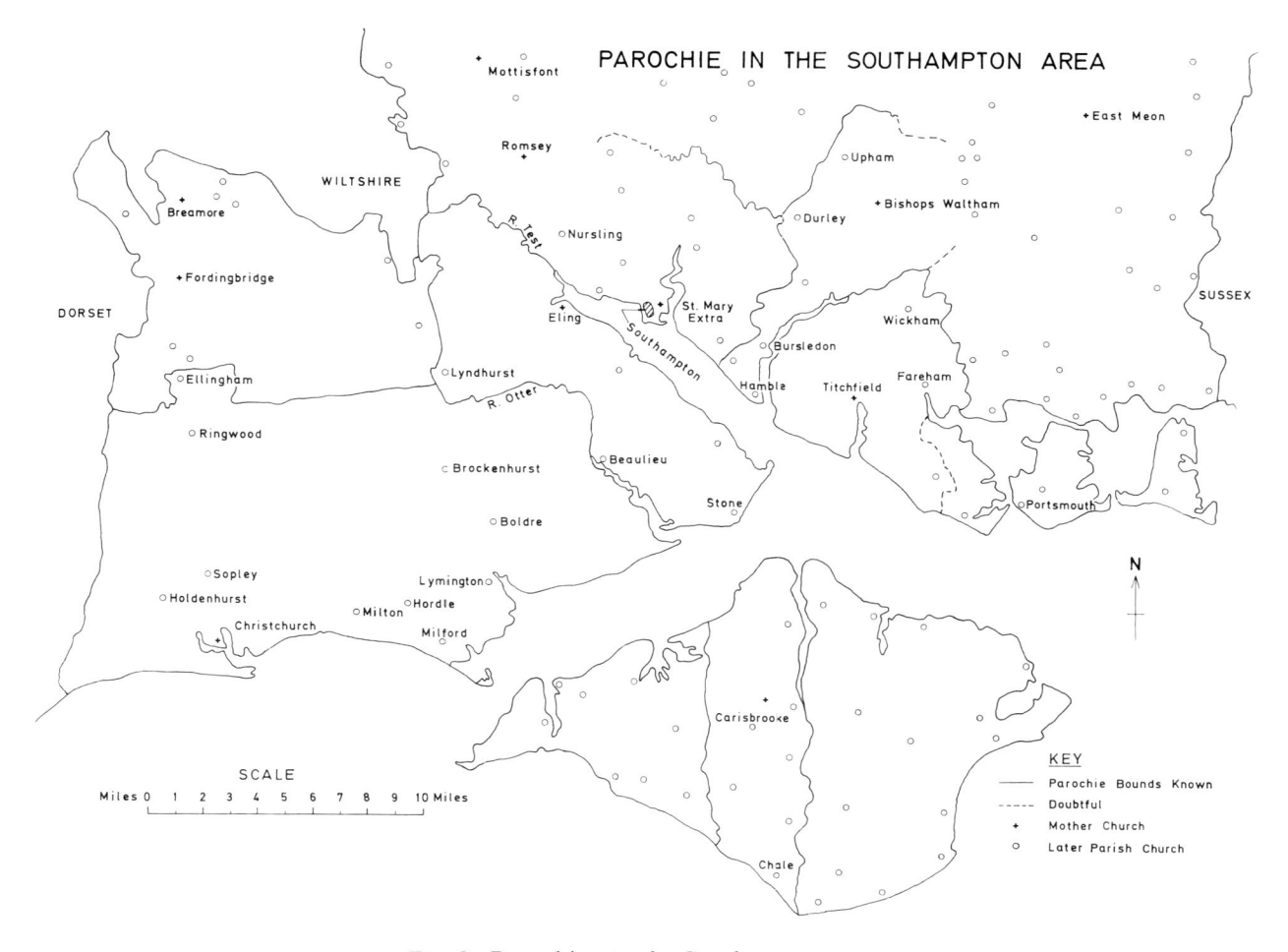

Fig. 9 Parochiae *in the Southampton area.*

Farnham hundred with the church founded at that date was a thank-offering to Bishop Hædde of Winchester by King Cædwalla on the occasion of his conquest of the area. At the least, however, the royal will seems of critical importance in the founding of both. Both Chertsey and Woking were collegiate when first mentioned; the land at Farnham was 'for the foundation of a minster' suggesting that this church, also, was collegiate.

The conclusion seems inescapable. In these two areas, Domesday Book shows ancient royal estates, each connected with a collegiate mother church and a hundred, with jurisdictional and religious districts which were essentially coterminous, forming a system covering the whole area. Given the dates briefly discussed above it is clear that this system was in existence by 700 or a little later. It is becoming widely accepted that the early kingdom of Wessex was administered internally below the county level as a network of sub-districts, each centred on a royal estate, the *villa regalis*, whose reeve administered the king's justice, collected the king's dues, maintained the king's hall and home-farm, and defended the king's men.[29] It seems clear that there was also a definite policy to attach to each *villa regalis* a mother church, to ensure that the social, political, judicial and religious life of the countryside centred on the same point, and that all were equally under the king's control. It is, perhaps, worth mentioning that such a system would make the hearing of ecclesiastical cases in the hundred court, as we know happened at least in the 11th century, quite understandable.

It may be worth speculating a little further. The conversion of Wessex was not a smooth affair. St. Birinus came to Wessex in 634. The king of Wessex, Cynegisl, was converted under pressure from Cynegisl's overlord, the Christian Oswald. Cynegisl was succeeded by his son Cenwalh in 642; Oswald's overlordship had ended with his death in 642, since when the dominant force in Wessex politics had been pagan Mercia, and Cenwalh had in consequence refused to accept Christianity. A quarrel with Mercia in 645 led to war, and four years during which Cenwalh was in exile and Wessex ruled directly by Mercians. Cenwalh was finally converted to Christianity during his exile, and, on his return to Wessex in 648, he supported the work of evangelisation, if without enthusiasm. However, he made no attempt to establish a cathedral church in Wessex until 662 (Birinus's see at Dorchester remained in Mercian hands from 645 onwards); he managed to quarrel with, and eject from his kingdom, both his second bishop (Agilbert, 650-60) and his third (Wine, 662-3), and he was prepared to leave his see vacant between 660 and 662, and again between 663 and 670. He did, however, found the cathedral church at Winchester in 662, and probably endowed it with the double hundred of Chilcomb. His death in 672 led to some twelve years of anarchy, with the kingdom dissolving into a number of quarrelling sub-kingdoms. It seems unlikely that much evangelisation in depth could have taken place in the stormy years between Cynegisl's death in 642 and Cædwalla's accession in 685, with the initially rather nominal Christianity of the king, the weak and at best intermittent episcopal presence, and the widespread political instability.

In these circumstances, the close relationship between Kings Cædwalla (685-8) and Ine (688-726) and the Church is entirely understandable. Both kings were strong and efficient, ruthless on occasion, determined, and intelligent. Under their rule Wessex could look to a period of stable and effective government, with kings who must have made the restoration of effective royal control at the local level a high priority. At the same time, both kings had a reputation for piety, and enjoyed the advice of saintly and learned bishops (St. Wilfred in Sussex and Wight, 680-6; St. Hædde of Winchester, 676-705; St. Eorcenwold of London in the latter part of his episcopate, 675-93; St. Adhelm of Sherborne, 705-9; Daniel of Winchester, 705-44, a man praised by Bede for his learning; and Forthere of Sherborne, 709-37, another man Bede praised for his learning). Cædwalla was notably generous to his bishops, and Ine's laws show clearly the influence on his policy of his senior ecclesiastical advisers. Both demonstrated the reality of their Christianity in their spectacular abdications and retirements to Rome. Clearly, under Cædwalla and Ine the Church in Wessex was subject to rulers who could provide the two factors essential to a conversion in depth but missing over the previous forty years — strong and effective royal rule, and a real commitment to the Church.

Furthermore, Cædwalla, Ine and their bishops also had the advantage of the powerful presence of Archbishop Theodore (668-90) rather than the less effective Archbishops Honorius and Deusdedit. Following the Council of Hertford (672), Theodore pressed for a more thorough conversion. This must have coincided not only with the views of the West Saxon bishops, but also with those of Cædwalla and Ine; the kings must have been as aware of the political value of a network of mother churches, one to each *villa regalis*, as the bishops were of the spiritual value of a widespread conversion of the countryside. It seems likely, therefore, that the establishment of a *system* of collegiate mother churches closely connected with the local royal jurisdictional system was an act of royal policy, essentially introduced by Kings Cædwalla and Ine in the years 685-726; and that this act of policy was designed both to enhance royal power in the countryside, and to complete a conversion which had not yet been properly consolidated.[30]

It should be stressed that this system, with one mother church in every *villa regalis* and with most mother churches founded by the king, is proposed here as essentially a West Saxon system. It is not the purpose of this paper to argue that identical, or even similar systems were established in other kingdoms, although evidence is now mounting that similar systems were not uncommon elsewhere.[31]

The Decay of the System

If we assume, as seems reasonable on the Southampton Water evidence, that 8th century Wessex was served by a network of royal mother churches, one to each *villa regalis*, then it is worth briefly considering the factors which strained this system and caused it to break apart in the 10th, 11th and 12th centuries.

In Hampshire, one of the most serious factors was the Monastic Reform movement of the 10th century. King Cenwalh had endowed the Old Minster with the double hundred of Chilcomb in 662, and King Cædwalla had added his thank-offering of Farnham in 685. These were probably the only estates held by the bishop and the Old Minster in the first few generations after the Conversion. Highclere was granted in 749, Calbourne in the Isle of Wight in 826, Nursling sometime before 872, Portchester before 904 and Alresford before 824 × 833. The vast bulk of the Bishop's and Old Minster's estates in 1086, however, were 10th- or 11th-century grants.[32]

It was, however, apparently felt in the 10th and 11th centuries to be inappropriate for any manor of the Old Minster or the bishop to be parochially subject to a mother church not in the bishop's control: each of these grants, therefore, tended to result in the foundation of a new parish church independent of the old mother church, and thus in a reduction of the pre-existing *parochia*. Thus, the grant of Fareham to the bishop (953 × 975) seems to have removed at least a quarter of the *parochia* of Titchfield, and the successive grants of Highclere, Burghclere, Hurstbourne Priors, St. Mary Bourne, Whitchurch, and Overton (respectively 749, 955 × 8, early 10th century, 900, 909 and 963 × 75) caused the old mother-church *parochiae* in the north of the county to disintegrate completely. There may originally have been three in this area, at Hurstbourne, Whitchurch and Kingsclere: but by 975 more than half the putative *parochia* of the first, almost all that of the second, and more than half that of the third was in ecclesiastical hands and outside the system, thus leaving hardly any signs of mother churches in this area to survive into the late 11th century.[33]

It would seem, too, that other vills in the hands of other religious in the 10th century were also, in many cases, taken out of the mother churches' control and made into independent parishes whose only mother church was the religious house owning the estate. Thus the establishment in the 10th century of the New Minster and the Nuns' Minster in Winchester, and royal grants to houses such as Abingdon outside the county, all helped to distort the older system by removing blocks of vills from the control of the old mother churches.

The other immediate effect of the Tenth-Century Reform on parochial history in Hampshire was the regularisation of the Old Minster. The double hundred of Chilcomb, Cenwalh's foundation grant of 662, must originally have been the area directly served from the cathedral as parochial mother church. However, this huge area (28 modern parishes, not including the urban parishes), could not be served effectively by a group of regulars. Seven to ten small vills in the suburbs of Winchester, and the urban area itself, could continue to be, and probably initially were, served from the cathedral, but the outer parishes needed a new solution.[34] Domesday Book shows almost all the village churches of the area in existence by 1086, and there can be little doubt that these foundations mostly date from the half-century following the regularisation, that is, from the late 10th or early 11th century.[35]

Another powerful factor leading to foundation of village churches within old mother-church *parochiae* was the difficulty of providing an adequate pastoral service for a substantial and thoroughly Christian population, on the basis of a system of mother churches designed for the much smaller, and much more nominally Christian, population of four centuries earlier. Mother churches with devout priests must have been anxious about the cure of souls of those villages which, though within their *parochiae*, were seven or ten miles from the mother church. Subordinate centres for such remote areas, served from and essentially part of the mother church, were the obvious answer; these can be seen in a number of Hampshire *parochiae* in the 11th and 12th centuries.[36] Of course, such subordinate centres, once founded, would tend to develop a life of their own and eventually develop into independent parish churches in their own right.

Thegnly families of respectable standing, living in the *parochia* of a mother church but at some distance from it, would be particularly anxious to have churches at the centres of their estates, both for their convenience and to enhance their secular status. It is clear that in the late 10th and 11th centuries it was a commonly accepted mark of a thegn-worthy man to have a church at his main residence, and this must have caused many churches to be founded.[37] It seems to follow from this that men who in all other respects were thegn-worthy had a *right* to have such churches. The thegn's church was not, however, necessarily an *Eigenkirche*, a proprietary church under the thegn's complete control. A church served from, and subordinate to, the mother church, similar to those subordinate churches built and served by the mother churches themselves in remote outliers of their *parochiae*, would provide all that the late Anglo-Saxon statements on the subject suggest. Nonetheless, once founded, such a thegnly church would clearly have a strong tendency to develop a life of its own.

Finally, mother churches were valuable to kings seeking income for royal clerks in need of patronage. A collegiate minster church, with income designed to support a group of priests — perhaps as many as 12 or 24 — would provide a very comfortable living for a royal clerk if the whole income was redistributed to only a few priests, or even to only one, with the actual parochial work delegated to one or two hired chaplains. Several mother churches in Hampshire were in the hands of individual royal or episcopal clerks by 1086, and it can be assumed that in most of these churches any traces of a collegiate structure had been extinguished by that date.[38] Obviously, a mother church in the hands of a royal clerk did not cease to retain its previous legal rights, and the proprietor could be expected to fight for the retention of any which were of direct financial significance to him. However, the establishment of independent parish churches within the *parochia*, which would reduce the ecclesiastical duties of the royal clerk, but which would at the same time increase his income (since he could demand to have his rights bought off), would be positively encouraged by such arrangements.

Christchurch provides a particularly valuable illustration of what could happen to a mother church when it was granted to a royal clerk. The history of this church from 1087 to 1146, written down and preserved there, centres on its fortunes after it was handed over to a great curial cleric (Rannulf Flambard), apparently for the first time, in or shortly after 1087.[39] Before Rannulf took the church over it was genuinely collegiate, with a communal religious life, and at least a partly communal lifestyle.

However, following the grant to Flambard he immediately reduced the number of canons sharply (from probably 25 to 13), by refusing to appoint a newcomer to replace any canon who died. He took the tithe income, some other ecclesiastical revenues, and the income from those estates not dedicated to the food and drink of the canons, and made it his own. This represented probably a quarter of the income from land, and perhaps half the total income of the church. Admittedly Flambard seems not to have used this money for himself but for the building of his great new church at Christchurch (Fig. 10), but the effect on the community was much the same as if he had used it for his own enrichment. Furthermore, he removed the canons from their residences adjacent to the church to new ones dispersed about the town, and allowed the

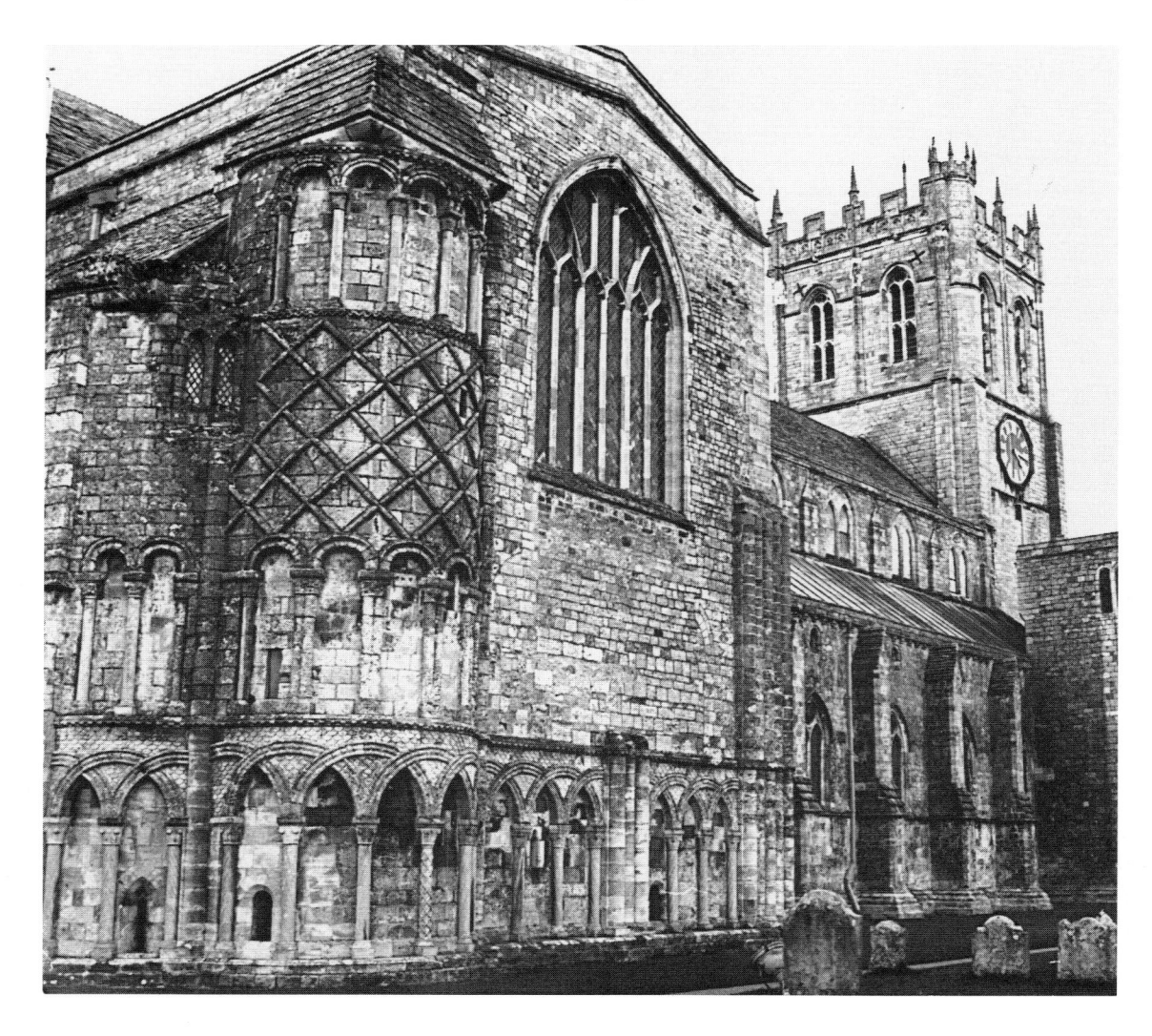

Fig. 10 Christchurch minster, Hants.: the Romanesque north transept. (Courtesy Conway Library, Courtauld Institute of Art.)

communal celebration of the daily hours to cease. He himself, of course, was not resident. By following these policies Flambard went a long way towards converting Christchurch from a genuinely collegiate church served by a community of canons into a church which, while still having a number of canonries attached to it, was no longer fully collegiate, a church whose communal life was seriously endangered, and where one non-resident cleric was in control of the bulk of the income.

Flambard's successor Gilbert de Dousgunels reduced the number of canons even further (to five). He also started to provide individual prebends for the remaining canons, most of them centred on the village churches dependent on Christchurch. This must have weakened the canons' ties to the mother church even further.

Peter de Oglander, the third Norman dean (probably during the 1130s) seems to have used the income taken by Flambard for his own enrichment, slowed down or stopped the work on the church, and surrounded himself with chaplains who were fed within his household, and who were thus presumably hired and not in receipt of any formal benefice. There is some evidence that the remaining canons were, at this date, living elsewhere than at Christchurch, at least for part of the time, in many cases at the churches on their new prebendal estates, leaving Christchurch more and more to the dean and his chaplains. The 'History' of the church mentioned above even suggests that during this period the remaining canons were effectively 'thrown out' of the mother church, with only the Dean's chaplains permitted to function there.

Thus within 45 years Christchurch changed from a genuinely communal mother church, with tightly controlled dependents, to what was little more than a single, very rich living for a single clerk, assisted by hired chaplains. Some few canonries remained, but the income of these canons was now secured to a large degree on the rectories of the previously dependent churches of the *parochia* plus some secular income; nor were the remaining canons apparently regularly resident in the mother church or living any sort of communal life there. In the 1140s a vigorous, reforming dean tried to return the church to its previous, genuinely collegiate state, and this must have slowed down the process of change. It is, however, clear from the Christchurch evidence how fast even a large and wealthy collegiate mother church with numerous dependents could become, once it had fallen into the hands of a clerical pluralist, just a wealthy rectory and a group of less wealthy ones with only vestigial collegiate links between them. Where no vigorous reformers opposed the process, and where no other impediments existed, these changes would have been completed very quickly indeed.

However, the forces leading to the breakup of the mother church system in the pre-Conquest period should not be exaggerated. Those Anglo-Saxon royal laws of the 10th and 11th centuries which discuss parochial rights assume, without exception, that the normal parochial system in England was the mother church with its dependent chapels.[40] Probably reality was more remote from this theory in some areas than in others, but in Wessex and Mercia at least, there are good grounds for thinking that the laws still approximated to contemporary circumstances. In Hampshire at the end of the 11th century the mother church system was still basically normal, although distortions in it were numerous, and although probably few mother churches were still collegiate by that date. The episcopal and religious vills which were entirely outside the system were liberties, exceptional grants to highly privileged religious bodies, and their independent churches were equally exceptional. The thegnly church with its cemetery was not outside the system, since it was, in the eye of the laws, dependent on the consent of the mother church. These royal laws were very close to the spirit of the canon law:[41] it can be confidently affirmed that the Church as well as the King remained convinced that the mother church system was right and proper, a system which ought to exist where no special considerations were involved.

Life in Late 11th-Century Mother Churches

Very little evidence of life in churches staffed by colleges of secular clerks survives for any area of England from before the mid 11th century, and very little even from then. The clearest cases are Harold's church at Waltham and the late pre-Conquest cathedral chapters. However, Waltham was a mid 11th-century foundation very closely connected with Earl Harold and the court, and is not necessarily good evidence for more ordinary mother churches dating from the 7th or 8th centuries and essentially parochial in character. Equally, it is dubious how far cathedral chapters can be assumed to be similar in life-style and constitution to local parochial secular minster churches. For these reasons, the post-Conquest evidence from Christchurch in Hampshire, which throws considerable light on the internal structure of that mother church and its *parochia*, is of exceptional interest.

There is no pre-Domesday documentary evidence for the existence of a church at Christchurch, though its cartulary preserves the texts of three late Anglo-Saxon royal charters in favour of laymen, two relating to small estates (each less than two hides) held by the canons of Christchurch in Domesday Book.[42] However, the plan of the Burghal Hidage *burh* of Twynham only makes sense on the assumption that the church and its cemetery were there before the *burh* was established in the mid 9th century. The site is the narrow peninsula of land between the Rivers Stour and Avon at their confluence on the northern side of Christchurch Harbour. The *burh* consisted of a ditch and bank running across the peninsula from river to river; its main street was laid out roughly parallel to the ditch, with the burgages running back to the foot of the bank. and with roads to east and west leading to the two river-crossings.[43] Obviously, to reduce the area requiring defence, it would have been sensible to place the ditch and bank as close to the tip of the peninsula as was feasible. This was not done. The whole of the tip of the peninsula, and all the land running back from it for a couple of hundred yards, was the cemetery and churchyard of Christchurch; the street of the *burh* and its defences were constructed beyond this, on the landward side of the churchyard. It is impossible to believe that the church was founded after the *burh* was laid out, and very difficult to believe that it was contemporary with the *burh*, because of the lavishness of the prime space occupied. Another suggestion of substantial age is the fact that the main church had a cluster of nine others around it (below p. 59), suggesting the 'multi-church' plans of other major early minsters. There were additional chapels standing in the cemetery at Eling and probably at St. Mary Extra also.

Thus it seems a fair presumption that Christchurch was, like the mother churches immediately to the east, around Southampton Water, a mother church dating back to the earliest Christian years. Like those churches, it is connected with a major royal manor and a group of royal hundreds.[44]

As we have seen, the church of Christchurch suffered badly in the post-Conquest years. Up to 1087 it seems to have continued to function as it had before 1066. Rannulf Flambard, on acquiring the church and manor from Rufus, reduced the community to raise money for his grand new church, the size of a moderate cathedral (Fig. 10).[45] Change culminated in outright exploitation under Dean Peter de Oglander, who diverted the income of the church to himself and his household clerks, and allowed the rebuilding to slow down or stop. This may have been a local reaction to the events of the civil war, in which the de Redvers family (patrons of

Dean Peter), were locally very active. Bishop Henry de Blois stepped in on Dean Peter's death (about 1140), ensuring that one of his own clerks, the energetic Hilary, later Bishop of Chichester, replaced Peter with a remit to bring the finances of the house back into order, restart the building work, and achieve the regularisation that Dean Gilbert had proposed. Dean Hilary achieved all these aims, although he had to retain the deanery for four years after his promotion to Chichester to do so.

Hilary started his internal reforms by demanding statements regarding the rights of the church before Rannulf Flambard took it over, and the fate of those rights in the intervening years. When he arrived at Christchurch two clerics at least, it would seem, remained alive whose memories stretched back to before Dean Rannulf's time: Ailmer, who seems to have remained throughout the period a canon at Christchurch, and Almetus, who was probably at Christchurch in the 1080s but who later moved to the prestigious post of priest of Carisbrooke and Dean of the Isle.[46] These two elderly priests provided statements which have survived in the Christchurch Cartulary, and it was probably one of them who produced the treatise on the history of the church from 1087 to 1146 which also survives there. Ailmer seems, in fact, not to have died until just before the regularisation in 1150, by which time he must have been into his late eighties.[47] It is these statements to Dean Hilary, probably made in the early 1140s, which give us the details of the post-Conquest but essentially pre-Norman way of life of this church.

The writer of the treatise on the internal history of Christchurch (hereafter called 'the History') stresses at the outset that, before Flambard took the church over, it was led by Godric, a man 'famous for his life and honesty'. Godric was not an autocratic leader like the later Norman Deans: he was *primus inter pares* ('leader and chief' — *patronus et senior*), resident in the church like the rest of the canons, elected by them, and like them dependent to a large extent on his share of the communally administered income of the church for his living. The History stresses that Godric celebrated every day 'the night hours and those of the whole day, from dawn to dusk' together with the rest of the canons. The History also implies that the main Mass each day was usually celebrated by Godric. It seems likely that the stress placed on these points is intended to show the respectability of the church. The late Anglo-Saxon laws enjoin both that in mother churches where the income was sufficient there should be 'right observance', which probably means that all the day and night hours should be celebrated communally, and that the priests should live as a celibate community.[48] It would appear that Christchurch met these requirements. It is interesting that Flambard seems to have allowed the full *horarium* to be dropped: at all events the History suggests that Dean Gilbert de Dousgunels had to reinstate it.

The canons had their houses built around the church in a close.[49] It would seem likely, though the History is not explicit on this point, that the 'outbuildings and domestic offices' of the canons which also stood in the close were held communally, and represent stables, barns and so forth for the community at large. Certainly the canons did hold some facilities in common: a school is mentioned in the early 12th century for instance.[50] Unfortunately the History is silent on the question of whether the pre-Flambard canons ate together in a refectory, and it is also unclear whether the income from the estates 'near the church' which was 'for food and drink' was distributed in the form of cash, or in the form of bread, beer, and other food, together with clothing and shoes. It is quite likely that at least part of the income from these estates was distributed in the form of bread and beer prepared communally, although it is, perhaps, unlikely that there was a refectory. At all events the church at Christchurch, with its full *horarium*, its presumably celibate priests, its resident leader, and its houses and outbuildings separated from the town and grouped around the church, is close to the Anglo-Saxon ideal of what a minster church should be.

The income of the estates of the pre-Flambard canons of Christchurch was divided, it would seem, into two. Most of it was not distributed into prebends, but was handled communally and distributed to the canons by way of an equal division. The History specifies that the income from the 'lands near the church' was distributed in this way, together with most of the alms received, and that this income was 'for food and drink', presumably meaning that it was for the necessary living expenses of the canons. These 'lands near the church' were contrasted with the 'external estates', which were therefore apparently not for food and drink and which were clearly handled differently. The 'lands near the church' were Hurn, Burton, and Preston. These were all estates lying within four miles of the church: Hurn four miles to the north-west, Burton one mile north, and Preston one-and-a-half miles west.

These estates form the Domesday $5\frac{1}{4}$ hide estate held by the canons in Twynham which had 'always been in the church'.[51] Domesday mentions a further one-hide estate in the Isle of Wight which had also 'always been in the church'. Unfortunately, this estate was also called Preston (in Shalfleet parish), and it is not clear if the History intends both Prestons or just the Christchrch Preston to be included within the 'lands near the church'. Nonetheless, it is clear that either $5\frac{1}{4}$ or, more likely, $6\frac{1}{4}$ of the $8\frac{3}{8}$ hides shown in the hands of the canons in Domesday Book was handled communally, and the income from this land distributed by equal division. This represents, if the 'lands near the church' include both Prestons, 25 virgates of land to support the probable 25 canons: an adequate but not excessively generous endowment, and one which recalls the frequently found endowment of a village church of one virgate for, presumably, one priest.

The remainder of the canons' land in 1086 must represent the 'external estates'. These were, it would seem, held by individual canons. Alsi the canon had held 1¾ hides at Bashley before the New Forest was formed, and Alnod the canon 1½ virgates at Borstall. Domesday states that both held 'of the King' although their land is entered under the estate of the canons. These two manors were presumably granted to the church in the 10th or 11th centuries following royal grants of them to named individuals: Bashley by King Edward in 1053, and *Borstealle* by King Æthelred in 985. A third Anglo-Saxon royal grant recorded in the Christchurch Cartulary, made by King Eadwig in 956, was of land at Zeals and Donhead in Wiltshire.[52] Domesday does not show any estate here held by the canons, but it is likely that they had some land in this area then since they later held some scattered small estates in South Wiltshire for which no later deed of grant can be shown. Equally missing from Domesday is the land at Piddleton in Dorset, held by the church 'of old' in the eyes of the early 12th-century Richard de Redvers.[53] It is very likely that this too was held by the canons in Anglo-Saxon times but without explicit reference in Domesday Book, perhaps because the canon holding the land was considered to hold 'of the king' like Alsi and Alnod and, as with most sub-tenants on royal estates in this part of England, was not mentioned separately by name.

However, it is clear that the total area of the external estates was small at best: perhaps a quarter of the total land of the church. Only a small minority of the canons can have held any of these external estates in addition to their share of the communally held land.

It is by no means clear that the 'external estates' were held by the canons as prebends, that is, as prebends were understood in later years. The classic prebend was a clearly delimited body of rights and income which a prebendary held in the same way that a rector held his church: with the exception that the prebendary could not alienate or waste the property, he was the absolute beneficial owner of it. The community to which a prebendary belonged could not, once the prebend had been handed over to him at his induction by the Bishop, claim back any part of it, nor direct how the income should be used, nor repartition the income into a new series of prebends.

At Christchurch in the late 11th century, the 'external estates' seem to have been something rather different. Bishop Flambard assumed that they were completely within the control of the community as a whole; while they were held by individual canons, this arrangement could be reconsidered at any time. He clearly felt that these 'external estates' could be more easily annexed to the building fund of the new church than could the 'lands near the church'. To get agreement to this diversion of revenues Flambard felt he needed to consult, not the individual canons holding these estates, but the community as a whole, which he accordingly called together in a meeting for the purpose. He obtained the community's agreement despite the vehement opposition of Godric, the leader of the canons, a man, presumably, who would himself have held at least some land of the external estates.

The 'external estates', therefore, if not dissimilar from prebends, were prebends in embryo only. They were, before 1087, economically peripheral to the community as a whole, with only a small part of the lands of the church included in them. Only a quarter of the canons at most, and probably less, can have held them; even if the leaders of the community enjoyed them, the church still essentially revolved around the management of a single common fund rather than around a congeries of separate estates. It is noticeable, too, how very small the individual 'external estates' were: the largest in 1066 was 1¾ hides, and that of poor-quality forest land,[54] and the only other estate with its area recorded in Domesday Book was a mere 1½ virgates. They would scarcely have provided much in the way of prebendal income.

The ecclesiastical income of Christchurch — tithe, customary offerings, and alms — was, it seems, divided along lines very similar to the income from land. Much of this ecclesiastical income seems not to have been distributed among the canons, but kept as a central reserve for spending on the needs of the community as a whole, in accordance with decisions taken by the community. Thus Flambard called all the canons together for a communal decision that he might use 'all ecclesiastical offerings from visitors, and all the offerings both of the living and the dead from the whole *parochia*', for the work of his new church.

Among the ecclesiastical income which was communally controlled in this way, and which was devoted to the work of the church following the meeting called by Flambard, was tithe. The History gives no hint of how the tithe income was used before Flambard and Gilbert de Dousgunels devoted it to the work of the church, and there is no evidence on the subject elsewhere in the Cartulary. Very possibly tithe income was used for the general communal expenses, especially the charitable expenditure, of the church.

By contrast, it seems that most of the alms offered at the church were set aside for the food and drink of the canons, and distributed among them together with the income of the 'lands near the church' by way of an equal divison. The History is explicit that the 'food and drink alms', whatever was included in that category, together with all other alms except Mass offerings, were distributed in this way. It is possible that these 'food and drink alms' represent all offerings made in kind; thus they may have included minor tithe and churchscot, which were mostly paid in kind, with only the major tithe being used originally for communal purposes and then later devoted to the work of the church by Deans Rannulf and Gilbert.

The History makes it clear, however, that while most ecclesiastical income was either distributed in equal shares with the income of 'the lands near the church' or else used for the communal purposes of the church in accordance with decisions of the community, some was held by individual canons: thus Mass offerings were retained by the celebrant at minor Masses and by the dean at major Masses. The History makes no mention of sepulture: this may also have been retained by the celebrant as with Mass offerings.

At all events, it is clear that the bulk of the ecclesiastical income was communally controlled: much was traditionally distributed in equal shares along with the income of the 'lands near the church' to meet the living expenses of the canons, and part was disbursed to meet other communal expenses. As with the income from land, only a small proportion was controlled and retained by individual canons.

Thus it seems that late Anglo-Saxon Christchurch did not operate under a semi-regular regimen of Chrodegangine type: there was no dormitory and probably no refectory, and the canons lived in individual houses arranged in a close. At the same time the income of the church was handled communally, the great bulk of it as a common fund which provided for the living expenses of the canons by way of equal distributions of cash and, probably, food and clothing among them. Other income, especially tithe, seems to have been controlled by the community, and spent in accordance with communal decisions. A small part of the income was handled in a semi-prebendal fashion, with small estates held by individual canons, but subject to control by the community as a whole. The canons seem to have lived as a celibate community and celebrated communally the full *horarium*, and they were lead by a resident 'leader and chief' elected from among themselves.

The regimen at Christchurch, therefore, seems very similar to those of the late pre-Conquest secular cathedral chapters and to that at Harold's church of Waltham.[55] At all these churches much of the income was distributed via a common fund, which provided for clothing, food and drink — in many cases by a distribution in kind — and which also met all the communal expenses of the church. Other income was distributed, in most of these churches, by way of embryo prebends. Most of the churches had their canons living in separate houses: where dormitories and refectories were found these all seem to have been the result of late pre-Conquest reforming bishops. At Waltham, apparently, some canons were married, but neither at Christchurch nor in the Cathedral chapters does this seem usual. The implication, perhaps surprisingly, is that Anglo-Saxon collegiate parochial mother churches had a lifestyle very similar to that of the greater churches: a mixed system in which elements of communal life and individual life are both notable, but in which the communal life, with its full *horarium*, tends to be the more significant.

The Cure of Souls in the Mother Church Parochia

The History of Christchurch does not discuss clearly the canons' provision for the cure of souls within their *parochia*. Luckily, a statement by Almetus and Ailmer preserved in the Christchurch Cartulary throws considerable light on the pre-1087 practice at this church.[56] The statement starts by outlining the bounds of the *parochia*, in only a few words ascribing to Christchurch the whole of the Hampshire coast from Beaulieu Harbour to Dorset and from the coast to deep in the New Forest: more than eleven modern parishes. Everything within this fifteen mile strip 'belonged' to Christchurch, and especially tithe, churchscot, alms and sepulture (Fig. 11).

Almetus's account of the dedication of the church at Milford shows the pre-1087 type of relationship between Christchurch and its dependent churches with exceptional clarity. At the time of Domesday Book Alvric the Small was one of the more important thegnly figures in the Christchurch area, where he probably held about 9¼ hides by 1079. Seven of these were lost when the New Forest was established in 1079, leaving him, with only 2¼ hides, perhaps the most seriously affected of all the local landlords by the afforestation. It may have been for this reason that the Conqueror granted him a half-hide estate just outside the Forest 'in exchange for (land lost to) the Forest'.[57] Before the afforestation Alvric probably lived at Brockenhurst, then his largest and richest manor, and Domesday records a church on his land there. Brockenhurst, however, was in the very heart of the Forest[58] and Alvric clearly preferred to move to his less exposed manor at Milford, the land newly granted to him by the Conqueror. Between 1079 and 1087, Alvric took steps to found a church at his new residence: presumably he or his predecessor had, a few decades earlier, done the same at the older residence.

The church which Alvric founded at Milford was very much not an *Eigenkirche*, yet it was, nonetheless, very much a church founded for his convenience. The dean of Christchurch agreed to send out a priest to say Mass there for Alvric (waiting for him 'as the greater man' before beginning). The priest was not resident at Milford — he was to be fed at Alvric's table — and, while it is likely that Mass continued to be said even when Alvric was not resident, the whole tenor of the document suggests that this was a bonus: essentially the church was for Alvric's convenience, and the priest was sent from Christchurch to serve him, not the village community of Milford. The personal connection between Alvric and his church is shown clearly by the dean's agreement that the priest sent to serve Milford church would accompany Alvric on his journeys to the hundred court.

The agreement between Alvric and the dean stipulated that a cemetery was to be provided at

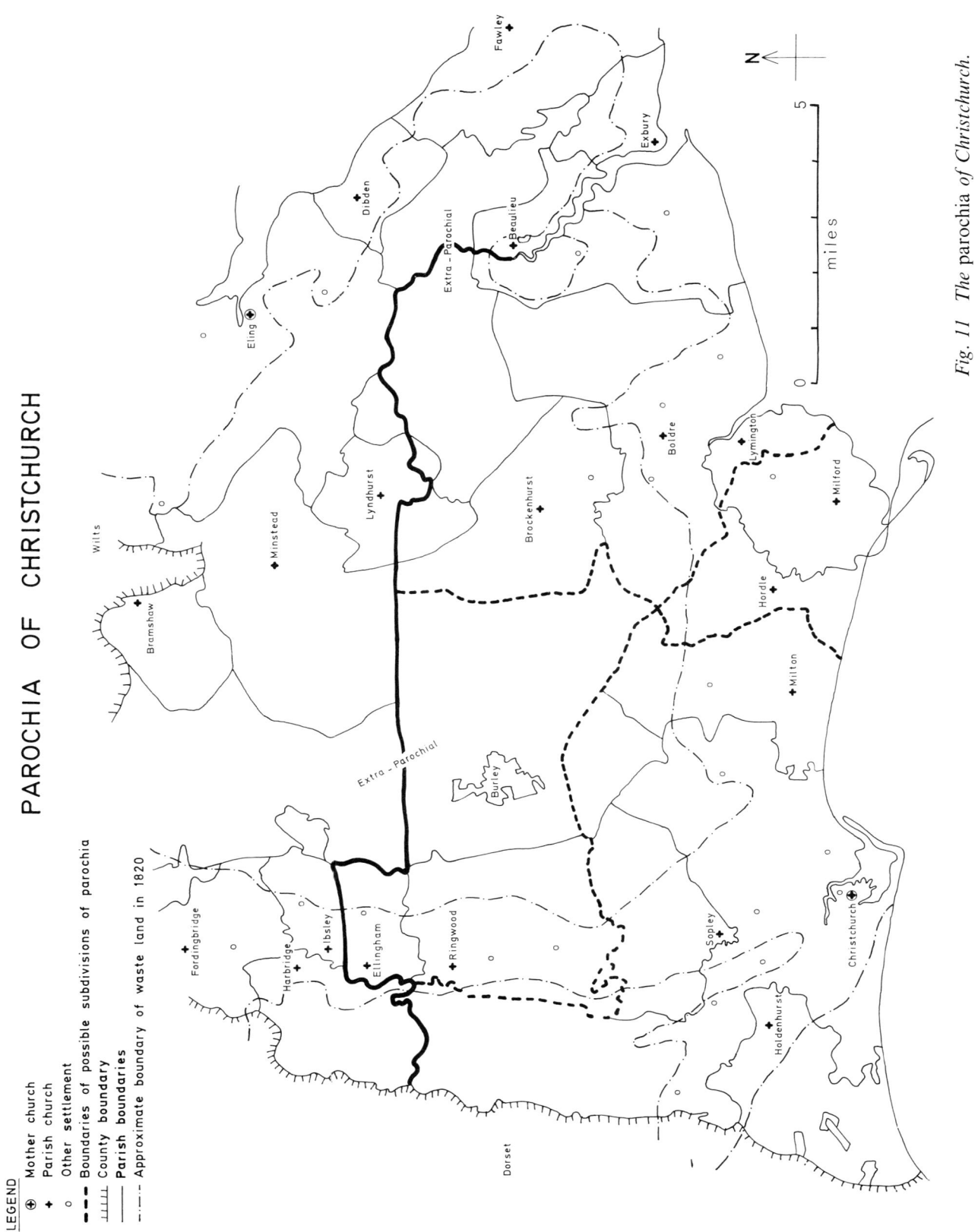

Fig. 11 The parochia of Christchurch.

Milford, but it was only to be used by 'Alvric's slaves and cottars', who were to pay 4*d.* as sepulture. All others were to be buried at Christchurch and pay the customary sepulture there. Almetus and Ailmer stated that similar arrangements governed the use of the cemetery at Boldre: only 'cottars and slaves of the manor on which that church is founded, who were so poor that they did not have the wherewithal to allow them to be carried to Christchurch', were to be buried there: all others were to be buried at the mother church.

At Boldre also it was stipulated that all men 'both free men and villeins' were to attend at the mother church on all feasts (presumably the priest normally sent to Boldre would remain at Christchurch for feasts) and to pay all their alms there. It seems likely that the same applied at Milford, although this is not stated. Both at Milford and at Boldre, and also at Brockenhurst, it is specifically stated that tithe and churchscot remained due to Christchurch: none was to be diverted to the new church.

Alvric was required to hand over half a virgate of land for this agreement. This was not, it seems, in any real sense glebe of the church at Milford, but land held by Christchurch to offset the costs of sending a priest to serve there: it is stated that Alvric handed over the land 'to Dean Godric and the canons of Christchurch'. It was probably only with the vicarage endowment of Milford imposed by Bishop Henry de Blois (1161–70) that this land became formally attached to the church of Milford.

A similar endowment of land can possibly be traced at another of the dependent churches in Christchurch *parochia*. Baldwin de Redvers I, in his confirmation charter to Christchurch on the appointment of Dean Hilary (probably 1140–1141),[59] mentioned that Earl Godwin had granted one virgate of land in Sopley to the church there, presumably on its foundation. After the Conquest the de Stanton family claimed to be the founders of Sopley church, and gave it to the Priory of Breamore: Christchurch only regained effective control following vigorous legal action by Dean Hilary. Once Hilary had regained control, he handed the church over to one of his canons, Sylvester, 'as a prebend': Sylvester presumably controlling the virgate in question as the bulk of his prebend and either travelling out to serve the church like Eilwi, the priest of Christchurch sent by Dean Godric to Milford, or else paying a chaplain to perform the necessary duties at Sopley.[60]

While the details of the dispute remain in part unclear, they are consistent with a mid 11th-century foundation by Earl Godwin along lines similar to those agreed between Alvric and Dean Godric: that is, with a church completely dependent on Christchurch, served from Christchurch, with no separate *persona* and with its 'glebe' held by Christchurch; followed by a post-Conquest refoundation by the de Stantons on standard Norman lines, in other words as an independent church with a resident priest. If such a development occurred, it might well have seemed to the de Stantons that the previous church had been little more than a mere private chapel, and that they, having put the church on a proper foundation, should have the right to endow it properly with the land which their predecessor had clearly intended for the church. If such a clash between Anglo-Saxon and Norman concepts did occur at Sopley, it is interesting that even in the mid 12th century the dean was able to win his case, and to get the land into the control of one of his canons. Equally, however, it is worth noting that about twenty years afterwards Bishop Henry de Blois ensured, by his formal vicarage endowment, that the canons' antiquated rights were modernised and the virgate handed over to the vicar, subject to an annual pension of 5*s.* to the mother church.

To return to Alvric's church at Milford, it is striking in the statement of Almetus and Ailmer how insignificant the bishop seems in the whole affair. Walkelin was not a weak or easy-going prelate, but it was not from him but from Dean Godric that Alvric sought permission to build his church, and it was Dean Godric not the bishop who eventually granted it. Walkelin's role seems to have been essentially to ensure fair play, to umpire the negotiations. Nothing could underline the real power of the Anglo-Saxon collegiate mother church more clearly than this evidence that, in a matter of vital importance to the cure of souls, the English head of a parochial minster was of more practical significance at the local level than an Anglo-Norman bishop of great power and magnificence.

Other early foundation documents of other Hampshire churches suggest much the same conclusions. At Bursledon, as late as the second quarter of the 12th century, it was only when the priest of the mother church of Bishops Waltham (an episcopal clerk, for this mother church had lost its collegiate status long before) requested it that the bishop gave the critical permission to allow Bursledon church to be built and, by implication for it to have a cemetery.[61] At Bursledon as at Milford, it was stipulated that the villagers were to attend the mother church on certain named feasts, to pay their alms there, and also their major tithe. The founders of Bursledon church were to pay a yearly pension of 4*s.* to the mother church (at Domesday values this is close to the value of a virgate, at mid 12th-century values perhaps to that of half a virgate), and were to present the priest who was to serve the new church, not to the Bishop, but to the priest of the mother church, who was presumably to induct him, and who could exact an oath of fealty from him.

Another foundation during Henry of Blois's episcopate was Wickham, within the *parochia* of Titchfield. The text relating to this is unfortunately not so detailed as that for Bursledon, and it does not make it clear whether in this case the consent of the mother church was sought: it merely states that the Bishop agreed with the lord of the manor that a church with cemetery should be founded and that the demesne tithe of the estate should be given to it.[62] Nonetheless, the Bishop required the newly built chapel to pay an annual pension to Titchfield mother church of no less than 20s.: the value, even at mid 12th-century prices, of about half a hide. Certainly this pension was of substantially greater value than the 40 acres ($\frac{1}{3}$ of a hide) granted to the new church, particularly if, as seems likely, the mother church was to receive not only the pension but the villein tithe as well.

In 1114 a full-scale dispute seems to have broken out in the Isle of Wight between the priest of Carisbrooke, Almetus, and Hugh Gernun, lord of Chale, on the foundation of a church at Chale.[63] Here the clash between Anglo-Saxon and Anglo-Norman concepts of proper parochial arrangements was certainly at least in part behind the dispute: Almetus claiming his full rights as priest of the mother church, Hugh Gernun claiming the right to do as he chose in his own fee. Bishop William Giffard, in the interests of peace, enforced a compromise, but it is striking how heavily that compromise was biased in favour of the mother church. The Bishop ruled that the mother church's rights were to be bought off by the transfer to it of half the land which Gernun had set aside to endow his new church, together with half the villein tithe and half the villein alms and sepulture. Even here, it was the priest of the mother church, not the Bishop, who gave the critically important permission which allowed the new church to have a cemetery.

These documents from Christchurch and elsewhere throw considerable light on the meaning of the 'lesser church with cemetery' which appears as one of the major categories of rural church in the late Anglo-Saxon laws.[64] Milford and Boldre can be taken to represent this sort of church: completely dependent on a mother church; served from that mother church by a non-resident or semi-resident priest; its endowment to a large degree merged with that of the mother church; its cemetery restricted to slaves and cottars; and subject to a requirement that the residents who normally worshipped there should return to the mother church on major feasts. At the same time, these two churches, with their close connections with the secular lords of the villages in which they stood, illustrate the sort of church that a West Saxon five-hide thegn could hope to have at his main residence.

Dependent churches of this type could not long survive the Conquest without major changes in their status. The severe restriction on the bishop's powers of control shown in the case of Walkelin at Milford would not have been acceptable to reforming 12th-century prelates; neither would the mediatising of control of the cure of souls from bishop to mother-church dean have been acceptable to the new canon law. The tendency to deny full ecclesiastical status to dependent churches, and to slow down the impetus to found village churches, must also have caused anxiety to reforming bishops. Anglo-Norman lords must, equally, have viewed with disfavour a system which denied them the power to found and endow at their free will churches on their own estates.

At Christchurch, the critical move from the mother church/dependent church system to a more modern parochial structure came in the middle of the 12th century. We have seen that Rannulf Flambard had reduced the number of canons and that the second Norman dean, Gilbert de Dousgunels, had reduced them even further and given each canon a formal prebend, with many of the prebends including control of one of the dependent churches of the *parochia*. There is some evidence that in this period the canons began to reside at their prebendal churches rather than at Christchurch, and that they had begun to depute their various duties in them to hired chaplains. This must have led not only to a decline in community life at Christchurch, but also to a decline in the dependence of the daughter churches. The relationship of the canons to the chaplains officiating in their prebendal churches must have led to a development of at least the beginnings of a rectorial/vicarial relationship. These tendencies were taken further and formalised in the third quarter of the 12th century by Bishop Henry de Blois. Thus, in Bishop Henry's vicarage endowments for the churches of Christchurch (Christchurch 1150–8, the dependent churches 1161–70) it is clear that before the date of the endowment, and probably therefore before 1150, the services conducted within the church of Christchurch were already the responsibility of a chaplain, the predecessor of the vicar whose status and income were now set down by the Bishop. In 1161–70, Thorley, Sopley and Milford churches had 'rectors' who were only to be replaced with formally endowed and instituted vicars on their deaths.[65] These 'rectors' can hardly be other than the secular canons who had held these churches as part of their prebends. The implication is that in the last decade before the regularisation in 1150 the dean was, with his chaplains, treating Christchurch itself more and more as his own personal church, while he allowed the daughter churches at least some *de facto* independence from it: each was subject to a rector who, while he remained in name a canon of Christchurch, was in fact no longer a member of a genuinely collegiate mother church. The use of the word 'rector' for the canons connected with the dependent churches certainly strongly suggests both a measure of independence for them and a tendency for the canons to reside at their prebendal churches at this date.

This vicarage endowment for the dependent churches dates from ten to twenty years after the regularisation, and it might be argued that these 'rectors' were a post-regularisation development. However, we hear elsewhere of a canon of Christchurch holding Sopley church 'as a prebend' in *c.* 1140,[66] and, at about the same date, of other canons holding

Piddleton church in Dorset[67] in the same way, suggesting that the arrangement dates from before the regularisation. Other prebends known during the 1140s are Stanpit just outside Christchurch (this prebend was held by the dean: after the regularisation it became the major holding of the Prior),[68] and Apse in the Isle of Wight.[69] Thus, given that there were only five canons by the 1140s, it seems likely that all of them were by then holding prebends; and that these were all (except for the dean's prebend at Stanpit) based on lands some way from Christchurch, although each canon probably continued to receive his share of the income of the old common-fund lands near Christchurch.

Bishop Henry's vicarage endowments, which are among the oldest surviving formal vicarage endowments in England, were on a pattern which became routine in later centuries. In some cases the vicar received all the glebe, tithe and other income, subject to a substantial annual pension to Christchurch; in others income was divided into rectorial (especially the greater tithe) and vicarial (most of the rest). The familiar nature of these endowments makes it easy to forget the revolutionary nature of Henry's actions. He was attempting to ensure that the basic income of the mother church was not affected, but that at the same time both its power over the dependent churches, and the power of the individual canons over the churches of their prebends, was limited. To do this, he gave to each of the previously dependent churches an independent *persona* and a fixed income, not subject to control by either the mother church or the prebendary, and he made the Bishop, not the mother church, responsible for induction of the vicar. Before these endowments, Christchurch was still, at least in theory, in full control of its *parochia*: the whole area 'belonged' to the mother church, which alone was responsible for ensuring an appropriate level of service, and any rectorial/vicarial relationships were informal and temporary only, although the establishment of prebends in the 1120s had gone some way, as we have seen, towards making the subordinate churches more independent. Afterwards, Christchurch controlled only its own parish, its rights over the rest of the *parochia* being reduced to a mere fixed income. By 1200 almost all mother church/dependent church relationships in Hampshire seem to have become converted into simple cash payments of this sort: action such as Bishop Henry's at Christchurch may have been more widespread than our present evidence suggests.

Fossilised relics of the older relationships did, however, survive here and there, probably more for the status which they conferred on the old mother church than for any other reason. In a number of places, processions to the mother church from its old daughter churches continued to take place on the patronal feast of the old mother church, and formal offerings were made of wax and cash in fixed amounts.[70] There is evidence for such processions to Christchurch, St.

Mary Extra Southampton, Carisbrooke and Bishops Waltham, and very similar arrangements are known from Winchester, Romsey and Wherwell.[71] At Bishops Waltham, the rector of the old mother church enjoyed an extraordinary archidiaconal jurisdiction (including the power to prove wills) over its old dependents down to the 18th century.[72]

Conclusion

Thus Hampshire provides a considerable body of evidence for the old mother church system. Obviously the evidence is thin and scattered, and it requires something of an act of faith to accept that each recorded case represents the normal situation rather than an anomaly. Nonetheless the Hampshire evidence does suggest four points of interest: first, that the system of collegiate mother churches probably resulted from an act of royal policy of the years 685–726 which linked the provision of parochial churches to the royal *villa regalis* system; secondly, that various forces placed increasing strain on that system in the 10th and 11th centuries and led to its almost complete collapse in the 12th, during which period remaining mother church rights were almost completely converted to cash payments; thirdly, that collegiate parochial mother churches were often run along lines similar to the greater Anglo-Saxon churches, with a semi-communal life, full *horarium*, a celibate community, and very little in the way of separate, prebendal income; and finally, that the mother church's control over the dependent churches of its *parochia* was very substantial in late Anglo-Saxon times: a dependent church having no independent *persona*, no tithe or glebe income separate from the mother church, and restricted rights of sepulture and of service. This evidence amplifies our picture of the thegnly lesser church with cemetery described in the late Anglo-Saxon laws.

Appendix: Documents relating to Mother Churches in Hampshire in the 12th Century

1. Internal history of the Mother Church of Christchurch, 1087–1146

(Christchurch Cartulary (Brit. Lib. MS Cott. Tib. D VI A) f.30b. Printed in W. Dugdale, *Monasticon Anglicanum* (London, 1661). ii, 177–8, and B. Ferrey and E.W. Brayley, *The Antiquities of the Priory of Christchurch, Hants* (London, 1834), Appendix i–iii)

Our orthodox forefathers — fathers, grandfathers and even great-grandfathers, lay and cleric — have told these things to those who came after them about the church of the Holy Trinity which is sited in the town called Twynham, in a completely trustworthy account.

At the time when William Rufus reigned in England there was a certain clerk named Godric in this church of Twynham — a man famous for his life and honesty. In accordance with their custom, Godric every day celebrated the night hours and those of the whole day, from dawn to dusk, together with the 24 canons of the church. Now at that time, his clerks treated this Godric not as dean, for they did not even understand that term, but as leader and chief.

It was the ecclesiastical custom of those canons that this Godric, the leader of the canons, should receive as his own the offerings of the Morrow Mass and of the High Mass, no matter who gave them, without anyone else sharing in them. Other offerings, however, that is to say those made before Mass, or between Masses, and those offered at Vespers, were shared out equally between the canons. The lands near the church, that is, Hurn, Burton and Preston, were treated in the same way, the income from them being distributed by division. Furthermore, any canon celebrating a Mass received all the offerings of that Mass without anyone sharing in them, that is to say, an offering made after he was vested in his cope.

At this point, as it chanced, Bishop Randulf begged this church, with the town, from King William. Since he saw that God had worked many miracles there on many occasions, he gave many kinds of precious things and relics of the saints to the church. Bishop Randulf wished to build a better church more fitted to religious use than the old church of the Holy Trinity at Twynham, and so he decided to make arrangements to tear the old church down. He called the whole community of the canons to a meeting, together with Godric, their leader, in order that they might grant him, for the completion of the future church, all ecclesiastical offerings from visitors, and all the offerings both of the living and the dead from the whole *parochia*, except for those offerings which were set aside for the food and drink of the canons; and further that they might also grant him their external estates so that he could assign them for this purpose together with the offerings, until such time as the church was fully built and perfect and dedicated to God. Since it seemed to them that their food and drink would be sufficient, all the canons complied with his wish and suggestion; Godric, however, the leader of the canons, recklessly objected to this proposal and argued against it for a long time, until he was forced to flee from the church, to be harried from one end of England to the other, getting neither help nor favour from either the King or his Bishop in this matter. Eventually he came back, begging for mercy from Bishop Randulf; beseeching him that he might be replaced in his original position among the canons subject to the Bishop.

The Bishop now tore down the old church of the place, and the nine others which stood about the cemetery, together with certain houses of the canons which stood near the cemetery of the church. In order that he might open up the site, he not only removed the outbuildings and domestic offices to new sites but also moved the canons into suitable accommodation in the town. Bishop Randulf, therefore, founded the church which now stands at Twynham, and the houses and outbuildings and domestic offices of all the clergy there. When any of the canons died he retained that canon's benefice in his power, not granting it out to any successor. He wished to distribute the prebends of every clerk that should chance to be overcome by death in his time to those remaining. Now Godric the leader of the canons died, and not long after him ten others from the community of canons. The Bishop therefore granted their prebends to the 13 remaining canons for the rest of their lives, as a supplement to their food and drink.

At this point, William, king of the English, died, and his brother Henry succeeded him as King. Bishop Randulf was gravely accused of many things by the King; he was captured and imprisoned in London. Following this, his church of the Holy Trinity of Twynham was disposed of, being granted in perpetual alms to a certain clerk called Gilbert de Dousgunels, but only after it had been despoiled by force and violence of all those precious things previously given to it by the Bishop. The church was granted to Gilbert de Dousgunels in its entirety, and he was to hold it on his own, for by this time death had seized all the canons except five. Gilbert, therefore, received the entire church, saving the liberty of the canons and all their rights, both in income for food and drink as laid down by Bishop Randulf, and in food and drink alms. He also continued the work required on the as yet unfinished church, using for this the external estates.

Since he saw that the site was adequate, and that the church now rising there was suitable to be used for religious purposes, Gilbert, with the assent of those five canons, went to Rome in order to get a licence and privilege from the Lord Pope to place in the church the order of canons regular, in accordance with the honour and standing of the church. However, as he was returning, he died.

When this happened, the elder Richard de Redvers, who had received the lordship of the church and the whole district from King Henry, gave this church of Twynham to a certain clerk, named Peter de Oglander. Peter de Oglander received the right to rule and the duty of completing the church, saving the position and rights of the canons, in accordance with what his predecessors Bishop Randulf and Gilbert had laid down.

This same Richard de Redvers gave to the work of the church and to the canons a certain manor in the Isle of Wight called Ningwood. One of his barons gave another manor, called Apse. Furthermore, all the parishioners gave all their tithes to the work of the church, as had been laid down by Gilbert. This same

Gilbert had also ruled that the community should celebrate together the complete day and night services, as is done now.

This Peter, however, overcome, alas! with evil ambition, took away all those things promised for the work of the church, whether set aside for it by ancient custom or else devoted to that end by the five canons. All those things granted as offerings for the completion of the church he took and distributed — not canonically but by an abuse of his power — to himself and to the household clerks he brought with him, granting them a table in his hall for the rest of their lives, and transferring to them the right to use this income. These intruder clerks, because of this grant, took council among themselves when Peter died, and, ganging up together, threw everyone else out, and occupied this table, craftily taking control of the offerings which should have been devoted to the work of the church, each giving testimony to the rest that this was something decreed, conceded, and confirmed by the dean. Thus they have fought up to the present in another's kingdom.

All these things which have been done since Randulf's time are thus still undecided and unsettled, and are left here to the consideration and judgement of the future as is the way of a good cleric, who, as his life draws to a close, should leave hidden many matters on behalf of the church (?).

Hilary, a clerk of the Bishop of Winchester, succeeded, a man famous for his honesty and life of humility. Hilary wished to change matters for the better, and so, by the providence of Divine Grace, he went to Rome, following the precedents which had been set by his predecessor. At Rome he was elected bishop by the Lord Pope and decorated with the fillet of Bishop of Chichester. It is his intention to consider carefully all these matters, to ensure that appropriate measures are taken for the future.

2. Rights of Christchurch over its Parochia

(a) Statement of Almetus and Ailmer on Rights over the Parochia *and on the Foundation of Milford Church*

(Christchurch Cartulary (Brit. Lib. MS Cott. Tib. D VI B) f.36a)

Almetus, Dean of the Isle, and Ailmer and many others testify that from the springs of a certain stream called Otter,[73] which rises at Lyndhurst in the virgate of Henry son of Herbert the Forester, and thence along that stream until it falls into the sea, everything is in the *parochia* of Christchurch, and all the churches which used to be or are still in the area from this side of that stream right across to Dorset belong to Christchurch, and also the tithe and churchscot.

They also testify that no-one should be buried at Boldre except cottars and slaves of the manor on which that church is founded. who were so poor that they did not have the wherewithal to allow them to be carried to Christchurch; both free men and villeins ought, one and all, to go to Christchurch on all feasts and pay there their tithe and churchscot and alms, and to carry their dead there for burial.

They also testify that the tithe of Brockenhurst belongs to the church of Christchurch.

Almetus also testifies that he was present at the dedication of the church of Milford and that Alvric the Small asked Dean Godric, and through him Bishop Walkelin, if he might build a church there, under condition that Christchurch should not lose any part of its ancient customs, that is, tithe and churchscot. Furthermore, Alvric gave half a virgate of land to the church when it was dedicated. At the same time, the Bishop and Alvric handed over the church and the land to Dean Godric and the canons of Christchurch free of services, by handing over the key. It was stipulated in the presence of the bishop that only Alvric's slaves and cottars should be buried there, and that they should pay 4*d.* as sepulture. Godric agreed that he would send a priest there, who should be fed at Alvric's table whenever he was resident there. The priest should wait for Alvric before beginning the service, he being the greater man, to a reasonable extent. The priest should accompany Alvric to the Hundred whenever he went there, but no further. Almetus also saw Godric send a certain priest of Christchuch there, by name Eilwi. Godric held the church in this way during his life, and after him his successors held it in the same way.

(b) Memorandum on Recognition Processions

(Christchurch Cartulary (Brit. Lib. MS Cott. Tib. D VIB) f.36b)

Note that the parishioners of Boldre, Brockenhurst and Lymington, Milton, Sopley and Holdenhurst must visit Christchurch as their mother church, on Ascension Day or on the Sunday following, with candles according to the number of parishioners, great and small, so that the parishioners of Boldre will bear a candle worth 3*s.* 6*d.*, those of Milford one worth 3*s.* 8*d.*, and those of Hordle one worth 2*s.* The tenants of the two estates at Hurn and of Bostall and the land near the Bridge shall offer on the same Ascension Day 16*s.* in lieu of candles. Those of Ringwood shall bring a candle worth 3*s.* 6*d.* and those of Ellingham one worth 2*s.* 6*d.* This is done in accordance with old and approved custom.

3. Foundation of the Church of Bursledon

(Winchester College Muniments No. 10629. Printed L. Voss, *Heinrich von Blois, Bischof von Winchester* (Berlin, 1932), p. 165–6)

Henry, by the Grace of God Bishop of Winchester, to the archdeacons, deans, and all the clergy and people of the diocese of Winchester, greeting:

Known you all that I have granted to the monks of Hamble, at the request of Walter my clerk who has obtained the parsonage of the church of St. Peter at Waltham, and with the assent of Christopher my clerk who by our generosity has succeeded canonically to the aforesaid Walter in the parsonage of this same church of Waltham, in perpetuity, all the tithe and offerings both of the living and of the dead from that hide of land which belongs to those monks, and also from the other hide of Bursledon, except for the tithe of salt.[74]

This grant is made on condition that the aforesaid monks shall pay to the church of St. Peter at Waltham 4s. each year as a recognition payment. The parishioners of the said hides shall pay Peter's Pence to the church of Waltham, and shall make a procession at Pentecost to the church of Waltham, and a visit there on the feast of St. Peter's Chains. I grant that the aforesaid monks may build a chapel at Bursledon for the convenience of the parishioners, which they shall serve well. The monks shall repair the chapel whenever work is needed. They shall collect their chrism from the parson of the church at Waltham. Furthermore, the priest who shall serve there shall be presented to the parson of Waltham by the aforesaid monks, and, if the parson of Waltham wishes, he shall swear fealty to him.

Witnessed by these: Ralph archdeacon of Winchester, Robert archdeacon of Surrey, William prior of the Hospital, Robert the Almoner, Robert of Clatford, Alberic Summarius, Robert of Limesia, Master Herbert, Master Nicholas, William Tirell, Bernard the Chaplain, Joseph, Alan, Martin Lamartre, clerks.

4. Foundation of Chale Church

(Carisbrooke Cartulary (Brit. Lib. MS Egerton 36667) f.22b)

In the Year of Our Lord 1114, on the first of December, this agreement was made between the church of St. Mary of Carisbrooke in the Isle of Wight and Almetus the priest of that church, and the church of St. Andrew of Chale and Hugh Gernun who had founded that church, in the presence of William Giffard, Bishop of Winchester, who had on that same day dedicated the church of Chale. At that dedication this agreement was discussed and agreed with many men witnessing it.

Almetus the priest claimed that the church of Chale was within the *parochia* of St. Mary of Carisbrooke. Hugh Gernun said that the men of his fee were not parishioners either of the church of Carisbrooke or of anywhere else but that, by ancient custom, alive they could go to whatever church they wished, and dead they could go wherever they wished for burial. He said that they could do this, and that they had done it. Almetus, however, denied this and offered proof of his accusation.

However, lest damage by caused between churches, and in order that peace and love be confirmed between them and their friends, this agreement was reached by the council of friends and by the grant and confirmation of the Bishop.

Hugh Gernun granted to the church of St. Mary of Carisbrooke half of all the land, tithe, sepulture and alms (except for those of his own house) which had been or would be given to the church of Chale, whether by men of his own fee or by anyone else.

As for the service of the church, and its upkeep, support and repair, this would be his responsibility without anyone else participating.

Hugh endowed the church with land, the tithe of his own ploughs, and, as mentioned above, the alms of his own house.

The priest of Chale would do all the duties of the church for the living and the dead, and keep the church in books and vestments, and he would be responsible for its support and repair, even if it were to fall down to the foundations, and he would do all these things without any help or assistance from the priest of Carisbrooke.

For this agreement Almetus allowed a cemetery to be provided at Chale.

The Bishop witnessed this agreement and signified his approval by fixing his seal on it, and confirmed it with a perpetual anathema, so that whoever should knowingly breach the agreement should be anathema.

With these witnesses: Richard, the Bishop's chaplain and Dean, Stephen the clerk, Roger de Melford, Ralph Mansell.

Notes

1. This article is developed from material discussed in greater detail in the author's unpublished PhD thesis, 'The Development of the Parish in Hampshire, Particularly in the Eleventh and Twelfth Centuries' (University of Cambridge, 1975), copies of which are in the University Library, Cambridge and in the Library of the Hampshire County Record Office, Winchester. In this article *Hampshire* means the county within its historic boundaries, not the present area so called.

2. Bede, *Ecclesiastical History of the English People* eds. B. Colgrave & R.A.B. Mynors (Oxford, 1969). Book iv, chapter xvi, p. 382. For date see *Anglo-Saxon Chronicle* ed. G.N. Garmonsway (London, 1953). *sub anno*.
3. Throughout this article *parochia* means the whole area parochially subject to a mother church; *parish* means the area subject to a single parish church, as shown in 13th century or later descriptions and maps. In other words, each *parochia* covers the area of a number of *parishes*.
4. The eastern bounds of the easternmost part of the *parochia* of Christchurch are spoken of in the Christchurch Cartulary (Brit. Lib. MS Cott. Tib. D Vl B f. 37., ?12th century) in one place as being also the western bounds of the *parochia* of Eling, showing that the whole western bank of Southampton Water lay in Eling *parochia*. The site where the princes were captured is called by Bede (loc. cit) *Ad Lapidem*, which has been located (e.g. by Colgrave and Mynors) at Stoneham, to the north-east of Southampton, and quite outside the Kingdom of Wight. Stone, within or at least close to the Kingdom of Wight, at the end of a Roman road from where a ferry crossed to the Isle of Wight and which was defended by a ditch and bank across the road, is almost certainly the correct site.
5. DB I 28b. The manor paid half a night's farm and had rather more than half the recorded population of the hundred, which was coterminous with the *parochia*.
6. It is so described in the *Hodoeporicon Willibaldi*, printed in *Mon. Germ. Hist. SS.* xvi, ed O. Holder-Egger (1887), trans. C.H. Talbot, *The Anglo-Saxon Missionaries in Germany* (1954).
7. For the early history of Southampton see O.G.S. Crawford, 'Southampton' in *Antiquity*, xvi (1942); L.A. Burgess, *The Origins of Southampton*, Univ. Leicester, Dept. of Local History Occasional Papers 16 (1964); P.V. Addyman & D.H. Hill, 'Saxon Southampton, a review of the Evidence' in *Papers and Proceedings of the Hampshire Field Club & Archaeological Society*, xxv (1968) and xxvi (1969); P. Holdsworth (ed.). *Excavations at Melbourne Rd. Southampton 1971–6* (1980); J.F. Cherry & R. Hodges, 'The Dating of Hamwih, Saxon Southampton, Reconsidered', *Antiq. J.* viii (1978); D.A Hinton, 'Hamwih' in J. Campbell (ed.) *The Anglo-Saxons* (Oxford, 1982), 102–3.
8. Winchester Cathedral Cartulary (*Codex Wintoniensis*, Brit. Lib. Add. MS 15350) f. 84b (S. 942; ed. J.M. Kemble, *Codex Diplomaticus*, No. 712)
9. A document of 1189 × 99 shows that the church was constituted at that date as a *precentor* and *clerici*, and that the *clerici* could make decisions for the church in the absence of the *precentor*. In about 1200 the arrangement was described as constituting a *custos* and *clerici*, and in 1258 as constituting a *custos* and *capellani et clerici*. In the mid 13th century the *clerici* were holding land in common near Southampton. In the early 16th century, the church was still headed by a *chaunter*. (St. Denys Cartulary, Brit. Lib., Add. MS 15314, f. 43; Winchester College Muniments No. 10662; St. Denys Cartulary. ff. 75 b, 16b, 78b.)
10. See author's PhD thesis (above, note 1), pp. 124–80, for details.
11. See above note 6.
12. Probably somewhat too much so, for Bishop Henry de Blois pulled it down and rebuilt it on a less 'humble and constricted' site further away from his castle: see Cartulary of St. Cross Hospital, Winchester (*Liber Primus Sancti Crucis*, Brit. Lib. MS Harl. 1616) f. 9a.
13. DB I 40a.
14. Winchester Cathedral Cartulary (*Codex Wintoniensis*, Brit. Lib. MS Add. 15350) f. 65b (S.372; J.M. Kemble, *Codex Diplomaticus*, No. 1085).
15. M. Hare, 'The Anglo-Saxon Church of St. Peter, Titchfield', *Papers and Proceedings of the Hampshire Field Club and Archaeological Society*, xxii (1976). It is interesting to note that the church at Titchfield, apparently built within one generation of Bede's church at Monkwearmouth, was almost identical to the Monkwearmouth building both in size and in plan.
16. Ibid., p. 8.
17. Winchester Cathedral Cartulary, Winchester Dean and Chapter Muniments, Vol. 1, f. 45b; calendared as No. 94 in A.W. Goodman, *Chartulary of Winchester Cathedral* (Winchester, 1927).
18. DB I 39a.
19. R. Rau, *Briefe des Bonifatius: Willibalds Leben des Bonifatius* (Ausgewaehlte Quellen zur Deutschen Ges. des Mittelalters, 1968), 466.
20. By, among others, E. Ekwall, *The Concise Oxford Dictionary of English Place-Names* (1960), *sub* Nursling; T. Schieffer, *Winfred-Bonifatius und die Christliche Grundlegung Europas* (1954); W. Levison, *England and the Continent in the Eighth Century* (1946); G.W. Greenaway, *St. Boniface* (1955); P. Wormald in J.Campbell (ed.) *The Anglo-Saxons* (1982). 82; T.A. Reuter, *The Greatest Englishman*, (1980); Rau, op. cit. note 19.
21. DB I 41a.
22. It is first mentioned in Domesday in the *Ibi ecclesia* form used for manorial churches on the Bishop's and Old Minster's estates.
23. There were three prebendaries: two whose prebends consisted of shares in the rectorial income of the parish altar, and a third whose prebend consisted of the church and some land at Edington in Wiltshire, some ten miles from Romsey. The Romsey rectorial canons served the parochial altar through hired chaplains until 1321, when a perpetual vicarage (at the joint presentation of the two Romsey rectorial prebendaries) was endowed (Register of Bishop Rigaud of Assier, f. 15b). The canons had a seat in the nuns' choir and a voice in chapter and in elections of abbesses. The nuns' chaplain was not appointed by the prebendaries. For the canons of Romsey see H.G.D. Liveing, *Records of Romsey Abbey* (Winchester, 1912), 125–41. There were similar groups of prebendaries serving the parochial altars in the Anglo-Saxon nunneries of Shaftesbury (Dorset) and Wherwell (Hants.), and canons were also found at the Nuns' Minster in Winchester. The prebends at the Nuns' Minster were all secured on various dispersed pieces of secular and ecclesiastical income owned by the nuns in various places in Hampshire, and clearly do not stem from a previous parochial mother church (there was no parochial altar in the Nuns' Minster, and the Nuns' Minster canons were more closely connected with the nuns than the other groups). At Wherwell, however, the four prebends were all secured on the income of the parochial altar, and on the income of the dependent churches of the *parochia*, and exercised mother church rights over the *parochia*. The way of life of the Wherwell prebendaries seems very similar to that of at least the two Romsey rectorial canons, and the much fuller information we have on the Wherwell canons (arising from a determined effort by the nuns to appropriate the prebends in the later 14th century) can be used to clarify information at Romsey. Cf. Wherwell Cartulary (Brit. Lib. MS Egerton 2104A) f. 39a *et seq.*, especially f. 41.
24. O.G.S. Crawford, 'Southampton', *Antiquity*, xvi (1942), 45 note, has, however, suggested that the two churches were one.
25. DB I 43b.
26. If the arguments sketched out here are unacceptable, it must be assumed that an early church at Nursling was very thoroughly sacked, perhaps by the Danes in their visits to Southampton and Winchester in 840 and 860 × 1, and that later this church was rebuilt, not at Nursling but on safer ground at Romsey, perhaps closer to the centre of the royal estate, so that when Nursling was granted to the Bishop at some time before 872 there was no church there. The present church at Nursling was already dedicated to St. Boniface in 1508 (it is so called in a will of that date: Baigent Papers Vol. 10 (Brit. Lib. MS 39968) f. 302a), suggesting not only a medieval tradition of a connection with St. Boniface, but also a dedication and presumably foundation

following his death. The church at Nursling is built half a mile north of a very small Roman settlement (*Onna*), which stood on the eastern bank of a ford over the Test used by the main Roman road from Winchester to Dorchester. The Roman road from Winchester to the Isle of Wight ferry at Stone crossed the Test at the present, Redbridge, crossing, i.e. went very close to Eling. Both Nursling and Eling are, therefore, perhaps likely sites for early Christian centres. But the tenurial and ecclesiastical insignificance of Nursling at all dates after the mid 9th century is so compelling that it is difficult to conceive of a mother church there unless it was very thoroughly destroyed at an early date.

27. Other churches clearly mother churches on 12th century evidence include: *Alton*, Neatham Hundred, and Neatham, a one night's farm estate — DB I 38a. The mother church and its glebe had been granted to the New Minster by the Conqueror. The glebe lands are included in Domesday Book but the church is omitted — D B I 43a; *Basing*, Basingstoke hundred, and Basingstoke, a third part of one night's farm estate — DB I 39a. The church stood at Basing which had been part of the royal estate in 951 × 5 (Will of King Eadred) but which had been divided off from Basingstoke and granted out before 1066. In 1086 Basing was held by Hugh de Port — DB I 45a. De Port had granted the church to Mont St. Michel, and it is consequently entered separately in Domesday Book — DB I 43a; *Andover*, Andover hundred and Andover, an estate for which 'they did not state the number of hides' — DBI 39a. The church is not mentioned in Domesday Book; *Mottisfont*, Thorngate (Broughton) hundred, and Broughton, a one night's farm estate — DB I 38b. The church had been granted to the Archbishop of York by one of the later Anglo-Saxon kings, presumably to give the Archbishop a residence near Winchester — DBI 42a; *Kings Somborne*, Somborne hundred, and Kings Somborne, an estate which 'belonged to the Kingship and had not been hidated' — DB I 39b; *Christchurch* (on this church see p. 51f.); *Carisbrooke*; the hundreds of the Isle of Wight are clearly in the process of being re-ordered at the date of Domesday Book; the estate is Bowcombe, a 4 hide (£20 valet) estate — D8 I 52a. The church had been granted to Lire after the Conquest — DB I 52a; *East Meon*, Meon hundred, and Meon a 72 hide (£60 valet) estate — DB I 38a. The church had been granted to the Bishop, possibly during Stigand's tenure of the royal manor — DB I 40b. Possible mother churches include: *Wherwell* (discussed above, note 23); *Breamore*, Fordingbridge hundred, and Breamore, an estate which 'had never gelded' — DB I 39a. The church is not mentioned in Domesday Book; *Odiham*, Odiham (*Edefele*) hundred, and Odiham, a 78½ hide £50 valet) estate — DB I 38a; *Kingsclere*, presumably as later Kingsclere hundred, and Kingsclere, a third part of one night's farm estate — DBI 39a. The Conqueror gave the Church here to the New Minster — DB I 43a. More doubtful possibilities include: *Hurstbourne Tarrant*, Hurstbourne (Pastrow) hundred, Hurstbourne, a third part of one night's farm estate - DB I 39a; and the two rich Old Minster churches of *Hurstbourne Priors* (holding 1 hide), Evingar, the Bishops franchisal hundred and Hurstbourne Priors, a 38–hide estate. This may, as discussed below, note 33, have been an old mother church — DB I 41a; and *Burghclere* (holding 1 hide), also in Evingar hundred, the estate was of 10 hides — DB I 41a; and the Bishop's rich church at *Houghton* (2 churches holding 1¾ hides), Somborne hundred and the bishop's estate of Houghton of 16 hides — DB I 40b. These last four churches have been included here because Blair, 'Secular Minsters' has taken a landholding of 1 hide attached to a Domesday church as indicating a likely mother church. In these cases, however, some other reason for this large glebe is likely. Hurstbourne Tarrant and Hurstbourne Priors seem likely to share between them an old mother church *parochia* (see below, note 33). Houghton was granted to the Bishop in, probably, 963 × 75 and was probably at that date cut out of the old mother church *parochia* of either Mottisfont or King's Somborne. Burghclere was similarly granted to the Bishop in 955 × 8 and probably at that date cut out of the old mother-church *parochia* of Kingsclere. The Bishop almost certainly founded new churches on these manors at these dates, with parishes covering the episcopal estates. The episcopal estates were quite large (Burghclere covered at least two later parishes), and it seems entirely likely that these new 10th century episcopal foundations were given the generous endowment of one hide at the date of foundation. These four cases are, therefore, very doubtful mother churches.

28. Grant of Farnham 'for the foundation of a minster' (S. 235); confirmation of grants of land by Frithuwold and Eorcenwold 'to the church of St. Peter Chertsey' (S. 1165). For the context and authenticity of these charters, see J. Blair, *Land-holding, Church and Settlement in Early Medieval Surrey* (Surrey Arch. Soc. forthcoming), ch. IV; P. Wormald, *Bede and the Conversion of England: the Charter Evidence* (the Jarrow Lecture, 1984), 9. Woking (with Bermondsey) was founded as a dependency of the Mercian monastery of *Medeshamstede* (Peterborough), and was probably, therefore, founded in an attempt to increase Mercian influence in Surrey during the period of Mercian dominance of the area (641–86). The monasteries of Woking and Bermondsey are mentioned in a privilege of Pope Constantine I (708–715) as subject to *Medeshamstede*. On the early history of Woking monastery see F.M. Stenton, 'Medeshamstede and its Colonies' in J.G. Edwards (ed.) *Essays in Honour of James Tait* (Manchester, 1933); Blair, *Early Medieval Surrey* ch. IV.

29. See J. Campbell in *The Anglo-Saxons* (Oxford 1982), 58, 61; Campbell, 'Church in Towns'; P. Sawyer, 'The Royal *Tūn* in Pre-Conquest England,' in P. Wormald et al. (eds.), *Ideal and Reality in Frankish and Anglo-Saxon Society* (Oxford, 1983); Blair, 'Secular Minsters'. Most of these writers mention a mother church as one of the usual appendages of a *villa regalis*: see especially Campbell, 'Church in Towns'; 121, on the 9th-century translator of Bede translating *urbana loca* as *mynsterstowe* in a context where *urbana loca* must mean *villae regales*. Other writers drawing attention to the frequent coincidence of hundred or other jurisdictional districts with mother-church *parochiae* include M. Deanesly, 'Early English and Gallic Minsters', *TRHS*, 4th ser. xxiii (1941); W. Page, 'Some Remarks on the Churches of the Domesday Survey', *Archaeologia*, lxvi (1914); Barlow, *Church 1000–66*, 184; and H.M. Cam, 'The Hundred and the Hundredal Manor', in *Liberties and Communities in Medieval England* (London, 1963), 84 ff.

30. This must not be exaggerated. *Some* conversion had taken place in the reigns of Cynegisl and Cenwalh. Eling, Chertsey, and probably Woking were in existence before Cædwalla's reign, as well as the cathedral at Winchester, and other churches such as Malmesbury in other parts of Wessex; the successful establishment by Cædwalla and Ine of so many new collegiate churches presupposes earlier conversions to provide the large number of priests required to man them. What was new was the systemisation and consolidation under Cædwalla and Ine of what must earlier have been a partial and intermittent process.

31. The other papers in this volume make this abundantly clear. Among previous writings, J. Campbell, *The Anglo-Saxons* (Oxford, 1982), 61, suggests that a similar system existed in Kent; Campbell, 'Church in Towns', 120, suggests that a similar system existed in 'all or most of England'; Blair, 'Secular Minsters', 116 suggests that such a system existed in 'some and possibly all of the English kingdoms ... by the early 8th century', although the same article (pp. 116, 118) suggests that many of the Mercian mother churches were originally aristocratic foundations which only later became closely connected with the (W. Saxon) royal family.

32. Among the 10th and 11th century grants in Hampshire are St. Mary Bourne (900); Bishops Waltham (by exchange for Portchester, 904); Whitchurch (909); Hurstbourne Priors (early 10th century); Chilbolton (934); Burghclere (955 × 8); Crondall

(before 955 × 9); Droxford (after 956); Exton (959 × 75); Alvarstoke (after 948); Wootton St. Lawrence (after 900); Havant (980); Crawley (963 × 75); Overton (963 × 75); Fareham (953 × 75); Houghton (probably 963 × 75); Ecchinswell (after 931); Candover (10th century); Stoneham (including Hinton Ampner, 1045); Hannington (after 1023); Hoddington (1046); Hayling (1052 × 3). Fawley, Meonstoke, and Wonston were probably also granted at this period, but documents do not survive. Most of the documents relating to these grants are in the Winchester Cathedral Cartulary (*Codex Wintoniensis*), Brit. Lib. MS Add. 15350; for details see S.

33. Whitchurch is already so called in 908, and a fine 9th-century gravestone survives in the church, suggesting, therefore, a considerable age for the 'White Church' there. The subordinate vills of the episcopal estate were later regarded as dependents of Whitchurch. Kingsclere church had a very large glebe (4¼ hides), and those few vills in the area which were not granted to the Old Minster/Bishop were regarded as its dependents. At Hurstbourne both Hurstbourne Priors (the Old Minster estate) and Hurstbourne Tarrant (the remaining royal estate) have churches with some mother church characteristics: probably an original mother church here split into two, with the two *parochie* following tenurial boundaries, and there is no clue as to which of the two churches was the earlier. Something similar may have happened at Whitchurch. Overton was probably originally within the *parochia* of Whitchurch. When Whitchurch was granted in 909 Overton must have become the centre of the remaining royal lands. Very probably a new church was established there with a *parochia* covering the remaining royal lands. When Overton in turn was granted in 963 × 75 it must have carried with it this new church: later Overton was considered the mother church of two chapels in nearby dependent vills.

34. In 1331 a full statement of the Old Minster's parochial rights over the city and suburbs was drawn up by Bishop Stratford (St. Swithun's Letter Book I, Winchester Dean & Chapter Muniments, f. 38). This document is very late, and records, therefore, only a very late stage of development, with earlier parochial rights fossilised into rights to collect income. However, it states that all the tithe of Chilcomb and Morestead (certainly including Weeke, Winnall, and Sparkford, and possibly also the other vills included in the Domesday manor of Chilcomb, i.e. Hursley, Sparsholt and Compton) were to go to the Old Minster, and that Littleton (probably including Lainston) was wholly appropriated to the Old Minster, and was to be served by hired chaplains. No burials were to take place in the city or immediate suburbs except at the Cathedral; in Chilcomb, Morestead, Weeke, Winnall and some suburban churches burials could take place, but all sepulture was to be paid to the Old Minster. All the city and suburban parishes, including Chilcomb, Morestead etc., were to pay pentecostals at the Old Minster and to get their chrism from there. At the more significant city and suburban churches (St. Maurice, St. Faith, St. Katherine, St. James, St. Giles and probably St. Anastasius) 'stations' were held on the feast-day of the church, when monks would go in procession from the Old Minster to the church, and would hold all the services of that day, taking all the alms offered back to the Old Minster with them. The religious houses within this area (Hyde Abbey, the Hospital of St. Cross, the College of St. Elizabeth) all paid pensions to the Old Minster to allow the residents of those houses to be buried within them. The Hyde Abbey pension was set out on the removal of the New Minster to Hyde in 1114, and the 1114 charter makes it explicit that the pension to the Old Minster (4 marks a year — the equivalent of the value of nearly 3 hides in Domesday, and of perhaps 2 hides at early 12th-century values) was payment for the Bishop freeing the Abbey's home parishes of Abbots Worthy and Hyde from the Old Minster's control of their tithe, sepulture and alms. The Hyde monks also had to attend the Old Minster 'station' at St. James, presumably in recognition of their original parochial subjection. See St. Swithun's Letter Book I f. 39, and Hyde Abbey Cartulary (Brit. Lib MS Cotton. Domit. A XIV) f. 22a. All this strongly suggests an Old Minster parochial mother-church control over the city and suburbs in the late pre-Conquest period.

35. DB I 40a, 41a–b. Nine churches are shown on the Chilcomb estate and one each on the Chilbolton and Worthy estates of the Old Minster, and churches are shown on the Bishop's manors of Alresford (3 churches). Twyford, Easton (2 *ecclesiole*), Bishopstoke, Kilmeston (*ecclesiola*), and Crawley — a total of 20 churches recorded for the 28 modern parishes in the area. The city and immediate suburban parishes are omitted from Domesday Book.

36. The clearest examples are those from the *parochia* of Christchurch discussed on pp. 54–6, but Basingstoke (within the *parochia* of Basing), perhaps Wallop (within that of Mottisfont), and Selborne (in that of Alton) are probably also foundations of this type.

37. Cf. the treatise *On Peoples Ranks and Law* para. 2, trans. *EHD*, 468.

38. E.g. the *presbyter* holding 2 churches with 2 hides at Odiham (DB I 38a); Vitalis the priest holding (the doubtful mother church of) Hurstbourne Tarrant with ½ hide (DB I 39a); Ralph the priest holding 2 churches with 2½ hides at Bishops Waltham (DB I 40a); Wibert the clerk holding (the doubtful mother church of) Houghton with 1¾ hides (DB I 40b); Alvric the priest holding Whitchurch with 1 hide and (the doubtful mother church of) Burghclere with 1 hide (DB I 4Ia–b); Lewin holding (the doubtful mother church of) Hurstbourne Priors with 1 hide (DB I 41a); and Richer the clerk holding 3 churches with 1 hide at Stoneham (DB I 41b). These Stoneham churches were St. Mary Extra and its two major dependents; Domesday Book does not suggest this, but we have seen that this church at least was certainly collegiate.

39. Christchurch Cartulary (Brit. Lib. Cott. Tib. D. VIB) f. 30b; printed W. Dugdale, *Monasticon Anglicanum* (London, 1661); ii, 177–178, and B. Ferrey and E.W. Brayley, *The Antiquities of the Priory of Christchurch, Hants* (London, 1834), Appendix i–iii. A translation is attached as Appendix (1).

40. II Edgar 1.1, 2.2, 2.3, 3, 5.2 (*C&S*, 97–102); VII Æthr. 4.1 (*C&S*, 377); I Cnut, 8–14 (*C&S*, 475–8). See also Cnut (1027 Proclamation) 16 (*C&S*, 512), and, for similar statements but less complete, V Æthr. 12.1 (*C&S*, 352); VIII Æthr. 8–14 (*C&S*, 391–3). I Æthelstan 4 (*C&S*, 46), and Ine, 4, 61, imply the same. Cf. also Alfred, 21, 5–5.2 (*C&S*, 29–30, 34–5) with its assumption that all priests normally live in communities. 'Edward and Guthrum', 6; I Edmund, 2; IV Edgar, 1.1–6 (*C&S*, 308–9. 62–3, 106–8) are also of interest. The laws allow practically no power to lay lords to found churches on their estates, but II Edgar 2 (*C&S*, 8), followed by I Cnut 11 (*C&S*, 477) allows a lay lord with a church with graveyard on his bookland to pay to it a third part of his demesne tithe.

41. Gratian 2.16 1.43–45: 'when a church is founded by episcopal consent the rights of the existing church where baptism is received to income and tithe must be safeguarded'; G2.16.1.54: 'within one boundary (*una terminatione*) there are not to be many baptismal churches, but one, with a number of chapels'; G2 16.1.56–59: 'laymen with churches on their estate are on no account to divert tithe, oblations, or land from the old church to their church'; G2 16.2.3.5–7: 'parochial status is indefeasible and not subject to prescription, except in areas where boundaries are unclear'; G2 16.2.4: 'no-one is to receive tithe which belongs to another'. Although the canon law also insisted that all villages over a certain size should have their own church (G2.10.3.3.1, G2.13.1.1) these were to be founded by episcopal consent, without harming the rights of the church of prior foundation, and with the lay founder having only the right of reporting misdeeds to the Bishop and the right of a ceremonial

reception at the church. It will be seen that the canonical rights of the church of prior foundation are very similar to the rights of the old minster under the Anglo-Saxon laws. The dates of these canons are rather doubtful, but they do at least represent the thinking of canon laywers during the 150 years before Gratian, even if they do not so clearly represent the thinking of the very early years to which they are formally ascribed by Gratian. See P. Thomas, *Le Droit de Propriété des Laiques sur les Eglises, et la Patronage Laique au Moyen Age* (Bibl. de l'Ecole des Hautes Etudes: Sciences xix, Paris, 1906).

42. Christchurch Cartulary (Brit. Lib. MS Cott. Tib. D VIA). f. 27b. (S. 637; J.M Kemble, *Codex Diplomaticus* No. 458): King Eadwig grants land at Zeals and Donhead to the huntsman Wulfric (956); Ibid. ff. 27b–28 (S.859; Kemble No. 647): King Æethelred grants land at *Borstealle* to his priest Wulfric (985); Ibid. f. 28 (S. 1024; Kemble No. 798): King Edward grants land at Bashley to his faithful *minister Lutrise* (1053). Despite the doubts cast on the last two there can be no doubt that all are basically poor copies of genuine charters.
43. For the topography of the *burh* see K.J. Penn, *Historic Towns in Dorset* (Dorset Nat. Hist. and Arch. Soc. monograph I, 1980), 38–44.
44. There are three Domesday royal estates in the area: Twynham (valet TRE £19), including the *burh*, which had 'always been part' of the royal estates; Holdenhurst (valet TRE £44) which 'had never gelded' and so is likely to be an ancient royal estate, but which TRE was held by Earl Tosti; and Ringwood (valet TRE £24), which had previously been hided as 28 hides, but which TRW was no longer hided. Probably this was originally one single royal estate from which Ringwood was detached in the 10th century (it was granted by Edgar to Abingdon in 961: S. 690) and which continued to be handled separately after its return to royal hands. Holdenhurst was probably divided off from Twynham to provide an estate for Earl Tosti: there is no evidence for two major royal manors in this area earlier than Domesday Book, and after 1086 the two estates were reunited. Domesday Book shows 6 hundreds in the area: Ringwood, Boldre, *Rodedic*, Shirley, *Egheiete*, and Througham. Of these, Througham is manifestly a copyist's error and can be ignored; Ringwood is just the two estates of Ringwood and Harbridge, and probably represents the liberty granted to Abingdon in 961. As for Boldre and *Rodedic*, the distribution of estates to these two hundreds only makes sense if the two names are alternative names for one hundred. This is probably also the same for*Egheiete* and Shirley. Later there were two hundreds – Christchurch and New Forest. Probably therefore Christchurch was originally connected with one major royal manor and two hundreds.
45. See History of Christchurch 1087–1146, translated as Appendix (1).
46. For Almetus at Carisbrooke, see the document translated as Appendix (2A) and (4).
47. The letter of Earl Baldwin de Redvers I to Bishop Henry de Blois announcing the regularisation of the church (1150), includes among the lands confirmed to the regular canons 'the other virgate which Ailmer the priest held', which suggests that Ailmer was only recently dead. Cartulary of Christchurch (Brit. Lib. MS Cott. Tib. DVIA) f. 13b, printed W. Dugdale, *Monasticon Anglicanum* (London, 1661), ii, 180, and Brayley and Ferrey op.cit, Appendix v.
48. V Æthr. 7 (C&S, 348–9); see Blair, 'Secular Minsters', 123.
49. Cf. Bampton, for which see ibid., 140.
50. It is mentioned in the general charter of Earl Baldwin de Redvers I (1140), for which see note 67.
51. DB I 44a.
52. See note 42.
53. It is so mentioned in the general charter of Richard de Redvers I (about 1130), for which see note 67.
54. One hide of the $1\frac{3}{4}$ had been lost to the Forest by 1087; DB I 44a.
55. On Waltham see Blair, 'Secular Minsters', 123; on the late pre-Conquest cathedral chapters see R.R. Darlingon 'Ecclesiastical Reform in the Late Old English Period', *Eng. Hist. Rev.* li,and K. Edwards, *The English Secular Cathedrals in the Middle Ages* (Manchester, 1967). 3 ff.
56. Christchurch Cartulary (Brit. Lib. MS Cott. Tib. DVIB). f. 36a, translated as Appendix (2A).
57. DB I 51b. Alvric the Small (Alvric parvus, Alvric Petit) is shown under that name as the holder TRE of 4 small manors totalling $3\frac{3}{4}$ hides (Througham $1\frac{1}{2}$ hides, Efford, $\frac{1}{2}$ hide, unnamed $\frac{3}{4}$ hide, Brockenhurst, 1 hide) valued TRE at about £7. He inherited Brockenhurst from his father and uncle, and is, therefore, probably the Alvric who inherited from his father and uncle an unnamed estate in Redbridge hundred of $\frac{1}{2}$ hide, valued TRE at 12*s*. He is probably the Alvric who held TRE 3 small manors totalling $1\frac{3}{4}$ hides and valued at £4 (*Wigarestun*, 1 hide, Pilley $\frac{1}{2}$ hide, *Godesmanescamp*, $\frac{1}{4}$ hide – this last is shown as owned by *Uluric*). He may be the Alvric who held a half-share of 2 hides at Battramsley with Saulf, the whole estate being valued TRE at £3, a third-share with two *alodiarii* of $1\frac{1}{4}$ hides at Otterwood, the whole being valued TRE at 30*s*., and a half-share with Agemund of $\frac{3}{4}$ hide in *Cocherlei*, the whole valued TRE at £3. These TRE estates suggest a total holding by Alvric of the equivalent of 7 hides $3\frac{1}{6}$ virgates. Alvric the Small had acquired $1\frac{1}{2}$ virgates in *Utefel* valued at 5*s*. and 1 virgate at an unnamed place valued at 6*s*. TRE between 1066 and 1079, and he is probably the Alvric who acquired 2 hides at *Oxelei* jointly with Wislac, valued at £2, between the same dates. He is probably (given the close ties between the New Forest and the Isle of Wight) also the Alvric who held $1\frac{1}{2}$ hides in the Isle TRE valued at 12*s*. jointly with Wislac. The total equivalent holding in 1079 is, therefore, 9 hides $1\frac{2}{3}$ virgates. Alvric is not a common name; elsewhere in the Hampshire Domesday it appears only three times: an Alvric held 2 manors in the north of the county; an Oluric held Lockerley between Southampton and Andover and was probably also the huntsman Uluric holding another small manor nearby; and lastly Alvric the priest who held the churches of Whitchurch and Burghclere.
58. DB I 51b.
59. See note 67.
60. Several of the documents relating to this legal process are printed from the Christchurch Cartulary in L. Voss, *Heinrich von Blois, Bischof von Winchester* (Berlin, 1932), 162–3.
61. Winchester College Muniments No. 10629, printed L. Voss. *Heinrich von Blois*, 165–6; translated here as Appendix (3). A photograph of this document is the frontispiece of the author's thesis – see note 1.
62. Winchester Dean and Chapter Muniments, Winchester Cathedral Cartulary, f. 29a, calendared as No. 67 in A.W. Goodman, *Chartulary of Winchester Cathedral* (Winchester, 1927).
63. Cartulary of Carisbrooke (Brit. Lib. MS Egerton 3667) f. 22b, translated here as Appendix (4).
64. VIII Æthr.S; I Cnut 3a; and also, for the basic idea, II Edgar 1.1 (C&S, 389–90, 98–8).
65. Bishop de Blois's vicarage endowments for Christchurch are printed in L. Voss, *Heinrich von Blois*, 159, 161–162. Voss, op.cit. 96–9 discusses the historical significance of these vicarage endowments, and also takes them as implying that the canons were not living communally at the mother church in the last years before the regularisation, but were more often to be found on their prebendal estates.
66. Christchurch Cartulary (Brit. Lib. MS Cott. Tib. D VI A). f. 58b; printed L. Voss, op.cit. note 61, 163; statement by Bishop Henry de Blois, 1169–1171, referring to events in the 1140s.
67. Christchurch Cartulary (Brit. Lib. MS Cott Tib. D VI A) f. 13a; printed W. Dugdale, *Monasticon Anglicanum*, ii, 179: general charter of Richard de Redvers I, date about 1130; and Cartulary f. 13a, printed Dugdale loc. cit. and Brayley and Ferry op.cit,

Appendix iv: general charter of Baldwin de Redvers I, date probably 1140.

68. Christchuch Cartulary (Brit. Lib. MS Cott. Tib. DV I A) f. 61a; quitclaim by Alice, daughter of Alvric the Small, of the land held by Dean Peter de Oglander at Stanpit 'as a prebend' on mortgage (1130s).

69. Ibid. f. 103a; grant of Apse by Roger de Estres (1130s) 'as a prebend'.

70. See, as an example, the record of the Christchurch processions, Christchurch Cartulary (Brit. Lib. MS Cotton Tib. DVIB) f. 36b, translated here as Appendix (2B).

71. On Christchurch see note 70. On Bishops Waltham, see note 66 and Appendix (3). For St. Mary Extra, see Cartulary of St. Denys (Brit. Lib. MS Add. 15314), f. 76b (all the churches within the walls of Southampton were to process to St. Mary Extra on the Dedication feast (the Assumption), on Ascension Day, and on the feast of St. Leger). For Winchester see the 'station' arrangements (note 34). For Carisbrooke see Carisbrooke Cartulary (Brit. Lib. MS Egerton 3667) f. 70b (parishioners of Shorwell to process to Carisbrooke on the Dedication feast of the Assumption). At Romsey the prebendaries and people were to process from the parochial altar to the High Altar on Palm Sunday (see Register of Bishop William of Wykeham f. 65b); and at Wherwell they were to do so on Palm Sunday, Candlemas, and on the Dedication feasts (St. Peter and Holy Cross), although it is not clear if this was just for the parishioners of Wherwell parish or those of the whole *parochia*: see Cartulary of Wherwell (Brit. Lib. MS Egerton 2104) f. 41. A particularly interesting recognition procession is that at Boldre. Boldre was probably the oldest of the dependent churches of Christchurch, and as such its parisioners had to make a recognition procession to Christchurch: see Appendix (2B). However, Boldre itself was regarded as a subordinate centre within the Christchurch *parochia*, with Lymington and Brockenhurst regarded as dependent on Boldre as well as on Christchurch; the parishioners of Lymington, therefore, were required to make recognition processions not only to Christchurch, but also to Boldre, with offerings of wax. This last procession was to take place on the anniversary of the date of the dedication of Lymington cemetery. See Christchurch Cartulary (Brit. Lib. MS Cott. Tib. D VI B) f. 81b. Even Lymington had a dependent chapel of its own, at Buckland.

72. *VCH Hants*. iii, 281, 284 note.

73. The Otter is now known as the Beaulieu Water.

74. Salt was treated as great tithe in a number of places near the Solent.

VI. The Fragmentation of the Minster *Parochiae* of South-East Shropshire*

Jane Croom

Introduction

It is now generally agreed that many minster churches were founded in the 7th and 8th centuries, in the secular administrative centres of *villae regales* or of *regiones* which were often co-terminous with the *parochiae* of the churches.[1] They were staffed by communities of clergy, who carried out missionary work in the extensive minster parishes. By the time of the 'Taxation of Pope Nicholas' of 1291, which provides the earliest systematic survey of the medieval English Church, ecclesiastical provision in England was very different: dioceses were divided into small parishes, each with a single church and priest responsible for one vill or small group of them. In order to understand the transition from the extensive *parochiae* of collegiate minster churches to the later parochial system of 'a church and priest in every village', it is of immense value to be able to reconstruct the middle Saxon land-units on which the *monasteria* were established, and to examine both the process of their fragmentation into smaller territorial units, and the foundation of local churches in the later Anglo-Saxon and Norman periods. It is possible to undertake such a study even in regions where pre-Conquest documentary material is lacking, and this paper will outline the methodology employed and present the results of work on the reconstruction of the minster *parochiae* of south-east Shropshire.[2] Following the Norman Conquest, Domesday Book and the more abundant documentation of the 12th and 13th centuries make possible the examination of the changing rôle and composition of the minster churches of the region at this period. Furthermore, something can be learned of their relations with the local churches founded within the area formerly under their ecclesiastical control, as the latter gained their parochial independence.

Villae Regales

The essential administrative and economic units into which the middle Saxon kingdoms were divided were *villae regales* and *regiones*, large royal estates and early tribal areas, each comprising a number of outlying settlements dependent on a central vill.[3] The royal vills were the foci through which the *feorm* and the services of their constituent settlements were rendered to the king, and the popular assemblies of the *villae regales* provided the basis for the maintenance of law and order and the administration of justice.[4] Helen Cam was able to show that post-Conquest groupings of hundreds centred on royal manors in Wessex had their origins in estates dependent on king's *tūnas*.[5] For example, the later medieval 'Seven hundreds of Cookham and Bray' may have been coextensive with the 7th-century *provincia* of the *Sunningas*.[6] P.H. Sawyer has compiled a list of the central settlements of pre-Conquest royal estates using a variety of criteria, and he remarks that minster churches were usually founded on, or near, royal vills.[7] Charters of the 7th and 8th centuries, granting land to, or for the foundation of, *monasteria*, convey to them extensive endowments. These estates were defined by anciently established boundaries within which were to be found all the natural resources necessary to life. They were frequently assessed at a large number of hides, and included a number of separate settlements dependent on the named central one.

The Break-up of the Villae Regales

The large estates of the 7th and 8th centuries broke up during the later Saxon period to produce the pattern of manors recorded in Domesday Book. The fission of the composite middle Saxon estates was the outcome of a number of developments.[8] One of the principal causes was the granting by kings and aristocrats of land, as a reward for service, to a rapidly expanding class of minor territorial nobility. The process of disintegration was further facilitated by the division of estates between a number of coheirs according to the custom of partible inheritance, by the giving of gifts of land to the Church, and by the inability of great churches to reclaim areas of land leased to tenants after the term of the lease had expired. There was thus a tendency for smaller tenurial units to develop, as the component parts of the *villae*

---

* I would like to thank Mr. S.R. Bassett and Dr. J. Blair for their advice and criticism of earlier drafts of this paper.

regales became tenurially separate estates, independent of the former central vills.

The tenurial fragmentation of the *villae regales* both led to and facilitated the break up of the coterminous *parochiae* into smaller 'parishes'. The provision of minster churches had been appropriate to the period of conversion, but once Christianity was established the need was felt for a more immediate clerical presence with churches and priests in local centres.[9] The basic framework of the early minster parishes had been modified during the middle Saxon period by the foundation of lesser minsters, whether by the king or as daughter houses of established *monasteria*.[10] Between the 9th and 11th centuries there were further changes, as chapels were established by churches and local lords to serve villages or private estates. These chapels were the private property of their owners, who were responsible for staffing them and for their endowments. The minster churches in the *parochiae* of which they were situated restricted their pastoral functions, but subsequently many sought and achieved full parochial independence. The creation of new parishes continued until the 12th and 13th centuries, but by 1200 reforms within the Church had frozen parish boundaries and subjected any subsequent changes to strict control.[11] By 1291, the majority of the parishes of the early 19th century were already in existence.

The two processes of fragmentation — tenurial and ecclesiastical — although closely linked in their inception, did not continue at a uniform rate. It is true that the creation of parishes was not complete by the late 11th century, and some manors recorded in Domesday Book seem to have covered the area of two or more 13th-century parishes. However, even by 1066, the area of many later medieval parishes must have encompassed that of several Domesday manors. And further manorial subdivisions and reamalgamations occurred after the fossilisation of the parochial pattern by about 1300.

Reconstructing the Middle Saxon Estates

In parts of Wessex, the ecclesiastical geography of the kingdom in the middle Saxon period can be inferred from the administrative arrangements recorded in Domesday Book. A close correspondence is apparent between minster churches and Domesday hundreds: there was usually only one minster church in each hundred, located near the hundredal *caput*, and the minster did not exercise any jurisdiction outside the bounds of the hundred.[12] In some regions of the Mercian kingdom, the Domesday hundreds may similarly have been coextensive with the ancient *villae regales*,[13] but in other parts of Mercia, including Shropshire, there appears to be no neat correlation between the two. This is usually explained on the grounds that the Mercian hundreds were artificial creations imposed from the outside by the West Saxon kings.[14] This does not seem to be the case in Shropshire where, rather, some reorganization of the ancient system of *villae regales* had taken place by the time of the Domesday Survey, as a result of the fragmentation and amalgamation of the earlier units. Potential estate centres can be recognised — for example, large royal, episcopal or comital manors in 1066; hundredal *capita* in Domesday Book; meeting places of the *witan* — and it is possible not only to reconstruct the middle Saxon estates dependent on them, but also to give the estates geographical definition.

Methodology

Middle Saxon *villae regales* were tenurial and administrative land units, and they may also have had an ecclesiastical identity as the *parochiae* of minster churches. The ecclesiastical relationships between minsters and the local churches founded within their districts were more enduring than links between manors and the administrative centres of the estates of which they once formed a part. Most manors had become tenurially independent of the royal vills by 1066, but the efforts of minster churches to retain over the local churches founded within their *parochiae* explicit rights, or at least recognition that such rights had once existed, can be traced throughout the later medieval period. The principal forms of evidence recording ecclesiastical relationships include: the designation of one church as a chapelry of another, for example in the 1291 Pope Nicholas Taxation, in the *Valor Ecclesiasticus*, or in episcopal charters; the record of a dispute about parochial status, usually as a result of a chapel breaking away from its mother church; and the attempt by a church to obtain its own cemetery and rights of burial there. These records may further be supplemented by other forms of evidence which may suggest a relationship between two churches but which do not in themselves prove it. The payment of a pension from one church to another may represent a former dependence, but it may merely have resulted from the appropriation of a church, or from a gift by a pious layman. Detached and interlocking parts of parishes may suggest the former unity of two or more land units, but the disposition of natural resources and arrangements for the payment of tithes must also be taken into consideration. Finally, the testimony of tenurial relationships may also be of some value. Manors belonging to a church in or before 1066 may represent a residual part of its original endowment and perhaps of its *parochia*, but they may equally have been acquired later either by purchase or as a gift. The evidence of the subordination of one church to another usually enables the identification of the mother church and of the chapels originally dependent on it (although in some cases the ancient relationship may subsequently have

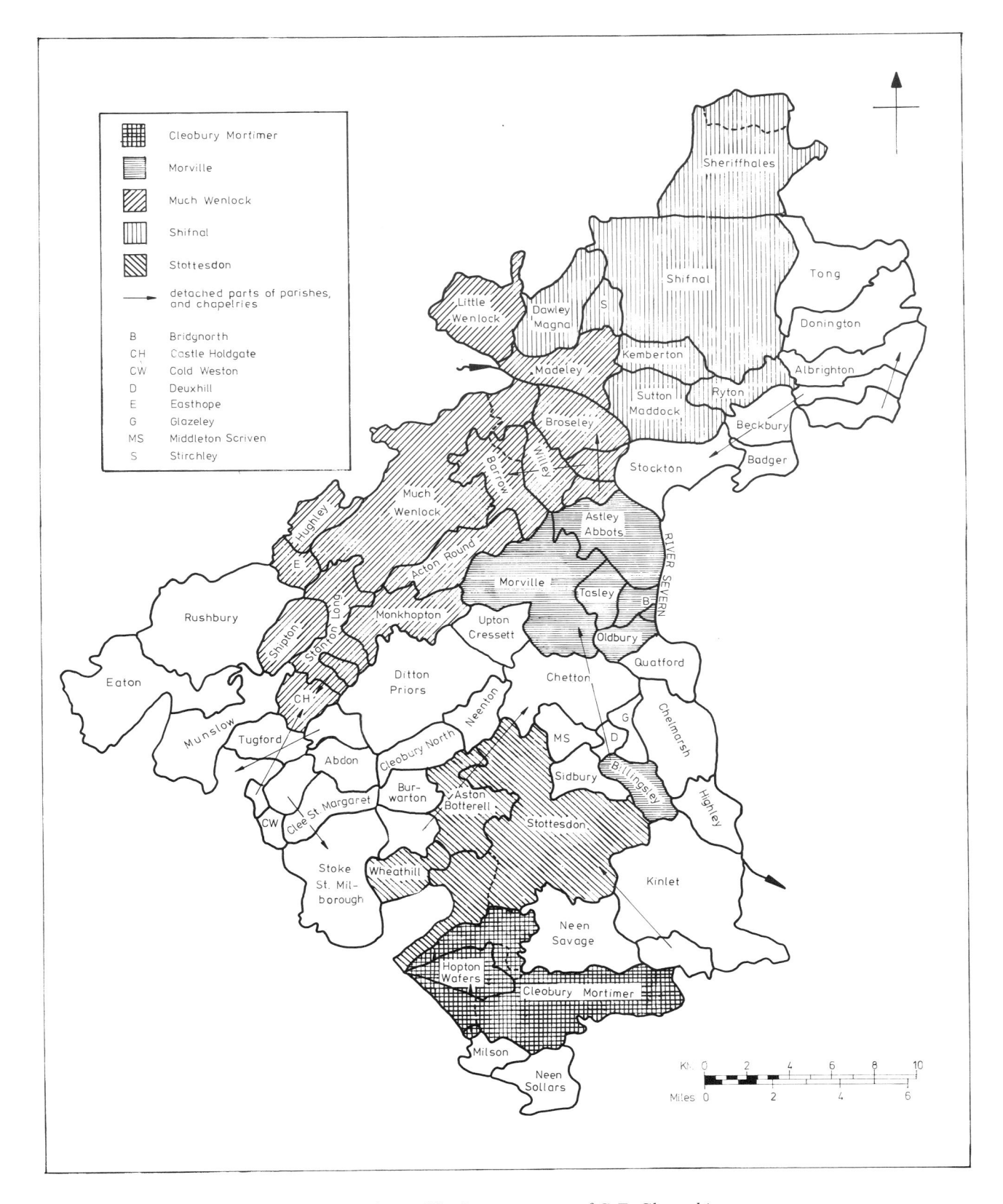

Fig. 12 The middle Saxon estates of S.E. Shropshire.

70   Jane Croom

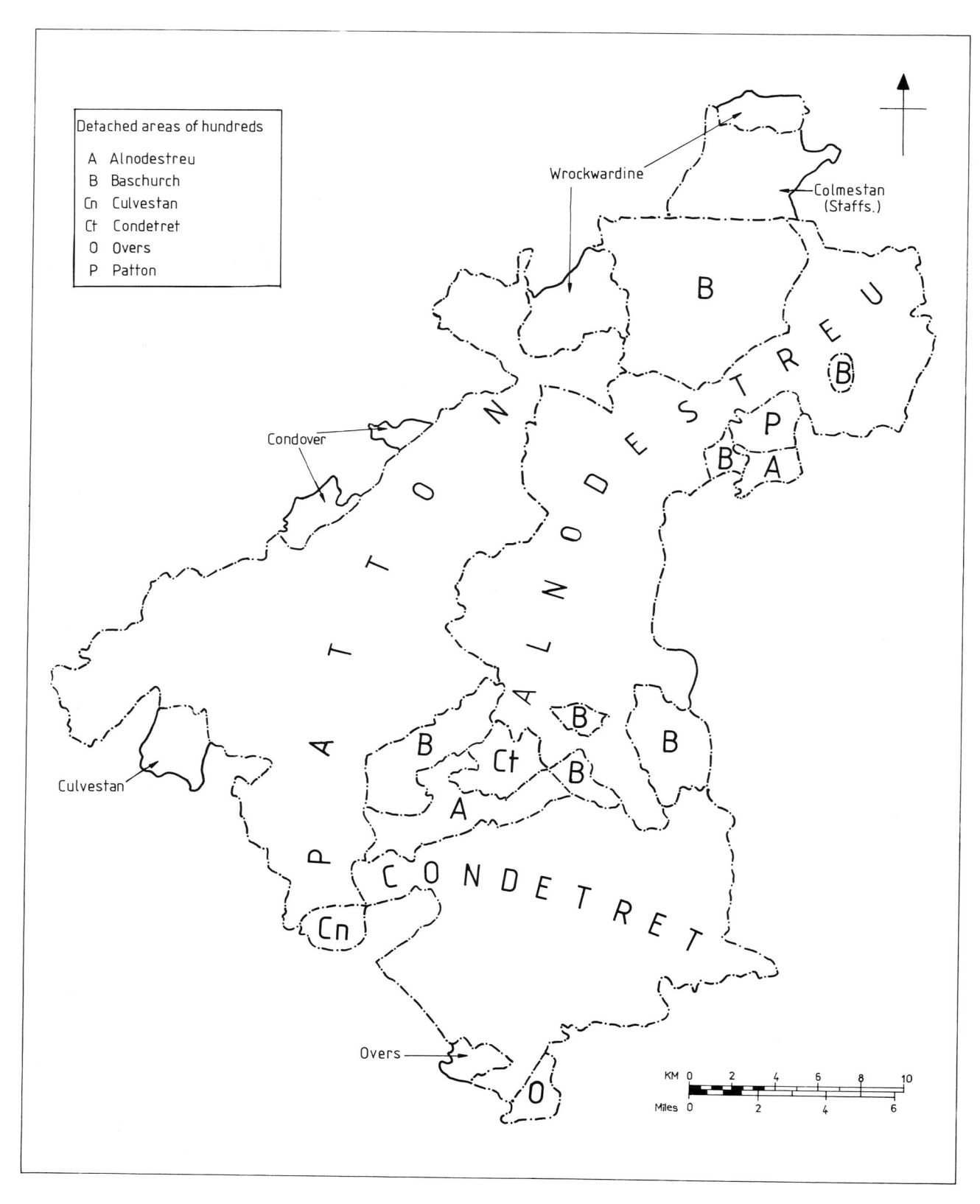

Fig. 13 The Domesday hundreds of S.E. Shropshire.

been reversed). The implication of this is that the parishes of the daughter churches must once have comprised part of the extensive *parochia* of the church to which they were subject.

It should therefore be possible to reconstruct topographically the earlier, larger minster-districts from the bounds of the parishes of their component chapelries. However, this raises the problem of the original extent of the medieval parishes. Only one Anglo-Saxon charter boundary clause survives for the whole of Shropshire,[15] so nothing is known from contemporary material about the pre-Conquest land units of south-east Shropshire. Elsewhere in England, the boundaries of Anglo-Saxon estates delimited in charters have often been shown to be coterminous with those of modern ecclesiastical parishes, and the parishes can be seen to have contained a number of separate land units which appear to correspond to Domesday manors.[16] The earliest representation of most ecclesiastical parish boundaries is usually that on the Tithe Maps of *c.* 1840. Given the apparently conservative nature of the boundaries of rural parishes, at least before the later 19th century, it can be assumed that the parishes depicted on the Tithe Maps were coextensive with those of *c.* 1300, and that the Tithe parishes and townships may have comprised one or more Domesday manors. Thus, by knowing the institutional relationships of churches, in particular between mother church and chapelry, it is possible to reconstruct the geographical layout of middle Saxon estates from the earliest known bounds of parishes.

The Minster Churches of South-East Shropshire

Figure 12[17] illustrates the minimal extent of the middle Saxon estates in the area of south-east Shropshire covered by the Domesday hundreds of *Alnodestreu*, Patton, *Condetret*, and detached parts of Baschurch (see Fig. 13).[18] The region chosen for this study thus had an administrative identity in the 11th century, but it also has a certain natural coherence.[19] One of the most prominent features of the area is Wenlock Edge, which lies along the north-western boundary of the study-area. It is one of a series of north-east to south-west running limestone escarpments and associated valleys: to the east are the Hope Dale, View Edge and the Corvedale. The two Edges rise to over 300m. The southern part of the area under study is dominated by the Clee Hill mass, a triangular platform sixteen kilometres long, bounded by the River Corve to the west, the Severn to the east and, south of the study-area, the Teme. This plateau stands at about 250m, and from it rise the two peaks of Titterstone Clee (530m), the southernmost, and Brown Clee (545m) to the north. The south-eastern boundary is formed by the river Severn below where it emerges from the Ironbridge Gorge. The deep and steepsided Gorge, fifteen kilometres long, cuts across the study area. The region to the north of the river is bounded by ridges rising to over 140m in the north-east, and in the north-west by higher land (*c.* 180m) out of which rises the Wrekin. Thus the area under study encompasses a wide variety of terrain but is bounded on most sides either by higher ground or by a major river.

The minster churches of the area can be identified as Much Wenlock, Morville, Stottesdon, Shifnal and, probably, Cleobury Mortimer, using the following criteria: pre-Conquest charter evidence; status as a 'superior' church in Domesday Book; location of the church on a manor which can be recognised as a king's *tūn*; and evidence of collegiate composition certainly by the late 11th century and probably pre-1066 also.

There is almost no pre-Conquest material relating to the minsters of south-east Shropshire, and the only church for which anything is known of its foundation is that of Much Wenlock. The church was founded in the late 7th century by Merewalh, king of the Magonsæte, for his daughter Mildburg, and copies of the charters endowing the *monasterium* have survived.[20] The church was a double monastery subject to an abbess,[21] and its community of priests would have served an extensive *parochia*. The community was still in being in 901, when Æthelred and Æthelflæd granted a charter to the *congregatio Wininicensis ecclesiae* (the monastic community of the church of Wenlock).[22] The *monasterium* was then no longer under the authority of an abbess, but of a male *senior*; however, the possibility that it was still mixed is suggested by the fact that five of the witnesses of the charter were women.[23] The church of Wenlock was enriched by Leofric, earl of Mercia (1023 × 32–57), and his wife Godgifu,[24] and was still a substantial land owner in Domesday Book, holding thirteen manors assessed in total at 73 hides in 1066.[25]

Morville and Stottesdon churches were of special status in Domesday Book, located on important manors. Since Morville was a royal manor TRE, and the *caput* of *Alnodestreu* hundred, it may probably be identified as a *villa regalis*.[26] The church of St. Gregory, Morville, was endowed with eight hides and served by eight canons before the Conquest.[27] Thus, St. Gregory's was probably an old minster church, founded on a middle Saxon royal vill. The manor of Stottesdon, assessed at nine hides in Domesday Book, was held by Edwin, earl of Mercia, in 1066.[28] It was situated in *Condetret* hundred; King Edward held no land in this hundred, and its *caput* can be inferred to be Stottesdon, although this is not recorded in the Domesday survey.[29] The church of the manor, together with two-and-a-half hides of land, was held separately in 1086 by Shrewsbury Abbey, having been granted to it by Roger de Montgomery, earl of Shrewsbury.[30] The church of St. Mary, Stottesdon, can be identified as a Saxon minster foundation, and several fragments of late Anglo-Saxon sculpture are reused to form a

Fig. 14 Stottesdon, Salop.: gravestone and other sculpture fragments re-set over W. door.

tympanum over an early Norman doorway at the west end of the nave (Fig. 14).[31]

The inadequacies of Domesday Book in recording some even of the 'superior' churches may be highlighted by the example of Idsall (Shifnal). The manor, held by Morcar, earl of Northumbria, in 1066 was then assessed at seven-and-a-half hides and valued at £15.[32] No mention is made in Domesday Book of a church or priest there, possibly because in 1086 the church was still in the hands of the same person as the manor. Idsall church was certainly in existence within ten years of the Domesday Survey, and it was probably in fact a pre-Conquest minster foundation. St. Andrew's was granted by Robert fitz Tetbald to Shrewsbury Abbey between 1086 and 1094, at which time it was prebendal.[33] It is likely that the *clerici* holding the prebends were the remnant of an Anglo-Saxon minster community.

The existence of a church at Cleobury Mortimer by the time of the Domesday Survey is implied by the presence of a priest on the manor,[34] but there are no indications that it then enjoyed a similar status to those of Morville and Stottesdon. There is indeed no firm evidence that Cleobury church was an old minster, beyond the circumstantial evidence that in the later medieval period the church itself was dependent on no other, and that it may have been a 'mother church' (see below). Cleobury Mortimer was situated in the same hundred as Stottesdon in Domesday Book; the manor was assessed at four hides and was held by Queen Edith in 1066.[35] It is possible that the church was founded within the middle Saxon *parochia* of Stottesdon, and that it gained its independence at such an early date that no signs of its former subordination survived.

The central vills of other middle Saxon estates in the vicinity of the study area can be listed as follows: to the north, Wroxeter and Wrockwardine;[36] to the west, Church Stretton, Lydbury North, Clun, Leintwardine; to the south-west, Corfham (Diddlebury), Stanton Lacy, Bromfield; to the south, Bitterley and Burford; and to the east Quatford. Many of these also probably had minsters surviving into the late 11th and 12th centuries. A church and two or more priests were recorded in Domesday Book for Burford, Lydbury North, Stanton Lacy and Wroxeter.[37] St. Mary's, Bromfield, was composed of twelve canons in King Edward's time, and it remained collegiate into the 12th century.[38] The churches of Corfham (Diddlebury) and Wrockwardine had been granted by Earl Roger to Shrewsbury Abbey before 1086 and these, too, were probably minsters.[39] A church and priest were also recorded at Bitterley and Church Stretton in 1086.[40] Quatford was a royal free chapel, which was transferred to Bridgnorth Castle by the earl of Shrewsbury *c.* 1102.[41] It is noticeable that an exceptionally large number of minsters seem to have gone on functioning into the Norman period in these parts.

The Reconstruction of the Parochiae of South-East Shropshire

The reconstruction of the *parochiae* of south-east Shropshire is based primarily on the evidence of ecclesiastical relationships, as outlined above. This evidence has been supplemented by that of other sources, including Anglo-Saxon charters, Domesday Book, place names and local topography. The individual estates will be discussed in detail.

The church of Holy Trinity is now responsible only for the parish of Much Wenlock, but it once served a much wider area, and its chapelries are likely to have encompassed at least a substantial part of the *parochia* of the Saxon minster church.[42] The following churches were accounted chapelries of Holy Trinity in the 13th and 14th centuries: Acton Round, Barrow, Benthall, Broseley, Hughley, Linley, Monkhopton, Posenhall, Shipton, Willey (see Figs. 12 and 18).[43]

From Fig. 12 it can be seen that Shipton would appear to have been a detached portion of the *parochia* of Much Wenlock. However, there is evidence to suggest that Easthope, Stanton Long and Castle Holdgate should also be included in the reconstructed estate. In 901, the church of Wenlock granted Easthope and Patton (in Stanton Long) to Æthelred and Æthelflæd in exchange for (*pro commutacione*) land in *Stantune*.[44] It is implied that the church of Wenlock had at an earlier date held the ten *cassatae* in *Stantune*, for the land is said to have been 'previously surrendered to the king's lordship in order to purchase the liberty of the minster' (*prius erat foras concessa in dominium regalem pro libertate illius monasterii*).[45] Three manors of *Stantune* are recorded in Domesday Book, all held by freemen in 1066.[46] Two of the manors were held in 1086 by Helgot under Earl Roger; the former had constructed a castle on one by the time of the Domesday Survey, and it is from this fortification that the distinctive place name Castle Holdgate is derived.[47] The third manor of *Stantune* was Stanton Long.[48] It can be suggested that the recurrence of the place name *Stantune*, '*tūn* on stony ground',[49] indicates that the three manors formerly comprised a single land unit. Moreover, their earlier unity is further emphasised by the interlocking nature of Stanton Long and Castle Holdgate parishes (see Fig. 12). It is possible that the whole of this area formed the estate of *Stantune* held by Wenlock church some time before the 10th century and after 901. Thus, Easthope, Stanton Long, Castle Holdgate and Patton (in Stanton Long) may have been possessions of the church of Wenlock before 901, and it can be surmised that they were part of its original *parochia* although no evidence of the former subjection of these churches to Holy Trinity survives.

Little Wenlock and Madeley, both Domesday manors of the church of St. Mildburg, Much Wenlock, may also have been included in the extensive middle Saxon parish of Wenlock.[50] The recurrence of the place name Wenlock suggests that Little Wenlock may be the remnant of a once-larger area of land called by that name, and the purchase of Madeley by the abbess Mildburg is recorded in a charter of 723 × 36.[51] Furthermore, the boundary of the medieval diocese of Hereford takes an anomalous course through this part of Shropshire, presumably to include Little Wenlock and Madeley in the same diocese as their mother church.[52]

There is evidence apart from the strictly tenurial to support the inclusion of Little Wenlock and Madeley in the middle Saxon estate of Wenlock, but problems arise over the other Domesday manors of the church, in particular those in Patton hundred. It may be safe to assume that the more distant, scattered manors held by the church in 1066, such as Sutton near Shrewsbury, Pickthorn (in Stottesdon), Deuxhill and Eardingon, were acquired by it during the later Saxon period as gifts or by purchase. However, there are three Domesday manors which may have been in its original *parochia*: Ticklerton (Eaton-under-Heywood), Stoke St. Milborough and Clee Stanton. The first two manors were in the same Domesday hundred as Wenlock church, that of Patton, and it is possible that Stoke St. Milborough and Clee Stanton were the land 'around *Clie* hill' granted to St. Mildburg in 674 × 704.[53] The churches of Eaton and Stoke would presumably have gained their parochial independence at an early date, since no evidence survives of their relationship with Holy Trinity church. If these Domesday manors of Wenlock church are to be included in the *villa regia* of Wenlock, this raises the possibility that the whole of Patton hundred may in fact have comprised this estate, although by 1066 many of the component parts were manorially independent, and no evidence of their ecclesiastical dependence has survived. Certainly, there were no other minster churches nor any royal vills in the hundred,[54] and Rushbury, at least, may have had its own church before the Norman Conquest.[55] However, it is also possible that the acquisition of Ticklerton, Stoke St. Milborough and Clee Stanton arose from the colonisation by the church of Wenlock of the less hospitable regions of Wenlock Edge and the Clee Hills. Wenlock Edge forms the natural western boundary to the hinterland of Much Wenlock, and the Clee Hills appear to have been an area of relatively late settlement (see below).

The former extents of the *parochiae* of St. Gregory's, Morville and of St. Mary's, Stottesdon are apparent from documents preserved in the cartulary of Shrewsbury Abbey. Chapels said to be attached to the mother church of Morville in 1138 × 48 were Aldenham (in Morville), Astley Abbots, Aston Eyre (in Morville), Billingsley, Oldbury, Tasley and Underton (in Morville)[56] (see Figs. 12 and 18). The Domesday manor of Morville covered the area not only of Morville, Astley Abbots, Tasley and Billingsley parishes, but also of Bridgnorth St. Leonard's.[57] A charter of 1186 × 90 records the dependent chapels of Stottesdon church.[58] They are said to be Farlow and Wrickton (both in Stottesdon), Wheathill, and Aston, probably Aston Botterell. The extent of both these estates is shown on Fig. 12.

The evidence for the bounds of the reconstructed *parochia* of Idsall (Shifnal) church is less straightforward, but nevertheless the principal component parts of the estate can be identified. Dawley church was recognised as a chapelry of Idsall in 1256, and pensions paid by the incumbents of Kemberton and Ryton churches to Shifnal church were probably in acknowledgement of their former position as chapelries of St. Andrew's.[59] Sheriffhales and Stirchley seem similarly to have been chapelries of Shifnal.[60] Sutton Maddock may also have been part of this estate, since its place name, 'the south *tūn*' presumably describes the settlement's location in relation to the estate centre to the north.

The parish of Cleobury Mortimer in the 19th century included the attached chapelries of Doddington and Earls Ditton. The middle Saxon estate centred on Cleobury Mortimer may also have included the area of Hopton Wafers parish, if the interlocking of these two parishes indicates they were once a single land unit.

Thus, there was a network of minster churches in south-east Shropshire in the middle Saxon period, serving extensive districts, and at least something of the extent of these *parochiae* can be reconstructed. It is apparent from Fig. 12 that there are a number of parishes in the area under study which cannot be assigned to the *parochia* of an old minster church. By the time of the earliest documentation these churches were already independent rectories, and some, like Glazeley, Chetton and Aston (Munslow), had priests recorded in Domesday Book, implying the existence of a church in 1086.[61] It is likely that many of these churches were in fact founded within the spiritual cure of a minster church, and that they gained independence from their mother church at a sufficiently early period for no evidence of their former subjection to survive. This may be the case with Easthope, Stanton Long and Castle Holdgate with respect to Much Wenlock, and with Sutton Maddock relative to Shifnal.

It is also possible that some parishes may have originated as detached chapelries, in particular in the area of Brown Clee Hill, which appears to have been a region of outlying hill pasture attached to a number of valley estates (see Fig. 15).[62] The Clee Hills are an upland area of rough pasture unsuited to arable agriculture, and they were probably one of the last areas locally to have been settled and divided into discrete land units. The region appears to have been colonised from several different centres, and in the 12th and 13th centuries a number of lowland estates still had an interest in the area. Bouldon was a detached part of Castle Holdgate, and Earnstrey township an outlying area of Diddlebury parish; Tugford and Abdon may have been chapelries attached to Morville, and Morville Priory also had an interest in Cold Weston; Cleobury North may perhaps have been an outlying member of Cleobury Mortimer, and Neenton of Neen Savage or Neen Sollars.[63] The Clee vills may have originated within a transhumant economy as summer shielings which later developed into permanent farms and which had gained manorial independence from their parent settlements by the time of the Domesday Survey. The parishes of the Clee Hill area are small, and the churches probably had their origins in manorial chapels. Some, such as Heath and Loughton, remained subject to their distant mother churches, but the majority had gained their parochial independence by the time that adequate documentation becomes available.

The Minster Churches in the 11th and 12th Centuries: changing conditions

The Domesday Survey shows that several Shropshire churches were still collegiate in 1086. These churches continued to be staffed by secular clerks holding individual hereditary prebends *quasi propria* for a period of up to fifty years after the Norman Conquest in the south-east of the county, but the 12th century witnessed the gradual extinction of the Anglo-Saxon colleges. A number of the minster churches of the region were granted to distant abbeys, their canons were replaced by regular monks, and the separate prebends were resumed by the church and communalized.

Earl Roger de Montgomery's new abbey of St. Peter at Shrewsbury was well-endowed with minster churches by its founder and early benefactors. Before 1086, the earl had granted the churches of Morville and Stottesdon to St. Peter's, and the abbey had also acquired Shifnal church before 1094.[64] The church of St. Gregory, Morville, was in King Edward's time served by eight canons and endowed with eight hides of the royal manor of Morville. The church was given by Earl Roger to Shrewsbury Abbey, and in 1086 St. Gregory's, now staffed by three priests, held only five hides of the manor. The remaining three were held by three chaplains of the earl, who were probably the remnant of the secular community. St. Peter's was granted the church with the provision that as the canons holding the prebends died, the land should revert to the monks of Shrewsbury,[65] but the abbey's rights to the prebendal estates did not go unopposed. When one of the chaplains, Richard de Meilnilhermer, died, his son Hubert claimed unsuccessfully his hereditary right to his father's prebend in 1108 × 14.[66] In the course of time, the abbey presumably gained possession of all the former prebends. Between 1138 and 1148, St. Gregory's was appropriated to Shrewsbury Abbey.[67] The monks were to staff the

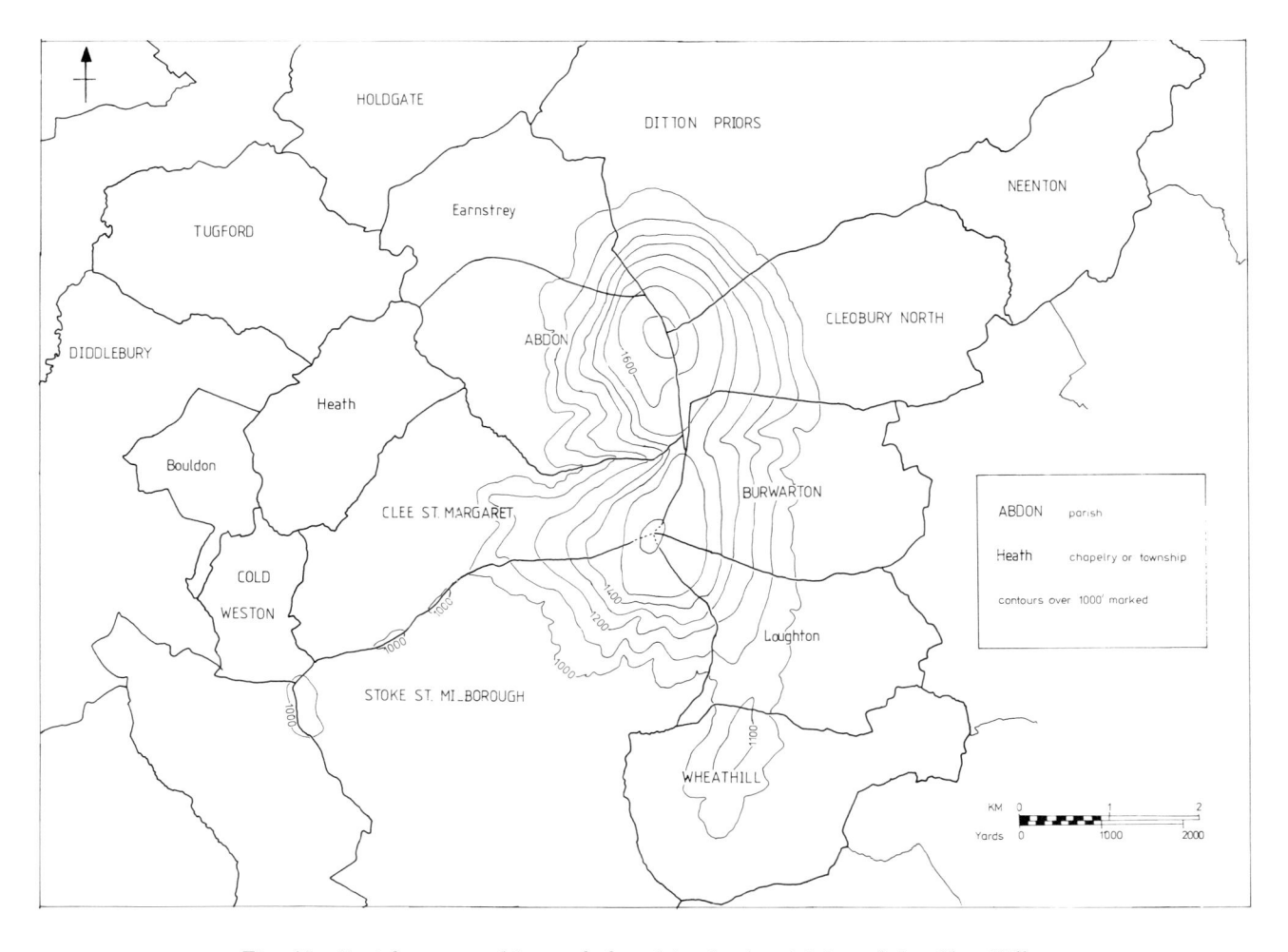

Fig. 15 Parishes, townships and chapelries in the vicinity of the Clee Hills.

church and provide hospitality there, and Morville Priory became a cell of St. Peter's.[68]

Similar arrangements to those made for the reversion of the prebends of Morville church were also made for Shifnal. When the church was given to Shrewsbury Abbey by Robert fitz Tetbald before 1094, the church was in the possession of secular clerks, but it was to revert to St. Peter's when the last of the prebendaries died.[69]

Domesday Book says of the church of Much Wenlock that Roger de Montgomery, earl of Shrewsbury, 'has made the church of St. Mildburg into an abbey': this refers to the subjection of the church to the Cluniac Priory of St. Mary of La Charité-sur-Loire.[70] There is no direct evidence that the minster church of Wenlock was still collegiate in 1086, but an entry in Domesday Book suggests that the secular clerks of the pre-Conquest church may have been recompensed when the church became a priory.[71] The manor of Stoke St. Milborough, which was in the possession of the church of St. Mildburg TRE, had been given by Earl Roger before 1086 to his chaplains, perhaps members of the minster community, 'although the church ought to have it'.[72] The manor of Stoke eventually reverted to Wenlock Priory, no doubt when the last of the clerks died.[73]

So although the minster churches of south-east Shropshire retained their collegiate constitution after the Norman Conquest, the communities of canons in those churches which became priories were replaced by regular monks during the late 11th and 12th centuries. However, not all minster churches were reformed and, in addition to the Royal Free Chapels which constitute a special case,[74] at least one in the vicinity of the area under study, Burford, persisted throughout the medieval period. Domesday Book records that on the manor of Burford there was a church and two priests, implying that the church was collegiate.[75] In 1253, Burford church consisted of three parts, and at the time of the *Valor Ecclesiasticus* there were still three portionists.[76]

The Minster Churches in the 11th and 12th Centuries: Continuing Rôle as Mother Churches

The minster churches of south-east Shropshire continued to exercise their rôle as mother churches

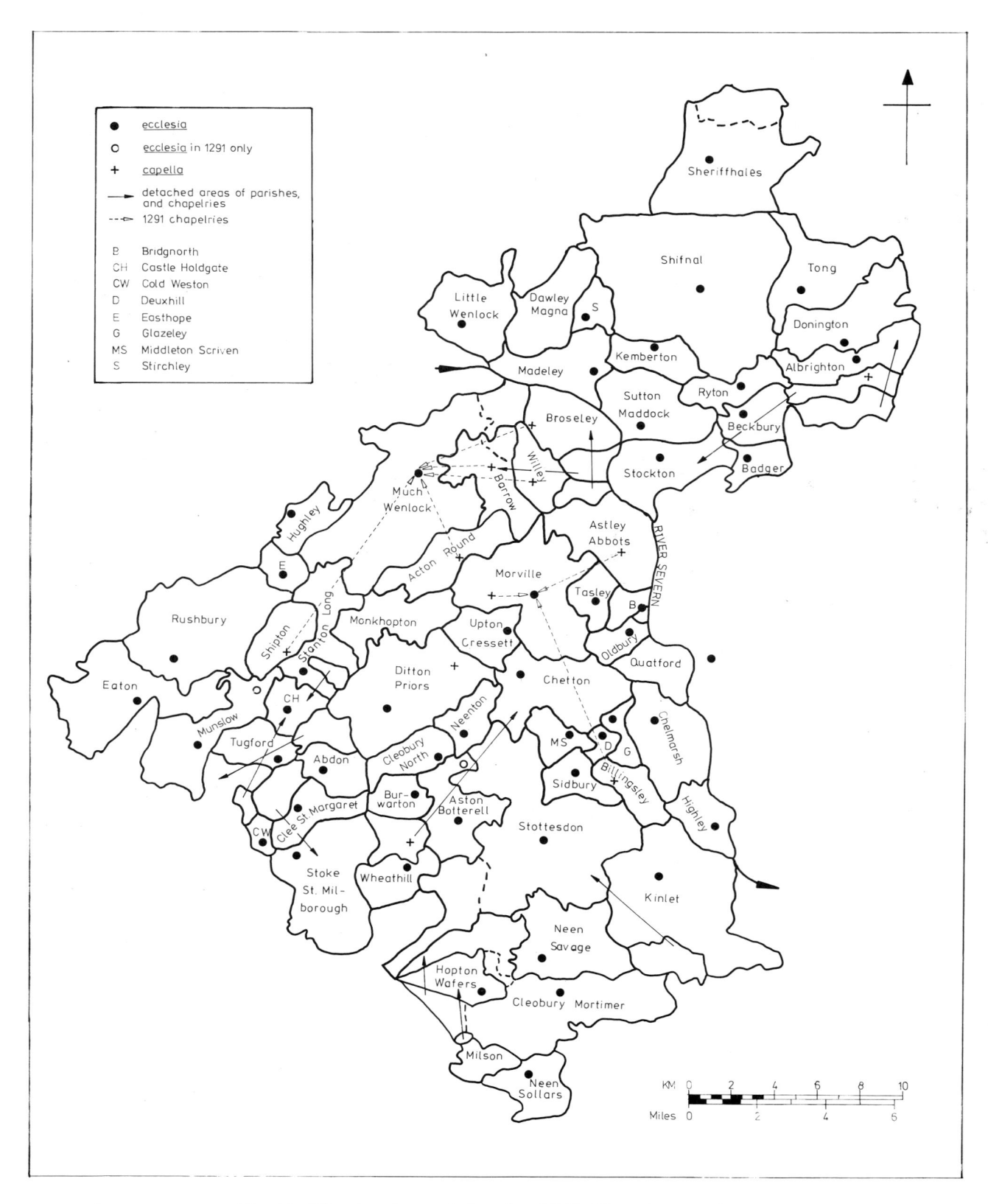

Fig. 16 The churches and chapels of S.E. Shropshire in 1291.

Fig. 17 Aston Eyre, Salop.: tympanum over S. door.

during the later middle ages, endeavouring to retain their rights over the local churches founded within their *parochiae* as the latter gained parochial independence. The date of the foundation of the parish churches, and the date by which the majority of them attained this status, can only be surmised. The majority of the early 19th-century parishes in the study-area were recorded in the Pope Nicholas Taxation of 1291;[77] those that were are shown on Fig. 16. However, not all of the churches were then designated *ecclesiae*, and some of the chapelries of Much Wenlock and Morville were still dependent on their mother church. It is likely that the late survival of minsters in south-east Shropshire retarded parochial development in the area. The retention of clerical staffs by the minster churches until *c.* 1100 may have made unnecessary the widespread foundation of local churches before then, or at least have prevented the cession of parochial rights to chapels founded by local landowners to serve their own estates.

There is only slight evidence to suggest that some of the lesser churches originated in the Saxon period. Barrow, a chapel of Much Wenlock, has a late Saxon chancel, but this may date from *c.* 1050–1100, and Rushbury church, possibly Saxo-Norman, could be 12th century.[78] On architectural grounds, supplemented by documentary material, the majority of the parish churches of the area would appear to be Norman foundations. Of the 62 churches in south-east Shropshire which were parochial by the early 19th century, 28 have surviving Norman features, and a further 15 are first recorded in documentary sources between 1086 and 1200.[79] In other words, nearly 70 per cent of the parish churches may have been constructed by the late 12th century, in addition to the known Anglo-Saxon foundations. Many of these churches may have been established *c.* 1080–1120, the period at which the minster system was at last breaking down in this area. During the 12th century, there are occasional references to the consecration of chapels, and to the conflict of interests between a mother church and its increasingly independent chapels. The example of St. Gregory's, Morville is especially informative, and it demonstrates the way in which local churches were initially subject to the minster, but gained greater autonomy as they were incorporated into the parochial system.

A charter issued by Robert de Betune, bishop of Hereford, in *c.* 1138 records the consecration of a number of chapels dependent on Morville: Oldbury, Billingsley, Aston Eyre, Aldenham and Underton.[80] The first three chapels received endowments from the lords of their respective manors, and it may be that the chapels were founded at that date by laymen to serve their own estates. However, there is evidence to suggest that the charter records the reconsecration of chapels already in existence or, more specifically, the consecration of graveyards perhaps newly attached to the chapels. The cemetery of Oldbury is mentioned in this charter, and a second one makes it clear that it was the graveyard which was dedicated at Aston.[81] Furthermore, the same bishop is said to have dedicated

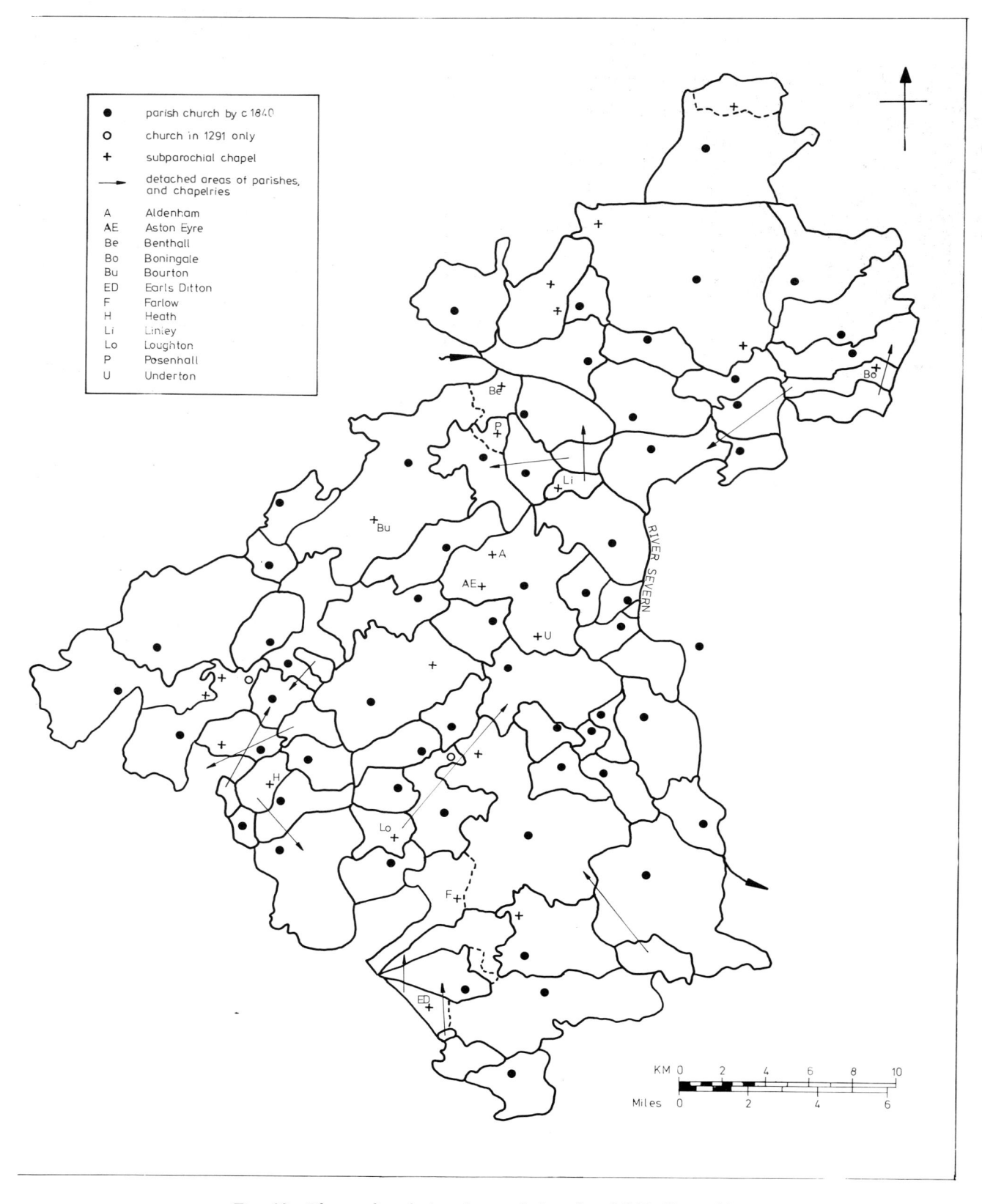

Fig. 18 The medieval churches and chapels of S.E. Shropshire.

the chapel and cemetery of Astley Abbots, with the proviso that the chapel should remain subject to Morville.[82] Burial rights were among those rights most coveted by chapels and most jealously guarded by mother churches. It would appear that these charters record not the initial foundation of churches, but a stage in their attempt to assume full parochial status. The Morville chapels were not wholly successful in this endeavour. Oldbury was an independent church by 1291, but Astley, which was given to the priory of Morville in 1217 × 9, was still dependent at the time of the *Valor Ecclesiasticus* although it was a parish church by 1561.[83] Aston Eyre remained in a subordinate position throughout the later medieval period, and did not become parochially separate until c. 1900. This case demonstrates, however, that a chapel could be handsomely upgraded in terms of its endowment and fabric, whilst continuing to be parochially dependent. The fine tympanum there, depicting the Entry of Christ into Jerusalem, has been described as 'the best piece of Norman carving in Shropshire' (Fig. 17).[84] It was presumably executed shortly after Robert fitz Aer gave his gifts to the church c. 1138, and may have reflected the increase in the importance of the chapel consequent upon the establishment of a graveyard there.

The efforts of manorial chapels to break away from the church in whose *parochia* they had been founded, gave rise to disputes over ecclesiastical rights. A number of disputes occurred at Aston Eyre between the fitz Aers, lords of the manor, and Shrewsbury Abbey which claimed authority over the church as a chapelry of Morville. In 1168 × 73, Robert fitz Aer lost his claim over the burial rights of Aston chapel, and agreed that the decision as to where inhabitants of Aston would be buried should rest with the church of Morville.[85] Robert was involved in a subsequent dispute over the rights of presentation to Aston chapel (1190 × 8). Fitz Aer was forced to acknowledge that the right of presentation belonged to Shrewsbury Abbey,[86] and when the abbot's nominee was admitted, the bishop of Hereford emphasised that all demesne tithes, burial rights and mortuary fees belonged to the mother church of Morville.[87]

In addition to the manorial chapels which eventually became full parish churches, there were many which remained sub-parochial. Fig. 18 shows the churches which were parochial by the early 19th century, together with all known medieval chapels. The history of most of these chapels is badly documented, but the general picture is one of diversity. During the later middle ages as a whole, there was a comparatively large number of sub-parochial chapels, but many would appear to have been short-lived and most have completely disappeared. The structures of those which survive indicate that some had their origins in, or by, the Norman period. Heath chapel is a perfectly preserved Norman chapel; the fine Norman tympanum can be seen at Aston Eyre; and at Boningale and

Fig. 19 Stottesdon, Salop.: this magnificent 12th-century font suggests that the former minster retained something of its old importance within its territory.

Bourton, parts of the Norman structure similarly survive.[88] Some of the chapelries were detached from the main area of the parish, and were therefore defined territorial areas. Several of these, in particular Heath, Loughton and Boningale, had a long history of parochial subjection but eventually became separate parishes in the late 19th century; and the same was true of some of the chapels founded in Domesday manors or townships, such as Aston Eyre, Benthall and Farlow. But of the remainder little is known: they were probably the private chapels of manor-houses with no cure, and most seem to have disappeared before 1500.

Conclusion

The most conspicuous characteristic of the parochial geography of south-east Shropshire in the 11th and 12th centuries is the large number of surviving minster churches which were still active then. The reasons for this are not easy to isolate. Part of the answer may be that the development of separate lordships in Shropshire was relatively less advanced than in other areas, and that vested aristocratic interests at the top were stronger. It would seem that the area was untouched by the reform movement of the 10th century, or that its effects were very short-lived. The non-regular minster communities persisted, and some were newly patronised during the earlier 11th century. The fact that the minsters were still functioning and not moribund in the late Saxon and early post-Conquest period may well have affected the chronology of local church foundation and the development of the parochial system in the area. Private chapels founded on small lay estates within the *parochia* of a forceful minster church would have been unable to infringe upon the ecclesiastical control of the minster over the population of the estate. Furthermore, the foundation of daughter churches by minsters may have been retarded so long as all parts of the *parochia* continued to be served by clergy from the central church. The minster system seems finally to have broken down in south-east Shropshire *c.* 1100. Many of the minster churches had been granted to distant abbeys, the secular clerks were being gradually replaced by regular clergy, and pastoral responsibilities were by then becoming differentiated from the monastic. The village churches and proprietary churches gained ecclesiastical rights and carved their own parishes from the *parochiae* of the minsters. The pattern of numerous local churches and small parishes which was established by *c.* 1300 was in marked contrast to the earlier one of a few minster churches each serving an extensive parish. Even so, the full development of the parochial system was not yet complete. It may be that the continued subordination of many small churches in south-east Shropshire during the later medieval period, was the consequence of their relatively late arrival on the scene.

Notes

1. C.N.L. Brooke, 'Rural Ecclesiastical Institutions in England: the Search for their Origins', *Settimane di Studi sull' Alto Mediovo*, xxviii.2 (1982), 685–711. This principle has been applied, apparently with success in, for example, C.C. Taylor, *Dorset* (London, 1970), 49–72. But for an alternative view, see D. Roffe, 'Pre-Conquest Estates and Parish Boundaries: a Discussion and some Examples from Lincolnshire', in M.L. Faull (ed.), *Studies in Late Anglo Saxon Settlement* (Oxford, 1974), 115–22. For further references to recent work on minsters and their *parochiae*, see Blair, 'Secular Minsters', 104 n 2, and above, p. 16 note 1.
2. This paper is based on research in progress for a Birmingham University doctoral thesis.
3. F.M. Stenton, *Anglo-Saxon England* (3rd ed., Oxford, 1971), 293–5; P.H. Sawyer, 'Anglo-Saxon Settlement: the Documentary Evidence', in T. Rowley (ed.), *Anglo-Saxon Settlement and Landscape*, BAR 6 (1974), 115–6.
4. Stenton, *Anglo-Saxon England*, 287–8; H. Loyn, 'The Hundred in England in the Tenth and Early Eleventh Centuries', in H.R. Loyn and H. Hearder (eds.), *British Government and Administration* (Cardiff, 1974), 3–4. For a similar system of organization, see G.W.S. Barrow, *The Kingdom of the Scots* (London, 1973), 7–68.
5. H. Cam, '*Manerium cum Hundredo*: the Hundred and the Hundredal Manor', and 'Early Groups of Hundreds', in *Liberties and Communities in Medieval England* (Cambridge, 1944), 64–106.
6. Ibid., 98–9; S.1165, dated 672 × 4.
7. P.H. Sawyer, 'The Royal *Tūn* in pre-Conquest England', in P. Wormald (ed.), *Ideal and Reality in Frankish and Anglo-Saxon Society* (Oxford, 1983), 273–99.
8. On which see T.H. Aston, 'The Origin of the Manor in England', in T.H. Aston et al. (eds.), *Social Relations and Ideas* (Cambridge, 1983), 1–44, especially 21–2, 24, 32–3.
9. Brooke, 'Rural Ecclesiastical Institutions', 696–7.
10. Ibid., 695–6.
11. C.N.L. Brooke, 'The Missionary at Home: the Church in the Towns, 1000–1250', in C.J. Cumming (ed.), *Studies in Church History*, vi (1970), 68–9.
12. W. Page, 'Some Remarks on the Churches of the Domesday Survey', *Archaeologia*, 2nd ser. xvi (1915), 66f.
13. For example, Gloucestershire and Oxfordshire: Cam, *Liberties and Communities*, 95–8.
14. Stenton, *Anglo-Saxon England*, 293, 298–9; Loyn, 'The Hundred in England', 2.
15. S. 723, granting six hides at Church Aston and at *Plesc* (963).
16. For example, C.D. Drew, 'The Manors of the Iwerne Valley, Dorset', *Proc. Dorset Nat. Hist. & Arch. Soc.* lxvi (1948), 45–50; Taylor, *Dorset*, 49–72; M. Reed, 'Buckinghamshire Anglo-Saxon Charter Boundaries', in M. Gelling, *The Early Charters of the Thames Valley* (Leicester, 1979), 168–87.
17. The map is based on one produced by the Shropshire Record Office showing the ecclesiastical parishes of the Tithe Maps.
18. Exceptions to this are: Clee Stanton (in Stoke St. Milborough) and Aston (in Munslow), which lay in *Culvestan* hundred; Tetsill (in Neen Sollars), which lay in Overs hundred; Hughley, and Wigwig (in Much Wenlock), which were in the hundred of Condover; Dawley, Stirchley, and Woodcote (in Sheriffhales), which were in Wrockwardine hundred; and Sheriffhales, which was entered under the Staffordshire hundred of *Colvestan*.
19. On the natural background of the area, see E.J. Howell 'Shropshire', in L.D. Stamp (ed.), *The Land of Britain: Report of the Land Utilisation Survey of Britain* (London, 1941), Part 66, 205–7; A.E. Trueman, *Geology and Scenery in England and Wales* (London, 1971), 246–8, 252; R. Millward and A. Robinson, *The Welsh Marches* (Basingstoke, 1971), 98–100, 129–33.
20. The charters are incorporated in 'Saint Mildburg's Testament', which has been transcribed and translated by H.P.R. Finberg, 'St. Mildburg's Testament', *ECWM*, 201–6. See also, A.J.M. Edwards, 'Odo of Ostia's History of the Translation of St. Milburga and its Connection with the Early History of Much Wenlock Abbey' (unpublished MA thesis, London, 1960). The charters can be accepted as genuine, but the narrative of the Testament is probably a tenth- or twelfth-century fabrication.
21. *ECWM*, 197. In a letter dated 716 St. Boniface refers to a 'brother' in the *monasterium* of Abbess Mildburg: *S. Bonifatii et Lullii Epistolae*, ed. Tangl (*Monumenta Germaniae Historica*), 8.
22. S. 221.
23. *ECWM*, 197 & n.1, 198.
24. 'Chronicon ex Chronicis', in Petrie (ed.), *Monumenta Historica Britannica*, p. 609.
25. Much Wenlock, Ticklerton, Madeley, Little Wenlock, Shipton, Petelie, Bourton, Stoke St. Milborough, Deuxhill, Pickthorn, Sutton near Shrewsbury, Clee Stanton, Hughley, Eardington: DB I, 252b, 254; *VCH Salop.* i, 312–3, 318.
26. DB I, 253; *VCH Salop.* 315.
27. Ibid., 7.
28. DB I, 254; *VCH Salop.* i, 318.
29. Stottesdon had a TRE value of £20 which was probably the income of the hundred as well as of the manor; by the twelfth century, Stottesdon was the *caput* of a hundred which

30. S.C. No. 35; DB I, 254; V.C.H. Salop. i, 318.
31. Personal observation. See N. Pevsner, *The Buildings of England: Shropshire* (London, 1958), plate 6a.
32. DB I, 256b; *VCH Salop.* i, 329.
33. S.C. No. 279 (p.256).
34. DB I, 260; *VCH Salop.* i, 345.
35. Ibid.
36. S.R. Bassett, pers. comm.
37. DB I, 252, 254, 260, 260b; *VCH Salop.* i, 311, 321, 344, 347.
38. DB I, 252b; *VCH Salop.* i, 313. See Blair, 'Secular Minsters', 128–31.
39. DB I, 253; *VCH Salop.* i, 315–6.
40. DB I, 254, 256b; *VCH Salop.* i, 317, 328–9.
41. *VCH Salop.* ii, 123–4. The royal free chapels of St. Mary Magdalene at Quatford and Bridgnorth are the subject of current research.
42. The late 11th-century Cluniac church overlies a Roman building, evidently with a history of continuous re-use from the 7th century onwards. Holy Trinity, which served the parochial functions, was rebuilt in the 12th century (*JBAA* cxl (1987), 76–87). For excavations at Much Wenlock see: D. Cranage, 'The Monastery of St. Milburga at Much Wenlock', *Archaeologia*, lxxii (1922), 107–31; E.D.C. Jackson and E. Fletcher, 'The pre-Conquest Churches at Much Wenlock', *JBAA*, 3rd ser. xxviii (1965), 16–38; H. Woods, 'Wenlock Priory', *JBAA*, cxl (1987), 36–75.
43. *Taxatio*, 167b; *Cal. Pat. R. 1348–50*, 188; S.R.O. 1224/2/11–13.
44. S. 221.
45. *ECWM*, 148. The charter appears to state explicitly that Æthelred and Æthelflæd were *regranting* the land to the church. The charter reads: *sed nos iterum ... comodavimus*. In this context *iterum* could signify 'on the other hand', but when taken in conjunction with the statement that the land had been surrendered to the king's lordship, the meaning 'again, a second time' seems more appropriate.
46. DB I, 256b, 258b; *VCH Salop.* i, 328, 337.
47. DB I, 258b; *VCH Salop.* i, 337; E. Ekwall, *Oxford Dictionary of English Place-Names* (4th ed., Oxford, 1960), 245.
48. DB I, 256b; *VCH Salop.* i, 328.
49. Ekwall, *DEPN*, 438.
50. DB I, 252b; *VCH Salop.* i, 312.
51. S. 1802; *ECWM*, 203, 206.
52. The diocese of Hereford was established by 676: J. Godfrey, *The Church in Anglo-Saxon England* (Cambridge, 1962), 133–4. The earliest date at which the boundaries of the medieval diocese can be reconstructed is 1291. The most prominent natural boundary line through Shropshire is the river Severn, and in the south-east of the county the diocesan boundary does follow the river, but at Madeley and Little Wenlock the boundary extends north of the Severn to include the two parishes. For a similar situation on the border of Gloucestershire with Worcestershire and Warwickshire, see C.S. Taylor, 'The Origin of the Mercian Shires', in H.P.R. Finberg (ed.), *Gloucestershire Studies* (Leicester, 1957), 17–51.
53. S. 1799; *ECWM*, 203, 205.
54. There were no royal manors in Patton hundred in 1066; the *caput* of the hundred was in fact King Edward's manor of Corfham in *Culvestan* hundred, of which it was also the *caput*: DB I, 253b; *VCH Salop.* i, 315–6.
55. Taylor & Taylor, ii , 526.
56. S.C. Nos. 333, 334.
57. R.W. Eyton, *Antiquities of Shropshire* (i–xii, London, 1854–60), i, 31, 83–4. Subject of current research.
58. S.C. No. 351b.
59. Eyton, *Antiquities of Shropshire*, ii, 88–9; iii, 7–8.
60. Ibid., ii, 330; viii, 123.
61. DB I, 254, 255; *VCH Salop.* i, 318, 322, 323.
62. This is contrary to R.T. Rowley, 'The Clee Forest – a Study in Common Right', *Trans. Shrops. Arch. Soc.*, lviii (1966), 48–67, where it is argued that the Clee Forest was an Anglo-Saxon estate. For a similar situation of outlying pastoral tracts attached to river-valley estates, see A. Everitt, 'The Making of the Agrarian Landscape of Kent', *Arch. Cant.*, xcii (1976), 1–31, and 'River and Wold. Reflections on the Historical Origin of Regions and Pays', *J. Historical Geography*, 3.1 (Jan. 1977), 1–19.
63. See Fig. 1; S.C. Nos. 333, 34; Ekwall, *DEPN*, 110–1, 337.
64. DB I, 253, 254 *VCH Salop.* i, 315, 318; S.C. Nos. 35, 279.
65. S.C. No. 1: *dum canonici que in ea prebendas habebant morte dificerent prebende in dominium monachorum devenerent.*
66. S.C. No. 1.
67. S.C. No. 334.
68. *VCH Salop.* ii, 29–30.
69. S.C. No. 279 (p. 256): *quia eandem ecclesiam tunc clerici habebant, precepit isdem Robertus, ut cum illi morentur, ecclesia in dominio Sancti Petri veniret.*
70. R. Graham, *The History of the Alien Priory of Wenlock* (London, 1965), 4.
71. *ECWM*, 198n.
72. DB I, 252b; *VCH Salop.* i, 312.
73. Eyton, *Antiquities of Shropshire*, iv, 7.
74. J.H. Denton, *English Royal Free Chapels 1100–1300: A Constitutional Study* (Manchester, 1970).
75. DB I, 260; *VCH Salop.* i, 344.
76. Eyton, *Antiquities of Shropshire*, iv, 321–2; *Valor Ecclesiasticus*, 214a.
77. *Taxatio*, 165–7, 247–8.
78. Taylor & Taylor, i, 49–51; ii, 526.
79. See relevant entries in Pevsner, *Shropshire*, and Eyton, *Antiquities of Shropshire*.
80. S.C. No. 333.
81. S.C. No. 346.
82. S.C. No. 348.
83. *Taxatio*, 166; S.C. No. 347; *Map of Shropshire with dates of commencement of parish registers*, published by the Institute of Heraldic and Genealogical Studies, 1983.
84. Pevsner, *Shropshire*, 64 and plate 6b.
85. S.C. No. 343.
86. S.C. No. 340, 314.
87. S.C. No. 342.
88. Pevsner, *Shropshire*, 64, 77, 78, 147.

VII. Some Aspects of the *Parochia* of Leominster in the 12th Century

Brian Kemp

While the Domesday account of Leominster contains none but the faintest clues on the status of its church,[1] the 12th-century evidence preserved in the Reading and Leominster cartularies proves conclusively that it lay at the heart of an ancient and extensive *parochia*. Moreover, although direct proof is lacking, there can be no reasonable doubt that the church was originally a minster church. Leominster had been the chief centre of Christianity in north-west Herefordshire since the 7th century. In addition to being the seat of two successive monastic communities during the Anglo-Saxon period, it seems throughout to have contained a group of secular clergy (whether collegiate in a strict sense or not) who served its large *parochia*. After the dissolution of the late Anglo-Saxon nunnery in or soon after 1046 the church and manorial complex of Leominster were granted to Queen Edith and, on her death, became Crown property until given by Henry I to his new abbey at Reading in 1121×23. Monks were sent to Leominster from Reading almost immediately and a fully conventual priory, strictly dependent upon the parent house, was established there in 1139.[2] The old minster church thus became monastic once again and, since there is no trace of any secular collegiate organisation surviving, the monks acquired a direct interest in its ecclesiastical rights.

These rights were still considerable in the early 12th century. The rather remote geographical position of Leominster, combined no doubt with the hold maintained by the nunnery and then by the Crown, meant that the formation of new parishes, so evident in southern and eastern England, had not gone far by that time. This is clear from an important charter of 1123 by Richard de Capella, bishop of Hereford, conceding and confirming the church of Leominster to Reading Abbey and listing thirty-nine places which, according to old and reliable men, lay within its *parochia*.[3] Thirty-five of the places listed can be certainly identified with modern ones, three others fairly confidently, and one not at all.[4] They form a broad, though not continuous, sweep of territory on all sides of Leominster, but with a lesser concentration to the west than on the other three sides. The most distant is Kinnersley, nearly 12 miles to the south-west, the most distant on the east being Edvin Ralph, about 10 miles from Leominster. Some development had clearly taken place in the old *parochia*, however, for the bishop's charter adds that the same witnesses declined to name several other places which were anciently included, because these were too old (i.e. presumably they had long been detached and could not now be regarded as part of the *parochia*). The *parochia* had thus been more extensive at an earlier date, and there are grounds for thinking that it originally covered the whole of the complex manorial lordship of Leominster described in Domesday,[5] which itself probably represented the bulk of the Anglo-Saxon nunnery's possessions.

Despite the bishop's charter, however, it is likely that the central church did not retain spiritual rights in all the places listed there. Some of the most outlying parts of the *parochia* were almost certainly not dependent upon Leominster in any real sense in 1123, and it seems best to regard the charter as containing those places which men were prepared to say were in the *parochia* or had been in the recent past. It would be rash to argue on this authority alone that all the places mentioned were in fact dependent in 1123 or became so as a result of the charter. For Dilwyn, Luntley (in Dilwyn), Sarnesfield, Edvin Ralph, Butterley (in Wacton), Whyle, Pudleston, Brockmanton and Ford (both in Pudleston) I have found no evidence that the church of Leominster had any spiritual rights after 1123, and all should probably be regarded as having been detached from the *parochia* before that date along with the other places on which the bishop's informants declined to commit themselves. To these should also perhaps be added Kinnersley and Titley, where the evidence for Leominster's continuing rights is very slight.[6] On the other hand, it is clear from later evidence that at least eight places not included in the charter were nevertheless in the *parochia* (some may, of course, have been parts of places that were named), namely, Docklow, Eyton, Hurstley (in Letton), Kimbolton, Lucton, Mileshope,[7] Orleton and Yarpole.[8] Despite certain losses, therefore, the *parochia* was still very extensive in 1123 and, having survived into the age of charters and episcopal *acta*, its subsequent history provides one of the best-documented examples of developments within the area of jurisdiction of an ancient minster. Moreover, although in 1123 the control of the mother church was better preserved in some parts than in others, the material value of its rights constituted sufficient

83

incentive for the monks to resist as far as possible any further weakening of ecclesiastical ties within the *parochia*. The evidence shows that to a considerable extent they succeeded.

What were Leominster's rights in the *parochia*? There are isolated references to its right to distribute chrism, to collect Peter's Pence and to compel the attendance of parishioners in the mother church on a certain day each year,[9] but to what extent these applied throughout the *parochia* is uncertain. Of the more important rights anciently belonging to mother churches, baptism is strangely never mentioned at Leominster, but it is impossible to believe that the right was not exercised or controlled over a good deal of the *parochia*. Leaving these aside, the spiritual rights which appear to have been of chief concern to the monks and which feature most prominently in the records were the receipt of tithes, the receipt of 'scrifcorn' and the right to bury the dead. Each of these will be considered in turn, but they cannot be separated entirely, since in the various settlements which ensued in the 12th century the monks not infrequently struck a bargain for the retention of one by agreeing to the surrender or modification of another.

(i) Tithes

The right to receive tithes was far and away the most valuable, but it was also the one most likely to be challenged. The monks had secular lordship in those parts of the *parochia* which came to Reading Abbey as members of the manor of Leominster, and in these it was comparatively easy to maintain tithe rights. However, many manors and estates were held by lay lords or had been given by them to different religious houses, and in certain of these some diversion of tithes away from the mother church had already taken place by 1123. In the late Anglo-Saxon period, according to the well-known law of King Edgar, all tithes from the *parochia* of a minster church were to be paid to that church unless a lord had a local church with a graveyard, in which case he was to devote one-third of his demesne tithes to his own church.[10] How far this law was obeyed we do not know, but in any case after the Norman Conquest manorial lords assumed a far greater freedom in the disposal of their tithes, often granting away to quite extraneous religious institutions two-thirds or sometimes the whole of their demesne tithes without reference to any ancient mother church.[11] Moreover, lords did not feel inhibited in so doing even if they had no church, chapel or graveyard on their land. Where two-thirds of the tithes were granted in this way, the remaining third seems normally to have gone to the parish church. If in such circumstances a former minster could maintain its right to be regarded as the parish church, despite the existence of a local church or chapel, then it would receive the third part of the tithes. By these means the legislation of Edgar on minster tithes was effectively reversed in the Norman period,[12] but with the added difference that the tithes which lords felt free to dispose of could and often did pass to religious houses entirely outside the bounds of an old *parochia*, a development certainly not envisaged in Edgar's law. In some parts of the *parochia* of Leominster these practices had clearly been in operation by 1123, and the mother church's receipts in tithes were markedly reduced in consequence.

The earliest ecclesiastical mandate concerning Leominster's tithes is by William of Corbeil, archbishop of Canterbury, to be dated probably 1127 × 31 during a vacancy in the see of Hereford. It orders the archdeacon of Hereford and his ministers to cause the tithes of all lands in the *parochia* to be paid to the church of Leominster, naming specifically Broadward, Wharton, Newton, Gattertop, *Achis*, Eaton, Hamnish (Clifford), Hatfield (Magna), Hatfield (Parva), Hampton (Mappenore), Risbury and Broadfield,[13] all of which had been included in the bishop of Hereford's list in 1123. However, although the gift of Leominster to Reading Abbey seems largely to have curtailed further diversion of tithes away from the mother church, by 1123 parts of the tithes of three places which were still within the *parochia* — Monkland, Hatfield Magna and Wharton — had certainly (or in one case probably) already come into the hands of other religious houses, and it is possible that the tithes of Broadfield had similarly been lost. All four cases are illuminating and will be dealt with in turn.

The earliest surviving tithe settlement in the *parochia* dates from 1137, when it was established before the bishop in the synod of Hereford that the abbot of Castellion paid to the church of Leominster 12*d*. annually for the third part of the tithe of Monkland.[14] The manor of Monkland had been given to the abbey of St. Peter of Castellion at Conches (Eure, Normandy) by Ralph de Tosny before 1086.[15] A chapel (or church) had been founded in the manor by then, or shortly after, and Castellion established a small cell there in the reign of William II.[16] The nature of the tithes in the 1137 settlement is unfortunately not made clear. They would certainly have included the demesne tithes, but possibly the tithes of villein land in the manor as well. At any rate, either by the terms of Ralph de Tosny's original gift or in its capacity as lord of the manor, Castellion was able to devote two-thirds of the tithes to itself, but could not deal in this way with the remaining third, which was claimed by Leominster as the superior 'parish' church. Under the terms of the settlement it secured the third part in return for an annual payment in recognition of Leominster's ancient right. Hatfield Magna is a rather similar case. The manor was acquired before 1127 by the priory of Great Malvern (Worcestershire),[17] a dependency of Westminster. A

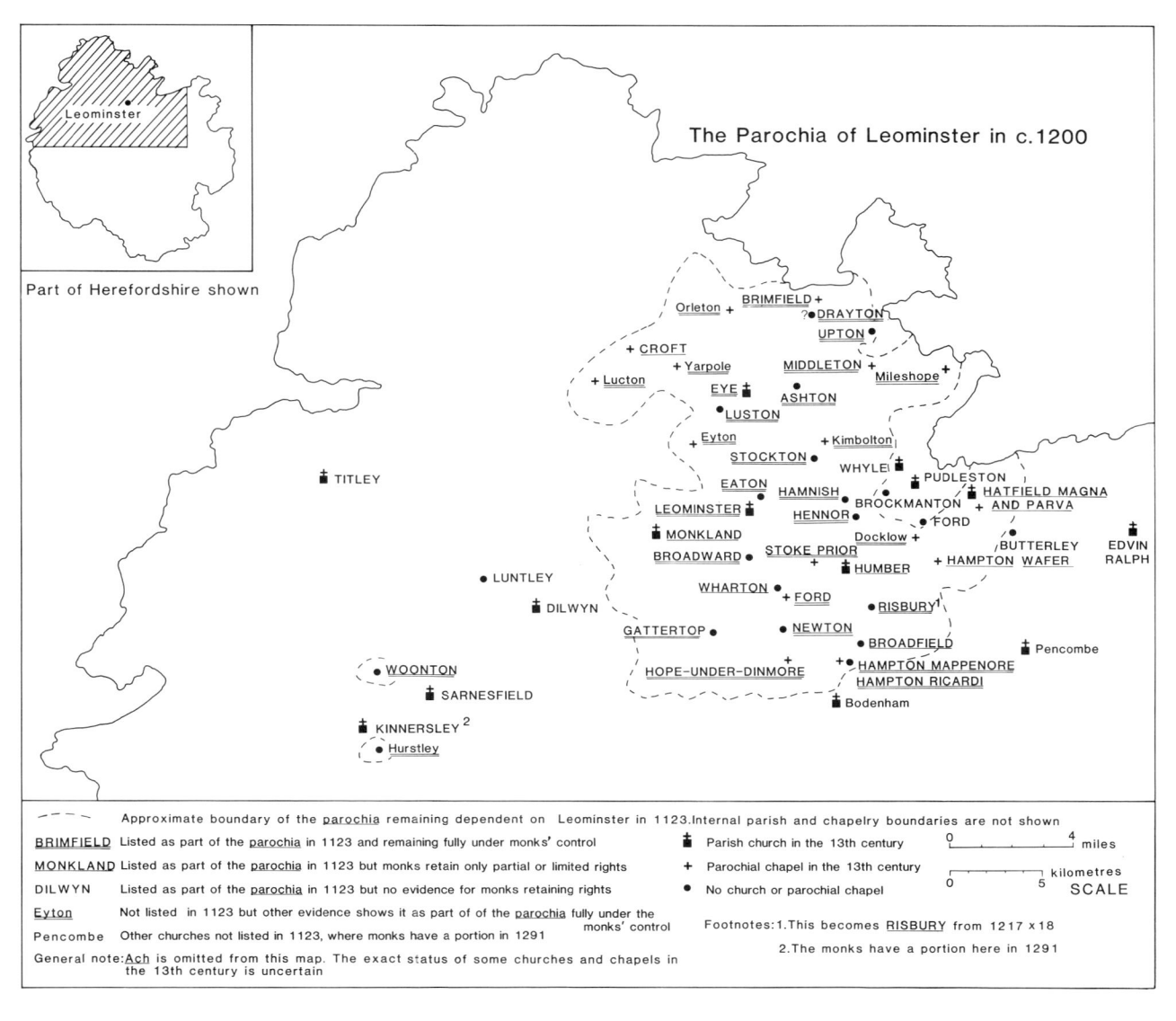

Fig. 20 The parochia *of Leominster in c. 1200.*

chapel had been established there by the late 11th century[18] and passed with the manor into the possession of the priory, to which it was paying a pension in 1291.[19] Apparently Great Malvern did not attempt to appropriate the tithes of Hatfield Magna, but nevertheless Leominster received only a third part, the other two-thirds going to the local chapel or, as it had become by the 13th century, the local church. This is clear both from an early 13th-century tithe settlement and from the Taxation of Pope Nicholas IV. In 1202 it was agreed between Great Malvern and its rector of Hatfield, on one side, and Leominster Priory, on the other, that the church of Hatfield should have the third part of the tithes in corn from the land of Nicholas of Bilfield (in Hatfield), as it had the other two-thirds, in return for which third the rector would pay annually to Leominster 1*lb.* of wax.[20] The natural inference from this is that normally two-thirds of Hatfield tithes belonged to the rector of the church, the remaining third going to Leominster in right of the old minster church; and this is supported by the valuations of 1291, when the prior of Leominster's portion in the church was exactly one-third of its value, the remainder being *ad pencionem prioris Maioris Malverne*.[21] Wharton is the third case, but of a slightly different type since, unlike Monkland and Hatfield, it had no chapel and was served from the church of Leominster, to whose immediate parish it continued to belong. Yet even here two-thirds of the demesne tithes were not paid to the mother church. The Domesday holder of Wharton, a certain Bernard, later gave two-thirds of his (demesne) tithes to the Cluniac priory of Thetford (Norfolk), founded in 1103 × 04, which he later still entered as a monk. The gift was confirmed by his son, Gilbert of Croft, in about 1130.[22] In 1189 Thetford leased the tithes in perpetuity to the canons of Oseney Abbey (Oxfordshire),[23] who were accordingly returned in 1291 as holding a portion of 13*s*. 4*d*. in Wharton.[24]

Monkland, Hatfield and Wharton are the only places where parts of the tithes of estates still within the *parochia* in 1123 had certainly or probably been acquired by other religious houses. It is possible, however, that a similar diversion of tithes had taken place at Broadfield, where, as at Wharton, there was no chapel. In 1131 × 37 a settlement was reached before the bishop in the synod of Hereford between the monks of Leominster and Miles the Constable over the 'parish' of the men of Broadfield, which the monks claimed as belonging to Leominster and which had been listed as such in 1123. It was agreed that Leominster would continue to receive scrifcorn, the corn of 2 acres of the demesne in August and Peter's Pence, all of which it had received previously, while the church of Bodenham would bury the dead and receive all other benefits.[25] Presumably the latter included tithes, since these were not specifically reserved to Leominster, and it may therefore be assumed that the church of Leominster had been deprived of Broadfield's tithes before this time.[26] Moreover, the church which received the tithes, Bodenham, was outside the *parochia* and had been given to Brecon Priory by its founder, Bernard de Neufmarché, early in the 12th century.[27] Broadfield was thus a further place where tithes from Leominster's *parochia* had been lost to an external religious house.

A similar loss of tithes probably occurred at Humber, but at a later date and subsequent to Reading Abbey's acquisition of Leominster. In 1148 × 54 Gilbert Foliot, bishop of Hereford, consecrated a cemetery at the chapel of Humber for the lord of the manor Walter del Mans and his wife, with the consent of the abbot of Reading and at the request of the monks of Leominster.[28] Burial rights were reserved to Leominster, however, and Walter and his wife gave the priory certain lands and rent, which were probably in lieu of tithes, since they intended to convey Humber church (as it soon became) with its tithes to Brecon Priory, which they had done by the autumn of 1155.[29]

Reading Abbey and its priory at Leominster clearly had to maintain constant watch on the tithe rights of the mother church. Periods of anarchy or disturbance in the area, such as the reign of Stephen, could lead to a detention of tithes by local lords which might threaten their permanent loss from the *parochia*. Such a situation arose on the manor known in the 13th century as Hampton Ricardi and now as Hampton Court, in Hope-under-Dinmore.[30] In the mid 12th century the lord of Hampton Ricardi was Gilbert of Hampton, *alias* Gilbert of Bacton,[31] who during the troubles of Stephen's reign (*tempore werre*) forcibly withheld the tithes of his Hampton, which the abbot of Reading claimed were by ancient right appurtenant to the church of Leominster. The dispute was settled in the chapter of Hereford before the bishop, Gilbert Foliot, in 1154 × 63, when the abbot was able to prove by sufficient testimony of clerks and laymen that the entire parochial right of the place belonged to Leominster.[32]

However, this was not the end of the matter, for by 1173 × 74 a new antagonist had appeared in the person of Roger son of Maurice, who claimed the demesne tithes of Hampton 'Gileberti' (i.e., Hampton Ricardi) as appurtenant to his church of Bacton (outside the *parochia*). This claim suggests the interesting possibility that, since Gilbert of Hampton/Bacton had held Bacton as well as Hampton Ricardi,[33] he too may have claimed the tithes of the latter as appurtenant to Bacton church. There was evidently an appeal to Rome, which resulted in the commission of the case to Robert Foliot, bishop-elect of Hereford, before whom Roger son of Maurice surrendered his claim to the tithes and delivered them into the elect's hands *tanquam ad ius ecclesie de Leominist[ria] pertinentes*. The abbot of Reading then granted the tithes to Roger for life for an annual pension of one gold coin,[34] but eventually in 1200 × 15 Roger surrendered them to Giles de Braose, bishop of Hereford, who conceded them in appropriation to the prior and monks of Leominster.[35] It is notable in this case that both in 1173 × 74 and in 1200 × 15 Leominster's title to the tithes was reinforced by the direct involvement of the diocesan, who took the tithes into his own hands before confirming them to the monks.

It was crucially important to Reading Abbey, as it was to other religious houses holding ancient minster churches with extensive *parochiae*, to obtain specific written confirmation of the rights of the mother church. In the case of Hampton Ricardi just mentioned, for example, Roger son of Maurice may have been assisted in his claim to the tithes in 1173 × 74 simply by the failure of the earlier settlement of 1154 × 63 to confirm them specifically to Leominster. The monks' need was, so to speak, to get the mother church's rights down on parchment. On the other hand, a not infrequent demand from lords of manors within the *parochia* was that they be allowed cemeteries on their lands, either with burial rights or, particularly in disturbed times, the more limited type of cemetery *ad refugium* without right of burial. Since burial rights in the *parochia* belonged essentially to Leominster, the monks were able to exploit such requests to secure the confirmation or restoration of the mother church's right to tithes in the places concerned.[36] In addition to the cemetery at Humber mentioned above, Gilbert Foliot consecrated cemeteries at Hampton Mappenore, Hampton Wafer and Risbury.[37] Only the first of these had a chapel, and at the others the cemeteries were merely *ad refugium*. Each place lay within the *parochia* and each cemetery was consecrated with the consent of the monks of Leominster in return for the grant to them by the local lords of the entire tithe of the demesne and tenants' land, although the lord of Risbury, Nicholas of Maund, would retain half his demesne tithe during his life. It will be necessary to return to these cemeteries later, but it is worth noting here that at each place the burial profits or full burial rights were also reserved to the mother church. These settlements, which were clearly so advantageous to the monks, reveal the controlling hand of Gilbert Foliot and the interest which he took in the Leominster *parochia*.

Other lords desired the convenience of private chapels in their lands, to be used only when they, their wives or their *familia* were in residence, and again the monks seized the opportunity to secure Leominster's tithe rights. Two cases are known. In the mid 12th century Reading Abbey allowed Walter de Clifford to have such a chapel at Hamnish (Clifford) in return for the grant to Leominster of the whole tithe of the place, both of the demesne and of the villeins, *scilicet de omnibus unde decime dantur tam de vivis quam de mortuis*.[38] In Henry II's reign Robert Malherbe, who had succeeded Nicholas of Maund at Risbury, was allowed a similar chapel there and gave to Leominster the tithe of his whole demesne in the same terms.[39] In this case the monks already had written title to the tithes, in Gilbert Foliot's charter concerning the cemetery *ad refugium* at Risbury, but, since that agreement had permitted the then lord of the manor to retain half the demesne tithes for life, the monks were now apparently making doubly sure that they obtained them after his death.

By such means as these the tithe rights of the mother church were bolstered by written confirmations. In each case it was the entire tithe which was confirmed or granted, a point which needs emphasising since, with the probable exception of Humber, Henry I's gift of Leominster to Reading Abbey seems virtually to have put an end to the practice by which two-thirds of demesne tithes could be diverted from the mother church, as had been done before 1123. The monks asserted Leominster's right to receive tithes within the *parochia* in full and apparently sought confirmation of this from Rome in the later 12th century, since William de Vere, bishop of Hereford 1186–98, in execution of a papal mandate ordered 'all chaplains and vicars belonging to the right of Leominster church' to see that all parishioners paid their entire tithe, of whatever kind, in full to the church of Leominster.[40] Moreover, a series of tithe disputes with other religious houses and ecclesiastics in the early 13th century shows Reading Abbey acting on the assumption that the mother church should receive tithes in full. In every case the monks' claim was vindicated, even though with two exceptions the parties which had been taking the tithes at issue retained them after recognising Leominster's right and agreeing to lease them for annual payments.[41]

(ii) Scrifcorn

One of the oldest and most enduring rights of ancient minster churches was their entitlement to church-scot. It was legally reserved to them in late Anglo-Saxon times and in many places survived the potentially disruptive effects both of changes in land-tenure following the Norman Conquest and of the erection of manorial chapels or churches within an old *parochia*.[42] It is at first sight surprising, therefore, that there is no evidence for church-scot at Leominster, but its absence is probably accounted for by the existence of another customary payment in kind called scrifcorn, which appears in many ways analogous to church-scot and which may have taken its place in the Leominster *parochia*. The name 'scrifcorn' almost certainly indicates an Anglo-Saxon origin and implies that the payment was originally made in recognition of Leominster's pastoral services to its parishioners, especially perhaps in penitential matters.[43] Be that as it may, by the 12th century it had become a standardised and obligatory annual render in corn from cultivated land in the *parochia*. Like church-scot, it has all the appearances of high antiquity, but it is not to my knowledge recorded elsewhere and seems to have been unique to the Leominster *parochia*. It was certainly unfamiliar to William de Vere, bishop of Hereford 1186–98, who described it as 'unknown to the general custom of the Church'.[44]

Scrifcorn is mentioned in Leominster's charters much less frequently than tithes, and how much of the *parochia* was still paying it in the early 12th century is unknown. It is not recorded, for example, in such places as Hatfield and Monkland, where chapel/churches were held by external religious houses. On the other hand, all surviving references to it occur in the context of stating or confirming the mother church's rights, directly or indirectly.

Scrifcorn is first mentioned in 1131 × 37, when, as part of the settlement over the 'parish' of the men of Broadfield discussed above, it was agreed that the monks of Leominster would continue to receive scrifcorn there as previously.[45] The earliest detailed description of the render occurs in an act by Bishop William de Vere in 1186 × 93, settling a dispute between the monks of Leominster and the 'vicar' who served in the central church.[46] According to this, previous vicars had been accustomed to receive from each virgate of land cultivated by the parishioners 12 sheaves of corn, commonly called scrifcorn, for which they had paid [the monks] an annual pension of half a mark. As a result, however, the tithes appropriated to the monks had been threatened with grave loss, because those collecting scrifcorn had maliciously seized the opportunity of diverting tithes as well. To solve the problem the bishop allowed the monks to appropriate the scrifcorn in return for an equivalent compensation to the vicar. This settlement makes quite clear the distinction between scrifcorn and corn tithes, but it may well be that previous vicars had acted as much from confusion as from malice in not always being able to distinguish between the two. The Leominster scrifcorn was again reserved to the monks in 1200 × 15 on the occasion of the presentation of a new vicar, who, unlike his predecessor, was to receive the bread of the principal feasts in place of scrifcorn.[47]

The only other references to scrifcorn occur in the 13th-century descriptions of various chapelries which were either certainly or probably dependent on the church of Eye, whose parish had been formed out of the *parochia* by the later 12th century and which remained in the monks' possession.[48] Most of the chaplains concerned made annual payments, presumably to Leominster, for their scrifcorn. Thus the chaplain of Eyton and Lucton received the entire scrifcorn of these places 'like the other chaplains of chapels' for 1 mark annually, the chaplain of Yarpole the entire scrifcorn 'as elsewhere' for 5s. 4d., the chaplain of Middleton (-on-the-Hill) similarly for 8s., the chaplain of Kimbolton had scrifcorn from both the free and the unfree for 12s. and the chaplain of Brimfield had scrifcorn from three men at Drayton (listed in 1123) apparently without making an annual payment. The chaplain of Mileshope (Hope *Milion*') received 5s. worth of maslin each year from the lord of the vill and his men, which may be scrifcorn in a different guise.[49] Finally, following these chapelry descriptions in the Leominster cartulary is a memorandum that each person rendering scrifcorn gave, for one virgate of land, 6 sheaves of wheat and 6 of oats and, for half a virgate, 3 sheaves of wheat and 3 of oats.[50] These figures tally exactly with the description of scrifcorn given by the bishop of Hereford in 1186 × 93. The receipts of scrifcorn which these chaplains were allowed no doubt represent assignments made out of the total scrifcorn from the *parochia*, which anciently belonged to the mother church.

(iii) Burial rights

In common with, every ancient *parochia*, the right of sepulture at Leominster belonged primarily to the mother church.[51] The right embraced the two basic aspects of burial of the dead in the central cemetery and the entitlement of the mother church to receive the burial offerings, or soul-scot. Mother churches endeavoured to preserve their hold on both aspects, but, where they were unable to prevent the consecration of local cemeteries, they were obliged to concede local burial and sought to retain their right to the offerings. There is some evidence to suggest that those old minsters which passed into monastic control were generally more successful than others in holding on to burial profits in these circumstances, and the Leominster evidence certainly supports this.

Discounting those parts of the *parochia* which had been detached by 1123, including probably Kinnersley and Titley, Leominster's sepulture rights in the remainder were virtually undisturbed when Reading Abbey acquired the church. The only possible exception known to us was at Broadfield, where, as was stated earlier, the monks of Leominster in 1131 × 37 agreed that the dead should be taken for burial to the church of Bodenham (outside the *parochia*), which would presumably receive the soul-scot as well.[52] Since the tenor of this agreement implies recognition of the *status quo* rather than a new departure, it seems likely that Leominster had already lost sepulture rights in Broadfield by this time and, given the monks' insistence on the mother church's rights elsewhere, possibly before 1123.

Otherwise Leominster's burial rights within the *parochia* appear to have held good and were to be strenuously defended by the monks, even where, as at Monkland and Hatfield, local chapels existed in the possession of other religious houses. As was noted above, the abbey of Castellion had a chapel at Monkland from well before 1123, but, in the absence of a cemetery, the parochial dead had to be taken for burial to Leominster. This is indicated by a rather ambiguous sub-clause in the 1137 tithe agreement discussed earlier,[53] the meaning of which is made clear by the terms of a settlement of the early 13th century. At that time Leominster's burial rights were tested when Hugh, incumbent of the neighbouring church of Stretford (outside the *parochia*), buried in his cemetery a parishioner of Monkland, who had died there. The prior of Leominster complained to the archbishop of Canterbury that this was to the prejudice of the church of Leominster. The archbishop appointed delegates to try the case, before whom the incumbent eventually confessed his fault and surrendered to the prior the dead body and the oblation of 11½d. which he had received at the funeral. At the instance of the archdeacon of Hereford, the delegates requested the prior to allow the corpse to remain buried at Stretford, since it had already been there for more than three months and 'would by now be stinking and horrible to look at' (*quia iam fetidum esset et horrendum aspectu*). To this the prior agreed, but he could legitimately have demanded the corpse's exhumation and reburial in the cemetery at Leominster in order fully to assert the mother church's right and to avoid the risk of a contrary precedent being established.[54] Just such a procedure was followed in an analogous case in Berkshire a century earlier, when Abingdon Abbey secured the reburial at its church of Longworth of a parishioner unlawfully buried at Pusey.[55]

The parishioners of Great Malvern's chapel at Hatfield had also to be taken to Leominster for burial until a cemetery was consecrated there in 1131 × 48 by Robert de Bethune, bishop of Hereford. However, although this altered the situation compared with that at Monkland, the terms of the bishop's *actum* were highly significant, for the cemetery was to be 'as an augmentation of the cemetery of Leominster' and all burial offerings, along with all dying bequests to the mother church of Leominster, were to go to the Leominster monks 'as though the dead were buried in the principal cemetery of Leominster'. Moreover, the chapel was to be regarded for diocesan purposes not as a parish church (*mater ecclesia*), but as a chapel.[56] In other words, although Hatfield's dead would henceforth be buried locally, the dependence of the chapel on the mother church was affirmed and the monks were to suffer no financial loss from the consecration of the cemetery.

Throughout the 12th century the monks asserted Leominster's sepulture rights with equal tenacity in the rest of the *parochia*, and their claims were generally upheld by the diocesan. A distinction needs to be drawn, however, between those areas where the monks also had manorial lordship and those which were held by lay lords. Where the monks were the manorial lords they had nothing to fear from the devolution of the mother church's burial rights to a local chapel/church which remained under their control. For example, by 1174 × 86 a cemetery with right of burial existed at the church of Eye, whose parish had been formed within the old *parochia* and where the monks had temporal lordship,[57] but how many others of this kind there may have been by the end of the 12th century is uncertain. The main threat to the mother church's rights came from the desire of other lords to have local cemeteries on their lands, but even here, although the monks agreed to some such requests, the effect on Leominster's position was minimal. Occasionally, as at Hatfield, local burial was conceded, but in each case the profits were reserved directly or indirectly to Leominster. Elsewhere two cemeteries *ad refugium* were allowed, but these by their nature entailed no diminution of the mother church's right either to bury the dead of the places concerned or to receive the offerings.

Apart from Hatfield, definite evidence exists for the consecration of a cemetery at Hampton Mappenore, apparently with right of burial, and of another at Humber with exceedingly limited burial right, and indirect evidence for the consecration of a third with burial right at Brimfield. In 1148 × 63 Gilbert Foliot consecrated a cemetery at Hampton Mappenore *ex mandato et voluntate domini abbatis Rading[ensis]*, but it was clearly for the convenience of the local inhabitants, and in return the lord of the manor, Peter de Mappenore, conceded to the mother church of Leominster the chapel situated within the cemetery, 40 acres of land and the whole tithe of his demesne and of his men 'with all parochial right'.[58] This cemetery probably had the right of local burial, since it was not described as merely *ad refugium*, but in any case all profits were retained by the monks through the cession of the chapel and the entire parochial right of the place to the mother church. The monks were here exploiting the request for a local cemetery to make good their title to the chapel and, as was noted above, the entire tithe of the place. The same bishop consecrated a cemetery at the chapel of Humber in 1148 × 54. He did so at the request of the Leominster monks and with the consent of the abbot of Reading, but again the initiative had come from the local lord Walter del Mans and his wife, who made over to the monks certain lands and rent, probably in place of the local tithes. An extraordinary condition was attached to this cemetery, however, since only one corpse was to be buried there, after which all others *cum divisionibus defunctorum* were to be taken as before to Leominster.[59] The reason for this strange stipulation is obscure, but it may have been somehow connected with Walter's intention to convey the 'church' of Humber to Brecon Priory, which had been carried out by the autumn of 1155.[60] Nevertheless, Leominster retained its right to bury the dead of Humber with one exception and, if one may read *divisiones defunctorum* in a broad sense, its right to the burial offerings as well. No notice survives for the consecration of a cemetery at Brimfield, but one was certainly in existence in 1174 × 86, when the abbot of Reading, at the request of the vicar of Eye, allowed that the poor parishioners of Brimfield chapel were to be buried there and not in the cemetery of Eye church, on which the chapelry was dependent, while the rest were to be buried at Eye at the discretion of the vicar.[61] Entitlement to the burial offerings was not specified, but, since the agreement was made *servata in omnibus indempnitate ecclesie de Leom[inistria] et de Eya*, they doubtless remained under the ultimate supervision of the monks.

The two cemeteries *ad refugium* were at Hampton Wafer and Risbury. They were consecrated by Gilbert Foliot, probably in 1148 × 54, with the consent of the Leominster monks, who, as we have seen, secured from the local lords, Robert of Hampton and Nicholas of Maund respectively, grants of the entire demesne tithe and tenants' tithe.[62] No chapel was mentioned at either place and the cemeteries were simply to provide a consecrated refuge, or sanctuary, for the inhabitants in time of trouble or disturbance. A cemetery *ad refugium* entailed no right of burial, as is made clear by a document of 1179 × 89 in the Brecon cartulary referring to a *cimiterium ... sine omni sepultura ad refugium pauperum tempore hostilitatis si ita contigerit*.[63] Leominster's burial rights were therefore not affected by the consecration of these cemeteries, as later evidence confirms. In 1186 × 98, when a settlement was reached over the advowson of Hampton Wafer chapel (first recorded on this occasion), 'the whole right of sepulture with the corpses of the dead' was reserved to the church of Leominster in perpetuity;[64] and in 1217 × 18 the abbot and convent of Reading, in agreeing that the men of Risbury were to attend divine service at Humber with their offerings, retained their right to the bequests of these men and their successors, 'which first and principally ought to be made to the church of Leominster', and to their corpses, 'which ought to be taken to the mother church of Leominster.'[65]

The Internal Development of the Parochia

Taken together the evidence on tithes, scrifcorn and sepulture reveals a remarkable degree of success for the monks in maintaining the ecclesiastical rights of the church of Leominster in the 12th century. It is true that some loss of tithes had occurred and that the records for scrifcorn are mainly limited to parts of the *parochia* which remained wholly under the monks' control, but, on the other hand, the preservation of Leominster's burial rights in a variety of potentially difficult situations is most impressive. There remains, however, the question of what all this amounted to in terms of parochial development in this period. By the 13th century the *parochia* (leaving aside those parts already detached by 1123) was largely divided up into parishes or chapelries, some of which remained directly or indirectly dependent on the mother church and others were largely in the control of other ecclesiastical or monastic authorities. The situation in the early 12th century is by contrast very uncertain. The Domesday account of Leominster mentions no churches or chapels, not even the central church itself,[66] and merely refers to a number of priests in the lordship, while the bishop of Hereford's charter of 1123 names only the church of Leominster and gives no clue as to how its appurtenant *parochia* was organised. Information on parochial developments in the 12th century comes mainly from subsequent charters and episcopal acts or, where such are lacking, from architectural evidence preserved in existing church buildings within the bounds of the old *parochia*.

According to Domesday, there were six priests in the composite lordship of Leominster in 1086 and two more in those parts of the lordship which had been alienated from the *caput* since the time of Edward the Confessor.[67] Although, as Mr. Lennard suggests,[68] the six priests in the demesne probably do not represent the survival of a collegiate establishment, even in the late 12th century a small group of assistant clergy appears to have been maintained at the centre, operating in that part of the *parochia* which was then served directly from Leominster. In 1186 × 93 the 'vicar' in the mother church had three chaplains to assist him 'on account of the scattered nature of the parishes' (*propter parrochiarum dispersionem*)[69] and when, a few years later, the living was appropriated to Leominster Priory, the bishop of Hereford enacted that the chaplains who were to celebrate for the people should be supported in the monks' *mensa*.[70] One chaplain seems to have served the chapel of Hope-under-Dinmore, which the vicar held with his living in the mother church,[71] but where the others operated is unclear, although their successors in the late 13th century served the chapelries of Docklow and Stoke (Prior), which were recorded with Hope-under-Dinmore as appurtenant to the church of Leominster in 1291.[72] The interesting point is, however, that the last remnants of a central clerical establishment would appear to have survived at Leominster until late in the 12th century.[73] On the other hand, most of the successors of the Domesday total of eight priests in the Leominster lands (to whom should perhaps be added an unknown number in those estates held under the manor T.R.E. which still lay within the *parochia*) probably did not reside in Leominster, but in the chapelries which they served.

The history of these chapelries and other parochial developments in the 12th century can most easily be understood by dividing the subject into two parts. The first concerns those areas where the monks retained full rights in the name of the mother church, comprising in fact the bulk of the *parochia* as it stood in 1123; the second those areas where the monks' rights were more or less limited by the interests of others.

Of the chapelries which remained dependent on Leominster the earliest for which documentary evidence survives were at Ford and Hampton Mappenore to the south of Leominster. They were certainly in existence by the late 1120s and were probably in origin in the same close relationship with the mother church as the later chapelries of Hope-under-Dinmore, etc., but shortly before 1130, that is only a few years after Reading had acquired Leominster, the link was threatened when the archdeacon of Hereford appointed clerks to the two chapels, 'which pertained to the church of Leominster', without the knowledge or consent of the abbot of Reading. The abbot appealed to the archbishop of Canterbury, who ordered the archdeacon to remove the clerks forthwith.[74] The outcome of this mandate is unknown, but it was apparently effective, since in 1148 × 63 Hampton Mappenore chapel was formally ceded to the monks by the lord of the manor in circumstances which suggest existing dependence on the mother church,[75] and in the early 13th century the bishop of Hereford confirmed to Leominster Priory half a mark annually from the chapel of Ford.[76] A few years later, in 1216 × 19, the monks obtained the appropriation of Ford chapel to the almonry of Leominster,[77] possibly in part to fend off a claim to it from the incumbent of the neighbouring church of Humber,[78] who, as we have seen, secured in 1217 × 18 the parochial suit of the men of Risbury, another part of the old *parochia*.

References to other chapels to the north of Leominster begin to occur in the later 12th century. None is mentioned before 1173 at the earliest and in only two cases is the architectural evidence sufficient to prove early foundation. Nevertheless, it appears that the whole area extending from the north-west round to the north-east of Leominster, which was by far the largest part of the *parochia* to remain dependent on the mother church, was organised into chapelries at an early date — or at least that the process began at an early date. Moreover, to judge from later evidence, the organisation of chapelries was centred on the chapel of

Eye, which was soon to become a parish church and was probably already long established by the last quarter of the 12th century.

Eye was undoubtedly the most important chapel in the area. The place was listed in the bishop of Hereford's charter of 1123, but the first mention of a chapel occurs in 1173 × 86, when Abbot Joseph of Reading granted it to Osbert son of Osbert to hold as his father had held it for an annual payment of 3 marks.[79] The formation of the parish of Eye within the *parochia* was clearly well under way by this time, since in two near-contemporary charters, dating from 1174 × 86, Eye is already described as a 'church'.[80] In 1216 × 18 the bishop of Hereford granted to Reading Abbey the appropriation of the church with all its chapels, although this was not carried fully into effect until 1254.[81] According to the 13th-century description of the vicarage of Eye in the Leominster cartulary,[82] the parish included Ashton and Luston, both of which had been listed in the 1123 charter. The chapelries dependent on the church at its appropriation were not named, and the *Taxatio* of 1291 refers simply to 'the church of Eye with its chapels'.[83] The earliest specific list of Eye's chapels known to me occurs in a Hereford diocesan survey of 1536, which names those of Eyton and Lucton, Orleton, Yarpole, Brimfield, Middleton (-on-the-Hill) and Kimbolton,[84] but the dependence of these chapels on Eye in the 13th century can probably be inferred from the particular selection of chapelry assessments entered in the Leominster cartulary.[85] In a single continuous sequence these comprise the vicarage of Eye followed by the chapelries of Eyton and Lucton, Yarpole, Orleton, Brimfield, Middleton, Kimbolton and Hope *Mililon'* (i.e., Mileshope, in Middleton).[86] These chapelries are not stated as being dependent on Eye, and one can only be certain of this for Orleton, Brimfield, Middleton and Mileshope, but, since no entries were made for the other chapelries in the monks' control, especially those of Hope-under-Dinmore etc. which were directly dependent on Leominster church in the 13th century, the entries appear to have covered only Eye and its chapels.[87] Of all the places concerned only Brimfield and Middleton were listed as parts of the Leominster *parochia* in 1123, but all clearly lay within it and most may have been considered at that date as parts of Eye. Moreover, four of the chapelries — Brimfield, Orleton, Kimbolton and Middleton — had certainly been founded by the end of the 12th century at the latest and were therefore among Eye's chapels at its appropriation. Brimfield chapel appears as appurtenant to Eye church in 1174 × 86, when, as noted above, the abbot of Reading allowed that the poor of Brimfield might be buried there and not at Eye;[88] and in 1239 the abbot made good a claim against the bishop of Hereford that the chapel was dependent on Eye church.[89] The present church of Orleton has a 12th-century nave,[90] and in the 13th century the chaplain of Orleton received the first offering from the dead there and the vicar of Eye the second, some at least of the corpses being buried at Eye.[91] The present church at Kimbolton contains work of the first half of the 12th century, and that at Middleton dates largely from the mid 12th century.[92] The antiquity of the other chapelries is uncertain, but the general pattern of development suggests strongly that, with the possible exception of Mileshope, they also originated in the 12th century; Yarpole was certainly in existence in the first half of the 13th century, when one of its chaplains was a son of the incumbent of Eye.[93] Finally, there is the possibility that Croft was originally dependent on Eye, for, although in 1291 it occurs as a separate chapelry, the 'rector' of Eye had a portion of 2s. there at that date.[94]

This network of chapelries no doubt evolved with the monks' blessing, and possibly encouragement, since they retained ultimate control, but elsewhere in the *parochia* developments took place which weakened links with Leominster. Although the mother church's rights were nowhere extinguished entirely, some places ceased to be fully dependent and in a few cases the monks failed to recover or retain the advowson of local chapels. Nonetheless, ignoring those parts of the *parochia* effectively detached by 1123, the losses in the 12th century, though significant, were not great and in no sense amounted to the fragmentation of the *parochia*.[95] They involved to a greater or lesser extent the chapelries of Monkland, Hatfield Magna, Humber and Hampton Wafer and the parochial suit of the hamlets of Broadfield and (in the early 13th century) Risbury. Most of these have already been mentioned, and it is largely a matter here of drawing the references together.

By late 1155 a total of three chapelries were in the hands of other religious houses. Castellion Abbey had held Monkland since the later 11th century and Great Malvern Priory had acquired Hatfield Magna before 1127. Both chapelries were well-established by the time Reading Abbey acquired Leominster and, although important tithe and burial rights were reserved to the mother church, their partial independence could not be reversed.[96] Monkland was still described as a chapel in the *Taxatio* of 1291,[97] but in an episcopal confirmation to Castellion in 1174 × 86 it was significantly already being called a church.[98] An episcopal act of 1131 × 48 insisted upon Hatfield Magna's status as a chapel,[99] but by the early 13th century it had become a church and, certainly by 1291, had its own chapelry at Hatfield Parva.[100] No chapel at Humber is recorded before 1148 × 54, when a cemetery was consecrated there, but by the latter part of 1155 the lord of the manor had given the 'church' of Humber to Brecon Priory, Leominster retaining only burial rights and compensation for the loss of other rights.[101] In this case, since Brecon was a dependency of Battle Abbey and the gift was confirmed by the earl of Hereford and sanctioned by Gilbert Foliot, it may be that powerful interests were at work which the Leominster monks were disinclined to oppose.

A different situation developed at Hampton Wafer in that the local lord rather than a religious house was involved. With the consent of the Leominster monks, Gilbert Foliot consecrated a cemetery *ad refugium* there probably in 1148 × 54.[102] No chapel was mentioned on this occasion, but one had certainly been founded by 1186 × 98, when the prior of Leominster was 'parson' and the advowson of the 'vicarage' was in dispute between him and the lord of the manor, Simon le Wafre. In settlement it was agreed that henceforth the perpetual vicar to be instituted in the chapel should be presented to the bishop jointly by the prior as parson and by the lord of the manor as patron (*advocatus*). The vicar was to pay the prior an annual pension of 2s. and swear faith to the church of Leominster, from which he was to receive chrism and to which full burial rights were reserved. These arrangements were confirmed by Bishop William de Vere.[103] Although the settlement represented a very modest adjustment of Leominster's position, it was in fact a stage in the parochial emancipation of Hampton Wafer, for by 1291 the chapel could be described as a church and, though still called a chapel in episcopal registers of the first half of the 14th century, its advowson was by then held solely by the lord of the manor.[104]

The other two losses concerned Broadfield and Risbury, which were never formed into chapelries. In the course of the 12th and early 13th centuries both places were for ordinary parochial purposes incorporated into the parishes of neighbouring churches. Broadfield was annexed to Bodenham in 1131 × 37, Risbury to Humber in 1217 × 18.[105] Bodenham had never been in the *parochia* of Leominster, and by 1217 Humber was in most respects outside it. Moreover, both churches were in the possession of Brecon Priory by the time of the respective annexations. Leominster retained very limited rights at Broadfield after 1131 × 37, and a decade or so later Gilbert Foliot, at the request of the local lord and the prior of Brecon, consecrated a cemetery *propter refugium* at Broadfield 'in the parish of the church of St. Mary of Bodenham' without reference to the ancient mother church.[106] A good deal more was salvaged at Risbury in 1217 × 18. Here a dispute had arisen between Reading Abbey (in the name of Leominster) and Adam, vicar of Humber, over the parochial suit (*sequela*) of the men of Risbury. On an appeal to the pope the case was committed to judges-delegate, before whom agreement was reached with the consent of the prior of Brecon. The men were to resort to the 'chapel' (*sic*) of Humber with all their due oblations *ad divinum officium ibi celebrandum et audiendum et ad spiritualia ibidem percipienda*, saving to Reading all tithes and burial rights. In return the vicar and his successors were to pay the monks 3s. annually on the feast of St. Peter and St. Paul (the dedicatees of Leominster Priory), on which day each year the vicar and all the men of Risbury were to come to the church of Leominster with their due oblations *ut eiusdem ecclesie parochiani*.[107] How long these arrangements endured in full is uncertain, but Risbury appears soon to have become absorbed into Humber parish, where in 1291 the prior of Leominster had a portion of 3s.,[108] presumably the annual payment made under the terms of the earlier settlement.

It is clear that developments were continuing to occur in the old *parochia* in the 13th century, but equally that these were of a comparatively minor nature. The later medieval pattern of parishes and chapelries, with their various relationships to the mother church, was largely complete by the end of the 12th century. But the most striking feature of the whole story is that, despite the losses and adjustments that had taken place by 1200, the *parochia* remained to a considerable extent intact and was still recognisably that of the bishop of Hereford's charter of 1123. The credit, if such it is, belongs chiefly to the monks of Reading and Leominster. It must be doubtful whether the mother church's rights would have been so effectively and consistently maintained, had the ancient church not come into the possession of so powerful a royal abbey as Reading.

Notes

1. See p. 90.
2. For Leominster in the Anglo-Saxon period, the gift to Reading and the establishment of the dependent priory, see B.R. Kemp, 'The Monastic Dean of Leominster', *Eng. Hist. Rev.* lxxxiii (1968), 505–6, 512–3.
3. *Reading Cartularies*, i, 287; *Mon. Ang.* iv, 56 (No. ii). However, the latter has, in place of *cum omni ad ipsam pertinente parrochia* as in the cartularies, the incorrect reading *cum omnibus ad ipsam pertinentibus parrochiis*. This has misled some scholars into thinking that the bishop was confirming a large number of dependent parishes (Lennard, *Rural England*, 400–1) or chapels (Brett, *English Church*, 154). It is clear, however, that the charter contains a list of places or estates belonging to the *parochia*, a number of which were not, and never became, chapelries or parishes. In 1158 × 61 the charter was confirmed by Gilbert Foliot in the same terms (*Gilbert Foliot*, 392–3) and by Archbishop Theobald with the slight variation: ...*ecclesiam de Leom[inistria] ... cum omnibus ad eam pertinentibus; parrochiam quoque de Bradeforda de Ach ... [etc.]* (A. Saltman, *Theobald, Archbishop of Canterbury* (London, 1956), 439–40).
4. The places listed are: Broadward, *Ach*, (Monk)land, Dilwyn first and second, Luntley, Kinnersley, Woonton, both Sarnesfields, Titley, Hope (-under-Dinmore), Wharton, New-

ton, Gattertop, Stoke (Prior), both Hatfields (i.e., Magna and Parva), Risbury, Humber, Edvin (Ralph), Butterley, Broadfield, both Hamptons (i.e. Mappenore and Ricardi), Ford, Hennor, Eaton (probably), Hampton (Wafer), Stockton, Ashton (probably), Brimfield, Upton, Middleton (-on-the-Hill), Drayton, Hamnish (Clifford), Whyle, Pudleston, Brockmanton, Ford (probably in Pudleston), Luston, Eye and Croft. In four cases (Dilwyn, Sarnesfield, Hatfield and the first Hampton) two places are specified, probably indicating separate hamlets or estates.

5. In 1066 Queen Edith held Leominster as 80 hides, made up of the *caput* and sixteen 'members', but in addition a number of tenants held dependent estates, from which they paid annual renders to Leominster. By 1086 the Crown's demesne was reduced to 60 hides, since some 'members' were wholly or partially in the hands of various important Herefordshire tenants, and most of the formerly dependent estates had been effectively detached from Leominster, although Domesday Book continued to treat them under that head (DB I 180a–b). Of the places listed in the bishop of Hereford's charter, Hennor, Drayton, Whyle, Ford and Eye are not mentioned in Domesday, but all the others, except Monkland, Kinnersley, Titley, Hope-under-Dinmore, Pudleston and Croft, either formed part of the manor and members of Leominster or had been held under Leominster T.R.E. The only places mentioned in 1086 as parts of the Leominster manorial complex which were not listed as parts of the *parochia* in 1123 or cannot be shown to have been parts of it are Aymestrey, Leinthall, Lye, *Wapletone*, Fencott, Wigmore and Farlow (the last being in Shropshire).

6. In 1291 the prior of Leominster had a portion of 6s. 8d. in Kinnersley church, which in 1317 was called *pensionaria ecclesie Leoministrie* (*Taxatio*, 160; *Registrum Ricardi de Swinfield, Episcopi Herefordensis*, ed. W.W. Capes (Canterbury & York Soc. vi, 1909), 522). The benefice was a rectory in the patronage of the lord of the manor (ibid., 522, 535, 543). In the absence of other evidence of Leominster's rights, it seems likely that the portion (or pension) was payable in respect of another part of the *parochia* not listed in 1123. In 1148 × 63 a dispute was settled before Gilbert Foliot between Leominster Priory and Serlo, priest of Kinnersley church, over the chapel and tithes of *Ewda* or *Eiwda* (now lost); Serlo renounced his claim to the chapel, conceding it 'to the church of whose territory it is known to be', and received it back for life for an annual payment to Leominster of 5s.; after his death the chapel and tithes were to return to the monks, to give to whom they wished or to retain in their hands at their discretion (*Gilbert Foliot*, 391). It may be, however, that the chapel's annexation to Kinnersley became permanent and that over the years the annual payment was raised to the 6s. 8d. recorded in 1291.

Reading Abbey claimed an annual payment in Titley 'chapel' in the later 13th century (*Reading Cartularies*, i, 141), but no portion or pension is recorded for the prior of Leominster in Titley 'church' in 1291 (*Taxatio*, 159) and no other evidence of Leominster's rights has come to light. The church was in existence by 1147 at the latest, when it was confirmed to Tiron Abbey (*Cartulaire de l'abbaye de Tiron*, ed. M.L. Merlet (Société Archeologique d'Eure-et-Loir, 1882–3), ii, 60) and was held by Titley Priory, a cell of Tiron founded 1120 × 1 (Knowles & Hadcock, 106–7).

7. See above, p. 91 and note 86.

8. In 1291 Docklow was a chapelry dependent on Leominster church (*Taxatio*, 159). Eyton and Lucton, Kimbolton, Mileshope, Orleton and Yarpole were chapelries certainly or probably dependent on Eye church in the 13th century (see above, p. 91). That Hurstley (in Letton) was in the *parochia* in the late 12th century is established by the fact that in 1173 × 86 the abbot of Reading allowed Roger of Letton to have a chapel there and to pay Leominster 2s. annually for the tithes of the vill (Brit. Lib., Cotton MS Domitian A iii (Leominster cartulary) [hereafter Cott. Domit. A iii], f. 120v).

9. In 1186 × 98 it was established that the vicar of Hampton Wafer chapel should receive chrism at Leominster (above, p. 92). In 1131 × 37 it was agreed that the monks of Leominster would continue to receive Peter's Pence (*Romescot*) from Broadfield, as previously (above, p. 86). In 1217 × 18, when the parochial suit of the men of Risbury was transferred to Humber church, they were required to come to Leominster church with their oblations annually on the feast of St. Peter and St. Paul (above, p. 92).

10. *C&S*, i, 97–9.

11. Brett, *English Church*, 225–6. For examples, see B.R. Kemp, 'Monastic Possession of Parish Churches in England in the Twelfth Century', *Journal of Ecclesiastical History*, xxxi (1980), 10–11.

12. The point is well made by Blair, 'Secular Minsters', 125.

13. *Reading Cartularies*, i, 288. The identification of Hampton as Hampton Mappenore rests on the fact that a chapel existed there by 1148 × 63 (above, p. 89), while one of the other Hamptons in the *parochia*, Hampton Ricardi, never had a parochial chapel and that at Hampton Wafer is not recorded before 1186 × 98 (above, p. 89).

14. *Concilia Magnae Brittaniae et Hiberniae*, ed. D. Wilkins (London, 1737), i, 413. The payment was still being made in 1419, although the chapel/church was then in royal hands (*Registrum Edmundi Lacy, Episcopi Herefordensis*, ed. J.H. Parry and A.T. Bannister (Canterbury & York Soc. xxii, 1918), 71, 72).

15. DB I 183; *Calendar of Documents preserved in France illustrating the History of Great Britain and Ireland, I, AD 918–1206*, ed. J.H. Round (London, 1899) [hereafter Round], 138–9.

16. No chapel/church is mentioned in Domesday and one cannot be sure from the bishop of Hereford's charter of 1174 × 86 (Round, *loc. cit.*) whether one existed at the time of Ralph de Tosny's gift to Castellion, but parts of the present church of Monkland probably date from the late 11th century (*Royal Commission on Historical Monuments, England: An Inventory of the Historical Monuments in Herefordshire*, iii (London, 1934) [hereafter *RCHM Herefordshire*, iii], 150). For the cell of Monkland, see Knowles & Hadcock, 84, 90.

17. *Mon. Ang.*, iii, 448 (No. iii).

18. Part of the nave of the present church dates from the late 11th century (*RCHM Herefordshire*, iii, 64).

19. *Taxatio*, 159.

20. Cott. Domit. A iii, ff. 110v–111r.

21. *Taxatio*, 159.

22. *Cartulary of Oseney Abbey*, ed. H.E. Salter (Oxford Historical Society, 1929–36), v, 111.

23. Ibid. 110

24. *Taxatio*, 159. This was the sum at which the tithes could be leased, for in 1246 Oseney leased their tithes in Wharton to Richard of Croft, rector of Letton (Herefordshire), for life for 1 mark annually, and in 1438 to Reading Abbey in perpetuity for the same amount (*Cartulary of Oseney*, v, 116, 118).

25. *Reading Cartularies*, i, 262–3.

26. There are, however, two notices which appear to contradict this. One of the surviving fragments of the Norwich Taxation (1254) records that the prior of Leominster had tithes of corn (*garbarum*) worth 20s. annually in the parish of Bodenham (*The Valuation of Norwich*, ed. W.E. Lunt (Oxford, 1926), 476–7), and in 1291 the prior had a portion of 3s. 4d. in Bodenham church (*Taxatio*, 158). It is likely, however, that the priory's receipts in corn represent the scrifcorn (on which see below) and the crop of 2 acres in August from Broadfield to which it was entitled in the agreement with Miles and which by the 13th century may have become confused with tithes.

27. *Mon. Ang.* iii, 264 (No. ii).

28. *Gilbert Foliot*, 386–7. By 1139 Miles of Gloucester held the 3½ hides in Humber which Roger de Lacy had held of the manor of Leominster in 1086 (*Herefordshire Domesday*, ed. V.H. Galbraith and J. Tait, Pipe Roll Society, new series, xxv (1950)

[hereafter *Herefs. Domesday*], 79). Walter del Mans was clearly the tenant of the manor, which became annexed to the honour of Brecon, since in 1242 × 3 a Matthew del Mauns held half a knight's fee in Humber of that honour (*The Book of Fees* (London, 1920–31), ii, 800, 813), which Miles had acquired by marriage in *c*. 1121 (*The Complete Peerage* (new edn., London, 1910–59), vi, 452).

29. For the gift to Brecon Priory of the church of Humber *cum omnibus pertinentiis suis, in decimis, in terris, in oblationibus et ceteris omnibus obventionibus*, see 'Cartularium Prioratus S. Johannis Evang. de Brecon', ed. R.W. Banks, *Archaeologia Cambrensis*, 4th ser. xiv (1883) [hereafter 'Cart. Brecon'], 33. The gift, made in the presence of Gilbert Foliot, was confirmed by him and by Roger earl of Hereford, who became a monk at Gloucester in the autumn of 1155 and died before the end of the year (*Gilbert Foliot*, 355; 'Cart. Brecon', 149; 'Charters of the Earldom of Hereford, 1095–1201', ed. D. Walker, *Camden Miscellany XXII* (Camden 4th ser. i, 1964), 9, 23).
30. *Book of Fees*, ii, 798.
31. *Herefs. Domesday*, 12, 85.
32. *Gilbert Foliot*, 391–2.
33. *Herefs. Domesday*, 42.
34. *Reading Cartularies*, i, 279–81, Nos. 344–5. In No. 345 the place is called Hampton *Gileberti* in allusion to the earlier tenure by Gilbert of Hampton.
35. Cott. Domit. A iii, f. 65r–v.
36. Cf. the deal struck by the monks of Winchcombe with William de Solers in Stephen's reign for a chapel at Postlip (Glos.) in return for a grant of the demesne tithes (*Landboc sive Registrum Monasterii ... de Winchelcumba*, ed. D. Royce (Exeter, 1892–1903), i, 81–3).
37. *Gilbert Foliot*, 387–9. See above, p. 89.
38. Cott. Domit. A iii, f. 77r–v. The monks' chaplain was to celebrate in the chapel, but when Walter was absent the villeins (*rustici*) were to come to 'their mother church of Leominster'.
39. Ibid., f. 80r. The deed is similar to the preceding, but here Robert's chaplain was to celebrate and there is no mention of the villeins attending the mother church at other times. For Robert Malherbe's succession to Nicholas of Maund in the 2 hides at Risbury held under Leominster T.R.E., see *Herefs. Domesday*, 13, 78 and cf. 105.
40. Cott. Domit. A iii, f. 64r–v.
41. The disputes concerned various greater tithes in Orleton, Lea (in Kimbolton), Bircher (probably near Winsley in Hope-under-Dinmore), Gattertop (in Hope-under-Dinmore), Broadward (near Leominster), Humber and *Akes*. In Orleton, Lea, Broadward and Humber the abbey claimed two thirds of of the greater tithes (since Leominster was already receiving the third part), and in Bircher, Gattertop and *Akes* all the greater tithes. Each case was taken on appeal to Rome and referred to judges-delegate in England, before whom the settlements were reached: Cott. Domit. A iii, f. 106r–v (Orleton), f. 108v (Gattertop, Broadward, Humber), f. 109r–v (Bircher), f. 110r–v (Lea), ff. 111v–112r (*Akes*). *Akes* has proved unidentifiable, but is clearly the same as *Ach* in the bishop's charter of 1123 (see note 4). In the settlement of this case in *c*. 1220 it became clear that the clerk who held the tithes owed his title ultimately to a gift from the lay lord of the demesne; after an acknowledgement that the tithes lay within the *parochia* of Leominster, they were resigned to the monks. This reveals a very significant change of attitude since the earlier post-Conquest period regarding a layman's freedom to dispose of his tithes.
42. F.M. Stenton, *Anglo-Saxon England* (3rd edn., Oxford, 1971), 153–4; Barlow, *Church 1000–66*, 195, 198.
43. The name ought probably to be rendered as 'shrift-corn', for it is clearly parallel to such words as 'shrift-silver' and 'shrift-shire' in which the element 'shrift' means either absolution or a payment or offering as a penance after confession (see *Oxford English Dictionary*, under 'shrift', section 10).
44. *Reading Cartularies*, i, 289–90.
45. Ibid., 262–3. See above, p. 86.
46. *Reading Cartularies*, i, 289–90.
47. Cott. Domit. A iii, f. 66r.
48. See below.
49. Cott. Domit. A iii, ff. 103v–104v.
50. Ibid., f. 104v.
51. This is clear from Edgar's legislation on minster tithes (see note 10). From that time onwards, and probably earlier, the presence or absence of a cemetery was a vital consideration in the 'grading' of a place of worship. Moreover, a mother church's possession of burial rights long remained an important test of a chapel's dependence, as is brought out very clearly in the record of a dispute over the chapel of Osmaston near Derby at the end of the 12th century; here the abbot of Darley was able to prove that the chapel pertained to the abbey's church of St. Peter, Derby, because 'the corpses of the dead of the said chapel are brought to the said mother church' (*The Cartulary of Darley Abbey*, ed. R.R. Darlington (Kendal, 1945), ii, 603). Cf. the reluctance of the Winchcombe monks in Stephen's reign to concede burial rights at the newly built church of Hailes (Gloucestershire), a manor which belonged to their *jus parochiale*; they were threatened by the local lord with starvation before they would agree (*Landboc ... Winchelcumba*, i, 65).
52. *Reading Cartularies*, i, 262–3.
53. See above, p. 84. The ambiguity arises in the following sentence, which contains the only reference to sepulture in the agreement: 'Sciatis quod abbas de Castaillons reddit singulis annis ad festum sancti Michaelis. xii. denarios ecclesie Leomen' pro tercia parte decime de Monekesleona, unde habent corpora.'
54. Cott. Domit. A iii, ff. 107v–108r.
55. *Chronicon Monasterii de Abingdon*, ed. J. Stevenson, ii (Rolls Ser., iib, 1858), 121–2.
56. Cott. Domit. A iii, f. 60r–v. The bishop's *actum* was confirmed by Gilbert Foliot (ibid., f. 61r; not in *Gilbert Foliot*) and by Archbishop Theobald (Saltman, *Theobald*, 440–1). See also Brett, *English Church*, 227 note 2.
57. For the church and cemetery of Eye, see above, p. 91. Eye was not mentioned in Domesday, but the later medieval manor of Eye, which first appears as such in the late 13th century, was made up of lands held of Reading Abbey in the 12th century (see B.R. Kemp, 'Hereditary Benefices in the Medieval English Church: a Herefordshire Example', *BIHR*, xliii (1970), esp. 3–9).
58. *Gilbert Foliot*, 388–9.
59. Ibid., 386–7.
60. See above, p. 86. It is possible that Walter wished to have a cemetery there, however limited the burial rights, before giving the church to Brecon. On the other hand, if the monks already knew of his intention, they may have thought it prudent to get the cemetery consecrated while the spirituality of Humber was still to some extent under their control and they could insist on Leominster's rights more easily than when the church had passed to Brecon.
61. The concession was confirmed by two acts of Bishop Robert Foliot, one of which quoted the abbot's charter (Kemp, 'Hereditary Benefices', 12; Brit. Lib. Add. Ch. 19585).
62. *Gilbert Foliot*, 387–8.
63. 'Cart. Brecon', 228.
64. Cott. Domit. A iii, f. 64r, f. 111r. See above, p. 92.
65. *Reading Cartularies*, i, 299–300. See above, p. 92.
66. Although the lack of reference to the mother church is perhaps puzzling, it does not appear to have had a large endowment separate from the lands of the former nunnery, which by 1086 were largely in the Crown's hands. Domesday's failure to mention any other churches that may have existed in the Leominster lands in 1086 is not surprising, given the low rate of recording or indicating churches in Herefordshire as a whole

67. DB I 180.
68. Lennard, *Rural England*, 401.
69. *Reading Cartularies*, i, 291.
70. Ibid., 292.
71. Ibid., 290–2. The vicarage was known as 'Leominster *ad crucem* and Hope' (see also the *acta* of Giles de Braose (1200 × 15) and Hugh Foliot (1226 × 34): Cott. Domit. A iii, f. 66r; *Reading Cartularies*, i, 295).
72. *Taxatio*, 159. See also Hereford Cathedral Archives, 1050a (see note 87 below).
73. Cf. the situation at Hartland (Devon), described by Lennard, *Rural England*, 301 and note 2.
74. *Reading Cartularies*, i, 277–8. For the identification of Hampton in the archbishop's act as Hampton Mappenore, see above, note 13.
75. See above, p. 89.
76. Cott. Domit. A iii, f. 66r.
77. The appropriation was granted by Bishop Hugh de Mapenore (ibid., ff. 67v–68r). His act was inspected and confirmed by Bishop Hugh Foliot in 1219 × 34 (ibid., ff. 68v–69r).
78. Bishop Hugh de Mapenore notified Adam, dean (and incumbent) of Humber, of the appropriation and ordered him to allow the priory to hold the chapel peacefully (ibid., f. 69v). Alternatively, however, he may have been informing Adam as rural dean, in which case one need not infer the latter's claim to the chapel.
79. Kemp, 'Hereditary Benefices', 11–12.
80. The two charters concerned the allowance of poor burial at Brimfield (see above, note 61)
81. For the grant of the appropriation, see Kemp, 'Hereditary Benefices', 13; for the date, see *Reading Cartularies*, i, 267. For the delay in fully implementing the appropriation, see Kemp, 'Hereditary Benefices', 6–9.
82. Cott. Domit. A iii, f. 71r, f 103v.
83. *Taxatio*, 159.
84. 'Registrum Edwardi Foxe, Episcopi Herefordensis' in *Registrum Caroli Bothe, Episcopi Herefordensis*, ed. A.T. Bannister (Canterbury & York Soc. xxviii, 1921), Appendix, 366.
85. Cott. Domit. A iii, ff. 103v–104v.
86. This chapelry is not recorded after the 13th century and no longer exists, but its location is the modern Mileshope, or Miles Hope, in Middleton parish (*RCHM Herefs*, iii, 149), a place which occurs in later Leominster charters as *Hopemile* or *Mileshope* or their variants. The name almost certainly derives from the Miles of Hope to whom Abbot Elias (1200–1213) and the convent of Reading granted 100 acres of land to assart in their wood of Hope and a further 108 acres in the same either to assart or to hold as wood (Cott. Domit. A iii, ff. 126v-127r). This Hope (not to be confused with Hope-under-Dinmore, 4 miles due south of Leominster) was in the demesne of Leominster in 1086 and accordingly, as several deeds in the Leominster cartulary show, came to Reading Abbey. As *Hopemile* or *Hop'myle*, Mileshope was confirmed to Reading by the pope in 1277 × 80 or 1288 × 92 as among the chapels of Leominster and Eye (*Reading Cartularies*, i, 141), and was described as a chapel of Eye in 1284 (Hereford Cathedral Archives 1050a — see next note).
87. There is a difficulty here, however, since a fragmentary record of a diocesan visitation in 1284 states that Middleton, Orleton and Mileshope were chapels of Eye, while Lucton, Eyton, Kimbolton, Brimfield and Yarpole were chapels of Leominster (Hereford Cathedral Archives 1050a), but, since this is certainly wrong in the case of Brimfield (see below), the evidence may be confused and, despite its official nature, must be treated with caution. Moreover, in a visitation of 1397 all these chapels, except Mileshope which had become defunct, reported at Eye and not at Leominster (Hereford Cathedral Archives, 1779, f. 15v; printed (inaccurately) 'Visitation Returns of the Diocese of Hereford in 1397', ed. A.T. Bannister, iii, *Eng. Hist. Rev.* xlv (1930), 100). In any case, it would be odd if chapels once dependent directly on Leominster were later transferred to Eye, where they were recorded in 1536. I am grateful to Professor P.E.H. Hair for drawing the Hereford manuscripts to my attention.
88. See above, p. 89.
89. Cott. Domit. A iii, ff. 96v–97r.
90. *RCHM Herefordshire*, iii, 155–6.
91. The allowance of the oblations of the dead is given in the assessment of Orleton chapelry, which refers to 'the garden of Hugh the clerk in the cemetery' (Cott. Domit. A iii, ff. 103v–104r), but according to one copy of the contemporary assessment of Eye vicarage the vicar was to receive 'the heriots of all corpses of Orleton that are buried in the cemetery of Eye' (ibid., f. 71r; see also n. 94).
92. *RCHM Herefordshire*, iii, 77, 147–8.
93. Cott. Domit. A iii, f. 147r–v. This is a charter by Philip the chaplain of Yarpole, son of Roger of Eye (incumbent of Eye), quitclaiming to Reading Abbey all his right in the lands and tenements which Walter his brother held in Eye and Yarpole (see Kemp, 'Hereditary Benefices', 6).
94. *Taxatio*, 159. This may be the annual payment in Croft chapel claimed by Reading Abbey in the later 13th century (*Reading Cartularies*, i, 141). Moreover, one copy of the 13th-century assessment of Eye vicarage implies that Croft may have been originally in Orleton, for it allows the vicar *herieta omnium corporum de Orleton que sepeliuntur in cymiterio de Eya exceptis heriettis corporum de Crofta de quibus non percipiet nisi medietatem* (Cott. Domit. A iii, f. 71r); the other copy has the same passage, but omits *de Orleton* (ibid., f. 103v). In the 1284 diocesan visitation Croft is called a church (Hereford Cathedral Archives, 1050a).
95. This remark excludes those places listed in 1123 which had been effectively detached from the *parochia* by then (see above, p. 83). Of these Dilwyn, Sarnesfield, Edvin Ralph, Pudleston, Kinnersley and Titley were either certainly or probably separate parishes by 1200, since either their churches are recorded before then or the present buildings contain 12th-century work. Whyle may also have been a parish, since its church, though now lost, is recorded in 1291 (*Taxatio*, 159). Even so, the total of separate parishes existing in 1200 within the old *parochia* as specified in 1123 was not great (about ten or a dozen) and, although several chapelries had also been formed, it would be wrong to suppose that the *parochia* had been completely parcelled out into parishes by the end of the 12th century.
96. For Leominster's tithe and burial rights at Monkland and Hatfield, see above, pp. 84–5, 88–9.
97. *Taxatio*, 159.
98. Round, 138. See also William de Vere's confirmation of 1186 × 98 (*Mon. Ang.*, vi (2), 1026).
99. See above, pp. 88–9.
100. *Taxatio*. 159.
101. See above, p. 89.
102. See above, p. 89.
103. Cott. Domit. A iii, f. 64r (de Vere's confirmation), f. 111r (agreement between the parties).
104. *Taxatio*, 159; *Registrum Ade de Orleton, Episcopi Herefordensis*, ed. A.T. Bannister (Canterbury and York Soc., v, 1908), 367. In Hereford episcopal registers Hampton Wafer is called a church between 1350 and 1453 (e.g., *Registrum Edmundi Lacy* (see note 14), 72), but from 1458 a free chapel (e.g., *Registrum Johannis Stanbury, Episcopi Herefordensis*, ed. A.T. Bannister (Canterbury & York Soc. xxv, 1919), 189). The 'church' was described as *diruta* in 1536 ('Registrum Edwardi Foxe' (see note 84), 366), and no longer exists.
105. See above, pp. 86, 89.
106. *Gilbert Foliot*, 353–4.
107. *Reading Cartularies*, i, 299–300.
108. *Taxatio*, 159.

VIII. The Secular College as a Focus for Anglo-Norman Piety: St. Augustine's, Daventry

M. J. Franklin

Recent work on pre-Conquest ecclesiastical organisation has pointed to the continuing vitality of some old minster *parochiae* into the 12th century and beyond. At the same time, the complexity of the Anglo-Saxon ecclesiastical structure on the eve of the Conquest has been emphasised.[1] *Eigenkirchen*, shrines, oratories and communities of all sorts are known to have intruded into the symmetery of the surviving *parochiae*. Indeed the churches which can be described as secular minsters at the end of the 11th century are diverse in origin. The refoundation of Waltham Holy Cross for a dean and twelve canons by Harold Godwineson in 1060 shows that the fashionable direction for pious patronage in this period was not always to the reformed Benedictine houses.[2] Great men also endowed secular colleges: these were still called minsters, but the inherent imprecision of that term, which could be applied to so many different types of institution, makes it important to grasp that these institutions were not *ipso facto* minsters with any sort of *parochiae* attached.

Earl Harold was not alone. Earl Leofric and Godiva seem to have patronised the minsters of Mercia, endowing, according to 'Florence' of Worcester, Leominster, Wenlock, Stow and both St. John's and St. Wereburh's in Chester.[3] Even if the view that the typical minster church of the last years of the Old English state was essentially cruciform, with tall aisleless nave, pair of north and south *porticus* and rectangular chancel[4] has been shown to be in need of modification,[5] so that it is no longer as easy to use architectural evidence as testimony to the continuing vitality of the secular tradition as some have thought, the fact of this vitality seems undeniable. '...Secular colleges were not mere relics in the Anglo-Norman world: they belonged to it more naturally than hindsight suggests...'[6] Kings, bishops and magnates continued to foster the clerical college as sources of maintenance for their clerical adherents. Hence, in London, St. Martin-le-Grand, the palace chapel, provided a living for the chief government servants of Henry I.[7] At South Malling (Sussex) the archbishops of Canterbury had a college which Theobald refounded *c.* 1150 for their clerks.[8] In Warwick *c.* 1120 the earl adapted the college of All Saints-in-the-Castle, which had run a school before the Conquest, and turned it into a larger college, the college of St. Mary.[9] In Leicester in 1107 Robert de Meulan rebuilt the college of St. Mary-in-Castro, which had been destroyed in the Conqueror's reign. This college endured after his son transfered it in 1143 to his own more fashionable foundation, the Augustinian abbey of Delapré.[10] Founders occasionally built entirely anew, or else refashioned more ancient institutions: this was the case with all four of the examples just cited. Yet this tendency, which was common to Normandy as well,[11] did not last long. The expansion of monasticism was the principal reason for this. 'From the end of the 11th century the Gregorian ideal, the growing pretensions of bishops and the advent of the regular Augustinian canons combined to achieve the eclipse of the seculars...'[12] Cluniacs, the new orders and above all the Augustinians, who appealed because of their involvement in the world, were all there to provide new *foci* for pious bequests. Many colleges, particularly those without patrons with vested interests to protect them, vanished completely, leaving scarcely a mark on the historical record, because their successors cared little for their predecessors' affairs.

Yet the England of Henry I contained many of these colleges. This paper aims to discuss the fate, and the motives behind that fate, of one of these underrated colleges, the college of Daventry (Northants.), in whose church Cluniac monks were placed *c.* 1108. It is based on a close study of the monks' 15th-century cartulary.[13]

The prevailing spiritual tastes of secular society inevitably influenced the nature of magnates' ecclesiastical patronage. Both magnates and their vassals were affected by the same sort of pressures. Hence while the Senlis earls of Northampton indulged their own taste for Cluniac monasticism by founding and maintaining the endowment of St. Andrew's, Northampton, Hugh the sheriff, an honorial baron, and steward perhaps to Matilda, wife to Earl Simon I and daughter of Earl Waltheof, founded Daventry Priory, also as a daughter of La Charité, next to his castle in Preston Capes.[14] The Priory had small beginnings and moved *c.* 1108 to Daventry.[15] The account of its origins actually inserted in the cartulary describes this as follows:

> Hugh of Leicester, called the sheriff ... removed the monks up to the vill of Daventry, with the licence of

Simon de Senlis the elder, earl of Northampton and lord of the town. He built the church of Daventry, where he set up the Priory for the second time and built the monastic buildings in honour of St. Augustine, apostle of the English, next to the parish church of the town. This contained four secular canons at this time, who each had their own prebends from the church. Two of them became monks, and two, remaining seculars, kept their prebends for the rest of their lives, by will of the patrons...[16]

Although this account is not by any means a contemporary record, it appears that a college of four priests, possibly with their own prebends and under the patronage of Earl Simon and his wife, had existed in Daventry.[17] The two canons who chose to retain their prebends are recorded in apparently genuine charters elsewhere in the cartulary. David I of Scotland, confirming the monks' possessions presumably as new lord of the honour, in a charter dated 1124 × 30, added 'And William and Hugh, who are canons of Daventry, are to hold their prebends freely and with honour, unless they change their habit or life....'[18] The lordship of the vill of Daventry came to form the *caput* of the marriage-portion of Matilda, daughter of Earl Simon I. This alienation from the honour, over which a loose form of overlordship only was retained,[19] must have been accepted by the earls of the Scots line, for the wife of Robert fitz Richard was pardoned 13*s*. 4*d*. of geld in the 1130 Pipe Roll, presumably for Daventry.[20] Matilda's progeny by Robert fitz Richard are described and treated in the Daventry cartulary as lords of Daventry and patrons of the Priory: they were one of a number of 'lords of far more than local distinction' in the honour.[21] The monks, not unnaturally, seem to have begun to look to the fitz Richards as being more able than the founder to give them the effective protection they needed, perhaps from difficulties caused by the well-known unwillingness of the later Scots lords of the honour to uphold earlier gifts. It is known that the founder's heir also contested some of his grants early in the reign of Henry II, for it was this which impelled the king to grant the monks the minster at Fawsley.[22] Hence it was to the lords of Daventry, and not the non-Senlis earls or the founder's family, that the monks increasingly turned at the end of Stephen's reign. Earl Simon de Senlis II issued a confirmatory charter in 1141 × 6.[23] No charters are known to have been issued by Robert fitz Richard, but it was his relict Matilda, the daughter of Earl Simon I, who provided the main stream of new benefactions to Daventry in the late 1140s, granting in a series of four charters, one of which was said to have been made for the soul of her first husband (who had attested Earl Simon II's charter), land and finally the church of Daventry.[24] This grant was later described by the monks, significantly, as being made 'in her widowhood, as patron and lord'[25] It must have occurred when Matilda was 'between' husbands, and should perhaps be understood as associated with the monks' need to look for a new, more powerful patron in the founder's declining years. Matilda had married Saer de Quincy by 1146: the latter, as lord of Daventry, attested the charter of Thomas de Braybrooke in which Thomas acknowledged his error in depriving the monks of Braybrooke church granted by his predecessors.[26] By *c*. 1150 even the amazingly long-lived Hugh the sheriff was certainly dead. Hugh Poer, his son, gave the monks the church of Cold Ashby: this lay on his fee held of the prior of Coventry, who assented to the transfer as superior lord of the fee in a charter dated 1150.[27]

Clearly then the 'minster' at Daventry was part of the comital estate which descended to the fitz Richard family. It need not necessarily have been a collegiate church of any great antiquity. In both England and Normandy magnates fostered the old secular tradition of the private college, though patronage rapidly came to be directed to more fashionable, and monastic, ends in step with Gregorian ideals. Nevertheless, before the advent of the Augustinians there is plenty of evidence that the need for a personal *monasterium* was sometimes satisfied, if no longer by the foundation of a new secular college, or the adaptation of an existing one, at least by its further transformation into an alien priory at the *caput honoris,* or a college at the castle gates. None of these colleges, apparently, had any basis of ancient parochial rights. The history of the church at Daventry may have close parallels with the history of William de Braose's college at Bramber castle in Sussex. Founded only in 1073, when he accompanied the Conqueror into Maine,[28] de Braose transferred it in 1080 to the priory of Sele, the most important of the English cells of Saumur Abbey, 'after the death of the canons now there, and one vacant prebend at once'.[29] That the monks actually took up residence in Daventry is the only significant difference. Perhaps the dedication of Daventry Priory to St. Augustine, apostle of the English, was something inherited from the college: it is an extremely unusual dedication for a Cluniac house. The fact that only one priest is recorded at Daventry in 1086[30] is not a reliable *terminus post quem* for the foundation of the college there: 'est ibi presbiter' in Domesday Book is inconclusive as negative evidence for a college of secular priests; for example, Great Paxton (Hunts.), well-known as a secular college, is so recorded.[31]

Did the monks of Daventry succeed to any parochial rights when they acquired the church of the college? And did the college thereupon dissolve spontaneously into a loosely federated body of separate priests in the *parochia* of the college?[32] It is clear that the church served by the canons of Daventry had had parochial functions: the account of the foundation speaks specifically of the planting of the monastic buildings cheek-by-jowl with the parish church,[33] and the proximity of monks to parishioners was to cause a series of problems throughout the medieval period. The

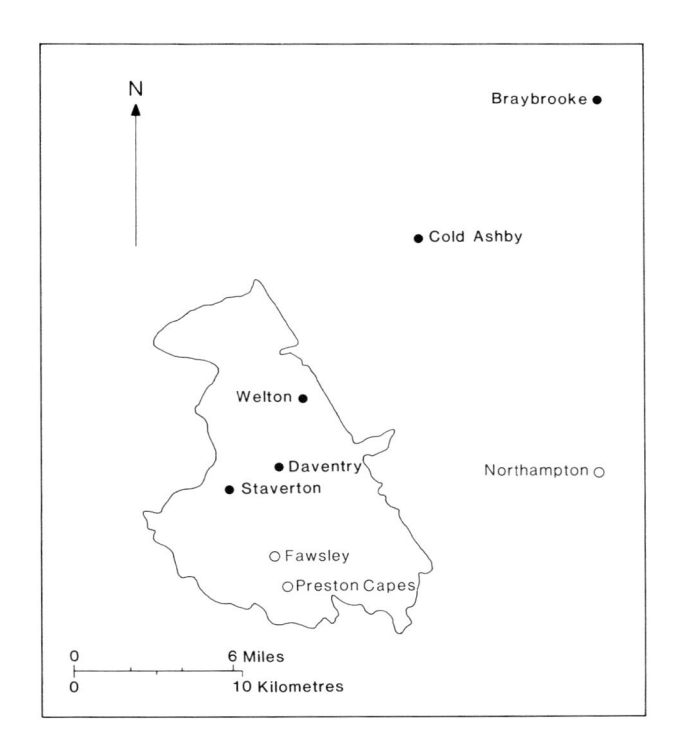

Fig. 21 The College of St. Augustine, Daventry: known endowment. The boundary shown is that of the hundreds of Gravesende and Alwardeslea. Names of places containing known College endowments are in heavy type.

cartulary in fact shows that both parishioners and monks used different parts of the same church. In 1390 the bells of the parishioners disturbed the convent to such an extent that John of Gaunt was called in to mediate,[34] and in 1374 Bishop Buckingham ruled in a dispute about the repair of a wall separating the parishioners from the cloister.[35] It has also been suggested that a similar dispute, mentioned in the records of Bishop Alnwick's visitation of Daventry in 1442, shows that the conventual church had a large south aisle used by the parishioners, with access through the outer court on the lines of the arrangements at Blyth Priory (Notts.).[36] No trace of the monastic building in Daventry now survives, since the parish church was completely rebuilt in 1752–8. However, the engravings of the fragments of the Priory surviving in 1729 confirm this, showing a north range of a cloister adjoining the parish church directly.[37] Whoever founded the college at Daventry may well have arranged exemption from the jurisdiction of the flourishing minster at Fawsley. When Henry II granted the latter to the monks of Daventry his grant included the churchscot of the two appendant hundreds 'from the places from which it was rendered in the time of King William and King Henry'.[38] Despite the fact that Fawsley is known to have maintained its claim to churchscot until as late as 1553,[39] Daventry is never recorded as being liable. This suggests that it was founded before the 'time of King William', that is

perhaps before the 1090s, or conceivably even before 1066. The church of Daventry also had at least one daughter chapel at Welton, whose existence is known in the 12th century.[40]

The data about Welton in the Priory cartulary allows two main points to be made, from which further inferences are possible: first, that Matilda de Senlis's charter granting Daventry church to the monks after 1147, though ostensibly a grant, was in reality merely adding her confirmation to a claim the monks already possessed; and secondly, that the canon William of Daventry in David I's charter is probably the same man as William de Neufmarché, lord of Welton, who was later revered by the monks as the donor of Welton church.[41] There are three important documents concerned with Welton. In the first it is recorded that William de Neufmarché (*de novo mercato*), in 1135 (*anno decessionis Henrici regis*), returned to the monks Welton chapel, which he and his father had unjustly taken from them: he laid himself open to this accusation by possession of the very key of the church (*verum eciam se reum clamitatis per clavem ipsius capelle eam saisivit*). Among the witnesses to the 'return' were the founder, Hugh of Leicester, Robert fitz Richard, and a certain William, *capellanus*, whose significance will become clearer later.[42] In the second, an *actum* of the suffragan Richard, bishop of St. Asaph, who acted for Bishop Alexander in the diocese between February 1141 and 1143,[43] is a report to the bishop of Lincoln: at the request of the lords, priest and parishioners of Welton, Bishop Richard had dedicated the chapel there, which had always been, and would remain, an appendage of the church of Daventry, as an *ecclesia*. He confirmed that no burials were to take place in Welton: the mother church was to retain all its rights. Before doing this he had received the public acknowledgement by William, the priest (*sacerdos*) of Welton, that Welton church was a part (*menbrum*) of the church of Daventry: no agency had intervened to make this so (*illi soli alio non participante pertinebat*). Interposing his authority between the prior and William *sacerdos*, Bishop Richard had supervised the latter's submission of the key of the church, the symbol of his authority, to the prior, and its regranting to William for his lifetime: a typical vicarage arrangement.[44] This implies that William had originally received the church from someone other than the prior. Bishop Richard further reported that William had also confirmed that he had been present in chapter at Daventry when William de Neufmarché had given Welton back to the monks (thereby equating the William *sacerdos* of 1141 × 3 with the William *capellanus* of 1135 and suggesting that he had been serving the church before 1135) and that Fulk Trussel, William de Neufmarché's nephew and heir, did not repudiate his uncle's charter.[45] The third is recorded in the cartulary as an *actum* of an archdeacon Simon of Northampton. No such archdeacon is known at this period, but this could simply be a scribal error for the unusual name Savaric (archdeacon from 1175).[46] It records the resolution of a dispute between the prior of Daventry and William, their 'curate' at Welton (*inter priorem et monachos de Daventre et Willelmum capellanum suum in Weltona*). William finally gave up his charge in return for six measures of corn and six of rye together with a stipend of one mark a year.[47]

Some idea at least of the nature of the endowment of the secular college at Daventry, if not its precise extent, can be gained from other references in the Priory cartulary. There is evidence that the canons possessed all the forms of revenue that might be expected: churches, lands and tithes. Robert, count of Eu, established a secular college from scratch in the castle at Hastings in 1090. Since the complete original endowment is known from a 12th-century confirmation charter, comparison with a 'typical' college endowment is possible, though the college at Hastings was clearly on a grander scale than Daventry. The college had ten prebends to which were attached churches, tithes, property and land in places as far away as West Thurrock in Essex.[48]

In a charter dated 1161 granting Staverton church to the monks, Stephen de Welton declared 'that this same church of Staverton pertained to the endowment (*ius*) of the church of Daventry and was part of it for many more years before this grant to St. Augustine'.[49] Of course this is not very specific: the charter refers to some vague time in the past when Daventry had had the church (a common enough claim in monastic cartularies and not a claim that inspires confidence in its veracity), and to Stephen realising his pious duty to restore to the monks their possessions. However, it is possible to proceed a little beyond this charter. The *Northamptonshire Survey* informs us that the holders of lands in Staverton were, as might be expected, Stephen de Welton (three hides) and, more significantly, William de Neufmarché (one hide).[50] Here is a hint that one of the canons of Daventry, whose rights were protected at the foundation, held land at least in Staverton well before the monks came to Daventry. If this identification is correct, we can picture the secular lord of Welton grabbing the right to present to Staverton church from a canon whose pre-occupations were becoming secular, or, and more likely, whose friends were no longer as important as they once had been. Such a context might well underlie the charter to the monks issued in 1161. Already this is informed speculation: but it is possible to hypothesise even further since in 1086 the same land units in Staverton already existed, though recorded as being on different fees (the three hides held by Alan of the Count of Mortain, the one hide by Osbern of Hugh of Grandmesnil, with only the three hides owing any soke to Fawsley).[51] As Staverton parish remained liable to pay churchscot to Fawsley until the 16th century,[52] it must therefore have had its ecclesiastical beginnings within the *parochia* of Fawsley. Hence if Staverton church had once been part of the endowment of the college of Daventry, and if William de Neufmarché was indeed canon of Daventry, this church must have properly pertained to the one-hide unit, not to Stephen de Welton's three-hide unit; and, as a corollary, the college must pre-date the Conquest, because otherwise the soke owed to Fawsley would have been recorded for that holding in 1086. We might then go on to argue that Osbern, who held a coherent estate in Welton, Thrupp and Staverton in 1086, and Baldwin, who had held the same in 1066,[53] were earlier canons, or possibly even heads, of the college (Baldwin had sub-tenants Leofric and Aluin), even though their priestly status is not mentioned in Domesday Book. Latent references to the many minsters which were still the cult centres of their regions are to be expected in Domesday Book.[54]

This is speculation indeed: but we are on firmer ground with other churches owned by the college. Braybrooke lies some 30 km north-east of Daventry; nonetheless, its church seems to have been given to Daventry in the immediate post-Conquest generation. In 1143 × 4 Robert fitz Viel finally allowed the monks of Daventry to possess all the churches of his barony of Foxton, one of which was Braybrooke. His charter, dated the ninth year of King Stephen, reports Prior Osbert's pleading before Bishop Alexander for the churches in the sixth year of Stephen (that is 1140 × 1) and Robert's final acknowledgement of his unjust possession from the year in which Archbishop Anselm died (that is 1109) till 1143.[55] His son's confirmatory charter also notes that his father gave all the churches in 1109,[56] but there is no charter of Robert in the cartulary explicitly granting all the churches. A confirmation by Robert's superior lord, Earl Simon I, addressed to Bishop Robert Bloet (?1109 × 11) is, however, preserved.[57] Clearly these events were happening in the very early days of the monks in Daventry: since, however, there survives a further charter of Robert granting Braybrooke church alone, and in this confirming the grant of Cetelbert,[58] about whom more is known, it seems very unlikely that Robert fitz Viel was, in the case of Braybrooke at least, merely confirming a recent grant by one of his own subtenants to the monks. It is much more likely that he was seeking to divert to the monks a grant made by someone else to the canons. For Cetelbert was probably that unusual man, the honorial tenant who survived the Conquest: he is explicitly named as tenant of Braybrooke under Countess Judith in 1086 and also as tenant in 1066.[59] The interpretation that Robert fitz Viel was merely confirming and augmenting, as superior lord, a grant recently made by an undertenant in c. 1109 would make Cetelbert improbably long-lived. In this event it would also be logical for the monks to preserve his charter or, at the very least, dignify him with the title of donor of Braybrooke in the list of benefactors. Neither of these things do they appear to have done.[60] The hypothesis that Cetelbert gave

Braybrooke church to the college of Daventry in, say, the reign of Rufus would make explicable the charters which the monks had.

And there does appear to be evidence for the canons holding land at this period. In the third year of the reign of Stephen (that is 1137 × 8) Rocius de Houghton granted back land in Welton and Thrupp to the monks 'which the same church [i.e. St. Augustine of Daventry] had held previously in the reign of Rufus'.[61] He would hold it henceforth at a rent of 10s. yearly. To persuade him to do this, the charter records, Hugh of Leicester (that is the founder and patron) and Prior Osbert gave Rocius 20s. The charter also notes that the founder 'had endowed the church of St. Augustine [not necessarily the monks of course] a long time before with this same land with the rest of his grants'.[62] This indicates either that Hugh of Leicester had supported the canons of Daventry as well as the monks, that is in the 1090s or before, or, possibly more likely, that he had intended these lands to go to the monks originally. However, there is other evidence which suggests that he had first supported the canons. In granting Elkington church to the monks, he reserved a life-interest in the church to Ivo son of John de Coldiun, and another life-interest in half his demesne tithes there to William, canon of St. Augustine's.[63] Hugh's longevity has been remarked upon,[64] but it seems incontestable. His grant to the monks of *terra Edrici* in Everdon[65] was confirmed by Earl Simon II, not Earl Simon I, since this confirmation is addressed to Bishop Alexander and archdeacon William of Northampton and witnessed by Robert fitz Richard:[66] it must date from c. 1141 × 6. But Hugh's usefulness to his monks as a patron must surely have declined with his advancing years: this might explain their need for a more effective patron. Hence the college of Daventry would seem to have possessed land near Daventry, at least one church and some tithes at some considerable distance.

There is no difficulty in suggesting that Matilda de Senlis II's charter to the monks concerning Daventry church, though ostensibly a grant, was in reality a confirmation. Since it is now accepted that coincident earldoms of Huntingdon, vested in the Scots line of descent from Matilda de Senlis I, and Northampton, vested in the senior Senlis line, existed at no time in the 12th century, and that the high politics of Anglo-Scots relations in reality determined whether or not the Senlis claimant obtained his patrimony through royal favour,[67] it follows that the attitudes of the various earls to the religious protégés of the respective lines would fluctuate according to which was in possession of the honour. It is known that the Scots earls gave ostensible charters of grant, rather than confirm their predecessors' benefactions, because, even though they did not accept the justice of the Senlis tenure, it was becoming increasingly difficult to dispossess the religious.[68] Hence the best way to deal with an adherent of the opposing line was to grant his lands to a religious house.[69] Hence when trying to interpret the documents in the 15th-century cartulary of Daventry it is important to remember that the house was a protégé of the Senlis line. The monks went from Preston Capes to Daventry with Earl Simon I's licence: we do not know that they definitely received the church of Daventry at this time, only that two of the members of the college there chose to join the monks. 'Monasteries were not only focal points of religious organisation; they were also centres of loyalties which were essentially secular and political.'[70] The remaining canons seem to have received protection from the Scots line.

Something analogous to what happened at Bromfield (Salop.) may have occurred, with the members of the college dissolving into a loose federation of village priests in the churches of the college.[71] Welton was always a possession of the church of St. Augustine, Daventry. The monks nurtured a claim to all the possessions of the old church, despite the fact that the rights of the canons to their prebends had been protected. Hence William de Neufmarché, almost certainly a priest because he laid himself open to the charge of abstracting the church from the monks by possessing its key,[72] was probably the canon William of King David's and Earl Henry's charters. Since the monks regarded both him and his father as being guilty of abstracting their property he must have inherited his claim after the monks moved to Daventry. Parallels exist for such a situation: at Morville (Salop.), which Earl Roger gave to Shrewsbury Abbey before 1086, the son of one of the minster priests claimed to have his father's prebend c. 1114.[73] The names of the canons of Daventry are not known until David I's charter of 1124 × 30: hence it could easily have been William's father who declined to become a Cluniac in 1108. In the year of Henry I's death, when loyalty to the Angevin cause represented by David I, the Scots earl of the honour, was an important issue, William de Neufmarché seems suddenly to have become convinced of the justice of the monks' claim to Welton church and openly acknowledged this, becoming its donor, despite the fact that it was more properly described as a direct dependency of Daventry.[74] A secular college might continue to exist for a variety of motives.

There remains one more aspect to be considered: the position of William, *sacerdos* of Welton recorded in 1141 × 3 and 1175 × 82. 'Vicars' of a sort are known to have served the dependent chapels of collegiate churches. Eilwi was sent out on a regular basis by Dean Godric of Twynham (Hants.) to minister in Milford church (above, pp. 54–6). However, he seems to have received almost a corrody from the local lord on the occasion of his visits: he did not gain any share of Milford church.[75] It is possible that William *capellanus* began his career in this mould: perhaps as the permanent resident 'curate' of William de Neufmarché. At any rate he was present at the latter's submission before Prior Osbert in chapter at Daventry in the year of Henry I's death, attesting the document recording this and warranting it before Richard of St. Asaph in 1141 × 3. In interpreting this *actum* we do well to remember that the honour of Huntingdon changed hands again in 1141, Simon de Senlis II being in tenure when the fight at Winchester had revealed King David's open support for the Angevin cause.[76] The monks might well choose this moment to seek to regularise the position of Welton church: the ecclesiastical heirarchy, imbued with Gregorianism, would be keen to give its assistance. Hence William was compelled to acknowledge that he held the church from the monks: in return he was safeguarded in possession of the church for his lifetime (*eandem dum vixerit habituram et servaturam suscepit*). Though described as William, *sacerdos* of Welton by Bishop Richard in 1141 × 3, and probably recorded attesting, as William, *sacerdos*, Rocius de Houghton's charter returning land in Welton and Thrupp to the monks in 1137 × 8,[77] by 1175 × 82 he was known as the monks' curate (*capellanus*) in Welton. It seems that the monks then tried again to acquire his church. On this occasion they succeeded, but only at the price of what amounted to a retirement pension for the rest of his life, apparently quite a considerable period. Again it is tempting to recall that Earl Simon de Senlis III, holder of the honour of Huntingdon from 1153 to 1157,[78] recovered it by the end of 1174 because of his services to Henry II during the Young King's rebellion: he 'had been recognised by Henry II as lord of the honour in the closing stages of the conflict "si illum adipisci posset"'.[79] William *sacerdos* seems to have been a man of longevity approaching that of Hugh of Leicester. After his retirement the church of Welton seems to have been served by Ralph, *capellanus*: nonetheless his family maintained an interest in Welton even though the college they had served had long since ceased to exist. William's son, Walter, who adopted the surname *Clerch*, is found involved in property transactions in Welton in the early 13th century. On receipt of three marks Prior Alelm of Daventry (1204 × 15)[80] granted 'to Walter *Clerch*, the son of William the priest, the messuage which Ralph the curate held next to the cemetery of Welton church' for a rent of 3*s*. a year.[81] It is tempting to equate this messuage with the parsonage house in Welton. Was this perhaps the family home, rented to Walter during a vacancy in the cure of Welton?

In microcosm the history of the college of Daventry shows how the potent forces of secular lordship, taste and Gregorianism could transform the ecclesiastical structure in an area. It was only through many vicissitudes that the simple pattern of the parish priest in his village church with his ordered place in the heirarchy beneath archdeacon and bishop was created. It is reasonably certain that this college's sphere of influence was carved out of the *parochia* of Fawsley. Apart from Daventry's position in the hundred of *Alwardeslea*, which is known to have been included in Fawsley's *parochia*, there is also the evidence of Domesday Book, which records that the king had soke over the holding which Leofric held of Countess Judith in Welton.[82] Fawsley is the nearest royal manor: it is unfortunate that the Domesday scribes did not choose to record the connection more explicitly. Whether the endowment of Daventry occured soon after the Conquest, or even perhaps before, is less clear. There is a possibility that it was before the Conquest. It is also tempting to draw attention to one further point: Barby and Ashby St. Ledgers are the only other parishes in the hundred of *Alwardeslea* whose liability to churchscot to Fawsley is not recorded.[83] The possibilty that this apparent exemption is connected with the endowment of the college is tantalising. Unfortunately virtually no comparable early data for these parishes is available to substantiate such a hypothesis. They appear to have ordinary village churches, proprietary in origin.[84] If they were a part of the endowment of the college, the monks of Daventry never managed to promote any claim to them.

The story of the end of the secular minster at Daventry was probably a common one. Honorial barons following the fashions of their magnate superiors would find the expense of founding a full monastery and maintaining it in a viable state beyond them. The surviving secular colleges provided a simple solution to this problem. The history of Daventry shows that it was not only the Augustinians who were the recipients of minsters. Cluniacs similarly received such institutions. But it was rarely a simple matter of the absorbtion of one body by another. The lists of honoured donors in monastic cartularies may conceal more complex stories. For the endowments of secular colleges were disparate in nature: many apparent donations may well have been resumptions of property lost by predecessors. Some colleges survived: many more did not. The lesson of the history of Daventry is that, for a variety of reasons, the repercussions of its end affected the environs of Daventry for a considerable time.

Addendum

Subsequent to the preparation of this paper Dr David Crouch of the SSMEA project, Institute of Historical Research, London, drew my attention to the connections of Welton with the honour of Leicester (personal communication). This evidence makes me incline less towards the identification of the William de Neufmarché of the *Northamptonshire Survey*, who seems to have been an adherent of Earl Robert II of Leicester surviving into the 1150s, with the William who became the donor of Welton to Daventry. But this latter William is unlikely to have been Earl Robert's adherent: he was almost certainly dead by the time of Richard of St. Asaph's involvement with Welton since in the *actum* issued by the Bishop William's heir, Fulk Trussel, was stated not to have repudiated his uncle's grant. However, given that, in this period, the possession of the key to a church does not necessarily indicate priestly status. it is possible to interpret the charters concerning Welton somewhat more simply with William canon of Daventry perhaps becoming by stages semi-independent *sacerdos* of Welton, under the patronage of another layman called William de Neufmarché and then, finally, the monks' vicar. The 'Leicester connection' also raises the further possibility that the politics of another honour, as well as the competing claims to the honour of Huntingdon/Northampton, determined the fate of the college at Daventry. These possibilities merely emphasise the difficulties in interpreting such fragmentary evidence.

Notes

1. Franklin, 'Identification of Minsters', 69–88; Blair, 'Secular Minsters', 104–42.
2. On Waltham see *The Foundation of Waltham Abbey*, ed. W. Stubbs (Oxford and London, 1861).
3. Florence of Worcester, *Chronicon ex Chronicis*, ed. B. Thorpe, 2 vols. (English Historical Society, 1844), i, 216. For their surviving charter to Stow (Lincs.) see *C&S*, i, No. 73.
4. Blair, 'Secular Minsters', 121 following C.A.R. Radford, 'Pre-Conquest Minster Churches', *Archaeol. J.* cxxx (1973), 120–40.
5. Franklin, 'Identification of Minsters', *passim*.
6. Blair, 'Secular Minsters', 131.
7. R.H.C. Davis, 'The College of St. Martin-le-Grand and the Anarchy', *London Topographical Record*, xxiii (1972), 25.
8. A. Hamilton Thompson, 'Notes on Colleges of Secular Canons in England', *Archaeol. J.* lxxiv (1917), 161. For the history of the college at South Malling see *VCH Sussex*, ii, 117–19.
9. Knowles & Hadcock, 442; *VCH Warwicks.* ii, 124.
10. Knowles & Hadcock, 429.
11. Cf. Blair, 'Secular Minsters', 133, on the 24 Norman seigneurial colleges of the period 960–1110, all of which were suppressed in the 12th century. See also L. Musset, 'Recherches sur les Communautés de Clercs Séculiers en Normandie au XIe Siècle', *Bulletin de la Société des Antiquaires de Normandie*, lv (1961 for 1959–60), 5–38, on which Blair's remarks are based.
12. Blair, 'Secular Minsters', 133.
13. Brit. Lib., MS Cotton Claudius D xii.
14. For the problems connected with the beginnings of Daventry see my forthcoming edition of the cartulary for the Northamptonshire Record Society. The single source which describes the founder as steward of Matilda, a preliminary leaf, not part of the main cartulary (Brit. Lib., MS Cotton Claudius D xii f. 2r, pd. *Mon.Ang.* v, 178, i) confuses 'Queen' Matilda, relict of Earl Simon I and subsequently wife to David I of Scotland and benefactor of the Priory, with Matilda, sister of Earl Simon II and wife successively to Robert fitz Richard (one of Henry I's new men) and Saer de Quincy I. Matilda and Saer de Quincy confirmed grants by 'Queen' Matilda in their joint charter to the monks (Brit. Lib., MS Cotton Claudius D xii f. 5r) so, though no separate charters of the latter to Daventry have survived, it is clear that both ladies acted in their own right. (For *acta* of 'Queen' Matilda to Lanthony and the canons of St. Giles-by-the-Castle, Cambridge cf. *Regesta Regum Scottorum*, ed. G.W. Barrow et al. (6 vols., Edinburgh, 1960–82), i, Nos. 2, 52). In consequence it is not possible to resolve this confusion, though the early date for the beginnings of Daventry seems correct.
15. Knowles and Hadcock, 99, following *Cartulary of the Mediæval Archives of Christ Church*, ed. N. Denholm-Young (Oxford Hist. Soc., 1951), vi. There had been only four monks at Preston: *Mon.Ang.* v, 178, i.
16. 'Hugo de Leycestre, dictus vicecomes...usque ad villam de Daventre ex licentia domini Simonis de Seynlitz senioris, comitis Norhampton et eiusdem ville domini removit. Ecclesiam de Daventre, ubi secundo fundavit prioratum, et monasterium construxit in honore beati Augustini Anglorum apostoli iuxta ecclesiam parochialem eiusdem ville, in qua tunc erant quatuor canonici seculares qui singuli habebant prebendas suas de eadem ecclesia, ex quibus duo susceperunt habitum monachalem et duo in seculo viventes retinuerant prebendas suas ad totam vitam illorum ex voluntate patronorum...': Brit. Lib., MS Cotton Claudius D xii f. 109r. There is a textual difficulty here: *Mon.Ang.* v, 178, ii prints this passage preferring the reading 'removit ad ecclesiam de Daventre...', but in the manuscript 'ad' is clearly an addition.
17. The usage of the term 'prebend' may not necessarily refect reality: cf. Franklin, 'Identification of Minsters', 73.
18. 'Et Willelmus et Hugo qui canonici sunt eiusdem loci prebendas suas omni vita sua libere et honorifice teneant nisi habitum suum vel vitam mutaverunt...': Brit. Lib., MS Cotton Claudius D xii f. 5r, pd. *Early Scottish Charters*, ed. A.C. Lawrie (Glasgow, 1905), No. LIX. A second charter, issued by Earl Henry February 1136 × January 1138, refers only to William, suggesting that the canon Hugh had died by that date: Brit. Lib., MS Cotton Claudius D xii f. 5r, pd. *Early Scottish Charters*, No. CXII. William is also mentioned in the founder's grant of Elkington church: Brit. Lib., MS Cotton Claudius D xii f. 142v, pd. *Cartulary of the Mediæval Archives of Christchurch*, ix.
19. Stringer, *Earl David*, 109.
20. *The Pipe Roll of 31 Henry I, Michaelmas 1130* (1929 facsimile reproduction of *Magnum Rotulum Scaccarii vel Magnum Rotulum Pipae...*, ed. J. Hunter, Record Commission, 1833), 85.
21. Stringer, *Earl David*, 127.
22. Brit. Lib., MS Cotton Claudius D xii f. 102v, pd. from later *inspeximus The Cartae Antiquae Rolls 1–10*, ed. L. Landon (Pipe Roll Soc., 1939), No. 173. Cf. also the account given to the escheator of the early history of the priory at an Inquisition sworn in 1270: Brit. Lib., MS Cotton Claudius D xii f. 111v. For discussion of the way Earl Simon II and later lords of the honour of Huntingdon habitually attended to the claims of the church on their patronage by granting manors encumbered by prior claims, see Stringer, *Earl David*, chs. 6 and 7 *passim* and especially p. 145 for the example of Potton (Beds.).
23. Brit. Lib., MS Cotton Claudius D xii f. 99v, pd. *Cartulary of the Mediæval Archives of Christ Church*, viii. Earl Simon II was acknowledged as earl from 1141 (Stringer, *Earl David*, 20), and Robert fitz Richard appears to have been dead by 1146 – see n. 26.
24. Brit. Lib., MS Cotton Charter xi.25, MS Cotton Claudius D xii ff. 5r–v.
25. 'Matilda Seynlitz...dedit nobis in libera viduitate sua tanquam patrona et domina, ecclesiam de Daventre': ibid, f. 109r.
26. Ibid, f. 156v.
27. Ibid, ff. 109r, 114v. For an example of the esteem in which a founder might be held by his monks cf. M.L. Colker, 'Latin Texts concerning Gilbert, founder of Merton Priory', *Studia Monastica*, xii (1970), 241–70, and for discussion of the proprietary character of several Anglo-Norman alien priories see Blair, 'Secular Minsters', 133, 138.
28. *Calendar of documents preserved in France...*, I, ed. J.H. Round (London, 1899), No. 1130, discussed Blair, 'Secular Minsters', 135.
29. *The Chartulary of the Priory of St. Peter at Sele*, ed. L.F. Salzman (Cambridge, 1923), 2, n. 1.
30. DB I 228c.
31. DB I 207a. Radford, 'Pre-Conquest Minster Churches', 133.

32. Cf. Bromfield, Salop.: *Historia et Cartularium Monasterii Sancti Petri Gloucestriae*, ed. W.H. Hart, (3 vols, Rolls Ser. 1863–7), ii, 213–14, discussed Franklin, 'Identification of Minsters', 74; Blair, 'Secular Minsters', 128–31.
33. Above, pp. 97–8.
34. Bodl., MS Dep. Deeds Ch. Ch. C.31 D.4.
35. Brit. Lib., MS Cotton Claudius D xii f. 25r.
36. *Visitations of Religious Houses II, a.d. 1436–1449*, ed. A. Hamilton Thompson (Lincoln Rec. Soc., 1918), 61, n. 3.
37. J. Bridges, ed. P. Whalley, *The History and Antiquities of Northamptonshire* (2 vols, Oxford, 1791), i, facing p. 49.
38. '... et churchseat de duobus hundredis ... concedo undecunque sibi redderetur temporis regis Willelmi et regis H ...': Brit. Lib., MS Cotton Claudius D xii f. 102v.
39. Franklin, 'Minsters and Parishes', 184–6.
40. Recorded as such in the *dimissio* for 1344: Lincolnshire Archives Office, Register VIIB f. 74r. In 1290 this status had been contested (Bodl., MS Dep. Deeds Ch. Ch. C.32 D.117) and in 1321 an indulgence for Welton described it as a *parochialis ecclesia*: Lincolnshire Archives Office, Register V f. 278r.
41. Brit. Lib., MS Cotton Claudius D xii f. 109r.
42. Ibid., f. 82v.
43. Cf. D.M. Smith, 'The Episcopate of Richard, Bishop of St. Asaph: a problem of Twelfth Century Chronology', *Journal of the Historical Society of the Church in Wales*, xxiv (1974), 11.
44. William is found in the 1140s attesting Prior Herbert's grant of half a virgate in Welton to Ketylbern: P.R.O., E40/7072, Brit. Lib., MS Cotton Claudius D xii f. 87r.
45. Ibid., ff. 83r–v.
46. J.Le Neve, *Fasti Ecclesiae Anglicanae 1066–1300: III: Lincoln* (comp. D.E. Greenway, London, 1977), 31; confirmed almost certainly by the appearance of Geoffrey, archdeacon of Berkshire in the witness list: he is recorded in 1175 × 9 (*HMC Wells*, i, 20). A similar error in the same cartulary produces the impossible 'Meluaritus', archdeacon of Northampton (Brit. Lib., MS Cotton Claudius D xii f. 83v). Since the subject of this *actum* would normally be the business of the diocesan, not the archdeacon, tentative limiting dates for this *actum* of 1175 × 82 can be assigned, that is during the tenure of the see of Lincoln by Geoffrey Plantagenet and before Savaric's temporary forfeiture for disloyalty 1182–4: see *Fasti*, 2, 31 and cf. *English Episcopal Acta: I: Lincoln 1067–1185*, ed. D.M. Smith (London, 1980), xxviii for discussion of the precise powers of Geoffrey both as un-confirmed and confirmed bishop-elect.
47. Brit. Lib., MS Cotton Claudius D xii f. 83r.
48. *VCH Sussex*, ii, 112–13 citing P.R.O., E210/1073.
49. '... hanc eandem ecclesiam de Staverton ad ius ecclesie Daventrensis pertinentem et menbrum eius pluris annis ante hanc donacionem sancto Augustino ...': Brit. Lib., MS Cotton Claudius D xii f. 72r.
50. *VCH Northants*. i, 371.
51. DB I, 223b, 224c.
52. Franklin, 'Minsters and Parishes', 184–6.
53. DB I, 224c.
54. Blair, 'Secular Minsters', 142.
55. Brit. Lib., MS Cotton Claudius D xii, ff. 145r–145v.
56. Ibid, f. 145v.
57. Ibid, f. 147r; *Mon.Ang*. v, 180, x.
58. Brit. Lib., MS Cotton Claudius D xii f. 156v.
59. DB I, 228c. Most manors changed hands between 1066 and 1086: P.H. Sawyer, '1066–1086: A Tenurial Revolution?', in idem (ed.), *Domesday Book: a Reassessment* (London, 1985), 71.
60. Brit. Lib., MS Cotton Claudius D xii f. 109r.
61. '... quam ipsa eadem ante tenuerat a tempore regis Willelmi iunioris ...' – ibid., f. 84r. Denholm-Young (*Cartulary of the Mediæval Archives of Christ Church*, vi) dismissed this as merely a vague reference, but he was concerned to deny the existence of Cluniacs at Daventry in the 1090s, not to analyse the endowment of the pre-existing college.
62. '... qui hanc eandem terram cum ceteris beneficiis ecclesie sancti Augustini longo tempore ante contulerat ...' – Brit. Lib., MS Cotton Claudius D xii f. 84r.
63. Ibid., f. 142r, pd. Denholm-Young, *Cartulary of the Mediæval Archives of Christ Church*, ix.
64. Ibid., vi.
65. Brit. Lib., MS Cotton Claudius D xii f. 99v, pd. *Cartulary of the Mediæval Archives of Christ Church*, vii.
66. Brit. Lib., MS Cotton Claudius D xii f. 99v, pd. *Cartulary of the Mediæval Archives of Christ Church*, viii.
67. On this point see Stringer, *Earl David*, which, naturally enough, concentrates on the later 12th century. For the view that the Senlis claimant, when not in tenure, tended to style himself *comes* without territorial designation, see for now idem, 'The Career and Estates of David, Earl of Huntingdon (d. 1219) with an Edition of the Surviving Charters', (unpub. Cambridge Ph.D. thesis, 2 vols. 1971), i, 93. This should be superseded by Dr Stringer's forthcoming edition of the Senlis *acta* for the Northamptonshire Records Society.
68. K.J. Stringer, 'A Cistercian Archive: the Earliest Charters of Sawtry Abbey', *Journal of the Society of Archivists*, vi (1980), 329–30. The fiction that Malcolm IV founded Sawtry Abbey, and not Earl Simon III, was maintained even by Henry II. Cf. idem, *Earl David*, 145, and on the difficulties for the secular tenants of the honour *Regesta Regum Scottorum*, i, 100–1.
69. E.g. Earl Simon II despoiled David Olifard, a Scots adherent, of Sawtry by granting it to his Cistercian foundation there: ibid, 129. Cf. ibid, 109 for other houses endowed with sequestered tenancies and ibid, 24 for St. Frideswide's complaints about their unjust exclusion from their manor of Piddington by Earl David in 1173/4.
70. Idem, 'A Cistercian Archive', 329.
71. For discussion of Bromfield see Blair, 'Secular Minsters', 128–31.
72. His heir was also his nephew – possibly significant.
73. Lennard, *Rural England*, 396. The claim was unsuccessful because Earl Roger had provided that the prebends should be appropriated by the abbey as their holders died off.
74. If we accept that the year of King Henry's death could run until Annunciation 1136 (Henry I died 1 December 1135), this argument is not compromised by the existence of the charter of Earl Henry confirming William the canon's rights (above, n. 18). David I resigned the honour in favour of Earl Henry in February 1136.
75. Franklin, 'Identification of Minsters', 74.
76. On the confused history of the honour in the period 1135–50 see *Regesta Regum Scottorum*, i, 102–3.
77. Brit. Lib., MS Cotton Claudius D xii, f. 84r.
78. Stringer, *Earl David*, 19; idem, 'A Cistercian Archive', 329, n. 23.
79. Stringer, *Earl David*, 28, citing *Gesta Regis Henrici secundi Benedicti Abbatis*, ed. W. Stubbs (2 vols., Rolls Ser. 1867), i, 71.
80. D. Knowles, C.N.L. Brooke and V.C.M. London, *The Heads of Religious houses: England and Wales 940–1216* (Cambridge, 1972), 117.
81. '... Waltero clerico filio Willelmi sacerdotis mesuagium quod Radulphus capellanus tenuit iuxta cimiterium ecclesie de Welton ...' – Brit. Lib., MS Cotton Claudius D xii f. 86v. The rubric to the next charter in the cartulary, which is Walter's grant to Richard, is 'Carta Walteri Clerch': this evidence justifies the translation of *clericus* in this context as a surname. This charter must be sometime later because the next charter, another *actum* of Prior Alelm for Welton, is the grant of the message next to Walter Clerk's – ibid.
82. DB I, 228d.
83. This is also true of Kilsby, but this parish was originally dependent on Barby – P.R.O., C146/11014.
84. An Anglo-Saxon window was nonetheless noted by Pevsner reset in the south aisle wall of Barby church – N. Pevsner, *Northamptonshire*, revised B. Cherry (2nd edn., London, 1973), 101. Ashby St. Ledgers church allegedly formed part of the foundation of Launde priory (*Mon.Ang*. vi, 188): this pre-1123 charter is however, manifestly false (cf. Knowles & Hadcock, 163).

IX. The Churches of Canterbury Diocese in the 11th Century

Tim Tatton-Brown

Introduction

Over fifty years ago Dr. Gordon Ward pointed out, in two important articles in *Archaeologia Cantiana*,[1] that over 400 of the parish churches of Kent are mentioned in lists that date from the late 11th century.[2] He went on to suggest that the majority of these were 'Saxon foundations', and gives compelling reasons for this. At the end of the 18th century Hasted[3] records 414 parishes in Kent (282 in Canterbury diocese and 132 in Rochester diocese), and to his list one can add perhaps another two dozen other parishes and parish churches that had disappeared in the preceding three centuries.[4] By far the most important document that Ward used was the 'Domesday Monachorum' lists of Kentish churches. A fine edition of Domesday Monachorum, with a useful introduction, was published by Professor David Douglas in 1944[5] and aspects of this document have been discussed more recently by Professor Frank Barlow.[6] In this article I shall examine in more detail the lists in Domesday Monachorum, and will try to show how they fit into the later parochial map of Canterbury diocese, which covers the eastern two-thirds of the county of Kent (Fig. 22).[7] I shall also look briefly at the meagre material remains of the late Anglo-Saxon churches in the diocese, as well as the new churches of the early Norman period.

Kent is unique in having within it two dioceses which both originate in the early 7th century, though in the 11th century in particular the bishop of Rochester often acted as a suffragan to the archbishop.[8] Canterbury diocese, though very small in area, was also the richest diocese in England, as Professor Barlow has pointed out,[9] and when combined with the diocese of Winchester (as under Stigand in 1052–70) it was an immensely important power-block covering all of the rich counties of Kent, Surrey and Hampshire. It is two late 11th-century documents, *Textus Roffensis* and Domesday Monachorum, which give us the factual basis of this wealth in Kent.

Domesday Monachorum

The first folio of the document known as Domesday Monachorum (recto and verso) contains five statements about Kentish churches: (i) a list of 88 churches from each of which a payment (probably mainly for chrism) is made at Easter; (ii) a description of the contributions due from St. Augustine's Abbey; (iii) a unique list of 12 major churches with lesser churches in the surrounding area which 'pertain' to them; (iv) an account of renders from the first 14 churches in the first list (this is described as 'the old arrangement (*institutio antiqua*) before the coming of the lord Lanfranc the archbishop', as distinct from Lanfranc's 'new arrangement', the simple money payments of the first list); and (v) a list of *Romscot* or 'Peter's Pence' payments from East Kent. Dependencies of major churches in the third list generally do not appear in the first list, presumably because they received chrism from their mother churches, not direct from Canterbury.

Altogether 212 churches are named; to these can be added another previously un-named 40 churches belonging to St. Augustine's, as well as quite a large number of other chapels, a few of which were certainly in existence by 1100.[10] This brings the total to nearly 300 named churches and chapels, which compares closely with the list of parish churches and chapels[11] of the later period. In fact, the provision of Kent with parish churches was virtually complete by the end of the 11th century, and few were added until the reforms of the mid 19th century. The Tithe Maps are therefore of great importance in studying the ecclesiastical geography of the late 11th-century diocese.[12]

The lists in Domesday Monachorum are therefore of very great interest as they tell us something of the Anglo-Saxon 'minster' (multi-priest) organization of the diocese as well as how Lanfranc was replacing it with the 'modern' (single-priest) system in the 1070s and 1080s.

The Late Anglo-Saxon Diocese

The fourth list in Domesday Monachorum, that giving the *institutio antiqua* before the coming of Lanfranc, lists 14 churches from which specified amounts of honey, sheep, bread and payments for wine and oil are given. This list, which is in the same order as the first list in Domesday Monachorum,[13] can be subdivided into three main groups (by the size of render). The first and biggest group give 1 sester of honey, 8 lambs, 60 loaves,

Key

1	Boxley	73	Stalisfield	142a	Bircholt	211a	Walmerstone
2	Maidstone	74	Charing	143	Smeeth	212	Adisham
3	Bearsted	74a	Pett	144	Sellindge	213	Godnestone
4	Otham	75	Pluckley	145	Aldington	214	Nonington
5	Langley	75a	Pivington	146	Lympne	214a	Ratling
6	Loose	76	Little Chart	146a	Berwick	214b	Shingleton
7	Linton	77	Hothfield	146b	Court-at-Street	215	Womenswold
8	Boughton Monchelsea	78	Bethersden	147	Eastbridge	216	Sibertswold or Shepherdswell
9	Chart Sutton	79	Great Chart	148	Burmarsh		
10	Sutton Valence	80	Woodchurch	149	Dymchurch	217	Barfreston
11	Marden	81	Shadoxhurst	150	Orgarswick	218	Wooton
12	Staplehurst	82	Orlestone	151	Blackmanstone	219	Lydden
13	Goudhurst	83	Warehorne	152	Seasalter	220	Swingfield
14	Cranbrook	84	Kenardington	153	Whitstable	221	Woolverton
15	Hawkhurst	85	Appledore	154	Swalecliffe	222	Alkham
16	Benenden	86	Ebony	155	Blean	223	Bilchester
17	Sandhurst	87	Stone	156	Hackington	224	Hawkinge
18	Rainham	88	Snave	157	Harbledown	225	Folkstone
19	Bredhurst	89	Snargate	158	St. Dunstan Canterbury	225a	Walton
20	Detling	90	Brenzett	159	Canterbury (17 urban parishes)	226	Capel-le-Ferne
21	Thurnham	91	Fairfield			227	Poulton
21a	Leeds	92	Brookland	159a	St. Mary Northgate	228	Hougham
21b	Aldington	93	Ivychurch	160	St. Martin Canterbury	229	Birchington
22	Broomfield	94	New Romney, St. Martin, St. Lawrence, and St. Nicholas	161	St. Paul Canterbury	230	Acol
23	East Sutton			162	St. Sepulchre	231	St. John-the-Baptist (Margate)
24	Headcorn			163	Thanington		
25	Frittenden	95	Old Romney	164	Milton	232	St. Peter-in-Thanet (Broadstairs)
26	Biddenden	96	Midley	165	Nackington		
27	Rolvenden	97	Broomhill	166	Petham	233	St. Lawrence-in-Thanet (Ramsgate)
28	Newenden	98	Lydd	166a	Swarling		
29	Upchurch	99	Luddenham	167	Lower Hardres	234	Minster-in-Thanet
30	Hartlip	100	Oare	168	Upper Hardres	235	Ash
31	Stockbury	101	Buckland	169	Waltham	236	Fleet
32	Hucking	102	Stone	170	Stelling	237	Stonar
33	Hollingbourne	103	Davington	171	Elmsted	238	St. Mary Sandwich
34	Harrietsham	104	Preston	172	Stowting	239	St. Peter Sandwich
35	Ulcombe	105	Faversham	173	Lyminge	240	St. Clement Sandwich
36	Boughton Malherbe	106	Norton	174	Monk's Horton	241	Staple
37	Smarden	107	Ospringe	175	Postling	242	Woodnesborough
38	High Halden	108	Throwley	176	Stanford	243	Worth
39	Tenterden	108a	Leaveland	177	Saltwood	244	Chillenden
40	Wittersham	109	Sheldwich	178	West Hythe	245	Knowlton
41	Lower Halstow	110	Selling	179	Hythe	246	Eastry
42	Newington	111	Badlesmere	180	Herne	247	Ham
43	Borden	112	Westwell	181	Hoath	248	Betteshanger
44	Bredgar	113	Challock	182	Sturry	249	Northbourne
44a	Bicknor	114	Molash	183	Westbere	250	Sholden
45	Wormshill	115	Eastwell	184	Fordwich	251	Deal
46	Frinsted	116	Boughton Alulph	185	Stodmarsh	252	Great Mongeham
47	Lenham	116a	Wilmington	186	Littlebourne	253	Tilmanstone
47a	Rayton	117	Kennington	186a	Garrington	254	Eythorne
48	Egerton	118	Ashford	187	Well	255	Waldershare
49	Iwade	119	Willesborough	188	Bekesbourne	256	Little Mongeham
50	Bobbing	120	Hinxhill	189	Patrixbourne	257	Sutton
51	Milton	121	Sevington	190	Bridge	258	Ripple
52	Tunstall	122	Kingsnorth	191	Bishopsbourne	259	Walmer
53	Sittingbourne	123	Mersham	192	Kingston	260	Ringwould
54	Murston	124	Ruckinge	193	Barham	261	West Langdon
55	Bapchild	125	Bilsington	194	Elham	262	East Langdon
56	Rodmersham	126	Bonnington	195	Denton	263	Oxney
57	Tonge	127	Newchurch	196	Acrise	264	Coldred
58	Kingsdown	128	St. Mary-in-the-Marsh	197	Paddlesworth	265	Beusfield (Whitfield)
59	Milsted	129	Hope	198	Newington	266	Guston
60	Wychling	130	Graveney	199	Beachborough and Asholt	267	West Cliffe
61	Minster-in-Sheppey	131	Hernehill	200	Cheriton	268	St. Margaret's-at-Cliffe
62	Elmley	132	Boughton-under-Blean	201	Reculver	269	Ewell
63	Eastchurch	133	Dunkirk (extra-parochial)	202	Chislet	271	River
64	Warden	134	Chilham	203	St. Nicholas at Wade	272	Buckland
65	Leysdown	135	Chartham	204	Sarre	273	Charlton
66	Harty	136	Godmersham	205	Monkton	274	St. Martin (with St. Nicholas and St. John), St. Peter, St. Mary, St. James, Dover
67	Teynham	137	Tremworth	206	Wickhambreux		
68	Lynsted	138	Crundale	207	Stourmouth		
69	Doddington	139	Wye	208	Preston		
70	Newnham	140	Brook	209	Elmstone	275	St. Mary-de-Castro, Dover
71	Eastling	141	Hastingleigh	210	Ickham		
72	Otterden	142	Brabourne	211	Wingham		

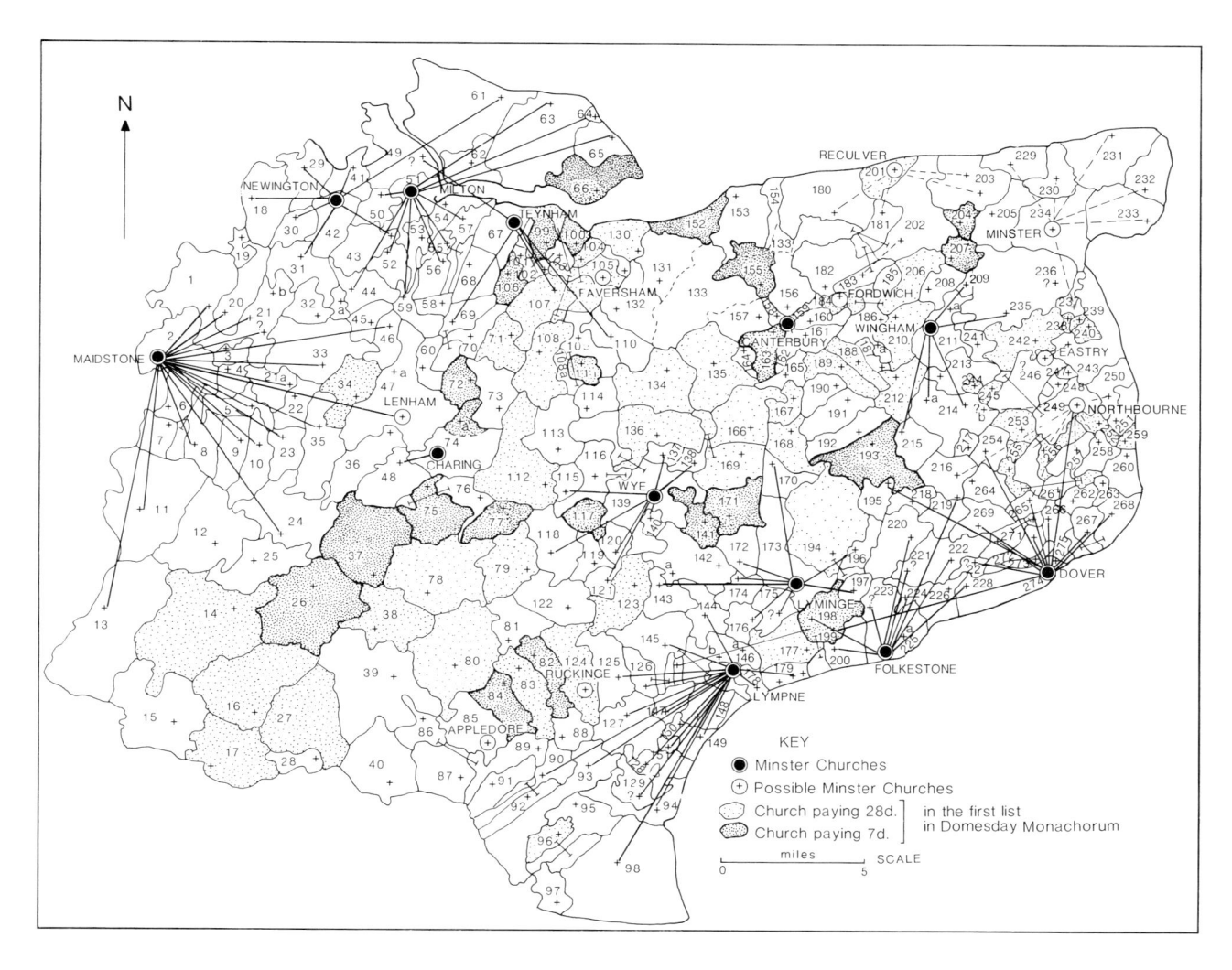

Fig. 22 Mother and daughter churches in E. Kent. See opposite page for key.

12d. for wine and 14d. for oil. These are from the churches of Milton (Regis),[14] Maidstone, Charing, Wye, Teynham, Wingham and Eastry. In the 'first list' (i.e. the changes to money payments brought about by Lanfranc), the payments are for 10s. less 4d., except Teynham and Wingham which only pay 2s. The second group, which render 1 sester of honey, 30 loaves, 2 sheep (or wethers) and 7d. for oil, are the churches of Lyminge, Appledore, Dover and Folkestone.[15] The latter two also render 600 pence, which is reflected roughly in the 'first list' payments of 55 and 50 shillings respectively.[16] Finally there are the two Boughtons and Ruckinge, which only render 4 lambs, 30 loaves and 13d. These three churches are clearly smaller than the others, and unfortunately there are four Boughton parishes in the diocese: Monchelsea and Malherbe near Maidstone, and Aluph and Boughton-under-Blean to the east. It is possibly the latter two which are meant.

Turning now to the list of 12 great churches with lesser churches pertaining to them (the 'third list'), many prove to be the same as those in the fourth list. These are named as St. Martin of Dover, Folkestone, 'Limen', Lyminge, Milton (Regis), Newington, Teynham, Wingham, Maidstone, Wye, Charing, and an unspecified church, which may be Eastry.[17] The new names added here are Newington (in the north-west corner of the diocese) and 'Limen', which must be Lympne and is almost certainly a new site on top of the cliff above the decayed late Anglo-Saxon seaport of 'Limen'.[18] This new site, which had a castle and church side-by-side, was given to the first Norman archdeacon of Canterbury (probably Ansketil) by Lanfranc. The large Norman parish church here, which is very close to a possible Norman tower,[19] is almost certainly a new church of the post-Conquest period. It is also possible that Lympne replaced Appledore as the 'old minster' church in the immediate post-Conquest period. With the added exception of Newington, which may originally have been part of Milton (Regis), we are left with ten certain 'old minster' churches in the diocese, as well as, of course, the Cathedral and St. Augustine's in Canterbury. These are:

Milton	Wingham
Maidstone	Eastry
Charing	Lyminge
Wye	Dover
Teynham	Folkestone

All of these were situated on ancient royal vills, although by the early 11th century several had been given to the archbishop and his community at Holy Trinity (Christ Church): Maidstone, Wingham and Eastry by the mid 8th century, and Charing and Teynham before *c.* 900.[20] Lyminge, Dover and Folkestone were very ancient double monasteries founded in the 630s, and though the monastic communities had almost certainly been destroyed at all of them by the Vikings in the 9th century, groups of priests still survived at Folkestone and Dover until the 11th.[21] Lyminge (as well as Reculver, another 7th-century monestery) came to the archbishop in the 10th century. Finally Milton (and Newington) were given to St. Augustine's Abbey, and Wye to Battle Abbey, by William the Conqueror.

The late Anglo-Saxon diocese was therefore made up of a series of head minsters with lesser churches attached to them, and it is only thanks to the third list in Domesday Monachorum that we know which of these lesser churches was attached to which head minster. For Maidstone, for example, they are: Boxley, Detling, Thurnham, Aldington (in Thurnham), Hollingbourne, 'Welcumeweg' (unidentified, possibly East Sutton), Lenham, Boughton (either Malherbe or Monchelsea), Ulcomb, Leeds, Langley, Sutton (Valence), Chart (Sutton), Headcorn, Frinsted, Goudhurst and Marden. The list is in roughly clockwise order (north, east, south: to the west is Rochester diocese), and all the churches lie around Maidstone. Of the later parishes in the area, only a few are missing (Bearsted, Otham, Hucking, Wormshill, Broomsfield, Loose and Staplehurst), and it is very likely that all of these parishes except Staplehurst (which still has a unique 11th-century door) were cut out of the parishes mentioned in the Domesday Monachorum later in the 12th century. They are all very small, and the topography of the parishes suggests that they are secondary.[22]

For Milton Regis and Newington, however, we have independent confirmation of the attached churches in the 'White Book of St. Augustine',[23] which also adds four churches missing from Domesday Monachorum: Murston and Sittingbourne, which were clearly originally part of Milton itself, and Bicknor, a small parish cut out of Bredgar. Elmley, the final addition, is described as 'a very small island', which it still is. It only pays 3½*d.* (all the rest pay 7*d.* for their chrism). Milton's churches in Domesday Monachorum are: 'Northcip' (Warden?) and Leysdown in Sheppey, Rodmersham, Milsted, Tunstall, Bapchild, Bredgar, Bobbing, Tonge, and Eastchurch in Sheppey, and together with the four mentioned above,[24] they make up a compact interlocking group of parishes. The churches under Newington in both Domesday Monachorum and the 'White Book' are: Hartlip, Rainham, Upchurch, Stockbury, (Lower) Halstow, Sexburgaminster (Minster-in-Sheppey, the 7th-century double monastery) and 'Niwecyrce' (Borden).[25] All these parishes make up another compact block,[26] and together with the parishes attached to Milton make up the ancient royal demesne (and later hundred) of Middleton.

The small group of churches attached to Teynham, immediately to the east, are Doddington, Stone, Selling and 'Aetwangeraede' (?Iwade). Here the situation is very different, and the next large royal demesne to the east, based on Faversham, appears to have been broken up by the very beginning of the 9th century.[27] Teynham and other detached estates (totalling 30 hides) went to the archbishop in 798, and it is presumably at this time that Teynham became a new 'head minster'. It is of interest to note that close to the large parish church of St. Mary at Faversham is a second parish church of Preston, the only other church 'within' Faversham itself. Like Faversham, Preston has at least two other detached portions of its parish 'without'. The subdivision here must also date from the early 9th century,[28] and the name Preston presumably comes from the priests attached to the head minster of Faversham.

A perhaps more recent (i.e. mainly 11th-century) group of churches are those listed as pertaining to 'Limen'. These are 'Laurentiuscirce' and 'Martin Ecclesia' (presumably the churches with those dedications in New Romney), Ivychurch, 'Bennedecirce' (perhaps Brenzett), Lydd, 'Siwold's circe', Newchurch, '2 churches in Hythe', 'Aelsiescirce' (Eastbridge), 'Blacemannescirce' (Blackmanstone), 'Mertumnescirce' (?Hope All Saints), 'Demancirce' (Dymchurch), 'Ordgarescirce' (Orgarswick), Bilsington, Bonnington, Aldington, 'Straeta' (the chapel at Court-at-Street near Lympne), Sellindge, 'Kingestun' (?Kingsnorth), 'Undetun', and 'Swirgildancirce'. Here many of the parishes have taken their names from the individual owners (and probably builders) of the churches. Two of them, Eastbridge (Aelsiescirce) and Blackmanstone, are clearly named after their owners in 1066, Aelfsige and Blaceman (T.R.E. in Domesday Book), and it is very likely that many of the churches in Romney Marsh proper (i.e. Newchurch, Eastbridge, Burmarsh, Orgarswick, Blackmanstone, St. Mary, Ivychurch, Brenzett, Snargate and Snave) are on land only reclaimed from the marsh in the 10th century.[29] South-west of the later Rhee 'wall', the land was perhaps only reclaimed from the late 11th century, hence the long thin strips of the parishes of Ivychurch and Brenzett, and the fact that the 'new' parishes there (Brookland and Fairfield) are not mentioned in the early lists. Lydd and Broomhill are, however, situated on the Dungeness shingle, which is documented (as Denge Marsh) from at least the 8th century.[30] Midley (i.e. the Middle Island), which is mentioned in the first Domesday Monachorum list, was perhaps also a new church in the mid 11th century. One other church nearby (St. Clement's, Old Romney) can also perhaps be dated by its dedication to the time of Cnut in the early 11th century.[31] Domesday Monachorum does not distinguish between the two Romneys, but dedications to St. Clement are, in Kent, usually only connected with urban centres (there are also churches with this dedication at Sandwich and Rochester which are also perhaps early 11th-century in origin).

Similar reasonably compact groups of churches are found attached to the head minsters of Dover, Folkestone and Lyminge, though quite a few of the names of the churches are obscure and a few of the churches are a long way off in the Weald (for example, Wittersham and perhaps St. Peter's Newenden, attached to Lyminge). Dover also has the odd entry of 5 *monasteria* within the *civitas*. These must be the five parish churches in the town, St. Mary, St. Peter, St. James, St. Martin, St. Nicholas and St. John, the last three of which were under the one roof of St. Martin-le-Grand after the Conquest (see below).

The churches attached to Wingham, ?Eastry, Wye and Charing are only a small number of the churches in the neighbourhood. In this great swathe of the diocese (running north-east to south-west), many of the later parishes are larger, and most of them are '28*d*. churches' mentioned in the 'first list' in Domesday Monachorum. These latter parishes range from the very large Wealden parishes (like Cranbrook, Beneden, Rolvenden, Woodchurch, High Halden and Bethersden) to the fairly large and certainly more ancient parishes, like Chilham, Chartham, Elham, Adisham, Woodnesborough and Wickham(breux) in East Kent, as well as many of the parishes cut out of the ancient royal demesne of Faversham mentioned above. Many of these churches must also have been attached to head minsters originally, i.e. to Wingham, Eastry, Wye and Charing, as well as perhaps Faversham; but by Lanfranc's time, and probably much earlier, they had become separate single-priest churches. This was perhaps partly because of the disruptions of the Viking invasions, and partly because of the proximity and control of Canterbury (in the sense that their 'head minster' was Canterbury Cathedral itself without an intermediate church).

Finally, there are the pre-Conquest churches belonging to St. Augustine's. Here again the White Book lists adds at least one other 'head minster' church, not yet mentioned. This is the church of Northbourne (near Eastry) which had as subordinate churches paying 7*d*. chrism fees: (Little) Mongeham, Sutton, Sholden, Sibertswold, Beusfield, Langdon, Shingleton and 'the chapel of Ripple'. There is also a cryptic reference in the White Book after Fordwich: 'but there are certain churches among these which pay chrism pence to the church of Our Saviour [i.e. the Cathedral] every year, but how this happens unless by our negligence is not known. These are the churches of Lenham, Fordwich, Faversham, Milton and Newington, and perhaps there are others'.[32] There is at least the suggestion here that Lenham (though later attached to Maidstone), Fordwich and Faversham were also ancient minster churches. The White Book, and much later St. Augustine's documentary evidence, also suggest that the former monastery of Minster-in-Thanet (given to St. Augustine's by Cnut in 1027) was also a 'head minster', with its attached chapels of St. Peter (Broadstairs), St. John-the-Baptist (Margate), St. Laurence (Ramsgate) and St. Nicholas at Stonar surviving as chapels into the later medieval period. It is also worth recording that the ancient monastery of Reculver, which passed to the archbishop in the 10th century, also had four chapels attached to it (Herne,[33] Hoath, St. Nicholas-at-Wade and Shuart) which did not acquire parochial status until the early 14th century.

The 'old minsters' of Anglo-Saxon Kent can therefore perhaps be listed as Milton, Maidstone, Charing, Wye, Teynham, Wingham, Eastry, Lyminge, Dover and Folkestone. To this can be added the perhaps 'late' old minster of Newington, and the churches of Northbourne, Minster-in-Thanet, Faversham and Reculver, as well as just possibly Fordwich, Lenham, Appledore, Ruckinge and the two Boughtons.[34] It is of great interest to see how many of these places were 7th-century royal vills, and that five out of the six old Kentish monasteries in the diocese were also probably 'head minsters' in the earlier arrangement. Only Minster-in-Sheppey (or Sexburgaminster, as it is called in Domesday Monachorum) is apparently downgraded in status later. This is possibly because Minster-in-Sheppey was always secondary to the great royal vill at Milton.

Anglo-Saxon Church Building in the Diocese

Apart from the Cathedral itself and St. Augustine's Abbey, Dr. Harold Taylor lists 23 possible Anglo-Saxon churches with surviving material remains in Canterbury diocese.[35] Of these, six churches have no real evidence to put them before the Conquest,[36] but three others can perhaps be added: Faversham, Preston-near-Wingham and Wormshill. It is also proposed to omit further discussion of Lydd, which is more likely to be Roman than Anglo-Saxon. One is therefore left with 19 churches,[37] which can be summarized as follows:

Aldington — Saxo-Norman north wall of nave and chancel.

Cheriton — Pre-Conquest west wall of nave with double-splayed window.

Canterbury (St. Martin) — 7th-century nave with earlier western part of chancel.

Canterbury (St. Mildred) — Late Saxon south and west walls of nave, and part of chancel south wall.

Dover (*St. Mary-de-Castro*) — Large cruciform church (*c*. early 11th century).
Faversham — Late Saxon west end of nave.
Lower Halstow — Late Saxon chancel with windows made of re-used Roman bricks.
Kingston — Saxo-Norman nave and western part of chancel.
Leeds — Pre-Conquest north wall of nave.
Lyminge — Remains of Anglo-Saxon church(es), with rebuilding of *c*. 1085.
Milton Regis — North wall of nave and chancel of large Anglo-Saxon church.
Minster-in-Sheppey — North wall of ?7th-century church.
Preston (Near Wingham) — Late Saxon west wall of nave and ?base of tower.
Reculver — Ruins of 7th-century church.
Richborough (in Ash parish) — Remains of Late Saxon chapel of St. Augustine.
Stone-by-Faversham — ?Early western part of chancel.
Stourmouth — Late Saxon north-west part of nave with double-splayed window.
Whitfield — Late Saxon nave and chancel remains with double-splayed window.
Wormshill — Late Saxon nave with double-splayed window in south wall.

By far the most important and impressive of these churches is St. Mary-de-Castro at Dover Castle, which, although heavily restored in 1860–2 by Sir George Gilbert Scott, is still one of the largest later Anglo-Saxon churches in England. It has been fully described by Dr. Taylor,[38] but no real attempt has been made to find a historical context for it. Much later historical sources[39] say that St. Martin's in Dover was founded 'in the castle' for 22 canons with prebends that were subject only to the King and Rome, and that this happened in the 630s. It was said to have been refounded by King Wihtred at the very end of the century and moved into the town. Wihtred confirmed St. Martin's prebends, possessions and liberties 'with a moiety of the toll of the port'. The early monastery was almost certainly founded inside the Roman Saxon shore fort[40] in the town (the only 'castle' in the 7th century), and attached to this fort on the west was a large trading settlement called the 'wic' (Wyke in the 16th century). The monastery (and its Abbots) are then documented[41] until the end of the 9th century when it was presumably destroyed by the Vikings. Nothing further is heard of the community until between 1017/20 and 1066 'Leofwine the priest and all the brotherhood at Dover' are mentioned in several charters,[42] and this community of canons and their prebends is well documented in the first folios of Domesday Book.[43] It seems highly likely that Leofwine and his canons were a refoundation of the early 11th century, and that the magnificent new church on the top of the hill inside the *burh* was built for them by Æthelred or Cnut, or just possibly by Earl Godwin himself who is known to have been involved later with Leofwine.[44] This hilltop stronghold (a late Anglo-Saxon *burh*) was of great importance to Earl Godwin, and some writers have suggested that it was a proto-'Norman' castle. It was certainly mentioned in 1051 and 1064–6, and in October 1066 William the Conqueror 'spent eight days in adding to it those fortifications which it lacked'. It was probably at this time, when the English were forced to evacuate their houses,[45] that the canons too were told that they would have to find a new site in the town (which was burnt in 1066). The result was the magnificent new Norman church of St. Martin-le-Grand. St. Mary-de-Castro is therefore likely to have been the original 'minster' church in Domesday Monachorum, and only after the arrival of Lanfranc in 1070 did it become 'St. Martin of Dover'.[46]

Of the other documented 'old minsters' of Kent, the remains of only two can with any certainty be ascribed to the pre-Conquest period. These are Milton Regis and Lyminge. Milton Regis is another large church which has very tall nave and chancel walls, and though no early windows or doors are visible, the north wall of the nave is made of distinctive unknapped large flints and Roman bricks, some laid herringbone.[47] It is also possible that Milton may originally have been a cruciform church, like Dover. Vestiges of a south transept (rebuilt in the 13th century) still survive.

Lyminge is another church that has been much discussed since the excavations there in 1874,[48] and it has been suggested that the present parish church of St. Mary and St. Ethelburga is the church rebuilt by St. Dunstan in *c*. 965 'for parochial needs' according to Goscelin (the nunnery of *c*. 633 had been destroyed by the Vikings in the 9th century). The nave and chancel of the present church, however, contain much Quarr stone in the quoins and elsewhere,[49] and the present writer feels that much of the fabric dates from the early Norman period, possibly *c*. 1085 when Lanfranc is known to have translated the relics of St. Ethelburga to St. Gregory's Priory in Canterbury. Nevertheless, some fragments of the lower south walls of the church do appear to be earlier, and may be part of St. Dunstan's rebuilding of the 'old minster' in the 10th century. Only re-excavation, however, will answer these points.

Of the other minster churches in Kent, much less survives. One, that at Maidstone, was completely rebuilt *c*. 1395 by Archbishop Courtenay for his college (the dedication was also changed from St. Mary to All Saints).[50] The parish churches at Folkestone (St. Mary and St. Eanswith), Teynham (St. Mary). Wingham (St. Mary), Eastry (St. Mary), Northbourne (St. Augustine), Faversham (St. Mary) and Minster-in-Thanet (St. Mary) all contain a basic core that is at least 12th-century in date, and it is noticeable how virtually all of them are dedicated to St. Mary and are cruciform in plan.[51] Perhaps the most remarkable plan, however, is that at Teynham parish church.[52] Here the earliest visible parts of the church date from the early Norman period; by the end of the 12th century at the latest, the church had two very long transepts (each with four spaced-out lancets in its east wall) and a long chancel (which contains some herringbone work in the north wall). The lancets in the transepts appear in places to be insertions, and it is not impossible that the long transepts actually date from the 11th century. The church was, however, an important building in the 12th century (the palace in which Archbishop Hubert Walter died in 1205 was immediately adjacent to the church on the south), and it is in equally possible that the transepts result from a 12th-century enlargement.[53]

Faversham church is another very large cruciform church, although sadly the central tower fell in 1755, revealing many reused Roman bricks.[54] The nave was completely rebuilt by George Dance senior in 1754–5, but at the west end are still the remains, in the north and south walls, of two large Romanesque arches with blocked clerestory windows above with their heads turned in Roman brick. A detailed examination of the fabric here is needed (preferably during restoration), but it is possible that this is all part of a very large late Anglo-Saxon aisled church.[55]

Of the lesser Anglo-Saxon churches in the diocese, little further will be said here, although as listed above at least a dozen churches have probable surviving remains above ground of pre-Conquest masonry. Most of the new churches and chapels of the later Anglo-Saxon period, however, are likely to have been of timber, and it is only after the arrival of Lanfranc as Archbishop that many of there 'private' churches were rebuilt in stone as parish churches.

The Early Norman Period

By the 12th century virtually every parish church in the diocese, as well as many other manorial chapels, had been built,[56] and by c. 1180 many of them were large aisled churches. This colossal programme of building and rebuilding started soon after Lanfranc's arrival in 1070, and very many of the parish churches in the diocese still exhibit early Norman features. Most striking of all, perhaps, is the use of Caen stone from Normandy, and to a lesser extent Quarr stone from the Isle of Wight, which is first imported in c. 1070. Quarr stone is no longer used after about 1120,[57] and is therefore a very useful tool for dating early churches of the Norman period.[58] Quarr and Caen are both used in large quantities for the new Cathedral and Priory and at St. Augustine's in Canterbury, as well as at St. Martin-le-Grand, Dover, but perhaps the finest surviving late 11th-century parish church in Kent using Quarr stone is that at Brook, near Ashford.[59] This church, which was built just before the end of the 11th century on an estate belonging to the Cathedral Priory, is remarkably well-preserved (it was hardly touched in the later medieval period). It has the fairly common plan of tower, nave and chancel, though the tower here is particularly massive (a miniature keep) and contains an upper chapel. Many other churches contain early Norman elements, and the commonest early Norman plan is just a simple two-celled structure with the rectangular chancel stepping in from the nave. A good example of this is the small parish church of St. Pancras Coldred (near Dover), which is situated inside the outer bailey of a probably contemporary motte-and-bailey castle. In the nearby parish of Sutton (originally another chapel attached to Northbourne) can be seen a slightly larger version of this with an apse on the end of the chancel.[60] The chapel of St. Leonard at Iffin manor, which was also perhaps built in the late 11th century and never became parochial, has the simplest plan of all, a plain rectangle.[61]

The 'first list' in Domesday Monachorum names about fifty churches paying 28*d*. at Easter. These must be the 'standard' local churches of the late 11th century, and at many of them there still survive the remains of the standard two-celled building, although most of them are larger than the examples mentioned above. An abnormal case here is the church at Godmersham, which has the usual nave and chancel but a north tower with an eastern apse attached to it. These churches are followed in the list by a further twenty or so which pay 7*d*. Most of these are still parish churches, but some were chapels which never reached full parochial status.

In the late 11th-century diocese of Canterbury we therefore have four main types of church:

(a) the great churches: the Cathedral, St. Augustine's Abbey, St. Gregory's Priory (Canterbury) and St. Martin-le-Grand (Dover).
(b) the old minsters, soon to become ordinary parish churches.
(c) the 'ordinary' churches, each paying 28*d*. at Easter.
(d) the chapels or 'field churches', each paying 7*d*., about half of which later acquire parochial status.

After Lanfranc's reforms few other major changes occurred in the parochial system, so that many anomalies persisted to the Reformation. St. Martin-le-Grand in Dover, for example, still had an 'archpriest' and two other priests serving three parochial altars under one roof until 1536.[62] Equally, quite a large number of detached manorial chapels survived to the Reformation, some of them even being allowed 'to celebrate all divine offices there except burial'.[63] The 11th century is therefore the critical period for the evolution of the parochial system in this diocese, which, with its exceptional documentation, has a special importance for any study of the origins of the parochial system in England.

112   *Tim Tatton-Brown*

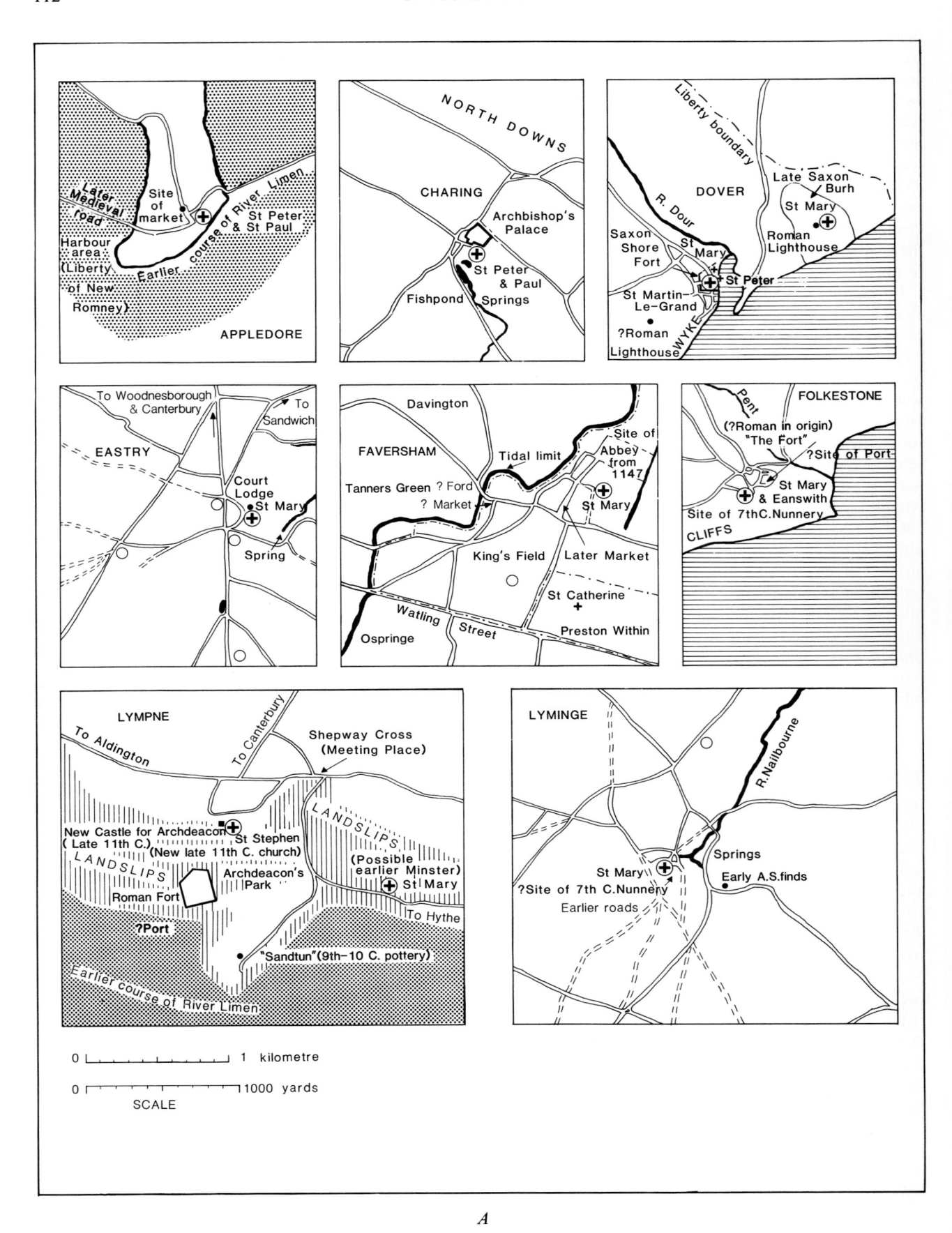

A

Fig. 23 The topographical setting of E. Kent minsters: A: Appledore to Lyminge; B: Maidstone to Wye.

The Churches of Canterbury Diocese

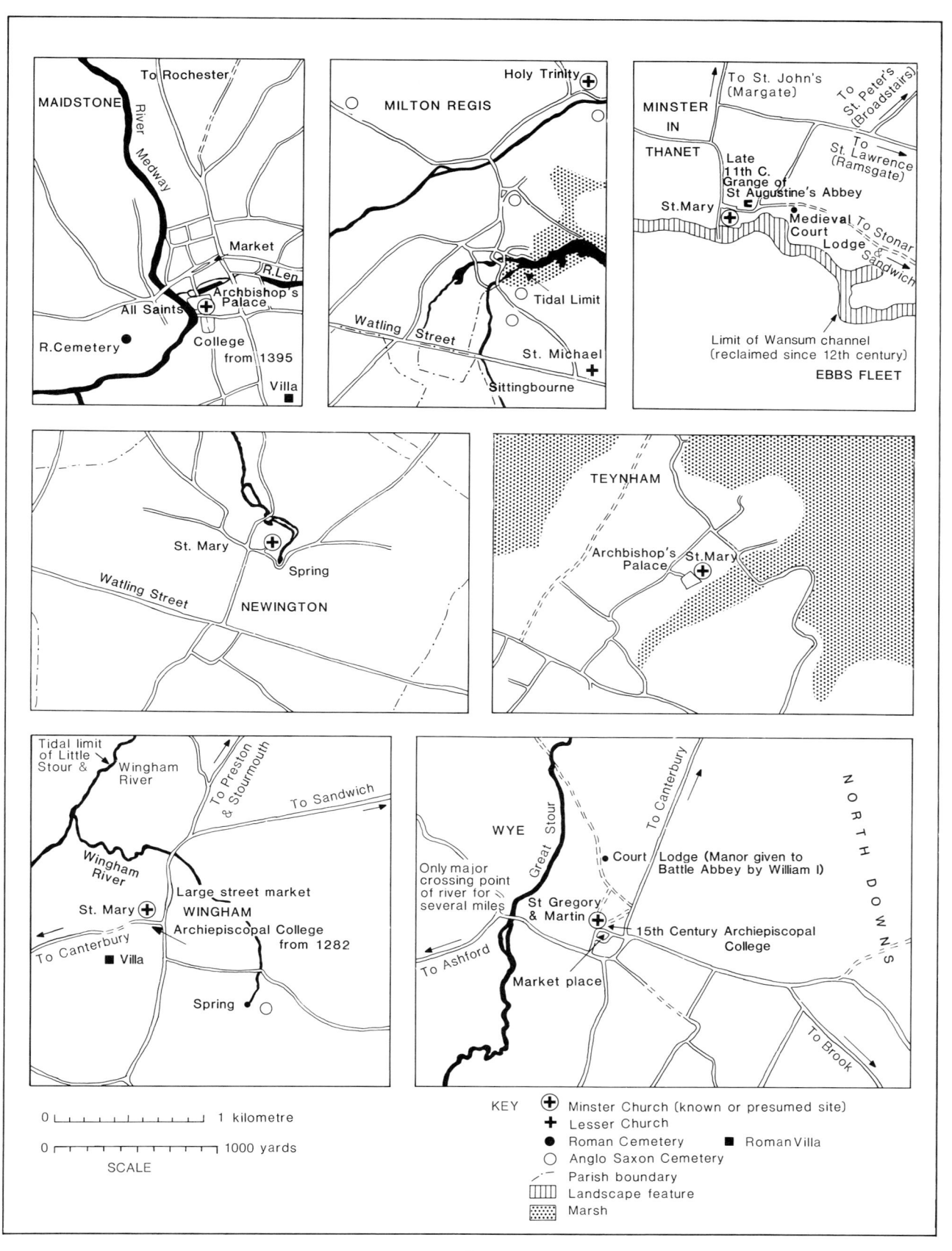

B

Appendix:
The 'Domesday Monachorum' and 'White Book of St. Augustine's, Church Lists

The numbers in brackets, after each entry, refer to the numbers on the map.

Domesday Monachorum [f.1, r–v]

I. These are the customs (*consuetudines*) of the archbishop at Easter from priests (*presbyteri*) and churches:

1. MIDDELTUNE (Milton Regis) 10s. less 4d. (5)
2. MÆGDESTANE (Maidstone) 10s. less 4d. (2)
3. CYRRINGE (Charing) 10s. less 4d. (74)
4. WY (Wye) the same. (139)
5. TÆNHAM (Teynham) 2s. (67)
6. WINGEHAM (Wingham) 2s. (211)
7. EASTREGE (Eastry) 10s. less 4d. (246)
8. LIMMINGES (Lyminge) 32d. (173)
9. APELDRE (Appledore) 7s. (85)
10. DOFORIS (Dover- ?St. Martin-le-Grand) 55s. (274)
11. FOLCESTANE (Folkestone) 50s. (225)
12. BOCTUNE (Boughton?Monchelsea) 28d. (8)
13. Other BOCTUNE (Boughton?Aluph) 28d. (116)
14. RUMENEA (Romney ?New) 32d. (94)
15. ROKYNGES (Ruckinge) 28d. (124)
16. SANDHYRSTE (Sandhurst) 28d. (17)
17. RULUINDÆNNE (Rolvenden) 28d. (27)
18. WNDECYRCE (Woodchurch) 28d. (80)
19. BINNIGDÆNNE (Benenden) 28d. (16)
20. SEALTWUDE (Saltwood) 28d. (177)
21. WODNESBEORGE (Woodnesborough) 28d. (242)
22. IEOCHAM (Ickham) 28d. (210)
23. BISCOPESTUNE (?Reculver) 28d. (201)
24. WELLE (Westwell) 28d. (112)
25. GRAUENEA (Graveney) 28d. (130)
26. BEREWIC (Berwick ??near Lympne) 28d. (146a)
27. PRESTENTUNE (Preston-next-Faversham) 28d. (104)
28. OSPRINGE (Ospringe) 28d. (107)
29. FÆURESHAM (Faversham) 28d. (105)
30. WICHAM (Wickhambreaux) 28d. (206)
31. CERTEHAM (Chartham) 28d. (135)
32. GODMÆRESHAM (Godmersham) 28d. (136)
33. CILLEHAM (Chilham) 28d. (134)
34. MUNDINGHAM (Great Mongeham) 28d. (252)
35. MERSEHAM (Mersham) 28d. (123)
36. CNOLTUNE (Knowlton) 28d. (245)
37. SANDWIC (Sandwich-?St. Mary) 28d. (238)
38. BURNA (?Bekesbourne) 28d. (188)
39. BURNA (?Patrixbourne) 28d. (189)
40. BRADEBURNA (Brabourne) 28d. (142)
41. CRANEBROCA (Cranbrook) 28d. (14)
42. WEALEMERE (Walmer) 28d. (259)
43. COLREDAN (Coldred) 28d. (264)
44. MIDDELEA (Midley) 28d. (96)
45. FORDWIC (Fordwich) 28d. (184)
46. WERHORNA (Warehorne) 28d. (83)
47. WEALDWARESCARE (Waldershare) 28d. (255)
48. CYLLINDÆNNE (Chillenden) 28d. (244)
49. TRULEGE (Throwley) 28d. (108)
50. ÆSLINGE (Eastling) 28d. (71)
51. ÆLHAM (Elham) 28d. (194)
52. HARDAN (Hardres, ?Upper or Lower) 28d. (167 or 168)
53. [A]DESHAM (Adisham) 28d. (212)
54. TILEMANNESTUNE (Tilmanstone) 28d. (253)
55. SMIÐATUNE (?Shingleton in Nonington) 28d. (214b)
56. HYRUUERÐESTUN (??Harrietsham) 28d. (34)
57. CERT (?Great Chart) 28d. (79)
58. BÆDERICESDÆNNE (Bethersden) 28d. (78)
59. HADMWOLDUNGDENNE (High Halden) 28d. (38)
60. WEALTHAM et PYTHAM (Waltham + Petham) 28d. (169 and 166)
61. RUMENEA (Romney?, Old, St. Clement) 31d. (95)
62. HAÐFELDE (Hothfield) 10d. (77)
63. PLUCELEA (Pluckley) 10d. (75)
64. NIWANTUNE (Newington by ?Sittingbourne or by ?Hythe) 7d. (42 or 198)
65. KYNIGTUNE (Kennington) 7d. (117)
66. SYRRAN (Sarre) 7d. (204)
67. HEORTEGE (Harty) 7d. (66)
68. BIDINDÆNNE (Biddenden) 7d. (26)
69. STURMUDE (Stourmouth) 7d. (207)
70. RÆTTE (??Richborough) 7d. (236)
71. SÆSEALTRE (Seasalter) 7d. (152)
72. BÆÐDESMERE (Badlesmere) 7d. (111)
73. HAMME (Ham) 7d. (247)
74. BEREHAM (Barham) 7d. (193)
75. OTTRINDÆNNE (Otterden) 7d. (72)
76. PYTTE (?Pett chapel Charing) 3d. (?7d.) (74a)
77. DENENTUNE (Thanington) 7d. (163)
78. LUDDENHAM (Luddenham) 7d. (99)
79. ORAN (Oare) 7d. (100)
80. PIUINGTUNE (Pivington, St. Mary in Pluckley) 7d. (75a)
81. BLEAN (Blean) 12d. (?7d.) (155)
82. NORÐTUNE (Norton) 7d. (106)
83. KYNARDINGTUNE (Kenardington) 12d. (?7d.) (84)
84. ELMESTEDE (Elmsted) 12d. (?7d.) (171)
85. EARDLANESTUNE (Orlestone) 7d. (82)
86. HÆSTINGELEGE (Hastingleigh) 12d. (?7d.) (141)
87. SINEREDÆNNE (Smarden) 7d. (37)

II. These are what are owed every year from St. Augustine to Christ Church. The sacristan of St. Augustine is to place seven pennies on the altar of Christ or shall give them into the hand of the sacristan of Christ Church. The abbot or he who shall be in the place of the abbot, by suitable servants, must send to Christ Church 30 loaves such that four are always worth one penny, and two of the best sheep, and three full amphoras, two of mead and the third of ale, and 600 pence. All these should be paid on Holy Thursday (*in cena domini*).

III. *These churches pertain to ST. MARTIN of DOFORIS [DOVER]:*

SAINT PETER'S (?Whitfield) (265)
SAINT MARY'S (?Poulton) (227)
Within the *civitas*, five *monasteria* (274)
CEORLETUN (Charlton) (273)
DENETUN (Denton) (195)
NIWANTUN (Newington, ?by Hythe or ??near Dover) (198)
ÆWELLAN 2 churches (?Temple Ewell + ?River) (269 and 271)
ITUN (Eythorne) (254)
ÆWELLAN (?Buckland) (272)
WALTUN (Walton – near Folkestone) (225a)
CLIUE (West Cliffe) (267)
BURNAN (?Northbourne) (249)
CLIUE (St. Margaret's-at-Cliffe) (268)
GUTIESTUN (Guston) (266)

To FOLCESTAN [FOLKESTONE] pertain:

AWOLUESCYRCE (??Hawkinge) Aethelwulf's church (224)
BILICEAN (??Beachborough in Newington or Bilchester in Hawkinge) (199 or 223)

CIRICETUN (Cheriton) (200)
SUMAFELD (Swingfield) (220)
EALHHAM (Alkham) (222)
FLEOTA (Fleet ?in Ash) (236)
HUHCHAM (Hougham) (228)
ACHALT (??Ashill, Folkestone or Asholt near Newington by Hythe) (199)
HLEODÆNA (Lydden) (219)
WULFERESTUN (?Woolverton in Alkham) (221)

To LIMENA [LYMPNE]:

LAURENTIUSCIRCE (St. Lawrence, New Romney) (94)
MARTINI ECCLESIA (St. Martin, New Romney) (94)
IUECIRCE (Ivychurch) (93)
BENNEDECIRC(E) (?Brenzett) (90)
HLIDE (Lydd) (98)
SIWOLDESCIRC(E) (?Siwold's church ?St. Mary-in-the-Marsh) (128)
NIWANCIRC(E) (Newchurch) (127)
In HYÐE 2 churches (?St. Mary, W. Hythe, and another) (178 and 179)
ÆLSIESCIRC(E) (Eastbridge) (147)
BLACEMANNESC(IRCE) (Blackmanstone) (151)
MERTUMNESC(IRCE) (??Hope All Saints) (129)
DEMANC(IRCE) (Dymchurch) (149)
ORDGARESC(IRCE) (Orgarswick) (150)
BILSWIÐETUN (Bilsington) (125)
BUNINGTON (Bonnington) (126)
EALDITUN (Aldington) (145)
STRÆTA (?Chapel at Court at Street) (146b)
SELLINGE (Sellindge) (144)
KYNGESTUN (??Kingsnorth) (122)
VNDETUN (?Wooton) (218)
SWIRGILDANC(IRCE) (??Swarling chapel in Petham) (166a)

To LIMMINGES [LYMINGE]:

WIHTRICESHAM (Wittersham) (40)
PETRI ECCLESIA (St. Peter, ?Newenden) (28)
MARTINESCIRCE (??Postling) (175)
STANFORD (Stanford) (176)
HORTUNE (Monk's Horton) (172)
STUTINGE (Stowting) (172)
BIRICHALT (Bircholt in ?Smeath or in ?Braborne) (142a)
STEALLINGE (Stelling) (170)
AQUS (Acrise) (196)
WEADLESWURÐE (Paddlesworth) (197)

To MIDDLETUNE [MILTON REGIS]:

NORÐCIP' (?Warden) (64)
LEGESDUN (Leysdown) (65)
RODMÆRESHAM (Rodmersham) (56)
MILSTEDE (Milsted) (59)
TUNSTEAL (Tunstall) (52)
BACELDE (Bapchild) (55)
BRADEGARE (Bredgar) (44)
BOBINGE (Bobbing) (50)
TANGA (Tonge) (57)
EASTCYRCE (Eastchurch) (63)

To NIWANTUNUM [NEWINGTON]:

HEORDYLP (Hartlip) (30)
RÆNHAM (Rainham) (18)
VPCYRCEAN (Upchurch) (29)
STACABERE (Stockbury) (31)
HALGASTAW (Lower Halstow) (41)
SEXBURGAMYNSTER (Minster-in-Sheppey) (61)
NIWECYRCE (?Borden) (43)

To TÆNHAM [TEYNHAM]:

DUDDINGTUN (Dodington) (69)
STANE (Stone-by-Faversham) (102)
CILLINGE (Selling) (110)
ÆTWANGERÆDE (?Iwade)

To WINGEHAM [WINGHAM]:

AESCE (Ash) (235)
NUNNINGITUN (Nonington) (214)
RYTLINGE (Ratling in Nonington) (214a)
WIMLINGWEALD (Womenswold) (215)
WIELMESTUN (?Walmerstone Fm. in Wingham) (211a)
EADREDESTUN (?Elmstone) (209)

To MÆGDESTANE [MAIDSTONE]:

BOXLEA (Boxley) (1)
DYTLINGE (Detling) (20)
THORNHAM (Thurnham) (21)
EALDINGTUN (Aldington in Thurnham) (21b)
HOLINGABURNA (Hollingbourne) (33)
WELCUMEWEG (??East Sutton) (23)
LEANHAM (Lenham) (47)
BOCTUN (Boughton ?Malherbe, or ?Monchelsea) (36 or 8)
WULACUMBA (Ulcomb) (35)
HLYDA (Leeds) (21a)
LANGALEA (Langley) (5)
SUÐTUN (Sutton Valence) (10)
CERT (Chart ?Sutton) (9)
HEDEKARUNA (Headcorn) (24)
FRIDENASTEDE (Frinsted) 46)
GMÐHYRSTE (Goudhurst) (13)
MÆREDÆN (Marden) (11)

To WY [WYE]:

ÆSCEDEFFORD (Ashford) (118)
CRUNDALA (Crundale) (138)
BROCA (Brook) (140)
DREAMWURÐE (Tremworth in Crundale) (137)
HÆNOSTESYLE (Hinxhill) (120)
BRIXIESTUN (Brixiston, ?Sevington) (121)
WYLLAN (Eastwell) (115)
HAUDKASHYRSTE (?Hawkhurst) (15)

To CYRRINGE [CHARING]:

EARDINGTUN (?Egerton) (48)

To [name missing, ?EASTRY]:

EBBENEA (Ebony) (86)
WYLMINGTUN (Wilmington ?in Boughton Aluph) (116a)
CEALUELOCA (Challock) (113)
BRYGGE (Bridge) (190)
BERHAM (??Bishopsbourne) (191)
other BERHAM (??Kingston) (192)
Monasterium aet HYRNAN (Herne) (180)
GARWYNNETUN (Garrington in Littlebourne) (186a)
NATINDUNE (Nackington) (165)
HARANHYLLE (Hernehill) (131)

IV. This is the old institution before the coming of the lord Lanfranc the archbishop:

From MILTON 2 sesters of honey, and 2 sheep and 8 lambs, and 60 loaves, and 12*d*., and at Pentecost 600*d*.

From MAIDSTONE 1 sester of honey, and 8 lambs, and 60 loaves, and 12*d*. for wine and 14*d*. for oil.

The same was given from CHARING, from WYE, TEYNHAM, WINGHAM, EASTRY.

From LYMINGE 1 sester of honey, and 2 wethers, and 30 loaves, and 7d.
From APPLEDORE 1 sester of honey, and 30 loaves, and 4 lambs and 7d. for oil and 6d. for wine.
From DOVER 1 sester of honey, and 30 loaves, and 2 sheep, and 7d. and 600d.
From FOLKESTONE 1 sester of honey, and 30 loaves, and 2 wethers, and 7d., and 600d.
From the 2 BOUGHTONS from each 4 lambs, and 30 loaves, and 13d.
Similarly from RUCKINGE.
But Lanfranc of blessed memory ordained and instituted as is before written.

V. ROMSCOTT from East Kent, from:

ST. AUGUSTINE'S 50s.
DOVER 10s.
HUGH DE MONTFORT 22s. 6d.
MAIDSTONE 10s.
LYMINGE 7s.
MILTON (Regis) 20s.
BISHOPSBOURNE 6s.
CHARTHAM 4s.
ALDINGTON 20s.
CHILHAM 3s. 8d.
BARHAM 2s. 9d.
MONKTON 7s. 3d.
GODWINESBOURNE (?Fairbourne in Harrietsham) 16d.
TEYNHAM 22d.
(?West)WELL 3s.
WICKHAM 12d.
ELHAM 2s.
THANET churches 6s. 5d.
SEASALTER 3s.
GODRICESBOURNE (Brabourne) 3s. 3d.
LITTLECHART and PLUCKLEY 2s. 7d.
NORTHWOOD of the Archbishop (Whitstable) 12s.
WINGHAM 14s. 4d.
STALISFIELD 12d.
WYE 7s.
EAST CHART (?Great Chart) 4s. 7d.
ICKHAM 5s.
STOWTING 2s.
GODMERSHAM 3s. 6d.
STURSÆTE (Westgate) 3s.
COLDRED 2s.
FAVERSHAM 7s.
CHARING 7s.
PETHAM 4s.
ADISHAM 12s. 8d.
THROWLEY 18d.
MERSHAM 2s. 8d.
EASTRY 11s. 2d.
BILICE (?Bircholt or Bilchester in Hawkinge) 4s.
FOLKESTONE 5s.
PRESTON 16d.
APPLEDORE 5s. 9d.
The city [of Canterbury] s.
BOUGHTON (?under Blean) 16d.
EARLES BOUGHTON (?Aluph) 8d.

The Churches of St. Augustine's Abbey

[From a late 11th-century list surviving as a transcript of c. 1200 in the 'White Book of St. Augustine's'; it therefore contains some 12th-century additions. Churches additional to the 'Domesday Monachorum' lists are indicated here with asterisks. See *Arch. Cant.* xlv (1933), 84–9).]

These are the churches of the tenure of St. Augustine, of Canterbury and beyond:

CANTERBURY: (159)
*St. PAUL the Apostle, before the gate of the monastery. (161)
*St. MARY before the gate of the castle, [given by William I, in exchange for Castle land].
*St. SEPULCHRE [Nunnery, but also parochial].
*St. LAURENCE Hospital [founded 1137]
*St. MILDRED
*St. JOHN
*St. MARGARET
*St. ANDREW, [given by William I in exchange for Castle land].
*ALL SAINTS

At NORTHBOURNE these are subordinate to the church of St. Augustine the mother church of the same vill:

*MONINGHAM (Little Mongeham) 7d. [chrism fee]. (256)
*SUTTANE (Sutton near Northbourne) 7d. (257)
*SCHOLDONE (Sholden) 7d. (250)
*SIBERDESWELDE (Shepherdswell) 7d. (216)
*BEAUWESFELDE (Beusfield) ?Whitfield 7d. (265)
*LANGEDUNE (East Langdon) (265)
SMEDETONE (Shingleton in Nonington) (214b)
The chapel of RIPPLE (Ripple) (258)
*LITLEBOURNE (Littlebourne) 7d. (186)
*STODMERCHE (Stodmarsh) 7d. (185)
FORDWICH (Fordwich) (184)
*STUREIE (Sturry) 7d. (182)
*CHISTELET (Chislet) 7d. (202)
*The chapel of BERE (Westbere) (183)
*St. MARY IN THANET (Minster) (234)
*St. PETERS (Broadstairs) 7d. (232)
*St. JOHN THE BAPTIST (Margate) 7d. (231)
*St. LAURENCE (Ramsgate) 7d. (233)
*St. NICHOLAS at STANORES (Stonar) (237)
*St. PETER at SANDWICH (239)
FAVERSHAM, [given by William I] (105)
*The chapel of CHELDEWICH (Sheldwich, [given by William I] (109)

MIDDLETONE with all its chapels by grant of the kings, namely William, Henry and Stephen. These are the chapels of the same church which there receive the chrism and there pay their pence:

Two churches in SCAPEI (Leysdown & Warden) (65 and 64)
*ELMELEIE is a very small island and pays 3½d. (Elmley) (62)
*MORINESTUNE (Murston) 7d. (54)
TANGES (Tonge) 7d. (57)
BACHECHILDE (Bapchild) 7d. (55)
RODMERESHAM (Rodmersham) 7d. (56)
MILSTEDE (Milsted) 7d. (59)
BREDEGARE (Bredgar) 7d. (44)
*SITHINGEBOURNE (Sittingbourne) 7d. (53)
BOBINGE (Bobbing) 7d. (50)
TUNSTALLE (Tunstall) 7d. (52)
*BIKENORE (Bicknor) 7d. (44a)

But they do not pertain to Middletone but there receive the oil and pay the pence. The mother church of Middletune pays 32d.
Again, there are chapels of NEWENTONE receiving the oil there, to wit [at] Middeltune, and paying pence:

Two churches in Sheppey (Minster & Eastchurch) (61 and 63)
RENHAM (Rainham) (18)
OPCHIRCHE (Upchurch) (29)
HALGESTOWE (Lower Halstow) (41)
STOKEBURI (Stockbury) (31)
HERLEPE (Hartlip) (30)
BORDENE (Borden) (43)
SCHELLINGE (Selling) (110)

*SWALCLIUE (Swalecliffe) (154)
*PRESTUNE (Preston-by-Wingham) (208)
LENHAM (Lenham) (47)
*The chapel of RATTUNE (?Rayton in Lenham) (47a)

KENINGTON (Kennington) (117). Item, be it remembered that the church of Keningtone pays to this church in one year and in the next year to the church of Holy Trinity; where it receives the oil, there it pays. Similarly also the church of SMEDETUNE (Shingleton) used to pay 7d. but by permission they [the pence]) are kept back.

*WIUELESBERGE (Willesborough) 7d. (119)
*BOREWAREMERCH (Burmarsh) (148)

*SNAVES (Snave) 7d. (88)
*BRKCHIRCHE (?Brookland) 7d. (92)
DEMCHERD (Dymchurch) (149)
*STONES IN OXONIAIE (Stone in Oxney) 7d. (87)
*TENTWARDENNE (Tenterden) 7d. (39)
*STRITHINDENNE (Frittenden) 7d. (25)

[The 'White Book' (c. 1200) also says, after the entry for Fordwich above: 'But there are certain churches among these which pay chrism pence to the church of Our Saviour [i.e. Christ Church] every year, but how this happens unless by our negligence is not known. These are the churches of LENHAM, FORDWICH, FAVERSHAM, NEWINGTON, and perhaps there are others.']

Notes

1. G. Ward, 'The List of Saxon Churches in the Textus Roffensis', *Arch. Cant.* xliv (1932), 39–59, and G. Ward, 'The Lists of Saxon Churches in the Domesday Monachorum and White Book of St. Augustine', *Arch. Cant.* xlv (1933), 60–89. Only about 180 churches and 6 chapels in Kent are mentioned in Domesday Book.
2. Even though the 'White Book of St. Augustine' was compiled in c. 1200 it is clearly copied from a late 11th-century list. There are, however, a few later additions like St. Lawrence in Canterbury (founded 1137).
3. E. Hasted, *The History and Topographical Survey of the County of Kent* I (2nd edn. 1797), 260–5.
4. Several medieval parishes, with either ruined or destroyed parish churches, survived until the 19th century (for example Sarre in Thanet or Midley, Eastbridge, Hope All Saints and Blackmanstone in Romney Marsh).
5. D.C. Douglas (ed.), *The Domesday Monachorum of Christ Church Canterbury* (1944).
6. Barlow *Church 1000–66*, 180–2.
7. I do not propose to examine the detached deanery of Canterbury diocese at Croydon in Surrey.
8. The best example is perhaps Gundulf (1077–1108) who not only acted as suffragan to Lanfranc and Anselm, but also 'looked after' the Canterbury diocese in the interregnum between 1089 and 1093 and during Anselm's exile. Only in 1238 did the Archbishop cease to hold the patronage of the Bishopric of Rochester: see J. Thorpe (ed.) *Registrum Roffense* (1769), 958.
9. Barlow, *Church 1000–66*, 208–9.
10. For example the churches and chapels given to the Canons of St. Gregory in its foundation charter of c. 1086, see A.M. Woodcock (ed.), *The Cartulary of the Priory of St. Gregory, Canterbury* (1956), 1–3.
11. Some churches remained chapels-of-ease right through to the 19th century; for example the churches in Hythe were chapels of Saltwood until 1844.
12. For example, the Wickhambreux tithe map of 1840 shows a detached portion of the parish to the west called Trenley Park. This is the deerpark created by Odo of Bayeux in the 1070s which was attached to his demesne manor of Wickham: see T. Tatton-Brown, 'Recent Fieldwork around Canterbury', *Arch. Cant.* xcix (1983), 117–19. Many of the 19th-century parishes are, in fact, identical with the 11th-century Anglo-Saxon estates in which they were created.
13. Except that 'Rumenea' comes before Ruckinge in the first list.
14. Milton, however, gives 2 sesters of honey, 2 sheep, 8 lambs, 60 loaves and 12d. as well as 600d. at Pentecost. In these lists, Milton perhaps also includes Newington (see below).
15. 4 lambs from Appledore (which also renders 6d. for wine).
16. Lyminge pays only 32d. and Appledore 7d. in the 'first list'.
17. However, unlike the dependencies of the other churches, the lesser churches which pertain to the un-named church are not a geographical entity. They are Ebony, Wilmington, Challock, Bridge, Barham, 'other' Barham, *monasterium aet* Herne, Garrington, Nackington and Hernehill.
18. The late Anglo-Saxon seaport was perhaps at West Hythe or 'Sandtun', and coins are minted at 'Limen' from the reign of Edgar (959–75). See T. Tatton-Brown, 'The Towns of Kent', in Haslam, *Towns*, 24–6.
19. See S. Rigold, 'Lympne Castle', *Archaeol. J.* cxxvi (1970), 260–1. The Archdeacon must have had an early castle comparable to the Archbishop's own castle at Saltwood, a few miles to the east.
20. For details see N. Brooks, *The Early History of the Church of Canterbury* (1984), 129–131.
21. In c. 1016–20 a priest of Folkestone witnessed a marriage: Brooks op.cit. note 20, 204. By the mid 11th century, Folkestone was in the hands of Earl Godwin.
22. Loose (along with Detling) was a chapel-of-ease to Maidstone until the 16th century.
23. G. Ward, 'The Lists of Saxon Churches in Domesday Monachorum and White Book of St. Augustine', *Arch. Cant.* xlv (1933), 86–7.
24. Only Kingsdown parish is missing from these lists, and it probably did not become a separate parish until the 12th century.
25. Eastchurch is attached to Newington, according to the 'White Book'.
26. Except that Iwade was apparently attached to Teynham.
27. Again the parishes (earlier estates) around Faversham are an interlocking group; see G. Ward, 'The Topography of some Saxon Charters relating to the Faversham District', *Arch. Cant.* xlvi (1934), 123–136.
28. Ibid. The main exchanges were in 811–2 between Coenwulf of Mercia and Archbishop Wulfred.
29. See N. Brooks, 'Romney Marsh in the Early Middle Ages', in R.T. Rowley (ed.), *The Evolution of Marshland Landscapes* (1981), 74–94.
30. Ibid., 86–88. Lydd church has a core in the north-west corner that is perhaps Roman. See E. Jackson and E. Fletcher, *JBAA*, xxxi (1968), 19–26.
31. See Erik Cinthio, 'The Churches of St. Clemens in Scandinavia', *Archaeol. Lund.* iii (1968), 103–116.
32. Ward op.cit. note 23, 80.
33. Domesday Monachorum also records a *monasterium* at Hyrnan (Herne). Was this just possibly the temporary inland refuge for the minster in the Viking period? For a note on the church, see N. Brooks, 'The Earliest Church at Herne', in K. McIntosh (ed.) *Hoath and Herne* (1984), 14.
34. From the first and fourth Domesday Monachorum lists.
35. Taylor & Taylor.
36. The churches of Coldred, East Langdon, Paddlesworth, St. Margarets-at-Cliffe, Willesborough and Bearsted, which are perhaps all early Norman.

37. St. Pancras's chapel east of St. Augustine's Abbey was always part of the Abbey.
38. Taylor & Taylor, i, 214–17.
39. Brit. Lib., MS. Cotton Jul. D.v. and Vesp. B. xi; see *Mon.Ang.* iv, 528, and *VCH Kent*, ii, 133.
40. See S. Rigold, 'The Shore Forts as Mission Stations', in D.E. Johnston (ed.), *The Saxon Shore* (1977), 73. Rigold, however, believed that the 630s monastery was in the *burh* (Iron-Age hillfort) and moved down to the Saxon-shore fort in the 690s.
41. See G. Ward, 'Saxon Abbots of Dover and Reculver', *Arch. Cant.* lix (1947) 19–28.
42. Ibid., 25–6.
43. Leuuin (Leofwine) held the prebend of Charlton, just outside Dover, T.R.E.
44. See S. 1472.
45. See R. Allen Brown, *Dover Castle* (3rd edn., 1983), 4–5.
46. It is only called this, as opposed to just 'Dover', in the third list in Domesday Monachorum. Domesday Book, of course, always calls them 'the Canons of St. Martin's'.
47. See Taylor & Taylor, i, 429. The internal dimensions of the nave are c. 65 × 31 feet (cf. Dover, 60 × 26 feet).
48. Ibid., 408–9, and H.M. Taylor, 'Lyminge Churches', *Arch. Jnl.* cxxvi (1971), 256–260. Also E. Gilbert, 'The Church of St. Mary and St. Eadburg, Lyminge', *Arch. Cant.* lxxix (1964) 143–8.
49. See T. Tatton-Brown, 'The Use of Quarr Stone in London and East Kent', *Med. Arch.* xxiv (1980), 213–5.
50. The church of St. Gregory and St. Martin at Wye was also largely rebuilt for a college in the mid 15th century by Archbishop Kemp, and the whole of the eastern part of the church was destroyed in 1686 when the tower collapsed.
51. See the plan of Minster-in-Thanet in *Arch. Jnl.* lxxxvi (1930), 269 for a typical example of how the core of a church of at least c. 1100 is suspected, which might also have been cruciform.
52. See the excellent article with plans by F.C. Elliston Erwood, *Arch. Cant.* xxxv (1921), 145–159.
53. Hubert Walter and his predecessors as Archbishop after the murder of Becket were heavily involved in new collegiate church building, at St. Stephen's Hackington (where there is also a cruciform 12th-century parish church) and later at Lambeth.
54. The church was also partly destroyed in 1301 when it was attacked by the townspeople.
55. From 1148, all building work at Faversham was concentrated a few hundred yards to the north where the great royal abbey for King Stephen was being built.
56. There were probably well over 300 churches and chapels in the diocese in the 12th century and about 500 in the county.
57. op.cit. note 49.
58. For example, Quarr stone is found in the quoins at Sholden church (a chapel attached to Northbourne), re-used at St. Nicholas-at-Wade, and in the excavations at Shuart church (both chapels to Reculver).
59. See S. Rigold, 'The Demesne of Christ Church at Brook' (with plan), *Arch. Jnl.* cxxvi (1970), 270–2; S. Heywood, 'The Ruined Church at North Elmham', *JBAA*, cxxxv (1982), 7–9 and Pl. III.
60. See G.M. Livett, 'Whitfield *alias* Beuesfeld', *Arch. Cant.* xl (1928), 141–158 for plans and a discussion of this.
61. See T. Tatton-Brown, 'Recent Fieldwork around Canterbury', *Arch. Cant.* xcix (1983), 119–124.
62. See F.C. Plumptre, 'Some Account of the Remains of the Priory of St. Martins' and the Church of St. Martin-le-Grand at Dover', *Arch. Cant.* xx (1893) 295–304.
63. See T. Tatton-Brown, 'The Topography and Buildings of Horton Manor, near Canterbury', *Arch. Cant.* xcvii (1982), 77–105.

X. Church and Parish in Norman Worcestershire

C. J. Bond

Introduction

Churches have a special interest for the landscape historian for a number of reasons:

(1) They represent known fixed points in the early medieval landscape, and therefore have an important bearing on topographical studies of routeways and of settlements.

(2) Their size may be at least partly a reflection of the size of the communities which they were expected to serve; enlargements or contractions to the building may, therefore, reflect the growth or decline of those communities.

(3) They represent focal elements in a form of territorial organisation, serving the religious needs of one or more communities within more or less fixed parochial boundaries; those boundaries themselves may sometimes fossilise the outlines of much older land-units, which antedate the parochial system as such.

(4) They are vehicles for the expression and development of architectural styles, which may either (i) be of a strongly indigenous regional or local character, or (ii) be subject to influences from outside the locality, which may themselves reflect a variety of different types of contacts.

(5) As consumers of building materials, especially of stone which may have a traceable source, they provide evidence for the distribution and organisation of contemporary extractive industry, and may also thereby be able to throw some light upon contemporary commercial or tenurial contacts and transport links, which sometimes operated over considerable distances.

The present paper, while attempting to take some account of all these topics, will pay particular attention to the origins and development of the parochial organisation and the nature of the buildings themselves.

In any examination of churches and ecclesiastical history it would be most logical to select a diocese or some other unit of ecclesiastical administration as the area of study. The anomalous use of the secular county of Worcestershire as the framework for the present paper is due solely to the author's background as a local government officer in the Museum service of Worcestershire County Council between 1969 and 1974, a post which provided both a brief and an opportunity to examine its ecclesiastical buildings; the adoption of a unit of secular administration for the present purpose has no academic justification whatsoever and does, moreover, present one or two special problems:

(1) The secular county does not all lie within the same medieval diocese; while most of it lay within the diocese of Worcester, a substantial portion of the north-west lay within the diocese of Hereford. This has certain implications for the availability of documentary sources, though these are perhaps less serious for the Norman period than they would be after the early 13th century, when the fine series of Worcester bishops' registers commences.

(2) As a land unit in the early middle ages, Worcestershire had a singularly tattered outline, being characterised not only by numerous deep gulfs and promontories, but also having nine detached exclaves scattered up to 15 km away from the nearest 'mainland' boundary, in addition to a couple of enclaves of neighbouring counties within its main perimeter. Many of these boundary anomalies are themselves a result of early medieval ecclesiastical organisation, a characteristic especially evident in the south, where lands belonging to the church of Worcester or to the abbeys of Pershore or Evesham were incorporated within Worcestershire, while those belonging to St. Oswald's or St. Peter's at Gloucester or to Winchcombe Abbey or Deerhurst Priory were given to Gloucestershire.[1]

The rationalisation of the tortuous medieval boundary began in the 1830s, and the outline of Worcestershire in its last years of independent existence up to 1974 represented a much tidied-up version of the medieval county. As far as the present study is concerned, it is the final boundary of 1974 which will provide the basic framework and the unit for statistical assessments (e.g. Fig. 24), but it would be inappropriate to impose these limits too rigidly, and the medieval bounds have been at least partly accomodated on most of the remaining maps.

Although there are some disadvantages in using the secular county as the study area, Worcestershire does, nonetheless, have some positive attractions as far as the present theme is concerned:

(1) For all the tortuous nature of its medieval boundary, in general terms Worcestershire comes closer to being a natural geographical entity than most counties. It may be likened to a great bowl of land drained by the Severn and Avon and their tributaries, and surrounded by a rim of hills. The crest of the

Malverns and the Redditch Ridgeway in particular form clearly-defined natural boundaries on the west and east respectively, while Kinver Edge and the Lickey Hills shut off the outside world to the north and the Cotswold scarp presents a barrier to the south-east. Only to the south, where the Severn valley opens into the Vale of Gloucester, is there no physical barrier, and only to the north-west, in the Teme Valley, is there a significant portion of the county extending beyond the encircling rim of upland.

(2) The Church was especially strong politically in Worcestershire, achieving a domination which is scarcely matched in any other area. At the time of the Domesday Survey, for example, 786 out of the 1200 hides in the county were in the hands of monastic or ecclesiastical authorities, compared with only 414 hides in the hands of laymen; the Church controlled seven of the twelve hundreds which made up the county.[2]

(3) As far as church buildings are concerned, Worcestershire has an unusually large proportion of its Norman work surviving. This is shown by Fig. 24, which has been produced, first, by assessing for each county in the south-west midlands the total number of churches and chapels which contain surviving medieval fabric (thereby excluding all churches totally rebuilt after the Reformation); and then by assessing the proportion within each county where the earliest recognisable standing masonry is of Norman date, as opposed to being of pre-Conquest origin or later medieval Gothic. For the purposes of this exercise, where the question of survival is of greater interest than that of replacement, only the structural fabric visible above-ground has been considered; the below-ground archaeological evidence and the presence of potentially moveable furnishings such as fonts and crosses have been deliberately excluded. Two significant points emerge:

(i) There is a lack of clearly-identifiable pre-Conquest masonry in Worcestershire churches,[2a] which is in sharp contrast to the considerable, and sometimes spectacular, remains in some of the neighbouring counties to the west and south.

(ii) By contrast, the proportion of churches with surviving Norman work is exceptionally high: no less than 102 out of the 161 medieval churches and chapels within the pre-1974 bounds of Worcestershire, that is, over 63 per cent of the total, include recognisable Norman structural fabric; this is appreciably more than the percentages derived for the counties to the west and south (59 per cent in Shropshire, 58 per cent in Herefordshire, 57 per cent in Oxfordshire, and 52 per cent in Gloucestershire) and dramatically greater than those for the counties to the north and east (39 per cent in Warwickshire, 36 per cent in Staffordshire).

In addition to those 102 wholly or partly extant Norman buildings, there are clear indications that there were at one time at least another 80 Norman churches and chapels in the county. The evidence includes:

(i) contemporary documentation, such as the Domesday record of a priest in Clifton-on-Teme,[3] where the present church displays nothing of recognisably earlier date than the 13th century;

(ii) the presence of loose preserved sculptural details, such as the 12th-century fragments at Wichenford, a church otherwise wholly rebuilt in *c.* 1320;

(iii) re-used material, such as the chevron-moulded stones incorporated in the nave when the church of Hampton by Evesham was rebuilt at the beginning of the 15th century, and the 12th-century ornament reused at the east end of the south wall of the nave at Upper Arley;

(iv) antiquarian descriptions of now-destroyed buildings, such as: the old church of Tardebigge, the south door of which, according to Nash, had, before its destruction in 1774, 'a circular arch ... with hatched mouldings, and the supporting columns had the common rude Saxon [*sic*] capitals'; the Norman chapel at Pensax, described by Noake after its demolition in 1829; the old church of Hallow, pulled down in 1830, where Prattinton discerned the north wall to be 'of considerable antiquity. It has a circular-headed door, now stopped, with pillars having Saxon [*sic*] capitals, and a narrow circular-headed window'; and the church at Doddenham, taken down after 1868, where Severn Walker's sketch shows a couple of 12th-century windows; also descriptions of individual sculptures, such as the lost tympanum which existed at Bayton before 1819;[4] and

(v) archaeological evidence discovered during alterations, such as the fragments of a late 12th-century arcade pier and doorway arch found beneath the north aisle wall of the 15th-century church at Claines during building operations in 1886–7.[5] The eventual total of Norman ecclesiastical buildings in Worcestershire may well be in excess of 200.

There is no simple explanation for the variations in experience from county to county. The first point which must be made is that the absence of recognisable pre-Conquest masonry in Worcestershire most certainly does not mean that there were no Anglo-Saxon churches. There are several dedications to local Anglo-Saxon saints — to St. Kenelm of Winchcombe at Clifton-on-Teme, Romsley and Upton Snodsbury, to St. Eadburga of Pershore at Abberton, Broadway and Leigh, to St. Ecgwin of Evesham at Church Honeybourne and Norton-by-Evesham, and to St. Mildburga of Much Wenlock at Offenham — and these are unlikely to be of post-Conquest origin. Fragments of Saxon crosses survive at Cropthorne, Frankley and Tenbury. There are many documentary records of churches and chapels in being before the Conquest. However, it is likely that many of the Anglo-Saxon churches which undoubtedly did exist were small and unsuited to later medieval needs. Probably a considerable proportion of these were of timber: the northern, central and western districts of Worcester-

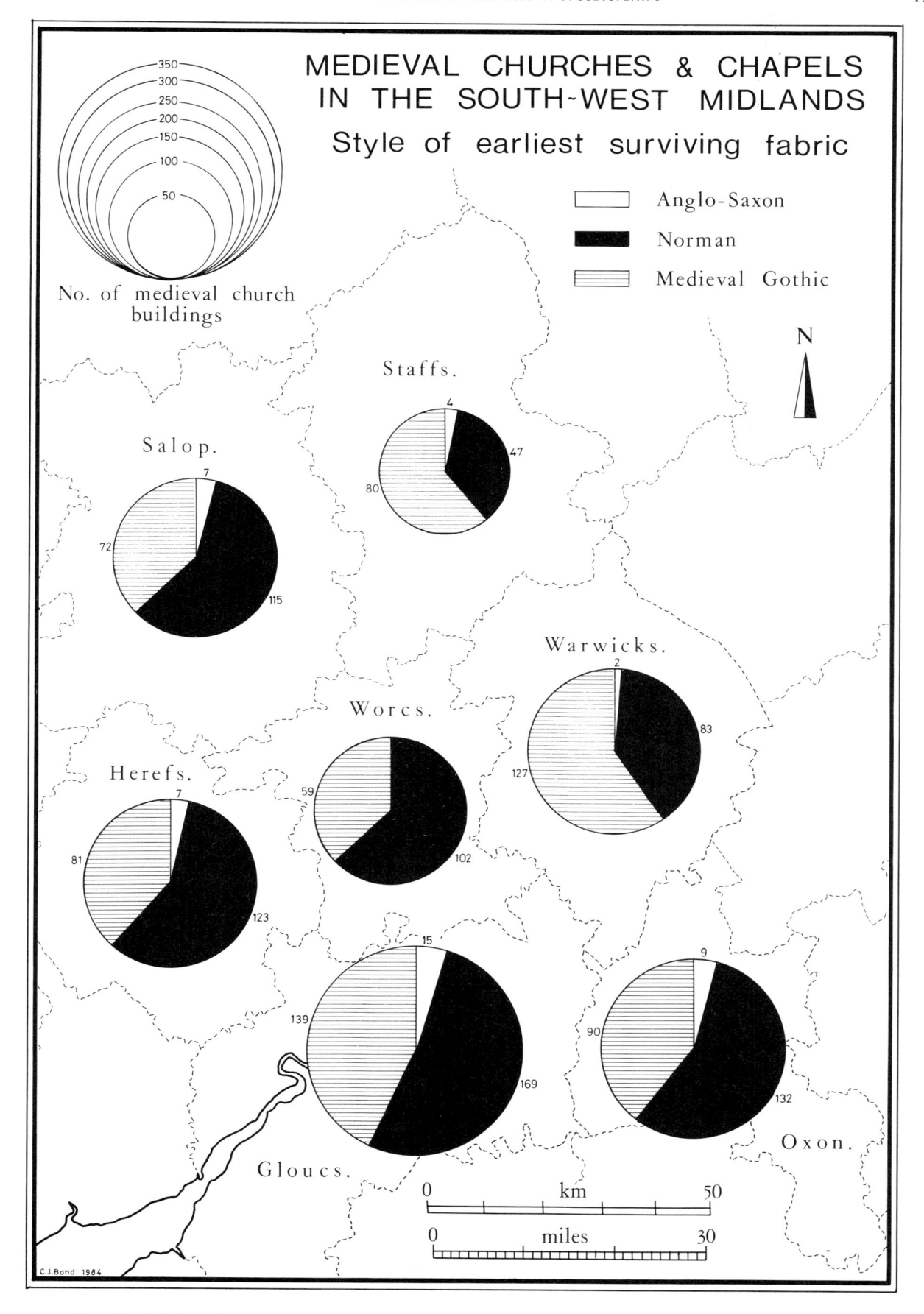

Fig. 24 Medieval churches and chapels in the S.W. Midlands: style of earliest surviving fabric.

122 C. J. Bond

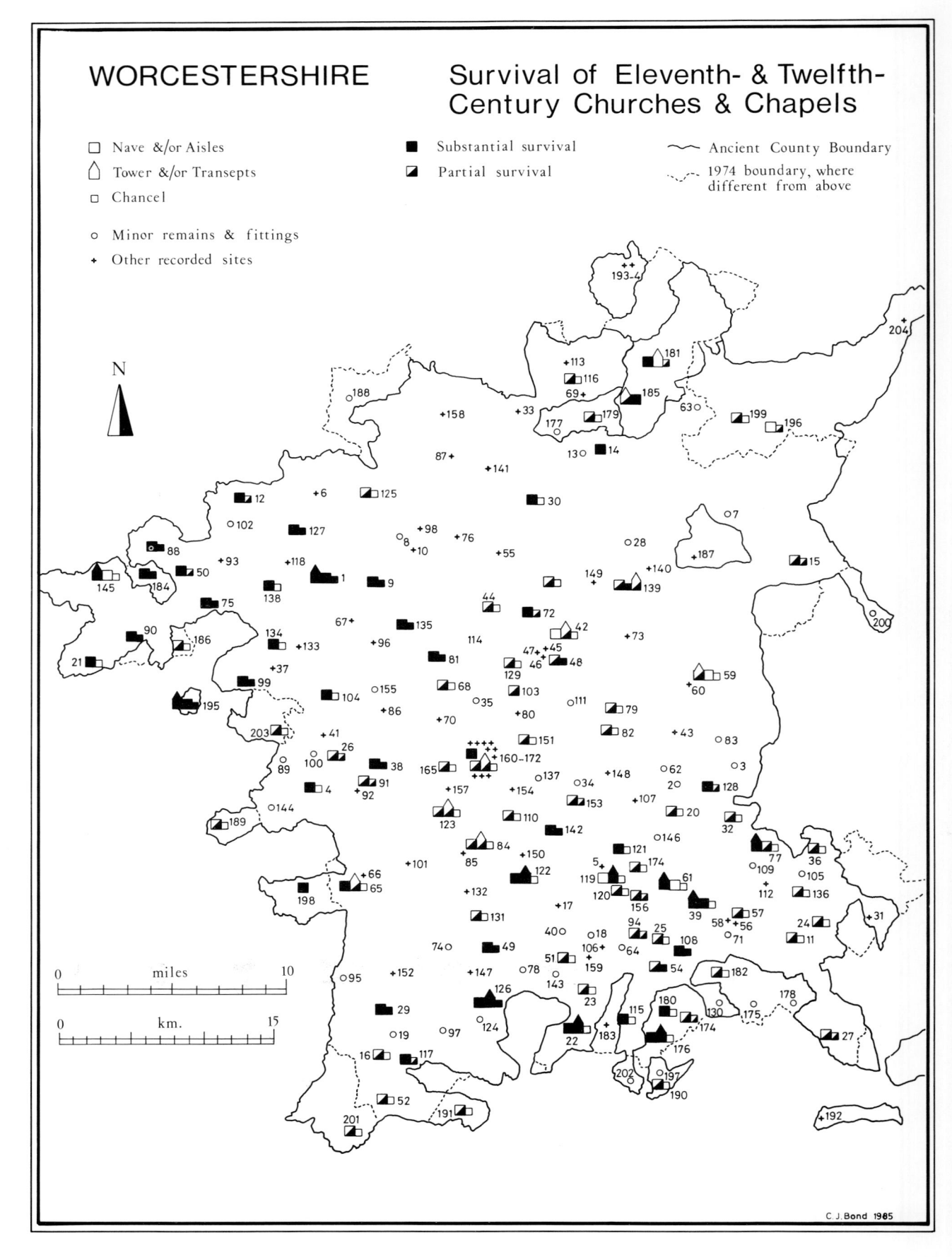

Fig. 25 *Distribution of surviving Norman church fabric in Worcestershire.*

Key to Fig. 25

1. Abberley — St. Michael (ruins) — Church
2. Abberton — St. Eadburga — Church
3. Abbots Morton — St. Peter — Chapel of Evesham Abbey
4. Alfrick — St. Mary Magdalene — Chapel of Suckley
5. Allesborough — St. Giles (site) — Chapel of Pershore Abbey
6. Alton (site) — ? Church
7. Alvechurch — St. Lawrence — Church
8. Areley Kings — St. Bartholomew — Chapel of Martley
9. Astley — St. Peter — Church & Alien Priory
10. Astley — Redstone Rock Hermitage — Hermitage
11. Badsey — St. James — Chapel of Evesham Abbey
12. Bayton — St. Bartholomew — Church
13. Belbroughton — Holy Trinity — Church
14. Belbroughton — Bell End Chapel — Private chapel
15. Beoley — St. Leonard — Church
16. Berrow — St. Faith — Chapel of Overbury
17. Besford — St. Peter — Chapel of Pershore St. Andrew
18. Birlingham — St. James — Chapel of Nafford
19. Birtsmorton — SS. Peter & Paul — ? Chapel of Longdon
20. Bishampton — St. Peter (now St. James) — Chapel of Fladbury
21. Bockleton — St. Michael — Church
22. Bredon — St. Giles — Old minster
23. Bredons Norton — St. Giles — Chapel of Bredon
24. Bretforton — St. Leonard — Chapel of Evesham Abbey
25. Bricklehampton — St. Michael — Chapel of Pershore St. Andrew
26. Broadwas — St. Mary Magdalene — Church
27. Broadway — St. Eadburga — Church
28. Bromsgrove — St. John Baptist — ? Old minster
29. Castlemorton — St. Gregory — Chapel of Longdon
30. Chaddesley Corbett — St. Cassian — ? Old minster
31. Church Honeybourne — St. Ecgwin — Chapel of Evesham Abbey
32. Church Lench — All Saints — Church
33. Churchill in Halfshire — St. James the Great — ? Church
34. Churchill in Oswaldslow — St. Michael — Chapel of Worcester St. Helen
35. Claines — St. John Baptist — Chapel of Worcester St. Helen
36. Cleeve Prior — St. Andrew — ? Old minster
37. Clifton-on-Teme - St. Kenelm — Church
38. Cotheridge — St. Leonard — ? Church or chapel of Wick Episcopi
39. Cropthorne — St. Michael — Old minster
40. Defford — St. James — Chapel of Pershore St. Andrew
41. Doddenham — St. Andrew (site) — Chapel of Martley
42. Dodderhill — St. Augustine — Church
43. Dormston — St. Nicholas — ? Chapel of Studley Priory
44. Doverdale — St. Mary the Virgin — Church
45. Droitwich — St. Andrew — ? Old minster
46. Droitwich — St. Mary-next-Witton (site) — Church
47. Droitwich — St. Nicholas (site) — Chapel
48. Droitwich — St. Peter de Witton — Church
49. Earls Croome — St. Nicholas — Chapel of Ripple
50. Eastham — SS. Peter & Paul — Church
51. Eckington — Holy Trinity — Church
52. Eldersfield — St. John Baptist — Chapel of Longdon
53. Elmbridge — St. Mary — Chapel of Dodderhill
54. Elmley Castle — St. Mary — Chapel of Cropthorne
55. Elmley Lovett — St. Michael — Church
56. Evesham — Abbey — Old minster/Benedictine Abbey
57. Evesham — All Saints — Chapel of Evesham Abbey
58. Evesham — St. Lawrence — Chapel of Evesham Abbey
59. Feckenham — St. John Baptist — Church
60. Feckenham — Chapel in royal lodge (site) — Private chapel
61. Fladbury — St. John Baptist — Old minster
62. Flyford Flavell - St. Peter — Church
63. Frankley — St. Leonard — Chapel of Halesowen
64. Great Comberton — St. Michael — ? Chapel of Pershore Abbey
65. Great Malvern — Priory — Benedictine Priory
66. Great Malvern — St. Thomas the Martyr (site) — Church
67. Great Witley — St. Michael & All Angels (site) — ? Chapel
68. Grimley — St. Bartholomew — Chapel of Worcester Priory
69. Hagley — St. John Baptist — Church
70. Hallow (site) — Chapel of Worcester Priory
71. Hampton-by-Evesham — St. Andrew — Chapel of Evesham Abbey
72. Hampton Lovett — St. Mary — Church
73. Hanbury — St. Mary the Virgin — Old minster
74. Hanley Castle — St. Mary — Church
75. Hanley Castle — All Saints — Chapel of Eastham
76. Hartlebury — St. James or St. Mary the Virgin — Church
77. Harvington-by-Evesham — St. James — Church
78. Hill Croome — St. Mary the Virgin — ? Chapel of Ripple
79. Himbleton — St. Mary Magdalene — Church
80. Hindlip — St. James the Great — Chapel of Worcester St. Helen
81. Holt — St. Martin — Chapel of Worcester St. Helen
82. Huddington — St. James — Chapel of Worcester St. Helen
83. Inkberrow — St. Peter — Church
84. Kempsey — St. Mary the Virgin — Old minster
85. Kempsey — St. Andrew's Chapel (site) — Private chapel
86. Kenswick — St. John Baptist (site) — Chapel of Worcester St. Helen
87. Kidderminster — All Saints — ? Old minster
88. Knighton-on-Teme — St. Michael — Chapel of Lindridge

89.	Knightwick — St. Mary (site)	Chapel of Grimley, subsq. of Martley	131.	Severn Stoke — St. Denis	Church
90.	Kyre Wyard — St. Mary	Chapel of Tenbury	132.	Severn Stoke — Hermitage (site)	Hermitage
91.	Leigh — St. Eadburga	Church	133.	Shelsley Beauchamp — All Saints	? Chapel of Martley
92.	Leigh — Manorial chapel (site)	Private chapel	134.	Shelsley Walsh — St. Andrew	? Chapel of Clifton-on-Teme
93.	Lindridge — St. Lawrence	Church	135.	Shrawley — St. Mary	Church
94.	Little Comberton — St. Peter	? Church or chapel of Pershore Abbey	136.	South Littleton — St. Michael the Archangel	Chapel of Evesham Abbey
95.	Little Malvern — St. Giles	Benedictine Priory	137.	Spetchley — All Saints	Chapel of Worcester Cathedral
96.	Little Witley — All Saints (now St. Michael)	Chapel of Worcester St. Helen	138.	Stockton-on-Teme — St. Andrew	Church
97.	Longdon — St. Mary the Virgin	Church	139.	Stoke Prior — St. Michael	Church
98.	Lower Mitton — St. Michael (site)	Chapel of Kidderminster	140.	Stoke Prior — St. Godwald's chapel, Finstall	Chapel
99.	Lower Sapey — St. Bartholomew	Chapel of Clifton-on-Teme	141.	Stone — St. Mary	Chapel of Chaddesley Corbett
100.	Lulsley — St. Giles (site)	Chapel of Suckley	142.	Stoulton — St. Edmund	Chapel of Kempsey
101.	Madresfield — St. Mary the Virgin (site)	Chapel of Powick	143.	Strensham — St. John Baptist (now SS. Philip & James)	Chapel of Pershore Abbey
102.	Mamble — St. John Baptist	Church			
103.	Martin Hussingtree — St. Michael & All Angels or St. Nicholas	Chapel of Pershore Abbey	144.	Suckley — St. John Baptist	Church
			145.	Tenbury — St. Mary the Virgin	Church
104.	Martley — St. Peter	? Chapel of Worcester St. Helen	146.	Throckmorton — Dedication unknown	Chapel of Fladbury
105.	Middle Littleton — St. Nicholas	Chapel of Evesham Abbey	147.	Upton-on-Severn — SS. Peter & Paul (site)	Chapel of Ripple
106.	Nafford — St. Katharine (site)	Church	148.	Upton Snodsbury — St. Kenelm	Chapel of Pershore Abbey
107.	Naunton Beauchamp — St. Bartholomew	Church	149.	Upton Warren — St. Michael	Church
108.	Netherton-by-Cropthorne (ruins)	Chapel of Cropthorne	150.	Wadborough — Hermitage (site)	Hermitage
109.	Norton-by-Evesham — St. Ecgwin	Chapel of Evesham Abbey	151.	Warndon — St. Nicholas	Chapel of Worcester St. Helen
110.	Norton-juxta-Kempsey — St. James the Great	Chapel of Kempsey	152.	Welland — St. James (site)	Chapel of Bredon
111.	Oddingley — St. James	? Chapel of Worcester St. Helen	153.	White Ladies Aston — St. John Baptist	? Chapel
112.	Offenham — SS. Mildburga & Mary	Chapel of Evesham Abbey	154.	Whittington — SS. Philip & James	Chapel of Worcester St. Helen
113.	Old Swinford — St. Mary the Virgin	Church	155.	Wichenford — St. Lawrence	Chapel of Worcester St. Helen
114.	Ombersley — St. Andrew	? Old minster	156.	Wick by Pershore — ? St. Laurence (now St. Bartholomew)	Chapel of Pershore St. Andrew
115.	Overbury — St. Faith	Church			
116.	Pedmore — St. Peter	Chapel of Old Swinford			
117.	Pendock — Dedication unknown	Church	157.	Wick Episcopi — St. Cuthbert (site)	Chapel of Worcester St. Helen
118.	Pensax — St. James (site)	Chapel of Lindridge	158.	Wolverley — St. John Baptist	Church
119.	Pershore — Abbey	Old Minster/Benedictine Abbey			
120.	Pershore — St. Andrew	Church	159.	Woollashull — St. Katharine's	Chapel of Nafford
121.	Pinvin — St. Nicholas	Chapel of Pershore St. Andrew	160.	Worcester — All Saints	Church
122.	Pirton — Blessed Virgin Mary & St. John Baptist (now St. Peter)	Church	161.	Worcester — St. Alban	Chapel of Worcester Cathedral
			162.	Worcester — St. Andrew	Church
			163.	Worcester — St. Clement (site)	Chapel
123.	Powick — St. Peter	Church	164.	Worcester — St. Helen	? former Celtic *clas* church
124.	Queenhill — St. Nicholas (now St. Laurence)	Chapel of Ripple	165.	Worcester — St. John-in-Bedwardine	Chapel of Wick Episcopi
125.	Ribbesford — St. Leonard	Church			
126.	Ripple — St. Mary the Virgin	Old minster	166.	Worcester — St. Margaret's Chapel (site)	Chapel
127.	Rock — SS. Peter & Paul	? Chapel of Alton	167.	Worcester — St. Martin	Church
128.	Rous Lench — St. Peter	? Chapel of Fladbury	168.	Worcester — Cathedral	Benedictine Cathedral Priory
129.	Salwarpe — St. Michael	Church			
130.	Sedgeberrow — St. Mary the Virgin	Church	169.	Worcester — St. Mary's Chapel (site)	Chapel

170.	Worcester – St. Michael-in-Bedwardine (site)	? Cemetery chapel
171.	Worcester – St. Peter the Great (site)	Church
172.	Worcester – St. Swithun	Church
173.	Wyre Piddle – Dedication unknown	Chapel of Fladbury

Churches and chapels in Worcesterhire in 1966–74, formerly in other counties

174.	Ashton-under-Hill – St. Andrew (now St. Barbara) (from Gloucs., 1931)	Chapel of Beckford
175.	Aston Somerville – Dedication unknown (from Gloucs., 1931)	Church
176.	Beckford – St. John Baptist (from Gloucs., 1931)	Old minster/Alien Priory
177.	Broome – St. Peter (from Staffs., 1844)	? Church
178.	Childswickham – St. Mary (from Gloucs., 1931)	Church
179.	Clent – St. Leonard (from Staffs., 1844)	Church
180.	Grafton (remains converted to domestic use) (from Gloucs., 1931)	Chapel of Beckford
181.	Halesowen – St. John Baptist (from Salop., 1844)	? Old minster
182.	Hinton-on-the-Green – St. Peter (from Gloucs., 1931)	Church
183.	Kemerton – St. Nicholas (from Gloucs., 1931)	Church
184.	Rochford – St. Michael (from Herefds., 1837)	Chapel of Tenbury
185.	Romsley – St. Kenelm's Chapel (from Salop., 1844)	Chapel of Halesowen
186.	Stoke Bliss – Dedication unknown (from Herefds., 1897)	? Church
187.	Tardebigge – St. Bartholomew (from Warwicks., 1844)	Church
188.	Upper Arley – St. Peter (from Staffs., 1895)	Church

Churches and chapels in Worcestershire in 11th and 12th centuries, subsequently transferred to other counties

(*) = Sites beyond eastern margin of Fig. 2.

189.	Acton Beauchamp – St. Giles (to Herefds., 1897)	? Church
(*)	Alderminster – SS. Mary & Holy Cross (to Warwicks., 1931)	? Old minster
190.	Alstone – St. Margaret (to Gloucs., 1931)	Chapel of Overbury
(*)	Aston Magna (remains converted to domestic use) (to Gloucs., 1931)	Chapel of Blockley
(*)	Blackwell (site) (to Warwicks., 1931)	Chapel of Tredington
(*)	Blockley – SS. Peter & Paul (to Gloucs., 1931)	Old minster
191.	Chaceley – St. John Baptist (to Gloucs., 1931)	Chapel of Longdon
192.	Cutsdean – St. James (to Gloucs., 1931)	Chapel of Bredon
(*)	Daylesford – St. Peter (to Gloucs., 1931)	Church
(*)	Dorn (remains converted to domestic use) (to Gloucs., 1931)	Chapel of Blockley
193.	Dudley – St. Edmund (to Staffs., 1966)	Chapel of Dudley Priory
194.	Dudley – St. Thomas (to Staffs., 1966)	Chapel of Dudley Priory
195.	Edvin Loach – St. Mary the Virgin (ruins) (to Herefds., 1893)	Chapel of Clifton-on-Teme
(*)	Evenlode – St. Edward (to Gloucs., 1931)	Church
(*)	Icomb – St. Mary the Virgin (to Gloucs., 1931)	Church
196.	Kings Norton – St. Nicholas (to Warwicks., 1911)	Chapel of Bromsgrove
197.	Little Washbourn – St. Mary the Virgin (to Gloucs., 1931)	Chapel of Overbury
198.	Mathon – St. John Baptist (to Herefds., 1897)	Church
199.	Northfield – St. Lawrence (to Warwicks., 1911)	Church
200.	Oldberrow – Blessed Virgin Mary (to Warwicks., 1894)	Church
(*)	Shipston-on-Stour – St. Edmund (to Warwicks., 1931)	Chapel of Tredington
201.	Staunton – St. James (to Gloucs., 1931)	Church
202.	Teddington – St. Nicholas (to Gloucs., 1931)	Chapel of Overbury
(*)	Tredington – St. Gregory (to Warwicks., 1931)	? Old minster
(*)	Tidmington – Dedication unknown (to Warwicks., 1931)	Chapel of Tredington
203.	Whitbourne – St. John Baptist (to Herefds., 1897)	? Church
204.	Yardley – St. Eadburga (to Warwicks., 1911)	Church

shire are known to have been well-wooded in the early middle ages, and timber-framing played a significant part in church building even into the later medieval period (there is one entirely timber-framed early 14th-century nave at Besford, timber towers of 13th- to 16th-century date at Cotheridge, Dormston, Kington, Pirton and Warndon, and a 15th-century timber arcade at Ribbesford). The evidence of widespread Norman reconstruction may reflect the influx of new wealth and energy, a dissatisfaction on the part of the new owners with the inadequacy of the buildings which already existed (either on practical or on artistic grounds), and perhaps the expansion of population allied with the reorganisation of the ecclesiastical system creating a need for larger churches. Equally, the extent of Norman survival in Worcestershire may also have several alternative explanations: either the quality of the Norman contribution was so high initially that it rarely required total replacement; or possibly that some areas of the county subsequently experienced a period of economic stagnation or population decline which meant that their churches never needed destructive wholesale enlargements later in the middle ages.

The Distribution of Norman Churches

The distribution of churches which contain Norman work is by no means an even one (Fig. 25), and it is of interest to compare it with other parameters of Anglo-Norman settlement. For all its many imperfections, the Domesday survey does enable us to make some sort of geographical analysis of agricultural resources, population distribution and other indices of wealth and prosperity. The entries relating to ploughteams and population are the most significant items of assessment for this purpose, and from the maps published in Darby's *Domesday Geography*[6] it is evident that the densities of both are at their greatest in the Vale of Evesham, and at their least in three widely-separated regions — Malvern Chase in the south-west, the Triassic sandstone areas in the north and parts of the Birmingham Plateau in the north-east. There is a very close correspondence between the *negative* areas on Darby's maps of Domesday ploughteams and population and the areas where Norman churches are rare or absent today: the reason for the lack of surviving Norman churches in Malvern Chase, the area around Kidderminster and the Stour Valley and the eastern central part of the county from the Forest of Feckenham into the Arrow Valley is very probably that these were genuinely underdeveloped areas, with a comparatively sparse population and little need of church buildings which were sufficiently substantial to stand much chance of survival. However, it is equally apparent that the area where the Domesday survey indicates the greatest concentration of wealth and prosperity, the Vale of Evesham, also has a relatively low occurrence of Norman churches. This is probably because the continuing prosperity of this region allowed much comprehensive rebuilding later on, and most of the evidence for older structures was torn down and replaced. Outside these two extremes, the areas which fall into the middle range of prosperity in the late 11th century include several significant concentrations of Norman survival. The most striking of these is in the north-west, in the Teme basin and on the plateaux west of the Severn. This group also includes some of the biggest and finest examples, such as Rock and Astley. In some respects this area may well have achieved a zenith of prosperity in the late 11th and 12th centuries which it never regained. A second significant concentration emerges in southern central Worcestershire, between the Severn and Bredon Hill. There are also several smaller groups, for example in the extreme south-west near the Gloucestershire border, to the north-east of Worcester in the rural parishes around Droitwich, and around the Clent Hills in the north-east.

Influences upon the Character of the Norman Church in Worcestershire

Insularity and English Continuity

Worcestershire lies deep in the English Midlands, geographically distant from foreign contacts and not especially accessible to sources of external influence. It has an inherent tendency towards insularity and conservatism, which was reinforced at the time of the Conquest by the presence of Bishop Wulfstan II of Worcester and Abbot Æthelwig of Evesham, two very powerful figures in local English monasticism, who were able to maintain their position long after the English hierarchy had been purged in most other parts of the country. Æthelwig had been appointed abbot of Evesham in 1059, had made a peaceful submission to King William, and was able not only to stay in his post, but also to win the king's confidence to such an extent that he was given judicial authority over no less than seven Mercian shires, namely Worcestershire, Gloucestershire, Herefordshire, Shropshire, Staffordshire, Warwickshire and Oxfordshire. Until his death from gout in 1077 he was able to foster and enhance the reputation of Evesham Abbey as a centre of Old English culture and tradition.[7] Wulfstan was a native of Warwickshire, born at Itchington in c. 1008, and educated at the abbeys of Evesham and Peterborough before entering the household of Bishop Brihteah of Worcester (1033–38); here he became first a monk and then prior of Worcester, and when Bishop Ealdred (1046–62) succeeded to the see of York and was forbidden by the pope to hold both sees simultaneously, Wulfstan took his place as Bishop of Worcester, chosing to be consecrated by Archbishop Ealdred rather than by Stigand of Canterbury. Along with Ealdred, he made his submission to King William soon after the Conquest and gave to Archbishop Lanfranc the profession of obedience which he had not been prepared to offer Stigand. Although he had been a close personal friend of King Harold, he seems to have recognised the inevitable, and did everything within his power to minimise the disruption within his own diocese. He managed to maintain the rights and authority of the Church despite the encroachments of voracious newcomers like Urse d'Abitot, the Norman sheriff, over its lands. He took an active part in the suppression of baronial rebellions in 1075 and 1088, when Worcester was itself threatened, and clearly retained the trust and confidence of both William I and Rufus. When Wulfstan died in 1095, he was the last survivor of the native Anglo-Saxon bishops.[8] It was due in no small measure to Wulfstan's policies that the diocese of Worcester escaped the destructive upheavals which had marred the transition to Norman rule in some other parts of the country.[9]

Continental Influences
It would be wrong, despite the unique position of Bishop Wulfstan, to overemphasize the insularity of the Church in Worcestershire (Fig. 26). Even before the Norman Conquest some of the English bishops had been well-travelled men of wide experience. Bishop Oswald (962–991) had been trained at Fleury, and was one of the leading figures of the English Benedictine revival. Ealdred, Wulfstan's immediate predecessor, had been on a mission to Cologne in 1054 to negotiate the return of Edward, son of Edmund Ironside, from Hungary, and had then journeyed to Rome in a fruitless attempt to persuade Pope Nicholas II to allow him to hold the archbishopric of York in addition to the sees of Worcester and Hereford. Two of the Norman bishops, Samson (1096–1112) and Theolf (1113–1123) had been canons of Bayeux, and the former was the brother of Thomas, the new Norman archbishop of York. At the very end of the period, Mauger, who succeeded to the bishopric in 1199, had been physician to King Richard I and had very probably accompanied him to Jerusalem. Evesham's connections were equally far-flung; the Chronicle records that in Æthelwig's time the abbey was frequently visited by 'many wanderers from Aquitaine, Ireland and many other countries'.[10] Three of its Norman abbots, who together ruled the abbey for over sixty years (though their exact chronology has been a matter of some dispute — the dates given here are those preferred by Knowles, Brooke & London[11]), had been trained in major continental monasteries which had been prominent in the Benedictine reform: Walter, Æthelwig's immediate successor (1077–1104), came from Cérisy-la-Forêt near Bayeux, and had been educated under Lanfranc at Caen.[12] Robert, who was abbot from 1104 to some time before 1130, came from the monastery of Jumièges near Rouen.[13] Abbot Adam (1161–89) was a Cluniac monk from La Charité–sur–Loire in Nivernais, France, who had been prior of Bermondsey before coming to Evesham.[14] In the time of William Rufus Evesham established a dependent cell in Denmark, sending twelve monks to Odensee.[15] Heads of other monastic houses tend to cease to bear English names by *c.* 1070–80, but generally little is known of the background of the new appointees. An exception is Walcher, prior of Great Malvern, who died in 1125; he was a Lotharingian, a noted astronomer and mathematician, who had certainly come to England by 1091.[16]

The Abbey of Westminster had acquired two-thirds of the estates of Pershore Abbey on its foundation shortly before the Conquest, and as a major landowner in the county it cannot be ignored as another source of influence from the continent. It too was ruled by Norman abbots within a decade of the Conquest: Vitalis, abbot from 1076 to *c.* 1085, had originally been a monk at Fécamp, and was abbot of Bernay before coming to England. His successor, Gilbert Crispin (*c.* 1085–1117), was a monk from the Abbey of Bec.[17]

Several Norman monasteries acquired estates in Worcestershire, and these were a third important source of continental influence. William FitzOsbern, earl of Hereford, wielded considerable power in the counties of Worcester, Gloucester and Hereford.[18] He had founded two new abbeys before the Conquest in what is the modern Departement of Eure, and subsequently endowed both with Worcestershire properties. St. Mary's Abbey at La Vieille Lyre, in the Risle valley, was founded in 1046. The Benedictine abbey of St. Mary at Cormeilles, 16 km north-east of Lisieux, was founded in about 1060, and FitzOsbern was himself buried there in 1071.[19] Lyre's Worcestershire endowments were mostly in the south-west, in Malvern Chase, where in 1086 the abbey had the tithes of Queenhill with half a virgate held by one villein, one virgate at Hardwick in Eldersfield occupied by another villein, and another tenanted virgate at Pull in Bushley.[20] By 1159–60 Lyre was also receiving the bulk of the tithes of Hanley Castle.[21] In addition, the Domesday survey records that the tithes of the manor of Feckenham, the church with the priest, and two virgates of land with one villein, had been given to the abbey of Lyre by Earl William;[22] the rectory belonging to Lyre subsequently included the large demesne of Astwood.[23] A confirmation charter of Henry II records the monks in possession of the church of Hanley Castle with its appurtenances, the tithes of the Forest of Malvern saving only the proceeds of the chase, the tithes of the whole demesnes of Queenhill chapelry and of Bushley, with small holdings of land in each, the tithes of the whole demesnes of Eldersfield and Feckenham, with a small holding at Eldersfield, and the church with a single ploughland at Feckenham.[24]

The possessions of Cormeilles were mostly in the north-west of the county. At the time of the Domesday survey the abbey held half a hide in Tenbury, worth 5*s.*, with one plough; there was already a priest here. It also held the church of Martley with its appurtenant lands and tithes, with two virgates of additional land farmed by two villeins; and the tithes of Suckley, with one villein and half a virgate of land.[25] A charter of Henry II subsequently confirmed to the abbey the churches of Suckley and Martley with all their chapels, tithes and appurtenances, together with other small holdings, with the tithes of Holloway in Feckenham and land at Tenbury.[26] The monks of Cormeilles later sold the Holloway tithes to the Cistercian abbey of Bordesley.[27] Earl William also gave to Cormeilles a couple of estates in the Carrant valley, which were then in Gloucestershire: 3 hides in Beckford, where 12 villeins had 5 ploughs, another property in Ashton-under-Hill, and the tithes and churches of these two places.[28] The church, chapels and tithes of Beckford with half a hide, and the church and tithes of Ashton-under-Hill with one virgate, were confirmed to Cormeilles by Henry II.[29]

It is of some interest that the descriptions of the possessions of Lyre and Cormeilles both include some of the very spasmodic Domesday references to churches. Both Martley and Feckenham were ancient royal demesne, and it is probable that the gifts of both churches are recorded because FitzOsbern, strictly speaking, had no right to grant them away.

While Lyre and Cormeilles were the principal continental monastic landowners in Worcestershire at the end of the 11th century, there were also a couple of smaller properties belonging to churches in Normandy and in France. The church of St. Denis on the northern outskirts of Paris had acquired considerable estates in Gloucestershire because of its absorption of Deerhurst as a dependent priory,[30] and it is probably through this connection that it acquired one hide in Droitwich, with 18 burgesses and a saltpan recorded by the Domesday survey.[31] The abbey of St. Evroult-Nôtre-Dame-des-Bois, in the Charentonne valley 45 km south-south-east of Lisieux, acquired by the gift of Ralph de Tosni in c. 1080 Alton with its church and all his lands in the Wyre Forest except for the *haia* of Bayton,[32] though this holding is not recorded in the Domesday survey.

There were two alien priories remaining under the domination of Norman houses, one early, one of comparatively late foundation. The Domesday survey records that Ralph de Tosni was lord of Astley, but that the abbey of St. Taurin at Evreux, 46 km south of Rouen, held it of him, and that four hides there belonging to the abbey were quit and freed from all dues formerly belonging to the king. The demesne included a church and a priest.[33] Soon after the Conquest the monks of St. Taurin established a dependent cell at Astley.[34]

Beckford, in Gloucestershire throughout the middle ages, was the site of a later alien priory founded in c. 1128 and attached to the Augustinian abbey of Ste. Barbe-en-Auge in Calvados.[35]

The ecclesiastical links with the Continent demand special consideration in the context of the present paper, but it should also be remembered that many of the secular Norman magnates retained estates in and contacts with their homeland for several generations.

Territorial Organisation of the Church

The territorial framework within which the Norman Church was organised was a complex one. Some of its elements were not only of pre-Conquest origin, but also pre-dated the formation of the shire system. The diocese of Worcester was one of those created in c. 680 by Archbishop Theodore to serve the sub-kingdom of the Hwicce when the vast Mercian diocese based on Lichfield was broken up. The organisation of monastic estates based upon Worcester, Evesham and Pershore goes back to the 7th and 8th centuries, and this not only exerted a strong influence upon the shape of the secular territory of the shire when this was created in the late 9th century, but also continued to dominate many aspects of the later medieval Church.

Other units of ecclesiastical administration do not appear to take shape until the 11th century (Fig. 27). Archdeaconries (at least, those outside the diocese of Canterbury) seem to have been established as one of the elements of Archbishop Lanfranc's reforms. Under Bishop Wulfstan there seems to have been only a single archdeacon, serving as the bishop's chief assistant; this post was held by an Englishman named Ailric, who witnessed Wulfstan's three known charters and was holding land at Bradley and Huddington from the Bishop at the time of the Domesday survey.[36] Soon after Ailric's death, during the episcopate of Samson or Theolf, the diocese of Worcester was divided into two archdeaconries: most of Worcestershire fell within the archdeaconry of Worcester, but a few parishes along the south-eastern fringe of the county came within the archdeaconry of Gloucester. The north-western part, in Hereford diocese, was part of the archdeaconry of Shropshire. The origin of the deaneries is a little more uncertain; Abbot Ælfward of Evesham is said to have appointed his prior Avitus or Æfic to be 'Dean of Christianity in the entire vale' (*Decanum Christianitatis totius vallis*) some time probably between 1021 and 1037;[37] and although this statement must be regarded with some suspicion, since the Chronicle claims that the creation of the deanery of the Vale was a result of Ælfward's having gained certain exemptions there from the jurisdiction of the bishop,[38] there is some independent evidence from one version of the Anglo-Saxon Chronicle that Æfic did indeed hold the position of dean of Evesham.[39] The deanery of Worcester must also have existed by the late 12th century, since the death of Roger Dod, dean of Worcester, is recorded in 1206.[40] The first positive statement of the bounds of both the archdeaconries and deaneries occurs in the records of Pope Nicholas IV's taxation of 1291,[41] but it seems likely that this record reflects a situation which

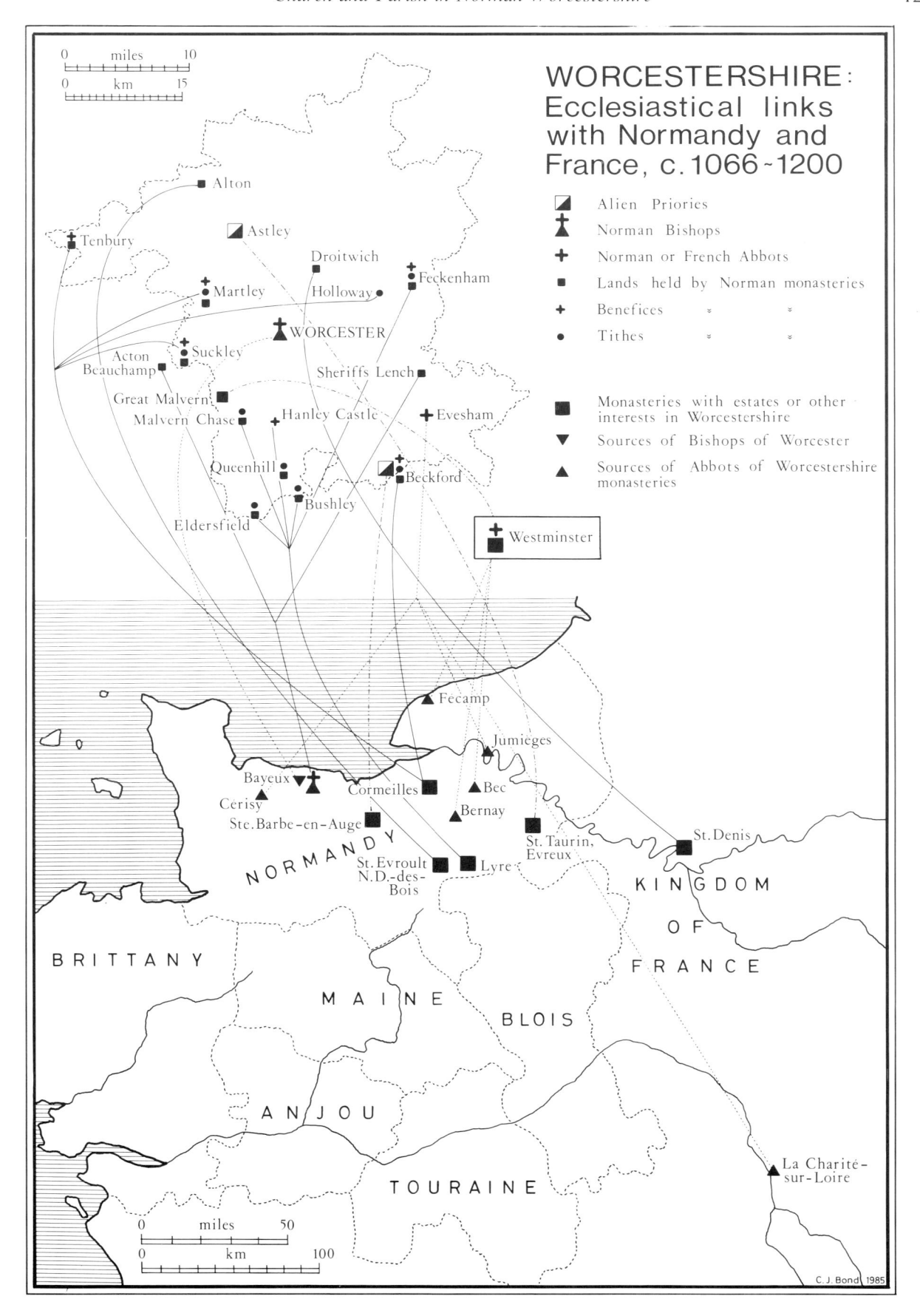

Fig. 26 Worcestershire: ecclesiastical links with Normandy and France, c. 1066–1200.

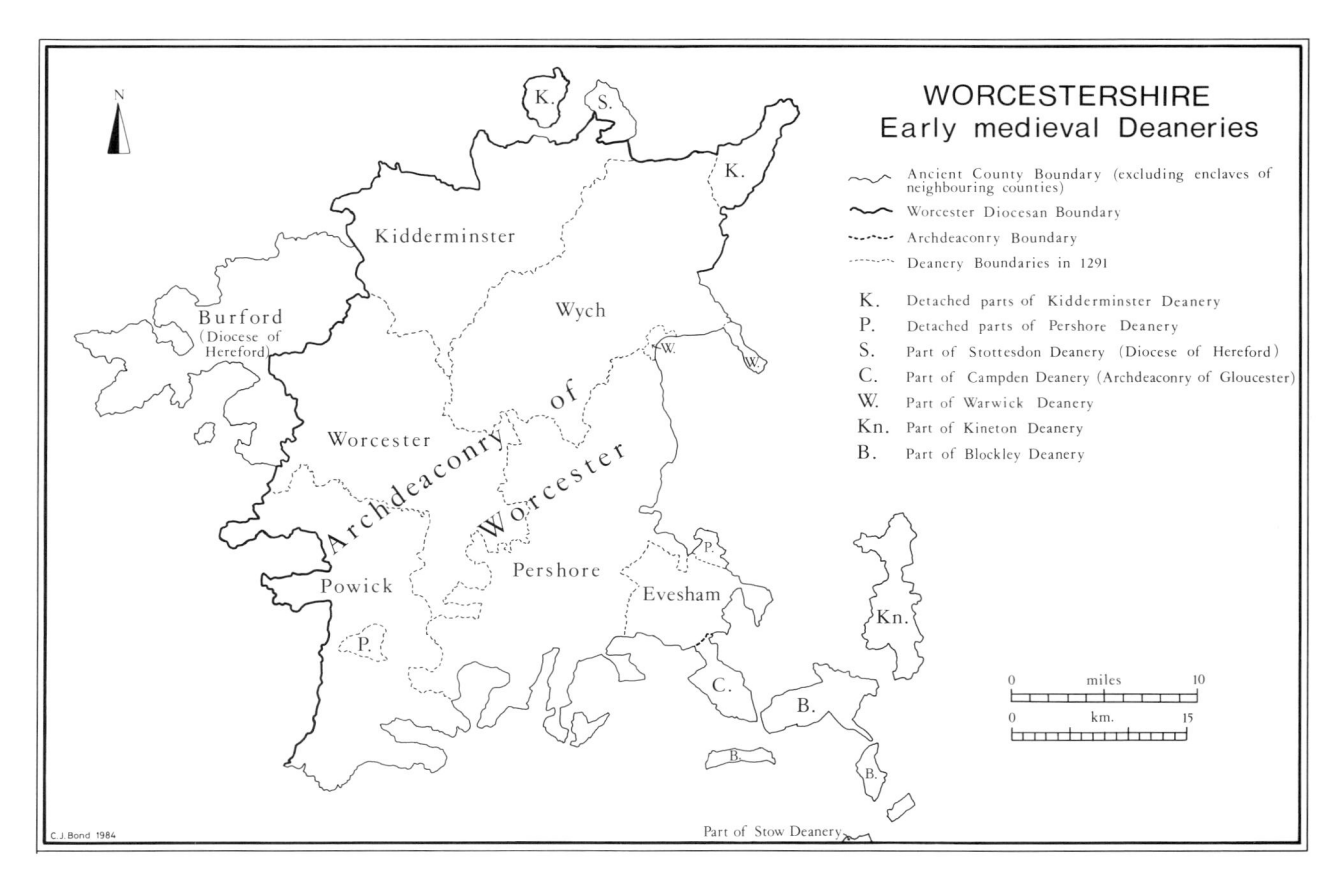

Fig. 27 Worcestershire: early medieval deaneries.

had been substantially stable for a considerable period.

It is with the organisation of the parishes, the smallest units in the system, that the biggest problems of investigation lie. It is difficult to detect any signs of parochial organisation as such before the 10th century, though some of the land-units onto which the system was grafted may have a very much older integrity. It is likely that the creation of ecclesiastical parishes was a complex and long-drawn-out process; although most of their essential features were well-established by the end of the 12th century (Fig. 28), their definition was probably not wholly complete until the mid 13th century.

Survival of Celtic Elements
Any account of the territorial organisation of the Church before the Conquest in the western parts of England needs to take account, not only of the Saxon Church itself, but also of possible undercurrents of Celtic survival.[42] Later accounts suggest that the former Roman town of Worcester may have been a centre of British christianity, served by a suffragan of Caerleon, and there is a tradition that a bishop from Worcester was amongst the delegation from the British church which met Augustine to resolve their doctrinal differences in 601.[43] The peculiar status of St. Helen's church in Worcester is worthy of further examination. It was claimed by both Leland and Habington to be the most ancient church in the shire,[44] and although these authorities are comparatively late, it seems likely that they were recording a much earlier tradition. The dedication to the Romano-British saint Helen is unique in Worcestershire and is generally rare in the West Midlands; her cult was not much favoured by the English Church.[45] Significantly, churches bearing this dedication in both York and Colchester have been found to have been built directly over Roman structures.[46] Before the Norman Conquest St. Helen's was the mother church of no less than eleven chapels, Churchill, Claines, Holt, Huddington, Kenswick, Warndon, Whittington, Wichenford, Wick Episcopi, Witley, and probably Oddingley, covering a considerable tract of land on both sides of the Severn, extending up to 11 km from the city; its territory may have been even more extensive, for it also received tithes from Martley until these were transferred to the Norman abbey of Cormeilles after the Conquest[47] (Fig. 29). In the 11th century it owned nine houses, which surrounded the church in a manner reminiscent of the oratories of a Celtic monastery.[48] As David Whitehead has pointed out, this bears all the hallmarks of a *clas* church, the mother-church in the Celtic system, served by a *clas*, or community of canons, which held pastoral responsibilities for a wide, but defined, area.[49]

In 960 the priest of St. Helen's agreed to become a Benedictine monk at St. Mary's in Worcester, and the

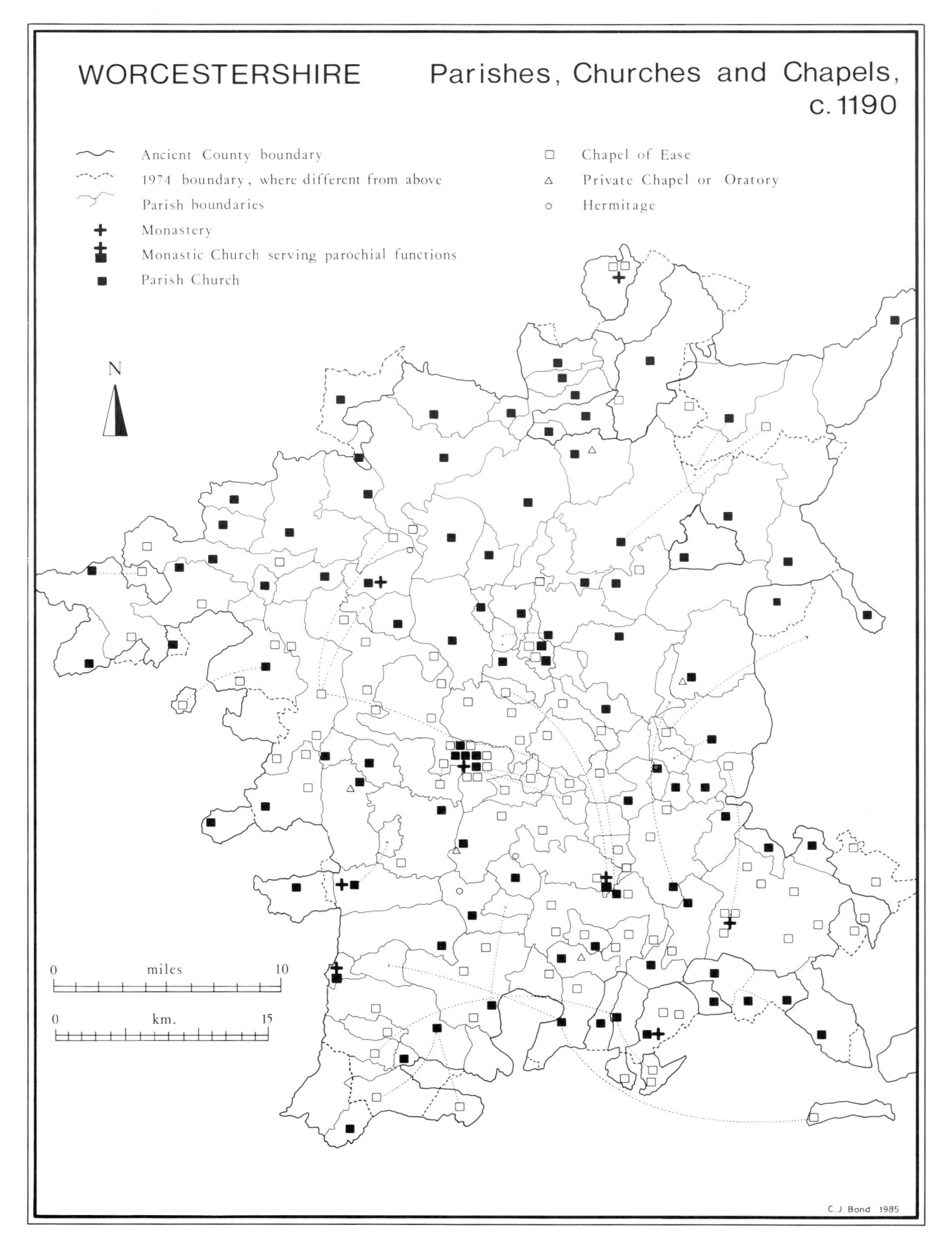

Fig. 28 Worcestershire: parishes, churches and chapels, c. 1190.

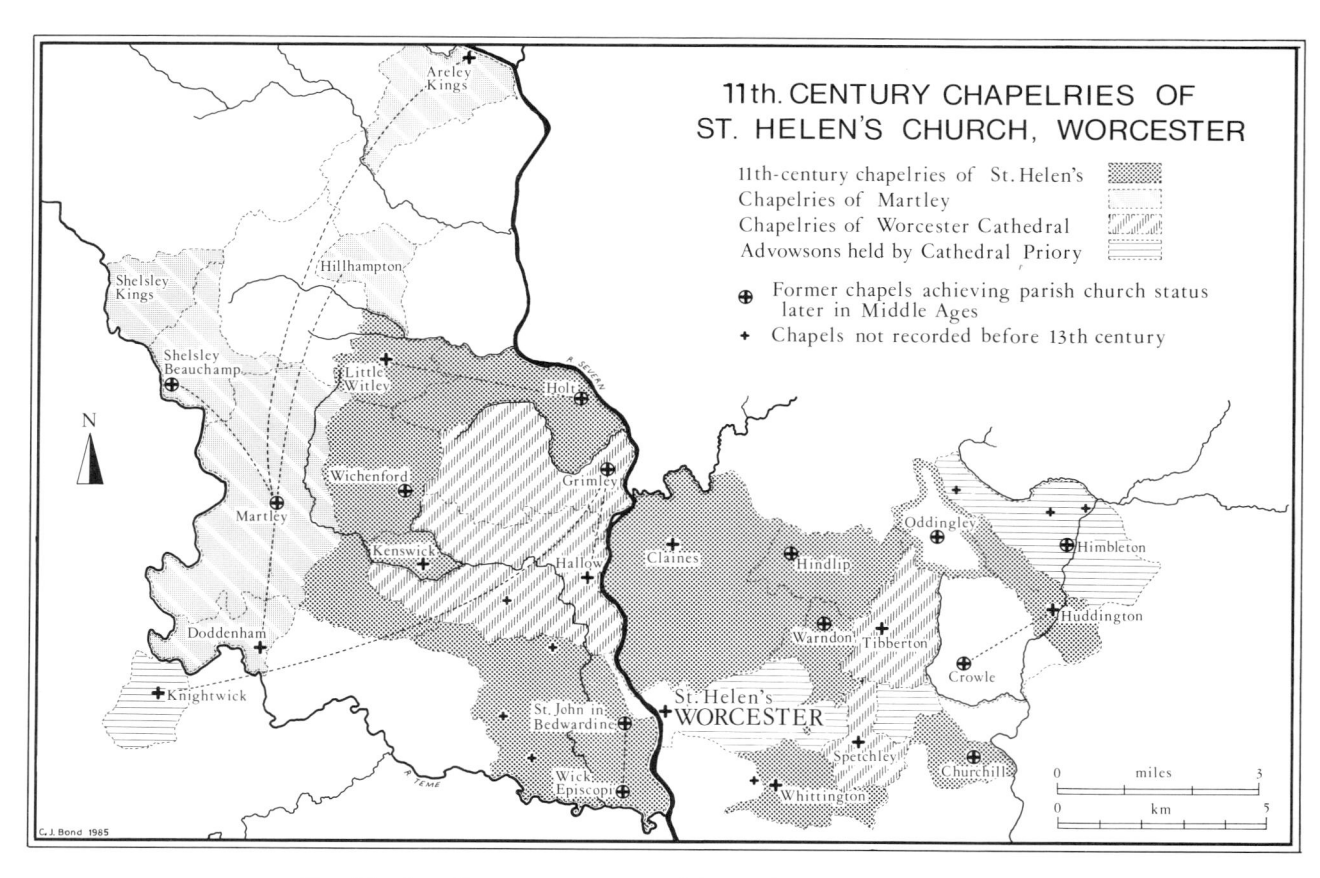

Fig. 29 Pre-Conquest territory of St. Helen's church, Worcester.

extensive possessions of this church came into the hands of the Cathedral Priory.[50] Thereafter the fragmentation of its vast territory seems to have begun, though it continued to contain a significantly high proportion of subordinate chapels. Martley, the most distant of the chapels originally subservient to St. Helen's, emerged as a mother church in its own right, with chapelries at Areley Kings, Doddenham and Shelsley Beauchamp, also including after the early 14th century the chapel of Knightwick which had previously belonged to Grimley. St. Cuthbert's at Wick Episcopi similarly for a time functioned as the mother church of chapels at Upper Wick, Laughern and St. John-in-Bedwardine. Little Witley became a chapel of Holt, while Huddington became annexed to Crowle. The lands, churches and chapels formerly attached to St. Helen's remained a constant source of disputes between the bishop and prior until 1234, when it was ruled by a commission that all the lands east of the Severn should belong to the bishop, and those to the west to the monks.[51]

It is significant that there were two other churches or chapels with dedications to Romano-British saints within the Roman defences of Worcester. St. Alban's, which belonged to Evesham Abbey, was a tiny church in a correspondingly tiny parish, bounded on the north by the Roman ditch.[52] Its priest figured in a dispute with the priest of St. Helen's, which was settled by the synod of 1092, which declared that St. Helen's had been a vicarage of the cathedral church since the foundation of the see.[53] St. Margaret's chapel was granted to Evesham Abbey along with St. Alban's in 721, and in about 1066 Abbot Æthelwig granted it to the rector of St. Andrew's church, as it had been built on land belonging to this church opposite *Wudestathe* (possibly Quay Street), in exchange for an annual rent of a pound of incense to the abbey sacrist. This chapel is last recorded in 1588–9; it never became the centre of an independent parish, and its very site is now uncertain, though there is a possibility that Spackman may have seen its remains early in the present century in the 'old tythe barn or chapel' containing 14th-century work in Grope Lane.[54]

There are other slight hints of Romano-British or Celtic christianity elsewhere, notably at Evesham, where William of Malmesbury claims that, before the foundation of the Saxon church there in 701, the site had been a wilderness occupied only by a small ancient church which was perhaps of British workmanship.[55] David Cox has argued persuasively that the central estates of Evesham Abbey, coinciding with the main block of the mid 10th-century hundred of *Fissesberg* and the Deanery of the Vale of Evesham, can probably be traced back to Ecgwin's foundation at the beginning of the 8th century; and, moreover, that the portion of the core estates on the south bank of the Avon, comprising Offenham, the Littletons, Bretforton, Aldington, Badsey and Wickhamford, was originally a single estate granted to the abbey in the early 8th century, which may itself have been made up from a nucleus of one or more discrete estates of Roman origin.[56]

Minster Churches

In the earliest period of Anglo-Saxon christianity the minster churches were the chief centres of pastoral organisation under the bishops, with large areas under their control; their functions were in many ways similar to those of the Celtic *clas* churches, though their territories would rarely be quite so extensive. There is not always a clear distinction at this stage between true monastic communities and colonies of secular clergy engaged in missionary activities.

Before the end of the 7th century there is evidence of minster churches with small colonies of monks or priests at Hanbury, Pershore, Ripple and Fladbury. During the following forty years further minsters were established at Evesham, Bredon and probably at Kidderminster, and there are subsequent references to minsters at Beckford, Kempsey and elsewhere.[57] In addition, the existence of several further probable minsters can be deduced from later sources. John Blair has recently defined several criteria by which churches of superior status can be identified within the Domesday record; the occurrance of two priests at Halesowen, Chaddesley Corbett, Ombersley and Droitwich in Domesday Book may represent a residual minster staff; and the endowment of a church with one or more hides, which occurs at Droitwich and Cleeve Prior, may also be significant.[58] At Droitwich two priests were said to have held one hide 'which has never paid geld and is in the abbot [of Westminster]'s demesne'.

The fate of the minster churches in Worcestershire was mixed. Some failed to survive in any shape or form. There are three pre-Conquest charter references to a church called *cadamunstre* or *cadan mynster*, 'Cada's Minster', which stood on the Cotswold scarp above Broadway;[59] but although its general location is clear, alongside a spring just outside the Willersey hill-fort, there is no evidence that any church survived on that spot after the Norman Conquest.

Others, like Evesham and Pershore, were re-founded during the Reform period as regular Benedictine monasteries. At Evesham the initial endowment of the church at the beginning of the 8th century consisted of a block of properties at the east end of the Vale, partly made up of discrete estates of even greater antiquity. Houghton suggested that the tithes of these properties, probably from the outset, were utilised for the general purposes of the Abbey, which in return appointed and paid secular priests to serve the Vale communities. This archaic system endured throughout the middle ages: the twelve churches of the Vale — All Saints and St. Lawrence in Evesham itself, Badsey, Bengeworth, Bretforton, Hampton, Church Honeybourne, Middle Littleton, South Littleton, Norton with Lenchwick, Offenham and Wickhamford — were all still *capellae*, or dependent chapels, of the abbey at the Dissolution, and they made up a peculiar which was exempt from the bishop's jurisdiction.[60]

At Pershore (Fig. 30) the situation was complicated by the seizure of two-thirds of the local abbey's estates by Edward the Confessor as an endowment for his new abbey of Westminster, which had resulted in the splitting of the town of Pershore itself into two separate parishes, Holy Cross serving the Pershore portion and St. Andrew's the Westminster portion. However, some elements of the original minster organisation still persisted:-

(i) Domesday Book records that payment of church-scot amounting to one horseload of grain on St. Martin's Day was still due to Pershore, not only from each of the hundred hides which it still held, but also from the two hundred hides which now belonged to Westminster.[61]

(ii) An enquiry into Pershore's ancient privileges after the accidental destruction of its registers by fire in the early 13th century established its claim to the ancient right of sepulture for all landholding persons dwelling in twenty surrounding manors, many of which had since passed into the hands of Westminster Abbey or other landowners. Landless persons from the same area, for whom no mortuary fee was payable, were interred at Little Comberton rather than in the abbey churchyard.[62]

(iii) Many of the original chapelries within the ancient minster territory of Pershore took a long time to acquire full parochial independence. Strensham acquired burial rights only in 1393, Martin Hussingtree in 1400, Upton Snodsbury as late as 1426, and then only upon payment of compensation to the abbey; and even then, the abbey retained a portion of the tithes. In the Westminster parish of Pershore St. Andrew's, the churches at Besford, Defford, Wick and Bricklehampton never did acquire their independence, and remained chapels throughout the middle ages; though the presence of 12th-century fonts at Bricklehampton and Pinvin indicates that they, at least, did acquire rights of baptism.[63]

Others of the early minsters never became monastic, and were progressively stripped of their pre-eminence. Houghton has traced the breakup of the 50–hide estate which formed the original minster territory of Cropthorne, with Bengeworth and Hampton falling into the hands of Evesham Abbey; Elmley Castle being seized by Robert le Despenser, brother of the Norman sheriff Urse d'Abitot, and becoming regarded as a separate parish under his successors the Beauchamps; and separate chapels appearing in Netherton by the mid 12th century and at Charlton by the 13th century, though these latter two remained subservient to the parish church of Cropthorne.[64]

Even in their reduced status after the Conquest, however, most former minsters still bore marks of special distinction long into the middle ages as the centres of unusually large parishes: Bromsgrove with King's Norton covered 9,894 hectares, Kidderminster 4,759 ha., Ripple 4,317 ha., Fladbury 3,557 ha. and Bredon 3,169 ha. Often, too, these large parishes contained several dependent chapels: up to seven in Fladbury, at least five in Bromsgrove, four or five in Bredon, and three in Beckford. The retention of mortuary fees, oblations and miscellaneous pensions from former dependencies is another distinguishing characteristic. At Fladbury the mother church not only continued to accomodate all burials from its own chapelries such as Throckmorton and Wyre Piddle, but also still received pensions from places which in all other respects were moving towards parochial independence: half the mortuary fees from Bishampton were paid to its rector in 1286, and an annual pension of 6s. 8d. was still being received from Rous Lench in 1535.[65] The former minster church of Ripple appears to have lost control of Upton-on-Severn by 1283, though its rector was still claiming tithes from tenements there; Croome d'Abitot and Hill Croome still paid pensions of 20s. and 6s. 8d. respectively in 1535; and the dead from Earl's Croome were still being interred at Ripple in 1541, the rector retaining half the mortuaries; the ancient minster territory also included the chapelry of Queenhill and the manor of Holdfast.[66] Within the territory of Kempsey, Norton-juxta-Kempsey did not acquire the privilege of sepulture until the mid 15th century, and Stoulton did not acquire full parochial independence for another three centuries.[67] Records of possession of burial rights, payment of tithes and other pensions serve to identify further early mother-churches which are not otherwise specifically documented as minsters, such as Clifton-on-Teme, which received pensions of 6s. 8d. from Lower Sapey, 3s. from Edvin Loach and 3s. from Shelsley Walsh in 1535, or Tenbury, which received pensions of 3s. from Rochford and 12d. from Kyre Magna in exchange for the privilege of those chapels having their own cemeteries.[68] Overbury, Powick, Longdon, Suckley and Inkberrow also emerge as churches with suspiciously large early parishes containing more than one dependent chapelry.

Proprietary Churches

From the late 7th century there are indications of lesser, local churches being built by families on their own properties, either to serve their tenants or as private oratories.[69] This process may well have accelerated in the 11th century. Bishop Wulfstan was active in building churches on his own estates, and he brought pressure upon other landowners in his diocese to do the same on their properties; he is recorded as consecrating several churches belonging to local thegns, one at Gloucester, one built by Ailsi at Longney-on-Severn (Gloucs.) and one built by his own archdeacon Ailric, in addition to others outside his own diocese, at Ratcliffe-on-Soar (Notts.) and Wycombe (Bucks.).[70]

The same process continued after the Conquest, and several examples can be recognised. The church of the Berrow in Malvern Chase is dedicated to St. Faith, a French martyr, suggesting a post-Conquest origin, and it is probable that it was built by Robert de Berrow, the local lord, on his own land in the 1170s;[71] some walling of about this period survives in the north wall of the nave. Similarly, Maurice de Ombersley, lord of Broome manor, is recorded as the founder of the church there after 1154.[72] Direct attribution of expenditure is comparatively rare; though when the church of St. Andrew in Pershore was rebuilt on a new site in 1147, this was said to be at the joint cost of Athelhard, the parson, and Edwin, the vicar.[73]

Domesday Book, though erratic in its recording of churches and priests, since details of these were not specifically required for the fiscal record, gives the impression that the normal status of the 11th-century priest was that of a member of the peasant community with his own land. 61 priests are recorded in 56 different places in Worcestershire. Two priests are recorded in five places, all of them subsequently large parishes with dependent chapelries; as suggested earlier, these may be ancient minsters, but it is also possible that some parochial chapels which are otherwise undocumented were already in existence by the 1080s. In 44 cases the priest is included in the enumeration of manorial tenants and their ploughteams: for example, on the royal manor of Bromsgrove, '20 villeins, the reeve, the beadle, the priest and 92 bordars between them have 77 ploughs'. In twelve cases the actual holding of the priest is given: eight of them had half a hide, the remainder a full hide. These may represent extra property in addition to their service-free land, which in theory should not have been assessable. In terms of its extent, the priest's land generally appears to have been comparable with the normal villein's holding. In exceptional cases the Domesday entry suggests a priest without land or ploughteams. At Kempsey and Abberley the priests are listed amongst the serfs, and at Nafford, where the land was waste (and where no church survives today), the priest was said to be without land or stock. Even more rarely, the Survey records an occasional priest whose position appears to have been markedly superior to that of the ordinary villager. At Besford William the priest held four hides as a subtenant of the abbot of Westminster, with his own men, one and a half ploughteams, and ten acres of meadow.[74]

The service-free land which had been allotted to the priest before the Conquest could not infrequently still be traced centuries later. In Stoke Prior, for example, in 1390 the vicar had half a virgate which, it was said, had

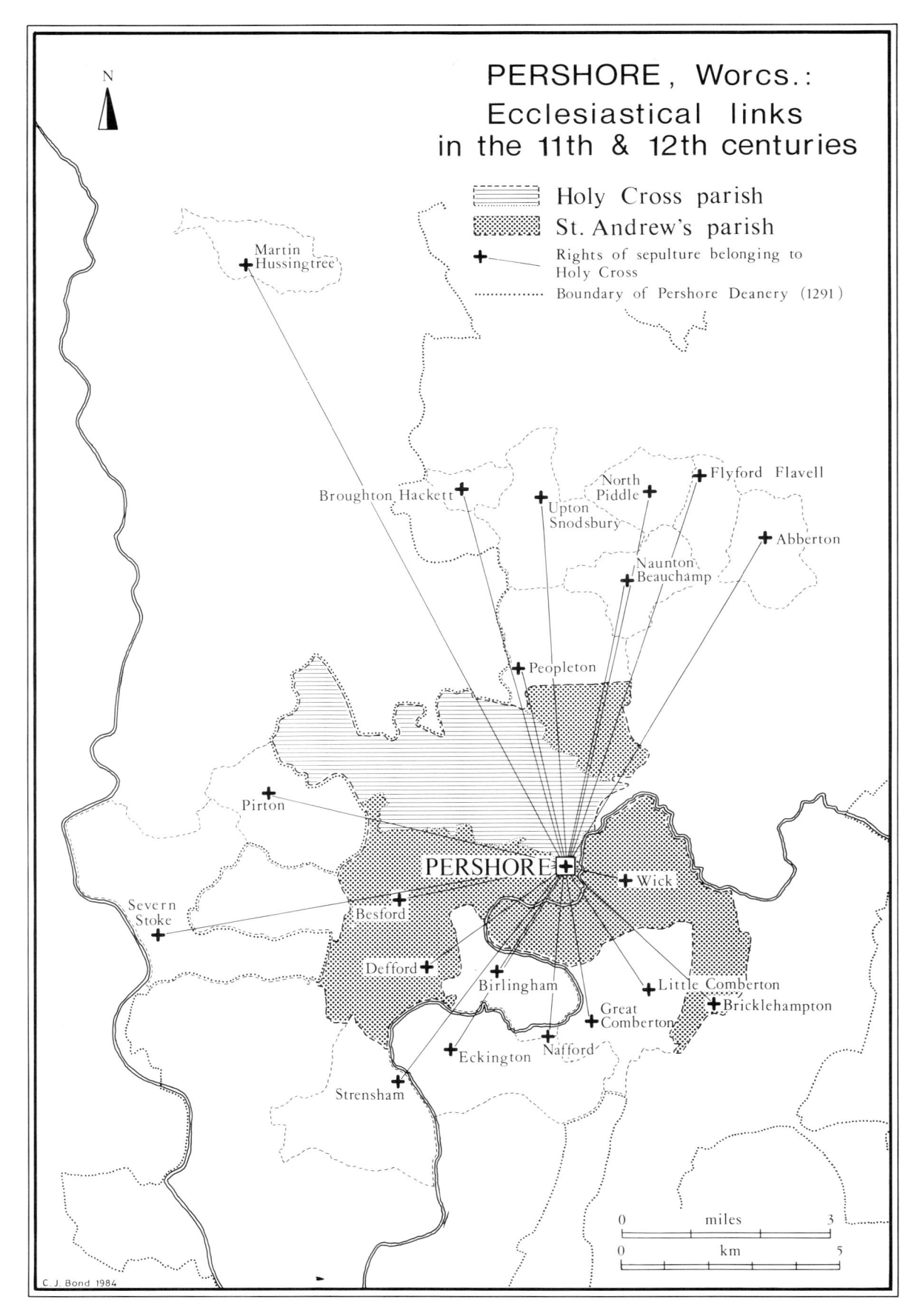

Fig. 30 Pershore: ecclesiastical links in the 11th and 12th centuries.

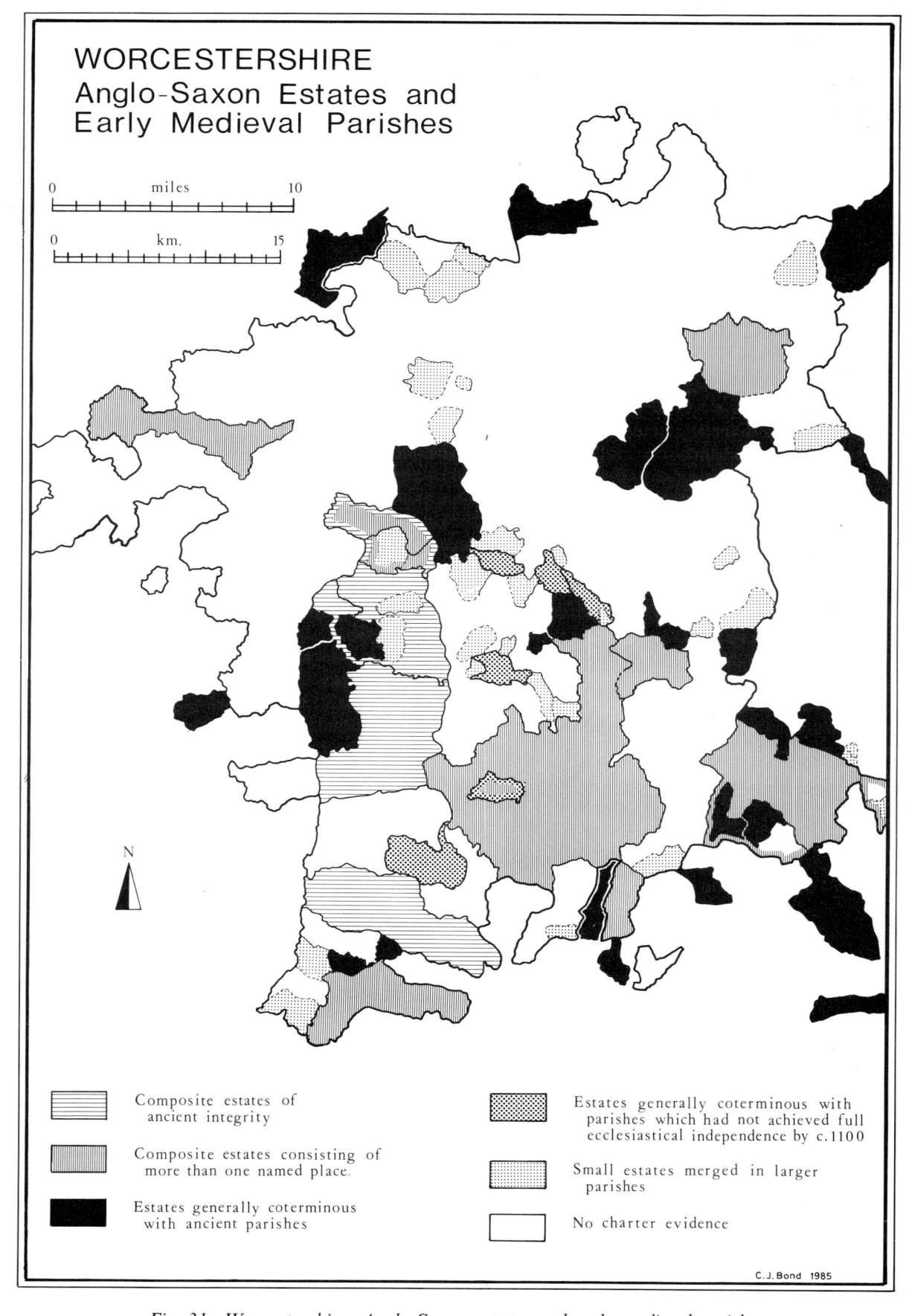

Fig. 31 Worcestershire: Anglo-Saxon estates and early medieval parishes.

'belonged to the church from ancient times'.[75]

The processes by which a parish priesthood emerged out of the sundry *ad hoc* provisions of minster clergy, domestic chaplains and peasant priests are difficult to document in detail. One significant factor was the practice of endowing local churches with tithes, which is first recorded in the 10th century. The tithe-payers were probably simply the tenants of the founding lord, and it would be unwise to assume that the areas from which tithes were to be collected were necessarily demarcated and stable from the outset. However, when parochial areas were eventually defined for tithing purposes they normally made use of more ancient estate and property boundaries. The charter evidence is unusually full for Worcestershire,[76] and it is possible to discern five different kinds of relationship between Anglo-Saxon estates and later medieval parishes (Fig. 31):

(i) Some of the larger estates described in charters, such as *Langandune* (Longdon) and *Poincgwic* (Powick)[77], may have possessed an ancient unity before they became broken up into smaller parishes.

(ii) Other large composite estates consist of several separately-named places from an early date. The 11th-century bounds of an estate bearing the single name of *Pensaxan* (Pensax) coincide with those attached to a late 8th-century charter which records a grant to St. Peter's, Worcester, of 15 *cassati* in *Cnihtatune* (Knighton-on-Teme), *Neowanham* (Newnham) and *Eardulfestun* (Eardiston); this multiple estate covered the whole of the present parishes of Knighton-on-Teme, Lindridge, Pensax and Stockton-on-Teme.[78] In 849 Bishop Ealhhun granted to King Berhtwulf of Mercia an estate consisting of 5 *manentes* in *Wearsetfelda*, 5 *cassati* at *Coftune* (Cofton Hackett), 5 *manentes* at *Wreodanhale* (Rednal), 2 *manentes* in *Weorsethylle* (Wast Hill) and *Hopwuda* (Hopwood), and 3 *manentes* in *Witlafesfeld*, which occupied the modern parish of Cofton Hackett with much of Alvechurch and parts of Kings Norton.[79] The spurious Evesham charter of 709 with two other sets of undated bounds of properties belonging to Evesham Abbey and the great Pershore charter of 972 are extreme examples of this practice.[80] These charters are describing estates which appear to represent an accumulation of formerly separate properties, perhaps over a period, in the hands of one individual or institution, and their later division into parishes need not represent their subdivision so much as a partial re-establishment of earlier bounds.

(iii) Some estates were directly translated into parishes with substantially identical boundaries: examples include *Swinford* (Old Swinford, which was only much later broken up into the smaller parishes of Upper Swinford, Stourbridge, Lye and Wollescote), *Bradanwege* (Broadway), *Beornothesleahe* (Leigh), *Mearnanclif* (Cleeve Prior), *Ambreslege* (Ombersley), *Penedoc* (Pendock) and *Stoke* (Stoke Prior).[81]

(iv) Some charters describe and give the bounds of individual estates which formed part of a larger ecclesiastical territory and did not achieve full parochial independence until later in the middle ages; examples include the 6 *mansae* at *Uptun* (Upton-on-Severn) described in 962 and the 5 *mansae* at *Crommam* (Croome d'Abitot) described in 969, both in the 12th century still chapelries of Ripple.[82]

(v) Sometimes a viable parish could only be created by the bringing-together of two or more small previously-independent estates, such as the additions of *Thorndune* (Thorne) to Inkberrow, *Poddanho* (Poden) to Church Honeybourne, *Sciran ac* (Shurnock) to Feckenham, *Wulfringctun* (the two Wolvertons) to Stoulton, or *Hwitanhlince* (Whitlinge) and *Waereslaege* (Waresley) to Hartlebury;[83] this process is sometimes suggested by boundary anomalies even where the charter evidence is lacking.

The coincidence of charter and parochial boundaries in any form cannot, however, be taken as evidence for the stability of local *parish* boundaries before the 12th century. The occurrence of such coincidences is more likely to be due to some secular land units retaining their identity over several centuries and still being available as a framework for parochial demarcation when this finally took place.

Lanfranc's reforms hastened the demise of the old minsters and encouraged the trend towards smaller churches serving individual parishes with a permanent priest. The position of the priest was now protected, (i) by prohibitions on monks and wandering clerics serving in parish churches and (ii) by limitations on the services which could be demanded of the priest by his lay patrons. Although the grading of churches was still remembered and still had a bearing upon the payment of dues like church-scot and sepulture, by the mid 12th century the contrast between the old minsters and the proprietary churches had become indistinct, and both were by then serving recognisable parochial functions.

Urban parishes are a rather different matter. Nigel Baker, who has examined the history of the Worcester churches, suggests that the formalisation of parishes in the city comes rather later there than in the countryside. The synod of 1092 which settled the dispute between the priests of St. Helen's and St. Alban's was still able to give the decision that 'there was no parish in the whole city of Worcester, save that of the Cathedral'; and, although there are signs of increasing parochial independence, it was not until the 12th or 13th centuries that indisputable evidence for the existence of the city parishes begins to emerge.[84]

Parochial Chapels
When the parish system did eventually crystallise, many already-existing chapels must have been subordinated to the charge of another church; and, unless the chapel's owner was prepared to continue to support it by maintaining the chaplain's stipend, or unless the lord of the manor or the rector of the new parish church was

Fig. 32 Grafton in Beckford, Worcs.: cottage incorporating remains of 12th-century chapel.

prepared to undertake the responsibility himself, such chapels must often have been reduced to occasional use only, or even in some cases abandoned altogether. At least 180 parochial chapels of various types are documented in Worcestershire between the 11th and 16th centuries, and of these over a hundred do not survive.[85]

Once the network of parish churches had been established, the inhabitants of more distant outlying hamlets not infrequently petitioned to have their own chapel, making much of the difficulties which they suffered in attempting to travel to a church perhaps several kilometres away. Such privileges were normally only acquired with some difficulty, and then only with the assurance that there would be no encroachment over the rights of the parish priest. Infringements against these rights were zealously sought out: in 1252, for example, the monks of Halesowen sued the chaplain of Frankley for burying a corpse there to the prejudice of the mother church.[86] Despite these safeguards, as we have already seen, quite a few once-dependent chapels were promoted to the status of parish churches later in the middle ages; while many of those which failed to achieve this advancement fell out of use, and often ultimately disappeared. However, field evidence of some examples may still be seen. At Grafton in Beckford the remains of the west, north and east nave walls of a mid 12th-century chapel, abandoned in about 1540, can still be recognised, though since converted to a cottage, and the foundations of the chancel have been excavated in the garden (Fig. 32).[87]

In a few cases the selection of the parish church proved abortive for one reason or another, perhaps because of subsequent movements of the population centre, and the ancient church was superseded as the parochial centre by one of its own chapels. In this way Nafford was replaced by Birlingham some time after 1305,[88] and in 1371 St. John-in-Bedwardine, in the western suburbs of Worcester, replaced St. Cuthbert's church at Wick Episcopi, which had itself earlier originated as a chapel of St. Helen's in Worcester.[89] Another possible example is at Rock, where the magnificent Norman church now standing may have replaced an earlier church at Alton. As we saw earlier, the church of Alton was given to the Abbey of St. Evroult in c. 1080, and a priest was recorded there in the Domesday survey; however, a St. Evroult document of 1292 mentions 'Avynton cum ecclesia de Hac' (i.e. Alton with Rock), which suggests that the two churches were identical and that a change of name has occurred.[90] The name 'Alton' is now retained only for a lodge and wood in the Wyre Forest, though it was clearly originally a habitative name.

Private Oratories

Private family chapels attached to manorial premises have a long tradition. A domestic oratory is said to have been built at the bishop's palace in Kempsey in 868.[91] Such chapels were still being built after the Conquest, remaining anomalous to the mainstream of the parochial system. In 1175–6 £19 10s. was spent on works in the chapel of the royal lodge at Feckenham,[92] and at the end of the 12th century Stephen Devereux, steward of the abbot of Pershore, acquired a licence to have a private oratory and chaplain at his house at Leigh.[93] It is probable that many other examples have left no trace in the documentary record.

Plan Types

More-or-less substantial Norman work can be recognised within the structural fabric of at least 102 Worcestershire churches. Often the remains are sufficiently coherent to give a reasonably clear indication of the plan of the building in the late 11th or 12th century. A variety of plan types is represented (Figs. 33–4).

Cruciform Plans

All of the principal Norman monastic churches (Worcester, Evesham, Pershore and Great Malvern) were of cruciform plan with transepts and a central tower. Worcester Cathedral may in addition have had a pair of western towers: the collapse of a tower there is recorded in 1175, and while most older authorities assumed this to be the crossing-tower, Brakspear argued that the immediately subsequent rebuilding of the western two bays of the nave strongly suggested that it was one of a pair of west towers which had collapsed, a view recently endorsed by Wilson.[94] Only five non-monastic churches present clear evidence of a Norman

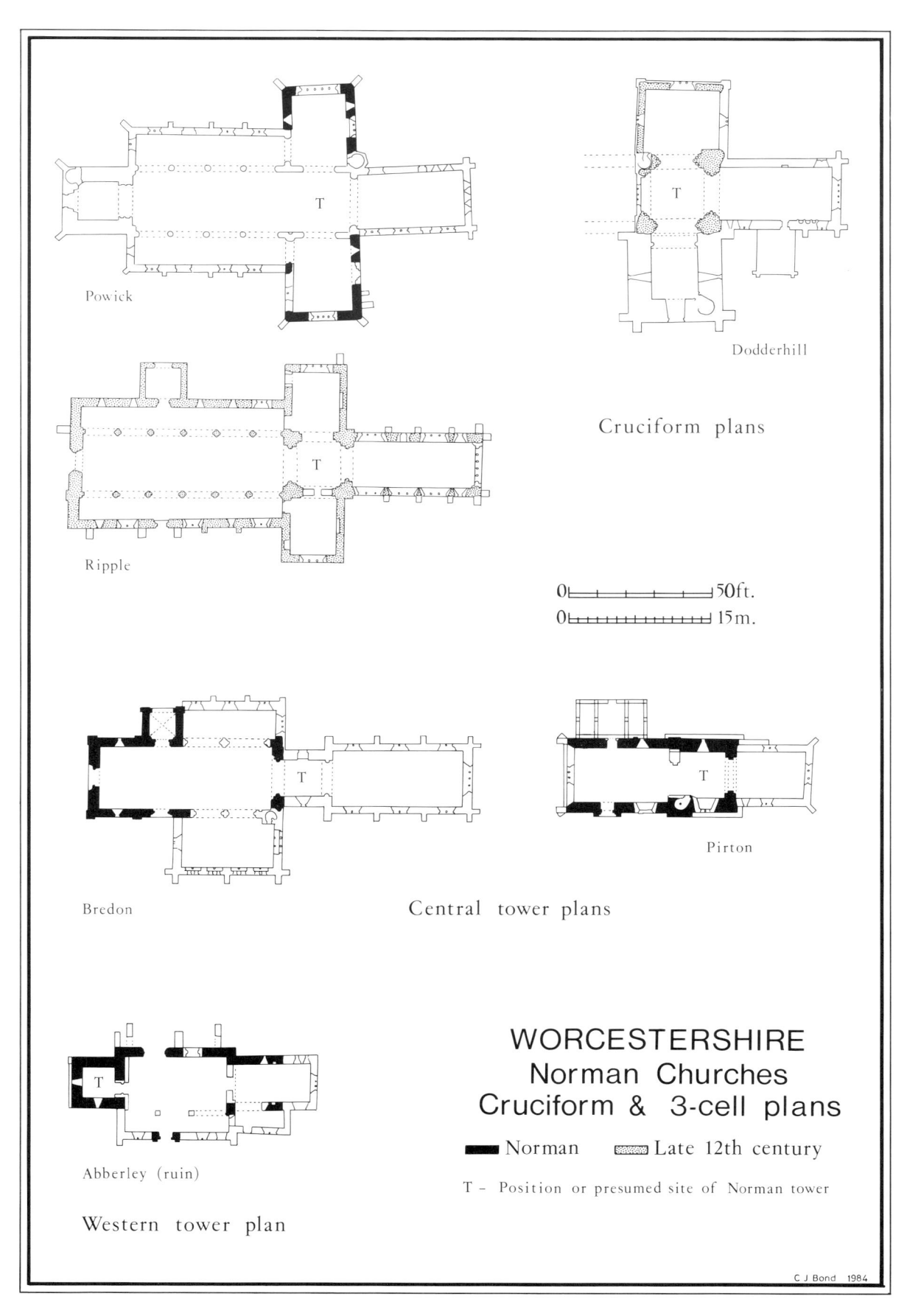

Fig. 33 Worcestershire Norman churches: cruciform and three-cell plans.

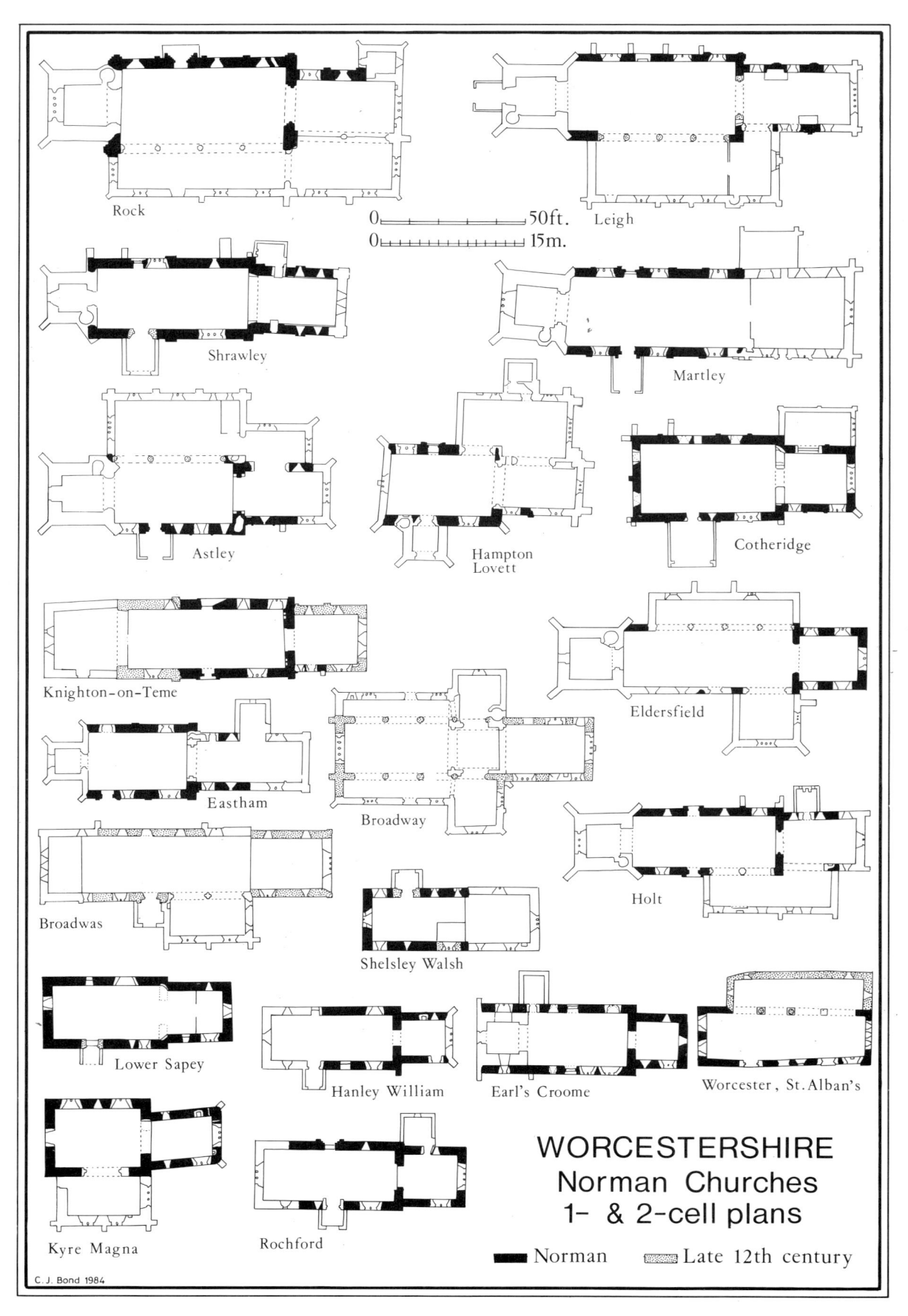

Fig. 34 Worcestershire Norman churches: one- and two-cell plans.

cruciform plan, and all of these are large churches which served extensive parishes and important manors; they are very likely to be of minster origin. The most complete surviving example is at Ripple, where the present building is largely late 12th century; it seems likely that this stands on earlier foundations, though further masonry has been encountered in grave-digging in the churchyard which, it has been suggested, may represent the remains of the 7th-century minster church on a different site.[95]

Three-cell Plan with Central Tower but no Transepts
There are at least half-a-dozen examples of a three-cell plan with western nave, central tower and eastern chancel, but with no evidence of original transepts. This plan-type occurs in large to medium churches, including some which were of minster origin, but does not appear to percolate down to the smallest churches. Examples include Beckford, where the lower part of the central tower is Norman, though it was heightened in the 13th century when the chancel was rebuilt; and Pirton (Fig. 44), where the central tower was taken down later in the middle ages, but has left clear traces of its former presence by the remains of a newel stair in a projecting bay on the south wall of the nave and by a step in the interior nave wall west of the chancel arch which marks the former position of the west wall of the tower. Another example is at Bredon, where only the nave and the west arch of the original central tower escaped later rebuilding. Bredon possesses one additional plan-feature of special interest, a rib-vaulted north porch which probably dates from about 1190. This is unique in Worcestershire, and stone porches appear to be generally rare in parish churches elsewhere before the 13th century.

Three-cell Plan with West Tower
There are also half-a-dozen examples of Norman churches with a west tower, central nave and eastern chancel. This is generally felt to be a later type of plan, but nonetheless western towers were already beginning to appear in Worcestershire by the first quarter of the 12th century. That at Harvington by Evesham survives to its full height. At Cropthorne and Fladbury only the lower stages are Norman, but these both have a distinctive feature which seems to be fairly local in its occurrence, an arrangement of pilaster-buttresses in which the buttress occupying the central position in the wall-space includes a small internally-splayed light. At Tenbury the west tower appears to be largely of mid 12th-century origin, and retains an original west doorway.

Two-cell Plans
Towerless churches consisting simply of a nave and chancel with a structural division between them represent by far the commonest plan-form in Worcestershire before the end of the 12th century, spanning a considerable range of sizes (Fig. 34), but being especially characteristic of medium and small parish churches such as Stockton-on-Teme, and of parochial chapels such as the abandoned example at Lower Sapey (formerly a chapel of Clifton-on-Teme) and the ruined example at Netherton (formerly a chapel of Cropthorne).[96]

Single-cell Plans
There are seven or eight surviving examples of small buildings with no structural division between nave and chancel. Most of these are subordinate chapels of various kinds. Perhaps the most complete example is the late 12th-century private chapel in the grounds of Belbroughton Hall, almost certainly built by the Belne family, who held the manor of Brian's Bell under the de Somerys.[97] Interestingly, there appears to be no medieval documentation whatsoever for the existence of this chapel, and it provides a salutory lesson in caution, if one were needed, for anyone attempting to rely upon documentary sources alone to assess the number of churches and chapels operating in the middle ages. In 1920 the foundations of a small single-cell 12th-century chapel were excavated near St. Katharine's Well on Bredon Hill, overlying the foundations of a still older building.[98] The identification of this building with any recorded structure is contentious, and the documentary sources are themselves confusing. Habington describes the 'ruinated church' of Nafford 'on the aspyringe heyght of Bredon Hyll', but also mentions that 'belowe Nafford on the same hyll is Wolashull's Chapell',[99] both of which may have been dedicated to St. Katharine. There is a record of a 'Chapel of Rupe' somewhere in this area in 1294, which may have been identical with one of the buildings mentioned by Habington, or may have been a different building altogether.[100] Fletcher took the remains to belong to the chapel of Woollashill,[101] but Buchanan-Dunlop preferred an identification with the church of Nafford, on the grounds that the excavator claimed the foundations to be no later than the 12th century, and the Woollashull chapel is said to have had an inscription in its east window recording its foundation by Richard Muchgros, *fl.c.* 1250.[102]

Size of Churches

Several writers have commented upon the very large size of some of the Norman parish churches in Worcestershire.[103] At Kempsey the floor area of the Norman nave is as much as 1731.4 sq.ft (161.7 sq.m). Rock, Halesowen and Martley all have nave areas in excess of 1500 sq.ft (*c.* 140 sq.m), Leigh, Stoulton, Bredon and Ripple in excess of 1300 sq.ft. (*c.* 120 sq.m.). The naves at the top end of the size-range have up to three times the floor-area of those at the bottom end of the scale, such as Kyre Magna (598.38 sq.ft., or

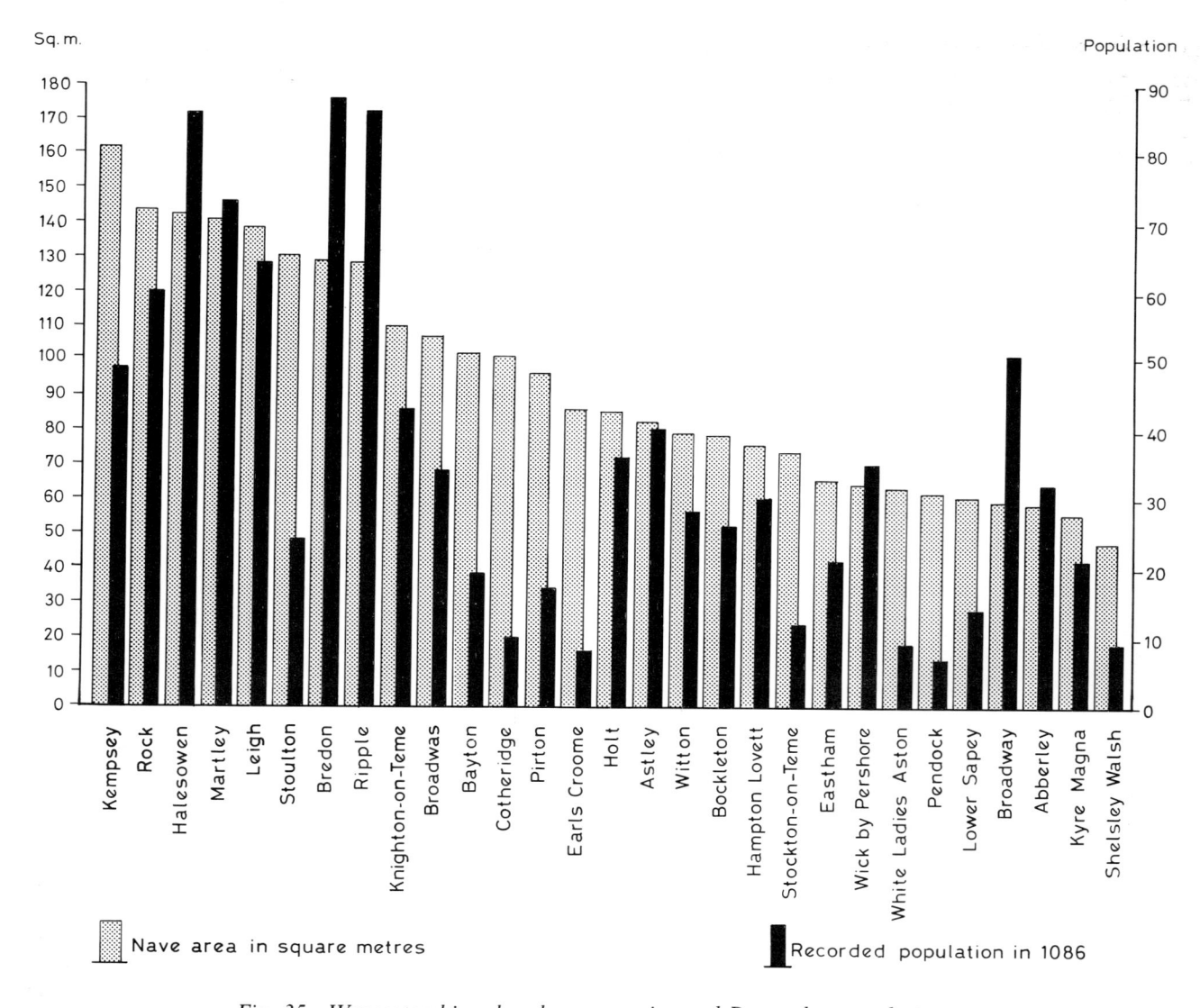

Fig. 35 Worcestershire churches: nave size and Domesday populations.

55.6 sq.m) and Shelsley Walsh (512 sq.ft., or 47.6 sq.m).

It is a not unreasonable assumption that the size of the nave will bear some relationship to the expected size of the contemporary congregation. Can this assumption be tested? No census of the 12th-century population exists, and the only near-contemporary source which sheds any light upon population is the Domesday survey. The problems of distilling meaningful information from this source are notorious, but since it is all we have, the attempt is worth making. Fig. 35 shows a sample of 29 Worcestershire churches ranked by nave size. The examples selected have been chosen because sufficient 11th- or 12th-century masonry survives for us to be reasonably certain either of the total extent, or, in cases where the west wall has been rebuilt, of the minimum extent of the nave at that date. Norman aisles have not been taken into account when assessing nave sizes: these are mainly 12th-century extensions, and it is felt that the nave alone, even if 12th-century in its present form, is likely to be closer to the size of the late 11th-century church. Over this ranking a histogram of the recorded Domesday population has been plotted. Some churches where the contemporary structural evidence is reasonably good have had to be omitted from the equation because no Domesday statistics are available: either they are not mentioned in the survey, like Castlemorton or Shrawley, or they are combined in joint entries, like Cropthorne and Netherton, in such a way that their respective populations cannot be disentangled. Elsewhere, even where population figures are available, many problems of interpretation remain. Rock, for example, is unnamed in Domesday (unless it is the otherwise unidentified *Halac*, which sounds as if it incorporates the same place-name element *ac*, meaning 'oak'), but the survey does record details for Lindon, Alton, Moor and Worsley, all localities, hamlets or farms which fell within the medieval parish of Rock; so the populations of these vills have been added, together with that of *Halac*, to produce a putative total for

Rock. Many other vills named in Domesday Book are not known to have had separate ecclesiastical provisions, or are thought to have acquired their own churches or chapels only after the late 11th century; so, in a number of cases, additional populations have been added to that of the named vill containing an extant Norman church in order to arrive closer to a theoretical 'original' congregation. The 86 people plotted under Halesowen, for example, include 5 listed in the survey under Lutley. The Bredon total includes 52 at Bredon itself, 31 at Mitton and Teddington, 3 at Westmancot and 2 at Bredons Norton. Similarly, the 30 people at Hampton Lovett include 6 at Horton and 14 at Thickenappletree. The general principle has been to exclude subsidiary vills from this process only where Domesday Book itself records a church or priest there, and even this has not been possible on every occasion. The total for Ripple, for example, not only includes stated populations of 12 from Hill Croome and 7 from Holdfast, but also an unknown proportion of the 67 people listed in the main entry who were living at Upton-on-Severn, and since that entry includes two priests, it is highly likely that there was already a separate church or chapel at Upton. Given the nature of the source, it is impossible to devise any method of presenting population figures which is wholly satisfactory. Nevertheless, it is hoped that the approach adopted overcomes at least some of the difficulties and provides a basis for assessment which is not wholly invalid.

The hypotheses that nave size reflects the size of the contemporary population, and that the Domesday statistics offer a means of checking this, does imply the adoption of several other assumptions:-

(i) That nave size will not be unduly inflated by factors other than the size of the congregation, such as the lord's or rector's desires to display their wealth in an unnecessarily ostentatious building; this assumption is probably justified, since quality of workmanship and lavishness of ornamentation are a more likely reflection of such motives than mere size alone, and the chancel is more likely to be the subject of prestigious display than the nave.

(ii) That the Domesday population figures did have some genuine basis in contemporary reality, and were not merely a fossilised record or an arbitrary fiction; this assumption is supported in principle by the records of King William's own instructions to his surveyors, as they were reported by the Peterborough Chronicler and by Bishop Robert of Hereford,[104] though allowances have to be made for errors in the original collection and presentation of the information.

(iii) That, leaving aside the obvious difficulties and anomalies outlined earlier, the bounds of the areas of land belonging to the vills and estates by which the Domesday record was organised usually bore some relationship to the bounds of the emergent contemporary parishes.

(iv) That there was no substantial proportion of the Domesday population which was served by other now-vanished and undocumented churches or chapels in the same vill; the evidence from sites such as Raunds (Northants.) shows that there is an element of risk in this assumption.[105]

(v) That there has been no major alteration to the size of the nave between the 1080s and the 12th century, the period of most of the extant structures; excavations in other parts of the country have suggested that, while the early phases of Anglo-Saxon churches were sometimes much smaller, by the mid to late 11th century the nave had attained a size which was likely to remain stable for some centuries.[106]

Any of the above considerations may unbalance the basic hypothesis, and it would be over-optimistic to expect a perfect correlation between nave size and Domesday population. Nonetheless, what emerges from Fig. 35 is that there does seem to be at least a broad correspondence between the two parameters. Although there are inevitably a few anomalies, all but one of the recorded Domesday populations of over 50 occur in places which also appear in the top eight of the size-ranked churches; Domesday populations of below 10 are correspondingly concentrated towards the lower end of the church size-scale. In general terms each Domesday household could have expected something like two or three square metres of nave floor space.

What, however, can be said of the places which deviate markedly from the norm, where the Domesday population is either greatly in excess of, or greatly below the church provision? The only major anomaly of excess is at Broadway, where a recorded population of 51 with their households was apparently expected to be accomodated in a nave of only 638 sq ft. (59.25 sq.m). Broadway church was almost entirely rebuilt in the last two decades of the 12th century, with aisles added on both the northern and southern sides of the nave in an attempt to cater better for its large population; but if the present nave approximates to the size of its late 11th-century predecessor, why was this initial provision so apparently inadequate? One possibility is that it was already beginning to be overtaken by commercial expansion. Broadway had belonged to Pershore Abbey since the mid 10th century, and lay in a key position between the Vale and Cotswold properties of the abbey; it already had a market by 1196, and although there is nothing distinctively urban in the Domesday record, it is possible that the beginnings of commercial expansion here had already inflated Broadway's population beyond the scale of a church built for a normal rural settlement, a process which also resulted in the increasing isolation of the church as the new market village began to develop along the main road above the abbey grange.

It is a much more frequent occurrence that the Norman nave is larger than might have been anticipated from the Domesday population. Stoulton, whose church ranks sixth in size of those in the sample, has a Domesday population of only 21, and this is stated to include the inhabitants of Mucknell and one of the Wolvertons; there were an additional three families recorded at the other Wolverton. At Bayton, Cotheridge, Pirton and Earl's Croome the churches are similarly larger than might have been expected. Stoulton lay within the Forest of Horewell, and all the other places in this group are situated in the western parts of the county where there are indications of rapid population expansion continuing after the Conquest. The next available source of statistics is the Lay Subsidy roll of c. 1280,[107] which records the tax upon moveable property paid by free householders. As this was assessed on a different basis and for a rather different purpose from the Domesday survey, comparisons between the two sources are somewhat hazardous. In particular, the Lay Subsidy roll lists only those above the taxable minimum, the proportion of which may vary considerably from place to place, and even among those liable there was widespread evasion, so the returns are an inadequate and unreliable source for total population. There are also considerable dangers in attempting to use a late 13th-century source as a guide to developments in the 12th century. Nonetheless, in default of any better alternative, it is worth comparing the numbers of people recorded in 1086 and c. 1280, while maintaining due caution. No returns for Cotheridge can be found in the Subsidy roll, but Earl's Croome, Pirton, Stoulton and Bayton show increases in recorded population of 74 per cent, 47 per cent, 42 per cent and 30 per cent respectively. Unlike Ripple and Kempsey, which also show increases of over 50 per cent, no additional chapels were built in these parishes during the period in question, as far as is known. These particular anomalies on Fig. 35 may, therefore, represent instances where assumption (v) was false, and where the existing 12th-century naves, regardless of the presence or absence of aisles, already themselves represent a considerable enlargement of the buildings which existed in the third quarter of the 11th century.

The Addition of Aisles
The lack of any further general population source before c. 1280 means that there is, therefore, no documentary basis for assessing population trends in the later Norman period. If it is accepted that the size of the nave of a church bears some relationship to the size of the congregation which it was originally expected to accomodate, then the incidence of enlargements by the addition of one or more aisles might be expected to reflect, however imprecisely, the size and chronology of subsequent population increases;[108] and for a period of nearly two centuries, the church fabric itself may well be the only source of evidence for such increases.

In Worcestershire the majority of churches where the evidence is still visible seem to have survived the Norman period without the addition of any aisles at all. Of the score of instances where aisles were added during this period, the majority were already medium to large-sized churches. Almost the only small church to be extended was St. Alban's in the city of Worcester, where a new north aisle was added in the late 12th century.[109] In 13 cases only a single aisle was added, and of these north aisles outnumber south aisles by a factor of 9 to 4, perhaps because of the preference for burying on the southern side, perhaps because of a reluctance to interfere unnecessarily with the normal access to the nave through the south door. In 8 cases aisles were added to both sides of the church, though not necessarily at the same time: at Chaddesley Corbett the north aisle was added early in the 12th century, the south aisle rather later in the same century.[110]

Unlike the monastic churches, few Worcestershire parish churches had acquired aisles before c. 1120, and the first major period of aisle-building activity occurs between c. 1180 and 1200, when the style was already becoming Transitional. At Bretforton, for example, the south arcade appears to precede the north arcade by a few years, but in both cases, while they feature round Norman-type piers, the intervening arches are already pointed.

Architecture and Sculpture
The next section of this paper will attempt to review the main developments in architectural and sculptural style which can be observed in parochial churches and chapels in Worcestershire, to distinguish features which have a special regional character, and to suggest some sources of influence.[111] It must be emphasized that chronology remains a major problem. Very few buildings are precisely dated, and even where approximate dates are cited, these are generally based upon art-historical criteria rather than upon solid archaeological evidence. A thorough re-examination of the buildings themselves, including stone-by-stone elevation drawings and analyses of building stones and mortars, backed up by selective excavations where critical evidence may be threatened by installation of drainage or underfloor heating systems, is highly desirable. Unless such a programme can be undertaken, much of the provisional chronology outlined below will continue to rest upon a fundamentally unsatisfactory foundation. However, on present knowledge, four major phases of building activity can be postulated:

Phase 1: Early Norman
William of Malmesbury, writing some sixty years after the Conquest, described how 'the Normans revived by their arrival the observances of religion, which were everywhere grown lifeless in England. You might see churches rise in every village, and monasteries in the towns and cities, built after a style unknown before'.[112]

The general results of this feverish building activity are described above by Richard Gem (pp. 21–30). Domesday Book provides a Worcestershire vignette in the entry for Offenham, where 'there are oxen for one plough, but they are drawing stone to the church', i.e. the rebuilding of Evesham Abbey.[113]

In the west Midlands the first generation of Norman churches were almost exclusively major monastic buildings, like Worcester, Pershore, Tewkesbury and Gloucester, built in the fashion of great Norman churches like Jumièges or Cérisy-la-Forêt with the type of apsidal ambulatory plan which seems to have its ultimate origin in central France. Bishop Wulfstan, as reported by William of Malmesbury, had mixed feelings about the replacement of the Anglo-Saxon cathedral: 'We miserable people have destroyed the work of saints, to attract praise to ourselves. Our predecessors did not know how to build pompous buildings, but could offer themselves to God under any sort of roof. We, by contrast, neglect our souls in order to pile up stones'.[114] Yet Wulfstan's crypt at Worcester, built between 1084 and 1092, is a major survival of this period, and is of particular importance as one of the few closely-dated structures.[115] By contrast, comparatively little work which can with confidence be attributed to the first few decades of the Norman occupation can be recognised in the smaller churches, a fact which suggests that most of what was done still followed the Anglo-Saxon tradition. Herringbone masonry is present in both the north and south chancel walls of Elmley Castle, and it also occurs in two former Worcestershire churches now transferred to other counties, Edvin Loach (Herefordshire) and Staunton (Gloucestershire);[116] though this technique of building is not confined to narrow date limits, it does generally appear in the West Midlands to be characteristic of the late Anglo-Saxon and early post-Conquest periods.

On present evidence there appears to be something of a pause in church-building during the first couple of decades of the 12th century, though this observation is made with considerable reservations, and this apparent hiatus may yet prove to be more illusory than real.

Phase 2: c. 1120–1150

Within sixty years of the Conquest the concepts and details of continental Romanesque architecture seem to have been fully absorbed by local architects, and are beginning to appear at all levels, not just in the prestigious major buildings. There remain many problems with dating, even where documentary sources suggest a contingent date. At Evesham the Chronicle of the abbey records that the precinct was first enclosed with a wall by Reginald Foliot, who was abbot from 1130 to 1149,[117] and the carriageway through the structure now known as Abbot Reginald's Gate contains a line of blind Romanesque arches. The block capitals are generally characteristic of the first half of the century, but some art-historians would put the work back to before 1120. Did Reginald perhaps incorporate an earlier gate into the alignment of his precinct wall, or was he simply building in a conservative style? Ironically the triple shafts below the capitals are generally more characteristic of the last decades of the 12th century[118], and on that evidence the whole structure may postdate Reginald's abbacy by thirty or forty years.

Doorways: Plain doorways with heavy roll mouldings were much used in this phase, but some were more elaborate, and some especially distinctive features appeared in north-west Worcestershire. Here many examples were set in a slightly projecting bay. The arch of the north doorway at Martley has a roll-moulding between two square orders, one ornamented with lozenges, the other with small saltire crosses, a pattern which will be discussed further below. The north doorway at Rock is probably a little later, with three orders of shafts and the arch decorated with chevron, crenellation and triple ray motifs. In addition to the projecting door bays, four Worcestershire churches, three in the extreme north-west and one near Pershore, have a very distinctive band of blank arcading over the door itself (Figs. 36–40). The simplest example is the most isolated one, at Stoulton, where the panel over the south doorway has two arches only. At Knighton-on-Teme there are four simple arches over the door. At Eastham the doorway itself is very similar to that of Martley, but the panel above has intersecting double arcading with very rudimentary capitals. The most extravagant displays are at Bockleton, where the south doorway has four interlaced arches with billet and cable ornament, the abaci and capitals grotesquely out of scale, and the north doorway is surmounted by five interlaced arches with billet, cable, embattled and saltire designs. Blank arcading as such is familiar enough as a Norman ornamental motif, occurring, for example, in buildings as widely spaced in locality and function as the White Tower of the Tower of London, Norwich Castle, Castle Rising, St. Botolph's Priory in Colchester, Lincoln Cathedral, the Lady Chapel of Glastonbury Abbey and the chapter-house of Much Wenlock Priory. Locally there is a band of intersecting arcading surrounding the interior wall of Worcester Cathedral's chapter-house, built *c.* 1120–30, and a panel of intersecting round arches inside the porch of the parish church on the Bishop's Gloucestershire manor of Bishop's Cleeve. The upper part of the south wall of the south transept of Pershore Abbey has a band of intersecting blank arcading over a string-course, which must be of mid 12th-century date, and Halesowen church, the advowson of which was held by Pershore Abbey between *c.* 1175 and 1199, has a similar intersecting blind arcade carried on cushion capitals on the exterior gable of the east end above the window.[119] There is also a band of blind arcading over the great

Figs. 36–40 Worcestershire 12th-century doorways under panels of blind arcading: 36: Stoulton (S. door); 37: Knighton-on-Teme (S. door); 38: Eastham (S. door); 39: Bockleton (N. door); 40: Bockleton (S. door).

round arch in the west front of Tewkesbury Abbey. It is very difficult, however, to find any direct parallels for the use of blind arcading in a panel over a projecting doorway, either elsewhere in Britain or in northern France. Curiously, the closest parallels so far discovered for both the projecting doorway bay and for the arcading over the lintel are Spanish. The incorporation of the doorway in a slightly projecting bay can be seen in a number of small Romanesque churches in northern Spain, where the fashion runs on into the early 13th century, for example San Pedro at Cervatos, San Juan at Raicedo and Santa Marīja del Yermo.[120] The blind arcading over the door is absent in the northern Spanish examples. There is, however, a remarkable similarity in concept between the Worcestershire doorways and several of the portals of the great mosque at Córdoba built by the Ummayad emirs and caliphs between c. 850 and 1008,[121] though the artistic details are naturally very different. The Moorish fashion for ornamental blind arcades over doorways survived the 11th-century phases of the Christian reconquest in New Castile, as is demonstrated by some of the Mudéjar works in Toledo, notably the outer face of the Puerto del Sol and the doorway of the church of Santiago del Arrabal. The query whether there may be some connection between these rather similar sets of doorways, occurring, as they do, in two widely separated and culturally very different areas, is put forward with the greatest possible circumspection. Nonetheless, some links are possible. The overland pilgrimage to Santiago de Compostella undertaken in about 1140 by Oliver de Merlimond, chief steward to Hugh de Mortimer, lord of Wigmore, is generally accepted as the occasion by which many of the architectural and sculptural patterns of the French and northern Spanish pilgrimage churches were transmitted to the English west Midlands and Welsh marches after the mid 12th century.[122] It is much more difficult to trace any direct links between western Worcestershire and Moorish Spain, though it is not impossible that some indirect trade connections may have existed through the Severn valley and the western seaways.[123] There are, moreover, clear indications of very strong Moorish influence in the Templars' church at Garway in Herefordshire. The four Worcestershire churches with the blank arcade motif over the doorway were all in different ownership in the 12th century, and although three of them were on estates which had belonged to the church of Worcester before the Conquest, there was no common link of patronage operating at the time the

38

39

40

present buildings were erected. As their similarity cannot be attributed to common patronage, it can only be related to the activities of a local school of masons working on a limited number of commissions carried out within a fairly short time-span. In view of the very restricted distribution of this type of doorway, it was almost certainly invented here in the Teme valley, by an unknown builder who perhaps had a second or third-hand knowledge of the Spanish prototypes.

At Knighton-on-Teme there are two additional pairs of blank arches or niches, each within a single round arch, flanking the chancel arch and facing west. Two pairs of blank arches survive in a similar position in the old church at Heythrop (Oxon.); and Deborah Kahn has recently drawn attention to a single arched niche on the southern side of the chancel arch at Halford (Warwicks.) which contains a defaced Romanesque standing figure; this was originally partnered by a similar niche on the northern side, of which only one jamb is still visible.[124] The height of these niches makes it unlikely that they served any function in relation to side altars, and it is equally difficult to see how they can relate to the Rood. Given the tradition of depicting the Annunciation across the span of an open arch or void

Figs. 41–3 Worcestershire tympana: 41: Ribbesford (N. door); 42: Beckford (S. door); 43: Beckford (N. door).

expanse, it is suggested at Halford that the surviving figure may represent the Virgin, with the corresponding northern niche designed to accomodate a representation of the Archangel Gabriel. It is difficult, however, to see how this interpretation can fit the pairs of arches flanking the chancel arches of Knighton or Heythrop, and perhaps these are to be regarded as a purely decorative feature analogous to the doorway arcades.

Another form of ornament which appears to have been favoured by the same group of masons is the covering of one or more orders of an arch with a finely-incised network of saltires or stars, sometimes incorporating small roundels. While this form of decoration is by no means peculiar to Worcestershire (examples may also be seen at Great Washbourn, Stratton and Leckhampstead in Gloucestershire, Bredwardine and Rowlstone in Herefordshire, and Great Rollright, Kencot and Newton Purcell in Oxfordshire, as well as further afield), in this county it is strongly localised in the Teme valley, where it was used with particular delicacy. It appears in the south doorway and chancel arch at Knighton-on-Teme, in the south doorway at Eastham, in the north doorway at Bockleton, above the tympanum at Rochford, and in the doorway already described at Martley.

Before leaving the Teme valley masons, one other highly-localised and distinctive device which can be attributed to them should be mentioned. At Eastham there are two small stone panels with low-relief carvings, one depicting the Agnus Dei within a round frame, the other a four-legged monster, set high on the east wall of the nave south of the arch, while outside on the south wall of the nave there are similar panels depicting Sagittarius and a crouching lion. There is a very similar series of panels at Stockton-on-Teme, with the Agnus Dei in a round-arched frame over the north side of the chancel arch and a wolf or lion over the south, together with a large winged quadruped over the south door. All these appear to be by the same hand.

Tympana: A number of interesting tympana are attributed to the second quarter of the 12th century. Re-set in the south wall of the ruined chapel at Netherton, but originally over the north door, is a tympanum with a single wyvern. At Rochford is a highly stylised Tree of Life, the only Worcestershire example of a pattern which was generally not uncommon in the west of England (Keyser[125] gives an incomplete list of 27 examples, and there are two similar depictions at High Ercall and Linley in Shropshire and two in Gloucestershire at Dymock and Kempley). The most elaborate and controversial tympanum is at Ribbesford (Fig. 41), which displays three figures: (i) A hunter with bare arms, wearing a full-length tunic and cap, shooting an arrow from a bow; (ii) A small quadruped running towards the hunter, variously interpreted as a doe or a greyhound; and (iii) A large, squat, nondescript creature with four short legs, two fins and a flat spade-like tail, which resembles nothing so much as a duck-billed platypus. It has been suggested that this last creature represents a salmon, and attention has been drawn to an incident in one version of the local legend of Robin of Horsehill, which relates that Robin, hunting in the riverside meadows after a night of over-indulgence, aimed his arrow at a deer on the opposite bank of the Severn below Blackstone Rock, but succeeded in hitting a salmon in the river instead.[126] This is an attractive story, but surely a local sculptor would have had a better idea of what a salmon looked like. Alternatively, it may represent a seal: the Legend for the festival of the Translation of St. Ecgwin records that on one occasion the monks of Evesham caught a seal in the Avon.[127] In the 12th century the Severn was tidal up to Worcester, and as late as 1875 two seals were caught at Gloucester.[128] A third alternative is a beaver. Gerald of Wales, writing in the 1180s, gives a long description of the beavers still living on the River Teifi in south Wales; and though he claimed that beavers were then extinct throughout England south of the Humber, there is nonetheless some evidence in the place-names of Bevere and Barbourne (*Beferburnan* in 904), both some ten miles below Ribbesford, and in a landmark described as *Befer pyttas* on the bounds of Pucklechurch (Gloucs.) attached to a charter nominally of the mid 10th century, that beavers had been present in the Severn basin perhaps not too long before.[129] John Ruskin, who visited Ribbesford in the summer of 1877, was amongst the first to draw attention to the tympanum,[130] and ever since there has been much speculation on its meaning. The legend of Robin of Horsehill, though probably owing a great deal to romantic embroidery in the 19th century in its recorded forms, does seem to be of some antiquity, and whether the monster is interpreted as a salmon, seal or beaver, the tympanum may be intended to portray some actual or legendary event. It may be a more general representation of the wealth of game in the locality — the villeins of Ribbesford had to furnish fish-weirs, nets and hunting equipment to Worcester Priory[131] — though if this was the intention it is odd that an unidentifiable monster should have been depicted in preference to more familiar and recognisable game. Another view is that the scene is purely allegorical, showing the human soul (the deer) fleeing from evil (the monster) and being saved by the intervention of Christ (the archer).[132]

Fonts: The devolution of the functions of the old minsters and the acquisition of baptismal rights by many local churches resulted in the manufacture of a large number of fonts in the 12th century. The baptismal rite had a fundamental importance in the medieval church, and the vessels associated with the sacrament seem to have been regarded with special reverence. The original font was often carefully preserved even when the rest of the church was totally rebuilt around it, so that the font is today frequently the oldest surviving feature of the building. Moreover, the old font was also often retained and cared for even when superseded by a later font in a more up-to-date style. As a result, a very high proportion of Norman fonts survives.

Stylistically the most primitive form is the plain tub font, examples of which are not uncommon in Worcestershire. Though these are not closely datable, there is no reason to suggest that any of them date from before the 12th century. Soon, however, the font became a vehicle for decoration and display, and it then becomes possible to identify schools of sculptors.

Two fonts in north-western Worcestershire, dated to about the middle part of the 12th century, are worth noting for their close similarities of style. That at Bayton has a circular bowl with cable-moulded bands and running strap ornament with dots, that at Rock has rosettes connected with clasps. These would appear to be the product of the same workshop, but no other obvious examples have survived locally.

Other features: The only piece of truly ambitious sculpture to survive from this period is the figure of Christ in Majesty at Rous Lench. This exhibits some similarities with sculptural work carried out at Ely in *c*. 1140; it is without local parallels, and may therefore be the work of a sculptor from eastern England. Many other churches have more modest details. The chancel at Shrawley, perhaps dating from *c*. 1120–30, has a zigzag- and cable-moulded string-course and a pilaster buttress pierced by a window, a local feature already noted in the towers at Cropthorne and Fladbury.

Phase 3: c. 1150–1180
After the middle of the 12th century Romanesque decoration becomes increasingly florid. Greater elaboration and variety affects even basic motifs such as chevron ornament, in which a typology broadly comparable with that defined by Alan Borg in Oxfordshire[133] can be observed. Sawtooth chevron-work pointing outwards, i.e. at right-angles to the plane of the wall, first appears at Rochford in about 1150, and may also be seen at Beckford, Bredons Norton, Earls Croome, Eldersfield, Great Malvern Priory, Pendock and Queenhill. At Castlemorton there is a tympanum depicting the Agnus Dei surrounded by furrowed sawtooth chevron-work, with alternate concave and convex ribs, a device which appears to be especially characteristic of south Worcestershire. At Shelsley Walsh a plain tympanum of tufa is also surrounded by furrowed chevron. At Holt (Fig. 45), built *c*. 1160–75, the chevron ornament is applied in steps, and is also beginning to be slightly undercut. The development of distinctive regional schools of sculptors and masons becomes more pronounced.

In north Worcestershire a certain amount of influence percolating through from the Herefordshire school is evident.[134] The classic work of the Herefordshire sculptors is best exemplified by Kilpeck or Shobdon, where the Anglo-Saxon and Scandinavian inheritances are blended with influences from western France and northern Spain assimilated through links with the Santiago pilgrimage route. Similar characteristics can be detected in the lively and distinctive work carried out in a number of Worcestershire churches, even if in some cases this may be merely the result of local men imitating the Herefordshire masters. One of the most accomplished Worcestershire churches of the third quarter of the 12th century is at Rock (Fig. 46),[135] where the chancel arch is a splendid example of the Kilpeck/Shobdon style, and the exterior of the chancel employs flat buttressing, a corbel-table and a string-course to divide up the wall space into compartments containing paired window spaces with shafts with scalloped capitals. One of each pair of windows appears to have been solid from the outset, creating a slightly curious effect on the exterior wall which has puzzled a number of commentators, and I am grateful to Dr. Warwick Rodwell for his suggestion that this was a method of compensating for the wall thickness in order to achieve a regular and symmetrical pattern of windows when viewed from the interior of the chancel, while still affecting a symmetry in relation to the other features on the external wall face. The south wall of the nave at Astley (Fig. 47), usually dated to *c*. 1150–60, displays similar motifs, the three eastern bays being divided vertically by engaged shafts and horizontally by a double-chamfered string-course at sill level, with a corbel-table below the eaves, a design very reminiscent of Kilpeck. The tympanum of St. Kenelm's chapel near Romsley includes a figure of Christ, crowned and seated, surrounded by angels, with an arc of loose interlacing with dragons' heads gnashing at each other, and a band of beakhead ornament on the arch above, a rare feature in Worcestershire, though it does also occur at Northfield (now in Birmingham) and Rock. There is a very similar tympanum at Pedmore, again depicting Christ crowned and seated within a beaded vesica, flanked by the symbols of the four Evangelists.[136] The splendid goblet-shaped font in St. Cassian's church at Chaddesley Corbett, with interlace on its base and rim, plaitwork on its stem and intertwining dragons on its bowl, is another item with strong Herefordshire links, being very similar in character to the fonts at Castle Frome and Eardisley (Herefs.) and Holdgate (Salop.).[137] Something of the same exuberant character lived on into the early years of the following century in the writhing monsters which adorn the base of the otherwise much later font at Elmley Castle.[138]

In south Worcestershire a different tradition, less distinctive and less well-defined, predominates. The key site here is Beckford (Figs. 42–3), which has the greatest range of sculpture surviving intact. Some of the work here has been claimed to have Italian parallels. The chancel arch is supported on round columns which are themselves carved with low-relief grotesque figures, including a centaur on the north shaft; this has been compared with work in the west door of San Ambrogio in Milan. The south door has furrowed zigzag and a tympanum supported by two-headed corbels (another Italian motif) with a depiction of two quadrupeds, a small bird and a roundel, probably representing the Adoration of the Cross, with a chain of interlocking circles symbolising eternity beneath. The tympanum of the north door has two corbels of Malmesbury type (see below), and shows the Harrowing of Hell, with Christ thrusting the Cross into the mouth of a dragon;[139] comparable designs appear at Shobdon (Herefs.) and Quenington (Gloucs.). Other significant details from this period in the south of the county include the tympanum at Little Comberton with an abstract design of eight whorls and a plain cross; and the font at Overbury, depicting a bishop with a nimbus holding a crozier, and a priest in vestments with a stole and maniple bearing a model of a church in his right hand.[140]

Roofs: Comparatively little evidence survives for the form of Norman roofs in parish churches. One exception which has recently been reviewed is at Halesowen, where the interior east wall of the chancel reveals a change from neatly-cut ashlar to rubble in an arc above the window; a similar change in masonry on the north wall indicates the springing-line of the vault, and the springer is also evident in the south-east corner. Light[141] concluded that the mid 12th-century chancel at Halesowen had a high tunnel or barrel vault. Pevsner[142] comments on the rarity of this feature, though Thurlby[143] has drawn attention to parallels at Kempley (Gloucs.) and Ewenny Priory (Glam.), in addition to the high barrel vaults formerly existing in the abbey churches of Tewkesbury and Pershore. Pershore Abbey held the advowson of Halesowen in the last quarter of the 12th century, which provides a significant link between the two buildings.

Phase 4: Transitional, c. 1180–1200
The characteristics of the final period, in which a last flourish of Romanesque details occurs alongside the emergence of Gothic features, have been defined by Neil Stratford,[144] and may be summarised as follows:

The patterns of undercut chevron-work, which were beginning to appear at Holt, become increasingly elaborate and sophisticated, and in its last phase of use at Bredon and Bricklehampton, chevron ornament is even found set diagonally to the plane of the wall. Chevron ornament retained its popularity late in the west of England, and may well have persisted in Worcestershire well after 1200. Trumpet-scalloped capitals begin to appear, the earliest examples probably being on the font at Pershore, c. 1175. Stiff-leaf capitals also begin to appear, used alongside trumpet-scalloped examples at Dodderhill, Stoke Prior and St. Andrew's in Droitwich. Triple shafts, which had already appeared in the gatehouse of Evesham Abbey, become more popular. However, the Gothic pointed arch was already beginning to emerge while many Romanesque details were in regular use. Progressive and reactionary features are often closely intermixed, and dating based on stylistic detail is extremely hazardous. For example, the capitals at Bretforton, which are employed alongside Norman-type round piers and pointed arches, while unlikely to be as early as 1180, could well be as late as c. 1220. One of the Bretforton capitals is of particular interest, depicting St. Margaret as a representative of female innocence being swallowed head-first by Satan, in the guise of a dragon, but being saved by the Cross on her staff, which has caused the dragon's abdomen to burst open to reveal the saint's head.[145]

The most significant parochial building of the last part of the 12th century is the nave at Bredon, which seems to have been constructed around 1180–90. The original west front survives here, with two massive square pinnacled corner turrets, which look like a rustic imitation of the similar turrets adorning the very much grander west front of Tewkesbury Abbey, just over 5 km away. At Bredon it has been clearly demonstrated that the architects and masons responsible for the larger cathedrals and abbey churches could also sometimes be employed on much smaller buildings. Its west doorway has continuous orders in its jambs and arches interspersed with orders having capitals and bases, a pattern which also appears at Bredons Norton, Ripple and Shrawley. The tower arch has trumpet-scallop capitals and chevron and lozenge ornament on the arch itself. This work is of very similar character to that in the western bays of Worcester Cathedral begun in the later 1170s, and since Bredon also belonged to the bishop, it is likely that the same master mason was employed. The distinctive features of the style used at Bredon had first emerged a couple of decades previously in the abbeys of Malmesbury and Keynsham, and were widely employed throughout central southern and western Britain up to about 1200.[146] Beasts'-head label-stops of Malmesbury type appear in the south doorway at Bredon, and also in the west doorway at Ripple, where they seem to be reused.

Building Materials

With the exception of the extreme south-east, Worcestershire is not especially well-endowed with building-stone of first quality, though many parts of the county had access to quarries producing material which was at least moderately serviceable. Apart from Canon Wilson's work on Worcester Cathedral,[147] little serious investigation of the building stone used in churches has yet been carried out in this area. Most of the comments

Figs. 44–7 Worcestershire 12th-century naves: 44: Pirton (S. side, showing base of former central tower); 45: Holt (S. side); 46: Rock (N. side); 47: Astley (S. side).

46

47

which follow are based upon casual observations of colour, texture and form, which should be moderately reliable in identifying most of the major types of stone in use during the Norman period; but no detailed petrological, mineralogical or palaeontological examinations which might pinpoint the sources more precisely have yet been undertaken.

The finest stone available was the yellow-grey oolitic limestone from the Cotswolds and Bredon Hill. Some of this material was of such quality that it was already being transported over distances of up to 90 km from its nearest available source by the 9th century. Oolitic limestone of Taynton type was used in the Anglo-Saxon cross shafts at Tenbury and Acton Beauchamp; the Taynton quarries in Oxfordshire are recorded in Domesday Book. Coarser-grained Inferior Oolite perhaps from Bredon Hill was used for the 9th-century cross-head at Cropthorne and for the early 11th-century sepulchral slab at Rous Lench.[148] Good-quality Inferior Oolite, probably from Guiting, Cutsdean, Campden, Broadway, Cleeve or Bredon, was used after the Conquest in the 1084 crypt and the tower staircase of Worcester Cathedral.[149] Oolitic rubble was used in the 11th-century herringbone masonry of the Elmley Castle chancel. By the 12th century the Cotswold and Bredon limestones were being widely used in the form of freestone throughout the Vale of Evesham, from Broadway westwards to Fladbury, Pershore, Bredon, Overbury and Beckford.

The orange-brown Middle Liassic marlstones, which are of some importance in north Oxfordshire and Warwickshire, are of limited occurrence in Worcestershire, though they were used for dressings in the early 11th-century church at Tredington (now in Warwickshire). The rubbly white, cream and blue limestones of the Lower Lias outcrop over a much wider area in the south-east, and were already being exploited by the later 10th century: the boundary perambulation attached to the great Pershore charter of 972 passes through a quarry (*stan gedelfe*) between Churchill and Broughton Hackett, where liassic limestones were quarried in a site still called Stonepit Copse.[150] They were used in Norman work on both sides of the Avon valley, though they were rarely valued sufficiently to be transported far from their source, and do not appear west of the Severn or north of the Bow Brook valley. The Liassic limestones were frequently used for rubble walling in combination with Oolite dressings, as in the Norman towers at Harvington and Cropthorne, or at Ripple. At Stoulton the nave was of Blue Lias, the flat buttresses of Bredon Oolite.

Of the Triassic materials, the Keuper Marl, which outcrops in a wide arc through Malvern Chase, the lower Teme, Laughern and Salwarpe valleys and parts of the Forest of Feckenham, contains occasional lenses of Arden Sandstone, a pinkish-grey stone of not especially high quality, which was nonetheless used locally, particularly in the extreme south-west at Berrow and Pendock. A single charter reference suggests that it was also being quarried near Kington in the early 11th century.[151] Across northern central Worcestershire the pinkish-red Lower Keuper Sandstone, which was quarried from an early date at Ombersley, Hadley and elsewhere, was quite widely used. It was capable of accomodating fine carving, and was used to good effect in the Norman naves at Astley and Holt and in the chancel at Shrawley, although its weathering qualities were not wholly reliable. At Martley the different sandstones are used quite deliberately in alternating bands of light pink and dark red to create a polychrome effect in the 12th-century nave. The Bunter Sandstones of the Stour valley and Clent region in the north are very soft, and were rarely used for major buildings.

The Carboniferous rocks of the Wyre Forest and Black Country fringes produce two main types of building stone, both from the Upper Coal Measures. The Halesowen Sandstones of the north-east and the corresponding Highley Sandstones of the Wyre Forest range from grey through yellow to greenish-grey hues. Charter evidence indicates that the Halesowen sandstones were being quarried on the bounds of Old Swinford near Wollescote before the Conquest.[152] The green Highley Sandstones, which have been quarried at Upper Arley, were employed in some of the Norman work in Worcester Cathedral, including the tower staircase, the shafts of the nave, and the chapter-house. The Alveley Sandstones, which have also been quarried in the Upper Arley area, are generally of a mottled red-brown colour, sometimes tending towards crimson, purple or mauve; they were used in the cathedral chapter-house below the seats.[153] The Upper Coal Measure sandstones were capable of taking fine carving, as may be seen in the outstanding church of Rock and the tympana of Pedmore and St. Kenelm's at Romsley.

The Old Red Sandstones of the Devonian provide the standard building material in the extreme west of the county, in the Teme Valley upstream from Clifton. They include a variety of pink, mauve, brown, grey and green sandstones, used either as rubble, as in the Tenbury tower, or as freestone, in the carvings around the doorways of Bockleton, Eastham and Knighton, and the tympana of Ribbesford and Rochford. Their weathering properties are not always very good, as the alarming condition of the Rochford tympanum demonstrates. Cradley stone was being used for the piers at Leigh in the late 12th century.

One of the most distinctive building stones used locally in the Norman period is the Calcareous Tufa, a grey stone of spongy appearance formed from deposits from springs rising from thin beds of limestone at the base of the Ditton Series within the Old Red Sandstone. This was available from the Southstone Rock near Stanford-on-Teme and from other localities in the Teme valley and north-east Herefordshire. At Shelsley

Walsh almost the whole church is built of tufa, though the chevron-work around the plain tympanum is carved in sandstone; it also appears at Eastham. The lightness of the tufa made it especially suitable for large roof vaults, and it was being used for vaulting at Worcester Cathedral by the end of the 12th century.

Few other building stones were exploited to any significant effect. Silurian limestones outcrop in a few very limited areas around Dudley, Martley, Alfrick and Suckley, and although they were used by the Norman builders of Dudley Castle, they do not appear to have been used in church building. The pre-Cambrian Gneisses of the Malverns provide irregularly-shaped blocks which were much-used in the 19th century, but which appear hardly to have been used at all in the middle ages.

Notes

1. Cf. C.S. Taylor, 'The Northern Boundary of Gloucestershire', *Trans.Bristol & Gloucs. Archaeol. Soc.* xxxii (1909), 109–39; C.S. Taylor, 'The Origin of the Mercian Shires' in H.P.R. Finberg (ed.), *Gloucestershire Studies* (Leicester Univ. Press, 1957), 17–51.
2. J.H. Round (ed.), 'The Domesday Survey', in *VCH Worcs.* i, 235–323.
2a. Since this was written a suggestion that the church at Sedgeberrow may contain upstanding Anglo-Saxon fabric has been put forward; however, while there is no doubt that the Liassic masonry in part of the west nave wall there antedates the documented dedication of Sedgeberrow church in 1331, there seems no overriding reason to attribute this to the pre-Conquest period. (E.A. Price & B. Watson, 'A Possible Anglo-Saxon Church at Sedgeberrow', *Trans. Worcs. Archaeol. Soc.*, 3rd ser., x (1986), 119–123).
3. *VCH Worcs.* i (1901), 313a.
4. T.R. Nash, *Collections for the History of Worcestershire*, ii (London, 1782), 408; J. Noake, *The Rambler in Worcestershire*, ii (London, 1851), 163–4, and *Guide to Worcestershire* (London, 1868), 252; E.A.B. Barnard, 'Some Old Worcestershire Churches and Parochial Chapels as Noted and Illustrated in the Prattinton Collections', *Trans. Worcs. Archaeol. Soc.* new ser. vii (1930), 86–7; J. Severn Walker, *Architectural Sketches...in Worcestershire and its Borders* (Worcester, 1862), 15; Noake, *Rambler in Worcs.*, iii (1854), 328.
5. *VCH Worcs.* iii, 304–7.
6. F.J. Monkhouse, *Worcestershire*, in H.C. Darby & I.B. Terrett (eds.), *The Domesday Geography of Midland England* (Cambridge, 1954), 215–69.
7. W.D. Macray (ed.), *Chronicon Abbatiae de Evesham* (Rolls Ser. xxix, 1863), 88–95; see also R.R. Darlington, 'Æthelwig, Abbot of Evesham', *Eng. Hist. Rev.* xlviii (1933), 1–22, 177–98.
8. R.R. Darlington (ed.), *The 'Vita Wulfstani' of William of Malmesbury*, Camden Soc. 3rd ser., xl (1928); see also W.F. Hook, 'The Life and Times of Wulfstan, Bishop of Worcester', *Archaeol. J.* xx (1863), 1–28, and J.W. Lamb, *St. Wulstan, Prelate and Patriot* (London, 1933).
9. A. Gransden, 'Cultural Transition at Worcester in the Anglo-Norman Period', in *Worcester B.A.A.*, 1–14.
10. I. Atkins, 'The Church of Worcester from the Eighth to the Twelfth Centuries', part 1, *Antiq. J.* xvii.4 (1937), 383–391; J.W. Willis Bund, 'Ecclesiastical History', in *VCH. Worcs.* ii, esp. 3–12; Macray, op.cit. note 7, 91.
11. D. Knowles, C.N.L. Brooke & V. London, *The Heads of Religious Houses, England and Wales, 940–1216* (Cambridge, 1972), 46–48.
12. Macray, op.cit. note 7, 96; N.E.S.A. Hamilton (ed.), *Willelmi Malmesbiriensis Monachi, De Gestis Pontificum Anglorum* (Rolls Ser. lii, 1870), 137.
13. Macray, op.cit. note 7, 98.
14. Macray, op.cit. note 7, 100; H.R. Luard (ed.), *Annales Monastici*, i (Rolls Ser. xxxvi, 1864), 49; ibid., iii (1866), 441.
15. Macray, op.cit. note 7, 325.
16. W. Thomas, *Descriptio Ecclesiae Maj. Malverne*, in *Antiqu. Prioratus Majoris Malverne* (London, 1725), 35; see also C.H. Haskins, 'The Reception of Arabic Science in England', *Eng. Hist. Rev.* xxx (1915), 56–9.
17. Knowles, Brooke & London, op.cit. note 11, 76–7.
18. W.E. Wightman, 'The Palatine Earldom of William Fitz Osbern in Gloucestershire and Worcestershire (1066–1071)', *Eng. Hist. Rev.* lxxvii (1962), 6–17.
19. Ordericus Vitalis, *Historia Ecclesiastica*, ii, 14, 235–6.
20. *VCH Worcs.* i, 322; for the location of the Eldersfield virgate at Hardwick, see *Book of Fees*, i, 140.
21. *The Great Roll of the Pipe for 6 Henry II, AD 1159–60* (Pipe Roll Soc. ii, 1884), 23–4.
22. *VCH Worcs.* i, 321.
23. Nash, op.cit. note 4, i (1781), 442.
24. *Mon. Ang.* vi (2), 1092–3.
25. *VCH Worcs.* i, 299, 320, 323.
26. *Mon. Ang.* vi (2), 1077–8.
27. *VCH Worcs.* i, 241n.
28. DB I, 164b.
29. *Mon. Ang.* vi (2), 1077.
30. *VCH Worcs.* i, 261.
31. Ibid., 299.
32. J.H. Round (ed.), *Cal. of Documents preserved in France* (H.M.S.O., London, 1899), 219; T. Hearne (ed.), *Hemingi Chartularium Ecclesiae Wigorniensis* (2 vols, Oxford, 1723), 255.
33. *VCH Worcs.* i, 310.
34. *VCH Worcs.* ii, 180–2.
35. *VCH Gloucs.* ii, 6, 52, 102; ibid., viii, 250–62; see also R.N. Sauvage (ed.), *La Chronique de Sainte-Barbe-en-Auge* (Memoires de l'Academie Nationale de Caen, 1906).
36. Darlington, op.cit. note 8, p.xxxvi.n.
37. Macray, op.cit. note 7, 83.
38. Cf. A. Gransden, *Historical Writing in England, c. 550 to c. 1307* (London, 1974), 519; Darlington, op.cit. note 8, p. xxxv.n.
39. D. Whitelock, D.C. Douglas & S. Tucker (eds.), *The Anglo-Saxon Chronicle: a Revised Translation* (London, 1961), 104.
40. H.R. Luard (ed.), *Annales Monastici*, iv (Rolls Ser. xxxvi, 1869), 395.
41. *Taxatio*, 165–6, 216–9, 223.
42. Cf. A.H. Williams, *An Introduction to the History of Wales*, I (Cardiff, 1969), Ch.5, 'The Celtic Church in Wales' and pp. 97–103, 'The Early Welsh Church'; C. Thomas, *The Early Christian Archaeology of North Britain* (Oxford, 1971); S.M. Pearce (ed.), *The Early Church in Western Britain and Ireland* (B.A.R. British Series no. 102, 1982). J.E. Lloyd, *A History of Wales* (3rd edition, London, 1939), 205, discusses the definition of the *clas* and lesser church in the laws of Hywel Dda.
43. D. Whitehead, *The Book of Worcester* (Chesham, 1976).
44. L. Toulmin Smith (ed.), *Leland's Itinerary in England and Wales* (London, 1964), ii, 90; J. Amphlett (ed.), *A Survey of Worcestershire by Thomas Habington*, ii, pt.3, Worcs. Hist. Soc., 1898), 419.
45. F. Arnold-Foster, *Studies in Church Dedications*, ii (1899),

181–9; F. Bond, *Dedications and Patron Saints of English Churches* (Oxford, 1914), 72–6.
46. J.D. Dawes & J.R. Magilton, *The Cemetery of St. Helen-on-the-Walls, Aldwark*, The Archaeology of York, 12/1 (London, 1980); J.R. Magilton, *The Church of St. Helen-on-the-Walls, Aldwark*, The Archaeology of York, 10/1 (London, 1980); W. Rodwell, *Historic Churches – a Wasting Asset* (C.B.A. Research Rep. xix, London 1977), 37–8; P. Crummy, *Aspects of Anglo-Saxon and Norman Colchester* (C.B.A. Research Rep. xxxix, London, 1981), 26–7, 47.
47. Hearne, op.cit. note 32, 427–8; W.R. Buchanan-Dunlop, 'St. Helen's Church, Worcester', *Trans. Worcs. Archaeological Soc.*, new ser. xvi (1939), 14–26.
48. Nash, op.cit. note 4, ii (1782), app., cxlv; Cf. C.A.R. Radford, 'The Celtic Monastery in Britain', *Archaeologia Cambrensis*, cxi (1962), 1–23; H.G. Leask, *Irish Churches and Monastic Buildings, i: The First Phases and the Romanesque* (Dundalk, 1955); V. Hurley, 'The Early Church in the South-West of Ireland – Settlement and Organisation', in S.M. Pearce (ed.), *The Early Church in Western Britain and Ireland* (B.A.R. British Ser. 102, 1982), 297–332.
49. Whitehead, op.cit. note 43, 17–18.
50. I. Atkins, 'The Church of Worcester from the 8th Century to the 12th Century', part 1, *Antiq. J.*, xx (1940), 12.
51. Luard, op.cit. note 40, 426
52. N. Baker, 'Churches, Parishes and Early Medieval Topography', in M.O.H. Carver (ed.), 'Medieval Worcester: an Archaeological Framework', *Trans. Worcs. Archaeological Soc.*, 3rd ser., vii (1980), 30–37.
53. The 1092 synod proceedings are quoted in full in V. Green, *The History and Antiquities of the City and Suburbs of Worcester* (London, 1795), I, 178–180, and more recently in *C & S*, ii, 635–9 (I owe the latter reference to Dr. Blair). The proceedings are discussed by I. Atkins in 'The Church of Worcester from the 8th Century to the 12th Century', part 2, *Antiq. J.*, xx (1940), 204–7.
54. N. Baker, 'The Urban Churches of Worcester: a Survey', in M.O.H. Carver, op.cit. note 52, 117; F.T. Spackman, *The Ancient Monuments and Historic Buildings of Worcester* (Birmingham, 1913), ii, 9.
55. Hamilton, op.cit. note 12, 296.
56. D.C. Cox, 'The Vale Estates of the Church of Evesham, c. 700–1086', *Vale of Evesham Hist. Soc. Research Papers*, v (1975), 25–50. The charter is a forgery (*ECWM*, 88–9), but may have some genuine basis.
57. *ECWM* Nos. 195, 196, 198, 201–5, 207–8, 211, 225–7, 233–4. Bredon was given in c. 716–7 to Eanulf, kinsman of King Æthelbald of Mercia, for the building of a minster, and Eanulf's grandson, Offa, added further endowments; in 736 Æthelbald similarly granted land in the province of *Husmerae* by the River Stour to his companion Cyneberht for the building of a minster, which was probably at Kidderminster.
58. Blair, 'Secular Minsters', 104–142.
59. W. de G. Birch, *Cartularium Saxonicum* (London, 1885–99), Nos. 125, 1282; J.M. Kemble, *Codex Diplomaticus Aevi Saxonici* (London, 1839–48) No. 1368; G.B. Grundy, 'Saxon Charters of Worcestershire', *Trans. Birmingham Archaeological Soc.*, lii. pt.i (1927), 42, 96, 103–4; D. Hooke, *Anglo-Saxon Landscapes of the West Midlands: the Charter Evidence* (B.A.R. British Ser. no. 95, 1981), 298.
60. F.T.S. Houghton, 'The Parochial and other Chapels of the County of Worcester, together with some Account of the Development of the Parochial System in the County', *Trans. Birmingham Archaeological Soc.*, xlv (1919), 32. During the course of Evesham Abbey's appeal to the Pope against the Bishop of Worcester in 1206 Thomas de Marleberge, Dean of the Vale and future Abbot of Evesham, argued that the Vale churches were not parochial despite their possession of fonts and baptismal privileges, but chapels of the Abbey, because (i) they received their chrism and consecrated oil from Evesham, (ii) the inhabitants of the Vale estates were buried at Evesham, and (iii) representatives from each household served by the Vale chapelries had to attend the Abbey church at Pentecost for payment of Whitsun farthings (Macray, op.cit. note 7, 184–9).
61. *VCH Worcs.* i, 305–6.
62. *Mon. Ang.* ii, 420; *VCH Worcs.* iv, 162–3.
63. *Cal. of Entries in the Papal Registers, Papal Letters*, iv, 499; v, 402; Nash, op.cit. note 4, ii, 440–3; Houghton, op.cit. note 60, 33–5.
64. Houghton, op.cit. note 60, 59–61.
65. J.W. Willis Bund (ed.), *Episcopal Registers, Diocese of Worcester: Register of Bishop Godfrey Giffard*, iii (Worcs. Hist. Soc. xiv, 1900), 287; J. Caley (ed.), *Valor Ecclesiasticus*, iii (Rec. Comm., London, 1817), 265.
66. Willis Bund, op.cit., ii (1899), 216; Caley, op.cit., iii, 266; see also Nash, op.cit. note 4, i, 266, 268.
67. *VCH Worcs.* iii, 456; Nash, op.cit. note 4, ii, 24.
68. Caley, op.cit., iii, 278–80; *Mon. Ang.* vi (2), 1094.
69. However, on the problems of early private churches see Blair, 'Local Churches in Domesday', 267–8.
70. Darlington, op.cit. note 8, 20–21, 32, 38, 40, 45, 55
71. Amphlett, op.cit. note 44, i (1893), 130; in 1194 Berrow was said to be a chapelry of Overbury (*VCH Worcs.* iii, 260, 477), where the church has the same dedication.
72. G. Wrottesley (ed.), 'Staffordshire Suits extracted from the Plea Rolls', in *Collections for a History of Staffordshire*, iii (William Salt Archaeol. Soc., 1882), 127–8.
73. T. Madox, *Formulare Anglicanum, or a Collection of Ancient Charters and Instruments of Divers Kinds* (London, 1702), no. cccxcix, 293; *Mon. Ang.* ii, 419ff.
74. *VCH Worcs.* i, 285–323.
75. Houghton, op.cit. note 60, 26, where other examples are also quoted.
76. See S. for a general guide. G.B. Grundy, 'Saxon Charters of Worcestershire', *Trans. Birmingham Archaeol. Soc.* lii, pt.1 (1927),1–183 & liii (1928), 18–131 translates most of the boundary perambulations and offers solutions, though his interpretations are not wholly reliable. For a reassessment see D. Hooke, *Anglo-Saxon Landscapes of the West Midlands: the Charter Evidence* (B.A.R. British Ser. no. 95, 1981).
77. Grundy, op.cit. note 76, i (1927), 172–5, and ii (1928), 43–7; but his suggested solutions both now require reassessment. My own experimental attempt to plot the Longdon charter bounds in R.T. Rowley (ed.), *The Evolution of Marshland Landscapes* (University of Oxford Dept. for External Studies, 1981), 98–100 & fig.2, was too heavily influenced by Grundy's interpretation, and failed to take account of the fact that the estate must have included the modern parishes of Castlemorton and Birtsmorton, in addition to Bushley; for comments on the bounds of the Powick charter see B.S. Smith, *A History of Malvern* (Leicester Univ. Press, 1964), 16–19.
78. Grundy, op.cit. note 76, i (1927), 170–2; Hooke, op.cit. note 76, 368–9.
79. Grundy, op.cit. note 76, i (1927), 54–60; Hooke, op.cit. note 76, 31.
80. Grundy, op.cit. note 76, i (1927), 88–112; Hooke, op.cit. note 76, 364–5; Grundy, op.cit., ii (1928), 30–40.
81. Grundy, op.cit. note 76, ii (1928), 72–5; i (1927), 40–43, 164–9, 52–4; ii (1928), 21–23, 25–30, 62–7; for a reinterpretation of the Pendock bounds, see Hooke, op.cit. note 76, 358–9.
82. Grundy, op.cit. note 76, ii (1928), 92–5; i (1927), 64–6, where *Crommam* is wrongly identified as Hill Croome; Hooke, op.cit. note 76, 29.
83. Grundy, op.cit. note 76, i (1927), 156–61, 146–7, 112–5; ii (1928), 67–72; i (1927), 129–35.
84. Baker, op.cit. notes 52 & 54, 31–7, 114–24.
85. Houghton, op.cit. note 60.
86. Ibid., 77.
87. W.H. Knowles, 'The Recently-Discovered Church at Grafton

near Beckford, and the Churches of Great Washbourne and Stoke Orchard', *Trans. Bristol & Gloucs. Archaeol. Soc.*, xlviii (1926), 287–300.
88. W.R. Buchanan-Dunlop, 'The Parish of Nafford with Birlingham', *Trans. Worcs. Archaeol. Soc.* new ser. xxxv (1958), 1–28.
89. *VCH Worcs.* iii, 501–10.
90. *VCH Worcs.* iv, 326.
91. H.R. Luard (ed.), *Matthaei Parisiensis, Monachi Sancti Albani, Chronica Major*, i (Rolls Ser. lvii, 1872), 391; Green, op.cit. note 53, (1795), i, 169.
92. *The Great Roll of the Pipe for 22 Henry II, AD 1175–6* (Pipe Roll Soc. xxv, 1904), 34.
93. *VCH Worcs.* iv, 110.
94. Luard, op.cit. note 14, iv, 383; H. Brakspear, 'A West Country School of Masons', *Archaeologia*, lxxxi (1931), 13–14; C. Wilson, 'The Sources of the late Twelfth-Century Work at Worcester Cathedral', in *Worcester B.A.A.*, 80–90.
95. E.F. Gray, *St. Mary's Parish Church, Ripple, Worcestershire* (5th edn, 1972), 12.
96. Houghton, op.cit. note 60, 111, 113.
97. Ibid., 48, 112.
98. Buchanan-Dunlop, op.cit. note 88, 3–4.
99. Amphlett, op.cit. note 44, i, 198, ii, 212.
100. Willis Bund, op.cit. note 65, iv (1901), 445; Houghton, op.cit. note 60, 65.
101. A.W. Fletcher, *Eckington: the Story of a Worcestershire Parish* (Oxford, 1933).
102. Buchanan-Dunlop, op.cit. note 88; F.T.S. Houghton, 'The Family of Muchgros', *Trans. Birmingham Archaeol. Soc.*, xlvii (1921), 8–9.
103. E.g. N. Pevsner, *The Buildings of England: Worcestershire* (Harmondsworth, 1968), 15.
104. Whitelock et al., op.cit. note 39; W.H. Stevenson, 'A Contemporary Description of the Domesday Survey', *EHR*, xxii (1907), 72–84.
105. A. Boddington & G. Cadman, 'Raunds: an Interim Report on Excavations, 1977–1980', in D. Brown, J. Campbell & S.C. Hawkes (eds.), *Anglo-Saxon Studies in Archaeology and History*, ii (B.A.R. British Ser. 92), 103–22.
106. See, e.g., J.P. Roberts & M. Atken, 'St. Benedict's Church (Site 157N)', Norwich Survey, 'Excavations in Norwich, 1971–1978', pt.i, *East Anglian Archaeol.* xv (1982), 11–29; J.G. Hurst, 'Wharram Percy: St. Martin's Church', in P. Addyman & R. Morris (eds.), *The Archaeological Study of Churches* (C.B.A. Research Rep. xiii, 1976), 36–39.
107. J.W. Willis Bund & J. Amphlett (eds.), *Lay Subsidy Roll for the County of Worcester, circa 1280* (Worcs. Hist. Soc., i, 1893).
108. Cf. L.J. Proudfoot, 'The Extension of Parish Churches in Medieval Warwickshire', *Jnl. of Historical Geography*, ix. pt.3 (1983), 231–246.
109. W.R. Buchanan-Dunlop, 'St. Alban's Church, Worcester', *Trans. Worcs. Archaeol. Soc.*, xxvii (1950), 1–14.
110. J. Roper, *A History of St. Cassian's Church, Chaddesley Corbett* (1969).
111. Earlier general reviews, from which I have drawn extensively, include J. Humphreys, 'Norman Work in the Churches of Worcestershire', *Birmingham & Midland Institute, Birmingham Archaeol. Soc. Trans. & Repts.*, xxxvii (1911), and, more recently, N. Stratford, 'Norman Sculpture' and other comments contributed to N. Pevsner, *The Buildings of England: Worcestershire* (Harmondsworth, 1968); the descriptions of individual churches included in the *V.C.H.* volumes are often still the fullest accounts available and remain useful, though they need to be used with some caution.
112. W. Stubbs (ed.), *Willelmi Malmesbiriensis Monachi, De Gestis Regum Anglorum*, ii (Rolls Ser., xc, 1889), 306.
113. *VCH Worcs.* i, 306b.
114. Hamilton, op.cit. note 12, 283; for a recent study of Wulfstan's new Cathedral, see R.D.H. Gem, 'Bishop Wulfstan II and the Romanesque Cathedral Church of Worcester', in *Worcester B.A.A.*, 15–37.
115. R. Willis, 'The Crypt and Chapter-House of Worcester Cathedral', *Trans. Royal Inst. of British Architects*, xiii (1862–3), 213–30; for a recent reassessment, see Gem, op.cit. note 114, 21–26.
116. Royal Commission on Historical Monuments, England, *An Inventory of the Historical Monuments in Herefordshire*, ii – *East* (H.M.S.O., London, 1932), 75; *VCH Worcs.* iv, 200–2, 274.
117. Macray, op.cit. note 7, 98.
118. Stratford, 'Norman Sculpture', in Pevsner, op.cit. note 103, 45, 47.
119. M. Thurlby, 'A Note on the former Barrel Vault in the Choir of St. John the Baptist at Halesowen and its Place in English Romanesque Architecture', *Trans. Worcs. Archaeol. Soc.* 3rd ser., ix (1984), 37–43.
120. E. Campuzano & F. Zamanillo, *Cantabria Artistica*, i: *Arte Religioso* (Santander, 1980), 15, 18, 19.
121. L. Torres Balbas, *La Mezquita de Córdoba* (Los Monumentos Cardinales de España, Madrid, 1952); T. Burckhardt (translated A. Jaffa), *Moorish Culture in Spain* (London, 1972).
122. G. Zarnecki, *Later English Romanesque Sculpture, 1140–1210* (London, 1953), 9.
123. For the sea route from the Severn estuary to Santiago de Compostella see E.G. Bowen, *Britain and the Western Seaways* (London, 1972), Ch.VII, 106–23.
124. D. Kahn, 'The Romanesque Sculpture of the Church of St. Mary at Halford, Warwickshire', *JBAA*, cxxxiii (1980), 64–73.
125. C.E. Keyser, *Norman Tympana and Lintels in the Churches of Great Britain* (London, 1904), 65. Keyser's plate of the Rochford tymanum (fig. 30) shows it in much better state than its present weathered and fragile condition.
126. J. Noake, *The Rambler in Worcestershire*, ii (1851), 144–5, and *Notes and Queries for Worcestershire* (London, 1856), 193–4; see also W. Salt Brassington, *Historic Worcestershire* (Birmingham, n.d., 150–3); and E. Lees, 'Description of some Curious Sculptures at Ribbesford Church, Worcestershire', *Assoc. Archit. Socs. Repts. & Papers*, xv (1879), 66–9.
127. Macray, op.cit. note 7, 33.
128. Gerald of Wales, *The Journey through Wales* (translated L. Thorpe, Penguin, 1978), 174–7, and *The Description of Wales* (ibid., 227–9).
129. A. Mawer, F.M. Stenton & F.T.S. Houghton, *The Place-Names of Worcestershire* (English Place-Name Soc. iv, Cambridge Univ.Press, 1927), 111 (though Lees, op.cit. note 126, 67, points to early forms of the name 'Evere' and 'Evereye', which may imply a different origin); G.B. Grundy, *Saxon Charters & Field-Names of Gloucestershire*, ii (Bristol & Gloucs. Archaeol. Soc., 1936), 213.
130. *Kidderminster Times*, July 27th 1877.
131. Hearne, op.cit. note 32, 256.
132. J.R. Burton, *History of Bewdley* (1883), 69–70; J. Romilly Allen, *Early Christian Symbolism in Great Britain and Ireland* (London, 1887), 285; Humphreys, op.cit. note 111, 88–9; Keyser, op.cit. note 125, p.xliii, Fig. 68.
133. A. Borg, 'The Development of Chevron Ornament', *JBAA*, 3rd ser., xxx (1967), 122–140.
134. Cf. G. Zarnecki, 'Regional Schools of English Sculpture in the Twelfth Century' (unpubl. Ph.D thesis, Univ. of London Courtauld Institute, 1950); G. Zarnecki, *Later English Romanesque Sculpture, 1140–1210* (London, 1953), 9–15; T.S.R. Boase, *English Art, 1100–1216* (Oxford Hist. of English Art, iii, Oxford Univ. Press, 1953), 75–83.
135. *VCH Worcs.* iv, 324–6; see also L. Richardson, 'The Church of SS Peter & Paul, Rock', *Trans. Worcs. Naturalists' Club* x. pt.2 (1945–7), 75.

136. Keyser, op.cit. note 125, p.lxii, Figs.113–4.
137. F. Bond, *Fonts and Font Covers* (Oxford Univ.Press, London, 1908), 50–55.
138. Illustrated by G. McN. Rushforth, 'The Font in Elmley Castle Church', *Trans. Worcs. Archaeol. Soc.* new ser. v (1927–8), 92–5, though this paper is more concerned with the later, upper part of the font.
139. Keyser, op.cit. note 125, p.xxiii, Figs. 21, 95; R.H. Martin, 'Beckford Church', *Trans. Birmingham Archaeol. Soc.*, liii (1928), 212–3; Pevsner, op.cit. note 103, 46, 76.
140. R.H. Martin, 'Overbury Church', *Trans. Birmingham Archaeol. Soc.* liii (1928), 214–6. The 11th-century date for the Overbury font suggested by *VCH Worcs.* iii, 473, is surely too early.
141. *VCH Worcs.* iii, 147.
142. Pevsner, op.cit. note 103, 179.
143. M. Thurlby, 'A Note on the former Barrel Vault in the Choir of St. John Baptist at Halesowen and its Place in English Romanesque Architecture', *Trans. Worcs. Archaeol. Soc.* 3rd ser., ix (1984), 37–43.
144. Stratford, 'Norman Sculpture', in Pevsner, op.cit. note 103, 47.
145. Romilly Allen, op.cit. note 132, Plate 117; J.E.H. Blake, 'Bretforton', *Trans. Birmingham Archaeol. Soc.* xliii (1917), 25–8, Figs iv & vii.
146. H. Brakspear, 'A West Country School of Masons', *Archaeologia*, lxxxi (1931), 1–18; C. Wilson, 'The Sources of the Late Twelfth-Century Work at Worcester Cathedral', in *Worcester B.A.A.*, 80–90.
147. J. Wilson, 'Some Notes on the Building Stones used in Worcester Cathedral, and on the quarries from which they were brought', *Assoc. Archit. Socs. Repts. & Papers*, xxxi (1911), 259–70.
148. E.M. Jope, 'The Saxon Building-Stone Industry in Southern and Midland England', *Med. Arch.* viii (1964), 106–7.
149. J. Wilson, op.cit. note 147, 261.
150. Grundy, op.cit. note 76, ii (1928), 39; Hooke, op.c.t. note 76, 274.
151. Grundy, op.cit. note 76, ii (1928), 41–2; Hooke, op.cit. note 76, 274.
152. Grundy, op.cit., note 76, ii (1928), 73; Hooke, op.cit. note 76, 274.
153. J. Wilson, op.cit. note 147, 262.

XI. Architectural Sculpture in Parish Churches of the 11th- and 12th-Century West Midlands: some Problems in Assessing the Evidence

J. K. West

> We must lift up our eyes and our understanding from the particular to the general, from the single building to the society which it served and which alone gave it meaning.[1]

Martin Biddle's call to archaeologists and historians for a broader-based approach to the study of parish churches raises a number of methodological questions. For art-historians, and particularly for those whose primary interest lies in architectural decoration, Biddle's exhortation invites some assessment of how the wider context of the material evidence should be encompassed, and in so doing, prompts certain questions about the criteria and methods which art-historians employ in their approach to the study of parish churches.[2]

Apart from the intrinsic artistic value of the material, the study of sculpture and the carved decoration of parish churches represents an important lead to a wider context of the building as a whole, both in terms of time and place. In order to identify certain iconographic and stylistic features of a given piece of sculpture, art-historians turn not only to other pieces in the same medium, but also to comparable works in other media to elucidate the subject of their research. Such a simple and accepted method self-evidently broadens the horizon of research and leads, to use Biddle's phrase, '... from the single building to the society which it served...'. It is not, however, without difficulties when applied to parish churches of the 11th and 12th centuries. Moreover, as part of a broader archaeological and architectural analysis of the fabric of parish churches, the study of sculpture can contribute a sometimes significant element to considerations of stylistic associations and chronology, or to the 'fine tuning' of possible dates derived from other types of analysis. It is therefore important to consider briefly some of the art-historical criteria used in the dating of architectural sculpture, and to review some of the underlying problems in assessing the single building of the 11th or 12th century in the context of its contemporary society.

Recent studies of the development of parishes and parochial organization have served to bring about a valuable reappraisal of many of the central issues and broader implications of the parish system in 11th- and 12th-century England.[3] Historians have once again been alerted to the limitations of the written record.[4] Whatever direction future studies take, there is a consensus that the surviving written evidence for parish churches before 1100 is scanty, and documentary accounts relating to the fabric of parish churches before the mid 13th century are few in number and often less informative than might be hoped.[5] References to parish churches in the form of charters and confirmations, which record the gift or confirm the ownership of a church and its appurtenances, are of great value; but for the architectural historian, such references often provide little more than evidence for the existence of a particular building at a particular moment in its building history. In view of these limitations, the fabric of parish churches, both above and below ground, becomes the primary document through which its architectural and sculptural history can be assessed.[6]

Central to the development of the parish and to the parish church itself is the part played by the patron or founder. In the absence of contrary indications, historians are obliged to conclude that it was the lord of the manor in which a church was founded who provided the financial impetus for new church building.[7] While this conclusion cannot generally be supported by written evidence, it is hard to imagine that the lord of the manor had no overall control of the types of building erected on his estates.[8]

In practice, one must assume that the commissioning of workshops and the day-to-day administration of building works in the larger or widely dispersed fiefs fell to stewards or obedientiaries of the seigneurial or monastic patrons; but firm evidence for the artistic rôle of patrons remains singularly elusive. In the area of the West Midlands, the invocation of such names as Robert of Lorraine, Gilbert Foliot or Robert of Meulan dispel any impression that the monastic inhabitants of the area were ignorant of cosmopolitan art and letters.[9] Nor can it be acceptable to assume that members of the local baronage like William fitzOsbern, Miles of Gloucester, the Lacys, Beauchamps or Beaumonts were significantly less cosmopolitan in outlook, taste or artistic patronage than their relatives or contemporaries in monastic orders. However, it is as much due to the nature and paucity of the written record as to the poor survival of secular art from the period, or to the difficulty of associating surviving objects with particular lay patrons, that lay patronage remains an ill-defined aspect of our knowledge of 11th- and 12th-century society.

Compared with the meagre remains of secular buildings and their furnishings,[10] the survival of parish churches of the immediately post-Conquest period is relatively rich. Nonetheless, ecclesiastical furniture and fittings in parish churches can only be assessed in the barest outline. While a large number of fonts survive from this period, it is primarily wall-paintings which, although fragmentary, allow the church archaeologist something approaching a clear idea of the 11th- or 12th-century parish church interior.[11] It would be interesting to know more not only of the type of artifact given by lay patrons to monastic houses, but also to what extent parish churches enjoyed similar patronage, or how far the foundation of a parish church required the patron to supply the paraphernalia which would enable it to serve its parish, replete with furnishings and ornaments.[12] The provision of roods and altars together with their ornaments, and possibly of vestments or the cloth from which they were made, were probably an integral part of the foundation of a parish church.[13] It is equally possible that the level of patronage reflected as much the status of the manor and that of the church within it, as it did the status of the patron. Adequate ecclesiastical provision, even lavish patronage of parish churches, might accrue wealth in Heaven and so sustain piety as the principal motivation of patrons; on the other hand, less elevated but pragmatic considerations of population and temporal power may have modified the spiritual investment and indirectly furnished benefits on earth.[14] Whatever the conclusions tentatively drawn about patronage from the written record, the relationship between patrons and workshops, and the freedoms and restrictions imposed in the execution of a given building project, remain a matter of inference and conjecture.

It would therefore be rash to draw any firm conclusions about the general appearance and contents of the 11th- and 12th-century parish church, or the immediate art-historical context of the architectural sculpture which has survived. The erosion of so much material evidence in the form of painted decoration, stone and wood carving, metalwork and textiles presents severe restrictions for the art-historian attempting to assess the wider context of the extant decorative work within a single building.[15] Not least among the casualties is the broad view of an artistic repertoire and the transmission of motifs at a purely parish level. This is not to dwell on the losses at the expense of the survivals. The passage of time, iconoclasm and simple material disintegration have taken their toll of all periods of art; but the restrictions that extensive losses place on the study of the 11th and 12th centuries have limited the value of the fabric of parish churches as 'documents' in their own right.

The 11th- and 12th-century diocese of Hereford and Worcester might be taken as a convenient definition of the West Midlands. Taken together, these two dioceses are bounded on their western flank by Wales and in the south-west by the diocese of Llandaff, and embraced, so to speak, on their eastern boundary by the dioceses of Lichfield, Lincoln, Salisbury and Bath & Wells — a perimeter which might be described by a semi-circle extending from Shrewsbury, through Warwick to Bristol. The area is varied topographically and geologically and, as a consequence, provides a variety of building materials of differing qualities, textures and colours; but perhaps more importantly, of differing potentials for constructional and decorative purposes. These range from some of the finest oolitic limestones to those of a shelly quality, less suitable for fine decorative carving; blue and white lias, rarely used in the 12th century but employed on a restricted scale subsequently; both old red and new red sandstones; and occasionally pockets of so-called 'marble', in reality hard fossiliferous limestones, in which some of the most delicate carving of the later 12th century was executed.[16]

The geological complexion of the West Midlands necessarily had a local effect in the building of parish churches. Not only did the types of stone employed have a determining effect on the physical appearance of church buildings, both in general form and architectural detailing; but it must also be assumed that the apparent expansion of stone church building in the late 11th and 12th centuries was, in no small measure, instrumental in the emergence of a class of skilled quarrymen and craftsmen able to respond to the demands of particular types of stone.[17] Furthermore, decorative carving in some of the smaller churches and field chapels, which seems inept, or lacking in refinement, may have been the direct result of the quality and potential of the stone itself, rather than of the status of the church or the manor in which it was situated.

In the West Midlands (defined in diocesan terms), the number of 11th- and 12th-century parish churches is in excess of four hundred. This total, which includes those churches where Romanesque remains are fragmentary, is not evenly distributed, nor is it possible to know if the surviving buildings are a representative sample of those built during the period. However, given the apparently high survival of parish churches, it is important to note the extensive losses of monastic buildings. Although some of the Romanesque fabric has survived in Hereford and Worcester cathedrals, with more extensive remains of the Romanesque buildings surviving in the abbey churches of Gloucester and Tewkesbury,[18] the loss of many monastic buildings in the area has effectively removed a body of material evidence which may have provided an armature of more or less fixed chronological points against which local developments in parish church buildings might have been measured. This is not to say that monastic buildings are *a fortiori* dated monuments,[19] but one cannot ignore the fact that in general terms, documentary sources for monastic houses and the *res gestae* of their dignitaries are often more forthcoming on the chronology of the fabric than is the case with the parish churches. It is when the direct and indirect references to monastic buildings can be married to surviving fabrics that a framework of more or less absolute chronological points can be established.[20] Consequently, there can be little doubt that the loss of such complexes of buildings as Abingdon, Evesham or Winchcombe of the Benedictine order, and Bristol, Cirencester, Keynsham or Wigmore of the Augustinian and Victorine orders, severely impoverishes the potential for establishing an absolute chronological framework for the region.[21] Furthermore, the loss of these and other monastic buildings coincidentally impairs our understanding of the possible interaction between workshops engaged in monastic building projects and those at work on seigneurial estates, as well as of the mobility of workshops from monastic to lay patrons and *vice versa*.

In view of these losses, and when so few parish churches have firm documentary dates for their construction or subsequent Romanesque modifications; how useful is stylistic analysis for dating parish churches, or the isolation of motifs for establishing the art-historical context of a building undated by other types of evidence? It was largely in response to this problem that the late Stuart Rigold proposed a system of dating based on working generations of artisans, which sought not to fix absolute dates, but to act as a '... convenient provisional grouping of works with some documentary credentials and no inconsistency of manner'.[22] Whatever the merits or otherwise of such an approach, before any conspectus of the art-historical context of parish churches can be achieved, art-historians need to assess the extent to which the architectural decoration of parish churches is comparable with that in monastic buildings. How much evidence is there, for example, of a 'two-tier' system of development between parish churches on the one hand, and monasteries on the other? It is probable that there is no single answer to this question and that the nature of patronage, as well as the mobility and interaction of workshops, varies regionally and from one generation to another.

In the decoration of the south door of St. Swithun's Quenington (Glos.), a distinctive form of clasp joins the jambs to the shafts flanking the door, and is continued around the arch enclosing the tympanum (Fig. 49).[23] This feature, which has a similar decorative function to the so-called beakhead, is also found in the decoration of the churches of Avington (Berks.) (Fig.

Fig. 48 Avington, Berks. S. door.

48), Chirton (Wilts.), South Cerney (Glos.) (Fig. 50) and Stoneleigh (Warks.).[24] Although it is unlikely that these examples represent the full extent of the 12th-century distribution of the motif, the examples cited occur in churches which neither conform to a single diocesan unit, nor do they reflect a pattern of related seigneurial estates.[25] St. Peter's Abbey, Gloucester, claimed to hold the church of Quenington through the gift of Hugh de Lacy I (before 1104);[26] but by the mid 12th century, the manor had been granted by Hugh's grand-daughter, Agnes de Lacy, to the Knights Hospitallers, who successfully contested the Abbey's claim to the church and secured their right to it.[27] Chirton and South Cerney were held by the Gloucester family, but neither of the manors or churches remained among the family's estates by the end of the 12th century.[28] Walter of Gloucester gave the church of South Cerney to Gloucester Abbey (before 1129), although in the mid 12th century his grand-daughter, Margaret de Bohun, had given the manor to her father's foundation of Lanthony Secunda by Gloucester.[29] Lanthony Secunda also benefited by a succession of gifts at Chirton from members of the Gloucester family, culminating in the gift of the church in 1167 by Margaret de Bohun.[30]

It might be argued that the use of this distinctive clasp motif at Quenington, South Cerney and Chirton reflects not only the activities of a single workshop or mason travelling from one project to another, but also the family ties and associations of the probable patrons

*Figs. 49–50 Gloucestershire 12th-century doorways:
49: Quenington (S. door); 50: South Cerney (S. door).*

who held either the churches, or the estates in which they were situated. The reasons behind the conflicting claims to the church of Quenington are uncertain; however, there was certainly a close association between the Lacy and Gloucester families, who held these estates, and further family associations with Gloucester Abbey, which held the churches of South Cerney and Quenington.[31] Although it would be misleading to base any firm art-historical conclusions on the evidence of a single motif, the underlying social framework behind church-building on these estates suggests that its use may be more than mere chance and is indicative of the transmission of motifs through patronage. There are, however, no apparent family or other links to associate these patrons with the holders of Avington and Stoneleigh. Avington was held in 1086 by Robert Puingiant and the church and manor may have descended in this family until c. 1166–7, when Richard de Camville held them.[32] The church of St. Mary at Stoneleigh, on the other hand, was founded on land held by Geoffrey de Clinton and granted c. 1123–1126 to Geoffrey's new Augustinian foundation at Kenilworth.[33] Even though the clasp motif used in the decoration of the chancel arch at Stoneleigh is the only element which links it with the other churches in the 'group', the south door at Avington shares with the south door at Quenington an equally distinctive hoodmould decoration, namely a palmette frieze enclosing balls (Figs. 48–9).[34] The very rarity of these motifs makes any conclusion drawn from their use somewhat speculative; but it is unlikely that either had any widespread currency in the decorative repertoire of 12th-century carvers. One might therefore infer, from the use of clasps and palmette friezes at Avington and

Quenington, that the transmission of motifs rests on the freedom of craftsmen to accept commissions from a variety of patrons without restriction.

The transmission of motifs through the mobility of workshops or individuals, whether the result of patronage or of freedom from constraints on the part of the artisans themselves, may have validity for both the particular and the general view of architectural decoration in parish churches. However, evidence of such mobility is not revealed through the written record; rather, it is an inference drawn by art-historians based on the stylistic analysis of surviving buildings. The occurrence of anomalies, such as at Stoneleigh, where only a single feature of the architectural decoration associates it with a group of churches sharing a more coherent repertoire, may also be understood in terms of the mobility of artisans. Alternatively, while there are a number of other possible solutions to this question, such anomalies might be plausibly explained by the interaction of workshops, or the influence of one workshop upon another.

The concept of 'influence' is by no means peculiar to art-history; but in this context it cannot be wholly divorced from the problems of repertoire, whether in terms of iconography, motif or stylistic traits. In view of the losses of 11th- and 12th-century buildings and their contents, the suggestion of influence remains, for the most part, a working hypothesis which recognizes a link between two or more buildings, but which does not necessarily identify a way in which the association was brought about. In general terms, certain types of decorative element found in 11th- and 12th-century parish churches are sufficiently widespread to constitute a part of a national or regional repertoire. The very size of the available sample of such decorative features as chevron mouldings, beakhead motifs or scallop capitals permits not only a typological appraisal, but also some assessment of regional variation and relative chronological development.[35] For the art-historian, stylistic analysis is further refined by the identification of idiosyncratic treatments of common elements. The apparently eccentric occurrence of a particular motif, or an idiosyncratic treatment of a common motif, in a building outside the locality where it has some common currency may indeed be evidence of artistic influence. The legitimacy of such a claim is supported by the fabric itself, but it rests on a number of assumptions about workshops and the nature of their individual repertoires.[36] While the postulate of influence of one workshop on another can rarely be substantiated from documentary sources, it represents, for the art-historian, a single solution in the interpretation of analogous features apparently unconnected through other types of evidence.

If the art-historical interpretation of parish churches calls for some degree of circumspection, less uncertainty attaches to the most celebrated instance of artistic influence in the 12th-century West Midlands. The pilgrimage of Oliver de Merlimond, high steward of Hugh de Mortimer, to the shrine of St. James at Compostela early in the 1130s, offers the most tangible of links between the churches of Western France and those of the so-called Herefordshire school of sculpture.[37] The repertoire of the school, in reality that of a highly-accomplished workshop, is a rich mixture of local and imported motifs and compositions,[38] importations which have been accepted by art-historians as a reflection of Oliver's pilgrimages. It is arguable whether the details of this extraordinary account of lay patronage would have been known at all, were it not for the fact that Oliver's journey had one other important by-product — the establishment of the first Victorine house in England.[39] Although the initial settlement at Shobdon was not wholly successful, and the canons later moved to Wigmore, the artistic impact of Oliver's pilgrimage on the later commissions of the Herefordshire school was decisive.

The introduction of radial voussoirs chracteristic of the Poitou and the Charente regions of western France, as at Shobdon or Brinsop (Fig. 51), must be attributed directly or indirectly to Oliver's intervention and influence. Similarly, the introduction of figures placed one above the other on a column as at Shobdon or Kilpeck, unprecedented in the earlier architectural decoration of the region, finds comparisons at Compostela and Maizailles. The churches along the route to Compostela may also have been influential in the iconography of the school, in particular the themes of Victory used to decorate the tympana at Brinsop (Fig. 51), Ruardean and Stretton Sugwas (Fig. 52). What is interesting to note is the way in which these several alien features have been absorbed by the Herefordshire carvers.

The almost inevitable choice of local sandstone by the sculptors may have dictated the presentation of forms, and determined a low-relief technique with an avoidance of high arrises. The effect is not that of western France transported to the West Midlands, but that of western French motifs transposed into a local Herefordshire idiom. The mode of transmission is entirely a matter for conjecture, for no firm evidence survives beyond the account of Oliver's pilgrimage to indicate how this was effected. Pattern books or an itinerant sculptor among Oliver's retinue or in his company remain plausible explanations;[40] but the conjectural nature of these solutions serves also to draw attention to just how little is certain about the nature and means of artistic transmission in the 11th and 12th centuries. Oliver's pilgrimage is not, after all, anything more than the story of the foundation of a small house of Victorine canons at Shobdon in Herefordshire. The account may open a door onto a deeper understanding of the nature of patronage; but stripped of associations, it provides only a plausible social context for artistic transmission, rather than producing firm evidence for the artistic rôle of patrons.

One must agree with the editor of the Chronicle of Wigmore, that it represents a '... type of medieval monastic literature which is as invaluable as it is rare'. It raises many interesting questions for the art-historian, not least the question of just how rare Oliver de Merlimond was as a 12th-century lay patron. The case of the Herefordshire school has become something of an art-historical *topos*, if for no other reason than that it leads from the single building to the society which it served. It would be an overstatement to say that it is an example in search of a context; but until further research into patronage and parish church building in the period has been undertaken, it is likely that Oliver's patronage will remain isolated and consequently of uncertain value. Without the support of written evidence, assessing the rôle of patrons in relation to the surviving fabric of parish churches is difficult, but it seems that matters of status can provide important leads. The value of the manor in which a church is founded or the status of a pre-existing church replaced after the Conquest may have as much importance in matters of size, plan or decoration, as the status and wealth of the patron or donor. This suggestion can only be verified by a broad study of which the art-historical and archaeological component would constitute a central part.

An example of the type of building which might be usefully selected for such a study is the church of St. Peter and St. Paul at Blockley. The church, now in the diocese of Gloucester, lay until recently in the diocese of Worcester.[41] The manor was an important one and was described by 'Florence' of Worcester as an episcopal vill (*villam episcopalem*),[42] a designation which suggested to the 18th-century historian William Thomas that there was at Blockley an episcopal palace of the bishops of Worcester.[43] While there is no evidence to support Thomas's assertion, the possibility that Blockley was the site of a minster church with an extensive *parochia* rests on firmer ground.[44] That the bishops of Worcester also held the advowson of the church identifies their proprietary rôle, but cannot be used to assert that church building on this or any other of their estates benefited from episcopal finance, artistic patronage or direction.[45] The lack of written records does not remove the possibility that like any other manorial lords, the bishops of Worcester may have responded to a building appeal.[46]

Turning from the details of the written record to the church itself one is confronted by a building dated, on stylistic criteria only, to the third quarter of the 12th century. The plan of the 12th-century building is that of a simple three-cell church with a western tower, an aisleless nave and three-bay chancel.[47] This is not to say that the church lacks distinction. Its ample proportions and the high quality of its decoration indicate a building with some pretensions. Whether the church was designed to reflect its status as a minster, or indeed the status of the lords of the manor, is an interesting speculation but not one that can be clarified from documentary sources.

Although much valuable evidence for the original form of the chancel interior was removed by plaster stripping in 1929, it is nevertheless clear that there was a vault of three bays supported on the extant wall-shafts with their elaborately carved capitals. The decoration of these capitals, together with the exterior corbel-table (Figs. 53–4), finds comparison with major monastic and parish church building in southern England rather than with parish churches of the region.[48] The fact that so many monastic buildings have been lost in the West Midlands may have falsified the art-historical context of Blockley. Even so, it would seem that the workshop responsible for the 12th-century building was well-informed on important developments in sculptural decoration, and certainly capable of realizing the types of capital being produced in progressive centres elsewhere.

The church, which has found no place in modern art-historical literature, deserves more detailed discussion than can be given here. The nature of patronage can only be inferred from the evidence of the fabric itself; but it seems to have been more cosmopolitan than local in taste. If this could be substantiated by further research, three questions would need to be addressed. Is there any evidence to demonstrate the proposition that churches of minster status rebuilt during the 11th and 12th centuries are distinguished by elaborate decoration? Are churches built on episcopal (or monastic) estates comparable with monastic styles of architectural decoration, whereas those on lay estates are not? Is there any significant change in the amount and quality of architectural decoration towards the end of the 12th century, that is after the main ecclesiastical provision of rural churches had been achieved?

The solutions to all these questions have ramifications for the social context of church-building, if only to throw some light on the men who built and decorated them as well as on those who might be supposed to have financed building projects. If the discussion of so rich a region has seemed to underline the shortcomings of the evidence and, in so doing, erred on the side of speculation and inference, it is because so little that affects architectural decoration in the period is certain. If, following the call from Martin Biddle, historians try to reach a firmer understanding of parish churches through the society which they served, it seems that there, too, much remains indistinct. There is therefore some justification for lifting up 'our eyes and our understanding from the particular to the general...'; but in doing so historians of whatever specialization must not lose sight of what is firm ground.

Figs. 51–2 Herefordshire tympana: 51: Brinsop; 52: Stretton Sugwas
(courtesy Conway Library, Courtauld Institute of Art).

Figs. 53–4 Blockley, Glos.: 53: N. chancel arch capital; 54: exterior corbel table, chancel S. side.

Notes

1. M. Biddle, 'The Archaeology of the Church: a Widening Horizon', in P. Addyman and R. Morris (eds.), *The Archaeological Study of Churches* (Council for British Archaeology Research Rep. No. 13, 1976), 70.
2. One line of approach, directed towards Anglo-Saxon buildings but applicable to those of other periods, was put forward by H.M. Taylor, 'The Foundations of Architectural History', in Addyman and Morris (eds.), op.cit. note 1, 3–9. See also, W. Rodwell, *The Archaeology of the English Church: the Study of Historic Churches and Churchyards* (1981), and review by R. Halsey in *JBAA*, cxxxvii (1984), 175–7.
3. P.H. Sawyer (ed.), *Medieval Settlement: Continuity and Change* (1976); Della Hooke (ed.), *Medieval Villages: A Review of Current Work* (Oxford University Committee for Archaeology Monograph 5, 1985); P.H. Sawyer (ed.), *Domesday Book: a Reassessment* (1985), especially, Blair, 'Secular Minsters', which also gives further bibliographical reference to regional studies.
4. D. Owen, 'Documentary Sources for the Building History of Churches in the Middle Ages', in Addyman and Morris (eds.) op.cit. note 1, 21–7; L.A.S. Butler, 'Documentary Evidence and the Church Fabric', Ibid. 18–19.
5. Butler, loc.cit, note 4.
6. Rodwell op.cit. note 2, 99–101; Halsey op.cit. note 2.
7. F. Barlow, *The English Church 1066–1154* (1979), 51; Lennard, *Rural England*, 295–8.
8. For discussion of the proprietary nature of the parish church see Lennard, *Rural England*, 319 et seq.; Barlow loc.cit. note 7.
9. M.T. Clanchy, *England and its Rulers 1066–1272* (1983), 177–8.
10. M. Wood, *Norman Domestic Architecture* (Royal Archaeological Institute Monograph, 1974).
11. A new survey of English medieval wall-paintings is currently being undertaken by D. Park of the Courtauld Institute (with funding from the Leverhulme Trust) in collaboration with the Royal Commission on Historical Monuments. For published surveys, see C.E. Keyser, *List of Buildings having Mural Decorations* (H.M.S.O. 1883); E.W. Tristram, *English Medieval Wall Painting: The Twelfth Century* (Oxford, 1944).
12. E. Mason, 'Timeo Barones et Donas Ferentes', *Studies in Church History*, xv (1978), 68–9, cites the gift to Westminster Abbey by Urse d'Abetot and the widow of Robert Despenser of a pair of silver candelabra, a thurible, a pallium and a tapestry. This gift symbolized the restoration of lands at Comberton (Worcs.), appropriated by Robert Despenser from Westminster. See also B. Harvey, *Westminster Abbey and its Estates in the Middle Ages* (Oxford, 1977), 74, 361. More light might be shed on this problem by the collection and analysis of citations of artifacts specified in wills; see for example the will of the Lady Wulfgyth (1042–53), D.C. Douglas and G.W. Greenaway (eds.), *English Historical Documents, II, 1042–1189*, (2nd edn., 1981), No. 187. Much valuable material on medieval wills is brought together in M.M. Sheehan, C.S.B., *The Will in Medieval England; From the Conversion of the Anglo-Saxons to the End of the Thirteenth Century* (Toronto, Pontifical Institute of Medieval Studies, 1963), especially 107–19, 298–300. I am grateful to Dr. Ann Williams for bringing this volume to my attention.
13. In addition to such late 11th- and 12th-century stone roods as Langford (Oxon.) and Barking (Essex), the only wooden rood to have survived from the Romanesque period is the head and foot of a rood from South Cerney (Glos.): G. Zarnecki, *English Romanesque Art 1066–1200* (Exhibition Catalogue, 1984) Cat. No. 113, and 'General Introduction' pp. 20–21. Precise information about altars in English parish churches will probably only be recovered through archaeological excavation and chance finds. The standard works on altars and altar ornaments remain: J. Braun S.J., *Der Christliche Altar*, 2 vols. (Munich, 1924); Idem., *Das Christliche Altargerät* (Munich, 1932). Braun, *Der Christliche Altar*, i, 105, draws attention to the reference in the *Vita Wulfstani* to St. Wulfstan's replacement of those wooden altars in parish churches of his diocese with stone altars. Although there is no indication of date in the *Vita*, it is probable that Wulfstan acted in accordance with the ruling of the legatine council held at Winchester in 1070 (*C&S*, ii, 575). In the wealthier manors, and churches of minster status, it is likely that altar ornaments, and in particular those associated with the Eucharist, were made of gold, silver or gilt-copper; conversely, in the poorer rural churches and field chapels, ornaments such as chalices and patens were probably made of tin or pewter. For the restrictions imposed on the use of certain materials for eucharistic vessels, see Braun, *Christliche Altargerät*, 30–47; for the use of base-metals see C. Oman, 'English Base Metal Church Plate' *Archaeol.J.* cxix (1962), 195–207. The position regarding the provision of vestments for parish priests remains unclear. As Brett, *English Church*, 221–9 has pointed out, textual accounts are too vague for any general conclusions to be drawn. *The Life of Wulfric of Haselbury by John Abbot of Ford* (ed. Dom Maurice Bell, Somerset Record Soc. xlvii, 1933), 109, contains an interesting passage in which Abbot John records that Godida, wife of the priest Brictric, made an alb for the church from some linen given to Wulfric. While this provides a charming cameo of parochial life, further research might clarify the question of provision related to foundations.
14. Brett, *English Church*, 221–9; Lennard, *Rural England*, 315–27; Mason, op.cit. note 12, 61, 71.
15. The decorative ironwork of the period is discussed by J. Geddes, *English Decorative Ironwork 1100–1350* (unpublished Ph.D. thesis, London University, Courtauld Institute 1978); see also idem., 'Decorative Ironwork', *English Romanesque Art 1066–1200* (Exhibition Catalogue 1984), 96–7.
16. The most accessible synopses of the geology of the West Midlands are to be found in the introductory matter of the relevant county volumes of the *Buildings of England* series, ed. N. Pevsner (Harmondsworth, Middlesex).
17. R. Morris, 'The Church in the Countryside: two Lines of Inquiry', in D. Hooke (ed.), *Medieval Villages: A Review of Current Work*, (Oxford University Committee for Archaeology Monograph No. 5, 1985), 53.
18. The extensive bibliography for these buildings cannot be recorded here; for recent studies with bibliographical references, see Zarnecki op.cit. note 13, Cat. No. 190 a–f; *Worcester B.A.A.*; *Medieval Art and Architecture at Gloucester and Tewkesbury: Brit. Archaeol. Assoc. Conf. Trans.* vii (1985).
19. S.E. Rigold, 'Romanesque Bases, in and South-East of the Limestone Belt', in M.R. Apted, R. Gilyard-Beer and A.D. Saunders (eds.), *Ancient Monuments and their Interpretation: Essays Presented to A.J. Taylor* (1977), 102.
20. The question of absolute and relative chronology is discussed further by R.D.H. Gem (above, Ch. II).
21. The survivals and losses of Cistercian buildings in the West Country in general is discussed by P. Fergusson, *Architecture of Solitude: Cistercian Abbeys in Twelfth-Century England* (Princeton University Press, 1984), 91–100, and *passim*.)
22. Rigold op.cit. note 19, 103.
23. The original dedication was to St. Mary; St. Swithun occurs after 1735, A.R.J. Jùrica, *VCH Glos.* vii, 127.
24. N. Pevsner and A. Wedgwood, *The Buildings of England: Warwickshire* (Harmondsworth, 1966), 405, describe this feature at Stoneleigh as '..., a kind of beakheads (sic) reduced to elementary geometry'. As yet its origins are obscure.
25. A further example occurs in the decoration of a gateway surviving at Newcastle, Bridgend, Glamorgan: D.B. Hague, *Glamorgan County History: iii: The Middle Ages* (1971), 432, pl.xx. The early history of the castle is unclear and evidence for the date of its 12th-century building phase is largely based on the stylistic date attributed to this gateway: B.H. St.J. O'Neil and

26. H.J. Randall, *Newcastle, Bridgend, Glamorgan*, (H.M.S.O. Guide, 1949), *sub* 'description', where a date of 1175–80 is proposed; see also D.J. Cathcart King, *Castellarium Anglicanum: An Index and Bibliography of the Castles of England, Wales and the Islands* (New York, 1983) i, 161. For a general history of the area including the military and political activities of the Earls of Gloucester, Lords of Glamorgan, see J. Beverley Smith, *Glamorgan County History: iii: The Middle Ages*, 30–9. The use of this motif in Glamorgan may be attributable to contacts between the earls of Gloucester and the family of the Gloucesters, earls of Hereford (after 1141). If O'Neil and Randall's proposed date is accepted, Newcastle Bridgend represents the latest use of the motif.
26. *Historia et Cartularium Monasterii Sancti Petri Gloucestriae*, ed. W.H. Hart (Rolls Ser. xxxiii (1), 1863) 109; C. Johnson and H.A. Cronne (eds.), *Regesta Regum Anglo-Normannorum*, ii (Oxford, 1956), p.410. The grant was made in the time of Abbot Serlo of Gloucester, died 1104 (Dom D. Knowles, C.N.L. Brooke and V. London, *The Heads of Religious Houses England and Wales 940–1216* (Cambridge, 1972), 52).
27. Júrica op.cit. note 23, 123, 126. Hart op.cit. note 26, ii (1865), 93.
28. D. Walker, 'The 'Honours' of the Earls of Hereford in the Twelfth Century', *Trans. Bristol and Glos. Archaeol. Soc.* lxxix (1960), 176.
29. Walker, op.cit. note 28, 198; R. Graham, *VCH Glos.* ii, 88. For Miles of Gloucester's foundation of Lanthony Secunda, see Walker, 'Miles of Gloucester, Earl of Hereford', *Trans. Bristol and Glos. Archaeol. Soc.* lxxvii (1958), 77; *VCH Glos.* ii, 87.
30. Walker, op.cit. note 28, 62, 69; J.H. Stevenson, *VCH Wilts.* x, 62, 69.
31. W.E. Wightman, *The Lacy Family in England and Normandy 1066–1194* (Oxford, 1966), 175–82; Walker, op.cit. note 28, 186–8. Walter de Lacy, abbot of Gloucester (1130–9) was succeeded by Gilbert Foliot (1139–48), a relative of Miles of Gloucester (Knowles, Brooke and London op.cit. note 26, 53; *Gilbert Foliot*, 37 and *passim*.) For Gloucester Abbey's claim to parochial jurisdiction over Gloucester castle, its castellans and inhabitants, see D. Walker, 'Gloucester and Gloucestershire in Domesday Book', *Trans. Bristol and Glos. Archaeol. Soc.* xciv (1976), 111–12.
32. H.J.E. Peake in *VCH Berks.* iv, 154, 162.
33. Johnson and Cronne op.cit. note 26, Nos. 1428, 1445; R. Hilton, *The Stoneleigh Ledger Book* (Dugdale Soc. xxiv, 1960), 7–8; see also J.T. Smith, *VCH Warwicks.* vi, 236 and pl. opp. 238. It may be important to note that Richard de Camville, holder of Avington, founded the Cistercian abbey at Combe near Stoneleigh in Warwickshire. For a synopsis of the remains of Combe, see Fergusson op.cit. note 21, 121–22 and *passim*.
34. The art-historical context of Avington has been shown to be closely associated with the work of Bishop Roger of Salisbury (1102–39) at Old Sarum and Sherborne Castle: R. Stalley, 'A Twelfth Century Patron of Architecture: A Study of the Buildings erected by Roger, Bishop of Salisbury 1102–1139', *JBAA*, 3rd ser. xxxiv (1971), 62–83, esp. 78–80. The only other example from 12th-century architectural sculpture of the palmette frieze enclosing balls occurs on the hoodmoulding fragment from Leeds Priory, Kent, of c.1160: see P.J. Tester, 'Excavations on the Site of Leeds Priory: part ii: The Claustral Buildings and other Remains', *Arch.Cant.* xciv (1978) 79 and Fig. 1.
35. Few studies have been undertaken which treat a single motif, its origins, distribution, development and variation; for beakheads, see Mlle. F. Henry and G. Zarnecki, 'Romanesque Arches Decorated with Human and Animal Heads', *JBAA*, 3rd ser. xx–xxi (1957–8), 1–34, reprinted with addendum in G. Zarnecki, *Studies in Romanesque Sculpture* (1979), No. VI. For chevron ornaments, see A. Borg, 'The Development of Chevron Ornament', *JBAA*, 3rd ser. xxx (1967), 122–40 (examples taken from Oxfordshire). For Romanesque bases, see Rigold op.cit. note 19. The enormous task of collecting and collating the various types of non-figurative capital has yet to be attempted.
36. Even though it can only be inferred, the possibility that influences were transmitted indirectly through pattern books cannot be ignored; see G. Zarnecki, *Later English Romanesque Sculpture 1140–1210* (Tiranti, 1953), 8; R. Scheller, *A Survey of Medieval Model Books* (Haarlem, 1963).
37. The art-historical importance of Oliver's journey to Compostela was first recognized by Professor G. Zarnecki, 'Regional Schools of English Sculpture in the Twelfth Century' (unpublished Ph.D. thesis, University of London, Courtauld Institute, 1950), 218 *et seq.*; Idem. op.cit. note 13, 147–8; Idem. op.cit. note 36, 9–15.
38. I. Wood, 'Areas of Tension' (review of *English Romanesque Art 1066–1200*), *Art History*, viii (2) (1985), 231, pointed to the Scandinavian element in the decoration of the school, and remarked on the relevance of a high proportion of Scandinavian personal names in Domesday entries for the area. I fail to see the force of Dr. Wood's comparison between the Eardisley Christ and the Jellinge crucifixion as an argument for a Scandinavian element in the repertoire of the school. For a parallel situation in Normandy, see M. Baylé, 'Interlace Patterns in Norman Romanesque Sculpture: Regional Groups and their Historical Background', *Anglo-Norman Studies*, v (1982), 1–20.
39. For a parallel text and translation of the Chronicle of Wigmore, see most recently J.C. Dickinson and P.T. Ricketts, 'The Anglo-Norman Chronicle of Wigmore Abbey', *Trans. Woolhope Nat. Hist. Field Club*, xxxix (1969), 413–46, esp. 413–16.
40. Zarnecki op.cit. note 13, 148.
41. M. Hollings in *VCH Worcs.* iii, 275.
42. Florence of Worcester, *Chronicon ex Chronicis*, ed. B. Thorpe, ii (1849), 92.
43. W. Thomas, *A Survey of the Cathedral Church of Worcester...* (1736), 107. This erroneous suggestion has gained considerable currency, but as yet no author has been able to verify Thomas's assertion.
44. S.207; Blair, 'Secular Minsters', map on p.108; W.J. Ford, 'Some Settlement Patterns in the Central Region of the Warwickshire Avon', in Sawyer, *Medieval Settlement* (op.cit. note 3), 286.
45. *VCH Worcs.* iii, 275. For a summary of the position regarding the proprietary status of parish churches see Lennard, *Rural England*, 319 and *passim*.
46. I would like to thank Mrs. Mary Cheney for her generous help over the discussion of the late 12th-century patronage of the bishops of Worcester.
47. A new plan, elevation and reconstruciton of the chancel have been prepared by R.A. Smeeton Esq. and published in the church guide: *The Church of St. Peter and St. Paul Blockley* (1980), 4–5.
48. Some comparative material may be listed as follows: Corbel table: St. Cross Winchester, Winchfield, Steyning. Capitals: Christchurch Canterbury, St. Bartholomew's Smithfield London, Ivychurch Priory, Shaftesbury Abbey, Durham Castle.

XII. The Round Towers of East Anglia[1]

Stephen Heywood

The circular western tower attached to an aisleless nave and chancel (Figs. 55, 56) is a common sight in the East Anglian landscape. The lack of parallels in other parts of Britain, and the use in some instances of archaic techniques of construction, have inspired local antiquarians[2] to make romantic statements about the origins of the East Anglian round tower and to claim extreme antiquity. As a local phenomenon characteristic of minor churches only it surely deserves serious study, if only as the manifestation of an otherwise undocumented cultural condition. This preliminary study will attempt first, to describe the round tower and the features associated with it from statistical, constructional and topographical points of view; secondly, to discuss the stylistic and constructional features which form virtually the only basis for dating; thirdly, to examine the widely-held view that the circular form may be explained by the paucity of freestone in the region; and finally, to place the phenomenon in a north European context.

I

There are 143 surviving round-towered churches in East Anglia including Essex and Cambridgeshire; 125 of these are in Norfolk, the greatest concentration being in the south-eastern quarter of the county from Norwich to the coast along the river Yare and along the river Waveney to Lowestoft. Elsewhere in Britain, there are three in Sussex along the river Ouse at Lewes, South Ease and Piddinghoe; there are two in Berkshire at Great Shefford and Welford;[3] one on Egilsay in the Orkney Islands; and there is evidence that two others existed at Ospringe in Kent and Tooting in Surrey[4] (Fig. 67).

Functionally, the round tower does not differ from the ordinary western tower except insofar as very few[5] round towers are provided with external doorways. This is probably only due to the difficulty of incorporating an entrance into a curved wall, which simply denies the majority of round-towered churches western processional entrances. In every other respect they are similar to square western towers, having monumental tower arches, and doorways above which connect the roof-space with the ringing-chamber and bell chambers to the top stages. Apart from these constants, the round towers vary greatly in quality of construction. The best-executed examples are at Little Saxham (Suffolk) and Haddiscoe (Norfolk) (Figs. 57–58): the former a regular cylinder, and the latter having a distinct batter. Both contrast with the majority which are less regularly formed.

Only the tower at Bramfield (Suffolk) was built as a free-standing bell tower. There are no examples of churches added to earlier towers, but 35 towers are additions to pre-existing naves. In a few instances, such as at Wramplingham (Norfolk), a complete tower is built up against an existing gable-end creating an excessively thick west wall. The more common method is to butt the tower against the west wall at ground level (Figs. 55, 59) and at the upper stage to build directly onto the gable (Fig. 60). In some cases, as at Beechamwell (Norfolk), an existing western doorway becomes the tower arch, whilst more often, as at Hales (Fig. 55), a new tower arch is cut through.

The quadrant pilaster, a fillet of masonry in the acute re-entrant angle between a round tower and the west wall of the nave (Figs. 55, 61), appears to be unique to East Anglia and occurs on 31 round-towered churches.[6] The feature is a purely aesthetic device, without any functional purpose apart from being a convenient way of filling an awkward angle. If its purpose had been to strengthen a potentially weak angle it would be most likely to occur on towers post-dating their naves; yet only 7 of the 35 added towers have quadrant pilasters. It is of considerable interest that quadrant pilasters also occur on the curious radiating chapels of Norwich cathedral (1096) and on the ruined church at North Elmham,[7] the only two instances not related to round-towered churches. Bishop Herbert de Losinga, the builder of the cathedral, may also have been responsible for the church at North Elmham, and it is significant that this minor yet very distinctive feature should be found on two of his buildings which may be closely related. The radiating chapels at Norwich Cathedral, each formed of a pair of intersecting circles in plan, are similar in concept to the round-towered church, and two possible explanations arise: that the common occurrence of quadrant pilasters on round towers should be attributed to the influence of Norwich Cathedral, or that East Anglian masons were involved in the design of the cathedral. There is insufficient evidence for a choice of explanation to be made, but at least there is proof of a correlation between the minor churches, designed and built by the indigenous population, and the principal church of the see, the vast creation of a foreign prelate.

A final feature which needs to be mentioned in this general description of round towers is the shallow undressed recessed blind arcading on three towers at Haddiscoe Thorpe and Tasburgh (Norfolk) (Figs. 61–2) and at Thorington (Suffolk). The stumps at ground level of what may have been similar blind arcading exist at Kirby Cane (Norfolk).

II

The round tower is not itself a dateable item, for examples can be found ranging from the 11th century to the 15th. However, by far the greatest number belong to the late 11th and the first half of the 12th centuries. That many scholars have been misled into claiming great antiquity for a number of these towers[8] may be explained first, by the fact that the round western tower is without parallels in Norman or French architecture; and second, by the survival in them of techniques of construction and decoration normally considered Anglo-Saxon, namely: rubble dressings, double-splayed windows, triangular-headed openings, strip-work, and tall, narrow openings. While some of these techniques may be indicative of Anglo-Saxon workmanship (which is, after all, to be expected), it is naive to assume that for this reason they must pre-date the Norman Conquest, as if every Anglo-Saxon mason was killed on the battlefield at Hastings. It would be lengthy and tedious to examine every claim of Anglo-Saxon date; it must suffice to illustrate the survival of these techniques with a few examples. As regards the use of rubble dressings, they are so common in an area without any local source of freestone that it seems pointless to cite examples; it is clear that the technique is in itself no more than an indication of rusticity.

The late use of the double-splayed window can be illustrated in a large number of examples;[9] of particular interest is Hales (Figs. 55–6), where two round double-splayed windows retaining the imprint of the original basketwork centring survive in a partially-blocked state (Fig. 63). As already mentioned, the tower and tower arch are later additions to a pre-existing church, which can be dated to the second quarter of the 12th century by its abundant mature Romanesque decoration. This consists of two elaborately-carved doorways of three orders with colonnettes, ashlar quoins with vertical angle rolls, one surviving window with nook-shafts and blind arcading around the chancel.[10] The quality of workmanship, and presumably the funds available, are obviously much higher in the original building than in the added tower, especially when the crudely carved denticle imposts and the triangular-headed upper doorway are taken into account. This illustrates not only the use of double-splayed windows towards the middle years of the 12th century, but also the danger of attempting to correlate date with quality.

Haddiscoe church,[11] of a similar date to Hales, illustrates the survival and adaptation of three Anglo-Saxon techniques: stripwork, triangular-headed openings and tall, narrow proportions (Figs. 58, 64–5). The twin bell openings have steep triangular heads formed out of large pieces of stone simply leant against each other. They are supported on octagonal mid-wall shafts with scalloped capitals[12] and the jambs are provided with nook-shafts. Each opening is surrounded by billet-moulded stripwork punctuated with blocks of square section and carved heads. The result is an amusing mixture of Anglo-Saxon and Norman: the twin bell openings with triangular heads and stripwork are clearly Anglo-Saxon survival, whilst the decoration and the shafts are of standard Norman type. Similarly, the tall, narrow tower arch reflects Anglo-Saxon taste, yet the technique, with neatly-cut voussoirs and simple chamfered imposts, is clearly Norman.

It remains to determine whether any of the round towers pre-dates the Norman Conquest. Even where there is Anglo-Saxon technique without any traces of Norman influence it is impossible to be certain of an Anglo-Saxon date, since these techniques survive up to eighty years after the Conquest. Bessingham (Norfolk) is a case in point (Fig. 66); the bell-openings are of the same type as Haddiscoe, but without any Norman decoration and without capitals or bases to the mid-wall shafts. No other features in the tower are obviously Norman in character, yet it is impossible to substantiate a date more precise than the second half of the 11th century.

III

The round tower is often explained as a practical method of avoiding the need for freestone quoins in an area where they are not locally available. This view is surely not acceptable in the light of the many square towers built virtually without freestone, such as Heigham (Norwich), Weybourne (Norfolk), Hethel (Norfolk), and Little Bardfield (Essex), or the round towers built out of materials more suited to square or rectangular structures, such as West Dereham (Norfolk), which is built with a ferruginous conglomerate facing, and the radiating chapels of Norwich Cathedral faced in ashlar. Furthermore, there are many areas in Europe with equally poor supplies of freestone which do not have round towers. Even in those areas with round towers the use of the cylindrical form often reduces the stability of the structure. The towers in the Schleswig-Holstein region of North Germany have square vaulted ground-floor interiors, which reduce buttressing mass where it is most needed. The effort required to lay out and construct a round tower and to incorporate it with a straight nave gable wall far

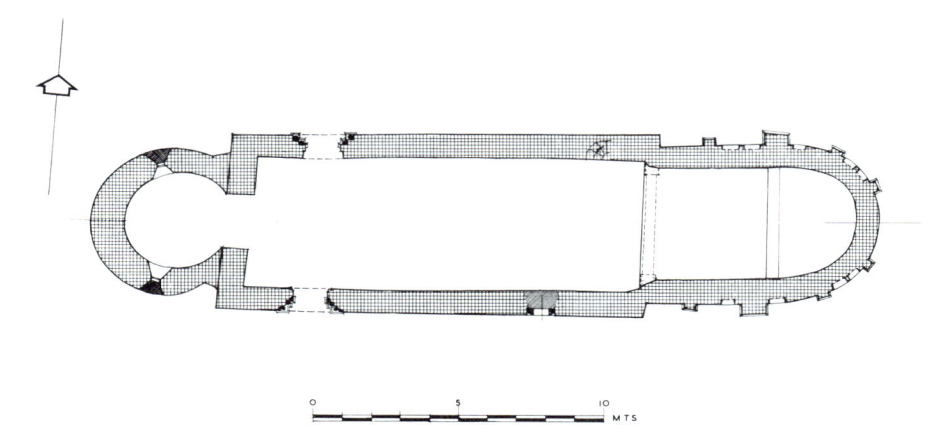

Fig. 55 Hales (Norfolk): plan, omitting post-Norman alterations.

Fig. 56 Hales (Norfolk), from S.E.

outweighs the difficulty of constructing a square eastern tower, whatever material is used. These arguments all point to the conclusion that the round tower as opposed to the square was the result of a free choice determined by aesthetic or cultural conditions.

IV

Round western towers are found in one other region of northern Europe, namely that bordering the Baltic and North Seas. The greatest numbers are found in north Germany, especially Schleswig-Holstein, and the area around Bremen and the Lüneburg Heath, with others in South Sweden and Poland (Fig. 67).[14] The Schleswig-Holstein group, for example Ratekau near Lübeck (Fig. 68), all have square vaulted ground floors with western entrances, and tribunes at the first floor gained by stairs in the thickness of the west wall. The top stage is occupied by bells. Despite these slight differences, the similarities with East Anglian round towers are striking, the round double-splayed window being common in both regions. It would appear that the towers closer to Bremen, for example the brick tower at Westen,[15] have circular interior spaces as well. The tower at Heeslingen,[16] in the same area, was unfortunately lost after being struck by lightning in 1897 but its diameter (probably external) was recorded as being 8 metres with a wall thickness of 1½ metres. This church is of particular importance because it has a

Figs. 57–8 Round towers: 57: Little Saxham (Suffolk); 58: Haddiscoe (Norfolk).

Fig. 59 Little Bradley (Suffolk): view from within tower, looking E.

Fig. 60 West Dereham (Norfolk): view from within tower, looking E. at first-floor level.

Figs. 61–2 Round towers: 61: Haddiscoe Thorpe (Norfolk); 62: Tasburgh (Norfolk).

documented date. Thietmar's chronicle says that Abbess Hathui (973–1013) replaced the earlier wooden church 'using stone of which there is very little in this land'.[17]

Given the extreme rarity of round western towers outside East Anglia and this part of northern Europe, and given the well-attested trading links which existed between the two regions,[18] it seems reasonable to assume that the two groups are related through the phenomenon of cultural exchange. The general popularity of round towers as stair-turrets *cum* bell towers on major buildings in the Empire from the Carolingian period until the end of the Middle Ages, and the early date of the tower at Heeslingen, suggest that the source for the East Anglian round tower lies in the Empire. The twin circular stair-turrets with bell openings at Möllenbeck[19] on the river Weser near Minden (Fig. 69) are a particularly good example of the sort of arrangement which might have inspired the use of single round western towers on minor churches.[20]

A final factor which confirms the close contact between the two regions concerns a detail in the field of architectural sculpture. A distinctive carved plait motif, commonly found as impost decoration on the 12th-century churches in Schleswig-Holstein (Fig. 70), exists on the hoodmould of the west door in the round tower of Great Leighs church (Essex) (Fig. 71), a form of decoration apparently unknown elsewhere in the Anglo-Norman context.

This study has tried to show how, after the Norman Conquest, the German Empire exerted influence not only on major projects such as the westworks of Ely Cathedral or Bury St. Edmunds Abbey, but also at the level of lesser churches. This implies a more widespread interaction of cultures: East Anglia can be seen as part of a northern European community where, in the design of churches, Anglo-Saxon, French and German forms combine.

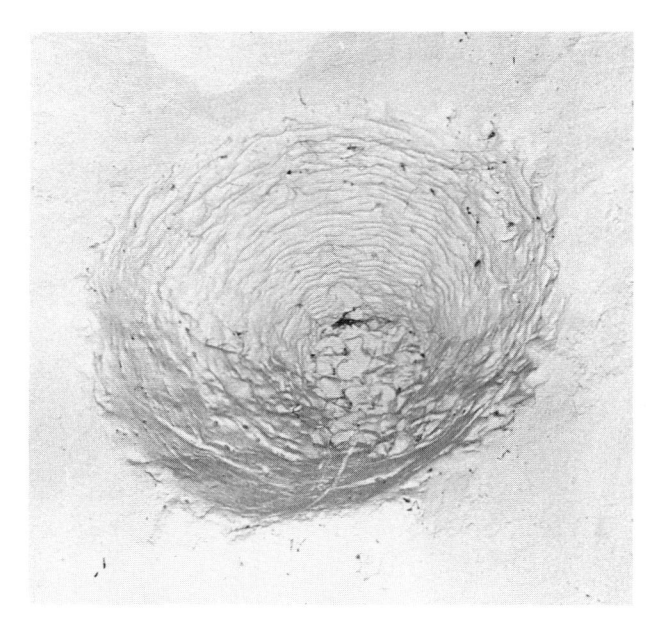

Fig. 63   Hales (Norfolk), double-splayed window.

Fig. 66   Bessingham (Norfolk): round tower.

Figs. 64–5. Haddiscoe (Norfolk): 64: bell opening; 65: arch into nave.

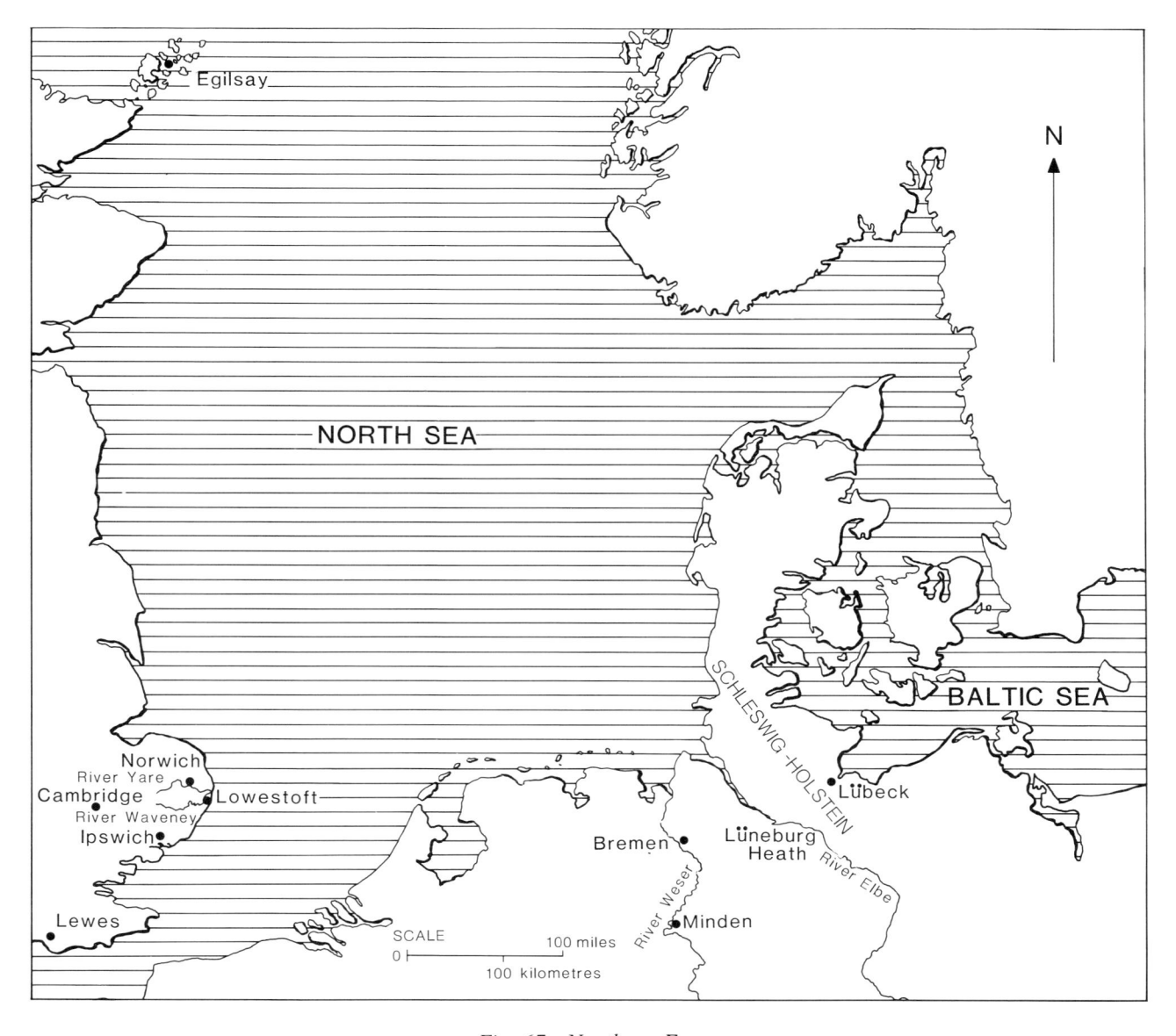

Fig. 67 Northern Europe.

Notes

1. The fieldwork for this paper was undertaken by the author in 1976/7 for an M.A. dissertation entitled 'Minor Church Building in East Anglia during the Eleventh and early Twelfth Centuries' (University of East Anglia, 1977).
2. See for example C.J.W. Messent, *The Round Towers to English Parish Churches* (Norwich, 1958). An admirably thorough recent work is W.J. Goode, *East Anglian Round Towers and their Churches* (Lowestoft, 1982).
3. Welford church was rebuilt in 1852–5. For an illustration of this church and several other round-towered churches see J. Gage, 'On the Ecclesiastical Round Towers of Norfolk and Suffolk', *Archaeologia*, xxiii (1831), 10–17.
4. For an illustration of Egilsay see G. Hay, *Architecture of Scotland* (2nd ed., Stocksfield, 1977), 25. The round tower at Ospringe fell in 1695. Drawings of the demolished tower at Tooting are in Brit. Lib., Crack.1. Tab.1. b.1, vol. xxiii, before and after p. 375; Brit. Lib., MS Add. 36389 f.87; Minet Library, LP25/713, SP25/713; see also M. Keulemans, 'Old St. Nicholas's Church, Tooting-Graveney', *Surrey Arch.Colls.* lvii (1960), 93–9.
5. Twelve.
6. At St. Julian, Norwich and Colney (Norfolk) a flat pilaster is used instead of the usual rounded feature in the re-entrant angle.
7. For North Elmham see S.E. Rigold, 'The Anglian Cathedral of North Elmham, Norfolk', *Med. Arch.* vi–vii (1962–3), 67–72, and S.R. Heywood, 'The Ruined Church at North Elmham', *JBAA*, cxxxv (1982), 1–10. Mr. Batcock (below, p. 190 note 4) contests the interpretation advanced in the second of these articles. He supports Rigold's belief that the Norman north and south nave doorways are insertations on the evidence of different mortars used. This question is discussed in the 1982 article (p. 3 note 7); to reiterate: the draw-bar hole uncovered by Rigold in the west jamb of the north doorway is 5 feet deep and it is unreasonable to assume that this was excavated out of the flint and mortar core. It is interesting to note in this context two instances of inserted draw-holes in Norfolk at the ruined church of St. Mary, Saxlingham Thorpe and in the basement of Castle Rising Castle. In both cases the draw-bar holes were inserted by cutting a channel into the wall and subsequently patching it with the draw-bar in position. There is no indication of disturbance

Figs. 68–9 Round towers: Ratekau (courtesy Landesamt für Denkmalpflege Schleswig-Holstein, Kiel); 69: Möllenbeck, from W. (courtesy Arthur Schultze-Naumburg, Fallingbostel).

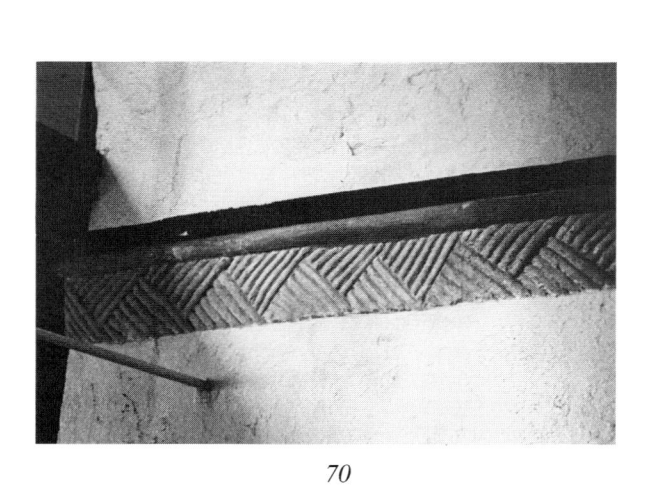

Figs. 70–1 Examples of plait motif: 70: Neukirchen (kreis Eutin), tower arch impost; 71: Great Leighs (Essex), W. doorway.

of this sort at North Elmham. The difference in mortar between the ashlar dressings and the surrounding masonry is not an indication of insertion because mortars can change with each mix and it is to be expected that the ashlar dressings of the doorways were erected before the rubble masonry to the sides. The 1982 paper also illustrates at considerable length how similar ashlar dressings were used elsewhere in the building. In support of his argument Batcock compares the continuous transept at North Elmham with Imperial cathedrals. The vast difference in scale and North Elmham's aisleless nave are enough to render the parallel invalid, and anyway, as is made clear in the 1982 paper, the entire North Elmham plan is without precise parallel in Europe at any date, supporting its private and personal nature. Batcock concludes his argument by stating that North Elmham is 'so dissimilar to other buildings which Bishop de Losinga is known to have constructed'. As indicated in the 1982 paper, de Losinga was probably responsible for the construction of the church at South Elmham adjacent to the manor which he bought there. The western towers at both buildings are strikingly similar — they are both of the same width as their naves and they both have attached semicircular stair turrets. In addition, Herbert's cathedral at Norwich and the chapel at North Elmham are the only two buildings without round western towers to use the distinctive East Anglian quadrant pilaster. There are several more arguments in favour of Bishop Herbert's authorship, and reference is duly made to the 1982 paper in which they are fully exposed.

8. Goode op.cit. note 2 has claimed a 9th-century date for some towers. More usually, dating is confined to the 11th century: see for example Taylor & Taylor.
9. 36 per cent of all churches with double-splayed windows in East Anglia have contemporary post-Conquest features. East Anglia has a far greater number of double-splayed windows than any other British region; for a distribution map see Taylor & Taylor, iii, 841.
10. It has been suggested that all the Norman work was inserted at a later date. For Hales see also Taylor & Taylor, i, 278–9; E.A. Kent, 'The Saxon Windows in Hales Church, Norfolk', *JBAA*, xxxiii (1927), 187–8.
11. For Haddiscoe see also Taylor & Taylor, i, 270, and S.R. Heywood, 'Haddiscoe Church', *Archaeol. J.* cxxxvii (1980), 310.
12. The shafts and capitals are modern replacements.
13. See A. Tuulse, *Scandinavia Romanica* (Vienna, 1968); A. Merhautová, *Romanische Kunst in Polen, der Tschechoslowakei, Ungarn, Rumanien, Jugoslawien* (Vienna, 1974).
14. See H. Ehl, *Norddeutsche Feldsteinkirchen* (n.d.); G. Dehio, *Handbuch der Deutschen Kunstdenkmaler Hamburg, Schleswig Holstein* and *Bremen/Niedersachen* (Deutscher Kunstverlag, 1971 and 1977). It is interesting to note that in this context, Egilsay in the Orkneys does not appear so remote.
15. See G. Meyer et al., *Die Kunstdenkmaler der Provinz Hannover*, ix (Hannover, 1908), 131–4.
16. See Ibid. 194–201, and F. Oswald, L. Schaefer and H.R. Sennhauser. *Vorromanische Kirchenbauten* (Munich, 1966–71), 410.
17. 'de lapidibus, qui in haec terra pauci habentur'.
18. E. Carus-Wilson, 'The Medieval Trades of the Ports of the Wash', *Med. Arch.* vi–vii (1962–3), 182–201.
19. This building has been dated from the early 10th century to the 11th; see Oswald et al. op.cit. note 16, 222.
20. The blind arcading is especially noteworthy in relation to the recessed arcading on the East Anglian round towers.

XIII. The Parish Church in Norfolk in the 11th and 12th Centuries

Neil Batcock

Norfolk is a very densely churched county. The vast majority of the county's parish churches are medieval, and some 650 of these still stand today. There is no precise information on the numbers of parish churches during the 11th and 12th centuries; but we do know that, by 1254, the county possessed at least 789 churches.[1] It seems likely that most of these were already in existence by the end of the 11th century, even though only 241 were listed in Domesday Book.

No church remains in the county antedate the 11th century. The reason for this may be very simple: before the 11th century, parish churches were constructed of flimsy, perishable materials, such as wood, wattle and clay. Where excavation of a church has taken place, the earliest masonry phase has invariably belonged to the 11th or early 12th century. Some of these may have been new foundations, the first church on the site. Overall, the impression is that, towards the middle of the 11th century, the small timber parish church began to be replaced by the small masonry church. This impression is strengthened by two documentary references (both written in the 13th century). First, John of Oxenede wrote, in his 'Chronicle of the Abbey of St. Benet's', that Abbot Ælfsige (1019–46) rebuilt the abbey church in stone, when it had been hitherto made of clay.[2] Thus St. Benet's Abbey, the most important pre-Conquest monastic foundation in Norfolk, possessed only a clay church until replaced by a stone one in the period c. 1020–1046. Unfortunately we know nothing about the form of this church. The second reference is a little more difficult to handle, since it is a thinly-veiled piece of episcopal propaganda in praise of the first bishop of Norwich, Herbert de Losinga. According to the First Register of Norwich Cathedral, the cathedral at Elmham was no more than a 'wooden chapel' before the see moved to Thetford (in 1071) and thence to Norwich.[3] If this is true, then the cathedral of the see of East Anglia, based at North Elmham, was a small timber structure: mere parish churches must have been insubstantial indeed. However, it is likely that the author of the First Register is guilty of a little exaggeration: the cathedral at Elmham may well have been wooden until the middle of the 11th century, but was then replaced by a masonry structure whose ruins (in the view of the present author) survive today.[4] A similar 'bending' of the facts, in the interest of promoting the reputation of Bishop Herbert, can be clearly demonstrated when the author of the First Register describes the foundation of Yarmouth parish church.[5]

The evidence from both the 11th and the 12th centuries gives the impression that Norfolk was a late starter, certainly so far as masonry church-building is concerned; but, from the middle of the 11th century, the county embarked on an astonishing campaign of building and rebuilding. Today, Norfolk can boast 293 parish churches which are known to possess 11th- and 12th-century fabric, and this represents only a fraction (perhaps one-third) of the total number of churches built during this period. With such a wealth of evidence, there are may avenues which this paper could explore: the lengthy period of 'Saxo-Norman overlap'; the architectural influences of Germany and Normandy; the relationship of major to minor architecture; and numerous others. In fact, I intend to look at three areas to see the light they respectively shed on the parish church in Norfolk during this period. These areas are: a village (Barton Bendish); a town (Thetford); and a patron (Herbert, Bishop of Norwich, and his successors).

A Village: Barton Bendish

South-west Norfolk, beteen Swaffham and Downham Market, is an area rich in deserted churches (Fig. 72). The map represents a 10 km square, containing, wholly or in part, 12 parishes (13 if we include the parish of Caldecote, absorbed into Oxborough long ago). Today, each parish possesses a single medieval parish church still in use; there is one fully-standing redundant church (Barton Bendish, St. Mary). In addition, there are three churches with visible ruins (Oxborough, St. Mary; Beachamwell, St. John and All Saints) and a further seven churches which have disappeared with little or no trace (Shouldham, St. Margaret; Marham, St. Andrew; Stradsett, site and dedication unknown; Fincham, St. Michael; Barton Bendish, All Saints; West Dereham, St. Peter; Caldecote, St. Mary). The decline has been very dramatic: from 21 parish churches in this area recorded in the Norwich Taxation of 1254, to a mere 12 today. Most striking of all is the number of

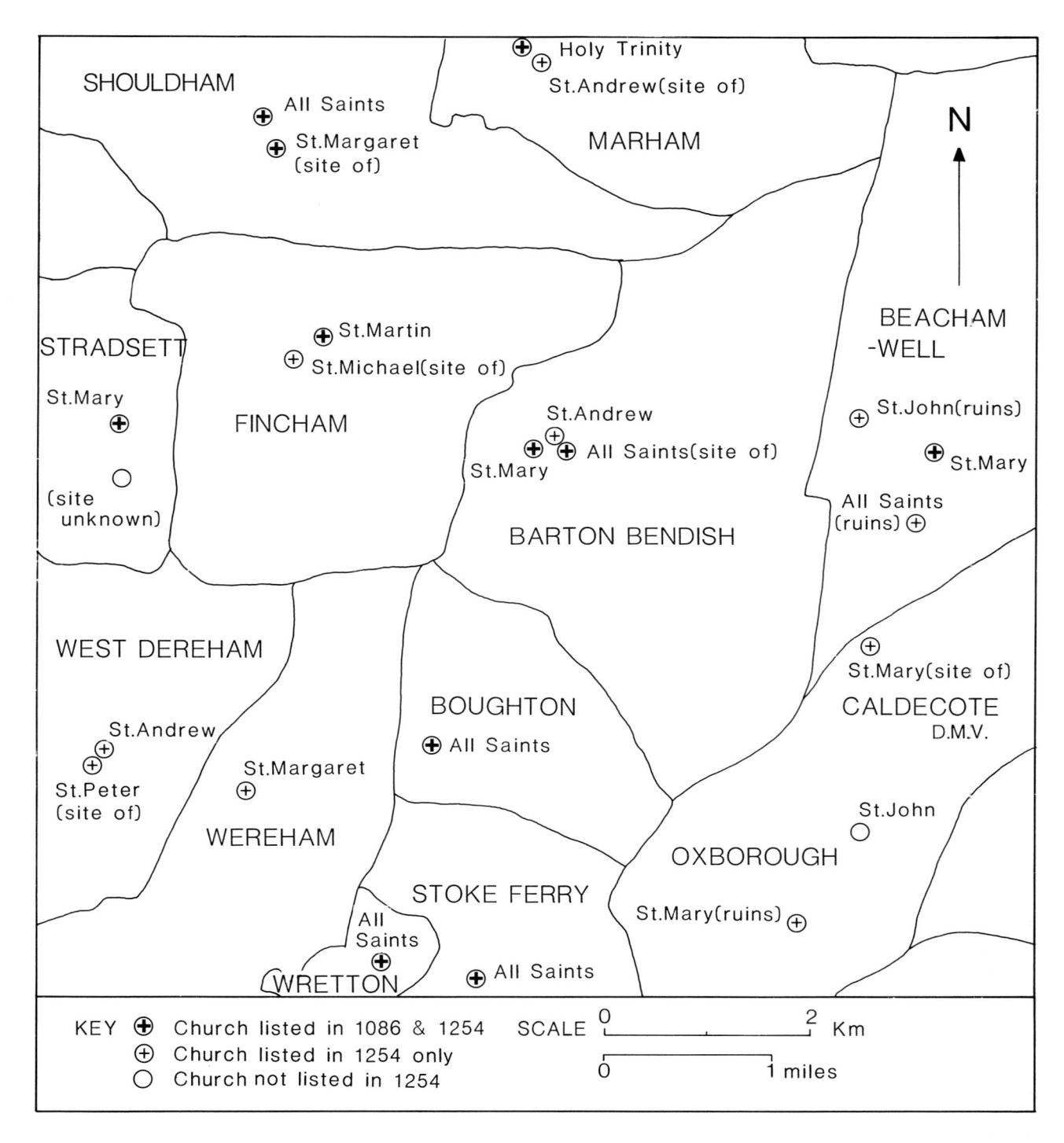

Fig. 72 Barton Bendish and neighbouring parishes.

parishes with more than one church: Shouldham, Marham, Stradsett, Fincham, Barton Bendish, Beachamwell, West Dereham, Oxborough. Indeed, Barton Bendish and Beachamwell possessed three churches each; but it would appear that Beachamwell All Saints belonged to the deserted village of *Wella*, later united with Beacham. It is equally noticeable how close these churches were to one another, although only West Dereham had both churches in the same churchyard (but nothing is known of the site of the second church at Stradsett).

Domesday Book records 12 churches in this area: one at Marham, one at Fincham, one at Boughton, and one at Beachamwell; but two at Shouldham, two at Stradsett, two at Barton Bendish, and two at Stoke Ferry (of this last pair, it seems probable that one subsequently became the separate parish of Wretton). Therefore, the practice of doubling, or trebling, the

All Saints'

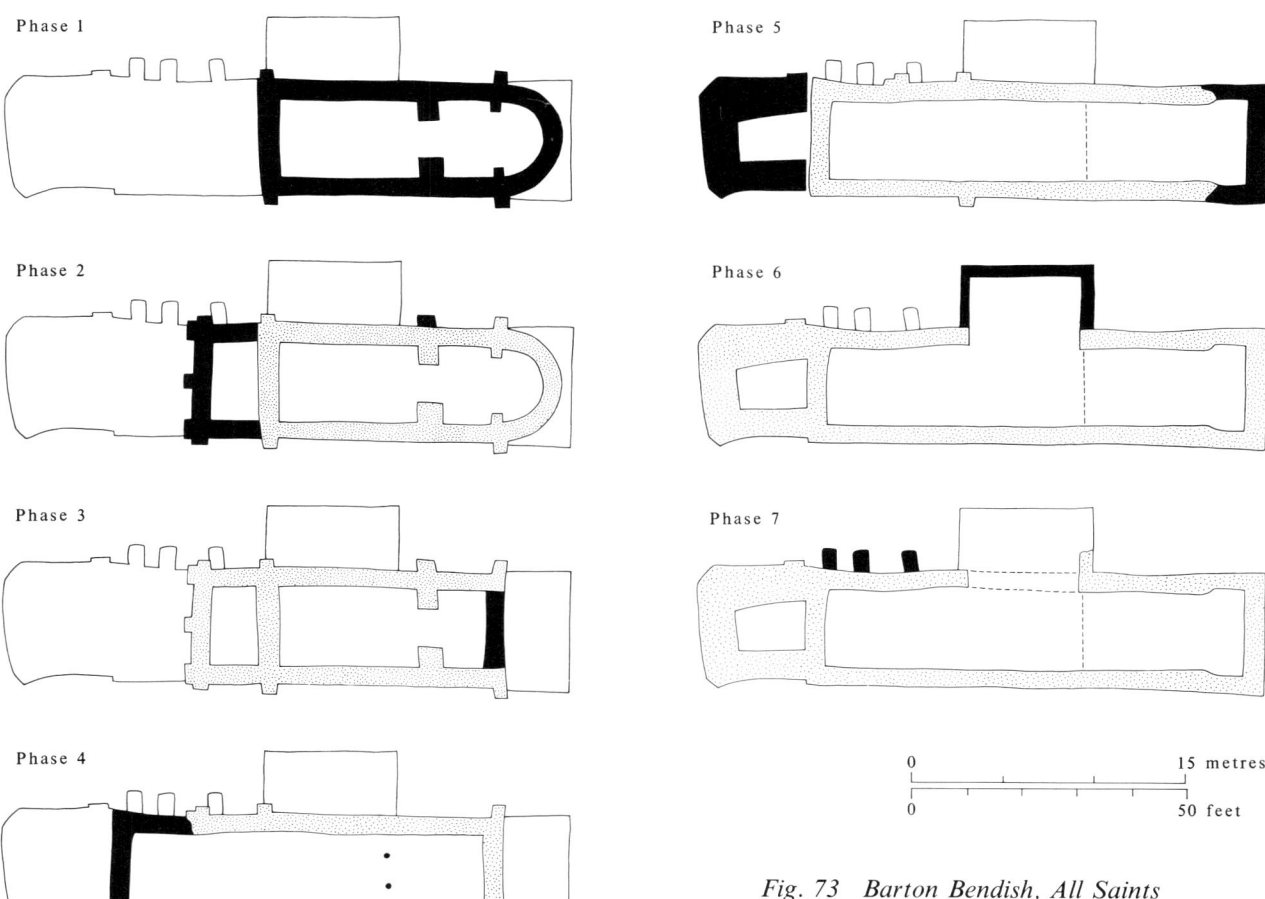

Phase 1

Phase 2

Phase 3

Phase 4

Phase 5

Phase 6

Phase 7

0 15 metres
0 50 feet

*Fig. 73 Barton Bendish, All Saints
(illustrator Steven Ashley).*

number of churches within a single village was common in this part of Norfolk from at least the 11th century. Dymond[6] has suggested that 'this practice seems to be the rural equivalent of the numerous closely-spaced churches which appeared in late-Saxon towns, such as Thetford and Norwich'.

All this helps to provide a context for Barton Bendish in the 11th and 12th centuries. This village maintained and used three parish churches until the 18th century, by which time All Saints had begun to fall into disrepair, and was therefore demolished in 1788. St. Mary's was declared redundant, and vested in the Redundant Churches Fund in 1976, leaving St. Andrew's as the sole parish church.

Two of the three churches are listed in Domesday Book, but which two? According to Blomefield[7] one of them was St. Mary's: in Domesday, a church with 12 acres of land belonged to Hermer of Ferrers; his manor was in Barton and was later held by the Lovels, along with the advowson of St. Mary's. John Lovel was buried in the middle of the church of St. Mary in 1372[8] and it seems probable that he was responsible for the rebuilding or the nave (and presumably the demolition, if any still remained, of the 11th-century church). All that stands today of St. Mary's (Fig. 76) is the chancel, of the 1340s, and the eastern part of the nave, of the 1360s; the west tower collapsed during the reign of Queen Anne[9] and no doubt demolished the western part of the nave too. Nothing above-ground survives of the church recorded in 1086.

It appears that the second church mentioned in Domesday was All Saints. In 1086, a church with 24 acres of land belonged to Ralf Bainard; Blomefield[10] pointed out the links between Bainard's manor and Dunmow Priory, the latter holding the advowson of All Saints in 1284/5. Despite the total demolition of All Saints church in 1788, we now know a great deal about it through Andrew Rogerson's excavation on the site in 1981.[11] Rogerson was able to show that, until its destruction, the church underwent seven distinct construction phases (Fig. 73). The Phase 1 church could be the one mentioned in 1086, although the three-cell plan with apse was still current in the first half of the 12th century. It remains an open question whether the apse was preceded by an axial tower; certainly, all the surviving examples of this plan in Norfolk do have a

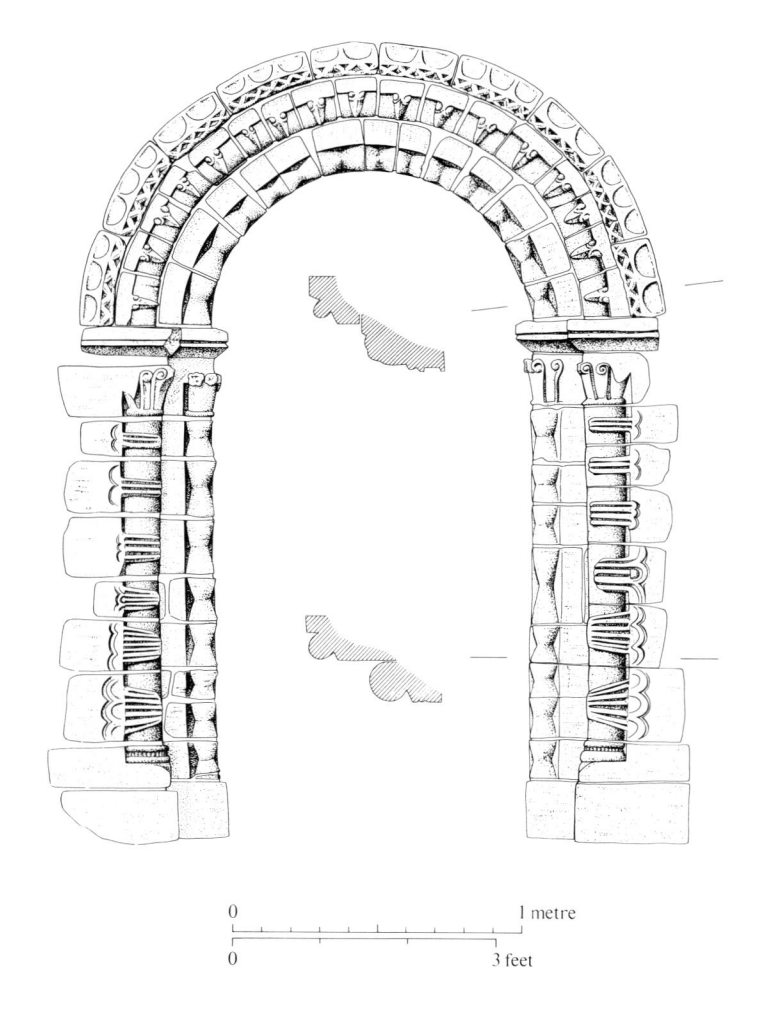

Fig. 74 Barton Bendish, St. Mary: W. doorway, formerly N. doorway of All Saints (illustrator Steven Ashley).

tower (e.g. Bawsey, Castle Rising, Great Dunham, Guestwick, Melton Constable, South Lopham). The rather short nave was extended westwards in the 1170s (Phase 2). One of the two portals belonging to this phase has survived, to become the west doorway of St. Mary's since 1789 (Fig. 74). Of equal interest is the history of the All Saints site before the construction of the Phase 1 church. This church was laid out on an earlier graveyard, with at least 49 burials in the immediate vicinity of the church pre-dating Phase 1. Pottery finds suggest that the graveyard came into use early in the 11th century. Prior to use as a graveyard, the site had been used for cultivation during the 10th century, with evidence of manuring and domestic refuse. Remains of a church built there before Phase 1 but after the foundation of the graveyard have not come to light. There seem to be three possible interpretations: that we are dealing with a cemetery with no church; or that a church associated with this graveyard was some way from the site of the later church, and remains unexcavated; or that a church stood on the same site, but was constructed of flimsy materials (wood, wattle etc.) which have left no trace after the rebuildings and robbings of several centuries. This last seems the most likely interpretation; indeed this 'undiscovered' church may be the one mentioned in Domesday. My hypothesis is as follows: the church was founded in the early 11th century, and built of timber; it was replaced with a masonry church in the late 11th century, and extended in the later 12th century.

Throughout the Middle Ages, St. Andrew's was the largest and wealthiest of the three churches. It is therefore strange that it should have escaped the attentions of the compilers of Domesday; and it is certain that a church stood here in 1086, as will be seen. Chancel and tower were built in the 14th century, but the large nave belongs to the early 12th century (Fig. 75). Two single-splayed windows survive in the north wall, the head of another in the west wall (cut by the tower arch). Most important for dating evidence is the south doorway; the capitals suggest an early date, though not too early, given the relative sophistication of the double angle-rolls of the arch: a date of *c*. 1110 would be acceptable. The masonry of the nave is

St. Andrew's

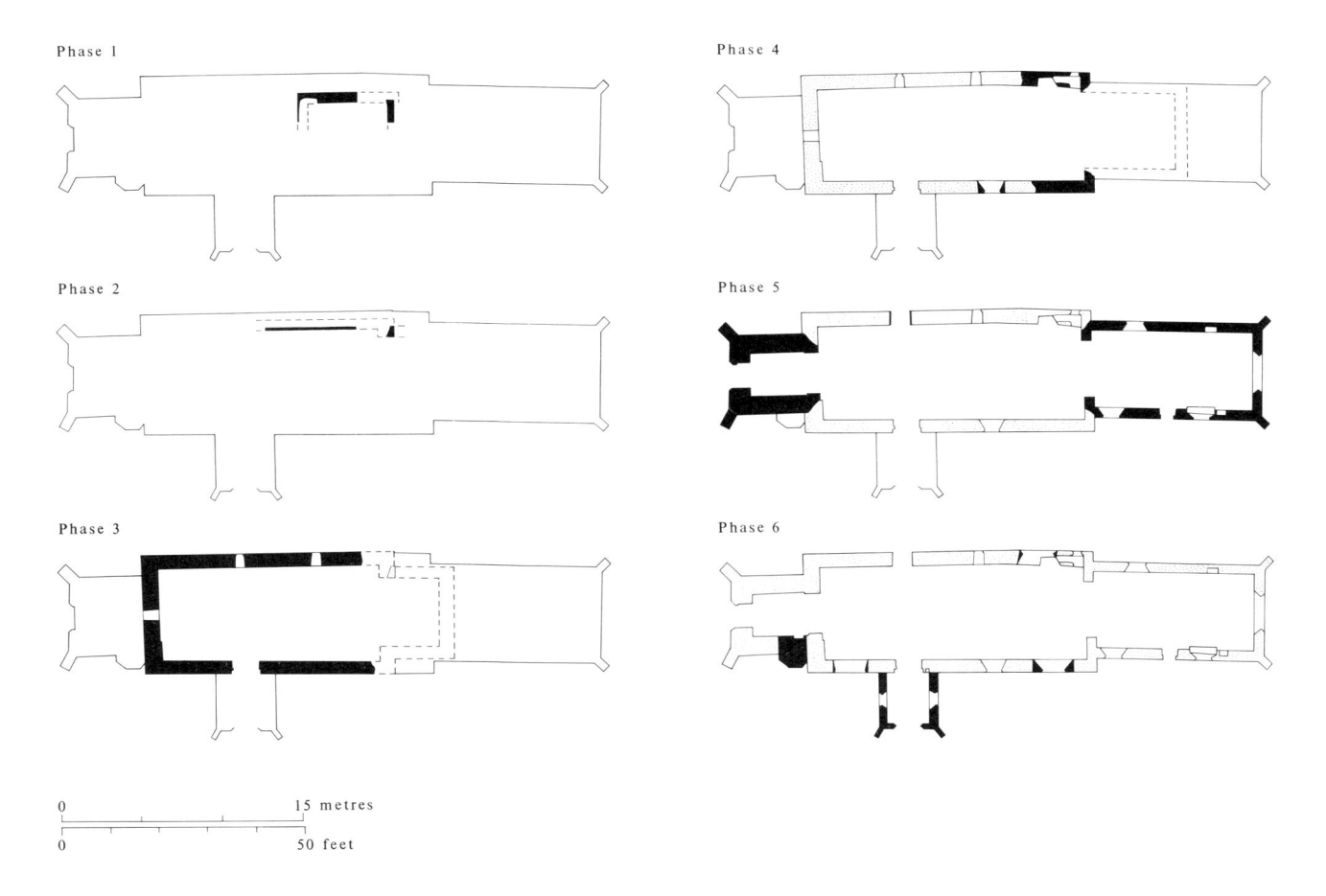

Fig. 75 Barton Bendish, St. Andrew (illustrator Steven Ashley).

principally of ironbound conglomerate, with quoins displaying an alternation of limestone (some rather large blocks) and conglomerate.

However, this merely represents Phase 3. Two earlier phases (Fig. 75) were discovered in 1982 when contractors were preparing to install a concrete floor. Phase 1 consisted of a foundation-trench filled with rammed chalk and flint, forming the north wall of a rectangular structure 4.6m long. This was partly cut through by Phase 2, of which the lowest courses of mortared flint survived; it is not certain how far the wall extended westwards. Nothing was found to date these features, save the fact that the Phase 2 wall was overlain by the internal plinth of the Phase 3 north wall; therefore both Phase 1 and 2 pre-date *c.* 1110. Probably they both belong to the 11th century, but it is hard to be specific; nevertheless, it seems likely that one of the two structures must have been in existence at the time of Domesday. Phase 1 seems to have been very small, a tiny cell, and presumably the first masonry church on the site.

Piecing together the various strands of evidence, we begin to form a picture of the development of Barton Bendish in the 11th and 12th centuries. All three churches were in existence by 1086, although only two were actually recorded in Domesday. All Saints began as a churchyard, probably with a timber church, in the early 11th century. It is not known how far back the principal church, St. Andrew's goes; but a tiny masonry church was built there, probably in the first half of the 11th century. Before the end of the century, it was replaced by a larger church, around which time All Saints received its first masonry church. We know nothing at all about the form of St. Mary's (Fig. 76) at this time, or its origins: merely that it existed in 1086. Lastly, St. Andrew's was replaced in the early 12th century by the large structure which still stands today. All Saints, however, was simply extended westwards later in the century, and given a very fine portal.

Clearly, it would be interesting to know more about the early history of the sites of St. Andrew's and St. Mary's, in order to present a more complete picture of the village. Barton Bendish is one of very few villages to have had three parish churches, and their inter-

St. Mary's

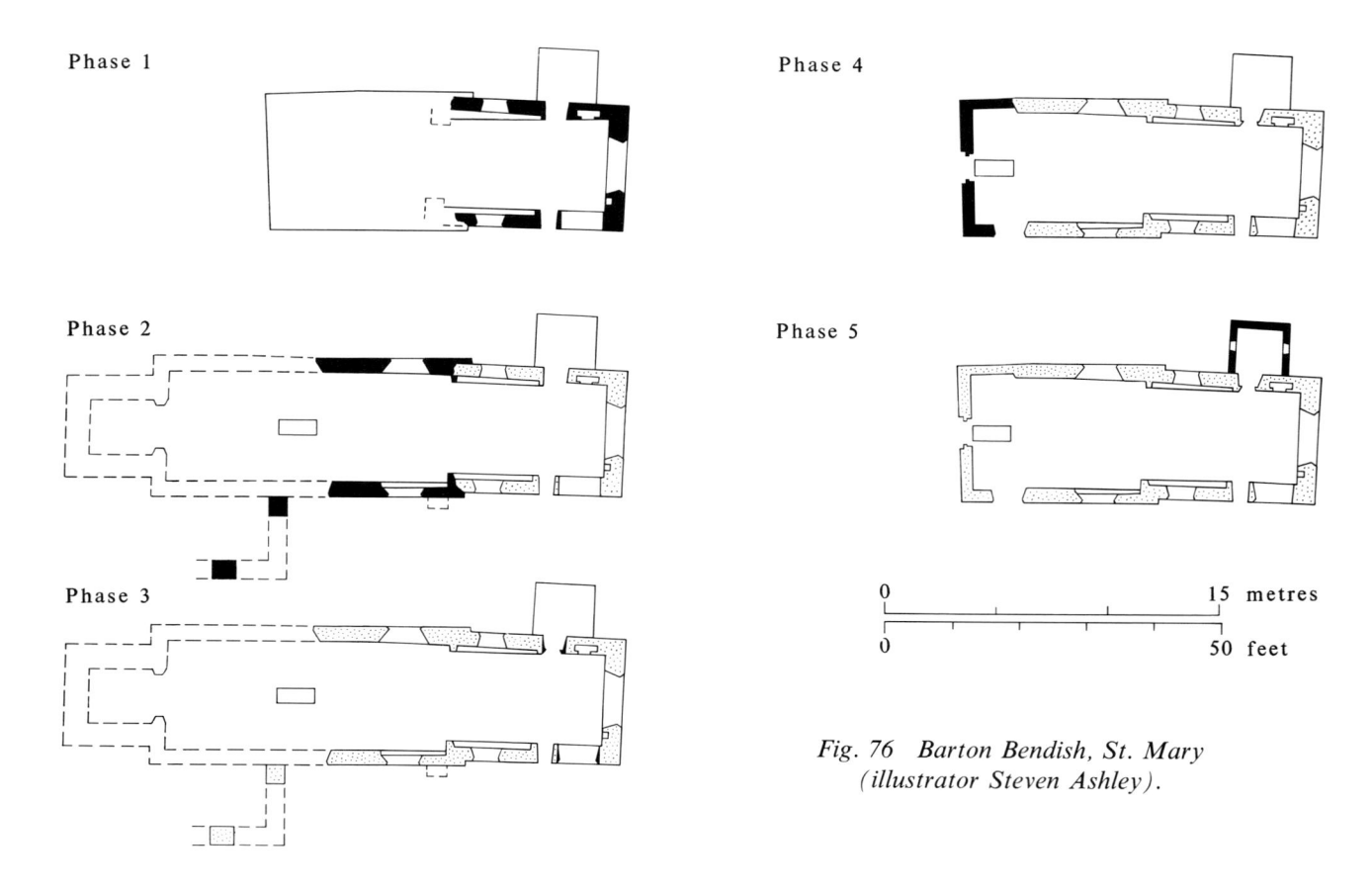

Phase 1

Phase 2

Phase 3

Phase 4

Phase 5

Fig. 76 Barton Bendish, St. Mary (illustrator Steven Ashley).

relationships throw an interesting light on parochial development in this part of Norfolk.

A Town: Thetford

Late Saxon Thetford was a large town, with 943 burgesses in 1066 (declining to 720 at the time of Domesday).[12] The town possessed at least 10 parish churches before 1066, and at least 11 churches and a cathedral at the time of Domesday.[12] St. Mary the Great became the cathedral after 1071, but it seems possible that this was a minster church before that. Domesday records that four churches were always attached to it: St. Peter, St. John, St. Martin and St. Margaret. Until recently, nothing was known about the architectural form of the churches of the late Saxon town; but now, four sites have come to light which give us some tantalizing glimpses of the type of parish church which Thetford was producing in the 11th century.

The first site has been identified as St. Michael's church, excavated by Davison and Mackey, with a brief published note in 1970.[13] The earliest of three phases shows a small timber church with square chancel and rectangular nave; this was later replaced by a masonry church, slightly larger but of similar disposition; finally, the church was extended to the west, to the east with (probably) an apsidal chancel, to the north with a chapel and to the south with a porch. Pottery finds suggest that the church was abandoned by the end of the 12th century. It seems probable that the apsidal chancel and nave extension are no later than mid 12th century. The first masonry church pre-dates this, and pottery finds indicate a date no earlier than the 11th century; this church suffered a period of abandonment, after which bells were cast in the nave. A limestone cushion capital formed part of the subsequent fill of the bell-pit. If the capital belonged to the original structure of this church, as seems likely, then we must date it to *c.* 1100. Earliest of all is the wooden church, which is likely to be early or mid 11th century.

A masonry church of identical plan was excavated at the Red Castle site at the western edge of Thetford by Knocker in 1957.[14] The details and dating are far from clear. However, it seems possible that, like St. Michael's, this church was preceded by a wooden structure of similar size. Unusually for Norfolk, the square chancel of the masonry church had pilaster buttresses at the corners. A mid to late 11th-century date is possible.

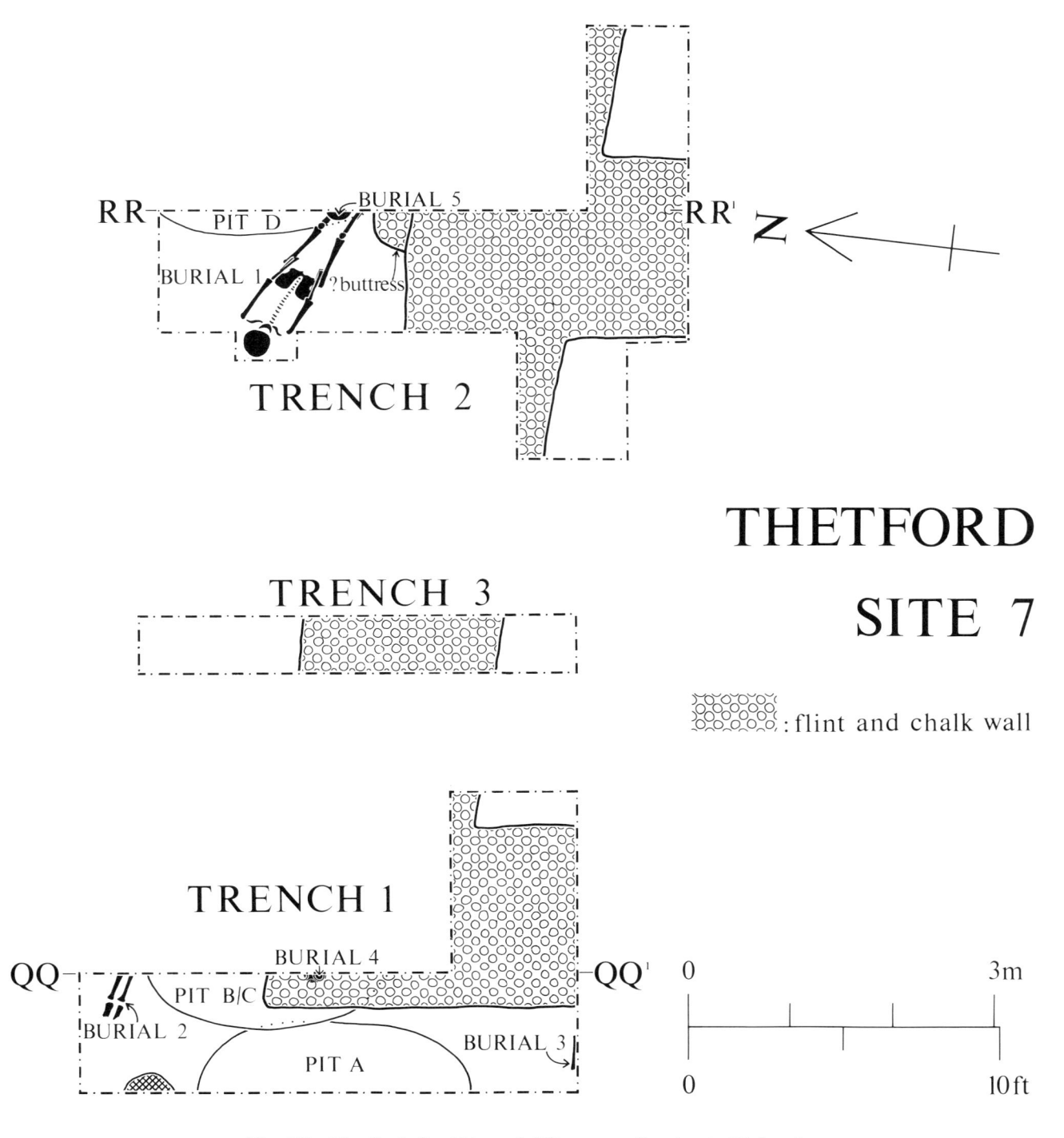

Fig. 77 Thetford, St. Edmund (illustrator Stephanie Rickett).

Fragmentary remains of a church, identified (probably wrongly) as St. Edmund's, have been excavated and published recently.[15] Only the flint and chalk foundations remained, a massive 1.8m thick (Fig. 77). Several inhumations were found in the vicinity, including one which was overlain by the church foundations. Associated pottery finds date these burials to broadly the 10th or 11th centuries. Presumably the church itself goes back to the 11th century. The size of the foundations suggest that the excavators uncovered a west tower, with a fragment of foundation continuing east in line with the tower north wall. This indicates that whatever abutted the tower to the east must have been the same width as the tower (or slightly narrower). This has led Heywood to postulate a tower-nave of Earls Barton type, with chancel directly adjoining west tower; but if this were the case, one would expect a chancel somewhat narrower than is indicated by these remains. A better interpretation would be that these foundations represent a west tower and the north-western corner of

Fig. 78 Snarehill church from S.W. Only the lower half of the wall is original. Note the S.E. quoins.

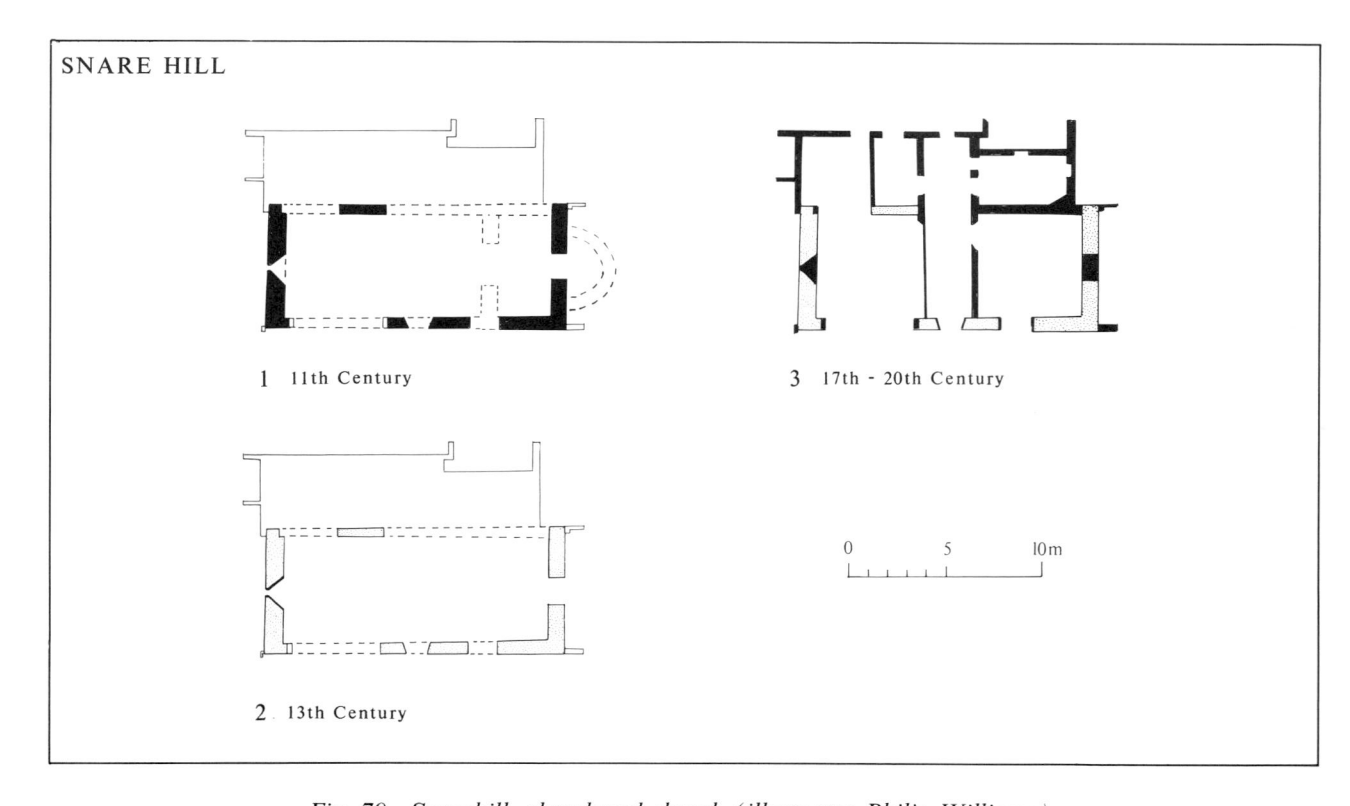

Fig. 79 Snarehill, abandoned church (illustrator Philip Williams).

Fig. 80 Snarehill church, S.W. corner of tower/transept, from S. Some of the stones have rather crude diagonal tooling.

a nave the same width as the tower: a feature also found at North Elmham cathedral. Perhaps we are dealing with a design current in the late-Saxon period (west towers the same width as the nave), suitable for a parish church as well as for a cathedral.

Finally, we come to Snarehill. Whilst it is true that the site of Great Snarehill lies outside Thetford proper, it is only 2km east of the centre of the town, and administratively was always considered part of Thetford. Today, Snarehill is an estate consisting of a stud-farm and large 18th-century house. North-west of the house there are some old stables, part of them used as a garage; the garage in fact occupies the nave of the former parish church of Snarehill, and incorporates some of the most important 11th-century remains in the whole of Norfolk (Fig. 78).

If St. Edmund's in Thetford possessed a rather curious plan, then the church at Snarehill is equally unusual. It is difficult to interpret the remains, but we seem to be dealing with a nave and some sort of transept/axial tower (Fig. 79). The chancel has gone, its site occupied by a 19th-century cottage which abuts the east wall of the transept/tower. There is no west tower, and the whole nave west wall has been incorporated into the end wall of a 17th-century timber barn. Since the 18th century, both nave and transept/tower have been used as stables; the eastern part continues to function as a stable, but the western part is now used as a double garage and has been provided with bright green sliding doors.

The outline of a tall, narrow chancel arch can be made out in the east wall of the transept/tower; the head of the arch no longer exists; the jambs are of limestone and have no mouldings. The east wall of the transept/tower survives to a height of some 4m, but the south wall only to 1m; neither west nor north walls survive. The south wall projects south of the nave south wall by some 6cms; it is thus a salient feature, if only just. But the southward projection of the tower/transept is emphasized by the presence of quoins at each corner, consisting of large limestone blocks, roughly squared, coarsely tooled, and set 'side-alternately' (Fig. 80). The intervening masonry is of coursed flint. Where it survives, the masonry of the nave south wall is of the same character. The nave west corner has quoins similar to those of the transept/tower, but a little more massive and set in 'upright-and-flat' fashion. Only the nave west wall stands entire. It is pierced by a deeply-splayed pointed window; high above (visible from the hay-loft of the adjacent barn) the gable of the west wall of the church can be made out. So much for the surviving remains: what form did the church take? It seems clear that a rectangular nave led into a transept/tower before proceeding through a tall, narrow arch into a chancel of undisclosed form (an apse is hypothetical). The fact that the transept/tower has thicker walls than the nave suggests that they rose higher than the nave; but it must have defined a space as much a transept as a tower (7m × 4.5m). Rectangular towers are not unknown: Surlingham, St. Saviour, in Norfolk, had a rectangular axial tower, as did Cluny II in France; but if Snarehill has a tower, it must be admitted that its plan is attenuated to an unusual degree. The only plausible alternative is that we are dealing with a transept: such a design would be unparalleled, unless comparison be drawn with North Elmham cathedral.

We must now move on to the problem of dating. There are three features which demand a late-Saxon or Saxo-Norman date for the church. First, there are the roughly-squared quoins, in upright-and-flat and side-alternate fashion. In England as a whole, such features occur from the later 10th century until the end of the 11th century, but probably not far beyond. Secondly, there is the tall, unadorned chancel arch; arches of this type can be found for minor openings well into the 12th century, but there can be very few (if any) used for chancel arches much after the Conquest. Lastly, there is the salient 'tower' (if it is a tower). The salient axial tower is a feature of several late-Saxon churches: Sherborne Minster (1045-58), Stow (mid 11th century), Norton (late 10th or early 11th century); there may have been the odd survival after the Conquest,[16] but it seems to be a late-Saxon design which had gone out of fashion by the end of the 11th century.

On balance, I think we are dealing with a mid 11th-century church at Snarehill, of late-Saxon rather than Norman (or even Saxo-Norman) type. In design, it is certainly very different from early Norman churches in the county (e.g. Castle Rising, Guestwick). Perhaps the plan of Snarehill represents a type of pre-Conquest

Fig. 81 Great Yarmouth, St. Nicholas, from S.E. Though restored, the lower part of the tower is Losinga's work.

parish church common in Thetford and its region (although none have survived). It is interesting that both the village and church of Great Snarehill seem to echo the fortunes of Thetford and its churches: at its greatest in the middle of the 11th century, depopulated and abandoned by the 16th.

It may be premature to make too many generalizations about the pre-Conquest architecture of Thetford. But the four churches we have looked at provide food for thought. Certainly the church designs show a variety and lack of uniformity, arguably in contrast with post-Conquest designs.

A Patron: Bishop Herbert and his successors

It is unlikely that any individual has had more impact on the ecclesiastical history (or, indeed, more influence on the human geography) of Norfolk than Herbert de Losinga, first bishop of Norwich. Not only did he establish the see at Norwich in 1094, but, through a policy which one can only call 'episcopal imperialism', he firmly imprinted the stamp of his authority throughout the county and diocese. He founded the new cathedral at Norwich in 1096, eager to be at the heart of the largest and most thriving town in his diocese, rather than in the already declining town of Thetford. He also built important new churches at Great Yarmouth and King's Lynn, and placed them under the authority of the priory he had established at Norwich. He built a large new parish church at North Elmham, next-door to the rather less imposing former cathedral. It is said that his munificence as a builder of churches was an act of penance,[17] to make amends for the bribe which he gave to the king in order to secure his appointment as bishop. But to secure a measure of strategic control over the two biggest ports and the largest town in the county suggests we are dealing with a man with a grasp of politics and economics rather than a man acting purely out of piety.

When the First Register of Norwich cathedral was written towards the end of the 13th century, the desire to approve the policies of the first bishop of Norwich led to a certain distortion of the facts. Herbert founded the church of St. Nicholas at Great Yarmouth on what, according to the First Register, was not much more than a deserted beach: 'And there was at that time on the sea shore at Yarmouth, a certain small chapel built, in which divine service was only celebrated during the season of the herring fishery, for there were not more than four or five small houses provided for the reception of the fishermen'.[18] Herbert duly built a new church there, having sought permission from the king; since the king in question was Henry I, the new church of St. Nicholas must have been constructed after 1100. The First Register would persuade us that, at this date, Yarmouth was no more than a scattering of fishing huts and a seasonally-used chapel. Yet Domesday Book makes clear that Yarmouth was a small town with as many as 70 burgesses, both in 1066 and 1086; furthermore, in 1066 the town possessed a church dedicated to St. Benedict, owned by the bishop of East Anglia. It is evident that some people did not like Bishop Herbert exercising his authority in the town in this way. Soon some merchants (*portenses*) drove away the chaplain appointed by the bishop, but Herbert restored his man by force of arms. Despite its continuing growth, Yarmouth never acquired further parish churches until the 19th century: Bishop Herbert and his successors maintained an unrelenting grip and prevented any subdivision of the parish. Thus the church of St. Nicholas, in order to house a growing population, came to be the largest parish church in England, with aisles wider than the nave of York Minster.[19]

Little remains of the St. Nicholas built by de Losinga, after so many enlargements and the bomb-damage of the last war. But what we know of it suggests that it was essentially a scaled-down version of Norwich cathedral:

Figs. 82–3 *North Elmham, St. Mary: 82: interior looking N.E.; it appears that Losinga's arcade was replaced in the 13th century and heightened in the 15th century; 83: interior looking S. across the (now) chancel: note the unblocked 12th-century window.*

cruciform in plan (although aisleless) with a large apsidal chapel projecting from each transept,[20] and with a crossing-tower decorated on the outside with shafts, capitals and arcading (Fig. 81).

An even larger church was established by Bishop Herbert at Lynn. The church of St. Margaret, like St. Nicholas's at Great Yarmouth, was given to the priory of Norwich soon after 1100, and served by a prior and three monks. The scale of this church is most impressive, with transepts, aisles and a two-tower facade. Equally impressive is the speed with which the 'Bishop's' Lynn expanded in the 12th century. Herbert's successor Eborard (1121–1145) built another larger church only 400 m east of St. Margaret's; it was dedicated to St. James, and remained a parochial chapel to St. Margaret's despite its apparent size: again, it had transepts, crossing tower and aisled chancel and nave.[21] Eborard's successor William Thurbe (1146–1174) continued this process by building a new parochial chapel, dedicated to St. Nicholas, in the 'Newland' north of St. Margaret's. Although mostly rebuilt in the early 15th century, this too was very impressive in scale for a mere chapel. Clearly, Bishop Herbert's successors were pursuing the 'Losinga doctrine' of diocesan politics.[22]

A similar desire to impress must lie behind Bishop Herbert's construction of a new parish church at North Elmham. After the transference of the see to Thetford from 1071, the cathedral at Elmham must have continued to function as the parish church of the village; its large graveyard continued in use until the beginning of the 12th century.[23] Losinga's new church was laid out, with surrounding churchyard, immediately south of the cathedral graveyard. No doubt the new parish church was the product of a desire by the bishop for more privacy for his manor, which adjoined the cathedral site. But there also may have been a desire to 'prove a point', a two-fold point in this case: that a Norman bishop could close down a former cathedral for public worship; and that he could replace it with a parish church larger and more magnificent than the late-Saxon cathedral.

We do not know the precise form of Losinga's church. Today, St. Mary's at North Elmham has a 6–bay arcade of the 13th century, with a further bay to the east. This further bay has responds of the Losinga period (Figs. 82–3). They have the appearance not of responds for an arch leading into a chapel, but of the first responds of an early 12th-century arcade.[24] At the very least the responds, undoubtedly *in situ*, establish the width of de Losinga's church; it was clearly a building of much grander scale than the adjacent former cathedral.

If, as seems likely, de Losinga built an aisled church at North Elmham, it shows that he regarded this as more than an ordinary parish church. Until the very late 12th century, when the great Marshland churches such as Tilney All Saints and Walsoken were being built, Norfolk parish churches were always constructed without aisles. The only exceptions were those which the parishioners shared with a monastic establishment, such as Binham or Wymondham. The churches at King's Lynn also had aisles; they also had monastic cells; and, like Elmham, they were under the patronage of the Bishops of Norwich. It is unlikely that Elmham in the early 12th century was so large a village as to require a parish church of exceptional size. It must be that Bishop Herbert required the new church at Elmham to dominate the former cathedral, to prove his right to the episcopate and his ability to rule.

We have looked at a village, a town, and a patron. It would be difficult to show that the examples chosen are typical of Norfolk as a whole. Nevertheless, such studies throw into focus some of the processes and influences at work in parish churches of the 11th and 12th centuries. It was undoubtedly a period of profound change, and of dramatic activity. At parish level, in a county like Norfolk, surprisingly little has changed since.

Notes

1. Bishop Walter de Suffield's valuation of 1253–4, printed W.E. Lunt, *Valuation of Norwich, 1254* (1926); the actual figure is certainly higher than 789, since no entries were made for Thetford, and only 29 for Norwich.
2. 'Huius abbatis tempore ecclesie Hulmensis lapidea, antea lutea, quae tempore Cnuti regis a fundamentis in honore sancti Benedicti abbatis fuerant inchoata, in construendi prosecutione opus non seguiter continuatur inceptum': Sir H. Ellis (ed.) *Chronica Jon. de Oxenedes monachi S. Benedicti de Hulmo* (Rolls Ser. xiii, London, 1859), 292.
3. H.W. Saunders, *The First Register of Norwich Cathedral Priory* (Norfolk Rec. Soc. xi, 1939), 23.
4. The author regards the thesis put forward by Heywood as unproven, and, despite certain shortcomings, Rigold's analysis as the more accurate: S.E. Rigold, 'The Anglian Cathedral of North Elmham, Norfolk', *Med. Arch.* vi–vii (1962–3) 67ff; S. Heywood, 'The Ruined Church at North Elmham' *JBAA*, cxxxv (1982), 1–10. Apart from the later medieval additions to the cathedral, the only features of undoubted post-Conquest date are the north and south doorways. Rigold (op.cit., p. 67) has demonstrated that these doorways are later insertions, since the mortar used for their construction is very different from that used in the rest of the building. Furthermore, the fact that diagonal tooling is found on quoins and jambs does not signify the certain evidence of a post-Conquest date: diagonal tooling is common in France from the late 10th century, and is found on pre-Conquest 11th-century structures in England (e.g. Sherborne Minster). If we are to look for analogies with Germany, North Elmham, with its continuous transept, has much more in common with cathedrals (e.g. Augsburg, Frankfurt, Halberstadt, Hildesheim, Colonge, Magdeburg, Mainz, Strasbourg, to name but eight). German bishops' chapels were of 'Doppelkapelle' type (as at Hereford), and did not resemble a small cathedral. North Elmham, on the other hand, does convincingly resemble a small cathedral of German type. Finally, the ruined church at North Elmham is so dissimilar to other buildings which Bishop de Losinga is known to have constructed (not least of which being the adjacent parish church of North Elmham), that it is very difficult to believe that he was responsible for the church on the site of the earlier wooden cathedral. [But cf. above, pp. 175–7 note 7: *Ed.*]
5. See below.
6. D. Dymond, *The Norfolk Landscape* (London, 1985), 82.
7. F. Blomefield, *Essay Towards a Topographical History of the County of Norfolk*, (1805–10), vii, 271.
8. Ibid. 271.
9. Ibid. 282.
10. Ibid. 285.
11. Rogerson's excavation is fully published in A. Rogerson, S.J. Ashley, P. Williams and A. Harris, 'Three Norman Churches in Norfolk', *East Anglian Archaeology*, xxxii (1987), 1–66.
12. R. Carr and S. Dunmore, 'The Late Saxon Town of Thetford', *East Anglian Archaeology*, iv (1976), 17.
13. D. Wilson and S. Moorhouse, 'Medieval Britain in 1970' *Med. Arch.* xv (1971), 130–1. It seems likely that the identification of the site as St. Michael's is erroneous; it may actually have been St. Benet's, but this is far from certain.
14. G.M. Knocker, 'Excavations at Red Castle, Thetford', *Norfolk Archaeology*, xxxiv (1967), 119–73.
15. S. Heywood, 'Discussion' in Excavations in Thetford, 1948–59 and 1973–80, *East Anglian Archaeology*, xxii (1984), 52.
16. E. Fernie, *The Architecture of the Anglo-Saxons* (London, 1983), 163.
17. E.M. Goulbourn and H. Symonds, *The Life, Letters and Sermons of Bishop Herbert de Losinga* (Orford and London, 1878)
18. A.W. Morant, 'Notices of the Church of St. Nicholas, Great Yarmouth', *Norfolk Archaeology*, vii (1872), 227.
19. It was only in 1714 that another church was built in Yarmouth: St. George's. Yet this remained a chapel-of-ease to St. Nicholas's.
20. 'The Rev. John Gunn believes that, when excavations were made during the alterations in 1847, he saw indications of two apsidal chapels opening from the eastern sides of the transepts as at Norwich Cathedral and Thetford Priory': A. W. Morant, op.cit. note 18, 216.
21. St. James's has had an unfortunate history. The nave was demolished in the 16th century, and the rest of the church used as a workhouse. The crossing tower collapsed in 1853, and the site demolished. A Methodist church stands on the site today. It has recently been discovered that some of the 12th-century remains were removed in 1854 and built into a house in the parish of Walpole St. Peter, some 20km away.
22. Further details found in E.M. Beloe, *Our Borough, Our Churches* (Wisbech, 1899); H.J. Hillen, *History of King's Lynn* (Norwich, 1907).
23. P. Wade-Martins, 'Excavations in North Elmham Park, 1967–72', *East Anglian Archaeology*, ix (1980), 3–11.
24. Fig. 83 provides convincing proof that the 12th-century responds belonged to nave arcades and not chapels or transepts: the presence of an original window above the responds makes the latter interpretation impossible: the window would either be masked by the chapel/transept east wall, or would have opened internally into the chapel space. The window is steeply splayed, and certainly looked onto exterior space.

XIV. Churches in York and its Hinterland: Building Patterns and Stone Sources in the 11th and 12th Centuries

Richard K. Morris

The argument of this essay is that while churches have been erected in England for the use of laypeople in every century from the 7th to the 20th, there was only one period during which the construction of such buildings in stone was practised as a general, national activity. The beginning of this period cannot be placed; it may centre around 1000, but the chronology is likely to vary from region to region and in some areas a date nearer 1050 might be argued for. The mass rebuilding came to an end in the second half of the 12th century. By this time almost all medieval parish churches existed. Here lies a clue to why so many of our parish church fabrics go back to an 11th- or 12th-century core, for this was the age when some parish churches were founded, and virtually all others were rebuilt, in stone, perhaps for the first time. Since there is evidence to suggest that many parish churches had predecessors which were already at least a century old at the time of their rebuilding, it becomes possible to propose a rule: that where the development of a stone building is additive, there will be a tendency for some fabric or configuration of the primary structure to persist.[1]

Once accomplished, the national rebuilding was never repeated. A minority of churches were entirely reconstructed; most others were enlarged, or underwent modification in some degree. But such changes were variable in their effects, and spread across centuries. A few churches escaped them. To illustrate this: out of the *c.* 560 parish churches which stood in medieval Yorkshire, only 19 appear on the list of churches claimed as Anglo-Saxon in whole or part by Dr. H.M. Taylor, and only two or three more might justifiably be added to it: a proportion of 3.5 per cent.[2] This level of survival may seem meagre, but it is not far from the average for England as a whole, which is around 3 per cent.

The figures to be derived from Domesday Book are more considerable, though nowhere near complete.[3] Domesday Book for Yorkshire records 47 churches, and a further 125 churches and priests. Priests mentioned at 13 places may possibly stand for churches, and there were five places called *Chirchebi* where presumably there were or once had been churches. In all, therefore, Domesday offers the possibility of a figure in the region of 190 churches: about 34 per cent of medieval provision.

Only seven of the 19 churches identified by Dr. Taylor as Anglo-Saxon were recorded in 1086. Leaving aside, for the moment, the question of whether some of these churches may have been founded *after* 1086, let us assume that the compilers of the Yorkshire Domesday ignored churches on a comparable scale throughout the region. In such circumstances, for every church noted, 2.7 churches would have been omitted. If this is what actually happened, around 82 per cent of local churches would have existed by 1086. More complete counts of churches which were undertaken in some other areas suggest that such a percentage may not be too high.[4] Nor is it necessarily inconsistent with the statement made by William of Malmesbury in *c.* 1125 that in Norman England one might see churches rise in every village: if *c.* 80 per cent of churches existed by 1086, it should follow that between 1000 and 2000 new churches were founded during the next 40 years.[5] Such concentrated building, coupled with the rebuilding, would have seemed impressive to those who lived through it.

In maybe four cases out of five, therefore, the old question of whether or not a given church could have existed before 1100, or 'might be Saxon', is hardly now worth the asking. Archaeology is beginning to show that even some parochial chapels were in being by this time.[6] A more vital topic is how much sooner local churches were founded. And was the process of foundation gradual, sporadic, or abrupt?

In Yorkshire, Dr. Taylor's 19 buildings take us as close as we shall get to a resolution of this issue from the study of upstanding fabrics alone. This essay is accordingly devoted to a brief review and tentative interpretation of the evidence they present.

Seven of the churches listed by Dr. Taylor contain evidence for ecclesiastical activity in the period *c.* 650–850. Collingham houses Anglian sculpture. So does Hackness, which was described by Bede as a dependency of *Streanaeshalch* and where the surviving nave embodies fabric for which a date in the first half of the 9th century has been suggested.[7] Hovingham possesses a stone 'frieze', carved around 800 and perhaps to be interpreted as the side of a reliquary shrine.[8] Kirby Hill incorporates architectural sculpture of disputed date, but arguably older than *c.* 900. The piece in question may not be *in situ*, but there are other architectural items re-used in the walls which collectively point to the presence of a masonry building on or near this site which preceded the church there now.[9] Kirkdale has two carved grave-covers of pre-Viking character, and the re-foundation inscription above the south door confirms that an earlier church stood here.[10] Ledsham has primary fabric, including architectural sculpture, which could date from the 8th century.[11] In York, pre-Viking sculpture, and an inscription of the 8th or 9th century, are provenanced to St. Mary Bishophill Junior.[12]

With the possible exceptions of Hackness and Ledsham, none of the foregoing buildings are in their present forms likely to be much older than 1000. It is their sites, not the fabrics we see today, that are likely to have been the scene of more ancient ecclesiastical use. Exactly how such use, or uses, should be characterised it is difficult to say, but in three cases there are strong indications that the churches had existed in monastic milieux.[13] It may well be that all these sites were once, in some sense, 'monastic'.[14] Such an interpretation would be in accord with the views which have recently been put forward by Eric Cambridge in his reassessment of pre-Conquest churches in County Durham. The essence of Cambridge's conclusion is that in the 7th, 8th, and 9th centuries the use of stone was restricted to churches of religious communities; that secular churches were generally timber-built until late in the pre-Conquest period; and that stone churches were accordingly still uncommon when the pattern of parishes began to assume its permanent shape.[15]

In Yorkshire as a whole, the ratio of parish churches for which a pre-Conquest monastic background is known or suspected, and those which seem to be of purely secular origin, is around 1:20. The present sample gives a ratio of 1:2.5. Since only two of our church structures are likely to be of monastic origin in themselves, this suggests that while the survival of late-pre-Conquest fabric may have been determined by factors operating haphazardly in later centuries, the *occurrence* of such fabrics is not likely to have been conditioned by chance. Small as it is relative to the total of parish churches in medieval Yorkshire, our group of 18 churches may therefore be of much greater statistical significance in relation to the population of comparable stone buildings which existed by, say, 1050. But this is no more than the rule of additive development should lead us to expect.

With Ledsham and Hackness now set to one side, reasons for claiming the remaining 19 buildings to be Anglo-Saxon must now be examined. The principal criteria have been tabulated (Fig. 84). The presence of megalithic side-alternate quoins emerges as the commonest criterion (11 buildings, 61 per cent). Next in frequency is the existence of a tower with double-belfry windows (8 buildings, 44 per cent). Among the nine churches which have two or more criteria in common, the conjunction of megalithic side-alternate quoins and double-belfry windows is the most usual (5 buildings, 28 per cent). No other permutations of the seven remaining criteria concern more than two churches at once. In five cases diagnosis rests on a single main criterion.

At least ten of the churches (55 per cent) share a further characteristic which was not recorded systematically by Dr. Taylor: some or all of the stones in their walls were derived from other buildings (Fig. 85). Direct evidence for the re-use of stone is provided by architectural components and earlier inscriptions. Monolithic window-heads, sometimes inverted and used simply as walling material, occur at Ryther, Hovingham, and Kirby Hill. Items such as this are most likely to be of Anglo-Saxon rather than Roman creation, but the willingness of masons to refashion Roman material is nicely shown at Ilkley, where excavations within the tower in 1982 disclosed two Roman altars which had been converted into the heads of single-splayed windows.[16] Roman inscriptions are rare.[17] A large stone with a formal border is set low down at the south-west angle of the tower at Kirby Hill. This is alleged to have carried an inscription, although nothing can now be read. There is a small stone with a drafted margin at the exterior of the south-west angle of the nave at Ledsham. This may have been a panel intended for lettering. Other signs of re-use include lewis-holes (sometimes off-centre, indicating the stone to have been re-cut), and the employment in a few places of small ashlars that are characteristic of Roman *opus isodomum* to be found in Roman centres such as York and Aldborough.[18] Predation by masons was not limited to Roman stone. The walls of quite a number of churches embody, or once embodied, pieces of pre-Conquest sculpture.[19]

Secondary evidence for re-use is provided by the large size and petrology of many of the stones that were taken. At Kirk Hammerton there are single stones weighing the best part of a ton. Blocks of similar magnitude are visible elsewhere, as at Skipwith and Kirby Hill. Fabrics of the 12th century display a growing preference for stones of more manageable proportions: often of a size that could be handled by one man. By contrast, earlier builders seem to have liked large stones, perhaps because they saw little purpose in the labour of splitting them up only to have to put them back together again in a wall. Large stones also reduced the quantities of lime mortar that were required for building.

Most of the megalithic material is Millstone Grit. Stone of this sort does not outcrop in the Vale of York. The nearest sources occur along the eastern flank of the Pennines. Outside Pennine areas gritstone was shunned by builders of churches after *c.* 1125. The material seems not to have been quarried again for general building purposes until the Industrial Revolution, when it returned to favour as being suited to the construction of such works as viaducts, bridges, and public buildings.[20]

CHURCH	Q.St.	R.St.	(C)PM	WD	A.Shfts		A.Shfts	WD	(C)PM	R.St.	Q.St.	CHURCH	(M)SAQ	DBW	Stp	MA	DSW	¾TSD	LS/E	MD	TSA
DARFIELD		+								+		RYTHER									+
RYTHER		+								+		MONK FRYSTON	+								
LAUGHTON		+										HORNBY	+								
BARDSEY		+										THORNTON STEWARD						+			
KIRBY HILL		+										BOLTON-ON-DEARNE						+			
SKIPWITH		+								+		LAUGHTON		−				+	+		
CRAMBE		+								+		MIDDLETON	+	−				+			
BURGHWALLIS	+	+								+		SKIPWITH	+	−	+	+					
YORK, ST MARY BISHOP	+	+	+			+	+	+		+		YORK, ST MARY BISHOP	+	−	−	+					
KIRK HAMMERTON	+		+	+		+	+	+		+		KIRK HAMMERTON	+	+	+		+				
HOVINGHAM	+		+	+		+	+	+		+		HOVINGHAM	+	+		+	+				
KIRKBY UNDERDALE	[+]	+	+	+		+	+				+	WHARRAM-LE-STREET	+	+	+						
CAMPSALL	+	[+]	+	+		+					+	APPLETON-LE-STREET	+	+							
LITTLE OUSEBURN		+	+							+		BARDSEY	+								
KIRKDALE		+		+	+					+		COLLINGHAM	+								
WHARRAM-LE-STREET	+			+	+				+	+		BURGHWALLIS	+								
APPLETON-LE-STREET	+			+						+		KIRBY HILL	+								
MIDDLETON				+			+	+		+		KIRKDALE	+								
OWSTON		+	+				+			+		LITTLE OUSEBURN	+								
KIPPAX		+								+		THRYBERGH	+								
PENISTONE		+								+		KIRK SANDAL	⸱ +								
KIRK SANDAL		+								+		DARFIELD	+								
THRYBERGH		+				+	+	+	[+]	+		KIRBY UNDERDALE									
BARWICK		+				+	+	+	[+]	+		CAMPSALL									
						+	+					OWSTON									
									+		CRAMBE									
						+					BARWICK									
						+					KIPPAX									
						+					PENISTONE									

Fig. 84 *Presence/absence chart of criteria used by Taylor (1978) "et al." for purposes of identifying pre-Conquest workmanship; and of other criteria, discussed in the text, which are applicable to a wider range of Yorkshire churches in the 11th and 12th centuries. Criteria conventionally regarded as indicators of pre-Conquest date are arranged in the right-hand column, where they are grouped, subjectively, by affinity. Criteria not hitherto considered in any systematic way are arranged in the central and left-hand columns, those on the left being grouped by affinity. Comparison of the two groups suggests that most of the usual criteria may have little or no strict chronological significance as between pre- and post-Conquest buildings. It will be noted that some of the highest scorers in the 'pre-Conquest' group also feature prominently on the left-hand side. KEY: Q.St.: quarried stone; R.St.: Roman stone, re-used; (C)PM: (counter-) pitched masonry; WD: west door; A.Shfts: angle shafts; (M)SAQ: (megalithic) side-alternate quoins; DBW: double belfry windows; Stp: stripwork; MA: megalithic arch and jambs; DSW: double-splayed window; ¾TSD: three-quarter-through-stone door; LS/E: long-and-short/Escomb-fashion quoins or jambs; MD: megalithic doorway; TSA: through-stone arch. Entries enclosed thus [ ] are uncertain. (Drawing: Malcolm Stroud.)*

It is not difficult to see why medieval masons soon came to regard Millstone Grit as unsuitable. As its name suggests, gritstone is coarse and granular. It is also hard, and does not carve easily. Jurassic and Permian limestones were more attractive, easier to work, and closer to hand. Millstone Grit is a heavy-duty stone, with an appeal to engineers rather than to master-masons in pursuit of artistic refinement.[21] However, it was just these properties of great tensile and compressive strength that rendered gritstone attractive to Roman artificers. They employed it for sarcophagi, podia, bases, column drums and monolithic columns, stylobate walls, the foundations of permanent defences, voussoirs of grand arches, and the vaults or lintels of culverts. If left alone, a great deal of the hard infrastructure of Roman places like York would have survived throughout the pre-Conquest period. With this cut stone already available, the first builders of stone churches had only to help themselves.[22]

It may be wondered, however, whether second-hand stone was ever acquired through casual or opportunistic robbing. Even derelict Roman buldings are likely to have had owners. Title to stone may therefore have been transferred by inheritance, gift, purchase, or even latterly as a reflex of site clearance ('We'll pay you to take it away'). Concerning this last possibility, there may be a connection between the development of York as a city, and the appearance of stone churches in its hinterland. Urban redevelopment in the 10th, 11th and 12th centuries, some of it involving expansion back across areas of former Roman occupation, and the

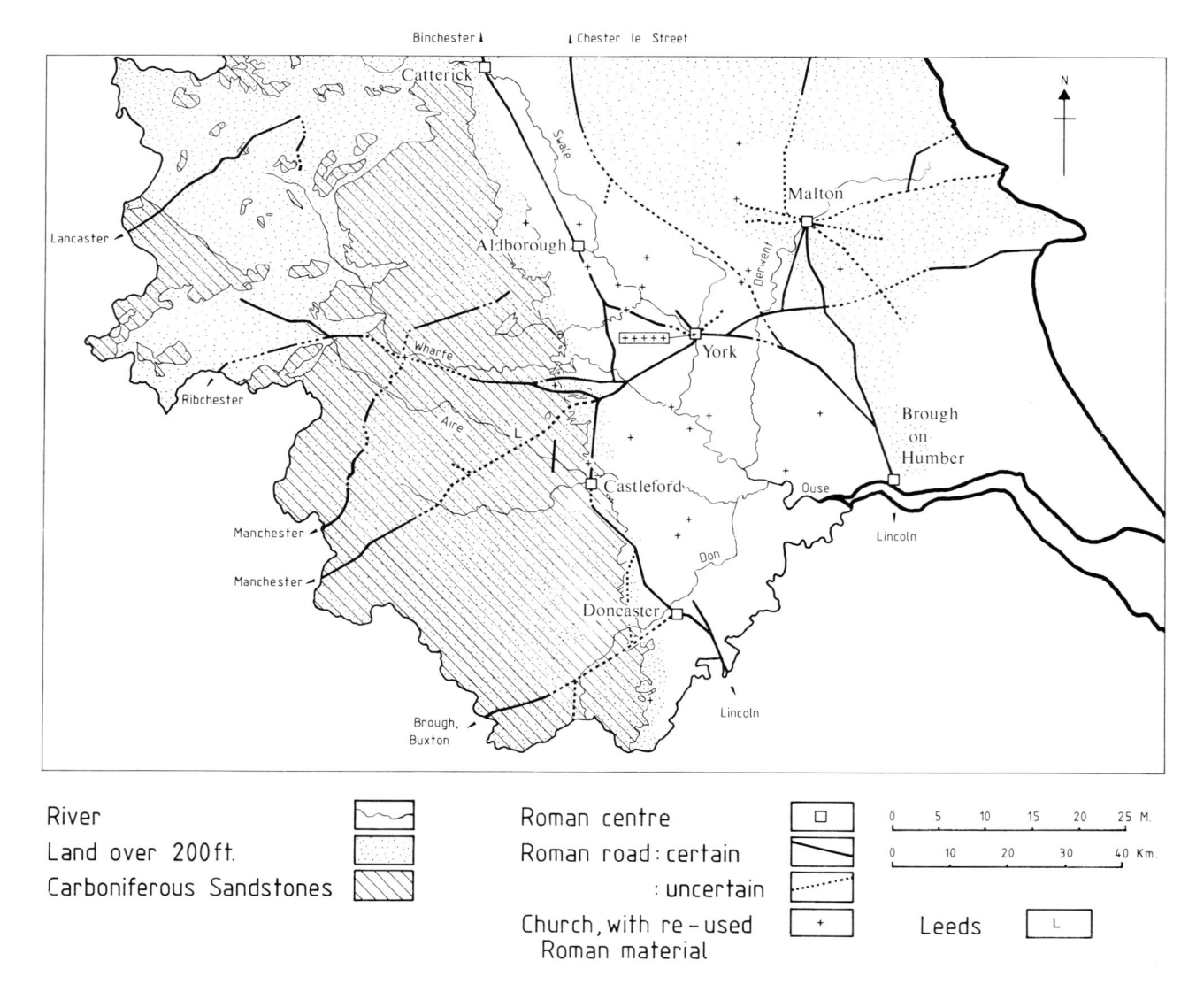

Fig. 85 Churches in Yorkshire containing re-used Roman building material, chiefly Millstone Grit. The source areas of gritstone are indicated. Not all churches in the region have been inspected by the author, who would be grateful for information about omissions. (Drawing: Malcolm Stroud.)

dismantling of defences on the eastern side of the old legionary fortress, may have released quantities of material.

Much of the stone which was re-used in church walls is of such a size that it could scarcely have been recovered from buildings other than of monumental character. This suggests that stone was fetched mainly from towns or important military installations, and it is noticeable that almost all the churches that have so far been observed as containing re-used material lie on a reasonably short radius from such places (Fig. 85). The main area of supply was in the vicinity of York, but there are signs of others in the vicinity of Aldborough, Castleford, and Malton. Some material may have been scavenged from villas, and perhaps especially bath-houses, but villas in Yorkshire do not as a rule seem to have incorporated much gritstone.[23]

Quite a number of churches in Yorkshire which were rebuilt after c. 1150 contain a certain amount of Roman stone. This is because the masons who undertook such rebuilding did not always discard materials from the structures that they were replacing. Stray chunks of gritstone occur in otherwise all-limestone fabrics at Bossall, Wistow, and Sherburn-in-Elmet. Gritstone is visible in the lower courses of the east wall of the chancel at Alne, and in the south wall of the nave at Holme-on-Spalding-Moor. A large amount was recycled in the nave of Howden Minster, especially in the lower register of the west front. In such instances we may be dealing with secondary, or even tertiary, re-use.

Outside York, the re-use of Roman stone seems to have lessened early in the 12th century, and to have ceased altogether by around 1150. Thereafter quarrying took over. The reasons for, and exact chronology of, this change of policy are not reported, but for reasons already touched upon it may be supposed that three factors were particularly influential. The unsuitability of gritstone for the purposes of 12th-century masons has been mentioned. A second drawback lay in the uneven distribution and limited number of places from which such material could be obtained. Thirdly, as more and more parish churches were built or rebuilt in stone, a point would have been reached at which all conveniently robbable Roman buildings had been picked clean. Meanwhile, the search for convenient sources of freestone was hastened by campaigns of monastic and cathedral building initiated by the Normans. At York, the cathedral begun c. 1080 by Thomas of Bayeux (1070–1100) seems to have had a horizontal division somewhere within its fabric, the lower portion being built with Roman stone, and the upper part being made of freshly-quarried material. This may mean that the extraction of magnesian limestone was resumed at some point between c. 1080 and 1100. Unfortunately, there is some doubt as to whether the fragments of Thomas's superstructure which survive lodged within the roof-space of the later cathedral are coeval with the primary campaign. However, even if they are somewhat later, this does not disturb the main argument here, which is that by the early 12th century supplies of Roman stone were either nearing exhaustion or were coming to be ignored, and that the needs of new building were to an increasing extent being met from quarries.[24]

Several churches listed in Fig. 84 appear to have been built from newly-quarried rather than re-used stone. They include Appleton-le-Street and Wharram-le-Street. This could indicate that some quarries were being opened up before the Conquest. But the evidence from York Minster does not support such a view, and a different explanation would be that the churches in question were not Anglo-Saxon at all, at least, not in any strictly chronological sense. In order to weigh up this possibility it is necessary to re-examine the criteria which have been used to establish the claims of our 18 buildings to be of pre-Conquest date.

It was noted above that the diagnostic features which occur with greatest frequency are double-belfry openings with mid-wall shafts, and megalithic side-alternate quoining. The credentials of these forms as indicators of pre-Conquest workmanship are not here contested.[25] What is in question is whether side-alternate quoining, and the double-belfry window with a mid-wall shaft supporting a through-stone slab, ceased to be employed after the Conqueror's decades: that is, after Dr. Taylor's period C3 (1050–1100).

Taking side-alternate quoins first, there can be no doubt that this form of construction was highly characteristic of pre-Conquest workmanship in northern England. It occurs both early (e.g. Jarrow), and late (e.g. Kirkdale). The technique may well have had continuous currency throughout the period c. 700–1100. However, there are examples of this type in buildings which on other grounds could be assigned to the 12th century, and in at least two of the present examples it occurs in conjunction with other criteria suggestive of a later date. Dr. Taylor regarded the tower of Appleton-le-Street as a structure of two periods, built within the range c. 950–1050. But there is a form of chevron ornament on the mid-wall shaft of the belfry opening in the upper stage, and internally this tower does not display signs of a two-stage development. The tower arch, regarded by Dr. Taylor as a probable Norman insertion, has yet to be proved as secondary to the body of the tower.[26] In this instance, therefore, such details as are available could point to a date in the first half of the 12th century.

At Burghwallis, all six quoins of the nave and chancel 'are of very large stones, well laid in side-alternate technique'. Other details, including a plain square plinth, and walls only 2'9" thick, combine 'to give a clear impression of Anglo-Saxon work, notwithstanding the use of herring-bone technique in the walls'.[27] By itself, herringbone or counterpitched masonry is not a criterion of date.[28] However, within certain regions counterpitching was practised more often in some periods than in others. In Yorkshire this technique was popular during the 50 years or so following the Conquest. Dated examples include Richmond Castle (1070s) and the Norman cathedral in York (c.1080–1100). Burghwallis is in fact but one of a large number of churches that embody counterpitched stones. Examples which occur nearby include Campsall, Owston, Kippax, Barwick-in-Elmet, and Marr. The church at Aberford, between Kippax and Barwick, had masonry of this type before its rebuilding in 1861. East of York, pitched and/or counterpitched stonework is to be seen at Hovingham, Bulmer, Terrington, Market Weighton and Kirby Underdale. In York itself, apart from the 11th-century cathedral, counterpitching occurs in the tower of St. Mary Bishophill Junior.

It will be noted that only three of the foregoing examples have been claimed by Dr. Taylor as Anglo-Saxon. While it is *not* suggested that counterpitched masonry is decisively diagnostic of post-Conquest workmanship, there seems to be no denying the popularity of this type of construction, in Yorkshire, in decades following the Conquest. The occurrence of counterpitching in well-dated buildings like York Minster, and in combination with 12th-century decorative details such as scalloped capitals and zig-zag, as at Kirby Underdale, suggests that the heyday of counterpitching lay in the years c.1070–1140. And if counterpitching *was* being practised in Yorkshire before the Conquest, the considerable use of this technique which was made in following decades would only suggest that pre-Conquest building methods were maintained well into the 12th century: a point which has implications for the chronological significance of other features, like side-alternate quoins or double-belfry windows.

A point about double-belfry windows which has

perhaps been given insufficient emphasis centres on the appearance in quite a number of them of architectural sculpture which is of conventional Anglo-Norman aspect.[29] The possible currency of the double-belfry form after the Conquest is not controversial: Dr. Taylor himself described the tower at Hornby as 'Saxo-Norman', and assigned that at Monk Fryston to period C3 (1050–1100). But it may be that more buildings with this feature should be placed after the Conquest, or even after 1100. Reasons for regarding Appleton-le-Street as a structure of the 12th century have been given: and this was one of the towers for which Dr. Taylor entertained a 10th-century date. At Hovingham, double-belfry windows occur in a tower which has a west doorway of Romanesque character set at its base. The door is overarched by a plump roll moulding, and flanked by angle-shafts: two features which would not be out of place around 1100. Hovingham, like Skipwith, has an extra diagnostic feature in the form of a large double-splayed window in the southern elevation of the tower. Windows of similar size occur in this position elsewhere, as at Little Ouseburn. But here the window is single-splayed, and although the tower has some megalithic quoins and re-uses Roman stone, the belfry openings have no throughstone slabs. Little Ouseburn's tower probably dates to the first half of the 12th century. The picture is thus of evolution rather than revolution.

Another building which could be described in these terms is Wharram-le-Street, where side-alternate quoins and double-belfry windows outlined by stripwork appear in company with mouldings and capitals of Norman type. Dr. Taylor has argued that Wharram-le-Street is an Anglo-Saxon building which was later trimmed with Norman detail.[30] Bilson regarded the Norman doorways and the jambs of the main arches as being coeval with the surrounding fabric: a view with which (the south door possibly excepted) the present author is inclined to agree.[31] This is an important case, for if the main shell of Wharram-le-Street is redated to after 1100, the stripwork which outlines the belfry openings must also belong to the 12th century: a conclusion which would in turn extend the time-range for a building like the tower of St. Mary Bishophill Junior, where counterpitched fabric has been noted.

Enough has been said to establish a *possibility* that at least eight and perhaps as many as eleven of the 'pre-Conquest' churches listed in Fig. 84 may be no older than c. 1050, and that many of them could have been built after 1100. Moreover, there are several features, not in themselves diagnostic of date, which occur in churches of both 'Saxon' and 'Norman' character. The large, south-facing window in the second stage of a tower is one such item. A west door to the nave or tower is another. At least six of the churches on Dr. Taylor's list have, or once had, such doors. So do towers which were built in the first half of the 12th century, like those at Little Ouseburn, Kirby Underdale, Leathley or Stonegrave.[32] If the issue of absolute date is set aside, it therefore becomes possible to admit a larger number of criteria (like the west doors and counterpitched masonry) which hitherto have been excluded from attention, but which arguably deserve a place in discussion of the use and design of churches in the 11th and 12th centuries. A sample list of 11 such churches has therefore been appended to the 'pre-Conquest' group in Fig. 84.

Two churches not so far discussed must now be mentioned: Kirkdale, and Kirk Hammerton. Both buildings contain between them many of the features which have already been considered. Kirkdale is of special importance because, unlike all the other churches which have been examined, it has a datable inscription built into its fabric. The inscription is fixed into the wall above the south door, and tells how Orm, the son of Gamal, bought St. Gregory's minster as a ruin and rebuilt it from the ground upwards, in the days of Edward the Confessor and Tosti. Tosti was earl of Northumbria from 1055 to 1065. It is widely assumed that this is the date of the inscription, and therefore of the fabric. This conclusion may well be correct. But there are two areas of uncertainty. The first is whether the inscription is in its original position.[33] The second is whether the inscription was cut at the time of the rebuilding and not, say, a few years later. Both queries may seem rather pedantic. In fact, they are rather important. For Kirkdale embodies Romanesque features.[34] If it can be shown that such details as angle-shafts had become fashionable in Yorkshire before the Conquest, then there is no reason to be taken aback by such precocity elsewhere — as at Hovingham or Kirk Hammerton. If on the other hand work stood incomplete in 1065, or had not even been started (one would like to know the contents of Orm's will), it may be that the dating of Kirkdale, and of other churches dated by reference to it, should be reviewed. A knowledge of the exact archaeological context of the inscription would not answer these questions, but it could help to narrow down, or widen, the options.

From all that has been said, the epithet 'late-Saxon' may now seem rather unhelpful, and possibly even misleading. In strictly chronological terms there might be no 'late-Saxon' churches in Yorkshire. 'Saxo-Norman' is more acceptable, provided that it is not held to betoken an idea that churches like Kirk Hammerton and Kirkdale were products of an obsolescent tradition. That this is unlikely is shown not only by the novelty of some features at these churches, but also by the fact that our survey has disclosed no surviving stone churches that can be regarded as having been immediately anterior to the 19 buildings on the list. On the whole, however, it seems best to avoid cultural and ethnic labels altogether and to use dates or age-ranges instead. Dates do not beg historical questions, and the less precise a date may be, the more important it is that such imprecision should be clearly acknowledged.

It therefore seems logical to look upon the churches singled out by Dr. Taylor in Yorkshire, and their Lincolnshire cousins, not as the last in a waning series, but as the *first* essays in a new tradition of stone-built village churches. These buildings display some features which were inherited from eve-of-Conquest or older practice and soon disappeared, but they also contain others, like the axial west door, which proliferated rather than died out during the next 50–75 years. If the inscription at Kirkdale is accepted at face value, then there is no reason why churches such as Hovingham and Kirk Hammerton should not have been built around 1050.

It is a question whether the local stone churches which appear in the 11th century were the first to have been built thus. Monastic churches of masonry had existed since *c.* 700. The fabrics of several, like Ledsham and Hackness, survived into the 11th century and seem to have been sufficiently sound to provide the structural nuclei of parish churches: the rule of additive development operating once again. Other monastic churches may have been dismantled, or more drastically restored, and their materials re-used in the parish churches that succeeded them.[35] Perhaps this explains why so many of the churches on our list had monastic ancestors, for the fact that they were among the first to be rebuilt in stone may be a function of the presence of an earlier masonry church which was available to be cannibalized.

A more difficult issue is whether ordinary secular churches of the 11th century were preceded by more primitive stone structures, or whether wooden churches were the norm until the mid 11th century.[36] The rule of additive development is no help in this, as it does not permit us to see beyond a complete rebuilding.[37] Archaeological excavation is the only way round the problem. Unfortunately, not enough churches in Yorkshire have yet been studied in this way to permit conclusions to be drawn, and where results are available the pattern is ambiguous. There is, for instance, the suggestion of a primary timber phase at Wharram Percy,[38] whereas the inaugural layout of St. Helen-on-the-Walls in York was apparently in stone.[39] Looking further afield, one point which does emerge from a comparison of church excavations, particularly those undertaken in towns since 1955, is how often the first stone phase is dated to the 11th century, and how often also the builders of such churches disturbed earlier burials, or purloined gravestones for use as building material.[40] In Yorkshire, carved stones of the 10th and earlier 11th centuries have been noted in at least a quarter of medieval parish churches.[41] In this region, at least, the local church may well have been a commonplace in the 10th century. The period *c.* 1050–1150 gives us a Great Rebuilding.

Within what sort of institutional framework were these churches accommodated? At first sight we appear to be dealing with a simple two-tier structure, comprising a handful of senior minsters[42] and many one-priest churches.[43] The intermediate category of old minsters which is so characteristic of late-Saxon ecclesiastical geography in parts of southern and western England seems to be missing.[44] If superior churches had existed in Yorkshire during the 10th and 11th centuries, however, disclosure of their presence could not be expected because hardly any written records of relevant type survive. Nor is Domesday Book much help, for in Yorkshire details of endowments were seldom given.[45]

It is interesting to compare this rather featureless picture with what can be found out about the disposition of the parish system in the 12th century, when documents become more abundant. There are signs that some churches were, or had once been, of greater status than their neighbours. For example, shortly after 1100 the churches of Driffield, Pocklington, Snaith, and Aldborough were granted by Henry I to St. Peter (of York) and the archbishop *cum omnibus suis capellis et soc et sac et consuetudinibus ad eas pertinentibus*.[46] That this was something more than a formula which could be applied to any parish church of the 12th century is revealed at Aldborough, where later sources depict the church of St. Andrew as a dominant *matrix ecclesia* which exerted authority over a constellation of dependent churches and chapels.[47] Miscellaneous marks of superior status have been noted elsewhere, as for instance at Dewsbury,[48] Ecclesfield and Conisbrough[49] (and cf. above. p. 10).

While more churches than we think may have approximated to the old minsters of Wessex and Mercia, it remains difficult to regard them as having been common, of even distribution, or of outstanding importance. Nor, on present evidence, is it possible to suggest whether such churches could be the vestiges of a network of minsters which had once been more extensive and was largely 'weathered down' in the 9th and 10th centuries, or the products of a more recent, limited programme of founding or upgrading.[50] Archaeology might furnish data which would help us to choose between these hypotheses, or to generate additional ones.[51] Nevertheless, even a cautious, provisional assessment would be that ecclesiastical organization in 11th-century Yorkshire was characterised by a greater measure of diversity than has sometimes been allowed.

Notes

1. H. Richmond, 'Outlines of Church Development in Northamptonshire', in L.A.S. Butler and R.K. Morris (eds.), *The Anglo-Saxon Church: Papers on History, Architecture and Archaeology in Honour of Dr. H.M. Taylor* (C.B.A. Research Rep. 60, 1986), 176–87.
2. Churches in Yorkshire not claimed as pre-Conquest by Dr. Taylor but likely to be so include Thornton Steward, N. Yorks., and Bolton upon Dearne, S. Yorks. For Bolton consult P.F. Ryder, *Saxon Churches in South Yorkshire* (S. Yorks. County Council Archaeol. Monograph 2, 1982), 17–20. Ryder makes a case for an early date for Conisbrough (45–52), but this is not a building which I have visited recently and it is excluded from discussion here.
3. Comments on the variations in completeness and presentation of ecclesiastical data in D.B. are made by Lennard, *Rural England*, 288–94; Blair, 'Secular Minsters', 106, 112–14; Morris, *CBA*, 68–71.
4. D.B. for Suffolk mentions at least 416 churches: about 75 per cent of the eventual medieval total for the county. The question of quantities is discussed, with undue caution, in R. Morris, 'The Church in the Countryside' in D. Hooke (ed.), *Medieval Villages* (Oxf. Univ. Committee for Arch. Monograph 5, 1985), 50–1, 53. Revised estimates are given in chapter 4 of my forthcoming book, *Churches in the Landscape*. A further sign of D.B.'s weakness as a guide to ecclesiastical provision in 11th-century Yorkshire is provided by the distribution of pre-Conquest sculpture, much of which is funerary. Outside York, only 45 of the 136 places with such stones were credited with a church in 1086: about one church in three. I am grateful to Dr. J. Lang, who kindly provided me with a list of sites in the county which have produced pre-Conquest sculpture.
5. Few can have been founded after *c*. 1130. By this time the enforcement of the legal definition of a parish was becoming effective; thereafter, intruders into the existing pattern of parish churches were seldom tolerated.
6. For an example in Yorkshire see P. Mayes, 'St James, Tong, West Yorkshire', *Bulletin of the CBA Churches Committee*, xii (1980), 20–1.
7. Bede, *H.E.* iv. 23; Taylor & Taylor, i, 268–70.
8. The date of the sculpture is discussed by R.J. Cramp, 'The Position of the Otley Crosses in English Sculpture of the Eighth and Ninth Centuries', in V. Elbern (ed.), *Kolloquium uber spätantike und fruhmittelalterliche Skulptur* (Mainz, 1971), 60. The function of the stone is considered by Prof. R.N. Bailey in a forthcoming study of Hovingham and its sculpture.
9. Taylor & Taylor, i, 354–6.
10. E. Okasha, *Handlist of Anglo-Saxon Non-Runic Inscriptions* (1971), Nos. 64, 87–8.
11. Taylor & Taylor, i, 378–84, esp. 383. See also R.N. Bailey, 'Ledsham', *Bulletin of the CBA Churches Committee*, xviii (1983, 6–8; articles by M.L. Faull and L. Butler in *JBAA* cxxxix (1986), 143–7, and cxl (1987), 199–203.
12. E. Okasha, *Handlist*, No. 148, p.132. For the provenance, consult D.H. Haigh, 'On an Inscribed Stone found at Yarm', *Yorkshire Arch. J.* vi (1881), 48.
13. Ledsham, Hackness, Hovingham. A possible monastic context for the site and surroundings of St. Mary Bishophill Junior is outlined in R. Morris, 'Alcuin, York, and the *Alma Sophia*', in Butler and Morris (eds.), op.cit. note 1, 85–6.
14. The socio-cultural context of monasticism in the period *c*. 650–850 is explored by P. Wormald, 'Bede, Beowulf and the Conversion of the Anglo-Saxon Aristocracy', in R.T. Farrell (ed.), *Bede and Anglo-Saxon England* (B.A.R. British ser. xliv), 49–58.
15. E. Cambridge, 'The Early Church in County Durham: A Reassessment', *JBAA*, cxxxvii (1984), 65–85, esp. 80–1.
16. *Med. Arch.* xxvii (1983), 211. The stones are displayed in the ground storey of the tower.
17. There were, however, a number re-used in the fabric of the late 11th-century cathedral at York: D. Phillips, *The Cathedral of Thomas of Bayeux. Excavations at York Minster: Vol. II* (1985), Pls. 51, 85, 86.
18. Such stones can be seen in the towers of St. Mary Bishophill Junior, York, and Little Ouseburn. They may also have been used at Burghwallis.
19. E.g. Bolton upon Dearne, Hovingham, Kirby Hill, Kirkdale, Little Ouseburn, Middleton.
20. Phillips op.cit. note 17, 183, n. 16, 17.
21. Ibid. 196.
22. P.C. Buckland, note in J.B. Whitwell, 'The Church Street Sewer and an Adjacent Building', in P.V. Addyman (ed.), *The Archaeology of York*, iii.1 (1976), 32–5.
23. Hovingham could be an exception.
24. Phillips, op.cit. note 17, 117, Fig. 19; 183–4.
25. The arguments were set out by the Taylors in Taylor & Taylor, i, 4–8, and refined by Dr. Taylor in Ibid. iii, 759–60, 762.
26. Taylor & Taylor, i, 29.
27. Taylor & Taylor, i, 119. Although it is often said that the walls of Anglo-Norman parish churches were thicker than those of pre-Conquest buildings, I am not aware of any systematic study which bears out this generalisation. Hence, while wall-thicknesses of pre-Conquest churches have been analysed by Dr. Taylor, there are no corresponding data for churches built in the period 1100–1150. Until such information becomes available, it may be unwise to place too much reliance upon the 'thin/thick' contrast.
28. J. and H.M. Taylor, 'Herring-bone Masonry as a Criterion of Date', *JBAA*, 3rd ser. xxvii (1964), 4–13.
29. E.g. Alkborough, Clee, Lincs., and St. Peter-at-Gowts, Lincoln, where Norman-derived capitals occur. I am grateful to David Stocker for information about the forms of capitals in these towers.
30. Taylor & Taylor, 647–53, esp. 651–2.
31. J. Bilson, 'Wharram-le-Street Church, Yorkshire, and St. Rule's Church, St Andrews', *Archaeologia*, lxxiii (1923), 55–72. The building sequence of the south wall and door requires further study. [And cf. above, pp. 28–9: *Ed*.]
32. Other examples of west doors in churches of the 11th and 12th centuries include Winterton, Scartho, Rothwell, Alkborough, all Lincs., Warnford, Hants., Shoddesdon, Heref., Barrow, Salop., Goodmanham, Humbs. (Yorks E.R.). Their frequency in the 11th and 12th centuries is presumably to be explained in terms of a pattern of use that required at least two entrances (south and west) often in close proximity. Not all the west doors led into towers.
33. Of all the exercises in church archaeology that await the undertaking, a meticulous study of this church and the context of its inscription must surely be among the most desirable.
34. Angle-shafts with bases and capitals; shafts against the jambs of the chancel arch. Eric Cambridge draws attention — and was responsible for drawing mine — to the significance of this in his essay on Beverley, forthcoming in the B.A.A. transactions of the conference on art and architecture in the East Riding of Yorkshire.
35. E.g. at Hovingham, Kirby Hill, where the re-use of window-heads points to earlier Anglo-Saxon builings.
36. Place-names in Yorkshire like Woodkirk ('church made of wood' or 'by the wood'?), Felkirk ('church made of planks') and Skewkirk (*skógr* 'wood') are suggestive: M. Gelling, 'The word 'Church' in English Place-Names', *Bulletin CBA Churches Committee*, xv (1981), 8. D.B. records an *ecclesia lignea* at Old Byland.
37. At Raunds, Northants., for example, the 11th-century church was a total rebuilding. The smaller, earlier church (10th-century?) would not have been detectable using methods outlined by H. Richmond (above, note 1). A. Boddington, 'A

38. J.G. Hurst, 'Wharram Percy: St Martin's Church', in *The Archaeological Study of Churches* (C.B.A. Research Rep. 13, 1976), 36–9. A preliminary statement about the revised chronology (wooden church later 10th century, first stone church 11th century?) appears in J.G. Hurst, 'The Wharram Research Project: Results to 1983', *Med. Arch.* xxviii (1984), 89–90. Excavations at Levisham, N Yorks, disclosed no predecessor to the first stone church, which has been assigned to the 12th century. However, the presence of earlier sculpture at this site suggests that ecclesiastical use was being made of it before the stone church was built (R.A. Hall & J.T. Lang, 'St. Mary's Church, Levisham, N Yorkshire', *Yorks. Arch. Jnl.* lviii (1986), 57–83).

39. J.R. Magilton, 'The Church of St Helen-on-the-Walls, Aldwark', in P.V. Addyman (ed.), *The Archaeology of York*, x.1 (1980). A date in the later 10th century is suggested for the first church (p.18), but there is some doubt about the precision of this, and it is a question whether the stone footings excavated were for a masonry building or a composite stone-and-timber structure.

40. E.g. St. Mark, Lincoln (B. Gilmour in 'Excavations at Lincoln. Third Interim Report: Sites Outside the Walled City 1972–77', *Antiq. J.* lxi (1981), 93–101); St. Benedict, Norwich (J.P. Roberts & M. Atkin, 'St Benedict's Church', in 'Excavations in Norwich 1971–1978', Pt. 1, *East Anglian Arch.* xv (1982), 11–29); St. Mary Bishophill Senior, York (H.G. Ramm, 'Excavations in the Church of St Mary Bishophill Senior, York', *Yorks. Arch. Jnl.* xlviii (1976), 35–68).

41. Yet only *c.* 33 per cent of these churches were recorded in D.B.: see note 4 above.

42. York (St. Peter, Christ Church), Beverley, Ripon.

43. Light is thrown upon aspects of clerical organization by 'The Northumbrian Priests' Law', *C & S*, i, 452–68.

44. Old minsters are surveyed by Blair, 'Secular Minsters'. See also Franklin, 'Identification'.

45. But see Blair, 'Secular Minsters', 117.

46. *Early Yorkshire Charters*, ed. W. Farrer (1914), Nos. 426, 427, 428. These were manors of Crown demesne. Further claims of Driffield as a royal centre are noted by P.H. Sawyer, 'The royal *tūn* in pre-Conquest England', in P. Wormald (ed.), *Ideal and Reality in Frankish and Anglo-Saxon Society* (1983), 293. The ancient parish of Snaith was large and important: Farrer op.cit., i, No. 472.

47. Farrer, op.cit., i, Nos. 509, 510.

48. *West Yorkshire: an Archaeological Survey to AD 1500*, eds. M.L. Faull & S.A. Moorhouse (1981), i, 216–18, Map 15.

49. P. Ryder, *Saxon Churches in South Yorkshire* (1982), 12–13. Catterick, Northallerton, Sherburn-in-Elmet and Howden are among other churches which have enjoyed some degree of superiority. According to Giraldus Cambrensis, Howden had been the burial place of the sister of Osred, king of Northumbria: (705–716): *Journey through Wales*, i.2. A large quantity of gritstone was recycled in the later medieval fabric.

50. cf. Cambridge, op.cit. note 15.

51. For example, some of the churches just discussed were rebuilt to a cruciform plan. This applies also to several churches which were in the hands of the archbishop (like Otley) or assigned as prebends (like Bossall). The functional significance of cruciformity at parish level remains obscure, but it is difficult not to think that it had to do with a need for more than one altar, and perhaps provision for important burials (cf the use of the north transept at Haddsock, Essex: W. Rodwell, 'The archaeological investigation of Hadsock Church, Essex: an interim report', *Antiq. J.* lvi (1976), 55–71), or even relics (cf. J. Blair, 'Saint Beornwald of Bampton', *Oxoniensia*, xlix (1984), 47–55).

Index of People and Places

Compiled by John Blair

Names of places where ecclesiastical buildings are mentioned are followed, in brackets, by abbreviations denoting status:

C church or chapel
CA cathedral
M minster

The following abbreviations denote counties (as existing before the 1974 boundary changes):

BDF	Bedfordshire	ESX	Essex	LNC	Lancashire	SOM	Somerset
BRK	Berkshire	GLA	Glamorgan	MDX	Middlesex	SSX	Sussex
BUC	Buckinghamshire	GLO	Gloucestershire	MON	Monmouthsire	STF	Staffordshire
CAM	Cambridgeshire	HMP	Hampshire	NFK	Norfolk	SUR	Surrey
CHE	Cheshire	HNT	Huntingdonshire	NTB	Northumberland	WAR	Warwickshire
CMB	Cumberland	HRE	Herefordshire	NTP	Northamptonshire	WLT	Wiltshire
CNW	Cornwall	HRT	Hertfordshire	NTT	Nottinghamshire	WML	Westmorland
DEV	Devon	IOW	Isle of Wight	OXF	Oxfordshire	WOR	Worcestershire
DOR	Dorset	KNT	Kent	RUT	Rutland	YOE	Yorkshire (East Riding)
DRB	Derbyshire	LEI	Leicestershire	SFK	Suffolk	YON	Yorkshire (North Riding)
DRH	Durham	LIN	Lincolnshire	SHR	Shropshire	YOW	Yorkshire (West Riding)

Aachen, palace chapel, 16
Abberley (C), WOR, 123, 135, 139, 142
Abberton (C), WOR, 120, 123, 135
Abbots Worthy (C), HMP, 64
Abbotsbury (M), DOR, 31
  gild, 31, 32, 34
Abdon (C), SHR, 69, 74, 75, 76
Aberford (C), YOW, 195
Abingdon (M, Abbey), BRK, 3, 5, 16, 49, 88, 161
Abitot, Urse d', 127, 133, 166
Ach (Achis, Akes), HRE, 84, 92, 94
Achalt, KNT, *see* Ashill and Asholt
Acol (C), KNT, 106
Acrise (C), KNT, 106, 115
Acton Beauchamp (C), HRE, 125, 129, 154
Acton Round (C), SHR, 69, 73, 76
Adam, Abbot of Evesham, 127
Adam, vicar and dean of Humber, HRE, 92, 95
Adisham (C), KNT, 106, 109, 114, 116
Æfic (Avitus), Dean of the Vale of Evesham, 128
Ælfflæd, daughter of Ælfgar, will of, 3–5, 6
Ælfgar, Ealdorman, will of, 3–4
Ælfric (homilist), 7, 8, 9
Ælfric the Small, lord of Milford (Alvric, Oluric, Uluric, and namesakes in Hampshire Domesday), 8, 54, 56, 60, 65
Ælfric the priest, 6
Ælfric (Alvric), Domesday priest, 64, 65
Ælfsige, Abbot of St. Benet's, 179
Ælfward, Abbot of Evesham, 128

Æthelbald, King of Mercia, 156
Æthelberht, King of Kent, 43
Æthelflæd, Lady of the Mercians, 3, 38, 71, 73, 81
Æthelflæd, daughter of Ælfgar, will of, 3–4
Æthelgifu, will of, 5, 6
Æthelmær, Ealdorman, will of, 33
Æthelnoth [priest?], 6
Æthelred, Ealdorman of Mercia, 71, 73, 81
Æthelred II, King, 8, 22, 53, 64, 65, 110
Æthelric son of Æthelmund, will of, 2–3
Æthelric, Bishop of Dorchester, 30
Æthelric the priest, 6
Æthelsige the deacon, 6
Æthelstan, King, 1, 3, 8, 42, 64
Æthelwig, Abbot of Evesham, 126, 127, 132
Ætwangeræde, KNT, *see* Iwade
Æwellan, KNT, *see* Buckland; Ewell, Temple; River
Aer, Robert Fitz (lord of Aston Eyre), 15, 79
Agemund (Domesday tenant), 65
Agilbert, Bishop of Wessex, 48
Ailmer, canon of Christchurch, 52, 54, 56, 60, 65
Ailric, archdeacon, 128, 134
Ailsi (Gloucestershire thegn), 134
Akes, HRE, *see* Ach
Alan, Domesday tenant, 100
Alan, clerk (witn. for Henry of Blois), 61
Albrighton (C), SHR, 69, 76
Alcuin, 198
Aldborough (M), YOW, 197
  Roman material from ?, 192, 194

Aldenham (C), SHR, 73, 77, 78
Alderminster (M?), WAR, 125
Aldhelm, Bishop of Sherborne, 48
Aldington [near Bonnington] (C), KNT, 106, 108, 109, 115, 116
Aldington [in Thurnham] (C), KNT, 106, 108, 115
Aldington, WOR, 133
Aldsworth (C), GLO, 11, 12
Alelm, Prior of Daventry, 102
Alexander, Bishop of Lincoln, 14, 99, 100, 101
Alfred, King, will of, 3
  laws of, 32, 64
  restoration of London by, 36, 38, 41, 43
  re-vitalisation of Church by, 38, 40, 42
Alfred, Ealdorman, will of, 3
Alfrick (C), WOR, 123
  stone from, 155
Alice, daughter of Ælfric the Small (q.v.), 66
Alkborough (C), LIN, 198
Alkham *(Ealhham)* (C), KNT, 106, 115
Allesborough (C), WOR, 123
Almetus, priest of Carisbrooke and Dean of the Isle of Wight, 10, 52, 54, 56, 57, 60, 61, 65
Alnod, canon of Christchurch, 53
Alnodestreu, SHR, hundred, 70, 71
Alnwick, William, Bishop of Lincoln, 99
Alresford (Cs), HMP, 48, 64
Alsi, canon of Christchurch, 53
Alsiescirce, KNT, *see* Eastbridge
Alstone (C), GLO, 125

201

Alton (M), HMP, 63, 64
Alton (M?), WOR, 123, 124, 128, 129, 138, 142; see also Rock
Aluin, Domesday tenant, 100
Alvarstoke, HMP, 64
Alvechurch (C), WOR, 123, 137
Alvescot (C), OXF, 11
Alvric see Ælfric
Alwardeslea hundred, NTP, 99, 102
Andover (M), HMP, 10, 63
    hundred, 63
    manor, 63
Anselm, Archbishop of Canterbury, 100, 117
Ansketil, Archdeacon of Canterbury, 107
Appledore (M?), KNT, 106, 107, 109, 112, 114, 116, 117
Appleton-le-Street (C), YON, 193, 195, 196
Apse, IOW, 58, 59, 66
Areley Kings (C), WOR, 123, 132
Arley, Upper (C), WOR, 120, 125
    quarrying at, 154
Arrow Valley, WOR, 126
Ash (C), KNT, 106, 115
Ashby, Cold (C), NTP, 98, 99
Ashby St. Ledgers (C), NTP, 102
Asheldham (C), ESX, 23
Ashford (C), KNT, 106, 115
Ashill *(Achalt?)* (C), KNT, 115
Asholt *(Achalt?)* (C), KNT, 106, 115
Ashtead (C), SUR, 11
Ashton, HRE, 85, 91, 93
Ashton-under-Hill (C), WOR, 125, 128
Ashwell (M), HRT, 5
Asser, Bishop, 3
Astley (C), WOR, 123, 126, 140, 142, 150, 152–3, 154
    Alien Priory, 123, 128, 129
Astley Abbots (C), SHR, 69, 73, 76, 79
Aston Botterell (C), SHR, 69, 74, 76
Aston, Church, SHR, 80
Aston Eyre (C), SHR, 15, 73, 77, 78, 79
Aston Magna (C), GLO, 125
Aston Munslow (C), SHR, 74, 80
Aston Somerville (C), WOR, 125
Aston, White Ladies (C), WOR, 124, 142
Astwood, manor, 127
Athelhard, priest of Pershore, 134
Augustine, St., 130
Auxerre Cathedral, 26
Avenbury (M), HRE, 5
Avington (C), BRK, 161–3
Avitus see Æfic
Avon, River, HMP, 51
Avon, River, WOR, 119, 132, 149, 154
Awolvescyrce, KNT, see Hawkinge
Aymestrey, HRE, 93

Bacton (C), HRE, 86
Bacton, Gilbert of, see Hampton
Badger (C), SHR, 69, 76
Badlesmere (C), KNT, 106, 114
Badsey (C), WOR, 123, 133
Bainard, Ralph, 181
Bakewell (M), DRB, 32
Baldwin, Domesday tenant [and canon of Daventry?], 100
Baltic Sea, round-towered churches near, 171, 175

Bampton (M), OXF, 5, 11, 13, 14, 16, 65, 199
Bapchild (C), KNT, 106, 108, 115, 116
Barbourne, WOR, 149
Barby (C), NTP, 102, 104
Bardfield, Little (C), ESX, 170
Bardsey (C), YOW, 193
Barfreston (C), KNT, 106
Barham (C), KNT, 106, 114, 116, 117
Barking (C), ESX, 166
Barnsley (C), GLO, 11, 12
Barrow (C), SHR, 69, 73, 76, 77, 198
Barton Bendish (3Cs), NFK, 7, 179, 180, 181–4
Barton-on-Humber (C), LIN, 23
Barwick-in-Elmet (C), YOW, 193, 195
Baschurch, SHR, hundred, 70, 71
Bashley, HMP, 53, 65
Basing (M), HMP, 63, 64
Basingstoke (C), HMP, 64
    hundred, 63
    royal manor, 63
Baslow (C), DRB, gild, 32
Battle Abbey, SSX, 91, 108
Battramsley, HMP, 65
Bawsey (C), NFK, 182
Bayeux Cathedral, Normandy, 127, 129
Bayeux, Odo of, 117
    Thomas of, Archbishop of York, 127, 195, 198
Bayton (C), WOR, 120, 123, 142, 144, 150
    haia at, 128
Beachamwell (3Cs), NFK, 179, 180
Beachborough *(Bilicean?)* (C), KNT, 106, 114
Bearsted (C), KNT, 106, 108, 117
Beauchamp, family, 159
Beaulieu (C), HMP, 47, 55
    Harbour, 54
    Water (Otter), 60
Beaumont, family, 159
Bec Abbey, Normndy, 127, 129
Beckbury (C), SHR, 69, 76
Beckford (M, alien priory), WOR, 125, 128, 129, 133, 134, 138, 141, 148, 150–1, 154
Bede, Venerable, 1, 48, 63, 191
Bedford (M), BDF, 5, 42
Bedwyn, Great (M), WLT, gild, 31
Beechamwell (C), NFK, 169
Bekesbourne *(Burna)* (C), KNT, 106, 114
Belbroughton (C), WOR, 123
    chapel, 123, 141
    Brian's Bell manor in, 141
Belne, family, of Belbroughton, WOR, 141
Benenden (C), KNT, 106, 109, 114
Bengeworth (C), WOR, 133
Bennedecirce, KNT, see Brenzett
Benthall (C), SHR, 73, 78, 79
Beoley (C), WOR, 123
Beornwald, St., 11, 199
Berham, KNT, see Bishopsbourne *and* Kingston
Berhtwulf, King of Mercia, 137
Berkeley (M), GLO, 16
Bermondsey (M, Abbey), SUR, 42, 63, 127
Bernay Abbey, Normandy, 26, 127, 129
Bernard (Domesday tenant), 85
    Gilbert his son, 85
Bernard the chaplain (witn. for Henry of Blois), 61

Berrow (C), WOR, 123, 134, 154, 156
Berrow, Robert de, 134
Berwick [by Lympne] (C), KNT, 106, 114
Besford (C), WOR, 123, 126, 134, 135
Bessingham (C), NFK, 169, 174
Bethersden (C), KNT, 106, 109, 114
Bethune, Robert de, Bishop of Hereford, 77, 88
Betteshanger (C), KNT, 106
Beusfield, KNT, see Whitfield
Bevere, WOR, 149
Beverley (M), YOE, 199
Bibury (M), GLO, 11, 12
Bicknor (C), KNT, 106, 108, 116
Biddenden (C), KNT, 106, 114
Bilchester [in Hawkinge] *(Bilicean?)* (C), KNT, 106, 114, 116
Bilice, Bilicean, KNT, see Beachborough, Bilchester *and* Bircholt
Billingsley (C), SHR, 69, 73, 76, 77
Bilsington (C), KNT, 106, 108, 115
Binham (C, Priory), NFK, 190
Bircher, HRE, 94
Birchington (C), KNT, 106
Bircholt *(Bilice?)* (C), KNT, 106, 115, 116
Birinus, St., 47
Birlingham (C), WOR, 123, 135, 138
Birmingham Plateau, 126
Birtsmorton (C), WOR, 123, 156
Biscopestune, KNT, see Reculver
Bishampton (C), WOR, 123, 134
Bishops Cleeve (C), GLO, 145
Bishopsbourne *(Berham?)* (C), KNT, 106, 115, 116
Bishopstoke (C), HMP, 64
Bitterley (C), SHR, 72
    manor, 72
Blacemannescirce, KNT, see Blackmanstone
Blackmanstone *(Blacemannescirce)* (C), KNT, 106, 108, 115, 117
Blackstone Rock, WOR, 149
Blackwell (C), WAR, 125
Blean (C), KNT, 106, 114
Blewbury (M), BRK, 5
Blockley (M), GLO, 15, 125, 164–5
    deanery, 130
Bloet, Robert, Bishop of Lincoln, 100
Blois, Henry of, Bishop of Winchester, 13, 52, 56, 57–8, 61, 62, 65
Blyth Priory (NTT), 99
Blythburgh (M), SFK, 4
Bobbing (C), KNT, 106, 108, 115, 116
Bockleton (C), WOR, 123, 142, 145, 146–7, 149, 154
Bodenham (C), HRE, 85, 86, 88, 92, 93
Bohun, Margaret de, 161
Boldre (C), HMP, 13, 15, 47, 55, 56, 57, 60, 66
    hundred, 65
Bolton-on-Dearne (C), YOW, 193, 198
Boniface, St., 46, 62–3, 80
Boningale (C), SHR, 78, 79
Bonnington (C), KNT, 106, 108, 115
Borden *(Niwecyrce?)* (C), KNT, 106, 108, 115, 116
Bordesley Abbey, WAR, 128
Borstealle, HMP?, 53, 65

Bosham (M), SSX, 27
Bossall (C), YON, 194, 199
Bostall, HMP, 60
Boston, LIN, gild, 33
Boughton (C), NFK, 180
Boughton Alulph (M?), KNT, 106, 107, 109, 114, 115, 116
Boughton-under-Blean (C), KNT, 106, 107, 116
Boughton Malherbe (C), KNT, 106, 107, 108, 115, 116
Boughton Monchelsea (M?), KNT, 106, 107, 108, 109, 114, 115, 116
Bouldon, SHR, 74, 75
Bourton (C), SHR, 78, 79, 80
Bow Brook Valley, WOR, 154
Bowcombe, IOW, manor, 63
Boxley (C), KNT, 106, 108, 115
Brabourne *(Godricesbourne)* (C), KNT, 106, 114, 116
Bradford-on-Avon (C), WLT, 27
Bradley, WOR, 128
Bradley, Little (C), SFK, 172
Bramber, SSX, castle, 98
  college, 25, 98
Bramfield (C), NFK, 169
Bramshaw (C), HMP, 55
Braose, Giles de, Bishop of Hereford, 86, 95
  William de, lord of Bramber, 25, 98
Braybrooke (C), NTP, 98, 99, 100, 101
Braybrooke, Thomas de, 98
Braughing (M), HRT, 5
Bray and Cookham, BRK, hundreds of, 67
Breamore (M?), HMP, 18, 47, 63
  Priory, 56
  royal manor, 63
Brecon, BRE, honour, 94
  Priory, 86, 89, 91, 92, 94
Bredgar (C), KNT, 106, 108, 115, 116
Bredhurst (C), KNT, 106
Bredon (M), WOR, 2, 123, 124, 125, 133, 134, 139, 141, 142, 143, 151, 154, 156
Bredon Hill, WOR, 126
  chapel near St. Katharine's well, 141
  stone from, 154
Bredons Norton, WOR, *see* Norton
Bredwardine (C), HRE, 149
Bremen, N. Germany, round-towered churches near, 171, 175
Brenzett *(Bennedecirce?)* (C), KNT, 106, 108, 115
Bretforton (C), WOR, 123, 133, 144, 151
Bricklehampton (C), WOR, 123, 133, 135, 151
Brictric, priest, 166
  Godida his wife, 166
Bridge (C), KNT, 106, 115, 117
Bridgend, GLA, gateway at Newcastle, 166–7
Bridgnorth (M), SHR, 72, 81
  castle, 72
  St. Leonard's church, 69, 73, 76
Bridlington Priory, YOE, 28
Brihteah, Bishop of Worcester, 126
Brimfield (C), HRE, 85, 88, 89, 91, 93, 95
Brinsop (C), HRE, 163, 165
Bristol Abbey, GLO, 161
Brixiestun, KNT, *see* Sevington
Brkchirche, KNT, *see* Brookland

Broadfield, HRE, 84, 85, 86, 87, 88, 91, 92, 93
Broadstairs (St. Peter-in-Thanet) (C), KNT, 106, 109, 116
Broadward, HRE, 84, 85, 92, 94
Broadwas (C), WOR, 123, 140, 142
Broadway (M?), WOR, 120, 123, 133, 137, 140, 142, 143
  estate, 137
  stone from, 154
Brockenhurst (C), HMP, 47, 54, 55, 56, 60, 65, 66
Brockmanton, HRE, 83, 85, 93
Bromfield (M), SHR, 11, 72, 101, 104
  manor, 72
Bromsgrove (M?), WOR, 123, 125, 134
  royal manor, 134
Bromyard (M), HRE, 5
Brook (C), KNT, 28, 106, 111, 115, 118
Brookland *(Brkchirche?)* (C), KNT, 106, 108, 117
Broome (C), WOR, 125, 134
Broomfield (C), KNT, 106, 108
Broomhill (C), KNT, 106, 108
Broseley (C), SHR, 69, 73, 76
Brough-on-Humber, YOE, Roman material from?, 194
Broughton, HMP, hundred, 63
  royal manor, 63
Broughton (C), LIN, 28
Broughton Hackett (C), WOR, 135
  stone-quarry at, 154
Brown Clee Hill, SHR, 71, 74
Buckingham, John, Bishop of Lincoln, 99
Buckland (C), HMP, 15, 66
Buckland [by Dover] *(Æwellan?)* (C), KNT, 106
Buckland [by Teynham] (C), KNT, 106
Buddlesgate, HMP, hundred, 46
Bulmer (C), YON, 195
Burford (M), SHR, 5, 11, 72, 75
  manor, 72
Burford, WOR, deanery, 130
Burghclere (M?), HMP, 48, 63, 64, 65
Burghwallis (C), YOW, 193, 195, 198
Burgred, King of Mercia, 3
Burley, HMP, 55
Burmarsh (C), KNT, 106, 108, 117
Burna, KNT, *see* Bekesbourne and Patrixbourne
Burnan, KNT, *see* Northbourne
Bursledon (C), HMP, 47, 56, 61
Burton, HMP, 52, 59
Burwarton (C), SHR, 69, 75, 76
Bury St. Edmunds (M, Abbey), SFK, 3, 4, 173
Bushley, WOR, 127, 129, 156
Butterley, HRE, 83, 85, 93
Byrhtnoth, Ealdorman, 6

Cadan Mynster (Cadamunstre) (lost M?), WOR, 133
Cædwalla, King of Wessex, 2, 45, 47, 48, 63
Caen Abbeys, Normandy, 25, 26, 127
Caerleon, MON, 130
Calborne, IOW, 48
Caldecote (C), NFK, 179, 180
Cambridge (M), CAM, 42, 103
  Castle, 103

Gild, 31, 32, 33, 34
Campden, GLO, stone from, 154
  deanery, 130
Campsall (C), YOW, 193, 195
Camville, Richard de, 162, 167
Candover, HMP, 64
Canterbury, Christ Church (CA), KNT, 13, 25, 105–18, 167
  St. Augustine's Abbey, 22, 25, 26, 105, 107, 108, 109, 111, 114, 116, 118
  St. Gregory's Priory, 110, 111, 117
  St. Laurence's Hospital, 116, 117
  churches, 106, 116
    All Saints, 116
    St. Andrew, 116
    St. Dunstan, 106
    St. John, 116
    St. Martin, 106, 109
    St. Margaret, 116
    St. Mary, 106, 116
    St. Mildred, 109, 116
    St. Pancras, 118
    St. Paul, 106, 116
    St. Sepulchre, 106, 116
  Archdeacon of, 107
  Gild of, 32
Capel-le-Ferne (C), KNT, 106
Capella, Richard de, Bishop of Hereford, 83
Carisbrooke (M), IOW, 10, 47, 57, 58, 61, 63, 66
  priest of, and Dean of Isle, 52
Carrant Valley, WOR, 128
Castellion, *see* Conches
Castle Frome (C), HRE, 150
Castle Holdgate (C), SHR, 69, 73, 74, 75, 76, 150
Castle Rising, NFK, 145, 175
  church, 182, 187
Castleford, YOW, Roman material from?, 194
Castlemorton (C), WOR, 123, 142, 150, 156
Catterick (M?), YON, 199
  Roman material from?, 194
Catteshall (C), SUR, 16, 17
Cenwalh, King of Wessex, 47, 48, 49, 63
Cérisy-la-Forêt Abbey, Normandy, 25, 127, 129, 145
Cerney, South (C), GLO, 161–2, 166
Cervatos, Spain, San Pedro at, 146
Cetelbert, Domesday tenant, 100
Chaceley (C), GLO, 125
Chaddesley Corbett (M?), WOR, 5, 123, 124, 133, 144, 150
Chale (C), IOW, 10, 47, 57, 61
Challock (C), KNT, 106, 115, 117
Charente region, architectural influence from, 163
Charing (M), KNT, 106, 107, 108, 109, 112, 114, 115, 116
Charité, La, sur Loire, Cluniac Abbey, 75, 97, 127, 129
Charlton (C), KNT, 106, 114
  prebend of, 118
Charlton (C), WOR, 133
Chart, KNT, *see* Sutton, Chart
Chart, Great (East Chart?) (C), KNT, 106, 114, 116
Chart, Little (C), KNT, 106
Chartham (C), KNT, 106, 109, 114, 116

Cheddar (M), SOM, 3
Chelmarsh (C), SHR, 69, 76
Cheriton *(Ciricetun)* (C), KNT, 106, 109, 115
Chertsey (M), SUR, 46–7, 63
  Abbey, 18
Chester (Ms), CHE, 6, 38, 42, 97
Chesterfield (M), DRB, 11
Chetton (C), SHR, 69, 74, 76
Chiddingfold (C), SUR, 15, 17
Chilbolton, HMP, 63, 64
Chilcomb, HMP, hundred, 48, 49
  manor, 64
Childrey (M), BRK, 5
Childswickham (C), WOR, 125
Chilham (C), KNT, 106, 109, 114, 116
Chillenden (C), KNT, 106, 114
Chirchebi, places called, in Yorkshire, 191
Chirton (C), WLT, 161
Chislet (C), KNT, 106, 116
Churchill in Halfshire (C), WOR, 123
Churchill in Oswaldslow (C), WOR, 123, 130, 132
  stone-quarry at, 154
Christchurch (Twynham) (M), HMP, 6, 8, 10, 12, 13, 15, 47, 49–66, 101
  burh, 51, 65
  hundred, 65
  royal manor, 65
Cirencester (M, Abbey), GLO, 12, 161
Ciricetun, KNT, see Cheriton
Claines (C), WOR, 120, 123, 130, 132
Clanfield (C), OXF, 16
Clatford, Robert of (witn. for Henry of Blois), 61
Clayton (C), SSX, 26–7
Clee (C), LIN, 198
Clee Forest, SHR, 74, 81
Clee Hills, SHR, 71, 73, 74
Clee St. Margaret (C), SHR, 69, 75, 76
Clee Stanton, SHR, 73, 80
Cleeve (C), HRE, 13
Cleeve Prior (M?), WOR, 123, 133, 137
  estate, 137
  stone from, 154
Clent (C), WOR, 125
Clent Hills, WOR, 126
  stone from, 154
Cleobury Mortimer (M?), SHR, 69, 71, 72, 74
  manor, 72
Cleobury North (C), SHR, 69, 74, 75, 76
Clerch [i.e. Clerk], family of priests at Welton, NTP, 102, 104
Cliffe *(Clive)*, St. Margaret at (C), KNT, 106, 114, 117
Cliffe, West *(Clive)* (C), KNT, 106, 114
Clifford, Walter de, 87, 94
Clifton-on-Teme (M?), WOR, 120, 123, 124, 125, 134, 141, 154
Clinton, Geoffrey de, 162
Clive, KNT, see Cliffe, St. Margaret at, and Cliffe, West
Clun, SHR, manor, 72
Cluny Abbey, Burgundy, 187
Cnut, King, 22, 32, 38, 64, 65, 109, 110
Cocherlei, HMP, 65
Coenwulf, King of Mercia, 117
Cofton Hackett, WOR, estate, 137
Cohhanleah, GLO/WOR?, 3

Colchester (M), ESX, 4
  Priory, 36, 145
  St. Helen's church, 130
Coldiun, Ivo son of John de, 101
Coldred (C), KNT, 106, 111, 114, 116, 117
Colney (C), NFK, 175
Combe Abbey, WAR, 167
Comberton, Great (C), WOR, 123, 135, 166
Comberton, Little (C), WOR, 13, 124, 133, 135, 151, 166
Coleshill (M), BRK, 5
Collingham (C), YOW, 191, 193
Colne, Earls (M), ESX, 6
Colvestan, STF, hundred, 70, 80
Compostella, Spain, Shrine of St. James, 146, 150, 163
Compton, HMP, 64
Conan son of Ellis, 19
Conches, Normandy, Abbey of Castellion, 84, 88, 91, 93, 94
Condetret, SHR, hundred, 70, 71, 80–1
Condover, SHR, hundred, 70, 80
Conisbrough (M), YOW, 197, 198
Constantine I, Pope, 63
Cookham and Bray, BRK, hundreds of, 67
Corbeil, William of, Archbishop of Canterbury, 84
Córdoba, Spain, mosque, 146
Corfham, SHR, see Diddlebury
Cormeilles Abbey, Normandy, 127, 128, 129, 130
Corve, River, SHR, 71
Corvedale, SHR, 71
Cotheridge (C), WOR, 123, 126, 140, 142, 144
Cotswolds, stone from, 154
Court-at-Street *(Straeta)* (C), KNT, 106, 108, 115
Courtenay, William, Archbishop of Canterbury, 110
Coutances, Walter of, Bishop of Lincoln, 14
Coventry, Prior of, 98
Cradley, HRE, stone from, 154
Crambe (C), YON, 193
Cranbrook (C), KNT, 106, 109, 114
Crawley, (C), HMP, 64
Cricklade (M), WLT, 39
  burh, 42
Crispin, Gilbert, Abbot of Westminster, 127
Croft (C), HRE, 85, 91, 93, 95
Croft, Gilbert of, 85
  Richard of, rector of Letton, HRE, 93
Crondall, HMP, 63–4
Croome d'Abitot (C), WOR, 134, 137
Croome, Earls (C), WOR, 123, 134, 140, 142, 144, 150
Croome, Hill (C), WOR, 123, 134, 143
Cropthorne (C), WOR, 120, 123, 124, 133–4, 141, 142, 150, 154
Crowle (C), WOR, 132
Croydon, SUR, deanery, 117
Crundale (C), KNT, 106, 115
Cullompton (C), DEV, 33
Culvestan, SHR, hundred, 70, 80
Cutsdean (C), GLO, 125
  stone from, 154
Cyneberht, Abbot of *Hreutford*, 45, 46
Cyneberht (companion of King Æthelbald), 156
Cynegisl, King of Wessex, 47, 48, 63

Damerham (M), WLT, 3
Dance, George, Snr. (architect), 111
Daniel, Bishop of Winchester, 48
Darfield (C), YOW, 193
Darley Abbey, DRB, 94
Daventry (M, Priory), NTP, 7, 11, 97–104
David I, King of Scots, 98, 99, 101, 102, 103
Davington (C), KNT, 106
Dawley Magna (C), SHR, 69, 74, 76, 80
Daylesford (C), GLO, 125
Deal (C), KNT, 106
Deerhurst (M, Priory) GLO, 2–3, 119, 128
Defford (C), WOR, 123, 133, 135
Delapré Abbey, NTP, 97
Demancirce, KNT, see Dymchurch
Dengie (M), ESX, 4
Denton (C), KNT, 106, 114
Derby (M), DRB, 42, 94
Dereham, West (2Cs), NFK, 170, 172, 179, 180
Despenser, Robert le, 133, 166
Detling (C), KNT, 106, 108, 115, 117
Deusdedit, Archbishop of Canterbury, 48
Deuxhill (C), SHR, 69, 73, 76, 80
Devereux, Stephen, 138
Devon, gilds in, 9, 31
Dewsbury (M), YOW, 197
Dibden (C), HMP, 55
Diddlebury (Corfham) (M), SHR, 72, 74, 75
  royal manor, 72, 81
Dilwyn (C), HRE, 83, 85, 92–3, 95
Ditton, Earls (C), SHR, 74, 78
Ditton Priors (C), SHR, 69, 75, 76
Docklow (C), HRE, 83, 85, 90, 93
Dod, Roger, Dean of Worcester, 128
Doddenham (C), WOR, 120, 123, 132
Dodderhill (C), WOR, 123, 139, 151
Doddington (C), KNT, 106, 108, 115
Doddington (C), SHR, 74
Doncaster, YOW, Roman material from?, 194
Donhead, WLT, 53, 65
Donington (M), SHR, 5, 69, 76
Dorchester (CA), OXF, 47–8
Dormston (C), WOR, 123, 126
Dorn (C), GLO, 125
Dousgunels, Gilbert de, Dean of Christchurch, 50, 52, 53, 57, 59, 60
Dover, St. Mary-de-Castro (M), KNT, 2, 6, 106, 107, 108, 109, 110, 112, 117
  St. Martin-le-Grand (M), 106, 107, 109, 110, 111, 112, 114, 116, 118
  churches (St. James, St. John, St. Mary, St. Nicholas, St. Peter), 106, 109, 114
  castle, 110
Doverdale (C), WOR, 123
Drayton, HRE, 85, 88, 93
Dreamwurthe, KNT, see Tremworth
Driffield (M), YOE, 197, 199
Droitwich (M), WOR, 5, 123, 126, 133
  St. Andrew's church, 151
  other churches (St. Mary, St. Nicholas, St. Peter), 123
  land and saltpan, 128, 129
Droxford, HMP, 64
Dudley (Cs), STF, 125
  Castle, 155
  Priory, 125
  stone from, 155
Dungeness, KNT, 108

Index of People and Places

Dunham, Great (C), NFK, 182
Dunkirk, KNT, 106
Dunmow Priory, ESX, 181
Dunstan, St., 110
Durham (CA), DRH, 25, 26, 27
   Bishop of, 38
   Castle, 162
   county, early churches in, 192
Durley (C), HMP, 47
Dymchurch *(Demancirce)* (C), KNT, 106, 108, 115, 117
Dymock (C), GLO, 149

Eadred, King, will of, 63
Eadredestun, KNT, see Elmstone
Eadwig, King, 53, 65
Ealdred, Bishop of Worcester and Archbishop of York, 126, 127
Ealhham, KNT, see Alkham
Ealhhun, Bishop of Worcester, 137
Eanulf (founder of Bredon minster), 156
Eardingtun, KNT see Egerton
Eardington, SHR, 73, 80
Eardisley (C), HRE, 150, 167
Eardiston, WOR, estate, 137
Earnstrey, SHR, 74, 75
Ease, South (C), SSX, 169
Eashing, SUR, 17
East Anglia, churches in, 2, 3–5, 8, 9–10, 32, 169–90
Eastbridge *(Ælsiescirce)* (C), KNT, 106, 108, 115, 117
Eastchurch (C), KNT, 106, 108, 115, 116, 117
Eastham (C), WOR, 123, 140, 142, 145, 146–7, 149, 154, 155
Easthope (C), SHR, 69, 73, 74, 76
Eastling (C), KNT, 106, 114
Easton (C), HMP, 64
Eastry (M), KNT, 106, 107, 108, 109, 110, 112, 114, 115, 116
Eastwell *(Wyllan)* (C), KNT, 106
Eaton, HRE, 84, 85, 93
Eaton (C), SHR, 69, 76
Eaton-under-Heywood, SHR, 73
Ebony (C), KNT, 106, 115, 117
Eborard, Bishop of Norwich, 189
Ecchinswell, HMP, 64
Ecclesfield (M), YOW, 197
Ecgwin, 132
Eckington (C), WOR, 123, 135
Edgar, King, 8, 12, 22, 36, 64, 65, 84, 94, 117
Edington (C), WLT, 62
Edith, Queen, 72, 83, 93
Edmund, King, laws of, 64
Edvin Loach (C), HRE, 125, 134, 145
Edvin Ralph (C), HRE, 83, 85, 93, 95
Edward the Elder, King, 3, 38, 41, 42, 45, 46
Edward the Confessor, King, 6, 10, 12, 16, 17, 32, 53, 65, 71, 133, 196
"Edward and Guthrum", laws of, 64
Edwin, Earl of Mercia, 71
Edwin, priest of Pershore, 134
Efford, HMP, 65
Egbert, King of Wessex, 3
Egerton *(Eardingtun?)* (C), KNT, 106, 115
Egheiete, HMP, hundred, 65
Egilsay (C), Orkney, 169, 175, 177
Eilwi, priest of Christchurch, 56, 60, 101
Eiwda, SHR, 93

Eldersfield (C), WOR, 123, 127, 129, 140, 150
Elham (C), KNT, 106, 109, 114, 116
Elias, Abbot of Reading, 95
Eling (M), HMP, 45, 46, 51, 55, 62, 63
   royal estate, 45
Elkington (C), LIN, 101, 103
Ellingham (C), HMP, 47, 55, 60
Elmbridge (C), WOR, 123
Elmham, North (CA?, bishop's chapel?), NFK, 9, 118, 169, 175–7, 179, 187, 189–90
   parish church, 188, 189–90
Elmham, South (C), NFK, 177
Elmley (C), KNT, 106, 108, 116
Elmley Castle (C), WOR, 123, 133, 145, 150, 154
Elmley Lovett (C), WOR, 123
Elmsted (C), KNT, 106, 114
Elmstone *(Eadredestun?)* (C), KNT, 106, 115
Ely (CA), CAM, 26, 27, 31, 33, 150, 173
Eorcenwold, St., Bishop of London, 40, 43, 46, 48, 63
Ercall, High (C), SHR, 149
Espec, Walter, 28, 29
   William (uncle of Walter and rector of Garton, YOE), 29
Essex, churches in, 18
Estres, Roger de, 66
Ethelburga, St., relics of, 110
Eu, Robert, count of, 100
Evenlode (C), GLO, 125
Everdon, NTP, 101
Evesham (M, Abbey), WOR, 2, 119, 120, 123, 124, 126, 128, 129, 132, 133, 137, 138, 145, 149, 151, 156, 161
   churches (All Saints, St. Lawrence), 123, 133
   Danish cell of, 127
   deanery of Vale of, 128, 130, 132
   Romano-Celtic Christianity, 132
   Vale of, 126, 133, 154, 156
   visitor to, from Ireland and Aquitaine, 127
Evingar hundred, HMP, 63
Evreux Abbey, Normandy, 128, 129
Ewda, SHR, 93
Ewell, Temple *(Æwellan?)* (C), KNT, 106, 114
Ewenny Priory, GLA, 151
Exbury, (C), HMP, 45, 55
Exeter (M, CA), DEV, 13, 42
   Castle, 25
   Gild, 31, 32, 33
Exhall (C), WAR, 8
Exton, HMP, 64
Eye (C), HRE, 15, 85, 88, 89, 90–1, 93, 94, 95
   hereditary priests of, 95
Eye (M), SFK, 4
Eynsham (M), OXF, 3, 5, 9
Eythorne (C), KNT, 106, 114
Eyton (C), HRE, 83, 85, 88, 91, 93, 95

Fairbourne *(Godwinesbourne?)* (C), KNT, 116
Fairfield (C), KNT, 10, 108
Fareham (C), HMP, 47, 48, 64
Faringdon (M), BRK, 5
Farlow (C), SHR, 74, 78, 79, 93

Farnham (M), SUR, 46–7, 63
   hundred, 46–7, 48
Faversham (M?), KNT, 106, 108, 109, 110, 111, 112, 114, 116, 117, 118
   royal manor, 108, 109
Fawley (C), HMP, 55, 64
Fawsley (M), NTP, 98, 99, 100, 102
   royal manor, 102
Fécamp Abbey, Normandy, 127, 129
Feckenham (C), WOR, 123, 127, 128, 129, 137, 154
   chapel in royal lodge, 123, 138
   Forest of, 126
Felkirk, YOW, 198
Fencott, HRE, 93
Ferrers, Hermer of, 181
Ferriby, North, Priory, YOE, 28
Fincham (2Cs), NFK, 179, 180
Finstall, St. Godwald's chapel (in Stoke Prior), WOR, 124
Fisseberg hundred, WOR, 132
Fladbury (M), WOR, 2, 123, 124, 125, 133, 134, 141, 150, 154
Flambard, Ranulf, king's priest and Bishop of Durham, 10–11, 49, 50, 51, 52, 53, 57, 59, 60
Fleet (in Ash) (C), KNT, 106, 115
Fleury Abbey, France, 127
Flitton (M), BDF, 5
Flyford Flavell (C), WOR, 123, 135
Foliot, Gilbert, Bishop of Hereford, 86, 87, 89, 91, 92, 93, 94, 159, 167
   Hugh, Bishop of Hereford, 95
   Reginald, Abbot of Evesham, 145
   Robert, Bishop of Hereford, 86, 94
Folkestone (M), KNT, 2, 106, 107, 108, 109, 110, 112, 114, 116, 117
Ford, HRE, 85, 93
Ford [in Pudleston] (C), HRE, 83, 85, 90, 93
Fordingbridge (M), HMP, 47, 55
   hundred, 63
Fordwich (M?), KNT, 106, 109, 114, 116, 117
Forthere, Bishop of Sherborne, 48
Fossard, Nigel (lord of Wharram-le-Street, YOE), 28
   Robert, son of Nigel, 28
Foxton, barony of, 100
Frankley (C), WOR, 120, 123, 138
Frinsted (C), KNT, 106, 108, 115
Frithuwold, sub-king, 46, 63
Frittenden *(Strithindenne)* (C), KNT, 106, 117
Frome, HRE, see Castle Frome

Garrington (C), KNT, 106, 115, 117
Garton-on-the-Wolds (C), YOE, 29
Garway (C), HRE, 146
Gattertop, HRE, 84, 85, 93, 94
Gaunt, John of, 99
Geoffrey, Archdeacon of Berkshire, 104
German Romanesque cathedrals, 190
Gernun, Hugh (lord of Chale, IOW), 10, 57, 61
Giffard, William, Bishop of Winchester, 11, 57, 61
Gilbert the Sheriff (founder of Merton Priory), 103
Gillingham (M), DOR, 5
Glaber, Ralph, 21

Glastonbury Abbey, SOM, 145
Glazeley (C), SHR, 69, 74, 76
Gloucester (M, Abbey), GLO, 38, 42, 94, 119, 145, 160, 161, 167
   St. Oswald's Priory, 119
   archdeaconry of, 128
   church dedicated by St. Wulfstan, 134
   Castle, parochial jurisdiction over, 167
Gloucester, Miles of, 93, 94, 159, 167
   Walter of, 161
   family, 162, 167
Gloucestershire, proportion of Romanesque church fabric in, 120–1
   church architecture in, 160–7
Godalming (M), SUR, 15–17
Godesmanescamp, HMP, 65
Godgifu (Godiva), Lady, 6, 71, 97
Godida, wife of Brihtric the priest, 166
Godiva *see* Godgifu
Godley, SUR, hundred, 46
Godmersham (C), KNT, 106, 111, 114, 116
Godnestone (C), KNT, 106
Godric, Dean of Christchurch, 52, 53, 56, 59, 60, 101
Godricesbourne, KNT *see* Brabourne
Godwin, Earl of Wessex, 56, 110, 117
Godwinesbourne, KNT, *see* Fairbourne
Goodmanham (C), YOE, 198
Goscelin of St.-Bertin, 21, 23, 110
Goudhurst (C), KNT, 106, 108, 115
Grafton (C), WOR, 125, 138
Grandmesnil, Hugh of, 100
Gratian (citations of Canon Law), 64–5
Graveney (C), KNT, 106, 114
Gravesende hundred, NTP, 99
Grimley (C), 123, 124, 132
Guestwick (C), NFK, 182, 187
Guiting, GLO, stone from, 154
Gundulf, Bishop of Rochester, 117
Guston (C), KNT, 106, 114

Hackington (C), KNT, 106, 118
Hackness (M), YON, 191, 192, 197
Haddiscoe (C), NFK, 169, 170, 172, 174
Haddiscoe Thorpe, NFK, *see* Thorpe
Hadleigh (M), SFK, 3, 4
Hadley, WOR, quarrying at, 154
Hadmwoldungdenne, KNT, *see* Halden, High
Hadstock (M?), ESX, 27, 199
Hædde, Bishop of Winchester, 47, 48
Hænostesyle, KNT, *see* Hinxhill
Hagley (C), WOR, 123
Hailes (C), GLO, 94
Halden, High (C), KNT, 106, 109, 114
Hales (C), NFK, 169, 170, 171, 174, 177
Halesowen (M), WOR, 5, 123, 125, 133, 138, 141, 142, 143, 145, 151
Halford (C), WAR, 147–9
Hallow (C), WOR, 120, 123, 132
Halstow, Lower (C), KNT, 106, 108, 110, 115, 116
Ham (C), KNT, 106, 114
Hamble (C), HMP, 47
   Priory, 61
   River, 45
Hambledon, SUR, 17
Hamnish Clifford (C), HRE, 84, 85, 87, 93
Hampshire, minsters, churches and parishes in, 2, 19, 45–66

Hampton, Gilbert of (*alias* Bacton), 86, 94
   Robert of, 89
Hampton Court, HRE, *see* Hampton Ricardi
Hampton-by-Evesham (C), WOR, 120, 123, 133
Hampton Gilberti, HRE, *see* Hampton Ricardi
Hampton Lovett (C), WOR, 123, 140, 142, 143
Hampton Mappenore (C), HRE, 84, 85, 86, 89, 90, 93, 95
Hampton Ricardi, HRE, 85, 86, 93, 94
Hampton Wafer (C), HRE, 85, 86, 89, 91, 92, 93, 95
Hanbury (M), WOR, 2, 123, 133
Hanley Castle (C), WOR, 123, 127, 129
   All Saints' chapel, 123
Hanley William (C), WOR, 140
Hanney, West (M), BRK, 5
Hannington, HMP, 64
Harbledown (C), KNT, 106
Harbridge (C), HMP, 55
Hardres, Lower (C), KNT, 106, 114
Hardres, Upper (C), KNT, 106, 114
Hardwick, WOR, 127, 155
Harold, Earl and King, 51, 54, 97, 127
Harrietsham (*Hyruuerthestun?*) (C), KNT, 106, 114, 116
Hartland (M), DEV, 95
Hartlebury (C), WOR, 123, 137
Hartlip (C), KNT, 106, 108, 115, 116
Harty (C), KNT, 106, 114
Harvington-by-Evesham (C), WOR, 123, 141, 154
Haslemere (C), SUR, 15, 17
Hastingleigh (C), KNT, 106, 114
Hastings, SSX, castle, 100
   college, 100
Hatfield Magna (C), HRE, 13, 84, 85, 86, 87, 88–9, 91, 93, 95
Hatfield Parva (C), HRE, 84, 85, 91, 93
Hatfield, ESX, 5
Hathui, Abbess of Heeslingen, 173
Havant, HMP, 64
Hawkhurst (*Haudkashyrste?*) (C), KNT, 106
Hawkinge (*Awolvescyrce?*) (C), KNT, 106, 114
Hayling, HMP, 64
Headcorn (C), KNT, 106, 108, 115
Heath (C), SHR, 74, 75, 78, 79
Heeslingen (C), N. Germany, 171–3
Helgot, Domesday tenant, 73
Hennor, HRE, 85, 93
Henley-in-Arden (C), WAR, 34
Henlow (M), BDF, 5
Henry I, King, 10, 35, 38, 59, 83, 87, 97, 99, 116, 188, 197
Henry II, King, 12, 14, 99, 102, 127–8
Henry son of Herbert the Forester (of Lyndhurst, HMP), 60
Herbert, Prior of Daventry, 104
Herbert, Master (witn. for Henry of Blois), 61
Hereford (CA, M), HRE, 5, 42, 160
   Archdeacon of, 84
   burh, 42
   diocese of, 73, 81, 119, 160
   Earls of, 91, 127, 167

   episcopal chapel, 190
Herefordshire, proportion of Romanesque church fabric in, 120–1
   church architecture in, 160–7
Herman, Bishop of Ramsbury, 6, 21
Herne (C), KNT, 106, 109, 115, 117
Hernehill (C), KNT, 106, 115, 117
Hertford, council of (672), 48
Hertingfordbury (M), HRT, 5
Hethel (C), NFK, 170
Heythrop (C), OXF, 147–9
Highclere, HMP, 48
Highley (C), SHR, 69, 76
Highworth (M), WLT, 5
Hilary, Dean of Christchurch and Bishop of Chichester, 52, 56, 60
Hillhampton, WOR, 132
Himbleton (C), WOR, 123, 132
Hincmar, Archbishop of Rheims, 32
Hindlip (C), WOR, 123, 132
Hinton Ampner, HMP, 45, 64
Hinton-on-the-Green (C), WOR, 125
Hinxhill (*Hænostesyle*) (C), KNT, 106, 115
Hitchin (M), HRT, 5
Hleodæna, KNT, *see* Lydden
Hlyda, KNT, *see* Leeds
Hoath (C), KNT, 106, 109
Hoddington, HMP, 64
Holbeach (C), LIN, 14
Holdenhurst (C), HMP, 47, 55, 60
   royal manor, 65
Holdfast, WOR, 134, 143
Holdgate, SHR, *see* Castle Holdgate
Hollingbourne (C), KNT, 106, 108, 115
Holloway, WOR, 128, 129
Holme-on-Spalding-Moor (C), YOE, 194
Holt (C), WOR, 123, 130, 132, 140, 142, 150, 151, 152, 154
Honeybourne, Church (C), WOR, 120, 123, 133, 137
Honorius, Archbishop of Canterbury, 48
Honorius of Autun, 33
Hope, Miles of, 95
Hope All Saints (*Mertumnescirce?*) (C), KNT, 106, 108, 115, 117
Hope-under-Dinmore (C), HRE, 85, 86, 90, 91, 92, 93, 94, 95
Hope Edge, SHR, 71
Hopton Wafers (C), SHR, 69, 74, 76
Hopwood, WOR, estate, 137
Hordle (C), HMP, 47, 60
Horewell, Forest of, WOR, 144
Hornby (C), YON, 193, 196
Horsehill, WOR, Robin of, 149
Horton, WOR, 143
Horton, Monk's (C), KNT, 106, 115, 118
Hospitallers, 161
Hothfield (C), KNT, 106, 114
Hougham (C), KNT, 106, 115
Houghton (M), BDF, 5
Houghton (M?), HMP, 63, 64
   manor, 63, 64
Houghton, Rocius de, 101, 102
Hovingham (C), YON, 191, 192, 193, 195, 196, 197, 198
Howden (M), YOE, 194, 199
Hoxne (M), SFK, 4
Hreutford (M) *see* Redbridge
Hucking (C), KNT, 106, 108
Huddington (C), WOR, 123, 128, 130, 132

Hugh of Leicester (Hugh the Sheriff), 97–8, 99, 101, 103
    Hugh his son, 98
Hugh, canon of Daventry, 98
Hugh, clerk of Orleton, HRE, 95
Hugh, priest of Stretford, HRE, 88
Hughley (C), SHR, 69, 73, 76, 80
Humber (C), HRE, 13, 85, 86, 89, 90, 91, 92, 93, 94, 95
Huntingdon, Earls of, 97–104
Huntingdon, Henry of (chronicler), 26
Hurn, HMP, 52, 59, 60
Hursley, HMP, 64
Hurst *(Whistley?)* (C), BRK, 8–9, 18, 32
Hurstbourne (Pastrow) hundred, HMP, 63
    royal manor, 63
Hurstbourne Priors (M?), HMP, 48, 63, 64
    manor, 63
Hurstbourne Tarrant (M?), HMP, 48, 63, 64
Hurstley [in Letton] (C), HRE, 83, 85, 93
Hurtmore (C), SUR, 15, 17
Husmerae, province of, WOR, 156
Hwicce, kingdom of, 128
Hyde (C), HMP, 64
Hyruuerthestun, KNT, see Harrietsham
Hythe (C), KNT, 106, 108, 115, 117
Hythe, West (C), KNT, 106, 108, 115, 117

Ibsley (C), HMP, 55
Ickham (C), KNT, 106, 114, 116
Icomb (C), GLO, 125
Idsall (M), SHR, see Shifnal
Iffin (C), KNT, 111
Ilchester (M), SOM, 5
Ilkley (C), YOW, 192
Ine, King of Wessex, 2, 32, 48, 63
Inkberrow (M), WOR, 123, 134, 137
Itchin, River, 45
Itchington, WAR, 126
Ipswich (M), SFK, 4
Ironbridge Gorge, SHR, 71
Ivychurch (C), KNT, 106, 108, 115
    Priory, 167
Iwade *(Ætwangerǣde?)*, KNT, 106, 108, 115, 117

Jarrow (M), DRH, 1, 195
John, Abbot of Ford, life of Wulfric of Haselbury, 166
Joseph, Abbot of Reading, 91
Joseph, clerk (witn. for Henry of Blois), 61
Judith, Countess, 100, 102
Jumièges Abbey, Normandy, 25, 127, 129, 145

Kemberton (C), SHR, 69, 74, 76
Kemerton (C), WOR, 125
Kemp, John Archbishop of Canterbury, 118
Kempley (C), GLO, 149, 151
Kempsey (M), WOR, 123, 124, 133, 134, 141, 142, 144
    St. Andrew's chapel, 123
    chapel in Bishop's Palace, 138
Kenardington (C), KNT, 106, 114
Kencot (C), OXF, 149
Kenilworth Priory, WAR, 162
Kennington (C), KNT, 106, 114, 117
Kenswick (C), WOR, 123, 130, 132
Kent, minsters and churches in, 2, 3, 10, 15, 105–18

Ketylbern, 104
Keynsham Abbey, SOM, 151, 161
Kidderminster (M), WOR, 123, 124, 126, 133, 134, 156
    deanery, 130
Kilmeston (C), HMP, 64
Kilpeck (C), HRE, 150, 163
Kilsby (C), NTP, 104
Kimbolton (C), HRE, 83, 85, 88, 91, 93, 94, 95
Kineton, WAR, deanery, 130
Kingestun, KNT, see Kingsnorth
Kingsclere (M?), HMP, 48, 63, 64
    hundred, 63
    royal manor, 63
Kingsdown (C), KNT, 106, 117
Kingsnorth *(Kingestun?)* (C), KNT, 106, 108, 115
Kingston *(Berham?)* (C), KNT, 106, 110, 115
Kington (C), WOR, 126
    quarrying near, 154
Kinlet (C), SHR, 69, 76
Kinnersley (C), HRE, 83, 85, 88, 92, 93, 95
Kinver Edge, WOR, 120
Kippax (C), YOW, 193, 195
Kirby Grindalythe (C), YOE, 28, 29
Kirby Hill (C), YON, 191, 192, 193, 198
Kirby Kane (C), NFK, 170
Kirby Underdale (C), YOE, 193, 195, 196
Kirk Hammerton (C), YON, 192, 193, 196, 197
Kirk Sandall (C), YOW, 193
Kirkdale (M), YON, 6, 28, 192, 193, 195, 196, 197, 198
Kirkham Priory, YOE, 28, 29
Knighton-on-Teme (C), WOR, 123, 140, 142, 145, 146, 147–9, 154
    estate, 137
Knightwick (C), WOR, 124, 132
Knowlton (C), KNT, 106, 114
Kyre Magna (C), WOR, 134, 140, 141, 142
Kyre Wyard (C), WOR, 124

Lacy, Agnes de, 161
    Hugh de, I, 161
    Roger de, 93
    Walter de, Abbot of Gloucester, 167
    family, 159, 162
Lainston, HMP, 64
Lamartre, Martin, clerk (witn. for Henry of Blois), 61
Lambeth (M?), SUR, 118
Lanfranc, Archbishop of Canterbury, 10, 105, 107, 109, 110, 111, 115, 117, 127, 128, 137
Langdon, East (C), KNT, 106, 109, 116, 117
Langdon, West (C), KNT, 106, 109
Langford (C), OXF, 27, 166
Langley (C), KNT, 106, 108, 115
Lanow (M), CNW, 9
Lanthony Priory I, MON, 103
Lanthony Priory II, GLO, 161, 167
Lastingham Abbey, YON, 28
Laughern (C), WOR, 132
    Valley, 154
Laughton (C), YOW, 193
Launde Priory, LEI, 104
Laurence (lord of Ashtead, Surrey), 11
Laurentiuscirce, KNT, see Romney, New

Lea, HRE, 94
Leatherhead (M), SUR, 11
Leathley (C), YOW, 196
Leaveland (C), KNT, 106
Leckhampstead (C), GLO, 149
Ledbury (M), HRE, 5
Ledsham (M), YOW, 192, 197
Leeds *(Hlyda)* (C), KNT, 106, 108, 110, 115
    Priory, 167
Leicester (M), LEI, 97
    Castle, 97
    Gild, 31
    honour of, 102–3
Leicester, Hugh of, see Hugh
    Earl Robert II of, 102–3
Leigh (C), WOR, 120, 124, 137, 140, 141, 142, 154
    manorial chapel, 124, 138
    estate, 137
Leighs, Great (C), ESX, 173, 176
Leinthall, HRE, 93
Leintwardine, SHR, manor, 72
Lench, Church (C), WOR, 123
Lench, Rous (C), WOR, 124, 134, 150, 154
Lenchwick, WOR, 133
Lenham (M?), KNT, 106, 108, 109, 115, 117
Leo IX, Pope, 21
Leofgifu, will of, 6
Leofric, Earl of Mercia, 6, 26, 71, 97
Leofric, Domesday tenant, 100, 102
Leofwine (Leuuin) priest of Dover, 110, 118
    Domesday priest, 64
Leominster (M), HRE, 2, 5, 6, 10, 12, 13, 15, 83–95, 97
    royal manor, 83, 93–5
Letton (C), HRE, 83, 93
Letton, Roger of, 93
Leuuin see Leofwine
Levisham (C), YON, 199
Lewes (C), SSX, 169, 175
Leysdown (C), KNT, 106, 108, 115, 116
Lichfield, STF, gild, 34
    diocese of, 128
Lickey Hills, WOR, 120
Limen, KNT, see Lympne
Limesia, Robert of (witn. for Henry of Blois), 61
Lincoln (CA), LIN, 26
    St. Mark's church, 199
    St. Peter-at-Gowts church, 198
Lincolnshire, churches in, 9, 197
    chapels in, 15
    estates and parish boundaries in, 80
Lindon, WOR, 142
Lindridge (C), WOR, 123, 124, 137
Linley (C), SHR, 73, 78, 149
Linton (C), KNT, 106
Littlebourne (C), KNT, 106, 115, 116
Littlechart (C), KNT, 116
Littleton, HMP, 64
Littleton, Middle (C), WOR, 124, 133
Littleton, South (C), WOR, 124, 133
Llanthony see Lanthony
Lockerley, HMP, 65
London:
    minsters, churches, parishes, wards, 3, 35–43
    minsters (certain and probable):
        All Hallows, 40, 41, 43
        St. Helen Bishopsgate, 40

St. Martin-le-Grand, 97
St. Mary Magdalen, 35, 36, 38, 40, 41, 42
St. Paul (CA), 39, 41
St. Peter ad Vincula, 13, 36, 39, 40, 41, 43
other parishes and parish churches:
St. Botolph, 35, 36, 39, 40, 41, 43
St. Dunstan, 40, 41, 43
St. Dunstan Stepney, 41, 43
Holy Trinity Minories, 43
St. Mary Matfelon, 43
religious houses:
St. Bartholomew Smithfield, 167
Holy Trinity Aldgate, 35, 36, 38, 40–1, 42
St. Katherine's Hospital, 43
St. Mary Graces, 143
Minoresses, 43
Westminster Abbey, 12, 22, 25, 26, 27, 84, 127, 129, 133, 134, 166
wards, sokes, gates:
Aldgate, 35, 36, 38, 39, 40, 41, 43
Bishopsgate, 39, 40, 41, 43
Ludgate, 39
Moorgate, 39
Newgate, 39
Portsoken, 35, 36, 39, 40, 41, 43
St. Olave Bread St., 40, 41
"St. Peter's Gate", 39–41, 43
Tower, 40
other locations:
Aldwych, 43
Baynard's Castle, 39
Canon Street, 39
Cheapside, 39
Eastcheap, 39
Great Tower Street, 39
Montfichet's Castle, 39
Ratcliffe Highway, 39–40
Shadwell, 40
Smithfield, 39, 40, 43
Stepney, 43
Tower of London, 39, 40, 145
gilds (incl. *Cnihtengild*), 32, 33, 34, 35, 36, 40, 42
restoration by King Alfred, 36
wic, 39, 42–3
Longdon (M?), WOR, 123, 124, 125, 134
estate, 137, 156
Longney-on-Severn (C), GLO, dedicated by St. Wulfstan, 134
Longworth (M?), BRK, 88
Loose (C), KNT, 106, 108, 117
Lopham, South (C), NFK, 182
Lorraine, of, *see* Losinga
Losinga, Herbert, Bishop of Norwich, 169, 177, 179, 188–90
Robert, Bishop of Hereford, 143, 159
Loughton (C), SHR, 74, 75, 78, 79
Lovel, John, 181
Lowestoft, SFK, 169, 175
Lucton (C), HRE, 83, 85, 88, 91, 93, 95
Luddenham (C), KNT, 106, 114
Lulsley (C), WOR, 124
Lüneburg Heath, N. Germany, round-towered churches near, 171, 175
Luntley, HRE, 83, 85, 92
Luston, HRE, 85, 91, 93
Lutley, WOR, 143

Luton (M), BDF, 5
"Lutrise", king's *minster*, 65
Lydbury North (M), SHR, 72
manor, 72
Lydd (C), KNT, 106, 108, 115, 117
Lydden *(Hleodæna)* (C), KNT, 106, 115
Lye, HRE, 93
Lye (C), WOR, 137
Lyminge (M), KNT, 2, 106, 107, 108, 109, 110, 112, 114, 115, 116, 117
Lymington (C), HMP, 15, 47, 55, 60, 66
Lympne *(Limen)* (M), KNT, 106, 107, 108, 112, 115, 117
Castle, 107
Lyndhurst (C), HMP, 47, 55, 60
Lynn, Kings (Cs), NFK, 188, 189, 190
Lynsted (C), KNT, 106
Lyre Abbey, Normandy, 127, 128, 129

Mâconnais, France, 7
Madeley (C), SHR, 69, 73, 76, 80, 81
Madresfield (C), WOR, 124
Magonsæte, Merewalh king of, 71
Maidstone (M), KNT, 106, 107, 108, 109, 110, 113, 114, 115, 116, 117
Maizailles, architectural parallel with, 163
Malcolm IV, King of Scots, 104
Malherbe, Robert, 87, 94
Malling, South (M), SSX, 97
Malmesbury (M, Abbey), WLT, 63, 151
Malmesbury, William of, 21–2, 132, 144, 145, 191
Malton, YON, Roman material from?, 194
Malvern Chase, WOR, 126, 127, 129, 134, 154
Malvern, Great, WOR, Priory, 84–5, 88, 91, 123, 127, 129, 138, 150
St. Thomas the Martyr C, 123
Malvern Hills, 120
stone from, 155
Malvern, Little, Priory, WOR, 124
Mamble (C), WOR, 124
Mans (Mauns), Walter del, 86, 89, 94
Matthew del, 94
Mansbridge, HMP, hundred, 45
Mansell, Ralph (witn. for William Giffard), 61
Map, Walter, 32
Mapenore, Hugh de, Bishop of Hereford, 95
Mappenore, Peter de, 89
Mare, Richard de la (lord of Alvescot, Oxon.), 11
Margate, St. John Baptist (C), KNT, 106, 109, 116
Marham (2Cs), NFK, 179, 180
Marleberge, Thomas de, Dean of the Vale and Abbot of Evesham, 156
Marr (C), YOW, 195
Martin Hussingtree (C), WOR, 124, 133, 135
Martinescirce, Martini Ecclesia, KNT, *see* Postling *and* Romney, New
Martley (C), WOR, 13, 123, 124, 128, 130–2, 140, 141, 142, 145, 149, 154
stone from, 155
Mathon (C), HRE, 125
Matilda, Queen, 35, 38
Matilda wife of Robert fitz Richard *see* Senlis

Mauger, Bishop of Worcester, 127
Maund, Nicholas of, 86, 87, 89, 94
Mauns *see* Mans
Meilnilhermer, Richard de, chaplain of Morville, 74
Hubert son of, 74
Melford (M), SFK, 4
Melford, Roger de (witn. for William Giffard), 61
Melton Constable (C), NFK, 182
Mendham (M), SFK, 4
Meon, East (M), HMP, 63
hundred, 53
royal manor, 47, 63
Meon Valley, 46
Meonstoke, HMP, 64
Merewalh, King of *Magonsæte*, 71
Merlimond, Oliver de, 146, 163–4
Mersea (M), ESX, 3, 4
Mersham (C), KNT, 106, 114, 116
Merton Priory, SUR, 103
Mertumnescirce, KNT, *see* Hope All Saints
Meulan, Robert de, 97, 159
Middleton, KNT, hundred, 108
royal manor, 108
Middleton (C), YON, 193, 198
Middleton-on-the-Hill (C), HRE, 85, 88, 91, 93, 95
Middleton Scriven (C), SHR, 69, 76
Midley (C), KNT, 106, 108, 114, 117
Milan, Italy, San Ambrogio in, 151
Milborne Port (M), SOM, 5, 6, 27
Mildburh (Milburga etc.), St., 71, 73, 80
Miles the Constable, 86, 93
Mileshope (C), HRE, 83, 85, 88, 91, 93, 95
Milford (C), HMP, 8, 13, 47, 54–6, 57, 60, 101
Milson (C), SHR, 69, 76
Milsted (C), KNT, 106, 108, 115, 116
Milton (C), HMP, 47, 55, 60
Milton (C), KNT, 106
Milton Regis (M), KNT, 106, 107, 108, 109, 110, 113, 114, 115, 116, 117
Minstead (C), HMP, 55
Minster-in-Sheppey *(Sexburgaminster)* (M), KNT, 106, 108, 109, 110, 115, 116
Minster-in-Thanet (M), KNT, 106, 109, 110, 113, 116, 118
Mitton, Lower (C), WOR, 124, 143
Molash (C), KNT, 106
Möllenbeck (C), N. Germany, 173, 176
Mongeham, Great (C), KNT, 106, 114
Mongeham, Little (C), KNT, 106, 109, 116
Monk Fryston (C), YOW, 193, 196
Monkhopton (C), SHR, 69, 73, 76
Monkland (C), HRE, 84, 85, 86, 87, 88, 91, 92, 93, 94, 95
Priory, 93
Monkton (C), KNT, 106, 116
Mont St.-Michel Abbey, Normandy, 26, 63
Montgomery, Roger de, Earl of Shrewsbury, 71, 72, 73, 74, 75, 101
Morcar, Earl of Nothumbria, 72
Moor, WOR, 142
Morestead, HMP, 64
Mortain, Count of, 100
Mortimer, Hugh de, lord of Wigmore, 146, 163
Morton, Abbots (C), WOR, 123

Index of People and Places

Morville (M), SHR, 11, 69, 71, 72, 73, 74, 76, 77, 79, 101
    Priory, 74, 75
    royal manor, 71
Mottisfont (M), HMP, 47, 63, 64
Muchgros, Richard, 141
Mucknell, WOR, 144
Munslow (C), SHR, 69, 76
Murston (C), KNT, 106, 108, 116

Nackington (C), KNT, 106, 115, 117
Nafford (C), WOR, 123, 124, 134, 135, 138, 141, 157
Naunton Beauchamp (C), WOR, 124, 135
Neatham, HMP, hundred, 63
    royal manor, 63
Neen Savage (C), SHR, 69, 74, 76
Neen Sollars (C), SHR, 69, 74, 76, 80
Neenton (C), SHR, 69, 74, 75, 76
Netheravon (M), WLT, 28
Netherton-by-Cropthorne (C), WOR, 124, 133, 141, 142, 149
Neufmarché, Bernard de, 86
    William de, 99, 100, 101, 102–3; *see also* William, canon of Daventry
Neukirchen (C), N. Germany, 176
New Forest, HMP, 53, 54, 65
    hundred, 65
Newchurch (C), KNT, 106, 108, 115
Newenden *(Petri Ecclesia?)* (C), KNT, 106, 109, 115
Newington [by Hythe] (C), KNT, 106, 114
Newington [by Sittingbourne] (M), KNT, 106, 107, 108, 109, 113, 114, 115, 116, 117
Newmarket *see* Neufmarché
Newnham (C), KNT, 106
Newnham, WOR, estate, 137
Newton, HRE, 84, 85, 92–3
Newton Purcell (C), OXF, 149
Nhutscelle (M) *see* Nursling *and* Romsey
Nicholas II, Pope, 127
Nicholas IV, Pope, Taxation of, 67, 68, 76, 77, 85, 91, 128
Nicholas, Master (witn. for Henry of Blois), 61
Ningwood, IOW, 59
Niwecyrce, KNT, *see* Borden
Nonington (C), KNT, 106, 114, 115, 116
Norfolk, churches in, 10, 169–90
North Sea, round-towered churches near, 171, 175
Northallerton (M?), YON, 199
Northampton (M), NTP, 99
    St. Andrew's Priory, 97
    Archdeacon of, 99–100, 101
    Earls of, 97–104
    Gild, 33
Northamptonshire, minsters and churches in, 8, 19
Northbourne *(Burnan?)* (M?), KNT, 106, 109, 110, 111, 114, 116, 118
Northchurch, KNT, *see* Warden
Northcip', KNT, *see* Warden
Northfield (C), WAR, 125, 150
Northwood, KNT, *see* Whitstable
Norton (M), DRH, 187
Norton (C), KNT, 106, 114
Norton, Bredons (C), WOR, 123, 143, 150, 151

Norton-by-Evesham (C), WOR, 120, 124, 133
Norton-by-Kempsey (C), WOR, 124, 134
Norton, Kings (C), WAR, 125, 134, 137
Norwich (CA, Priory), NFK, 169, 170, 175, 179, 188, 189
    St. Benedict's church, 157, 199
    Heigham church, 170
    St. Julian's church, 175
    multiple churches, 181
    Castle, 145
Norwich Taxation (1254), 180
Nostell Priory, YOW, 28, 29
Nursling (*Nhutscelle*, M?), HMP, 46, 47, 48, 62, 63

Oare (C), KNT, 106, 114
Oddingley (C), WOR, 124, 130, 132
Odensee, Denmark, cell of Evesham Abbey, 127
Odiham (M?), HMP, 63, 64
    hundred, 63
    royal manor, 63
Offa, King of Mercia, 42, 156
Offenham (C), WOR, 120, 124, 133, 145
Oglander, Peter de, Dean of Christchurch, 50, 51–2, 59, 60, 66
Oldberrow (C), WAR, 125
Oldbury (C), SHR, 69, 73, 76, 77, 79
Olifard, David, 104
Oluric *see* Ælfric
Ombersley (M), WOR, 5, 124, 133, 137
    estate, 137
    quarrying at, 154
Ombersley, Maurice de, 134
Onna, HMP, Roman settlement, 63
Ordgarescirce, KNT, *see* Orgarswick
Ordric, priest of Cullompton, 33
Orgarswick *(Ordgarescirce)* (C), KNT, 106, 108, 115
Orlestone (C), KNT, 106, 114
Orleton (C), HRE, 83, 85, 91, 93, 94, 95
Orm son of Gamal (builder of Kirkdale minster), 196
Osbern, Bishop of Exeter, 27, 33
Osbern, Domesday tenant [and canon of Daventry?], 100
Osbern, William fitz, Earl of Hereford, 127–8, 159
Osbert, Prior of Daventry, 100, 101
Osbert son of Osbert, 91
Oseney Abbey, OXF, 11, 85
Osmaston (C), DRB, 94
Ospringe (C), KNT, 106, 114, 169
Osred, King of Northumbria, 199
Ostia, Odo of, *History of the Translation of St. Milburga*, 80
Oswald, King of Northumbria, 47
Oswald, Bishop of Worcester, 127
Otham (C), KNT, 106, 108
Otley (C), YOW, 198, 199
Otter, River, HMP, *see* Beaulieu Water
Otterden (C), KNT, 106, 114
Otterwood, HMP, 65
Ouse, River, SSX, 169
Ouseburn, Little (C), YOW, 193, 196, 198
Overbury (M?), WOR, 123, 124, 125, 134, 151, 154, 156
Overs, SHR, hundred, 70, 80

Overton, HMP, 48, 64
Owston (C), YOW, 193, 195
Oxborough (3Cs), NFK, 179, 180
Oxelei, HMP, 65
Oxenede, John of (chronicler), 179
Oxford, St. Frideswide's (M), OXF, 5, 39, 104
Oxfordshire, proportion of Romanesque church fabric in, 120–1
Oxney (C), KNT, 106

Paddlesworth (C), KNT, 106, 115, 117
Pastrow hundred, HMP, 63
Patrixbourne *(Burna)* (C), KNT, 106, 114
Patton, SHR, 73
    hundred, 70, 71, 73, 81
Paxton, Great (M), HNT, 98
Pedmore (C), WOR, 124, 150, 154
Pencombe (C), HRE, 85
Pendock (C), WOR, 124, 137, 142, 150, 154
    estate, 137, 156
Penistone (C), YOW, 193
Penkridge (M), STF, 5
Pennines, stone from, 192
Pensax (C), WOR, 120, 124,
    estate, 137
Peopleton (C), WOR. 135
Pershore (M, Abbey), WOR, 2, 6, 12, 13, 119, 120, 123, 124, 127, 128, 133, 135, 137, 138, 143, 145, 151, 154
    St. Andrew's church, 123, 124, 133, 134, 135
    Holy Cross church, 133, 135
    deanery, 130
Petelie, SHR, 80
Peterborough (M, Abbey), NTP, 63, 126
Petham (C), KNT, 106, 114, 116
Petri Ecclesia, KNT, *see* Newenden *and* Whitfield
Pett *(Pytte?)* (C), KNT, 106, 114
Philip, son of priest of Eye and chaplain of Yarpole, HRE, 95
Pickthorn, SHR, 73, 80
Piddinghoe (C), SSX, 169
Piddington, OXF, 104
Piddle, North (C), WOR, 135
Piddle, Wyre (C), WOR, 134
Piddleton (C), DOR, 53, 58
Pilley, HMP, 65
Pinvin (C), WOR, 124, 133
Piperham (C), SUR, 17
Pirton (C), WOR, 124, 126, 135, 139, 141, 142, 144, 152
Pivington (C), KNT, 106, 114
Plantagenet, Geoffrey, Bishop of Lincoln, 104
Plegmund, Archbishop of Canterbury, 38
Plesc, SHR, 80
Pluckley (C), KNT, 106, 114, 116
Pocklington (M), YOE, 197
Poden, WOR, 137
Poer, Hugh, 98
Poitou region, architectural influence from, 163
Poland, round-towered churches in, 171, 175
Portchester, HMP, episcopal estate, 45, 48, 63
Portsmouth (C), HMP, 47

Posenhall (C), SHR, 73, 78
Postling *(Martinescirce?)* (C), KNT, 106, 115
Postlip (C), GLO, 94
Potton, BDF, 103
Poulton (St. Mary's?) (C), KNT, 106, 114
Powick (C), WOR, 124, 134, 139
  deanery, 130
  estate, 137, 139
Preston, HMP, 52, 59
Preston, in Shalfleet, IOW, 52
Preston [by Faversham] (C), KNT, 106, 108, 114, 116
Preston [by Wingham] (C), KNT, 106, 110, 116, 117
Preston Capes Priory, NTP, 97, 99 101
  Castle, 97
Pucklechurch, GLO, 149
Pudleston (C), HRE, 83, 85, 93, 95
Puingiant, Robert, 162
Pull, WOR, 127
Pusey (C), BRK, 88
Pytte, Kent, *see* Pett

Quatford (M), SHR, 69, 72, 76, 81
  manor, 72
Queenhill (C), WOR, 124, 127, 129, 134, 150
Quenington (C), GLO, 151, 161–3
Quincy, Saer de, 98, 103

Rætte, KNT, *see* Richborough
Raicedo, Spain, San Juan at, 146
Rainham (C), KNT, 106, 108, 115, 116
Ralph, Archdeacon of Winchester, 61
Ralph, chaplain of Welton, NTP, 102
Ralph, Domesday priest, 64
Ramsgate (St. Lawrence-in-Thanet) (C), KNT, 106, 109, 116
Ratcliffe-on-Soar (C), NTT, dedicated by St. Wulfstan, 134
Ratekau (C), Schleswig-Holstein, 171, 176
Ratling (C), KNT, 106, 115
Raunds (C), NTP, 23, 143, 198
Rayton (C), KNT, 106, 117
Reading Abbey, BRK, 12, 19, 83–95
Reculver *(Biscopestune?)* (M), KNT, 2, 106, 108, 109, 110, 114, 117
Redbridge *(Hreutford)* (M), HMP, 45, 63
  hundred, 45, 65
Redditch Ridgeway, WOR, 120
Rednal, WOR, estate, 137
Redstone Rock Hermitage (in Astley), WOR, 123
Redvers, family, 51–2
  Baldwin de, I, 56, 65, 66
  Richard de, I, 53, 59, 65
Regenbald, king's priest, 6, 27
Remi, bishop of Lincoln, 26
Rhee Wall, KNT, 108
Ribbesford (C), WOR, 124, 126, 148, 149, 154
Richard, suffragan bishop of St. Asaph, 99, 102
Richard, Bishop's chaplain and Dean (witn. for William Giffard), 61
Richard, Robert fitz, 98, 99, 101
Richborough *(Rætte?)*, in Ash (C), KNT, 110, 114
Richer, Domesday priest, 64
Richmond Castle, YON, 195

Rievaulx Abbey, YON, 29
Ringwood (C), HMP, 47, 55, 60
  hundred, 65
  royal manor, 65
Ringwould (C), KNT, 106
Ripon (M), YOW, 199
Ripple (C), KNT, 106, 109, 116
Ripple (M), WOR, 2, 123, 124, 133, 134, 137, 139, 141, 142, 143, 144, 151, 154
Risbury (C), HRE, 84, 85, 86, 87, 89, 90, 91, 92, 93, 94
Rivenhall (C), ESX, 23
River *(Æwellan?)* (C), KNT, 106, 114
Robert, Bishop of St. Andrew's, 29
Robert, Abbot of Evesham, 127
Robert the Almoner (witn. for Henry of Blois), 61 Robert, Archdeacon of Surrey, 61
Robin of Horsehill, 149
Rochester, Bishop of, 105
Rochford (C), WOR, 125, 134, 141, 149, 150, 154, 157
Rock (M?), WOR, 124, 126, 138, 140, 141, 142, 143, 145, 150, 152–3, 154
  see also Alton
Rodedic, HMP, hundred, 65
Rodmersham (C), KNT, 106, 108, 115, 116
Roger, Earl of Hereford, 94
Roger, Bishop of Salisbury, 167
Roger, incumbent of Eye, HRE, 95
  Philip and Walter his sons, 95
Roger son of Maurice, 86
Rollright, Great (C), OXF, 149
Rolvenden (C), KNT, 106, 109, 114
Romney, New, KNT, churches, 114, 117
  St. Martin *(Martini Ecclesia)*, 106, 108, 115
  St. Lawrence *(Laurentiuscirce)*, 106, 108, 115
  St. Nicholas, 106
Romney, Old, St. Clement (C), KNT, 106, 109, 114
Romney Marsh, KNT, 108, 117
Romsey *(Nhutscelle?)* (M), HMP, 46, 47, 58, 62, 66
Romsley (C), WOR, 120, 125
  St. Kenelm's chapel, 150, 154
Ross-on-Wye (C), HRE, 13
Rothwell (C), LIN, 198
Rowlstone (C), HRE, 149
Ruardean (C), GLO, 163
Ruckinge (M?), KNT, 106, 107, 109, 114, 116, 117
Rupe (C), WOR, *see* Bredon Hill
Rushbury (C), SHR, 69, 73, 76, 77
Ryther (C), YOW, 192, 193
Ryton (C), SHR, 69, 74, 76

St. Albans (M), HRT, 5, 6
St. Andrews, St. Rule's C., 29, 198
St. Asaph, suffragan bishop of, 99
St. Barbe Abbey, Normandy, 128, 129
St. Benet's Abbey, NFK, 179
St. Denis Abbey, France, 128, 129
St. Evroult Abbey, Normandy, 128, 129, 138
St. John Baptist, KNT, *see* Margate
St. Keus, honour of, CNW, 18
St. Lawrence-in-Thanet, KNT, *see* Ramsgate
St. Margaret's, KNT, *see* Cliffe

St. Mary's, KNT, *see* Poulton
St. Mary Bourne, HMP, 48, 63
St. Mary-in-the-Marsh *(Siwoldescirce?)* (C), KNT, 106, 108, 115
St. Nicholas-at-Wade, KNT, *see* Wade
St. Peter's, KNT, *see* Newenden *and* Whitfield
St. Peter-in-Thanet, KNT, *see* Broadstairs
St. Teath (M), CNW, 9
Saltwood (C), KNT, 106, 114, 117
  castle, 117
Salwarpe (C), WOR, 124
  Valley, WOR, 154
Samson, Bishop of Worcester, 127, 128
Sandhurst (C), KNT, 106, 114
Sandtun, KNT, 117
Sandwich, KNT, churches:
  St. Clement, 106, 109
  St. Mary, 106, 114
  St. Peter, 106, 116
Sapey, Lower (C), WOR, 124, 134, 140, 141, 142
Sarnesfield (C), HRE, 83, 85, 92–3, 95
Sarre (C), KNT, 106, 114, 117
Sarum, Old, WLT, castle, 167
Saulf (Domesday tenant), 65
Saumur Abbey, France, 98
Savaric, Archdeacon of Northampton, 99–100
Sawtry Abbey, HNT, 104
Saxham, Little (C), SFK, 169, 172
Saxlingham Thorpe (C), NFK, 175
Scapei, KNT, *see* Leysdown *and* Warden
Scartho (C), LIN, 198
Schleswig-Holstein, round-towered churches in, 170, 171, 173, 175
Seasalter (C), KNT, 106, 114, 116
Sedgebarrow (C), WOR, 124, 155
Selborne (C), HMP, 64
Selby Abbey, YOW, 28
Sele Priory, SSX, 98
Sellindge (C), KNT, 106, 108, 115
Selling (C), KNT, 106, 108, 115, 116
Senlis, Matilda de, 98, 99, 101, 103
  Simon de, I, Earl of Northampton, 97–8, 100, 101, 103
  Simon de, II, Earl of Northampton, 98, 101, 102, 103, 104
  Simon de, III, Earl of Northampton, 102, 104
Serlo, Abbot of Gloucester, 167
Serlo, priest of Kinnersley, HRE, 93
Severn, River, 69, 71, 81, 119–20, 126, 130, 149, 154
Severn Stoke (C), WOR, 124, 135
  Hermitage, 124
Sevington *(Brixiestun?)* (C), KNT, 106, 115
Sexburgaminster, KNT, *see* Minster-in-Sheppey
Shadoxhurst (C), KNT, 106
Shaftesbury (M, Abbey), DOR, 5, 167
  Nunnery, 62
Shefford, Great (C), BRK, 169
Sheldwich (C), KNT, 106, 116
Shelsey Beauchamp (C), WOR, 124, 132
Shelsley Kings, WOR, 132
Shelsley Walsh (C), WOR, 124, 134, 140, 142, 150, 154–5
Shepherdswell, KNT, *see* Sibertswold
Sheppey, Isle of, KNT, 108

Sherborne (M), DOR, 5, 187
  Castle, 167
Sherburn-in-Elmet (M?), YOW, 194, 199
Sheriff, Hugh the, see Hugh
Sheriffhales (M?), STF, 5, 69, 74, 76
Sherrifs Lench, WOR, 129
Shifnal (M), SHR, 11, 69, 71, 72, 74, 75
  manor, 72
Shingleton *(Smithatune?)* (C), KNT, 106, 109, 114, 116, 117
Shipston-on-Stour (C), WAR, 125
Shipton (C), SHR, 69, 73, 76, 80
Shirley, HMP, 65
Shobdon (C), HRE, 150, 151, 163
Shoddesdon (C), HRE, 198
Sholden (C), KNT, 106, 109, 116, 118
Shorwell, IOW, 66
Shouldham (2Cs), NFK, 179, 180
Shrawley (C), WOR, 124, 140, 142, 150, 151, 154
  estate, 3
Shrewsbury (M), SHR, 42
  Abbey, 71, 72, 74–5, 101
  Earl of, see Montgomery
Shrivenham (M), BRK, 5
Shropshire, minsters and churches in, 2, 67–81
  archdeaconry of, 128
  chapels in, 15
  hundreds in, 70
  proportion of Romanesque church fabric in, 120–1
Shuart (C), KNT, 119
Shurnock, WOR, 137
Sibertswold (Shepherdswell) (C), KNT, 106, 109, 116
Sidbury (C), SHR, 69, 76
"Simon", Archdeacon of Northampton, 99–100
Sittingbourne (C), KNT, 106, 108, 116
Siwoldscirce, KNT, see St. Mary-in-the-Marsh
Skewkirk, YOW, 198
Skipwith (C), YOE, 26, 28, 192, 193, 196
Smarden (C), KNT, 106, 114
Smeeth (C), KNT, 106
Smithatune, KNT, see Shingleton
Snaith (M), YOW, 197, 199
Snarehill (C), NFK, 186-8
Snargate (C), KNT, 106, 108
Snave (C), KNT, 106, 108, 117
Solers, William de, 94
Somborne, Kings (M), HMP, 63
  hundred, 63
  royal manor, 63
Sompting (C), SSX, 27, 30
Sonning (M), BRK, 9, 19, 32
Sopley (C), HMP, 47, 55, 56, 57, 60
Southampton, St. Mary Extra (Stoneham) (M), HMP, 45, 46, 47, 51, 58, 62, 65
  wic, 42
Southampton Water, HMP, 2
Southstone Rock, WOR, stone from, 154
Southwark (M), SUR, 42
Spain, architecture in, 146–7, 150
Sparkford, HMP, 64
Sparsholt (M), BRK, 5
Sparsholt, HMP, 64
Spetchley (C), WOR, 124, 132
Stafford (M), STF, 42

Staffordshire, proportion of Romanesque church fabric in, 120–1
Stalisfield (C), KNT, 106, 116
Standlake (C), OXF, 19
Stanford (C), KNT, 106, 115
Stanpit, HMP, 58, 66
Stanton, family, 56
Stanton Lacy (M), SHR, 11, 72
  manor, 72
Stanton Long (C), SHR, 69, 73, 74, 76
Staple (C), KNT, 106
Staplehurst (C), KNT, 106, 108
Staunton (C), GLO, 125, 145
Staverton (C), NTP, 99, 100, 104
Stelling (C), KNT, 106, 115
Stephen, King, 86, 116, 118
Stephen, clerk (witn. for William Giffard), 61
Steyning (M), SSX, 167
Stigand, Archbishop of Canterbury, 105, 126–7
Stirchley (C), SHR, 69, 74, 76, 80
Stockbury (C), KNT, 106, 108, 115, 116
Stockton, HRE, 85, 93
Stockton (C), SHR, 69, 76
Stockton-on-Teme (C), WOR, 124, 137, 141, 142, 149
Stodmarsh (C), KNT, 106, 116
Stoke Bliss (C), WOR, 125
Stoke Edith (M), HRE, 5
Stoke Ferry (C), NFK, 180
Stoke-by-Nayland (M), SFK, 3–5, 6
Stoke Prior (C), HRE, 85, 90, 93
Stoke Prior (C), WOR, 124, 134, 137, 151
  estate, 137
Stoke St. Milborough (C), SHR, 69, 73, 75, 76, 80
Stonar (C), KNT, 106, 109, 116
Stone, HMP, 45, 47, 62, 63
Stone (C), WOR, 124
Stone-by-Faversham (C), KNT, 106, 108, 110, 115
Stone-in-Oxney (C), KNT, 106, 117
Stonegrave (M), YON, 196
Stoneham (M and Cs), HMP, see Southampton
  royal manor, 45, 62, 64
Stoneleigh (C), WAR, 161–2, 163
Stottesdon (M), SHR, 15, 69, 71, 72, 73, 74, 76, 79, 80–1
  deanery, 130
  manor, 71
Stoulton (C), WOR, 124, 134, 137, 141, 142, 144, 145, 146, 154
Stour, River, HMP, 51
Stour, GLO/WOR, 3
Stour Valley, WOR, 126, 156
  stone from, 154
Stourbridge (C), WOR, 137
Stourmouth (C), KNT, 106, 110, 114
Stow (M), LIN, 6, 22, 26, 27, 97, 187
Stowmarket (C), SFK, 4
Stowting (C), KNT, 106, 115, 116
Stradsett (2Cs), NFK, 179, 180
Straeta, KNT, see Court-at-Street
Stratford, John, Bishop of Winchester, 64
Stratford-on-Avon (Cs), WAR, gild, 31
Stratton (C), GLO, 149
Streanaeshalch (Whitby?) (M), 191
Strensham (C), WOR, 124, 133, 135

Stretford (C), HRE, 88
Stretton, Church (C), SHR, 72
  manor, 72
Stretton Sugwas (C), HRE, 163, 165
Strithindenne, Kent, see Frittenden
Studley Priory, WAR, 123
Sturry (C), KNT, 106, 116
Stursæte, KNT, see Westgate
Suckley (M?), WOR, 123, 124, 128, 129, 134
  stone from, 155
Sudbury (M), SFK, 3, 4
Suffolk, churches, in, 169–78
Sumafeld, KNT, see Swingfield
Summarius, Alberic (witn. for Henry of Blois), 61
Sunningas, province of, 67
Surlingham (C), NFK, 187
Surrey, conversion of, 46–7
  minsters and churches in, 3, 18
  chapels in, 15
  Archdeacon of, 61
Sutton [by Northbourne] (C), KNT, 106, 109, 111, 116
Sutton [near Shrewsbury], SHR, 73, 80
Sutton, Chart (C), KNT, 106, 115
Sutton, East *(Welcumeweg?)* (C), KNT, 106, 108, 115
Sutton Maddock (C), SHR, 69, 74, 76
Sutton Valence (C), KNT, 106, 108, 115
Swalecliffe (C), KNT, 106, 117
Swarling *(Swirgildancirce?)* (C), KNT, 106, 108, 115
Sweden, round-towered churches in, 171, 175
Swinford, Old (C), WOR, 124, 137
  estate, 137
Swinford, Upper (C), WOR, 137
Swingfield *(Sumafeld)* (C), KNT, 106, 115
Swirgildancirce KNT, see Swarling
Sylvester, canon of Christchurch, 56

Tackley (M?), OXF, 18
Tardebigge (C), WOR, 120, 125
Tarragona, Gild, 34
Tasburgh (C), NFK, 170, 173
Tasley (C), SHR, 69, 73, 76
Taynton, OXF, stone from, 154
Teddington (C), GLO, 125, 143
Teme, River, 71, 120, 126, 147, 149, 154
Templars' church at Garway, HRE, 146
Tenbury (M?), WOR, 120, 124, 125, 127, 128, 129, 134, 141, 154
Tenterden (C), KNT, 106, 117
Terrington (C), YON, 195
Test, River, 45, 46, 63
Tetbald, Robert fitz, 72, 75
Tetsill, SHR, 80
Tettenhall (M), STF, 5
Tewkesbury Abbey, GLO, 145, 146, 151, 160
Teynham (M), KNT, 106, 107, 108, 109, 110–11, 113, 114, 115, 116, 117
Thanet, KNT, churches in, 116
Thanington (C), KNT, 106, 114
Thatcham (M), BRK, 16
Theobald, Archbishop of Canterbury, 92, 94, 97
Theodore, Archbishop of Canterbury, 2, 48, 128

Theodred, Bishop, will of, 4
Theolf, Bishop of Worcester, 127, 128
Thetford (M, CA), NFK, 4, 184, 188
 multiple churches, 7, 179, 181, 184-8
 Priory, 85
 town, 184
Thickenappletree, WOR, 143
Thomas, Archbishop of York, 28
Thorington (C), SFK, 170
Thorley (C), HMP, 57
Thorne, WOR, 137
Thorney (M), SFK, 4
Thorngate, HMP, hundred, 63
Thornton Steward (C), YON, 193, 198
Thorpe, Haddiscoe (C), NFK, 170, 173
Throckmorton (C), WOR, 124, 134
Througham, HMP, 65
 hundred, 65
Throwley (C), KNT, 106, 114, 116
Thrupp, NTP, 100, 101, 102
Thrybergh (C), YOW, 193
Thurbe, William, Bishop of Norwich, 189
Thurnham (C), KNT, 106, 108, 115
Thurrock, West, ESX, 100
Tibberton (C), WOR, 132
Ticklerton, SHR, 73, 80
Tidmington (C), WAR, 125
Tilmanstone (C), KNT, 106, 114
Tilney All Saints (C), NFK, 190
Tirell, William (witn. for Henry of Blois), 61
Tiron Abbey, France, 93
Titchfield (M), HMP, 46, 47, 48, 56-7, 62
 royal manor and hundred, 46
Titley (C), HRE, 83, 85, 88, 92, 93, 95
 Priory, 93
Titterstone Clee, SHR, 71
Todenham, GLO, 3
Tofig the Proud, 38
Toledo, Spain, buildings in, 146
Tong (M), SHR, 5, 69, 76
Tong (C), YOW, 198
Tonge (C), KNT, 106, 108, 115, 116
Tooting Graveney (C), SUR, 169, 175
Tosny, Ralph de, 84, 93, 128
Tostig, Earl, 65, 196
Tredington (M), WAR, 7, 125, 154
 estate, 7
Tremworth *(Dreamwurthe)* (C), KNT, 106, 115
Trenley Park, KNT, 117
Trussel, Fulk, 99, 103
Tuesley (M), SUR, 15, 17
Tugford (C), SHR, 69, 75, 76
Tunstall (C), KNT, 106, 108, 115, 116
Twyford (C), HMP, 64
Twynham (M), HMP see Christchurch

Ulcombe (C), KNT, 106, 108, 115
Uluric see Ælfric
Underton (C), SHR, 73, 77, 78
Undetun, KNT, see Wooton
Upchurch (C), KNT, 106, 108, 115, 116
Upham (C), HMP, 47
Upton, HRE, 85, 93
Upton Cressett (C), SHR, 69, 76
Upton-on-Severn (C), WOR, 124, 134, 137, 143
Upton Snodbury (C), WOR, 120, 124, 133, 135
Upton Warren (C), WOR, 124

Urgel, Gild, 34
Urki (of Abbotsbury), 31, 32, 34
Utefel, HMP, 65

Valdès of Lyon, 33
Vere, William de, Bishop of Hereford, 87, 92, 95
Viel, Robert fitz, 100
View Edge, SHR, 71
Vitalis, Abbot of Westminster, 127
Vitalis, Domesday priest, 64

Wacton (C), HRE, 83
Wadborough Hermitage, WOR, 124
Wade, St. Nicholas (C), KNT, 106, 109, 118
Wærferth, Bishop of Worcester, 38
Wafere, Simon le, 92
Walcher, Prior of Malvern, 127
Waldershare (C), KNT, 106, 114
Wales, Gerald of, 149, 199
Walkelin, Bishop of Winchester, 56, 57, 60
Wallop (C), HMP, 64
Wallop, Nether (M), HMP, 6, 18
Walmer (C), KNT, 106, 114
Walmerstone *(Wielmestun?)* (C), KNT, 106, 115
Walpole St. Peter, NFK, 190
Walsoken (C), NFK, 190
Walter, Abbot of Evesham, 127
Walter Clerch, 102
Walter, clerk of Henry of Blois, 61
Walter, son of priest of Eye, HRE, 95
Walter, Hubert, Archbishop of Canterbury, 111, 118
Waltham (C), KNT, 106, 114
Waltham, Bishops (M), HMP, 45, 46, 47, 56, 58, 61, 63, 64, 66
 episcopal manor and hundred, 45
Waltham Holy Cross (M), ESX, 6, 35, 38, 42, 51, 54, 65, 97
 burh, 38
Walton [by Folkestone] (C), KNT, 106, 114
Wantage (M), BRK, 5
Wapletone, HRE, 93
Warden *(Northcip')* (C), KNT, 106, 108, 115, 116
Wareham (M), DOR, 39
 Holy Trinity C., 39
 St. Martin's C., 39
Warehorne (C), KNT, 106, 114
Warelwast, William, Bishop of Exeter, 11
Waresley, WOR, 137
Warndon (C), WOR, 124, 126, 130, 132
Warnford (C), HMP, 198
Warter Abbey, YOE, 28
Warwick (M), WAR, 97
 Castle, 97
 deanery, 130
Warwickshire, proportion of Romanesque church fabric in, 120-1
Washbourn, Great (C), GLO, 149
Washbourn, Little (C), GLO, 125
Wasthill, WOR, estate, 137
Waveney, River, NFK, 169, 175
Wearsetfelda, WOR, estate, 137
Weaverthorpe (C), YOE, 28, 29
Weeke, HMP, 64
Weighton, Market (C), YOE, 195
Welcumeweg, KNT, *see* Sutton, East
Welford (C), BRK, 169, 175

Well (C), KNT, 106
Wella, NFK, *see* Beachamwell
Welland (C), WOR, 124
Welle, KNT, *see* Westwell
Welton (C), NTP, 11, 99, 100, 101, 102, 104
Welton, Stephen de, 100
Welwyn (M), HRT, 5
Wenlock Edge, SHR, 71, 73
Wenlock, Little (C), SHR, 69, 73, 76, 80, 81
Wenlock, Much (M, Priory), SHR, 2, 3, 6, 11, 69, 71, 73, 74, 75, 76, 77, 80, 81, 97, 120, 145
 Holy Trinity C, 73
Wereham (C), NFK, 180
Wessex, conversion of, 47-8
 royal manors and hundreds in, 67
Westbere (C), KNT, 106, 116
Westen (C), N. Germany, 171
Westgate *(Stursæte)* (C), KNT, 116
Westmancot, WOR, 143
Westminster *see* London
Weston (M), HRT, 5
Weston, Cold (C), SHR, 69, 74, 75, 76
Westwell *(Welle)* (C), KNT, 106, 114, 116
Weybourne (C), NFK, 170
Whaplode (C), LIN, 14
Wharram Percy (C), YON, 23, 157, 197, 199
Wharram-le-Street (C), YOE, 28, 29, 193, 195, 196, 198
Wharton, HRE, 84, 85, 86, 92, 93
Wheathill (C), SHR, 69, 74, 75, 76
Wherwell Nunnery (M?), HMP, 58, 62, 63, 66
Whistley, BRK, *see* Hurst
Whitbourne (C), HRE, 125
Whitby *see Streanaeshalch*
Whitchurch (M), HMP, 48, 63, 64, 65
Whitfield (St. Peter's?, Beusfield) (C), KNT, 106, 109, 110, 114, 116, 118
Whitlinge, WOR, 137
Whitstable (Northwood) (C), KNT, 106, 116
Whittington (C), WOR, 124, 130, 132
Whyle (C), HRE, 83, 85, 93, 95
Wibert, Domesday priest, 64
Wican, WOR, 7
Wichenford (C), WOR, 120, 124, 130, 132
Wihtred, King of Kent, 110
Wick Episcopi (C), WOR, 123, 124, 130, 132, 138
Wick-by-Pershore (C), WOR, 124, 133, 135, 142
Wick, Upper (C), WOR, 132
Wickham (C), HMP, 47, 56-7
Wickham (C), KNT, 116, 117
Wickhambreux (C), KNT, 106, 109, 114, 117
Wickhamford, WOR, 133
Wielmestun, KNT, *see* Walmerstone
Wigarestun, HMP, 65
Wight, kingdom/Isle of, 45, 62, 63, 65
Wigmore, HRE, 93
 Abbey, 161, 163, 167
Wigwig, SHR, 80
Wilfrid, St., 48
Willersey Hillfort, WOR, 133
Willesborough (C), KNT, 106, 117
Willey (C), SHR, 69, 73, 76
William I, King, 10, 13, 22, 38, 39, 63, 110, 116, 126

William II, King, 11, 51, 59, 91, 127
William, Prior of [St. Cross?] Hospital, 61
William, Archdeacon of Northampton, 101
William, Domesday priest of Besford, WOR, 134
William, canon of Daventry, 98, 99, 101, 102–3; *see also* Neufmarché, William de
 Walter (Clerch) son of, 102
William, chaplain of Welton, NTP, 99, 100, 101, 102
Willibald, St., 45
Wilmington [in Boughton Alulph] (C), KNT, 106, 115, 117
Wilton (C), HRE, 13
Wilton (M), WLT, 5
Wimborne (M), DOR, 16
Winchcombe (M, Abbey), GLO, 94, 119, 120, 161
Winchester, Old Minster (CA), 48, 49, 58, 63, 64, 65
 New Minster, 38, 49, 63
 Nuns' Minster, 49, 62
 Hyde Abbey, 64
 St. Cross Hospital, 64, 167
 St. Elizabeth College, 64
 churches (St. Anastasius, St. Faith, St. Giles, St. James, St. Katherine, St. Maurice), 64
 Archdeacon of, 61
 gilds, 32, 33, 34
Winchester, Herbert of (lord of Weaverthorpe, YOE), 28
 William of (brother/son of Herbert), 28
Winchfield (C), HMP, 167
Wine, Bishop of Wessex, 48
Wing (M), BUC, 27
Wingerworth (C), DRB, 11
Wingham (M), KNT, 106, 107, 108, 109, 110, 113, 114, 115, 116
Winnall, HMP, 64
Winsley, HRE, 94
Winson (C), GLO, 11, 12
Winterton (C), LIN, 198
Wislac (Domesday tenant), 65
Wissett (M?), SFK, 4
Wistow (C), YOW, 194
Witlafesfeld, WOR, estate, 137
Witley, Great (C), WOR, 123
Witley, Little (C), WOR, 124, 130, 132
Wittering (C), CAM, 26–7
Wittersham (C), KNT, 106, 109, 115
Witton (C), WOR, 142
Woking (M), SUR, 46–7, 63
 hundred, 46
Wollescote (C), WOR, 137
Wolverhampton (M), STF, 5

Wolverley (C), WOR, 124
Wolverton, WOR, 137, 144
Womenswold (C), KNT, 106, 115
Wonston, HMP, 64
Woodchurch (C), KNT, 106, 109, 114
Woodcote, SHR, 80
Woodkirk, YOW, 198
Woodnesborough (C), KNT, 106, 109, 114
Woollashull (C), WOR, 124, *and see* Bredon Hill
Woolverton (*Wulferestun?*) (C), KNT, 106, 115
Woonton, HRE, 85, 92
Wooton (*Undetun?*) (C), KNT, 106, 108, 115
Wootton St. Lawrence, HMP, 64
Wootton Wawen (M), WAR, 34
Worcester (CA, M, Priory), 3, 5, 23, 124, 126, 128, 129, 130, 137, 138, 145, 146, 149, 151, 154, 155, 160
 St. Helen (M), 2, 13, 123, 124, 130–2, 137, 138
 other churches:
 All Saints, 124
 St. Alban, 124, 132, 137, 140, 144
 St. Andrew, 124
 St. Clement, 124
 St. John-in-Bedwardine, 124, 132, 138
 St. Margaret, 124, 132
 St. Martin, 124
 St. Mary, 124
 St. Michael-in-Bedwardine, 125
 St. Peter the Great, 125
 St. Swithun, 125
 formation of parishes in, 137, 156
 Gild, 34
 Romano-British Christianity in, 130–2
 Grope Lane, 132
 Quay St. (*Wudestathe?*), 132
 bishops of, 126–7
 diocese of, 119, 128, 160
 archdeaconry, 128
 deaneries, 128, 130
Worcester, 'Florence' of, 97, 164
Worcestershire, minsters and churches in, 2–3, 8, 10, 119–58
 chapels in, 15, 137–8
 church architecture in, 160–7
 proportion of Romanesque church fabric in, 120–1
Wormshill (C), KNT, 106, 108, 110
Worsley, WOR, 142
Worth (C), KNT, 106
Worth (M?), SSX, 18
Worthy, HMP, 64

Wramplingham (C), NFK, 169
Wrekin, the, SHR, 71
Wretton (C), NFK, 180
Wrickton (C), SHR, 74
Wrockwardine (M), SHR, 72
 hundred, 70, 80
 manor, 72
Wroxeter (M), SHR, 72
 manor, 72
Wulfgeat of Donington, will of, 5
Wulfgyth, will of, 166
Wulfred, Archbishop of Canterbury, 3, 117
Wulfric of Haslebury, 166
Wulfric, Abbot of St. Augustine's Canterbury, 22
Wulfric, king's priest, 65
Wulfric, king's huntsman, 65
Wulfstan, Archbishop of York, 7, 9
Wulfstan, Bishop of Worcester, 10, 23, 126–7, 128, 134, 145, 166
Wych, WOR, deanery, 30
Wychling (C), KNT, 106
Wycombe (C), BUC, dedicated by St. Wulfstan, 134
Wye (M), KNT, 106, 107, 109, 113, 114, 115, 116, 118
Wyllan, KNT, *see* Eastwell
Wymondham (C, Priory), NFK, 190
Wynflæd, will of, 5
Wyre Forest, WOR, 128, 138
 stone from, 154
Wyre Piddle (C), WOR, 125

Yardley (C), WAR, 125
Yare, River, NFK, 169
Yarm, DRH, 198
Yarmouth, Great (Cs), NFK, 179, 188–90
 town, 188
Yarpole (C), HRE, 83, 85, 88, 91, 93, 95
Yeovil (M), SOM, 5
Yermo, Spain, Santa Marija del, 146
York (CA), 28, 195, 197, 198, 199
 St. Mary's Abbey, 28
 churches:
 St. Helen-on-the Walls, 130, 197
 St. Mary Bishophill Junior, 29, 192, 193, 195, 196, 198
 St. Mary Bishophill Senior, 199
 use of Roman material from, 9, 192, 193–4
Yorkshire, minsters and churches in, 2, 6, 9, 10, 15, 191–9

Zeals, WLT, 53, 65

Select Subject Index

Compiled by John Blair

abbess, as head of minster, 71
Adoration of the Cross, on tympanum, 151
Agnus Dei, in sculpture, 149, 150
aisles, 189, 190
    addition of, 15, 143, 144
alms, paid to minsters, 3–5, 32, 53–4, 57, 59, 61, 64
altars, 160, 166
Ancient Demesne land, as definiton of parochial area, 13
Annunciation, over chancel arch, 147–9
apses, 111, 145, 170, 171, 181, 184, 189, 190
arcading, blind, 27, 145–7, 170
archdeaconries, 128, 130
architecture, Anglo-Saxon, 6, 9–10, 24–30, 46, 109–11, 170, 192–6
    Romanesque, Continental, 21–7, 127–8
    Romanesque, Anglo-Norman, 6, 9–10, 14–15, 22–30, 49–50, 111, 120–2, 144–55, 159–67, 170, 192–6
    proportion of in West Midland counties, 120–2, 126
    see also ornament, technology
archpriest, as head of ex-minster, 2, 111
ashlar masonry, 25–9, 170, 192
Augustinian canons, replacing minster-priests, 35–6, 51–2, 59, 97

baptism, control of, 13, 19, 64, 84, 116, 149–50
    see also fonts
baptismal oil (chrism), distribution of from minsters, 2, 13, 61, 64, 84, 92, 93, 105, 108, 109, 116, 156
    received by minster from cathedral, 107, 116, 117
basketwork, as centring for double-splayed windows, 170, 174
beaver, possibly shown in sculpture, 149
bell-pit inside church, 184
bishop and priest depicted on font, 151
bishops, rôle of in parochial formation, 2, 10–11, 13–14, 19, 48, 51–2, 56, 57–8, 64–5, 77–9, 83–92, 93, 99, 100, 188–90
blood-feuds, 32–3
    deterring parishioners from visiting minster, 9
boundaries, *see* parishes
bread, paid by minster to cathedral, 105, 107, 114, 115, 116
building materials, *see* stones
building practice, *see* masonry techniques
burhs, see towns
burial, at minsters, 3, 5, 11, 13, 31, 32, 54, 56, 60, 86, 88–9, 91, 99, 133, 134, 156
    at local churches, 7, 14, 88–9, 95, 138
    in alternate graveyards, 13
    carried out by gilds, 31–2
    as contentious issue between minsters and local churches, 8, 10, 13, 39–40, 79, 88–9, 138
    exhumation after illicit, 13, 88, 138
    freedom from control of, 10, 41, 61
    of the poor, slaves, etc., 13, 54–6, 60, 91, 133
    in Winchester, confined to the Cathedral, 64
    see also graveyards
        buttresses, pilaster, 150, 184
        pierced by windows, 141, 150

Caenais masonry, 25
candles, carried to minsters, 60, 66
Canon Law, application of to parochial matters, 14, 15, 51, 64–5

canons, regular, *see* Augustinian canons
canons, secular, *see* priests in minster communities
capitals, carved, 28, 151, 164–5, 167
castles, minsters and colleges associated with, 39–40, 72, 97–8, 100, 107, 110, 111, 116, 167
cathedrals, rebuilding of, 21–2, 145, 179, 188–90, 195
Celtic church organisation, *see* Romano-British church organisation
cemeteries, *see* graveyards
centaur, as sculpture motif, 151
chalices, 160, 166
chancel arch, niches over, 147–9
    tall and narrow, 187
chapels, 15, 73–4, 77, 78, 87, 90–2, 107, 109, 111, 137–8, 141
    built because of inconvenience of visiting mother church, 8–9, 11, 13, 32, 34, 54–5, 74, 138
    built and maintained by gilds, 31–2, 34
    built and maintained by monasteries, 61
    built to be served from minsters, 7, 8, 11–12, 49, 54–8, 90
    built during the Anarchy, 19, 77
    hierarchies of, 11–12, 15–16, 90–2, 132
    lost, 15, 16, 79, 111, 132, 138, 141
    only tenants of founding lord to hear mass in, 11
    only to be used by tenants when lord present, 94
    only used during herring fishery, 188
    reversal of hierarchy with mother church, 15, 138
    to serve 12th-century 'Newland', 189
    timber, 15, 17
    in west tower of church, 111
    see also churches, parishes, priests
chaunter, as head of ex-minster, 62
chrism, *see* baptismal oil
Christ in Majesty, sculpture, 150
    on tympanum, 150
Chrodegang, Enlarged Rule of, 6, 54
churches, local/parish:
    abundance of, in 11th cent., 9–10, 21–3, 105–9, 120–1, 179, 191–7
    adoption of as devotional focus, 7–9
    adulterine, destruction or subjection of, 10–11
    appropriation of, 90, 95
    as attributes of thegnly status, 8, 49, 57, 58, 134
    building of, 7, 9–10, 21–30, 111, 120–2, 126, 144–55, 179, 191–7
    burial in, *see* burial
    clay, 179, 197
    consecration of by bishops, 10, 11, 22, 77, 99
    contiguous with, or contained within, monastic/minster churches, 46, 62, 98–9, 110, 111, 141, 188, 190
    economic and demographic context of, 7–9, 74, 108–9, 126, 141–4
    foundation/control/endowment/patronage of, by bishops, 134, 167, 188–90
        corporate, 8–9, 15, 32, 34
        by laity, 7–9, 10, 13–14, 22–3, 49, 51, 54–8, 134
        by monasteries, 9, 13–14, 28–30, 48–9, 91, 99–102, 134, 161–2
        by parson and vicar jointly, 134
        under licence from minsters, 8, 11, 86, 90–2, 94
        restricted by minsters, 77, 79–80
    furnishings and fittings of, 160, 166
    hierarchies of, 22, 66, 90–2, 111
    lost, 117, 179–84, 186–8

Select Subject Index

maintained by parish priest, 61
multiple, in one township or parish, 10, 179–84
named after lay owners, 108
Norman Conquest, effects of on, *see* Norman Conquest
payments from to cathedral, 107, 114–17
plans, of, 15, 111, 138–41
    standardised, 10
size of, in relation to Domesday population, 141–4
timber, 23, 120, 126, 179, 182, 183, 184, 197, 198, 199
two in one churchyard, 180
urban, 35–43, 109, 132, 137, 184–90
see also chapels, minsters, parishes, priests
churchscot, 8, 11, 12, 19, 53, 54, 56, 60, 87, 99, 100, 102, 133, 137
    see also scrifcorn
churchwardens, advent of, 15, 33
churchyards, *see* graveyards
clas churches, 130–3
clergy, *see* priests, minsters
Cluniac monks, replacing minster-priests, 97–102
colleges of canons, *see* minsters; priests in minster communities
colonnettes, *see* shafts
column figures, 163
Conversion, establishment of minsters a consequence of, 45–8
corbel-tables, 150, 164–5, 167
corpses, *see* burial
cottars, not obliged to be buried at minster, 13, 55–6, 60
counter-pitched masonry, *see* herringbone
cross, on tympanum, 148, 151
crosses, Anglo-Saxon, *see* sculpture
cruciformity, significance of for status of church, 14–15, 19, 26–7, 97, 110, 111, 118, 138–41, 189, 199
custos, as head of ex-minster, 62

Danegeld, possible effects on minster endowments, 3, 18
dean, as head of minster, 49–50, 52, 59–60, 97
'Dean of Christianity', 128
deaneries, rural, 128, 130
decoration, *see* ornament
dedications, notable or unusual:
    Holy Cross, 35
    St. Alban, 132
    St. Andrew, 74
    St. Augustine, 98
    St. Boniface, 62–3
    St. Clement, 109
    St. Cuthbert, 132
    St. Eadburga, 120
    St. Ecgwin, 120
    St. Faith, 134
    St. Gregory, 71
    St. Helen, 130–2
    St. Kenelm, 120
    St. Margaret, 132
    St. Mary, 110
    St. Mildburga, 71, 73, 120
    St. Peter-ad-Vincula, 40, 43, 61
Domesday Book, references to minsters and churches in, 4–5, 9, 23, 29, 45, 49, 52–3, 54, 62–5, 67–75, 83, 90, 98, 100–1, 102, 110, 120, 126, 127, 128, 134, 145, 180–5, 188, 191, 198
    population data in relation to church sizes, 141–4
Domesday Monachorum of Christ Church Canterbury, 105–18
doorways, western, 28, 151, 169, 171, 193, 196, 197, 198
'double' minsters, 3, 71, 108

elder *(senior)*, as head of minster, 2, 3, 52, 59, 71
Entry into Jerusalem, on tympanum, 77, 79
estates, breakup of, 7, 18, 67–8
    correspondence of with parishes, 117, 130, 132–3, 136–7, 142–3
    royal, episcopal, *see* vills
exhumation, *see* burial

'field-churches', 22, 111
fonts, 13, 15, 79, 133, 149–50, 150–1, 160
    see also baptism
'food and drink alms', 53, 59
French architectural influence, 21–7, 127–8, 150, 163
funeral rites, 8, 31

gates, town, parishes and wards formed around, 35–43
gilds, parochial, 2, 9, 13, 31–4
    urban, 32, 34, 35–43
gild-houses, 32, 34
glebes, of local churches, 8, 10, 52–3, 56, 58, 60, 77
    held free of service, 134–7
gravestones, Anglo-Saxon, *see* sculpture
graveyards, 7, 8, 13, 14, 18, 19, 22–3, 36, 42, 56–7, 61, 77–9, 88–9, 182, 185, 189
    consecration of by bishops, 13, 19, 77–9, 88–9, 91, 92
    for refuge in time of war (i.e. without burials), 13, 86, 87, 89, 92
    to receive only one corpse, 13, 89
    pagan Saxon, abandonment of, 45
    for the poor, slaves etc. only, 13, 54–6, 60, 91, 133
    see also burial
Gregorian Reform, effects of, 7, 13–16, 33, 97–8, 102

Harrowing of Hell, on tympanum, 151
Herefordshire school of masons, 150, 163–4
heriots, *see* soulscot
herringbone (pitched, counter-pitched) masonry, 25, 110, 111, 145, 154, 193, 195, 196
hillforts, minsters in or near, 110, 118, 133
honey, paid by minster to cathedral, 105, 107, 115, 116, 117
hundred court, minster-priest to attend thegn at, 54, 60
hundreds, in relation to minster parishes, 2, 3, 38, 45–9, 51, 63, 67–71, 99
hunting scene, on tympanum, 149

inscriptions, dedication, 7, 28, 192, 196
ironwork, decorative, in churches, 108, 160, 166
Italian influence on sculpture, 150–1

key of church, as symbol of proprietorship, 11, 60, 99, 101, 103

laity, *see* churches, foundation etc. by laity; minsters, foundation etc. by laity; patrons; parishes, local, corporate activity in
Laws, Anglo-Saxon and Anglo-Norman, references to churches in, 8, 9, 22, 51, 57, 58, 64, 84, 94

masonry techniques, *see* ashlar, Caenais, herringbone, *opus reticulatum, opus isodomum, petit appareil*
masons, local schools of, 10, 28–9, 144–55, 159–67, 195–6
megalithic masonry, 192–5
minsters:
    abandonment of as devotional foci, 7–9, 57–8
    annexation of to royal clerks, 6, 27, 49–51
    architectural character of, 14–15, 19, 26–7, 97, 110, 111, 118, 138–41, 199
    bequests to, 2–6
    burial at, *see* burial
    communities in, *see* priests in minster communities
    decline of, 6–7, 10–11, 48–60, 74–9, 105, 111
    definition of, 1
    disappearance of, 133
    disendowment of, 3, 49–51, 73–5, 133–4
    division of one into two, 64
    duty of parishioners to visit, *see* processions
    estates of, 2–3, 6–7, 45–7, 51–4, 59, 71, 73, 74–5
    foundation/control/endowment/patronage of, 2–3, 6, 40, 45–8, 67, 128, 133
        by bishops, 4, 12, 164
        by kings, 1, 3, 6, 10, 45–8, 53, 65, 73, 97, 197, 199

by monasteries, 12, 16, 46, 74–5, 83–92, 97–9, 102, 127–8
by laity, 2–6, 71–2, 97–102
gift of to monasteries, 72, 74–5, 83–92, 108, 128
gilds associated with, 2, 31–2
groups of churches dependent on, 11–13, 54–8, 74–80, 90–2, 105–9, 114–17, 132, 133, 134, 135, 197
heads of, 2, 3, *and see* archpriest, chaunter, *custos*, dean, elder, precentor
hierarchies of, 7, 18, 22, 38–41, 68
houses of priests surrounding, 49, 52, 59, 130
hundredal, 3, 16, 38, 68
identity of, after the 12th century, 2, 14–15, 75–80, 111, 134
internal life of, 6–7, 10–11, 49–60, 62
invaded by household clerks, 50, 60, 74–5
multiple churches at, 51, 59
Norman Conquest, effects of on, *see* Norman Conquest
obligation of to stable royal horses, 3
parish churches in or adjoining, 46, 62, 98–9, 110, 111, 141, 188
pastoral work of, 1–6, 7, 8, 10–11, 54–8, 77, 90, 98–9, 101–2
rebuilding of in 11th and 12th cents., 6, 14–15, 21–3, 26–7, 49–50, 59, 107, 110–11, 164
regularisation of, 35–6, 49, 51–2, 59, 65, 74–5, 97–9, 102, 133
revenues and rights owing to, 2, 5, 8, 12–13, 68, 83–92, 105–9, 114–17
reversal of hierarchy with daughter churches, 15, 138
sculpture associated with, 191–2
siting of, 110–13, 118, 130–3
stone building possibly confined to before 10th cent., 192, 197
urban, 3, 35–43, 112–13, 143
see also monasteries, parishes, priests
monasteries, definition of, 1
rebuilding or building of, 21–2, 145, 160–1
as landowners, 127–8
Norman, 84, 91, 127–9
see also minsters
monks, in minsters, 3, 16, 74–5, 83, 97–102
serving parish church, 189
Moorish influence on West Midlands architecture, 146–7
mortuaries, *see* soulscot
mouldings, Romanesque, 25–7, 145, 170, 182, 196

naves, size of, in relation to Domesday population, 141–4
niches over chancel arch, 147–9
Norman Conquest, effects of on churches, 6–7, 10–11, 21–30, 49–51, 97–102, 105, 111, 126–9, 133–4, 137
see also architecture, Romanesque
nuns, in minsters, 3, 16, 46, 62, 71, 83

one-cell churches, 111, 140–1
opus isodomum masonry, 192
opus reticulatum masonry, 27
ornament, architectural, 144–55, 159–67
balls, 162, 167
beakheads, 150, 160, 167
billet, 145, 170, 174
cable, 145, 150
chevron, 26, 29, 120, 145, 150, 151, 155, 167, 176, 195
clasps, 160–3
crenellation, 145
cushion capital, 184
denticle, 170, 174
lozenges, 145, 151
palmettes, 162, 167
plait, 173, 176
rosettes with clasps, 150
roundels, 149
saltire crosses, 145, 149
scallops, 170, 195
stars, 149
stiff-leaf, 151

straps, 150
triple rays, 145
trumpet-scallops, 151
oxen hauling stone to build church, 145

palaces, royal, minsters used as, 3
parishes:
minster, boundaries and extent of, 10, 46, 54–5, 60, 62, 64, 83, 85, 133
breakup of, 1, 8–13, 67–80, 83–92
definition of, 1, 8, 22
formation of, 1–2, 45–8, 128
relationship to royal vills and territories, 2, 45–8, 67–71, 83, 132–3, 199
urban, 13, 35–43, 64
local, boundaries of, 10, 14, 39, 41, 64, 71, 130, 136–7, 179–81
corporate activity in, 15, 31–4
correspondence of with estates, 117, 130, 136–7, 142–3
defined in terms of lordship, 11, 56, 61, 94
detached portions of, 14, 68, 74, 117
extra-mural, in relation to urban parochial structure, 39
formation of, 1, 7–9, 10, 13–15, 68, 130, 137
urban, 35–43, 49, 64, 137, 184–90
see also churches, minsters, priests
parishioners, *see* parishes, local, corporate activity in
parochiae, *see* parishes, minster
pastoral work, *see* minsters, priests
patrons of churches, influence of on architecture, 15, 23–9, 79, 144–51, 159–67
patronus, as head of minster, 52, 59
'Peace of God' associations, 32–3
pensions, from daughter to mother churches, 56–7, 58, 61, 64, 68, 74, 85–7, 92, 93, 134
pentecostals, paid to Old Minster Winchester, 64
Peter's Pence, paid to minsters, 61, 84, 86, 93, 105
petit appareil masonry, 25
pilaster strips, *see* stripwork
pilasters, quadrant, 169–70
pilgrimages, 33, 146–7, 150, 163
pitched masonry, *see* herringbone
plough-alms, 8
pointing, ribbon, 25
polychrome masonry, 154
poor, not obliged to be buried at minster, 13, 55–6, 60, 91
population (1086) in relation to church sizes, 141–4
porch, late 12th-century, 141
porticus, west, 46
portioners, in ex-minsters, 75
prebends, 6–7, 18, 46, 49, 50–4, 56, 57–9, 62, 72, 74–5, 97–8, 100, 101, 110, 199
precentor, as head of ex-minster, 62
priest and bishop depicted on font, 151
priests, local, 7–9
advent of in 11th century, 9
education of, 9
election and dismissal of, 32
employed by gilds, 32
forbidden to serve two churches, 9
as heads of parish gilds, 9, 31
houses of, beside churchyards, 95, 102
in lay households, 8
obliged to maintain church, 61
status of in 1086, 134
priests in minster communities, 1, 2, 3, 6–7, 10–11, 46, 49–60, 62, 71–2, 74–5, 83, 90, 97–8, 100, 108, 110
celibacy of (or lack of it), 52, 54
decline of, 6–7, 10–11, 48–60, 74–9
houses of, 49, 52, 59, 130
service of, and devolution to, local churches by, 8, 10, 11, 49, 50–1, 54–8, 90, 98, 101–2, 133
to wait for thegn before saying mass, 8, 54, 60

Select Subject Index

to accompany thegn to hundred court, 54, 60
to be fed at thegn's table, 8, 54, 60
see also churches, minsters, parishes
priories, alien, 84, 91, 93, 97–8, 127–8
processions, from daughter churches to minsters, 2, 11, 56, 58, 60, 61, 64, 66, 84, 92, 93

quarrying of stone for churches, 111, 151–5, 192–5
quoins, ashlar, 170, 190
    'Escomb-fashion', 193
    long-and-short, 193
    megalithic, 192–3, 195, 196
    rubble, 170
    side-alternate, 187, 192–3, 195, 196

re-used stone, as criterion of date, 192–5
Romano-British: building material re-used in 11th-century churches, 9, 110, 111, 192–5, 196
    church organisation, survival of, 130–3
    churches re-used as parish churches, 109, 130
    monuments, roads and settlements, 39–40, 64, 193–5
    towns and forts, minsters and churches sited in, 110, 112, 118, 130–2
Romescot, *see* Peter's Pence
roods, 160, 166
roofs, church, 151
Royal Free Chapels, 72, 75, 81
Rules, for canonical life, 6–7, 18, 51–4

Sagittarius, in sculpture, 149
St. Margaret, depicted on capital, 151
salt, tithe of, 61
salt-pans in Droitwich, 128
Scandinavian influence on sculpture, 150, 167
schools, associated with minsters, 38, 42, 52, 97
scrifcorn (Leominster version of churchscot), 2, 12, 84, 86, 87–8
sculpture, Anglo-Saxon, 8, 64, 71–2, 120, 154, 191–2, 197, 198, 199
    Romanesque, 15, 72, 77–9, 120, 144–51, 159–64, 196
    see also ornament
senior, *see* elder
sepulture, *see* soulscot
services, religious, *see* minsters, internal life of
services, owed from a chapel, 16
settlement, nucleation of, 7
shafts, angle/nook, 26–8, 151, 170, 193, 196, 198
sheep, paid to minster or by minster to cathedral, 42, 105, 107, 114, 115, 116
shrift-corn, *see* scrifcorn
slaves, not obliged to be buried at minster, 13, 55–6, 60
soulscot (heriot, *sawelscættas*, mortuary, sepulture) paid to minsters, 5, 8, 13, 32, 39–40, 42, 53, 60, 61, 64, 79, 88, 95, 133, 134, 137
Spanish influence on West Midlands architecture, 146–7, 150
stair-turrets, 173
'stations', *see* processions
stones, used in building:
    Alveley Sandstone, 154
    Bunter Sandstone, 154
    Caen, 111
    Calcareous Gritstone, 28
    Calcareous Tufa, 154–5
    Ferruginous Conglomerate, 170
    Gneisses, 155
    Halesowen Sandstone, 154
    Highley Sandstone, 154
    Keuper Marl, 154
    Keuper Sandstone, 154
    Liassic, 154, 160
    'Marble', 160
    Millstone Grit, 192–5
    New Red Sandstone, 160
    Old Red Sandstone, 154, 160
    Oolitic limestones, 154, 160
    Quarr, 110, 111, 118
    Silurian limestones, 155
    Taynton, 154
    Triassic, 154
    Upper Coal Measure Sandstone, 154
stripwork (pilaster strips), 28–9, 170, 193, 196
sundials, inscribed, 28, 196

technology, Anglo-Saxon, 6, 9–10, 23–5, 170, 192–6
    Anglo-Norman, 6, 9–10, 23–5, 192–6
    see also architecture, masonry techniques
Tenth-Century Reform, attitude of to minsters, 1, 2, 6, 48–9, 127
thegns, as church-owners, *see* churches, foundation etc. by laity; minsters, foundation etc. by laity
    gild of, 31
three-cell churches, 29, 139, 141, 164, 181, 186
through-stone masonry, 193
tithes, to be paid to minster, 8, 11, 53, 54, 56, 57, 60, 64, 79, 84–7, 133, 134
    diverted from minster to local church or to monastery, 9, 84, 86, 127–8, 137
    in return for pension, 58, 61, 64, 85, 93
    two-thirds demesne, diverted from minster, 12–13, 84–5
    half, diverted to local church, 57, 61, 87, 101
    one-third demesne, diverted to local church, 8, 13, 64, 84–5
    freedom to alienate unacceptable after mid 12th cent., 87, 94
    leasing of, 93
    obligation to pay acknowledged in return for licence to found chapel, 86–7, 94
    payable to minster from Ancient Demesne land, 13
    of salt, reserved to minster, 61
    withheld during Anarchy, 86
tolls of port, assigned to minster, 110
tooling, diagonal, 187, 190
    Roman, 192
towers, axial or central, 141, 181–2, 186–7, 189
    with salient angles, 26, 27, 187
    over N. transept, 111
    round, 9–10, 169–77
    timber, 126
    western, 28–9, 111, 141, 164, 169–77, 185–7, 195–7
towns, Anglo-Saxon, 3, 32, 35–43, 45, 51, 109, 110, 112–13, 137, 143, 184–7, 188
transepts, continuous, 177, 187, 190
transhumance, in relation to parish formation, 72, 81
Tree of Life, on tympanum, 149
tunas, royal, *see* vills
two-cell churches, 111, 140–1, 181–4
tympana, 15, 77, 78, 120, 148–9, 150, 151, 154, 163, 165

vaulting, 151, 155, 170, 171
vestments, 160, 166
vicarages, establishment of, 13, 14, 56, 57–8, 65, 90–2
Victorine canons, architecture of, 161, 163
Victory, depicted on tympanum, 163
Vikings, alleged effect of on minster system, 2, 3, 36–8, 45, 62, 108, 109, 110, 117
vills, episcopal, and estates, in relation to minsters, 43, 45, 63, 164
    royal, and estates, in relation to minsters, 2, 18, 38, 45–8, 51, 63, 65, 67–72, 83, 93, 102, 108, 109, 199
voussoirs, radial, 163

walls, thickness of, 195, 198
wall-paintings, 160, 166
wards, urban, 35–43
Whitsun farthings, 156

wills, Anglo-Saxon, references to minsters in, 2–6
windows, belfry, twin openings, 28–9, 170, 192–3, 195–6
    blind, 150
    double-splayed, 25, 30, 109, 110, 170, 171, 177, 193, 196
    piercing buttresses, 141, 150
    round, 170, 171
    south-facing, in second stage of tower, 196
    triangular-headed, 25, 170
wine, received by minster from cathedral, 107, 115, 116
wyvern, on tympanum, 149